INTRODUCTORY
SOCIOLOGY

D0170788

PAUL H. LANDIS

State Professor of Sociology
Washington State University

THE RONALD PRESS COMPANY • NEW YORK

5

Library of Congress Catalog Card Number: 58–6660

PRINTED IN THE UNITED STATES OF AMERICA

Preface

The uniqueness of any new textbook for introductory sociology courses must be largely in its organization, emphasis, and student appeal. In this book I have tried above all to make sociology a vital subject in the student's experience. It is my conviction that the introductory course should be one of the most humanizing influences in the college curriculum. A genuine culture consciousness is the best foundation for tolerance and provides the most discerning perspective for world leadership, the task with which American youth is challenged as no generation has ever been.

With this objective in view, the book begins with a consideration of the concept of culture. Classroom experience has shown that this concept is unusually fresh and revealing to beginning students, providing as it does a new insight into their own interrelationships. In brief, my approach follows a sequence which aims at the following. (1) to develop culture consciousness; (2) to give insight into group interaction; (3) to build an understanding of the social structure and its operations; (4) to interpret personality and its problems in a group context; (5) to make students aware of social control, disorganization, and planning; and (6) to introduce them to a study of basic institutions.

A thorough understanding of these topics has an important place in the education of every student. It provides the essential background and orientation for those who will take more specialized courses in sociology. For the terminal student, it lays the groundwork for the insight and tolerance needed by every citizen in an everexpanding, interdependent world.

A special feature of the book is the emphasis on social structure, an area of increasing importance to sociology which can no longer be ignored or given only cursory attention. I have, therefore, not been content with presenting class and caste as the complete framework of the status structure, but have also given attention to religion, race, age, sex, and occupation as other contributing factors.

iii

Much attention has been given to pedagogical effectiveness. For the most part, the treatment proceeds inductively from interesting case example to principle, from description of situation to definition. This I have found to be the most effective technique for challenging interest and building understanding. Almost every chapter reproduces brief and pointed excerpts such as are found in source books. In addition to chapter-end bibliographies, there are special chapter-by-chapter reference lists built around standard books of readings. If the appropriate reading is found in more than one source book, duplicate listings are made. A film list appears at the end of the first chapter of each Part.

I am indebted to J. B. Lippincott Company for permission to parallel at certain points paragraphs from my *Social Control;* also to my colleagues Joseph B. Perry and Edgar G. Epps for a critical reading of and suggestions on certain chapters, and to Vernon Davies for criticism and suggestions on the Student Introduction.

PAUL H. LANDIS

Pullman, Washington
February, 1958

Contents

v

The Role of the Sociologist

Sociology is a body of *tested knowledge* having to do with man's behavior in all kinds of group situations from the pair relationship of marriage to the interactions of nations. It is the last great area of human knowledge to be examined scientifically, and the most significant. It competes at many points with folk knowledge, since every man considers himself to be his own sociologist. This does not mean that all folk knowledge is in error or that, say, pawnbrokers and ministers of the gospel lack understanding of how human beings interact with their fellows.

The difference is that, to merit a place in sociology, folk belief must have been put to the test of scientific verification. If the pawnbroker claims women are more likely to pawn diamonds than are men, it is probably the conclusion he has reached from his limited experience with customers and that of his known business associates. If the sociologist makes such an observation about the fair sex, it will be after having tabulated the records of a random sample of pawnbrokers' customers in offices scattered over a considerable number of cities.

The evangelist may declare boldly "all men are sinners." Before the sociologist could, as a scientist, accept this hypothesis, he would have to define "sinner" in specific terms and then set out to discover whether all men fit the definition.

He would begin with a more definable term, say "lawbreakers," that would describe all men. This concept is more clearcut in definition. From this point, he would assemble proof. He might deal with arrest records or use a questionnaire in which he asked direct questions regarding lawbreaking in general, or about specific illegal acts, like entering an intersection without coming to a complete stop. If he did ask such questions, he should require that the questionnaire not bear the respondent's name, since research shows people are most honest where there is no danger of identification. He might well find that all men are lawbreakers, or that 95 per cent or 98 per cent are. When he made his declaration about lawbreakers, it would be an utterance based not on folk belief or on limited personal experience but on tested knowledge.

This is not to say that all tested knowledge has to be reduced to statistical terms, even though the sociologist makes extensive use of tabulated data, calculating machines, and tabulators. The case history of an individual or of a group of individuals may reveal a great deal about human behavior. How much will depend on the skill, sociological insight, and understanding of the person reporting and interpreting the case.

The late Charles H. Cooley, first-generation sociologist who spent his professional life at the University of Michigan, developed a profound understanding of human nature, its origin and shaping, by observing his own children as they grew from infancy. Conclusions he reached about the social self, its origin, and its identity with the primary group are valid still. He observed well and reported his tested knowledge with great accuracy.[1]

Frederic M. Thrasher used the *participant-observer* technique in studying Chicago teenage gangs. For seven years he associated intimately with them and saw society as they saw it. His report on gang life is scientific in the same sense that a chemist's report of an experiment is scientific.[2] So is a similarly conducted study of Chicago hobo life by Nels Anderson.[3]

Thomas and Znaniecki used the personal letter between newcomers and home folk as one research source in trying to understand the adjustment problems and attitudes of the Polish peasant immigrant in American cities.[4] The author, similarly, has used files of a promotional land office as one phase of a study of new settlers in Washington and their aspirations.[5] A recurrent theme was their great desire for wood, water, and a garden, which reflected their tragic experience in the arid Great Plains, where they lacked fuel, a sure domestic water supply, and natural rainfall for garden and farm crops.

[1] Charles H. Cooley, *Human Nature and the Social Order* (New York: Charles Scribner's Sons, 1902).

[2] Frederic Thrasher, *The Gang* (Chicago: University of Chicago Press, 1927).

[3] *The Hobo* (Chicago: University of Chicago Press, 1923).

[4] *The Polish Peasant in Europe and America*, 3 vols. (Boston: Chapman & Grimes, Inc., 1918–1920).

[5] *The Drought Farmer Adjusts to the West*, Washington Agricultural Experiment Station Bulletin No. 378 (Pullman, Wash., 1939).

THE LABORATORY TECHNIQUE NOT THE PRIMARY ONE

In the physical and natural sciences, except astronomy, geology, and meteorology, the laboratory technique has become the primary method of study. In the physical sciences particularly, the laboratory provides ideally controlled conditions for manipulating matter to learn its properties and behavior. In the natural sciences the physical properties of creatures, particularly of dead ones, can be as rigorously controlled, although to learn about behavior, more flexible conditions must be dealt with, or as the scientist says it, variables are more difficult to control.

The "Real-Life" Laboratory. In sociology, more than in any other field of science, it is difficult to simulate laboratory conditions and to control all variables by laboratory techniques. One of the critical problems here is that to control the behavior situation is to create artificial behavior. Research results tend to be unrealistic and do not reflect how groups actually behave.

This does not rule out experiments entirely, however. It does require that they be carried out under lifelike conditions by the use of a portion of a population universe. Various inventions, such as the one-way screen and the tape recorder, today permit the intrusion of the observer without his presence being known. For example, much research in recent years has been concerned with human behavior in small groups. The Carnegie Corporation has helped finance at the University of Minnesota a unique conference-type classroom. Unknown to the group is the presence of an observer in an adjoining room petitioned off by a one-way glass screen, invisible from the classroom side. Here the observer can record small-group behavior interactions under natural conditions, just as can the biologist who observes hens in a pen and records the pecking order which they establish over each other in determining rank and dominance. (For more detail on pecking order, refer to pages 286–87. For similar observations about wives of managers in industry, see page 366.)

Many industries are now able to manipulate people in such a way as to provide a "real-life" laboratory. The Western Electric Company sponsored some of the most significant early research in small-group behavior in industry by manipulating work arrangements under sociological observation to see how such arrangements affected the attitudes and work output of the workers. (A brief report of this research appears on page 178.) Since that time, industry has become more research-minded in the sociological area. Sociologists are called upon to set up experiments and to report results.

Although research in sociology can seldom use controlled laboratory methods, studies of animals often reveal behavior parallel to that of humans. Make the maze too complicated, change the route too often or make it impossible, and any creature with a nervous system can in time suffer such frustration as to give up—first in defeat and then in despair. Neurosis is the result of such frustration in man when the human maze becomes too complicated, ventures too unpredictable, outcomes unrewarding or highly risky. War has taught us that every man has his breaking point, no matter how well-adjusted he may have been at the outset. (University of California, Berkeley)

to a life situation created in the laboratory

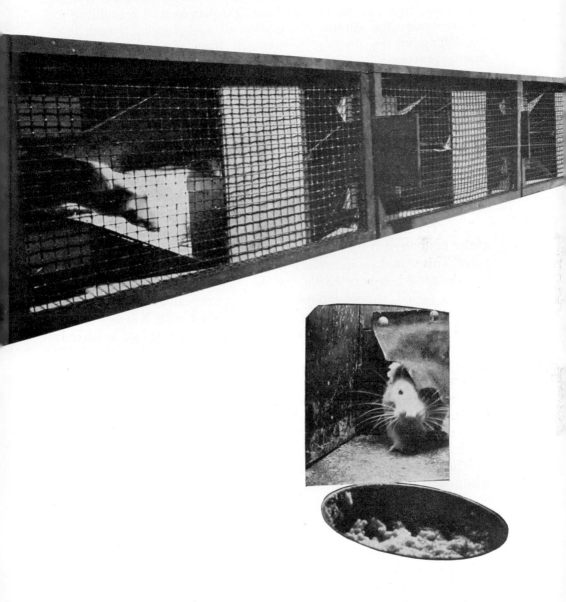

The Rand Corporation has in process a sociological experiment today in a remote Brazilian area where it has established a coffee plantation. In a community of about 500 people it is rebuilding a society under the careful observation of sociologists, remodeling everything in the group's environment from plumbing to child-rearing practice.

The Army was persuaded by sociological research workers during the war to try out experiments in life situations with limited groups to see what would really happen in the area of racial attitudes. Although many persons felt that if Negroes were to be drafted and exposed to the risks of war the same as white men it was morally obligatory on the nation to accord them equal status, even the Army feared that integration would be disastrous. Sociologist Samuel Stouffer, serving the army while on leave from his university position, reports the experiment and its results:

". . . The Army tried out in Europe the radical idea of placing an entire platoon of Negro volunteers in a white infantry combat company. This was done in several divisions, most of which saw several months of subsequent battle. At the end of the campaign, interviewers polled sample groups of men in several divisions to find out how the attitudes of men who had served with Negroes compared with those of men who had not. In divisions that had no mixed companies, 62 per cent of the soldiers said they would dislike very much to serve in the same companies as Negroes. Of white infantrymen who had fought in the same divisions but not the same companies as Negroes, only 20 per cent said they would dislike it very much. And among white infantrymen who had actually been in the same companies as Negroes, only 7 per cent said they disliked it very much.

"There was another very interesting finding. Two-thirds of the white men in the mixed companies, when polled after the experience, said that they had been opposed to the scheme beforehand and had thought it would fail. This was almost exactly the same proportion of opponents as was found in divisions that had not experienced the plan; in other words, the retrospective answers about attitudes corresponded closely to those of groups reporting current attitudes, so one finding tended to confirm the other. . . ."[6]

The ultimate result of this experiment was integration within the armed forces. This integration predated the Supreme Court decision

[6] Samuel A. Stouffer, "A Study of Attitudes," *Scientific American*, 180: 11–15 (May 1949).

The pilot plant model dam, shown above, is used to test the principles involved in the gigantic structure to be built. Below is the Grand Coulee Dam—three and a half times the masonry of the Great Pyramid. (WSC Photo, State College of Washington)

(1954) concerning school integration and led to none of the hubbub and disturbance which followed school integration in some communities.

It was another social science experiment which ultimately led to the revision of the traditional army physical conditioning program:

"A committee of physical educators had proposed a new physical-conditioning program for the Army, based on modern experience in training football players and other athletes. They believed that the traditional Army regimen of setting-up exercises and hikes was uninteresting to the men, time-consuming and generally inefficient. A Research Branch survey of samples of troops throughout the country, using tests of physical proficiency devised by the committee, confirmed the criticism. It showed that men who had been in the Army six months to a year [and] had been subjected to the old-fashioned conditioning system made little better scores on tests of strength or of stamina than did new recruits. That the tests were valid measures of physical condition was confirmed by the fact that paratroopers, initially selected for ruggedness and subjected to particularly rigorous physical training, were able to make high scores on them.

"A controlled experiment was then set up. Two samples of new recruits, matched on initial proficiency tests, were selected. One sample was put through the conventional Army course of calisthenics and hikes. When retested the group showed only a slight improvement over its initial scores. The other group was given the rigorous new program of training. After six weeks, its proficiency scores were far superior, almost as high as those of the paratroopers. Moreover, the men getting this training liked it better than did those in the traditional program. The results persuaded the Army to scrap its traditional procedures and introduce the new program on an Army-wide basis."[7]

STATISTICS IN SOCIOLOGICAL ANALYSIS

Modern social institutions are given to compiling elaborate statistical records dealing with number of members, classifications of members by age and sex, with costs of operation, and in many cases with behavior characteristics of persons allied with the institution. Each member of a college student body not only is registered, but his age, sex, address, previous schooling, religious affiliation, his parents or guardian and their location, and other such factors are recorded. Each patient entering a hospital must record detailed information on

[7] *Ibid.*

The sociologist manipulates statistics to provide information which will help him understand human behavior as it manifests itself in groups. Such statistical research in social science has been mechanized, and vast quantities of data can be handled with little manpower. (Tommy Weber)

parentage, parent's age at death if deceased, cause of death, his own prior illnesses, his operations, his age, his religious affiliation, his bank or credit references, etc. Even an involuntary resident of an institution, for example, a criminal entering prison, becomes a member of a card file bearing information about personal characteristics and outlining a behavior record involving previous convictions and commitments.

For the sociologist, more than any other social scientist, the environment is teeming with statistical data, data which he can make significant by using it to answer sociological problems. Then, too, the sociologist can, by asking innumerable questions of human beings of various groups, classes, and stations in life, accumulate statistics about large groups to pursue his inquiry further, or in directions where no systematic data are accumulated by institutional bodies. It is little wonder that statistics and machines for manipulating them have become the most important research aids to the sociologist.

The statistical approach, like all research, tends to take the following steps: (1) An *hypothesis* based on observation and general knowledge of the phenomenon to be studied is formulated. (2) Then follows more critical observation involving the *collection and analysis of statistical data*. (3) Such data, if the sample is representative of some universe, permit the third step, *generalization*, or the formulation of a principle applicable to the universe represented. (This is often called projection or prediction, in research terminology.) (4) Science rarely is content with findings from a single study, no matter how adequate the sample seems to be. Repeat studies are entered into for the final step, *verification* of the truth or falsity of the principle.

Take the statistical research involved in the study of the relationship of age at marriage to success, reported in the chart below. Folklore holds that the more youthful a person, the more adjustable he is. This alone might be accepted as a beginning hypothesis. Or one who had inquired into the experience of relief agencies, marriage clinics, and divorce courts, on the basis of his limited observation might well formulate the opposite hypothesis: that youthfulness is a handicap to marital adjustment. Starting with either premise, a vital sociological problem is to be answered, and the statistical approach offers a valid means.

In this instance, the researchers chose to study in great detail the marital history of over 500 couples by questionnaire. Data so collected provided the information for statistical analysis of the age factor, and many others affecting the outcome of marriage.

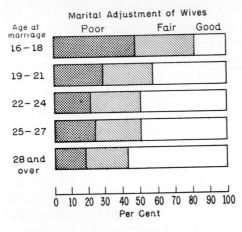

At What Age Is It Safe To Marry?

The chart shows the results of one of the first sociological studies that tried to answer this question scientifically. A study of 526 married couples by age at time of marriage showed that almost half of the women who married at under 19 had a poor adjustment and less than 20 per cent made a good adjustment. Univac could give even more conclusive results with cards on thousands of marriages selected by random sampling.

Folk wisdom says, "The younger one is when married, the more adjustable he is likely to be." Fact here says almost half of the women who married young failed. As economic conditions have improved, people are marrying at younger ages than when this study was made. Perhaps they are adjusting better too. Sociological study must be a continuing enterprise if human behavior as it manifests itself currently is to be understood. (Data from E. W. Burgess and L. S. Cottrell, Jr., Predicting Success or Failure in Marriage, p. 117. Copyright, 1939, by Prentice-Hall, Inc. Reprinted by permission of the publisher.)

Having found a clear, in fact, striking relationship between age of marriage and success or failure in husband–wife adjustment, generalization in these terms was justified: Marriage of girls under 19 greatly increases the risk of failure. The older the girl at time of marriage, the greater the likelihood of her making a successful adjustment. Such generalization is often called, in statistical terminology, *prediction*, in that it provides for forecasting outcome of future relationships of couples on the basis of the way past marriages have turned out. In statistical research, prediction, or as the writer prefers to call it, generalization, is stated in terms of statistical probability. For example, in the case above, generalization (prediction) would be stated thus: It is probable that about half of marriages of girls under 19 years of age will lead to poor adjustment, and that only about 15 per cent will lead to good adjustment. Those marrying at 28 or older have almost a 60 per cent chance of good adjustment, and less than a 20 per cent chance of poor adjustment.

To be fully certain of the validity of this conclusion, a larger sample involving a greater diversity of the population is required. If extensive verification should prove this ratio correct, one could set up dependable norms for measuring the probable marriage success of those to be married. (The researchers who did the study described here did build a "marriage prediction scale," using age of marriage, happiness of parents' marriage, and other such factors as indexes of probable success or failure.) Ultimately sociologists hope to develop tests with norms based on diverse enough samples so that a young person or couple taking such tests will know what their percentage chance of success or failure is, just as one does now on such matters as probable college success as shown by the college entrance examinations, and probable success in a particular vocation as shown by vocational aptitude tests.

Statistics and Statistics. Statistics do not answer questions except as they are applied to a realistic problem and handled with a critical and logical mind. Mathematical formulae are a great help, but are at best mechanical devices which answer questions correctly only when used in connection with logically sound hypotheses and in relation to meaningful social relationships.

The correlation technique has been used extensively in social science research; it is a frequently used mathematical procedure for showing the degree of relationship between two logically related sociological phenomena. One can obtain a very high correlation between the infant death rate and softness of asphalt pavements. Yet it would be quite senseless to conclude that soft asphalt pavements have anything to do with the infant death rate, even though it is true that dysentery and other infant diseases flourish in very hot weather and that asphalt pavements get soft in very hot weather.

Neither can any degree of mathematical refinement of data make these data tell more than they told at their source. Sir Josiah Stamp tells of a young man in India who quoted Indian statistics to a judge. The judge was not impressed. He said, in substance, "Young man, when you are a bit older and have had more experience with Indian statistics, you will not quote them with such assurance." He then commented on how the government, keen on amassing statistics, not only collected them but added them, "raised them to the nth power," took the cube root, and made of them wonderful diagrams. But they forgot that the statistics originated in distant villages where some village watchman puts down "what he damn pleases."[8] Sociologists never need three decimal points to express their findings. Neither can any degree of statistical manipulation save the researcher the obligation of a cautious and critical interpretation of findings. Some amateurs come out with conclusions about as valid as that of the deaf man who gave a hearing aid a two weeks' trial. It "improved" his hearing a great deal, yet he had never turned on the battery. Actually, it did not improve his hearing ability at all—it only made those conversing with him talk louder.

Even though statistics are often used as a crutch for a lazy mind, sociology would accomplish very little in solving the problem of understanding human behavior without them.

SOCIOLOGISTS AS SOCIAL PLANNERS

The sociologist, when he becomes a planner, has entered the province of social engineering and social reform. He is working as an applied sociologist. This kind of activity, within the mores of the "sociologist as a researcher" clan, is considered less respectable sociology. The primary reason, no doubt, is that as social planner the sociologist has to exceed his tested knowledge by projecting inferences beyond the boundary of definite proof. He must venture and speculate in charting change. As a sociologist he should do better at this kind of thing and act more wisely than, say, politicians, but he has left the realm of what is known as "pure" sociology.

8 Sir Josiah Stamp, *Some Economic Factors in Modern Life* (London: Staples Press), as quoted in Victor Boedicke, *Introduction to the Theory of Statistics* (New York: Harper & Brothers, 1953), p. 258.

This does not mean that such sociological activity is without merit, or that it should not be entered into. Few sociologists reject the planner–consultant role when it is offered to them. They welcome the role for the opportunity it gives to put their knowledge and techniques to the test of real life, and as an opportunity to test their judgments in competition with politicians, statesmen, and administrators.

For many years sociologists studied success of probation and parole by analyzing records of success and failure of different types of criminals on parole. By assembling a large body of facts about the criminal experience and personal characteristics of successes and failures, they were eventually able to develop a scale which could measure an untried criminal's statistical chances of failure or success. This instrument, if valid, should help prison parole boards take a lot of the guesswork out of parole.

It is not surprising that sociologists have welcomed the opportunity to act as members of parole boards and try out their tests and put their general sociological knowledge of criminal behavior to the life test. They have accepted such appointments in several states. During recent years three different sociologists in the state of Washington have served on the prison parole board.

The sociologist's educative function is often best served by switching from the research to the administrative or consultant role. Thus he proves to administrators the worth of his tested knowledge.

ADMINISTRATIVE RESEARCH

A step between the planner–engineer and the pure research sociologist is the sociologist whose research activity is oriented primarily toward solving administrative problems. Today, an increasing number of farsighted administrative officials in government, school, church, industry, and business understand the importance of sociological knowledge to wise administrative policy. They employ the research sociologist to assemble facts, figures, opinions, and other information by which they as administrators may be guided. The opinion poll is one of the familiar devices, as is the questionnaire, the census, and the periodic statistical report.

"Administrative research," as it is often called, differs from pure research in that the problem to be solved is not one of theory or principle in the area of human social behavior but rather a concrete administrative problem of how this or that situation can be most intelligently manipulated, perhaps to win an election, gain support for a public policy, seek the greatest welfare, avoid crises such as strikes,

What Do You Think?

Citizens' views on particular questions may be vital in determining the political climate or the morale of citizens in wartime—and they serve many other uses in business, politics, and war. The Pittsfield Project, begun in 1952, has focused on many aspects of political behavior processes in Pittsfield, Massachusetts. The survey has included a historical-sociological analysis of the community, eleven sample surveys, quantitative content analyses of various communication media, and a series of intensive case studies of leading individuals and groups in the city. Shown here is a typical interview and the subsequent processing and filing of the data obtained. (Roper Public Opinion Research Center)

or, as in the case of the census, to establish a basis for knowing how many schools, churches, highways, and manufacturing plants will be needed to meet the demands of the new generation.

The United States Reclamation Service provides a good example of the worth of administrative research. The Service has experienced a high rate of failure among first settlers in irrigated areas. How to eliminate failures by more careful selection of settlers is a vital problem. How can sociological research help in settler selection? By interview, the sociologist assembles information on settlers who have succeeded and those who have failed. From sufficient information of this character, he is able to build a scale which will provide insight concerning the likelihood of an untried settler's eventual success or failure.

Such administrative research has been used extensively in western irrigated areas. Sociologists have also helped with planning land patterns and farm layouts as they affect the economics and sociability of the new community life established. (The proposed settlement pattern for much of the million acres of Columbia Basin irrigation now being developed is discussed on page 192.)

THE SOCIOLOGIST AND SOCIAL REFORM

Sociology deals with *what is,* not *what ought to be.*

The sociologist may be personally gravely concerned about the rise in the divorce rate curve; he may try to learn why and seek measures to correct the trend. Yet he leaves to others pronouncements such as "divorce is sin," "the family is doomed." If he makes such pronouncements, he has at the time abandoned his role as a sociologist and speaks as a religionist or moralist. This he has a perfect right to do.

But the terms *good* and *bad* are not in his sociological vocabulary. As a sociologist, he is quite as much at home in studying the factors in social environment which lead to prostitution as he is in studying the background factors which lead to a happy marriage.

Even though the sociologist in his research is not a reformer as such, his findings often threaten existing regimes. The Army soon learned this and forbade all sociological surveys dealing with attitudes of enlisted men. Finally one exception was made, and the survey proved to be as disturbing as expected, perhaps even more disturbing. Fortunately the Army leaders into whose hands it fell were willing to face the facts and use them to advantage. Here is Stouffer's account of the sociological survey and of the reform it initiated.

"In July, 1941, the Secretary of War issued an order prohibiting surveys of attitudes of enlisted men. If their attitudes were critical of the Army, the order said, a survey would be 'destructive in its effect on a military organization where accepted responsibility on the part of every individual is fundamental.'

"Five months later, an exception to this rule was permitted. With the personal backing of Chief of Staff George C. Marshall, a group of psychologists and sociologists used anonymous questionnaires to sound out the attitudes of a representative cross section of 1,500 enlisted men in one infantry division in training. The study was made the day after Pearl Harbor. For the first time in any modern army, the new methods of social science research had a chance to show their power in comparison with the reports of visiting officers, who had to get their impressions from haphazard and biased samples of informants.

"The report was critical, all right. Straight from the pencils of the men came frank and documented indictments of the training methods, the leadership system, and other activities of an army which was enmeshed in ancient tradition and only beginning to awake to the needs of modern mechanized war. The complaints were not just idle gossip and griping. For example, statistical tables and charts proved that the men were discriminating in their criticisms: some practices were condemned by nine out of ten; some were approved by almost as large a proportion.

"General Marshall himself read the report on this division. So did many of the officers on the General Staff. One general started reading it at midnight and said the next day that it was so exciting and revealing that he did not put it down until three o'clock in the morning. A considerable number of changes were instituted as a result of that one study, including a revision of plans for the new Officer Candidate Schools. Most important of all, the War Department put such research on a permanent basis. Between Pearl Harbor and the end of the war, the Research Branch of its Information and Education Division made more than 200 surveys of representative samples aggregating over half a million U.S. enlisted men and officers.

"The Army had opened up a new channel of communication. The top command now could replace guesswork about some of the morale problems with evidence. To be sure, not all officers welcomed it. There was always opposition, but skepticism diminished as the war progressed. The standard argument that it would 'upset a man's morale' to give him a chance to say frankly what he thought without fear of reprisal was easy to refute with evidence.

"Moreover, it was possible to show that these surveys, using the best methods available to social science, got down to some solid realities. They proved to be of value in predicting the performance of groups of men in combat. For example, before the Normandy invasion all the enlisted men in the 108 rifle companies in four divisions were studied in England. An attitude or morale index was constructed for each company. After two months of fighting in Normandy, each company's record was compared with its prebattle attitude index. The criterion of its behavior under the stress of combat was taken to be its noncombat casualty rate, because many if not most of the noncombat casualties at this period were psychiatric in character, and some companies had much higher noncombat casualty rates than others. Comparing the three rifle companies with the worst attitude index with the three rifle companies with the best index in each regiment, we found that on the average the companies with the worst indexes before combat had 60 per cent more nonbattle casualties in Normandy than the companies with the best.

"The surveys were applied to hundreds of problems, many of which do not loom large in the perspective of total war, but were important at the time. Why did men in malarial regions fail to use Atabrine as regularly as they should? What attitudes and practices were associated with trench foot? Which of two kinds of huts did men in Alaska prefer? What were the favored types of winter clothing among front-line troops in Belgium, Luxembourg, and Germany? What radio transcriptions did men want? What did they like most to read in *Yank* magazine? What about needs for athletic equipment? What could be done to improve a difficult laundry situation in Panama? What were the sources of difficulties in soldiers' relations with the French? Such inquiries were routine and were made in increasing numbers.

"Some of the larger-scale enterprises were: studies of soldiers' postwar plans, which provided a factual basis for drawing up the GI Bill of Rights; studies of psychiatric screening, which led to the development by the Research Branch, in cooperation with the Surgeon General, of a test that was used routinely in all induction stations in the last year of the war; special surveys of the Air Forces and of other large components of the Army such as the infantry (the idea of the Combat Infantryman's Badge grew out of one of the studies); analyses of problems of occupying troops, which led to changes in occupation policy in Germany."[9]

[9] Stouffer, *op. cit.* The materials in this article were later used in *The American Soldier,* 4 vols. (Princeton: Princeton University Press, 1950).

Again and again sociological research disturbs administrators, political regimes, all kinds of institutional regimes and vested interests. They do not always respond with the cooperative spirit shown in the Army case described above. Often they respond by criticism, fighting the research man, going after his job, or flatly denying his results. Unlike the physicist, whose findings may directly concern no one, the sociologist's findings of necessity concern some person, or more likely groups of persons, for the sociologist deals with human life and group behavior itself.

As Robert Redfield has said, social science research results are not "morally indifferent"; they are "morally significant."[10] The sociologist, therefore, constantly challenges things as they are. If he finds, for example, that fee-splitting is common among doctors and surgeons, it is not neutral knowledge.[11] The public has far too much at stake to ignore such findings. If the sociologist finds, as he does, that there is a common pattern of parental neglect and abuse, a denial of love, in the background of most prostitutes, that practically all of them reflect deficiencies in personality development that relate to a certain type of family pattern, then this is not neutral knowledge.[12] It is of great human concern and may inspire social action in the direction of replacing penal treatment by psychiatric treatment.[13] The sociologist may become so concerned about his research findings that, by writing or participating as consultant or planner, he takes an active part in reform. He may and does frequently pass from the role of sociologist to reformer, just as the chemist may shift from his laboratory role to that of factory consultant to help provide "better things for better living."

Sociology is a tested body of knowledge, not the techniques of social welfare, social policy-making, or social reform. It studies social problems and social change but promotes social welfare and social change only indirectly, in that its findings may suggest the need for certain action.

By sticking to an objective approach in his role, the sociologist's counsel is more valid than that of the evangelical reformer and in

[10] "Prospects for the Scientific Study of Human Relations," University of Chicago Round Table, Dec. 28, 1947, p. 13.

[11] Edwin H. Sutherland, "White Collar Criminality," *American Sociological Review*, 5: 1–12 (Feb. 1940). This was Sutherland's presidential address before the American Sociological Society.

[12] See John M. Murtagh and Sara Harris, *Cast the First Stone* (New York: McGraw-Hill Book Co., Inc., 1957).

[13] For an experiment in the nonpunitive handling of the prostitute, see Ernest G. Lion, *et al.,* "An Experiment in the Psychiatric Treatment of Promiscuous Girls," Psychiatric Service, San Francisco Department of Public Health, 1945.

the end his views become the foundation for a new approach to the problem. For example, sociological knowledge of cause and effect in the area of personality has completely changed our society's approach to many age-old problems. No longer does the sociologically-wise court punish the juvenile; rather, it seeks to educate and rehabilitate, to improve the family and community setting. To understand that social factors form the juvenile delinquent, just as they form the model boy, is to cease to rely upon punishment. It calls for rehabilitation to repair the damage that a given set of social circumstances has wrought in the personality of the child.

Although sociologists are not reformers, they have perhaps had more influence on social change since the 1930's than has any other group of scientists, with the possible exception of chemists and physicists, and in the long view of history, perhaps even more influence than these. Although sociologists have struggled with inefficient research instruments and often used the ones they have poorly; although they, compared with natural and physical scientists, have had only the crumbs of finance that dribble down from the budgets of universities and government bureaus, they have nonetheless contributed to a profound new insight into human personality, motivation, character development, and group understanding.

Take the field of criminal behavior. Although sociology as a scientific approach to man's social behavior is only now in its second generation, the first generation of sociologists having died within the last decade and a half, its insight has remodeled thinking and practice in the field of penology and correction. Sociology has demonstrated beyond doubt that the roots of crime are not in the germ plasm, but rather in the family–social setting in which the child is reared.

A society which knows this can no longer be punitive and be just. Society itself is before the bar of justice as long as a punitive approach is employed. This is sound and accepted sociological knowledge. It is far from being in universal application in penal practice, but reformation is in process. It began with the humane tactics of the juvenile court and is being extended to the area of adult rehabilitation.

Sociological knowledge has helped spark slum clearance and the playground movement, and has bolstered reform in divorce law. It has helped destroy the old type of orphanage, which formed the plot of many a novel of earlier days—a plot in which a witchlike character dominated the formation of personality in the child. It has exposed the reasons for the black market in babies; shown how people act in marriage as they build in the direction of happiness or of the divorce court; provided data which acts as a guide to wise mate selection; and in a thousand other areas of human behavior has provided information and insight that is by and large so far superior to folk wisdom that no one familiar with the general body of sociological knowledge can doubt that it has scientific validity.

This is not to claim that the sociologist never reaches erroneous conclusions. All scientists do. Sometimes their basic premise is wrong; sometimes their techniques. This happens in physics. It happens in chemistry. It happens even more often in sociology. In addition to these common errors of all scientists, the sociologist is more closely identified emotionally with the phenomenon he is studying and must always fight his own folk wisdom.

The writer would be the last to claim that sociology has "arrived" in any final and complete sense. If there is any science standing only on the threshold of a vast field of potential knowledge, certainly it is sociology. Scientists in all areas feel that this is true of their specialty because the area of the unknown is so much greater than the known that they work about the brink of a great chasm of the unknown. Then, too, a single new theoretical approach may undermine much that has been thought to be known and break the ignorance barrier for the next generation. This has happened again and again in geology, astronomy, physics, chemistry. It has happened and will happen in sociology.

The development of the culture concept, with which this book begins the study of sociology, has revolutionized sociology during the years since the 1920's. That the dominating influence of culture on group life, so obvious on every hand, could have been overlooked by the first generation of sociologists seems preposterous, and yet again and again the research-minded person, like the inventor, overlooks the obvious. But as "Boss" Kettering, inventive genius of General Motors, has said, in substance, "You fail 999 times, but if you succeed on the thousandth try, you're in."

Sociology is "in" in the sense that it has opened a vast field of knowledge and behavior to study and has already provided a flash of insight into human behavior previously denied to man. Introductory sociology tries to share this insight, and to give the student some of the conceptual tools and vocabulary by which he may sift folk knowledge with some critical sense in such areas as race, nationality, class relationships, sex statuses, child training practices, personality problems, institutional behavior, world relations, social control, and social change.

SOURCEBOOK READINGS

FREEDMAN, RONALD, AMOS H. HAWLEY, WERNER S. LANDECKER, GERHARD E. LENSKI, and HORACE M. MINER. *Principles of Sociology* (rev. ed.). New York: Henry Holt & Co., Inc., 1956.
  1. STOUFFER, SAMUEL A., "A Study of Attitudes," pp. 12–22.
  2. LAZARSFELD, PAUL F., BERNARD BERELSON, and HAZEL GAUDET, "The People's Choice," pp. 34–52.
  3. LIKERT, RENSIS, "Public Opinion Polls," pp. 52–61.

GITTLER, JOSEPH B. *Social Dynamics*. New York: McGraw-Hill Book Co., Inc., 1952.
  4. GITTLER, JOSEPH B. With illustrative quotations on scientific observations under conditions of starvation from Martin Gumpert, "Sociology, Common Sense and the Scientific Method," pp. 14–19.

KOENIG, SAMUEL, REX D. HOPPER, and FELIKS GROSS. *Sociology: A Book of Readings*. Englewood Cliffs, N.J.: Prentice-Hall, Inc., 1956.
  5. BAIN, READ, "Sociology as a Natural Science," pp. 1–4.
  6. BIERSTEDT, ROBERT, "Social Science and Social Values," pp. 5–10.
  7. BOWMAN, CLAUDE C., "Science Can Evaluate," pp. 10–14.

LEE, ELIZABETH BRYANT, and ALFRED MCCLUNG LEE. *Social Problems in America* (rev. ed.). New York: Henry Holt & Co., Inc., 1955.
  8. SUTHERLAND, EDWIN H., "White-Collar Criminality," pp. 302–7.
  9. BARRON, MILTON L., "The Delinquent: Society or the Juvenile," pp. 307–10.
  10. COHEN, OSCAR, "Social Research and Intergroup Relations," pp. 445–48.
  11. BIERSTEDT, ROBERT, "Social Scientist *and* Citizen," pp. 461–63.
  12. CLARK, KENNETH B., "The Social Scientist as an Expert Witness in Civil Rights Litigation," pp. 470–71.

O'BRIEN, ROBERT W., CLARENCE C. SCHRAG, and WALTER T. MARTIN. *Readings in General Sociology* (2d ed.). Boston: Houghton Mifflin Co., 1957.
  13. GREENWOOD, ERNEST, "Social Science and Social Work: A Theory of Their Relationship," pp. 12–18.
  14. SHAW, CLIFFORD R., "A Delinquent Boy's Own Story," pp. 18–22.
  15. WHYTE, WILLIAM FOOTE, "Corner Boys: A Study of Clique Behavior," pp. 33–39.
  16. CADWALLADER, MERVYN L., "An Experiment in Crisis Interaction," pp. 40–44.
  17. WITMER, HELEN L., and EDITH TUFTS, "The Cambridge-Somerville Youth Study," pp. 44–47.
  18. *U. S. News and World Report*, "Some Practical Consequences of the 1950 Population Changes," pp. 62–65.

SCHULER, EDGAR A., DUANE L. GIBSON, MAUDE L. FIERO, and WILBUR B. BROOKOVER. *Outside Readings in Sociology*. New York: The Thomas Crowell Co., 1956.
  19. LUNDBERG, GEORGE A., "The Transition to Science in Human Relations," pp. 14–20.
  20. RADCLIFFE-BROWN, A. R., "On the Concept of Function in Social Science," pp. 20–25.
  21. STOUFFER, SAMUEL A., "A Study of Attitudes," pp. 25–33.
  22. LAZARSFELD, PAUL F., "What Do Attitude Surveys Tell Us?" pp. 32–35.
  23. USEEM, JOHN, "Recent Trends in Sociology," pp. 36–39.
  24. LEWIS, MYRON F., "Careers in Sociology," pp. 851–59.
  25. "Social Work as a Profession," pp. 859–67.

WILSON, LOGAN, and WILLIAM L. KOLB. *Sociological Analysis*. New York: Harcourt, Brace & Co., Inc., 1949.
  26. WEBER, MAX, "Science as a Vocation," pp. 5–16.
  27. GLUECK, SHELDON, and ELEANOR T. GLUECK, "Predictability and Criminal Justice," pp. 30–43.
  28. STOUFFER, SAMUEL A., "Social Science and the Soldier," pp. 44–51.

FILM LIST

A list of film sources appears at the end of the book as an appendix. The most inclusive current information can be found in the *Educational Film Guide,* published by the H. W. Wilson Company, New York.

Science and Superstition—10 minutes—sound
Illustrates use of the scientific method in showing the inaccuracy of certain superstitions about groundhog day, the rabbit's foot, etc.
Source: Coronet Films.

Scientific Method—12 minutes—sound
Describes the major steps in the process of thinking known as the scientific method; the principles of thought employed by all scientists; the utilization of these principles in everyday living.
Source: Encyclopaedia Britannica Films.

Part I

CULTURE

Chapter 1

The Culture Concept

The ways of men are unique and varied. Although few would quarrel with this observation, still the life of other people seems peculiar and somehow less real and genuine than one's own. To be formed by a culture is to be partial to it. Yet any man could have been formed entirely otherwise, as can be seen from the following remarks.

"A child born and raised among the Hottentots will acquire the habits, the attitudes, the morals of the Hottentots. If a boy is brought up among the head hunters, he will likewise become a head hunter. If he is born and bred in the United States, he will take on the characteristics and peculiarities that distinguish the American. Of course, there is a greater variety of customs and other educational influences among the people of the United States than among the Hottentots or head hunters, but that does not change the principle involved. Furthermore, it does not make much difference whether the child is of the same stock as the people among whom he is raised or not; he will become one of them just the same. . . .

"If now we should make a list of all the beliefs, habits, morals, and institutions of which we have a record as existing and having existed, we will find that at one time or another almost any conceivable practice has been tolerated and even glorified and also been condemned and suppressed. This bewildering diversity of morals and institutions admits of but one explanation, namely, that the decisive factors in molding our conduct are not unchangeable attributes of human nature, but habits acquired under the influence of environment."[1]

For centuries man explored the geographical environment, and the heavenly space beyond. During the last half of the nineteenth

[1] Herman Hilmer, "The Out-look for Civilization," *The Pedagogical Seminary,* Sept. 1924, pp. 247, 248.

century, he undertook the scientific study of the human organism, its functioning, its forces of life and growth, its hereditary potential. Then psychology came of age to probe man's nervous mechanism and delve into his capacities. Psychology learned to measure his potentialities and to understand his performance as a behaving organism.

Psychology made its main contribution during the first twenty-five years of this century. Since then the newer behavior sciences of sociology and anthropology have come of age to explain man as both a culture builder and as a culture product. The culture concept has proved to be the most revolutionary concept of this half-century, comparable in its influence on human thought to the evolutionary hypothesis of the Darwin-produced age in natural science.

The discovery of culture has made man aware, in a sense that he never had been, of moral relativity; that group-approved behavior patterns, the morals of man, are matters of time, place, and circumstances. As suggested by the quotation above, and as William Graham Sumner, author of *Folkways,* declared, the culture of a people can make anything right or anything wrong. And anthropology has shown, by a comparison of cultures, that in one place or another almost anything one can imagine is right, and in still other places, this same behavior is wrong.

The culture concept has also made it clear that what a people is, their culture has made them. To understand them, one must understand their culture, and to understand their culture is to cease to blame them for what they are.

Little wonder that the culture concept, as a philosophical approach to life and human understanding, has been rated the most dynamic invention in the intellectual climate of this century.

Here an anthropologist, Kluckhohn, raises and answers some typical questions about human differences:

Why do the Chinese dislike milk and milk products? Why would the Japanese die willingly in a Banzai charge that seemed senseless to Americans? Why do some nations trace descent through the father, others through the mother, still others through both parents? Not because different peoples have different instincts, not because they were destined by God or Fate to different habits, not because the weather is different in China and Japan and the United States. Sometimes shrewd common sense has an answer that is close to that of the anthropologist: "because they were brought up that way." By "culture" anthropology means the total life way of a people, the social legacy the individual acquires from his group. Or culture can be regarded as that part of the environment that is the creation of man.[2]

[2] By permission from *Mirror for Man* by Clyde Kluckhohn, p. 17. Copyright, 1949, McGraw-Hill Book Co., Inc., New York.

Culture is such an important factor in human life that the study of sociology has become focused about it, and even history must be understood in terms of it. Today, at Yale University, there exists a Cross-Cultural Index, in which the traits of numerous cultures from various parts of the world are catalogued. From this index one can see how alike and how vastly different are the patterns of life by which human beings live. One can find how, for example, many people trace descent through the mother, others through the father, others through both.

These files of the Cross-Cultural Survey show that at least seventy-five of the cultural practices listed—for example, "marriage cere-monies," "life crisis rites," "incest taboos"—are found in every one of the hundreds of cultures analyzed. Yet no two peoples are quite alike in their practices or their reasoning concerning the necessity for the practice. Similarity of patterns here is explained by the fact that members of all human groups share the same bodily structure. And furthermore, as Kluckhohn notes, "All men undergo the same poign-ant life experiences such as birth, helplessness, illness, old age, and death. The biological potentialities of the species are the blocks with which cultures are built. Some patterns of every culture crystal-lize around focuses provided by the inevitables of biology: the dif-ference between the sexes, the presence of persons of different ages, the varying physical strength and skill of the individuals. The facts of nature also limit culture forms."[3]

Even though languages differ, there is a biological limit to sounds the vocal apparatus can make; so there is also some similarity. A language may be built of twenty sounds, or it may use forty; but all languages are built within the limitations of the human vocal ap-paratus.

But it is in their differences that cultures are distinctly human creations. Canaries of similar breed sing much the same tune the world over, for they have only limited capacity for training. So don-keys and cattle "speak" the same language everywhere. But the funeral dirge of the American will make the Eskimo roll in laughter. And the wooing words of the American will leave the South Seas maiden quite unmoved—for she does not know their meaning, unless they are accompanied by certain gestures, and even these may lack meaning there.

Cultural diversity is the result of trial-and-error adjustments made by different peoples in their adaptation to life as they experience it in their different environments. So peoples develop various approved

[3] *Ibid.,* p. 20.

Cultural Traditions
Become Part of Group Life

Rally speeches at a pajama parade

Rally bonfire before the game

Students of the school which loses the game walk to the other school's campus

The meaning of traditions must be understood in their local setting and in a particular aspect of group life. Traditions are always in the making. Herodotus tells of the meeting of two kings. One said, "Let us drink wine together." "But it is not customary for kings of our nations to drink together," the other replied. "A custom must begin somewhere," said the first, and they drank their wine together. (WSC Photo, State College of Washington)

ways of meeting life, and these become for them the meaningful way of life. Their discoveries are then passed on as a heritage to their children.

Culture is the mold into which the human being is cast. It can be any one of many thousands that exist in the world today, and whatever the mold is he will fit it and not any other. Culture is the conditioning mechanism employed by the local group in the building of personality. Here is a striking example of this basic principle of culture, presented by Clyde Kluckhohn.

Some years ago I met in New York City a young man who did not speak a word of English and was obviously bewildered by American ways. By "blood" he was as American as you or I, for his parents had gone from Indiana to China as missionaries. Orphaned in infancy, he was reared by a Chinese family in a remote village. All who met him found him more Chinese than American. The facts of his blue eyes and light hair were less impressive than a Chinese style of gait, Chinese arm and hand movements, Chinese facial expression, and Chinese modes of thought. The biological heritage was American, but the cultural training had been Chinese. He returned to China. Another example of another kind: I once knew a trader's wife in Arizona who took a somewhat devilish interest in producing a cultural reaction. Guests who came her way were often served delicious sandwiches filled with a meat that seemed to be neither chicken nor tuna fish yet was reminiscent of both. To queries she gave no reply until each had eaten his fill. She then explained that what they had eaten was not chicken, not tuna fish, but the rich, white flesh of freshly killed rattlesnakes. The response was instantaneous—vomiting, often violent vomiting. A biological process is caught in a cultural web.[1]

Culture can instill in man such patterns of living and belief, during a brief span of time, that one without anthropological experience or knowledge might well conclude that nature has built in man an elaborate framework of mechanistic patterns that prepare him well for life. During the era of "instinct" psychology, and before Americans had so much opportunity to observe the ways of other peoples, many thought that much of what is now known to be learned was built-in by nature.

The genius of man's achievement, of his ability to improve his life and extend his range in the natural environment, lies in his culture-building potentiality, not in inborn mechanisms. In fact, man's very superiority in nature is attributable to the culture-building propensity. Change such as nature takes millions of years to accomplish in animal life through mutation, culture can accomplish very quickly. The bird's pattern of nest-building goes on and on in instinct, and only a biological mutation can change it, but man's

[1] *Ibid.,* p. 19.

home-building has assumed almost an infinite variety of patterns, and the end is not yet. New styles appear constantly to modify past patterns.

In a real sense culture emancipates man from his biological heritage, helps him rise above its limitations and supplement it by invented devices. Culture is the distinctly human reality which makes man the master of his universe and which helps him rise above the biological limitations of other creatures.

If man is destroyed, it will not likely be by natural calamity. Of all creatures on earth, he is the most competent to mediate and manage nature and its elements. But he is at the mercy of his culture. This fact has been vividly portrayed by an imaginative writer who, some years ago, visualized modern urban man stripped of his culture. Here is his account:

> If the earth were struck by one of Mr. [H. G.] Wells' comets, and if, in consequence, every human being now alive were to lose all the knowledge and habits which he had acquired from preceding generations (though retaining unchanged all his own powers of invention, and memory, and habituation), nine-tenths of the inhabitants of London or New York would be dead in a month, and 99 per cent of the remaining tenth would be dead in six months. They would have no language to express their thoughts, and no thoughts but their revery. They could not read notices, or drive motors or horses. They would wander about, led by the inarticulate cries of a few naturally dominant individuals, drowning themselves, as thirst came on, in hundreds at the riverside landing places, looting those shops where the smell of decaying food attracted them, and perhaps at the end stumbling on the expedient of cannibalism. Even in the country districts men could not invent, in time to preserve their lives, methods of growing food, or taming animals, or making fire, or so clothing themselves as to endure the northern winter. An attack of constipation or measles would be invariably fatal. After a few years mankind would almost certainly disappear from the northern and temperate zones. The white races would probably become extinct everywhere. A few primitive races might live on fruit and small animals in those fertile tropical regions where the human species was originally evolved until they had slowly accumulated a new social heritage.[5]

Today, man has in hand a single invention capable of destroying much of civilization and rendering life on earth impossible. It is the product of western-industrial culture—an invention of man.

In a day of world-wide contacts, of extensive travel by ordinary citizens, and of governmental and economic activities carried out on a global scale, the culture concept is important to understanding in dealing with other peoples. To understand that other peoples are

[5] Graham Wallas, *Our Social Heritage* (New Haven: Yale University Press, 1921), p. 80.

a product of their culture, as we are of our own, is the beginning of wisdom in dealing with others.

During World War II, many flyers who parachuted into strange places, whether jungles or distant islands, learned the significance of the culture concept very quickly. For they found themselves among peoples whose language they did not understand, whose ways of life they did not know; yet they had to make their wants known and learn to adjust. Survival itself depended on their willingness and ability to understand and to fit into a new culture, and to accept the native ways of dealing with the local environment.

Young people going into the army or entering the foreign service need to understand the culture concept. The traveler, tradesman, scientist, teacher, and government official who is aware of culture differences is more likely to be sympathetic, curious, and interested about the ways of life of people everywhere than to be critical, stand-offish, haughty, or condescending. If he applies the culture concept intelligently, he will become aware that other peoples consider him just as peculiar, because of his way of life, as he once considered them, and, if he is sufficiently objective, he will have to conclude, as he observes patterns of life of various people in far-off places, that particular elements of their culture may be a better adaptation to their time and place than his own culture could possibly be.

Even among the most primitive of peoples, there is amazing ingenuity and cleverness employed in attacking the environment, and in working out a system of life and human relationships that is effective and that maintains coordinated social interaction.

The culture concept is an essential tool in this day when the United States is undertaking world leadership. Those who comprehend the culture concept can approach different peoples with an understanding previous administrators could not command.

Understanding the culture concept, seeing and appreciating the meaning of the culture of other peoples, is necessary to an understanding of one's own culture and its importance. Only those who have been made culture-conscious can truly analyze their own culture and see its meaning for them. As anthropologist Ralph Linton has said, "Those who know no culture other than their own, cannot know their own."[6]

Finally, the culture concept is a key to self-understanding. One who understands the culture concept will see that many of his own attitudes, activities, habit patterns, tastes, and aspirations are derived

[6] Ralph Linton, *The Study of Man* (New York: Appleton-Century-Crofts, Inc., 1936).

from the unique cultural system of his own line of ancestors, particularly that of his own family, for every family in a certain sense is the product of a unique family culture. Of course, he will also find in his own behavior the unique "subculture" of his own sex. The United States, even with its approach to sex equality, still is a world in which there is a distinct male subculture and a female subculture, and to be a male is to be to some extent an outsider to female culture, and vice versa.

Because of its importance and significance, this study of sociology begins with the study of culture, a thing of man's making, which in turn shapes him and his destiny.

FILM LIST FOR PART I

A list of film sources appears at the close of the text as an appendix. The most inclusive current information can be found in the *Educational Film Guide*, published by the H. W. Wilson Company, New York.

African Tribes—12 minutes—sound—color
Shows four tribes of Africa: Bamburi, Ifi Pygmies, Mangbetu and Rendilli. *Source:* Simmel-Meservey, Inc.

A Giant People (The Watussi of Africa)—11 minutes—sound
Depicts cultural development of a pastoral–agricultural tribe in the Rwanda region of Africa. *Source:* Encyclopaedia Britannica Films.

A People of the Congo (The Mangbetu)—11 minutes—sound
Detailed study of the cultural development of primitive agricultural group. Shows their food, homes, art work, music, dancing, etc. *Source:* Encyclopaedia Britannica Films.

Pygmies of Africa—22 minutes—sound
Illustrates the folkways and mores of an extremely primitive group of African Pygmies. *Source:* Encyclopaedia Britannica Films.

People of the Potlatch—19 minutes—sound—color
Well-photographed sequence of how West Coast Indians live. Shows costumes, dances, music, totems, and includes the potlatch celebration, a native tribal feast. *Source:* Ideal Pictures Corporation.

Hausa Village—22 minutes—sound
Daily life and customs of Mohammedan villagers in Northern Nigeria; wedding ceremony and building a house. *Source:* British Information Service.

Man and His Culture—15 minutes—sound
Excellent illustrations of variability and uniformity and all the major cultural concepts and processes. *Source:* Encyclopaedia Britannica Films.

Ancient World Inheritance—10 minutes—sound—color
Illustration of the inheritance of modern civilization from older civilizations such as the Egyptian, Babylonian, and Assyrian. Relates modern to ancient civilization. *Source:* Coronet Films.

Walkabout—17 minutes—sound—color
Australian aborigines. *Source:* Australian News and Information Bureau.

American Anniversary—15 minutes—sound
Shows the rise of an immigrant to a place of significance in his community. *Source:* National Association of Manufacturers.

Greenie—10 minutes—sound

A Polish refugee boy becomes part of the American scene. *Source:* Teaching Film Custodians, Inc.

The Town—2 reels—sound

A film visit to Madison, Indiana, revealing the many ways in which American customs are related to the rest of the world. *Source:* Office of War Information.

Last of the Pagans—14 minutes

Deals with native customs, including marriage by capture in French Polynesia. *Source:* Teaching Film Custodians, Inc.

String of Beads—20 minutes

A story of life on a tea plantation in Assam, showing work and play, betrothal, marriage, and family life. *Source:* United World Films, Inc.

Chapter 2

The Nature of Culture

From the preceding chapter, it may be concluded that:

1. Culture is man's distinctly human attribute. It is beyond the physical, beyond the mental, beyond the social; it is a creation of man passed on and continuous, giving his experience continuity through the generations. It is superorganic (beyond the organic). Peoples may come, peoples may go, but culture goes on forever.

2. In the unique world of devised patterns and invented material objects, man lives his social life on a level above the beasts of which he is a part by physical heritage. With his culture, he mediates the geographical environment, inhabiting the most inhospitable areas and warping nature's resources to his will.

3. Finally, man is man because of culture. In the culture is his religion, his political system, his technological empire. Culture is the gigantic matrix in which is cast the form, not only of man's personality, but of his social relations.

It will now be seen that culture is a unique aspect of the life of every people on earth. It molds them to its peculiar pattern. Because it does so, they understand each other and live a common life. Because it does so, they cannot be fully understood by any other people, nor can they accept as proper and appropriate the ways of peoples of other cultures.

CULTURE AS ENVIRONMENT

One of the classics of English literature is that of Daniel Defoe which takes his character, Robinson Crusoe, and places him on an island where he is almost completely removed from his cultural environment. With the few tools he was able to salvage from the ship, without companions except the cat he rescued, he begins life on the island. With his tools and memory he starts building a cultural environment like that he has known before—a shelter, a boat, a garden, and later, when he captures Friday, he is building an Englishman by teaching the savage the English language, manners, and religion.

In this story, Defoe showed the tremendous importance of the cultural environment by indicating how a man misses it when it is taken from him. As long as he has all the material objects of his civilization—for us, automobiles, chairs, tables, pencils, typewriters, houses and ships, books and art, to mention but a few of the thousands at our convenience—their possession seems so natural that he scarcely realizes that he lives in an environment of things made by man himself. He takes with equal naturalness the language, etiquette, customs, and laws that provide for him a framework of intangible man-made patterns by which his life is regulated. *Culture* is a collective name which embraces this entire man-made environment—language, art, science, custom, morals, religion, tools, machines, houses, and domesticated plants and animals.

Material and Nonmaterial Culture. The cultural environment is divided into two aspects: (1) *material culture,* which is composed of tools and machines, all man-made tangible objects; and (2) *nonmaterial culture,* which consists of the customs passed down by man from generation to generation through training, all man-made intangible patterns for living.

Among primitives the cultural environment is relatively simple. A bow and arrow may be the most dangerous weapon of war. Compare this with the weapons of modern nations which consume billions of dollars, which call for the inventive genius of the best trained scientists, and which are capable of such destruction as taking the lives of tens of thousands in a single explosion. Among primitives, customs and traditions are uniform throughout the group and are administered by a chief. Among moderns there are innumerable laws enforced by administrative bodies; for each activity there are customs which vary for each segment of society; and such an elaborate code of etiquette is maintained that it must be recorded in guidebooks.

In comparing cultures, a person superficially acquainted with them is likely to rate them in terms of superior material culture. For example, an American soldier in Los Negros of the Admiralty Islands during World War II wanted to find out how the native rated the Americans and the Japanese, both of whom had been there. Reticent at first, his native friend finally gave him this answer: "Jap no good. Him no gottum truck. He work hard."

CULTURE AS CIVILIZATION

Culture is another word for *civilization*. Sociologists would have no reason to use the former were it not that the latter has come to have a more narrow meaning in many circles. People have come to think of the word civilization as being applicable only to those peoples who represent the higher levels of cultural development. Actually, all peoples are civilized if one is thinking of civilization in terms of man's creating material objects and nonmaterial patterns. All peoples have culture. Many peoples have no machines, only the simplest of tools. They may be called savages or primitive (pre-literate) by more advanced peoples, but even savages have a culture. They are often highly advanced in skills of handicraft, perhaps in hand-wrought art, such as pottery or weaving. They may have no written language, yet their traditions are passed on by word of mouth through centuries.

CULTURE AS A HERITAGE

Culture is the heritage which man passes on from generation to generation through training. It is also the heritage of material goods accumulated in the handiwork of man by which each new generation profits from the efforts of the old.

Humanity throughout the ages has been leaving to its descendants its lifetime accomplishments, the results of all its former handiwork, material objects built by each succeeding generation. Man improves upon the inventions of his forebears and passes them on in turn to his children. Similarly, he passes on a philosophy of life, religion, and welfare which his children will use and pass on again.

Because culture is passed on from generation to generation, with such additions and modifications as each new generation makes, it is often called the *cultural heritage*. It is, in fact, a rich heritage which lifts man above the level of beasts in that animals begin life where their forebears began, as far as behavior patterns are concerned, and, for the most part, as far as material objects are concerned. Man, on the other hand, begins with the rich accumulation of all of the patterns and material cultural objects that the ingenuity of his ancestors has provided.

The uses of fire come down from the distant past. Through centuries man tinkered with the making of fire and developing of improved methods for handling it. Through its use he is able to live in many natural environments which would otherwise be hostile to him. Consider the metals used for all the numerous gadgets and devices which are so much a part of modern civilization. The use of metals dates back to the time when man found that copper could be shaped and used more efficiently than stone. Then came iron, steel, and all the other metals of current usage. Think of the wheel and its importance in our daily life. If one stops to analyze, he finds that the modern cultural environment is full of wheels. They are the basis of a timepiece no less than of factories and transportation. History does not go back far enough to tell us who first developed the wheel, but the author has hunted with African natives who still do not use it. They move on foot and carry burdens on their backs, with a bark strap across their foreheads to support the load.

Take the matter of reckoning time. It remained for modern timepieces to develop great precision in this field. Yet the calendar far predates our epoch of history. It is a part of a long cultural heritage.

One could go on to discuss the various domesticated animals which are so important to modern man, and the numerous plants which he has learned to cultivate. These are the culmination of husbandry practiced by remote peoples. In all of these aspects of cultural environment modern man is a debtor to the past. But he also adds to the cultural heritage which will be passed on to posterity. Thus it is constantly being enriched, with each generation, now as always, inheriting more culture than they create.

Someone has said that although Aristotle, the Greek philosopher, was the greatest mind of his day, he knew less than the average eighth-grade schoolboy of today. If the writer was thinking of knowledge in terms of laws of engineering, such as the transmission of sound through the ether waves, or of the numerous scientific principles that find usage in our everyday mechanical devices, then there is no question that the eighth-grade schoolboy has a field of understanding greater than that of Aristotle. The example is a striking way of pointing out the difference in the cultural heritage on which Aristotle had to draw and that of the youth of today.

Our forefathers dreamed of flying. Modern man does it. Not that he is smarter than they, but technical knowledge has accumulated since their time, and man today profits from these additions to the culture heritage. The rate at which the cultural heritage is built today makes certain that the children of tomorrow and their children after them will perform feats in the air and on the earth that will make present means of transportation seem as ancient to them as horse-and-buggy travel now seems.

THE ORIGIN OF CULTURE

Man's first task in any environment is to live. Through trial and error he must learn to provide himself with food and, if the climate

is rigorous, with clothing and shelter. In his attempt to meet the
needs of life in any environment, he immediately begins to invent.
If he is near water and the water is teeming with fish, the problem
is to catch the fish for food. He may attempt numerous methods.
Perhaps he throws stones at them, if the water is shallow, and succeeds in dazing one now and then and capturing it. If the task is
more difficult, he may resort to religious incantations and ritual of
various sorts in order first to win the favor of the gods and enlist their
help. Then he may resort to new physical methods of attacking fish.
He may try clubs for beating the water, but if the water is deep this
will prove futile. And so he sharpens a stick and jabs at them with his
crude spear. If this works, spearing may become his method of catching fish. If the water is very deep, however, this too will fail. In this
case, he may try to coax them to the surface by feeding them. This
may not work. If the climate is warm, he may try to dive after them
and catch them in his hands. But fish are elusive. If he has learned to
make cord of bark strips and has any kind of metal or bone in his
culture, he may try to shape a hook, put bait on it, and catch fish in
that manner. If he has learned basket-weaving and the weaving of
nets, he may try to chase or bait fish into the basket or net. The
knowledge which he gains from his experiments is the beginning of
a new element of culture.

Folkways. If the people are intelligent and have sufficient culture
traits to try various methods of fishing, sooner or later they will learn
how to catch fish, for fish have never yet been able to consistently
outwit man. The usual consequence of success is that the tribe adopts
the particular method or methods that have proved effective in meeting this need. Such adopted methods are called by sociologists *folkways*, meaning the ways of doing things which become customary in
a particular group of people or folk.

Folkways of mankind are as diverse as the tribes of people that inhabit the earth because through trial and error, in various environments, peoples have stumbled upon different effective ways of meeting their needs of life. Man tends to keep the ways of doing things
that have proved effective for him and for his ancestors, and to stop
trying new methods because he already has a system that works.

This is, of course, much more true of pre-literate peoples, who may
fear the new once a workable method has been found, than it is of
peoples in a culture like our own where we tend to encourage invention through scientific research. But even modern peoples often cling
to folkways when it would be quite easy to develop new and better
ways of doing things if they were not already prejudiced by the folk-

Dishes- and Clothes-Washing Folkways of Java

Though not up to our standards of convenience and sanitation, these methods are as old as human history. Dishes and clothes must be cleaned—and folkways for washing them develop everywhere. (Standard Oil Company, N.J.)

ways. Folkways not only become man's habitual ways of doing things, but sooner or later, as custom accumulates and the established folkways are passed from one generation to another, they come to be considered the right way.

There is some logic in clinging to old ways, especially among pre-literate peoples, where to experiment with the new often is to court

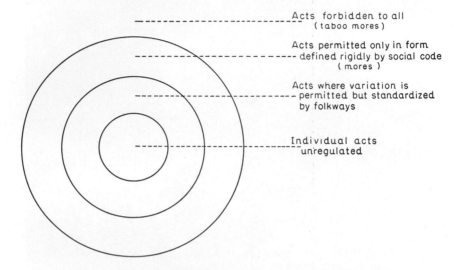

Acts forbidden to all
(taboo mores)

Acts permitted only in form
defined rigidly by social code
(mores)

Acts where variation is
permitted but standardized
by folkways

Individual acts
unregulated

How Culture Defines Human Liberties

danger and sometimes even disaster. Modern man, with a scientific approach to natural phenomena, tends to experiment on a small scale, thereby protecting himself from catastrophe. If he wants to know what will happen when he mixes two types of elements together, he uses only a small quantity so that if the thing is going to explode it will explode in such quantity that no harm will be done. Primitives have no such means of laboratory experimentation; hence, to tinker with new ways of handling nature is often a risk. There are also psychological elements involved. Being *animistic* in religious philosophy—that is, attributing life and spirit to inanimate objects—primitives feel that their tinkering with nature invites the special hazard of offending the gods and courting their displeasure.

Mores. Certain folkways become elevated to the position of *mores*. Mores (the word is always used in the plural) are ways of doing things which carry with them an element of obligation. They differ from folkways in that a folkway is optional; it is considered the proper way to do things, the most efficient way, and the accepted way. But mores involve a sense of obligation not a part of folkways.

To state it somewhat differently, mores are folkways that have been rationalized to the point where they are identified with the welfare of the group. They become the philosophies of welfare. Mores may take the form of *taboos*, which forbid the doing of certain things, perhaps eating a certain food or carrying out certain practices: for example, the Jewish taboo on the eating of animals with cloven hoof unless they chew a cud; or the Puritan taboo against carrying on certain types of work or social activities on the Sabbath.

Mores may also be positive in that they require specific kinds of behavior. Among certain early primitive tribes, for example, men were required by the mores to go into a dark cave before the hunt and carry on religious ceremonies before a drawing of the animal to be hunted. Any man who would go out to hunt a dangerous wild beast without first observing this religious ceremony would be considered an enemy, as he would be disregarding group welfare by risking the disfavor of the gods, which could bring disaster not only on himself but on all his hunting companions.

Or, to take another example, among the Plains Indians the mores forbade hunting buffalo alone. If a scout spotted a herd of bison, he was obligated to report to the tribe. Underlying this practice was the fact that an individual hunter could as readily scare away an entire herd of bison as could the entire tribe. And the tribe itself might perish from hunger as a result. The solution was to organize a hunt and surround the herd. From that point on, each individual was free to kill as many bison as he could.

Comparable in logic are the mores of Reno, Nevada, today with regard to the residence period for obtaining divorce. In watching the "divorce mill" there, one gains the impression that the lawyer representing the client and the client himself are extremely careless in formulating the reasons they believe a divorce should be granted. But there is one point on which the court always demands absolute accuracy: the period of residence in the state of Nevada. A lawyer who is convicted of perjury on this point is likely to be sent to prison for a long term, for to permit perjury here would "kill the goose that lays the golden egg." The court, the divorce lawyers, the hotels, the gambling resorts and other recreational centers, the merchants and rooming-house owners—all depend on the residence period for their income.

Today, after centuries of rationalization, modesty is in the mores, yet clothes did not first originate for modesty's sake, but for art's sake. It is so much easier to ornament the body with clothes than to have to do it by tattooing the skin or painting it as savages without clothes do. To the extent that modern women have exposed their bodies, they have had to resort to increased ornamentation of the body itself: with open-toed shoes, painted toenails are necessary; with ungloved hands, painted fingernails; with the unclothed shoulder in the evening gown, tints and powders to add luster to the skin and to give it that "love-to-touch" softness.

Whether logical or not, every people has a set of mores which are identified with group welfare. Whether or not they are actually related to group welfare is beside the point. If the group thinks so, it makes the behavior compulsory for all individuals. In modern cultures many mores have been incorporated into laws, which are more formal definitions of what an individual must or must not do. Penalties follow violation as they always follow disregard of mores. The most effective laws are those backed by mores, by universal attitudes on the part of people that certain types of acts are against group welfare and, therefore, to be condemned. Our mores thus condemn infanticide (that is, taking the life of infants), the eating of human flesh, and bigamy.

Where laws are passed running counter to the mores, enforcement is very difficult. The desegregation issue shows this clearly. In the Deep South segregation is in the mores.

William Graham Sumner, originator of the concepts of folkways and mores, held that the mores of a people can make anything right or wrong. To state it somewhat differently, anything is right in a culture that is so designated by its mores. Here are Sumner's views on the matter.

"At every turn we find new evidence that the mores can make anything right. What they do is that they cover a usage in dress, language, behavior, manners, etc., with the mantle of current custom, and give it regulation and limits within which it becomes unquestionable. . . .

"The mores come down to us from the past. Each individual is born into them as he is born into the atmosphere, and he does not reflect on them or criticize them any more than a baby analyzes the atmosphere before he begins to breathe it. Each one is subjected to the influence of the mores, and formed by them, before he is capable of reasoning about them.

". . . We learn the mores as unconsciously as we learn to walk and eat and breathe. . . . The justification of them is that when we wake to consciousness of life, we find them facts which already hold us in the bonds of tradition, custom and habit.

". . . We must conceive of the mores as a vast system of usages, covering the whole of life, and serving all its interests; also containing in themselves their own justification by tradition and use and wont, and approved by mystic sanctions until, by rational reflection, they develop their own philosophical and ethical generalizations, which are elevated into "principles" of truth and right. They coerce and restrict the new born generation. They do not stimulate to thought, but the contrary. The thinking is already done and is embodied in the mores. They never contain any provision for their own amendment. They are not questions, but the answers, to the problem of life. . . ."[1]

The building of folkways and tools to carry them out, and the development of philosophies of welfare—mores—illustrate the way the cultural environment has been gradually built. The process is far more ancient than recorded history and will continue to the end of man.

TRAITS, THE UNITS OF CULTURE

The simplest unit of culture is the *culture trait*. In so breaking down culture to its smallest part, the sociologist is doing what all science does. Biology begins with the simple unit called the living cell, and physics with the atom and its parts, electrons and protons. Psychology begins with the neuron. A culture trait may be a material object, such as the lead of a pencil, or a nonmaterial trait, such as the superstitious fear of a black cat crossing the road.

Culture traits have three distinct characteristics: (1) Each trait has a history. Its history may be short or long depending on when the trait was invented. (2) Traits are *mobile*, that is, they tend to spread as human beings who use them scatter over the face of the earth or contact peoples at a distance. (3) Culture traits tend to form clusters known as culture complexes.

History of Culture Traits. Inside the band of a man's straw or felt hat is a little bow at the place where the inner leather band joins. It serves no purpose today, but if one were to trace its history, he would follow it back to a time when hats were made in only one size and there was a drawstring in the band which could be let out or pulled up to make the hat fit the man. The culture trait survives even though today it has no purpose except a questionable ornamental one. There is a buttonhole in the lapel of a man's coat. It is usually sewed shut, so one can scarcely insert even a rose stem in it. This culture trait harks back to a time when coats were drawn about the neck and buttoned. The niche in the lapel of a man's coat dates back to the same practice. It left room for the dandy to show his shirt and tie.

[1] W. G. Sumner, *Folkways* (Boston: Ginn & Co., 1906), pp. 76–79, 521. Used by permission of Ginn & Co.

If such incidental and nowadays useless culture traits have such an interesting history, what of such an important culture trait as building fire? Indeed, its history goes back many millenniums to the time when fire was started by friction, and before that to a time when it was preserved and carried when lightning or other natural causes had started a blaze. Today if one were to study the history of fire-making he would have to study its improvement throughout the centuries until the time when the sulphur match was invented.

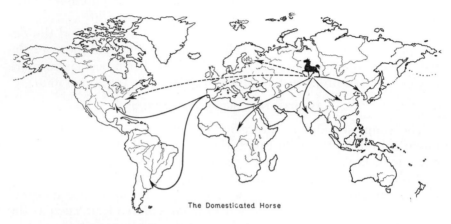

The Domesticated Horse

Diffusion of a Culture Trait Throughout the World

Adapted from Man and Culture, *by Clark Wissler, p. 120. The Thomas Crowell Co., 1923.*

Diffusion of Culture Traits.[2] Culture traits tend to be mobile, that is, to spread or diffuse beyond the point of origin. Take the domesticated horse as a case in point (see map). It is believed that the horse was first domesticated in Syria or Babylonia, certainly in the Near East. The use of the domesticated horse spread westward till the Spaniards, probably De Soto's band, introduced it during the conquest of America to the southern plains of the United States. Being well adapted to the Great Plains, the horse multiplied in a wild state until it had spread throughout the area. Whether the Indians learned to domesticate the horse from early conquerors or developed domestication on their own is a debated question. But certainly when the white man met and attempted to conquer them, he found them already using the fleet-footed Indian pony as a means of attack and escape.

[2] Diffusion is the topic of Chapter 5.

THE CULTURE COMPLEX

Culture traits tend to *cluster into complexes*. They rarely have much usefulness to man individually, but grouped into units of human use they are of great value. Man no sooner domesticates the horse than he improves his riding by building some kind of saddle. Later, he develops one device or another to make the horse a beast of burden. The Indians, not having a wheel in their culture, developed the travois, which was made of two sticks joined together and laid across the horse's back with the down ends dragging the ground. This permitted the horse to bear greater burdens than could ordinarily be placed on its back. The Englishman, with the wheel in his culture, developed the wagon and carriage to be powered by the horse, thus developing a more elaborate travel–transportation complex. When a group of culture traits are clustered in such a way that they have a key place in human use, they are called a *culture complex*.

A cluster of related culture traits is seen today in the American football game. The football complex involves not only the material culture traits such as the ball, the field, the goal posts, the bleachers, the stadium, tickets, the trinkets, scorecards, and chrysanthemums that are sold in connection with the game, and so on, but also an elaborate set of rules, customs, folkways, and even superstitions that center around the great American college game.

Modern culture has developed what may be termed a "punctuality complex." A primitive will be content to say, "We meet tomorrow when the sun is so high," as he points to the horizon. He will not be disturbed if he has to wait two or three hours until his friend appears. Not so with modern man. He has exact timepieces, punch clocks, speedometers, and split-second radio timing. The punctuality complex tends to make us all anxiety-prone. One of the best descriptions of the effects of this culture complex on modern man is that of a former railroad man turned sociologist. He writes:

. . . All those who have direct responsibility for the actual operations of trains must carry a fine timepiece which will gain or lose not more than forty seconds in two weeks and which must be cleaned and regulated twice a year by a railroad watch inspector. A delay of thirty seconds in leaving a terminal calls for explanation, five minutes' delay means investigation, and a half hour gives apoplexy to every official from the superintendent to the lowest foreman. On single-track roads where trains meet at passing tracks, thirty seconds' delay means that one of the trains will be almost a half mile from a passing track when the other reaches it, and that means delay of a second train, with possible misunderstanding and resultant disaster. . . .

As "time marches on," its rhythm is set, not by organic impulse, but by the clacking of wheels on rail joints, the clatter of a telegraph key, and the distant whistle of a train departing "on time."[3]

One could list hundreds of culture complexes in modern culture, all of which represent an elaborate grouping of related culture traits—the "baked-bean complex," if one lives in Boston, for example; or the "harvest complex," if one lives in a wheat-growing area; and so on with numerous groups of related cultural traits which involve material objects and a set of customs and traditions representing the practices and beliefs that center around a particular set of social activities.

Some complexes also could be broken down into components; for example, the transportation complex could be broken down into numerous minor complexes: air travel, boat travel, rail travel, automobile travel, etc.

THE CULTURE PATTERN

Culture complexes tend to form a *culture pattern*. Every culture is unique because within it certain clusters of traits are exaggerated out of proportion to their development in other civilizations. These outstanding culture complexes become the distinguishing features by which the major cultures of the world can be identified.

If one were to point out the particular kinds of complexes in American culture that distinguish it from other cultures, he would probably mention three or four complexes which stand out in bold relief—democracy with universal education, efficient assembly-line methods of production, and Christianity. If one, similarly, wanted to characterize the culture of Indians, he would mention Hinduism and the philosophy of nonresistance which made Gandhi a powerful figure in his day. He might also cite the primitive hoe methods of land cultivation.

If, on the other hand, one were describing a culture pattern of the original Plains Indians, he would have to do it in terms of the "buffalo complex" around which their manner of life was built. If one were thinking of the culture pattern of the civilization of the Indians of the Pacific Northwest, he would have to describe it in terms of the "salmon complex," for most of their customs, religious ceremonies, and material traits were built around the catching of salmon. Even multiple births are significant in this culture com-

[3] W. F. Cottrell, "Of Time and the Railroader," *American Sociological Review*, 4: 190–98 (April 1939).

plex, for today the British Columbia Indians think twins are gifted with uncanny power to attract the migratory salmon into the nets.

A visitor to East Africa today would find the life and ceremony of most of the tribes centering in cattle. Brides are purchased with cattle. A man's prestige and wealth are measured in terms of head of cattle owned. Cattle enter into eating, religious, and burial ceremonies in most tribes. The following from anthropologist Melville J. Herskovits's study of this area is illustrative.

"The Nandi (one of several tribes studied) . . . are also known for their cattle. They do agricultural work, but there may be no mixing of the two kinds of food (plants and meat of cattle). They are careful in the extreme that these do not mix in the stomach, for should this happen, the cows would be materially harmed. The Nandi young men care for the cattle, living by themselves at the grazing grounds away from the married people. When an animal is slaughtered, or when one dies, and there is meat to be eaten, it cannot be consumed in a vulgar way. There are special huts, placed in the woods, to which the men repair for their feasts. All the agricultural work is done by the women, although the men clear the ground for them. The ceremonies attendant on [the] . . . capture [of cattle] or when they have been struck by lightning, the part they play in the occasions of crisis in the lives of their masters, and the constant care and thought given to them, show their importance for an understanding of the culture of these people."[4]

The culture pattern, then, refers to the arrangement of complexes within a civilization which makes the civilization unique or distinctive. It is the design of a civilization. Sociologists often use the term *ethos* to describe the peculiar characteristics of a civilization that set it apart from all others.

THE UNIVERSAL CULTURE SCHEME

If one were to travel around the world, he would gain the impression that in no two places are manners of life alike. And it is true that cultures differ in almost every detail with regard to the peculiar manner in which man expresses his social life and his general behavior. Culture has great variability from place to place and people to people. But are there uniformities within a broad framework by which cultures can be classified?

Clark Wissler, an American anthropologist, developed the fol-

[4] Melville J. Herskovits, "The Cattle Complex in East Africa," *American Anthropologist,* 28:259 (Jan.–March 1926).

lowing classification according to which most cultures, whether primitive or advanced, can be grouped:

The Culture Scheme[5]

1. Speech
    Languages, writing systems, etc.
2. Material Traits
    a. Food habits
    b. Shelter
    c. Transportation and travel
    d. Dress
    e. Utensils, tools, etc.
    f. Weapons
    g. Occupations and industries
3. Art
    Carving, painting, drawing, music, etc.
4. Mythology and Scientific Knowledge
5. Religious Practices
    a. Ritualistic forms
    b. Treatment of the sick
    c. Treatment of the dead
6. Family and Social Systems
    a. The forms of marriage
    b. Methods of reckoning relationship
    c. Inheritance
    d. Social control
    e. Sports and games
7. Property
    a. Real and Personal
    b. Standards of value and exchange
    c. Trade
8. Government
    a. Political forms
    b. Judicial and legal procedures
9. War

It is immediately recognized that in advanced civilizations such an outline has comparatively little meaning because some of these broad categories include so many things that one would have to break them down into a dozen subclassifications to make them meaningful. Nonetheless, Wissler's universal culture scheme does suggest a uniformity in outline of cultures in all times and places.

This classification would be valuable not only to any student who was going to study a primitive tribe but also to one approach-

[5] Clark Wissler, *Man and Culture* (New York: The Thomas Crowell Co., 1923), p. 74. Wissler called it the universal culture pattern, but this term is too confusing here where culture pattern has been used with a different meaning.

ing a study of his own modern civilization.[6] To study modern culture, he would probably want to add to this list education, which certainly is on a par with many of the other major culture complexes listed here. Presumably Wissler omitted it because education, as something separate from family and social life, scarcely exists among primitive peoples. One might well wonder also whether mythology and scientific knowledge have not become so widely separated in the modern world that there is little logic in classifying them together. Perhaps today one should also include a classification for technology, since it has become so prominent a phase of western culture.

SIMILARITY OF CULTURE PATTERNS

At Yale University, anthropologist George P. Murdock and his staff have studied hundreds of cultures, past and present, and indexed them under the headings of housing, finance, funeral practices, sex patterns, education, religion, etc. Microfilm copies of this Cross-Cultural Index are used by researchers and students in key libraries throughout the country. This project effectively employed the universal culture scheme in its work.

Why is there such standardization in all cultures? Human beings everywhere possess the same biological capacities. Culture-building is limited to particular kinds of activity and takes a certain direction, regardless of the accidents of history or of variations in local geographical circumstances. Human biology sets the limit to invention and therefore dictates that only certain culture complexes are possible. Anthropologist Murdock has assembled a list of cultural items found in all cultures studied in his attempt to cross-index civilizations. Here are some of the items: age-grading, athletic sports, bodily adornment, calendar, cleanliness, training, community organization, cooking, cooperative labor, cosmology, courtship, dancing, decorative art, divination, division of labor, dream interpretation, education, eschatology, ethics, ethnobotany, etiquette, faith healing, family, feasting, fire-making, folklore, food taboos, funeral rites, games, gestures, gift-giving, government, greetings, hair styles, hospitality, housing, hygiene, incest taboos, inheritance rules, joking, kin-groups, kinship, nomenclature, language, law, luck superstitions, magic, marriage, mealtimes, medicine, modesty concerning natural functions, mourning, music, mythology, numerals, obstetrics, penal sanctions, personal names, population policy,

---

[6] The Lynd studies actually followed the Wissler scheme with modifications; see Robert Lynd and Helen Lynd, *Middletown* (New York: Harcourt, Brace & Co., Inc., 1929), and *Middletown in Transition* (New York: Harcourt, Brace & Co., Inc., 1937).

postnatal care, pregnancy usages, property rights, propitiation of supernatural beings, puberty customs, religious ritual, residence rules, sexual restrictions, soul concepts, status differentiation, surgery, tool-making, trade, visiting, weaning, and weather control.[7]

The germ plasm necessarily limits man's ability to vary the scheme of culture-building, but the fact remains that the present hereditary characteristics carried in the germ plasm are sufficient to provide a variety of cultures so complex and so different from one part of the world to another that no man could begin to encompass their variety, even in a limited field like language, in a lifetime.

THE DEVELOPMENT AND SIGNIFICANCE OF DIVERSE CULTURES

Origin of Diverse Cultures. Assuming that man originated at one particular place on the face of the earth, which is the accepted view, the question may well be asked, "How has the almost infinite diversity of cultures been developed in various parts of the world?" The answer is: by *migration* and subsequent *isolation.*

As the various tribes spread out over the surface of the earth, they took with them the original folkways and mores of their people. But in each new natural environment they encountered new situations. In working out their problems of obtaining shelter, food, and clothing, they developed new methods of conquering their environment. In one part of the country, where there were no trees, they could no longer use wood to build shelters. Perhaps they used sod, or, if it was a hilly country, took over caves in the rocky hillsides as dwelling places. In another part of the world, where animals were plentiful, they developed tentlike structures of skins which met their needs, especially if their life was nomadic. They could quickly erect a dwelling, take it down again and carry it with them.

In one part of the world their customs were built around the use of certain types of animal life for food. In other parts of the world they built their culture around fishing, since fishing provided the main source of food supply. In certain locations they struggled with devices for improving land transportation and succeeded in domesticating a particular animal of their environment, perhaps the dog. In other locations they were concerned primarily with navigation, because water travel was the problem to be solved. Through trial and error in various environments, a people who started with a given culture heritage soon developed one far different than the parent cul-

7 George P. Murdock, "The Common Denominator in Cultures," in Ralph Linton, *The Science of Man in the World Crisis* (New York: Columbia University Press, 1945), pp. 123–25.

ture. Through centuries of isolation and further migration, numerous culture patterns developed over the face of the earth.

Anthropologist Ruth Benedict has described this process in this way.

"The course of life and the pressure of environment, not to speak of the fertility of human imagination, provide an incredible number of possible leads, all of which, it appears, may serve a society to live by. There are the schemes of ownership, with the social hierarchy that may be associated with possessions; there are material things and their elaborate technology; there are all the facets of sex life, parenthood and post-parenthood; there are the guilds or cults which may give structure to the society; there is economic exchange; there are the gods and supernatural sanctions. Each one of these and many more may be followed out with a cultural and ceremonial elaboration which monopolizes the cultural energy and leaves small surplus for the building of other traits. Aspects of life that seem to us most important have been passed over with small regard by peoples whose culture, oriented in another direction, has been far from poor. Or the same trait may be so greatly elaborated that we reckon it as fantastic."[8]

CULTURE AREAS

The term *culture area* refers to a geographical territory over which a characteristic culture pattern extends. In the world today, if one would classify most broadly, there are two great culture areas: (1) the *Euro-American culture area*, which consists, as the term implies, of the European and American civilizations where such culture complexes as mechanical development, population control, Christianity, and world trade have become the characteristic patterns of the civilization; and (2) the *Oriental culture area*, which includes the great overpopulated area of the globe, India and China, where human reproduction is relatively unrestrained by birth control, where the masses till the soil by hand and with oxen, where peoples are relatively immobile, and where ancient traditions characterize the civilization.

Using the concept of culture area less broadly, one can designate two major culture areas within our own nation which in many respects are distinct: the North and the South. The North is a great industrial area, progressive and forward-looking in matters of business and finance. Agriculture there is prosperous, and the work of machines has replaced horsepower on farms to a great extent. The South

[8] Ruth Benedict, *Patterns of Culture* (New York: Houghton Mifflin Co., 1934), p. 22.

designates the eleven southeastern cotton states where slavery once existed, where hoe-and-mule farming of corn and cotton long persisted, where the poor white and Negro have subsisted under a system of sharecropping, and where great industries are only now being built. There, the birth rate of the rural population is still the highest in the nation, and migration outward is still the dominant pattern of the population flow.

We may also characterize the East and the West as distinct culture areas for certain purposes, because they are quite different in traditions and customs. One could even name much smaller areas as representing unique cultures, for example, the mountain areas as contrasting with the Great Plains.

It is clear from this discussion that the use of the term culture area by the sociologist is a flexible one (this is equally true of other sociological concepts as well). It is used to describe for certain purposes large and very general areas of cultural distribution, and for other purposes to designate more localized areas of cultural distribution.

ETHNOCENTRISM

All peoples have a distinct loyalty to their own culture patterns and culture areas which tends to make them prejudiced against all others. The philosophy of many primitives is: We alone are people, our ways of life are best. This is paralleled in modern times by a philosophy of certain religious groups which assumes that their particular religious culture is the one and only one that will assure a person ultimate salvation.

A feeling of intense loyalty to one's culture is called *ethnocentrism,* ethnos meaning culture, centrism meaning centeredness. It is logical that a person should consider his culture superior. It is the one he has known since birth. The familiar ways always appeal to him; the unfamiliar seem strange and often ridiculous. One tends to think that what has been, among his own ancestors, must be what is right and useful. Moreover most persons, unless they have traveled widely, have little familiarity with cultures other than their own. They do not realize with what satisfactory logic many peoples in other culture areas do things in ways exactly opposite to theirs. The American considers a person with lice as dirty, filthy, and unkempt, but according to the theory of Greenlanders, it is a sign of health, for vermin will leave a dying man as rats leave a sinking ship. To be louseless is to be anxious about one's health and well-being.[9] It is hardly for us to pick lice from another's hair and crush them between our teeth. But

---

[9] Robert H. Lowie, *Are We Civilized?* (New York: Harcourt, Brace & Co., 1929), p. 235.

this can be a very sociable activity, especially for lovers in courtship, if the culture accepts it.

The rationality and logic of given practices are dependent on one's cultural orientation, as is his scheme of values. J. S. Slotkin, an anthropologist, illustrates the working of ethnocentrism in a typical college class by illustrating how its logic is determined by customary practice. He begins by reading this passage on the Caribou Eskimo: "An underfrock . . . of short-haired skin with the hair inwards is worn next to the body. When the weather is warm enough, it is worn without any outerfrock and is therefore usually ornamented in various ways."[10] Then he begins a dialogue with his female students that runs about as follows:

Q. What do you think of wearing the fur side inside?
A. It's peculiar.
Q. Why?
A. It would make my flesh creep.
Q. Do any of you have fur coats?
A. Yes.
Q. Why do you wear them?
A. To keep warm.
(This time the laughter had a pitying ring to it, for it was obvious that only a professor who does not know much about life could ask such a quaint question.)
Q. What part of the fur coat keeps you warm?
A. The skin.
Q. Does the fur on the outside help keep you warm?
A. No.
Q. Then why not wear a leather coat? It's cheaper.
(Laughter at the absurdity of the idea.)
Q. Then why don't you do it?
(Again laughter.)
Q. If you buy a fur coat to keep you warm, and only the leather actually does so, but you insist on having fur on the outside, why not buy a cheap rabbit coat rather than one made of mink, let us say?[11]

Slotkin reports that, although the Eskimo practice is much more rational than ours in terms of utility, students rationalize the American practice, which is, of course, primarily motivated by status rather than practical considerations.

Those who have traveled widely and studied the customs of many peoples are more likely to be tolerant toward foreign ways. Even primitives who live close by other tribes of different customs are in-

[10] J. S. Slotkin, *Social Anthropology* (New York: The Macmillan Co., 1950), pp. 71–72.
[11] *Ibid.*

clined to be tolerant toward them. They excuse the other person by simply saying, "He has his customs; we have ours."

SUMMARY

Culture has been defined as the man-made, consisting of material traits such as tools and machines and nonmaterial traits such as folkways and mores which are passed from generation to generation as the cultural heritage. The simplest unit of culture is the culture trait. All traits have a history; they are mobile; they tend to group into useful units called culture complexes. The emphasis given to particular complexes in a culture gives a civilization its design or pattern. Culture patterns have a special distribution, the extent of a particular culture pattern's dominance being called a culture area. Cultures have great diversity; yet all have certain basic complexes. They are built according to a common scheme determined by human biological limitations. Through migration and isolation, diverse cultures developed as men struggled to survive in different environments. But molded by its own culture pattern, each people considers its pattern the best, thus displaying ethnocentrism.

DISCUSSION AND REVIEW QUESTIONS

1. What is culture? Of what does it consist?
2. Distinguish between and illustrate material and nonmaterial culture.
3. Discuss culture as a heritage from the past.
4. Discuss trial and error as a factor in the origin of culture. What ways are kept to become culture?
5. Distinguish between habit and folkways; between folkways and mores.
6. Give an illustration of a folkway. Illustrate mores.
7. What are prohibitive mores called?
8. Define and distinguish the various units of culture: the trait, complex, and pattern.
9. Name and explain some characteristics of culture traits.
10. Illustrate the concept *culture complex*.
11. What unique culture complexes give the American culture pattern its distinctiveness? the Indian?
12. Are cultures standardized? In what sense? Present evidence.
13. What are the major classifications in Wissler's universal culture scheme?
14. Through what historical experience did cultures become different? Illustrate.
15. What is a culture area? Illustrate.
16. Would you say that ethnocentrism is universal? Do you see any cure for it?

SOURCEBOOK READINGS

LANDIS, JUDSON T., and MARY G. LANDIS. *Readings in Marriage and the Family.* Englewood Cliffs, N.J.: Prentice-Hall, Inc., 1952.
   1. MURDOCK, GEORGE P., "A Cross-Cultural Picture of Sex Codes," pp. 403–8.

O'BRIEN, ROBERT W., CLARENCE C. SCHRAG, and WALTER T. MARTIN. *Readings in General Sociology* (2d ed.). Boston: Houghton Mifflin Co., 1957.
    2. BENEDICT, RUTH, "The Diversity of Cultures," pp. 142–47.

SCHULER, EDGAR A., DUANE L. GIBSON, MAUDE L. FIERO, and WILBUR B. BROOKOVER. *Outside Readings in Sociology.* New York: The Thomas Crowell Co., 1956.
    3. KLUCKHOHN, CLYDE, "The Concept of Culture," pp. 57–70.
    4. SUMNER, WILLIAM GRAHAM, "Fundamental Notions of the Folkways and of the Mores," pp. 258–68.

WILSON, LOGAN, and WILLIAM L. KOLB. *Sociological Analysis.* New York: Harcourt, Brace & Co., Inc., 1949.
    5. MURDOCK, GEORGE PETER, "The Cross-Cultural Survey," pp. 64–72.
    6. SUMNER, WILLIAM GRAHAM, "Characteristics of the Mores," pp. 72–80.

SELECTED READINGS

BENEDICT, RUTH. *Patterns of Culture.* New York: Penguin Books, Inc., 1946.

CHASE, STUART. *The Proper Study of Mankind.* Rev. ed.; New York: Harper & Brothers, 1956, chaps. 6–10, 13.

GRAHAM, SAXON. *American Culture.* New York: Harper & Brothers, 1956.

HERSKOVITS, MELVILLE J. *Man and His Works.* New York: Alfred A. Knopf, Inc., 1949.

KRONENBERGER, LOUIS. *Company Manners: A Cultural Inquiry into American Life.* Indianapolis: The Bobbs-Merrill Co., Inc., 1954.

LINTON, RALPH. *The Study of Man.* New York: Appleton-Century-Crofts, Inc., 1936.

MEADOWS, PAUL. *The Culture of Industrial Man.* Lincoln, Neb.: University of Nebraska Press, 1950.

SHAPIRO, HARRY L. (ed.) *Man, Culture and Society.* New York: Oxford University Press, Inc., 1956.

SUMNER, WILLIAM GRAHAM. *Folkways.* Boston: Ginn & Co., 1906.

THOMPSON, LAURA, and ALICE JOSEPH. *The Hopi Way.* Chicago: University of Chicago Press, 1944.

WHITE, LESLIE. *The Science of Culture.* New York: Farrar, Straus & Cudahy, Inc., 1949.

Chapter 3

Cultural Continuity

Man is not only a culture-builder. His culture outlives its maker. As Clark Wissler has said, "Tribes may come and tribes may go, but culture goes on forever."

Man's persistent cultural past is his greatest environmental asset. Through it he has dominion over material things and over all creatures of nature. Because of it each new generation begins where the preceding one left off, building still more elaborately the great superstructure of folkways, mores, institutions, and invented material devices.

PERSISTENCE OF PAST CULTURE

Culture may change, but it rarely disappears. It may have little meaning, and yet it survives. For example, in modern cultures, the bow and arrow is no longer the basic weapon that it was for thousands of years, and yet bows and arrows are about as numerous as they ever were. Except among primitives, they are now used for recreation and sporting, rather than for war and hunting. In their hobby use they have even become a method of hunting wild game again. Many states now have special bow and arrow hunting seasons for the sportsman who wants to pit his wiles against nature with the weapon of his distant ancestors. Even so, it is a more effective weapon than weapons made by primitive man anywhere.

So culture has continuity. It lives on. And this is not true merely of material culture. It is equally true of ceremony and ritual. Whole books have been written about the customary practices that have developed in connection with the Christmas celebration. There has come down through centuries the religious lore of this holiday. Much of the ceremonial practice, even in this connection, predates the birth of Christ. There is a tree, which had its origin somewhere in

34

Europe, and the stocking, the candles, the giving of gifts, and then the more recent custom of the greeting card, the use of which is no longer confined merely to friends or close relatives, but which also has become an instrument of business promotion. Practically all businesses send everyone with whom they have had contact Christmas greetings. These greetings are hardly sent in the religious spirit. They are assumed, in most cases, to have a business connotation.

So one might go on indicating how the Christmas celebration has accumulated traits from antiquity but is being added to from generation to generation, as the Christmas celebration persists into the future.

This persisting cultural influence shapes us even to our attitudes and prejudices. This idea is strikingly developed in the following passage.

". . . beyond your flesh and blood are ten million years of biological evolution, ten million years of adaptations, survivals, and selections, ten million years during which the germinal bases of your essential self have been slowly and inexorably fashioned. And beyond your mind—that baffling complex of sensations, perceptions, emotions, feelings—that mysterious unity of wishing, aiming, purposing, resisting, striving, competing, which some psychologists still vaguely name the ego is an incredibly vast and complicated and ancient social heritage from which practically the entire content of your mind has been unconsciously derived.

". . . Nine-tenths of all you do or say or think or feel from the time you get up in the morning until the time you go to bed at night is done and said and thought and felt, not in independent self-expression, but in uncritical, unconscious conformity with rules, regulations, group habits, standards, codes, styles, and sanctions that were in existence long before you were born. You wear clothes of a certain cut not because your individuality compels you to, but because that cut is in style. You take off your hat to a lady of your acquaintance, not because your ego demands it, but because the social code prescribes it . . . You praise this man and denounce that one; you like this man and dislike that one; you accept this article of religious faith and reject that—and, if you think about these evaluations and preferences, you will be forced to the conclusion that practically all your standards and criteria have been socially created."[1]

It is through the culture heritage, and it alone, that man's pattern of life itself has continuity. Suddenly blot out culture, and man is

[1] Russell Gordon Smith, *Fugitive Papers* (New York: Columbia University Press, 1930), p. 23.

bankrupt, for nature has not provided through built-in mechanisms a pattern for man's social life and material achievement. The significance of this essential fact is underscored in the following passage.

"Take a few ant eggs of the proper sexes—unhatched eggs, freshly laid. Blot out every individual and every other egg of the species. Give the pair a little attention as regards warmth, moisture, protection, and food. The whole ant "society," every one of the abilities, powers, accomplishments, and activities of the species, each "thought" that it has ever had, will be reproduced, and reproduced without diminution, in one generation. But place on a desert island or in a circumvallation two or three hundred human infants of the best stock from the highest class of the most civilized nation; furnish them the necessary incubation and nourishment; leave them in total isolation from their kind; and what shall we have? The civilization from which they were torn? One tenth of it? No, not any fraction; nor a fraction of the civilization attainments of the rudest savage tribe. Only a pair or a troop of mutes, without arts, knowledge, fire, without order or religion. Civilization would be wiped out within these confines—not disintegrated, not cut to the quick, but obliterated in one sweep. Heredity saves for the ant all that she has, from generation to generation. But heredity does not maintain, and has not maintained, because it cannot maintain, one particle of the civilization which is the specifically human thing."[2]

Need one say more to demonstrate the supreme importance of cultural continuity to human life?

OUR KNOWLEDGE OF THE PAST

Every person who has finished the fifth grade today knows that culture has great antiquity, that it goes back through hundreds of centuries; yet this idea in Western civilization is scarcely a hundred years old. Before that time Archbishop Ussher's chronology of human history, which placed the date of creation at 4004 B.C., was generally accepted. The Orient has long recognized that the world is much more ancient than that, and that human life extends back over a much longer period. But it remained for a scientific age to open the eyes of the West to a new conception of the immensity of time and of the long history of man.

The science of geology, through a study of rock formations of the earth's surface, established the great antiquity of the world in which we live. Paleontology dated skeletal remains of extinct animal species by the geological strata in which they were found. Anthropology did

2 A. L. Kroeber, "The Superorganic," *American Anthropologist*, April–June, 1917. Also, reprinted by the Sociological Press, Hanover, N.H., 1927.

the same for man from skeletal remains found in the earth's surface. Archeology sought *artifacts* (invented devices like flint arrow points) of early cultures, and also dated them by geological periods. Although geological ages are not dated with the specific exactness of contemporary history, it is believed that the history of man goes back not less than 750,000 years. Some would say much longer, some a shorter time. But even the shortest period places the earliest man millenniums prior to 4004 B.C.

The study of ancient man employs, as has been implied, the time sequence of geology which reckons time in terms of eons and ages and millenniums rather than years. Skeletal remains give something of the history of early man, abbreviated and inexact though it may be, and artifacts remaining in various layers of the earth's surface give some idea of the more durable tools and some of the customs of early man. The main artifacts, of course, are those of stone, although bone instruments are also quite durable. And in the sheltered caves, paintings which give some index of man's art and of his religion date back at least 15,000 years.

The long perspective of man's past is a cultural perspective in the strictest sense. There is no evidence of a physiological change in man which could explain the improvement in his culture during the last 10,000 to 15,000 years or longer. Cultural growth is, therefore, not dependent on new improvements in man brought about by mutation or other biological changes. Cultural accumulation and cultural growth go on because of man's inventive capacity and mental ingenuity, not because he has become suddenly a better animal creature by virtue of hereditary mutation.

HOW CULTURE IS BUILT

Presumably man has always been a culture builder. In ancient cultures, where it is possible to trace the progress of culture in stone-working, evidence of *cultural continuity* has been found. Man began with the stone provided by nature, and gradually through the centuries improved his stone implements until he had the finished flint arrow or spear point. Through the study of such artifacts chronologies of culture are built. The *eolithic period* (dawn) is the earliest known stone age. During that age man was working with tools so undeveloped that they were of the crudest fashion. The *paleolithic period* (ancient) marks the middle period in the development of man's use of stone. The *neolithic period* (new) brought the stone age to its climax. Polished implements of stone and efficient bone implements were used. Thus is seen the gradual continuity and improvement of a culture trait.

Although it cannot be demonstrated, nonmaterial culture has presumably also had, from the earliest period of history, a thread of continuity that binds past and present. Family and social systems, customs, traditions, and religious systems have undoubtedly grown in much the same way as material culture.

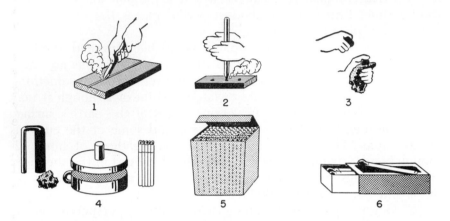

Development of the Match, an Example of Cultural Continuity

1 Stick in groove	*2 Fire drill*	*3 Striking fire*
4 Tinder box, flint, steel, and sulfur-tipped splinters	*5 First friction chemical matches, sold in blocks*	*6 Box of modern safety matches*

Although the modern match seems unrelated to the early fire drill, history shows the match to be the direct descendant of the most primitive method of making fire. (Drawings adapted from Stories of Useful Inventions, by S. E. Forman, pp. 5–12. Copyright, 1911, the Century Co. Reprinted by permission of Appleton-Century-Crofts, Inc.)

Streams of Culture History. It is known that, first in Central Asia and North Africa, and later in Western Europe, culture-building began many centuries ago and passed through the stone age to the bronze age, then entered the age of iron. More recently the fact has been established that culture-building of a high order went on in lower Mexico, Yucatan, Central and South America. At least 5,000 years ago natives of this area passed the stone age and developed copper-working. Their religion had reached a level of complexity that called for the building of great temples such as command the respect of even our age of masonry and steel.

Certainly during the period of written history all evidence supports the accepted thesis of the cultural anthropologist and the sociologist that culture has persistence, that it has continuity, that the present is built out of the past.

The western world has passed rapidly, relative to the long period of history, from the iron age to the steam age to the electrical age, and perhaps is now entering the atomic age. In this era the progress of civilization is measured not by the perfection of stone-working or even by the working of higher metals, but by the harnessing of natural sources of power, steam, electricity, and now the atom.

Man's Nonmaterial Past. The reconstruction of man's nonmaterial past, which consists of language and religion, philosophical systems, and social institutions is a problem of history, not of sociology. But historians, cultural anthropologists, and sociologists are agreed that there is continuity in the development of nonmaterial as well as material culture.

In every field of human culture—the development of social organizations, of religious systems, of literature, of material traits—one thing paves the way for another. Thus a trend of cultural development may be studied as it evolves century after century in various cultures. This trend gives a consistency of meaning to the past and the present, and also assures that there will be a certain consistency of meaning in the culture traits developed in the future. This continuity of pattern not only affects the culture traits which are invented in a particular area but also affects what a people will borrow from the outsiders in the way of innovations.

MAN, A TIME-BINDING CREATURE

Plants are merely cell-binding creatures; animals are space-binding; man is more than either of these: he alone is time-binding.[3] It has been cleverly stated that "birds and beasts inhabit the world, only man inhabits the universe."[4] Man alone looks beyond the earth to the outer immensities. The birds and beasts live in the present moment; only a man broods over the past and the future. As has been stated, as civilization has advanced man's conceptions of history have reached further and further backward. His conception of the future extends into millenniums of geological ages and perhaps eons of astronomical ages ahead. The more he knows about himself, the more man realizes that his destiny as a culture-builder is of his own making, that he is born and nurtured in the warp and woof of a

[3] Alfred Korzybski, *The Manhood of Humanity* (2d ed.; Lakeville, Conn.: Institute of General Semantics, 1953).

[4] Charles Johnson, in Willey and Wallis, *Readings in Sociology* (New York: Alfred A. Knopf, Inc., 1930), pp. 600–01.

Acres of floor space . . .

tons of books . . .

thousands of index cards . . .

cultural fabric which has not been woven primarily by his own generation, but by a thousand generations that have preceded him.

Man is so much of a time-binding creature that Wissler has stated, in *Man and Culture,* that culture has continuity just as does the germ plasm. Throughout history, he believes, cultures have had their life cycle like individuals. They have grown and matured, begot other cultures, declined, and eventually died.

Man's Time-binding Achievements. The human group, like the individual, has the capacity to store up experience. The individual does it by the process of learning—*habit and attitude* formation; the group does it by accumulating devices that man has made and customs that become his guide for living. This experience of the race is accumulated not only for a generation, but for many generations, since it is passed on down beyond the lifetime of those who invented it. Thus the cultural heritage accumulates not only through the centuries but through the millenniums. Culture is in this sense man's past affecting his present.

Man makes extensive use of the past. His traditions are as vital to him as is the biological mechanism itself. Even peoples without any written language have an abundance of tools and folkways and mores which constitute a system of life as important to them as are the instincts with which nature has equipped animals or the trophic responses she has provided plants. Because man is time-binding, that is, because he looks to the past and draws from its experiences, he also looks into the future. He is a planner in a sense that no other animal is, projecting the course of civilization into the days and years ahead.

and miles of film . . . are used to store the cultural heritage of modern man.
(*WSC Photo, State College of Washington*)

In less rational moods he takes his past for granted. He uses fire in its many forms but never stops to think what a marvelous invention it is or even raises the question as to who discovered its use or when. So it is with much of his culture. He goes on building new things without realizing that they are rooted in the groundwork of what inventors have achieved through the centuries, and in his pride he often claims uniqueness for his own inventiveness, failing to credit his numerous predecessors without whom he could not have taken the first step.

SUMMARY

Man is effective to the extent that he has been able to carry on with him a rich and useful past. Peoples most advanced, peoples most inventive, peoples most free from the restrictions of environment, are those who have been able to bring forward from the past a rich and enduring cultural heritage. To have been able to do so has required not only inventiveness, not only a natural environment rich with resources for tool-creation and for manufacture, but also a culture rich in contacts, flexible in borrowing, adapting, and using the cultures of many people, and in working out from them a complete way of life.

Because culture has continuity, man now has attained a level of living beyond anything that earlier man might have dreamed of. And it is on this foundation of all the past that the new and better culture of tomorrow is built. Culture thus is a never-ending stream, which provides man with the pattern for his life and the environment for his being.

Culture's eternal persistence is not an unmixed blessing. Although it adds an important element of stability and continuity to man's experience, cultural inertia is often a drag on the present. Survivals of old culture traits add needless baggage, and lagging elements of culture are one source of maladjustment, particularly in an age where certain aspects of the culture are more dynamic than other aspects. The liabilities of cultural continuity will be discussed in detail in Chapter 6.

DISCUSSION AND REVIEW QUESTIONS

1. What is meant by the concept "cultural continuity"? Cite examples.
2. In what sense is man's ability to accumulate culture a factor in making him human?
3. Discuss briefly the period of time over which culture had accumulated. What evidence has helped establish this new time perspective on culture?

4. Cite some high points in man's cultural development.

5. In what three areas of the world has culture developed to a high level?

6. Discuss the phrase "Man is time-binding."

7. What is meant by the concept "cultural accumulation"? Illustrate from the evidence of history.

SOURCEBOOK READINGS

O'BRIEN, ROBERT W., CLARENCE C. SCHRAG, and WALTER T. MARTIN. *Readings in General Sociology* (2d ed.). Boston: Houghton Mifflin Co., 1957.

    1. GILLIN, JOHN, "The Old Order Amish of Pennsylvania," pp. 147–55.

    2. LYND, ROBERT S., "Assumptions in American Life," pp. 155–56.

    3. LINTON, RALPH, "One Hundred Per Cent American," pp. 157–58.

SELECTED READINGS

BENEDICT, RUTH. *Patterns of Culture.* New York: Penguin Books, Inc., 1946.

GRAHAM, SAXON. *American Culture.* New York: Harper & Brothers, 1956.

HERSKOVITS, MELVILLE J. *Man and His Works.* New York: Alfred A. Knopf, Inc., 1949.

LINTON, RALPH. *The Study of Man.* New York: Appleton-Century-Crofts, Inc., 1936.

POTTER, DAVID M. *People of Plenty: Economic Abundance and the American Character.* Chicago: University of Chicago Press, 1954.

SHAPIRO, HARRY L. (ed.). *Man, Culture and Society.* New York: Oxford University Press, 1956.

SUMNER, WILLIAM GRAHAM. *Folkways.* Boston: Ginn & Co., 1906.

THOMPSON, LAURA, and ALICE JOSEPH. *The Hopi Way.* Chicago: University of Chicago Press, 1944.

Chapter 4

Culture Change by Invention

The folklore saying that "necessity is the mother of invention" has been widely questioned by sociologists, who are inclined to make it read something like this: "Culture is the mother of necessity."

Peoples need what their existing culture has taught them to need. Peoples who have never had a wheel sense no need for it. They carry their burdens on their heads or on their backs, or, if further advanced, on the backs of domesticated animals. But peoples who have the wheel are constantly sensing a need to employ it in more and more complicated devices. Thus the wheel comes to be used, not only for bearing burdens, but also for telling time, lifting weights, and in a thousand other ways.

In the following quotation a sociology-minded author with a vivid imagination challenges the idea that inventions spring full-blown from the mind of any man. He gives a truer picture of invention, and one much more acceptable to the sociologist, than does the folklore belief that inventions are momentary creations of some genius.

" 'Blessings on the man who invented sleep,' said the classic Sancho Panza; and the English balladist:

> So I wish in heaven his soul may dwell
> Who first found out the leather bottell.

"Perhaps, indeed, he was thinking more of the inner spirit of the bottle, than of its outer integument. Anyway these old-timers express a thought that is common today, the rule even, and which not even a single social scientist has shaken himself sufficiently free from, viz., that the great inventions were made by certain great men. . . .

"Who invented the telegraph? Any American who has been

44

through the eighth grade knows that it was Morse and Vail, in 1844. But there was an English commercial line seven years earlier, and the Germans credit the telegraph to Sommering, of Munich, in 1809, and in Switzerland there was an electric telegraph in 1774, and one was proposed in Scotland in 1753. The matter becomes rather confusing for the eighth grade. . . .

"The chief reason for this confusion of parentage is that the process of making a great invention is totally different from the common understanding about it. A great invention is not a completed product, issuing at one time from the brain of one inventor. It is a multitudinous collection of little inventions, and is a growth of centuries. Had a single inventor to make the whole, he would need more hands than a monkey, more lives than a cat and more inventive genius than Pallas, Hermes, and Loki combined. . . ."[1]

INVENTION, KEY TO CULTURAL CHANGE

In the preceding chapter discussion centered about the tendency of culture to persist and to accumulate from age to age. This is one of its important aspects. It explains the great residue of the past which carries on into the present of human experience.

But culture is also dynamic, for man is an eternal tinkerer. He is never quite content to leave things as he found them; he invents. The child when he first begins to explore his environment takes things apart to see what they are made of. So, also, man throughout the ages has been taking apart the cultural heritage left by his ancestors to see not only what it is made of, but what he can make of it. Thus change comes about. Through the process of invention the cultural heritage is reworked. New combinations of culture traits are made and new principles, laws, and codes of behavior are discovered.

It is in this broad sense that *invention* will be discussed, that is, *the process by which the cultural heritage is remade,* or in the broader sense, *the process by which new culture, both material and nonmaterial, comes into being.* Thus the term invention, as used by sociologists, refers to the development not only of new material culture traits like microfilm or electric shavers, but also of nonmaterial culture traits such as a new law, a new folkway, a new system of etiquette, or a new superstition. The split-T formation in football is as much an invention under this definition as is the self-starter on the automobile.

Probably no significant invention in the realm of ideas or techniques has ever been made by man and widely adopted without its causing widespread change in related aspects of culture, as well as

[1] S. C. Gilfillan, "Who Invented It?" *Scientific Monthly,* 25:529–34 (Dec. 1927).

The Race of the Iron Horse and the Horse Car

New inventions often must prove themselves in the face of skepticism. The old and the tried seem more safe and, to most, more satisfactory—particularly in cultures accustomed to a slow rate of change. (Association of American Railroads)

in aspects of society. New material devices such as new machines, for example, very obviously produce widespread changes in various aspects of social institutions and various customs, even at times creating new problems of morality.

It is a little less easy to demonstrate that marked changes in non-material culture so readily revolutionize material culture, and yet it is commonly argued that even the inventions of pure science, which represent the highest type of theoretical reasoning, often produce revolutionary effects in the technological world where they are sooner or later applied. New theories of genetics lead to the development of new plant and animal species; the discovery of new laws of the atom led to the invention of the atom bomb with all the possible industrial applications lying ahead. The development of the theoretical principle of electricity opened the road for the application of this new force to numerous types of machines for the making of numerous types of technological devices.

The point of the discussion is that fundamental inventions, either in nonmaterial or in material fields, have far-reaching implications for many aspects of culture, often starting a series of changes that vibrate throughout the entire cultural structure of a people which adopts the new invention. Contemporary students of culture have been inclined to rate the appearance of new technological inventions as being the major force of cultural change in our time and have called attention to the lag of various social institutions, mores, and folkways in the trail of these material developments. Perhaps the case has been overstated, but, on the other hand, certainly technological invention has moved the industrial culture forward at a rapid pace, often leaving numerous problems of social adjustment behind.

It is perhaps also true, although this is less easy to demonstrate, that technology at many points lags behind our best knowledge of natural science, that many of the laws of science have not yet been applied to certain aspects of production to increase its efficiency and to bring it to the highest level of human usefulness. The technocrats of the 1930's raised a lot of argument about industries withholding important inventions because they could make more money by producing goods under the old scheme, at least as long as they had a monopoly on the old process. How much of this goes on in industry is, of course, not known.

Basic Inventions. Obviously, some inventions are relatively insignificant, affecting very few aspects of culture and requiring few personal adjustments. Others are so far-reaching that they require widespread personal adjustments, provide avenues for extensive changes in ideology and attitudes, and often require changes in related aspects of technology itself. They may be referred to as basic inventions.

William F. Ogburn, University of Chicago sociologist and outstanding student of invention as a phase of cultural change in the modern world, has summarized 150 broad social effects of the radio as an invention in American culture.[2] He finds that the radio has been a major factor in the spread of culture traits in the modern world. It has widespread effects on recreational habits, on transportation, education, religion, business, and industry. It has made possible a new series of occupations; it has come to play a leading part in government. It has provided stimulus for many new related inventions which deal in intangible forces of the air. The social effects of television are perhaps even more profound.[3]

INVENTORS AND THE CULTURE HERITAGE

The culture heritage is produced by invention. The amount any one inventor contributes to the culture heritage is very small indeed compared to the total of culture that has accumulated through the ages. Moreover, every inventor must work with the culture heritage which is at hand.

The African genius at best will invent a better drum, a better method of handling fire for cooking, a new religious ritual for gaining favor with the gods, or make some other simple addition to culture that to us seems childish and unimportant. But in the light of his cultural heritage, the invention may be a great achievement. Men in primitive cultures could not make incandescent light bulbs, talking pictures, or any other of the many gadgets which an Edison made in our culture; but neither could an Edison, placed in a primitive African culture, have made the talking machine.

This brings us again to an observation which has often been overlooked in discussing inventions. Some have said "necessity is the mother of invention"; others that "inventions are a product of genius." It would be more correct to state that "culture is the mother of invention."

Inventors and the Culture Base. There must be a certain accumulated *culture base* in order to make any new invention possible. *By culture base is meant the total existing culture on which an inven-*

[2] For a list of these 150 traits see W. F. Ogburn and Meyer F. Nimkoff, *Sociology* (3d ed.; Boston: Houghton Mifflin Co., 1955), chap. 26.

[3] See such works as Leo Bogart, *The Age of Television* (New York: Frederick Ungar Publishing Co., 1956), and Charles A. Spielman, *Radio, Television and Society* (New York: Oxford University Press, 1950).

tor may draw. Given the necessary culture base, men of ability will make the new combinations of cultural traits which we call inventions. Lacking an adequate culture base, no man of genius will produce a particular device that must wait another age. Many traits must be present in the culture base before any genius can reproduce the human voice.

Given a motion picture and a talking machine in the same culture, it is logical that sooner or later some inventor will think of putting the two together to produce a talking picture. Given a high-pressure combustion gas engine of light weight which is capable of producing high speeds on land, sooner or later someone will put this engine in a machine attempting to overcome the force of gravity and fly a heavier-than-air craft. Inventions, when they actually appear, often seem very simple indeed, because all of the elements required for their making had already existed in the culture base.

Today the richness of the culture base is measured by the number of symbols present. The making of an invention is facilitated greatly where the specific and exact language of science has come into wide usage, where the even more abstract symbols of mathematics, chemical formula, engineering blueprints, and other such devices for clear-cut and abbreviated communication permit a man to accumulate a great deal of knowledge concerning the cultural heritage and become an expert in its use. The more a particular man of genius has mastered these various fields of culture that have been reduced to special scientific symbols, the more freely he can manipulate a large field of culture, bring it within his grasp, and make the new combinations of culture traits which are inventions.

Necessity as a Factor in Invention. There is little question that need enters into the inventive process, especially in times of crisis when men are made aware by impending danger that some new approach to situations must be found. Certain kinds of inventions, for example, are much more prominent in wartime than in peacetime. Nations facing destruction by foreign opponents are willing to pour unlimited wealth and scientific skill into the kinds of inventions that will save them. In peacetime the same invention probably would have come over a period of possibly a quarter- to a half-century, whereas it may come in a period of two to five years when a nation faces crises. On the other hand, need alone leaves man still wanting unless he has the cultural elements with which inventors can work. It is this point that the student of culture wishes to stress rather than simply to overthrow the myth of necessity itself being sufficient to explain the appearance of new culture traits.

As man acquires new cultural elements by invention and becomes habituated to their use, they become for him necessities in maintaining prestige among his fellows. The idea is of merit; necessity is, after all, a relative thing. Peoples who have no tractors don't need them, at least not from their point of view. Most American farmers consider a tractor an absolute necessity. Forks are handier than fingers only if one has learned to use them. Most peoples have not found them necessary, but those peoples who have already possess them.

Invention as a Process. This raises another point often overlooked by those who have not made a special study of culture-building. *Invention is an accumulative process rather than an individual act.* By this is meant that seldom does a single inventor produce an invention out of whole cloth, and seldom does he bring it to the place of final completion in his lifetime. The inventor usually works with an understanding of what many men before him have tried to do and sometimes have done more or less successfully. Through his lifetime he may continue to improve the thing he has made, and others for many generations afterward may continue to add improvements.

The automobile was, appropriately enough, first called the horseless carriage. Its inventors simply added a gasoline engine and cogs for propelling it to the old rubber-tired buggy. Some early builders, in order to cater to culture inertia (natural public resistance to culture change), mounted a false horsehead on the dashboard. But was the invention of the automobile completed by those who first claimed to have created the horseless carriage? It was not and is not, even today. Millions are spent annually making mechanical improvements and style changes in the automobile, and the process will go on for years to come as new engineering knowledge and better devices are accumulated in the culture to improve the automobile.

So it is with basic inventions; they are a contribution of many inventors through many generations rather than the product of some one genius in a moment of time.

It is true that some inventions are in the nature of major discoveries and that some of the simpler inventions are relatively perfect at the time of their invention. Some also have their short day and disappear from human use, but generally speaking, the process of invention must be described as a long-time accumulative process to which many contribute. Culture-building, as a consequence, does not stop because a particular inventor has died.

One writer has said that the talking machine would have been invented even had the great Edison died of the whooping cough when he was three years old.[4] It probably would have been. It might not have been invented in exactly the same way or at exactly the same time, but the elements for such an invention were present in the culture base of Western man. It is likely, therefore, that someone would have invented the talking machine.

In the field of nonmaterial culture, concrete demonstration of the process of invention is less easy, but it is common knowledge that most traditions have accumulated and been added to through the centuries as have most ceremonials. Ceremonies connected with the Christmas celebration, with marriage, and with religious observance are examples. New generations will modify and add to them. So, also, has the accumulation of law been a slow process extending through many centuries, indicating that the inventions of nonmaterial culture follow a course parallel to that of material inventions.

Duplicate Inventions. It has been implied that invention is dependent upon the accumulated cultural heritage, the culture base, of a particular time and place. Proof for this hypothetical notion is found in the fact that many significant inventions have appeared within the same general cultural area from the hand of different inventors at about the same time. Lawsuits over patent rights are a common occurrence; yet in many cases the claimants have worked independently.

Consider the following examples from a list of 148 duplicate inventions:

Introduction of decimal point. By Burgi (1592), Pitiscus (1608–12), Kepler (1616), and Napier (1616–17)

Hypothesis as to arrangement of atoms in space. By Van't Hoff (1874), and Le Bel (1874).

Telescope. Claimed by Della Porta (1558), Digger (1571), Lippershey (1608), Johannides, Metius (1608), Drebbel, Fontana, Janssen (1608), and Galileo (1609).

Photography. By Daguerre-Niepce (1839), and Talbot (1839).

Pendulum clock. Claimed by Burgi (1575), Galileo (1582), and Huygens (1656).

Telegraph. Henry (1831), Morse (1837), Cooke-Wheatstone (1837), and Steinheil (1837).

Telephone. By Bell (1876), and Gray (1876).

Theory of natural selection and variation. By C. Darwin (1858), and Wallace (1858).

Some results of heredity. By Mendel (1865), DeVries (1900), Correns (1900), Tschermarck (1900).

Theory of mutations. By Korschinsky (1899), and DeVries (1900).

Theory of emotions. By James (1884), and Lange (1887).

[4] Gilfillan, *op. cit.*

Northern Pacific's first locomotive—the Minnetonka

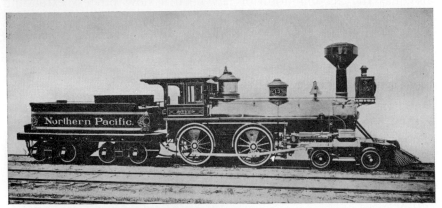

Northern Pacific locomotive No. 13

The first North Coast Limited

Invention Is a Social Process

In a sense, a modern invention is never complete. It moves through steps of increasing efficiency and eventually turns to competition on the aesthetic level.

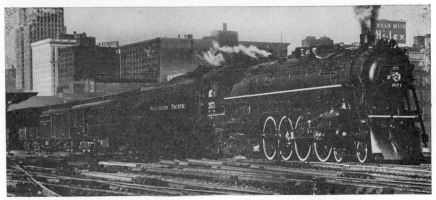

A pre-streamliner North Coast Limited

The Yellowstone—for many years the world's largest steam locomotive

The Vista-Dome North Coast Limited

The development of the train engine from 1870 to the present is an example of this process. (Northern Pacific Railway)

Sewing machine. By Thimmonier (1830), Howe (1846), and Hunt (1840).

Flying machine. Claimed by Wright (1895–1901), Langley (1893–7), and others.

Reapers. By Hussey (1833), and McCormick (1834).

Steamboat. Claimed by Fulton (1807), Jouffroy, Rumsey, Stevens, and Symmington (1802).

Use of gasoline engines in automobiles. By Otto (1876), Selden (1879?), and Daimler (1885).[5]

The point need not be labored, but certainly it is clear that particular inventions require more than men of genius. To develop a given invention, the genius must work within the framework of a cultural heritage which already provides most of the elements for the new invention. The fact that many traits developed by different inventors appear independently in different parts of the same culture area would seem to demonstrate the fact that, regardless of any particular man, inventions would probably appear. This is also a strong argument against the view held by some anthropologists to the effect that all culture originated at one point of origin. It is, in fact, one of the strongest proofs for the theory of independent invention.

Fortunate indeed is the man who makes the peculiar combination of existing culture traits to produce a new and usable idea or product. Actually in the modern world the inventor is a person who brings a new device or gadget to the point where he can secure a patent or copyright and profit commercially from it. Ball-point pens, for example, had been experimented with by many companies in Europe and the United States over a long period of time, but Reynolds, who succeeded in making them work at least enough to fool the public, got the invention on the market quickest and coined a fortune.[6]

The inventor of today has all past knowledge readily available in any field of invention he wishes to enter. He may visit the United States Patent Office in Washington, D.C., ask for the file of patents in any one field or all fields related to the one in which he wishes to work, and study them in planning his own. He may, for a charge of twenty-five cents per copy and without even visiting the Patent Office, have photostatic copies of all the drawings and descriptions mailed him, and study and work with them in his own home or shop. By this method the wise inventor can save himself much waste trial and error and greatly simplify his own labors. He can also avoid duplicating an invention already patented.

[5] From W. F. Ogburn, *Social Change* (rev. ed.; New York: The Viking Press, Inc., 1950).

[6] Lawsuits over patent rights were involved in this invention, as in so many others.

INVENTIONS, FOLKWAYS, HABITS, AND TECHNICWAYS

When the automobile began to be used extensively it became necessary to signal when one was going to turn right or left. This was unnecessary in the slower transportation of horse-and-buggy days. When cars became closed for year-around travel, the electric turn signal was developed to keep one from having to open the window in wintertime. So man is constantly modifying his behavior pattern by the development of new culture traits. These traits in turn become folkways and traditions and thus become a part of the social heritage which is passed down to the next generation. Such changes in the folkways require the building of new habits on the part of the individual. The development of new traditions similarly requires the modification of the attitudes of the individual living in the culture.

The late Howard W. Odum, sociologist at the University of North Carolina, suggested that in Western culture, where inventions requiring changes are so frequent, the term *technicways* would be more appropriate than the term folkways to describe the new group behavior patterns that develop.[7] There is considerable logic in this. Sumner, inventor of the folkways concept, considered folkways as the unplanned patterns that developed over long periods of time primarily in adjusting to natural environment to meet the needs of life.[8] Technology, the product of rational processes, often requires an immediate rational adjustment in behavior to meet the new conditions developed in the cultural environment.

Odum also suggested that in an age of planning and policy-making, where government plays such an important part in the affairs of men, it would be appropriate to use the term *stateways* to cover that aspect of the culture having to do with government-developed patterns for doing things. Obviously here, too, are consciously created culture patterns, contrasted with Sumnerian unconsciously evolved mores.

Certain it is, regardless of the terminology used, that we live in a time when invention is a deliberate and conscious activity of major proportions. Man must reckon with the numerous changes it produces. So far he does not do so with the degree of intelligence and foresight with which he might. Far too often he waits until new inventions have created widespread maladjustments before doing anything about it. While one cannot foresee a time when all the numerous consequences of particular inventions will be anticipated in

[7] Howard W. Odum, "Notes on Technicways in Contemporary Society," *American Sociological Review*, 2:337–41. 1937.

[8] William Graham Sumner, *Folkways* (Boston: Ginn & Co., 1906).

advance and difficulties thereby avoided, foresight is possible and practicable.

THE CYCLE OF INVENTION

Some writers have likened invention to a compound-interest curve because of the fact that cultural adaptation and borrowing both tend to speed up the inventive process. They add new elements to the culture which cause spurts of new invention. Thus the inventive process is accumulative, much like money to which the interest is added periodically. There is no doubt a great deal of truth in this analogy, but a more scientific approach to invention in particular fields probably would indicate that spurts in cultural growth tend to be confined to certain areas, and also tend to be clustered about certain key culture traits which open up new fields of innovation, making rapid growth in culture possible. Such research would also demonstrate that there are vast differences in the significance of various inventions from the standpoint of their effect on future inventions. Some key traits, like the use of steam or electricity for power, produce spurts in cultural invention which make the inventive "compound interest curve" multiply at 100 per cent rather than a normal 5 or 6 per cent. Other traits have little or no ability to stimulate further invention.

F. S. Chapin, a sociologist at the University of Minnesota who has a gift for reducing complex sociological phenomena to concrete mathematical terms, has measured the growth curve of invention in specific fields in an attempt to arrive at a law concerning invention.[9] His evidence, produced in connection with certain material and non-material traits, indicates that when a new invention comes into being there usually follows a spurt in inventions until eventually a climax is reached, after which the rate of inventions clustering around the new trait declines. The three stages are (1) a slow beginning, (2) a period of growth leading to the relative perfection of the invention, and (3) a slow addition of minor inventions. He has shown, for example, that the invention of the sulky plow led to an accelerated rate of accretion of new inventions, which led to the perfection of the plow. There followed then a decline in the addition of new culture traits. Specifically, from 1855 to 1859 thirty-five new patents were issued on the sulky plow. The rate increased until the period 1880 to 1884, when 164 patents were issued. The rate of accretion then fell off rapidly, until in 1920 to 1923 only three patents were added. In nonmaterial culture Chapin studied city government, and shows a similar curve of addition of new government functions.

9 F. S. Chapin, *Cultural Change* (New York: Appleton-Century-Crofts, Inc., 1928), chap. 12.

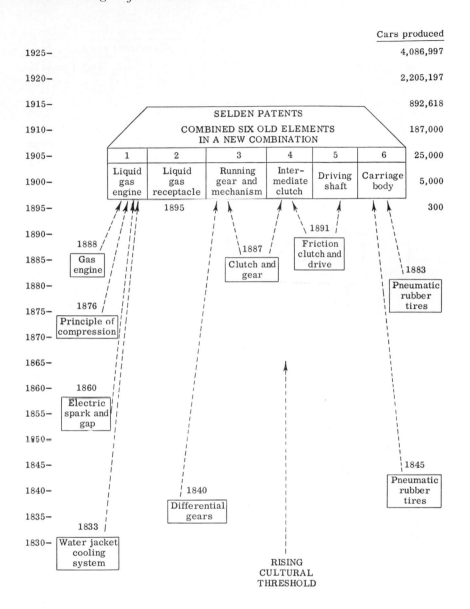

Invention of the Automobile

The chart depicts the integration of six known culture traits into a new pattern. (Adapted from Cultural Change, *by F. Stuart Chapin, p. 336. Copyright, 1928, The Century Co. Used by permission of Appleton-Century-Crofts, Inc.)*

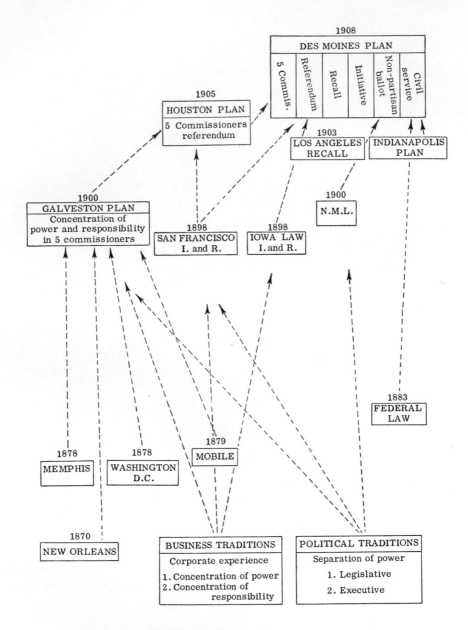

Invention of the Commission Plan of City Government

This chart shows the integration of a new pattern of political structure. (Adapted from Cultural Change, *by* F. Stuart Chapin, *p. 339. Copyright, 1928, The Century Co. Used by permission of Appleton-Century-Crofts, Inc.)*

Elmo Caulkins holds that the third stage in invention is really a stage where additions are mainly artistic.[10] For example, once kitchen devices have been made practical they tend to be made ornamental. Even the basement furnace eventually takes on symmetry and ornamentation. The bathtub cannot be improved beyond a certain point, as far as fitting the space of the bathroom and the human body are concerned, but tints of color can be added.

POOLED RESEARCH IN INVENTION

Among primitive peoples invention is in large part an answer to a problem faced in coping with the natural environment. In modern society invention is becoming increasingly a product of cooperative thought. During World War II, as never before, the mentality and genius of the nations in certain fields, particularly physics, were pooled to produce new inventions needed to help the nations through a crisis. This greatly speeded inventions such as radar.

The pattern for pooled research had already been established in the universities, medical centers, and in industries, but it reached its fullest development during the war years. The results of pooled research during World War II were so far-reaching in their significance that government subsidy of research has been a major issue in Congress since the termination of the war. There has been little question that natural-science research was worth the expenditure of vast sums of money, much of it in government research centers, colleges, and universities, but there has been considerable debate as to whether social science would justify such expenditures or produce equally significant results.

There is little doubt that in all fields of science the pooling of talent and economic resources offers a practical way of speeding up cultural change in the direction of the desirable goals. This is vaguely realized even by the general public, but perhaps not sufficiently so to command the financial support necessary. Time will tell. Scientists are agreed that almost anything in the way of a foreseeable development in both nonmaterial and material fields is possible through well-organized projected research programs. For example, it is now believed that an understanding of the cause of cancer, and thereafter a development of the cure, is possible if sufficient scientific talent is pooled in a gigantic research effort with adequate funds to carry out the necessary program.

INVENTION AND PERSONALITY

From what has been said concerning the laws which determine the rate of cultural invention, it may well be concluded that the world

[10] Elmo Caulkins, "Beauty in Business," *Atlantic Monthly*, 147:145–46 (1927).

today is witnessing a much more rapid rate of cultural invention than at any previous time. As one looks into the future, he can be sure that invention will increase, thus speeding up further cultural changes in Western society.

How fast man's culture can change while allowing man to maintain his peace of mind and equilibrium becomes an important question. Ogburn, in wrestling with this question, has suggested that man has three alternatives: (1) He can slow down the rate of cultural change if the pace should become too great for the biological organism to stand. (2) He can direct invention so that it will better fit the human organism, causing less warping of the animal creature which has to live and develop within the cultural framework. (3) He can confine his attention to correcting maladjustments which develop once culture traits are invented and cause unexpected personality strain.[11] By the latter alternative he would gradually improve his culture by correcting when they develop those problems which he cannot foresee.

There is this encouraging fact about the situation as one peers into the future. Studies of cultural anthropologists made among primitives and studies of sociologists made among moderns demonstrate the fact that man is remarkably malleable. His original nature can be shaped into numerous forms. His shoulders can be loaded with numerous cultural burdens, and yet man survives and lives reasonably happy and satisfied with himself. So he has done under numerous culture patterns, even though following the same general universal scheme.

This, of course, is not to argue that man should make no effort to improve his culture. Certainly the more needless baggage he can drop by the wayside and the more culture he can develop which will make his life easier, better adjusted, and more effective, the better. Science, especially social science, can help in this, as social science challenges man's values and tries to establish for him new values and goals in invention, as in other fields.

SUMMARY

Invention, the basic process of cultural change by which new material and nonmaterial culture traits are produced by man, has been covered. Some inventions are of only incidental significance, while others are basic in the sense that they initiate a whole series of inventions, which together may in the end revolutionize many aspects of human life.

11 Ogburn, *op. cit.*, pp. 336–46.

An invention is the product of men of genius working within the framework of a given culture base. What they can and will invent depends on the richness of this social heritage on which they have to draw. Building on the inventions of others, inventors push the creative process a step further. So the process goes on into the future, few major inventions ever being in any final sense completed. There is the slow beginning in the inventive process, the rapid-growth stage, the slower final stage that leads to artistic rather than practical additions.

A favorable attitude toward innovation is important to the inventive process. Western society is more tolerant than most toward the new; is quite ready, in fact, to replace folkways by technicways, to consider social policies to replace outworn folkways of government administration. Government research as a means of pooling inventive talent and so speeding up the process of cultural creation is now accepted practice.

Can the rate of culture change become too fast for man? There is no answer yet. We do know, however, that man is remarkably malleable.

DISCUSSION AND REVIEW QUESTIONS

1. What factors lie back of an invention?
2. Show how invention makes culture dynamic.
3. Does the term *invention* apply to nonmaterial as well as material culture?
4. Discuss basic inventions and their influence on cultural change.
5. Discuss the place of the inventor in cultural change. In what respect is he limited?
6. What do we mean when we say that invention is a social process rather than an individual act?
7. Would invention go on in the absence of any particular individual—for example, Edison? Explain.
8. What do duplicate inventions tend to prove?
9. Explain how social attitudes toward innovation affect the inventive process.
10. Discuss the term "technicways"; "stateways."
11. Discuss Chapin's cycle of invention.
12. What seems to be the final stage in the invention of material objects?
13. Discuss pooled research as a new system of invention.
14. Discuss the possible effects of rapid change through invention on personality.

SOURCEBOOK READINGS

FREEDMAN, RONALD, AMOS H. HAWLEY, WERNER S. LANDECKER, GERHARD E. LENSKI, and HORACE M. MINER. *Principles of Sociology* (rev. ed.). New York: Henry Holt & Co., Inc., 1956.
1. COTTRELL, W. F., "Death by Dieselization: A Case Study in the Reaction to Technological Change," pp. 220–29.

GITTLER, JOSEPH B. *Social Dynamics.* New York: McGraw-Hill Book Co., Inc., 1952.
    2. WOODWARD, W. E., "Boston Three Hundred Years Ago; Boston Today," pp.
      245–47.
KOENIG, SAMUEL, REX D. HOPPER, and FELIKS GROSS. *Sociology: A Book of Readings.* Englewood Cliffs, N.J.: Prentice-Hall, Inc., 1956.
    3. GILFILLAN, S. C., "The Process of Invention," pp. 513–19.
    4. DAVIS, KENNETH S., "The Machine Age Transforms the Farmer," pp. 533–38.
    5. RIDENOUR, LOUIS N., "Mechanical Brains: The Second Industrial Revolution,"
      pp. 538–46.
    6. OSBORN, FREDERICK, "Can We Control Atomic Energy?" pp. 546–49.
LEE, ELIZABETH BRYANT, and ALFRED McCLUNG LEE. *Social Problems in America*
   (rev. ed.). New York: Henry Holt & Co., Inc., 1955.
    7. OGBURN, WILLIAM FIELDING, "The Social Impact of Technological Changes,"
      pp. 48–59.
O'BRIEN, ROBERT W., CLARENCE C. SCHRAG, and WALTER T. MARTIN. *Readings in
   General Sociology* (2d ed.). Boston: Houghton Mifflin Co., 1957.
    8. BENDINER, ROBERT, "The Age of the Thinking Robot," pp. 172–80.
SCHULER, EDGAR A., DUANE L. GIBSON, MAUDE L. FIERO, and WILBUR B. BROOKOVER.
   Outside Readings in Sociology. New York: The Thomas Crowell Co., 1956.
    9. OGBURN, WILLIAM FIELDING, "The Process of Adjustment to New Inventions,"
      pp. 770–81.

SELECTED READINGS

ALLEN, FRANCIS R., HORNELL HART, DELBERT C. MILLER, WILLIAM F. OGBURN, and
   MEYER F. NIMKOFF. *Technology and Social Change.* New York: Appleton-
   Century-Crofts, Inc., 1957.
BARNETT, H. G. *Innovation: The Basis of Cultural Change.* New York: McGraw-Hill
   Book Company, Inc., 1954.
DRUCKER, PETER F. *The Future of Industrial Man, a Constructive Approach.* New
   York: John Day Co., Inc., 1942.
————. "America, Next Twenty Years," *Harper's.* "I. The Coming Labor Shortage."
   Nov., 1954, pp. 67–78; "II. The Promise of Automation." April, 1955, pp. 41–47;
   "III. The New Tycoons." May, 1955, pp. 39–44.
GILFILLAN, S. C. *Sociology of Invention.* New York: Follett Publishing Co., 1935.
HOCKING, WILLIAM E. *The Coming World Civilization.* New York: Harper & Brothers,
   1956.
HUGH-JONES, E. M. (ed.). *The Push-Button World: Automation Today.* Norman:
   University of Oklahoma Press, 1956.
KROEBER, A. L. *Configuration of Cultural Growth.* Berkeley: University of California
   Press, 1944.
MALINOWSKI, BRONISLAW. *The Dynamics of Cultural Change.* New Haven: Yale
   University Press, 1945.
MEAD, MARGARET. *Cultural Patterns and Technical Change.* New York: United Na-
   tions Educational, Scientific, and Cultural Organization, 1955.
OGBURN, W. F. *Social Change.* New York: The Viking Press, Inc., 1950.
————. *The Social Effects of Aviation.* Boston: Houghton Mifflin Co., 1946.
ORWELL, GEORGE. *Nineteen Eighty-Four.* New York: Harcourt, Brace & Co., 1949.

Chapter 5

Culture Change by Diffusion and Borrowing

The tendency of culture traits to spread has been mentioned in Chapter 2. Of this fact both the anthropologist and sociologist make much, for the diffusion of culture is one of the phenomenal processes of human history. Were it not for this process, civilization on the grand scale that exists today would be unknown. The borrowing of culture between peoples has pushed man forward both in material achievement and in patterns of behavior. No peoples fully admit their debt to other peoples, for people of all cultures are ethnocentric. Yet even the most self-assured 100 per cent American lives, acts, and thinks in an environment of culture, which Linton says is 90 per cent borrowed. Read him in the following convincing account:

"The service of diffusion in enriching the content of individual cultures has been of the utmost importance. There is probably no culture extant to-day which owes more than 10 per cent of its total elements to inventions made by members of its own society. Because we live in a period of rapid invention we are apt to think of our own culture as largely self-created, but the role which diffusion has played in its growth may be brought home to us if we consider the beginning of the average man's day. . . .

"Our solid American citizen awakens in a bed built on a pattern which originated in the Near East but which was modified in Northern Europe before it was transmitted to America. He throws back covers made from cotton, domesticated in India, or linen, domesticated in the Near East, or wool from sheep, also domesticated in the Near East, or silk, the use of which was discovered in China. All of these materials have been spun and woven by processes invented in the Near East. He slips into his moccasins, invented by the Indians of the Eastern woodlands, and goes into the bathroom, whose fixtures are a mixture of European and American inventions, both of recent date. He takes off his pajamas, a garment invented in India, and washes with soap invented by the ancient Gauls. He then shaves, a masochistic rite which seems to have been derived from either Sumer or ancient Egypt.

"Returning to the bedroom, he removes his clothes from a chair of southern European style and proceeds to dress. He puts on garments whose form originally derived from the skin clothing of the nomads of the Asiatic steppes, puts on shoes made from skins tanned by a process invented in ancient Egypt and cut to a pattern derived from the classical civilization of the Mediterranean, and ties around his neck a strip of bright-colored cloth which is a vestigial survival of the shoulder shawls worn by the seventeenth century Croatians. Before going out for breakfast he glances through the window, made of glass invented in Egypt, and if it is raining puts on overshoes made of rubber discovered by the Central American Indians and takes an umbrella, invented in southeastern Asia. Upon his head he puts a hat made of felt, a material invented in the Asiatic steppes.

"On his way to breakfast he stops to buy a paper, paying for it with coins, an ancient Lydian invention. At the restaurant a whole new series of borrowed elements confronts him. His plate is made of a form of pottery invented in China. His knife is of steel, an alloy first made in southern India, his fork a medieval Italian invention, and his spoon a derivative of a Roman original. He begins breakfast with an orange from the eastern Mediterranean, a canteloupe from Persia, or perhaps a piece of African Watermelon. With this he has coffee, an Abyssinian plant, with cream and sugar. Both the domestication of cows and the idea of milking them originated in the Near East, while sugar was first made in India. After his fruit and first coffee he goes on to waffles, cakes made by a Scandinavian technique from wheat domesticated in Asia Minor. Over these he pours maple syrup, invented by the Indians of the Eastern woodlands. As a side dish he may have the egg of a species of bird domesticated in Indo-China, or thin strips of the flesh of an animal domesticated in Eastern Asia which have been salted and smoked by a process developed in northern Europe.

"When our friend has finished eating he settles back to smoke, an American Indian habit, consuming a plant domesticated in Brazil in either a pipe, derived from the Indians of Virginia, or a cigarette, derived from Mexico. If he is hardy enough he may even attempt a cigar, transmitted to us from the Antilles by way of Spain. While smoking he reads the news of the day, imprinted in characters invented by the ancient Semites upon a material invented in China by a process invented in Germany. As he absorbs the accounts of foreign troubles he will, if he is a good conservative citizen, thank a Hebrew deity in an Indo-European language that he is 100 per cent American."[1]

THE SIGNIFICANCE OF DIFFUSION AND BORROWING

Just as winds, waters, animals, and human beings spread the seeds of various plants over the face of the earth, so also has the movement of people by land, water, and later by air, spread the different inventions of man.

Diffusion and borrowing have gone on throughout the course of history, as the introductory quotations show so clearly. In early days, when a day's journey was limited to perhaps 20 miles on foot, borrowing was confined to a small geographical space. So cultures developed great diversity in meeting the needs of men in different environments. And the exchange of what man learned in his trial and error —adjusting to his local environment—has been limited. Now, with air travel, diffusion goes on on a worldwide scale, and borrowing between peoples on opposite sides of the earth is possible. Philosopher Arnold J. Toynbee, writing in 1947, tries to look back on 1947 from 100 years in the future, and then from 2,100 years. He comments as follows:

"Future historians will say, I think, that the great event of the twentieth century was the impact of the Western Civilization upon all the other living societies of the world of that day. They will say of this impact that it was so powerful and so pervasive that it turned the lives of all its victims upside down and inside out—affecting the behavior, outlook, feelings, and beliefs of individual men, women and children in an intimate way, touching chords in human souls that are not touched by mere external material forces—however ponderous and terrifying. This will be said, I feel sure, by historians looking back on our times even from as short a time hence as A.D. 2047. . . .

". . . The historians of A.D. 4047 will say that the impact of the Western Civilization on its contemporaries, in the second half of the second millennium of the Christian Era, was the epoch-making event of that age, because it was the first step toward the unification of mankind into one single society. By their time, the unity of mankind will perhaps have come to seem one of the fundamental condi-

[1] Ralph Linton, *The Study of Man* (New York: Appleton-Century-Crofts, Inc., 1936), pp. 325–27.

tions of human life—just part of the order of nature—and it may need quite an effort of imagination on their part to recall the parochial outlook of the pioneers of civilization during the first six thousand years or so of its existence. . . ."[2]

In the two accounts just presented are pictures of culture as it is related to the past and to tomorrow. The first account shows that exchange of culture has been a major process of history. Yet one sees today a world of vastly different patterns, in spite of all this. This is largely because of the relative isolation of peoples from each other. They have borrowed much, but it has taken long periods of time for culture traits to spread over the earth. Most traits have not gone far. Few have become universal. In isolated areas of the globe, borrowing has been confined to peoples a day's walk away. Many local cultures have harbored their unique inventions, and they have found little place in the larger world outside.

The second article is a picture of tomorrow. It foresees cultural uniformity throughout the world as cultures meet and blend in this age of easy mobility and globe-girdling travel.

If diffusion has been a major process of human history, how much more is it going to be in this day of Olympic games, international "atoms for peace" conferences, world trade fairs, international student exchange, and intercontinental airlines.

So, although culture traits come into being only by invention, the culture of any particular people is the sum total of what it has borrowed and what it has invented. Diffusion and borrowing are, therefore, as the sociologist sees it, major sociological forces in human history.

The term *diffusion* applies to *the spread (mobility) of a culture trait or culture complex from a center of origin;* the term *borrowing* refers to *the taking over by a people of a culture trait that is not a part of their native culture area.* For example, the spread of a culture trait from America to Europe, such as the use of tobacco, would be described by the term diffusion. From the European point of view, the process would be described as borrowing from the New World.

DIFFUSION AMONG CULTURE AREAS

Today, with numerous contacts between various peoples of the world, any particular group of people is likely to borrow more than it invents. In fact borrowing, under certain circumstances, becomes a major competitive process. It would be interesting indeed to know the number of spies that the various nations are using for their at-

2 Arnold J. Toynbee, "Encounters between Civilizations," *Harper's Magazine,* 194: 290 (April 1947).

tempts to borrow—steal, we call it when referring to the other nation —various aspects of the inventive process in the making of bombs, guided missiles, submarines, rocket ships, and other nuclear and hydrogen-powered war-making devices. Any nation knows that it can save years of work and millions of dollars if it can borrow some of the secret steps of manufacture of these new sources of motive power.

Except for such secrets, so important in the competitive strength of nations, modern nations try to hasten the borrowing process by intentional diffusion, that is, by making every attempt possible to spread new ideas and inventions. To expedite this process, modern nations have scientific journals in which new discoveries are reported. In order that the candidate for the Ph.D. degree (the degree designed for those specializing in research) may become acquainted with the scientific discoveries reported in the journals of other nations, he is required to have a reading knowledge of two foreign languages. The usual languages required of the American scholar are French and German, the two foreign cultures in which scientific developments have been most frequent.

In the field of invented gadgets, radio and television have become the most effective devices of diffusion of all history. In America alone there are some 150,000,000 radios, and television is also on the way to becoming universal. Millions are spent in heralding the merits of a new product over the airwaves. Complementing this means of diffusion are the advertisements in national magazines and metropolitan newspapers. In a matter of days or weeks almost every housewife knows about almost any new gadget.

In the borrowing of culture, people in close contact often take over a whole complex rather than an isolated trait. Thus the Pilgrims took over the Indian maize complex in almost every detail. They planted corn in hills as the Indians did. Where fish were available, they planted a fish in the hill to fertilize it. They hoed dirt up around the hills. They even planted beans and pumpkins in the hills with the corn. They used a wooden pin to pull open the husks. When the maize culture trait spread to England, however, it went as an isolated trait rather than a culture complex. The Europeans planted the corn in rows exactly as they planted the other cereal grains and cultivated it in the same way.

BORROWING AMONG SOCIAL CLASSES

Culture traits may spread not only from their original area but also from secondary areas in which they have been adopted. They may spread not only horizontally, that is, geographically, and from one class to a class on the same general economic and social level, but especially in an open-class system like our own they may spread vertically, that is, from one social class to another, up or down the scale. For example, in the United States, where opportunity has been equalized to such a great extent, a new style in dress is about as quickly adopted by the clerk in the ten-cent store or the girl in the farm community as by the wealthy matron in Boston. So also songs and tunes, dances, new games, and other traits tend to diffuse through all social classes regardless of the class by which they were initiated or the class that first borrowed them. Brought from abroad, certain slang phrases and vulgarities perhaps still remain uniquely lower class, but most innovations in America tend to become the possession of all classes. Even a trait like birth control, which began among the upper classes, has gradually sifted downward until few remain today, even among the lowest classes, who have deep inhibitions or religious taboos restricting their practice of birth control. Because of limited dwelling space and lack of bathroom facilities, those among the lower classes probably do not practice it as effectively as those in the upper classes, but the trait has diffused down to them.

DIFFUSION VERSUS INDEPENDENT INVENTION

Some leading anthropologists have taken the position that all culture originated in one major center from which it spread out over the face of the earth. Others are convinced that cultures have originated independently in various parts of the world without any contact with the original inventors of the trait. Those who hold the first view will argue that the similarity between the pyramid of Egypt and the mounds of the mound-builders in the lower Mississippi Valley of Illinois exists because at some time lost to history the mound-builders' ancestors migrated from the original culture center of the Middle East to reproduce the culture they originally learned in the far distant land. On the other hand, those who believe in independent invention would say that through trial and error, the accidents of history, and the similarities of geography, various peoples building culture in different parts of the world sometimes develop traits that have great similarity.

Our only interest in this controversy is that it affects the interpretations of history from time to time. Even if we chose to do so, we could not settle the argument. However, there seems to be little support for the view that all inventions of a similar nature must have originated from one source. As has been pointed out, inventions of a similar nature are developed today, independently of each other,

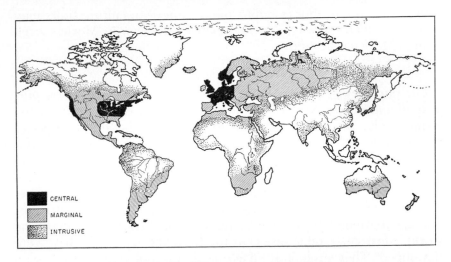

The Spread of Euro-American Culture

The European white man's civilization has been spread throughout much of the globe. (From Man and Culture, *by Clark Wissler, p. 346. The Thomas Crowell Co., 1923.)*

in various parts of the world in which the culture base is adequate. Since that type of development is going on today, it is logical to assume that it has been going on throughout history. The working of bronze or the development of weapons of iron could have come about entirely independently where migrating peoples found these natural resources in the environment.

THEORIES OF DIFFUSION

Some sociologists think of the process of diffusion as being like a pebble dropped into the water about which waves spread out in concentric circles in an ever widening zone. Others think of it as water seeking its own level, that is, traits tending to diffuse out from the center of origin along the line of least resistance. Some nearby areas, where the culture is compatible, will accept the new trait. Other areas, which for some reason are resistant to or disinterested in the culture trait, may not accept it. It is the later analogy that would seem to describe more aptly what actually happens in the diffusion of culture traits.

In the modern world, however, it is doubtful whether either of these pictures is fully adequate. Culture traits today, because of effective means for travel and communication, may jump from one area to another far distant. For example, many American culture traits may take root much more readily in Japan today than in Mexico, even though Mexico is next door.

TYPES OF DIFFUSION

For purposes of convenience, diffusion may be classified as *purposeful* and *nonpurposeful*. This distinction means exactly what the terms imply. Some traits are spread by the deliberate attempts of people in the culture which possesses them. Other traits spread without anyone's intending that they find a place in another culture.

The Christian and Moslem missionary movements have been among the major agencies of purposeful diffusion in the field of religion. In fact, these missionary movements represent the greatest organized attempt ever made by man to spread a religion to all the world. Most early religions were for the tribe in which they were developed. They excluded outsiders; it was not part of their plan to take outsiders in. Even the Jews considered themselves a peculiar people chosen of God; they had no intention of converting the rest of the world to Judaism.

Business, which promotes by advertising and salesmanship, represents another great agency in the purposeful diffusion of the modern world. Products are advertised and sold by planned campaigns, the intention being to spread new inventions in the field of technology and material culture to as many people as can be induced to purchase. On a worldwide scale trade and commerce have been agencies for purposeful diffusion.

Throughout history, wars of invasion and conquest have often been motivated in part by the idea among one people of spreading their culture or some particular phase of it to other peoples. Before World War I Germans considered their culture to be the best in the world, and a part of the rationalization that motivated the initiation of both world wars was to spread this culture first to nations surrounding Germany, and then to the world. Soviet communism embodies the idea of purposeful diffusion, attempting to organize communistic units throughout the world and gradually stir up conflict and revolution until the time when Communists will be able to take over the weakened and "degenerate" capitalistic system.

A certain amount of nonpurposeful diffusion always accompanies the promoted or purposeful diffusion. In many historic wars of conquest the conquerors brought home women whom they married, only to have their own culture changed by the outsiders they had incorporated into their own group. Travelers and tourists today visit the Orient or other foreign shores and bring home souvenirs.

These find their way to the mantelpiece, and from this display a fad in decoration may start. This nonpurposeful diffusion is often the more effective. For example, book publishers do their best to promote a novel by advertising and salesmanship, but it is quite generally recognized that the word-of-mouth gossip of women's groups, "Have you read this?" and other such informal means of diffusion are probably the most important phase of making a best seller. It has even been suggested that book companies might find it profitable to give away the first hundred thousand copies of a novel.

Joel V. Berreman, University of Oregon sociologist, has made an analytical study of the comparative effect of advertising and gossip on the sale of books.[3] His study of *Goodbye, Mr. Chips* indicates that although there was relatively little advertising, the book was a surprise success. Its sales seemed to have resulted from factors apart from the conscious efforts of publishers to promote it. Apparently it contained homely elements that inspired a great deal of discussion and gossip among women's groups. It rapidly rose to the point of being a best seller and continued to be so over a long period of

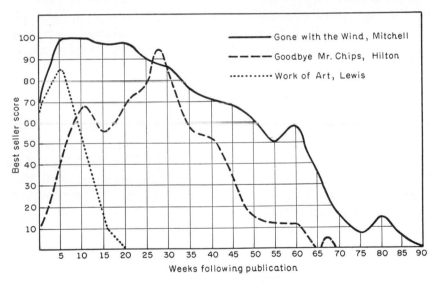

What Makes a Best Seller?

The sales of Gone With the Wind *resulted from effective purposeful diffusion by publisher promotion plus nonpurposeful diffusion by informal means; sales of* Goodby, Mr. Chips *resulted primarily from nonpurposeful diffusion; and sales of* Work of Art *resulted primarily from purposeful diffusion. (Data by J. V. Berreman, University of Oregon.)*

[3] Ph.D. thesis, Stanford University.

time. *Gone With the Wind* was heavily promoted by advertising and book reviews and soon rose to a high peak of sales, but the high sales level continued long after heavy promotion was terminated, indicating that probably after a certain point gossip or other non-purposeful factors in diffusion were responsible for the continuing high level of sales. Finally Berreman takes Sinclair Lewis' book, *Work of Art*, as an example of a case where a very aggressive sales campaign failed to produce notable results. There apparently was little in this book to inspire gossip, and even though Sinclair Lewis had previously published notable best sellers, such as *Main Street*, little interest in the book could be stimulated. (See chart.)

Many fads in America, like slang phrases, hit songs, or transient forms of recreation, such as miniature golf, seem to spread without much purposeful diffusion on anybody's part.

THE RATE AND DISTANCE OF DIFFUSION

Traits spread with different speeds and for different distances from a center of origin. Historically some important traits like Indian corn (maize) spread very rapidly through the European continent, and then much further. Christianity spread rapidly, being a religion propelled by purposeful diffusion. The intent of its founders was to make it a possession of all humanity, and with missionary zeal they carried it to all lands. Mohammedanism spread even faster, forwarding its spiritual message by the sword.

The horse, without any purposeful intent on anybody's part, spread rather quickly over the face of the earth. This diffusion probably happened because the horse is adapted to a wide range of geographical territory and because, being a fast traveler able to cover much more distance than man could on foot, and being able also to bear heavy burdens, it lent itself to many uses as a domestic animal. Copper and bronze working, on the other hand, spread very slowly, probably in part because they require complicated skills and in part because the basic metals are available only in certain natural environments.[4]

Some culture traits never get beyond their original area; in fact, some never spread far within the culture area in which they are invented. For example, when the automobiles first appeared, a Hibbing, Minnesota, inventor built a large clocklike speedometer to be attached to the radiator so that everyone in front of the automobile could see how fast it was moving. The local newspaper heralded this as a great invention that would not only restrain drivers to

[4] Clark Wissler, *Man and Culture* (New York: The Thomas Crowell Co., 1923), chap. 8.

socially acceptable speeds but would also warn the pedestrians how fast the oncoming car was traveling so they might plan their escape. As significant as the invention was then considered to be by the inventor and the local newspaper, it has never been heard of since. On the other hand, the small speedometer on the dashboard inside the car, which the driver and occupants of the car alone can observe, has spread wherever automobiles are used.

Just why the one invention spread and the other did not is a matter for speculation. Probably the prime reasons are that the latter mechanism, being less expensive, less subject to damage from flying obstacles, and less exposed to the weather and dirt damage, was more practical than the former. Perhaps drivers also prefer to have their speed known only to occupants of the car.

FACTORS AFFECTING THE SPREAD OF CULTURE TRAITS

Characteristics of the Traits Themselves. Students of culture hold that each culture trait or complex tends to have its own dynamics insofar as rate and distance of spread are concerned. What is it about the trait itself that may affect its spread?

It has already been suggested that the *practical appeal* of a culture trait affects its spread. The comparative practical appeal of the two kinds of automobile speedometer cited may explain why the one survived and the other disappeared. Practical appeal is no doubt a major factor today in the spread of most gadgets and other material inventions. Millions of dollars are spent annually diffusing information concerning material culture traits. Modern advertising has become the major vehicle, and one of its main appeals is on the basis of utility.

A second factor about a trait which affects its spread is its *sensory appeal*. Traits with definite sensory appeal may spread widely over the surface of the earth. No better example can be cited than tobacco, the weed that was in use among the American Indians when the white man came and which today has spread through every part of the world. It has become so important in the habit systems of many peoples that it becomes a medium of exchange more important than money during periods of privation in warring nations. Such was the case in both world wars, when the cigarette ration of an American soldier could get him almost anything he wanted in a conquered country.

Other culture traits make an *intellectual appeal*. Take the theory of evolution. It so challenged the imagination of man that he read its implications into every field of scientific thought. Even though the theory challenged traditional religion, its interpretation of life and the universe has become known wherever man has achieved the higher levels of learning throughout the world.

Another factor in culture trait diffusion is its *artistic appeal.* Many works of art are spread widely. For example, the motion picture is a modern art form which has spread from the movie capital of the world in Hollywood throughout all modern nations. Or consider the spread of works of art through history. The finer pieces of painting and music have been preserved through the centuries. Such items are relatively timeless and diffuse widely, finding eventually a place in many cultures in many lands. Art is, of course, one of the major appeals in modern diffusion by advertising. The beauty of the new model is stressed to motivate the buyer.

A fourth type of appeal is *comic appeal.* In a day of radio and television, jokes spread rapidly throughout the nation. They may even spread to other culture areas where a similar sense of humor exists.

Influences Outside the Traits. Outside culture traits themselves, there are factors which affect their diffusion. *Geographical factors* definitely affect the spread of culture traits. Geographical barriers, mountains, rivers, and in the earlier days, oceans, blocked the spread of traits, because there was no way for man to cross back and forth readily, and there were no indirect means of communication which made for the spread of traits or complexes in the absence of travel. Geography always limits the spread of traits that are closely allied to soil, climate, or topography, for being adapted only to a particular part of the earth's surface, they must remain there. Corn, for example, will probably never spread to most parts of Alaska, because the geography forbids its planting.

Political barriers often hinder the spread of culture traits. Some nations forbid travel across their boundary or restrict it rigidly, trying to keep out new ideas or to keep their own activities from being known to the outside world.

In the modern world the Soviet Union has set up many barriers to hinder the diffusion of culture. It erects barriers to keep the outside world from knowing conditions and attitudes in Russia, and barriers to keep the Russian people from learning much about the real standard of living in capitalistic countries such as the United States. No doubt Soviet leaders secretly agree with a statement attributed to the late President Roosevelt. He is reputed to have said that the thing which would win Russia from Communism in the end was the Sears and Roebuck catalog.

Political ideologies may also close the minds of a people to the acceptance of many culture traits from the outside. Most political philosophies under nationalistic regimes create an atmosphere of ethnocentrism which automatically leads to the rejection of cultural traits which are not compatible. Communists find no place in their culture for many of the traits of a capitalistic economy. Neither can a capitalistic country, which takes its capitalism seriously, find a place in its system for many ideologies which are vital to communism.

Language, of course, is one of the major barriers to diffusion of culture traits, especially of a nonmaterial sort. In order to accept many culture traits in the field of ideology, one must understand the language. Many have dreamed of a day when there will be a universal language, such as Esperanto, which will make it possible for ideas to become the property of all peoples alike, thus stimulating similar thinking and the ultimate development of a worldwide culture pattern.

Affecting the acceptance of a trait by a new area is the factor of *cultural preparedness* in the area itself. This has been implied above. If the culture area can find a place for the diffusing trait, it will likely be adopted. If it is contrary to the culture pattern of the area, it is likely to be rejected or simply passed by as being unimportant.

One could scarcely expect a primitive tribe, for example, which has not yet had any experience with the wheel, to adopt any complex phase of our culture like lubrication oil, which is essential to all of our engines with fast-moving wheel parts. If they did borrow it, they would have to use it in some way quite different from that in which we use it, perhaps to grease their bodies for ornamentation or to use as hair oil.

Mohammedan culture, in spreading westward, could hardly be adopted by the Euro-American culture area because of its characteristic traits such as polygyny, the veil, the unequal status of women, and the rest of the patterns that go with that religious and family social system.

So it is seen that each culture pattern has within it a sense of fitness and unity which is not to be disturbed by the acceptance of contrary ideas. New culture traits of a political, economic, or social nature have to penetrate slowly and gradually, acting as leavening influences, transforming the whole social-political system slowly. This kind of diffusion takes generations. It cannot ordinarily come suddenly and catastrophically like the acceptance of the automobile or some material trait or complex which may, in the course of a few years, entirely transform the external nature of a civilization.

Effect of New Traits. It is usually assumed that culture traits or complexes, once borrowed, are modified by the borrowers to fit into the trend of their own culture. Jules Henry, professor of sociology and anthropology at Washington University, has challenged this view.[5] He suggests that borrowed culture complexes, rather than being molded to fit into the existing trend of cultural development of a people, may in actuality drastically and swiftly transform a culture pattern and start a new trend of development. In support of the thesis he cites the tremendous new industrial developments in Japan resulting from contact with Western culture. He concludes that what took place in Japan was "not so much the transformation of capitalism by the Japanese 'culture pattern,' as the anthropologists love to put it, but rather the transformation of Japan by a new cultural entity introduced from across the sea."

He goes on to apply this hypothesis to many other such broad changes that are taking place in the world today and concludes

. . . it is not so much that old, local "cultural patterns" are determining what changes shall take place in the world today, but rather that irresistible forces are pushing the world toward a goal that shall be very much the same for many of us regardless of our traditions. Wherever we go, wherever we shall arrive, will be a place of no return. For the old ways will be gone, and the changes that occur will bring about a new alignment of human relationships.

ISOLATION AND CONTACT IN BORROWING

The most important determiner of the trend of cultural history is the extent of a people's contact with others. If there has been rather complete isolation, because of geographical or cultural barriers, there will be relatively little change, for opportunities for borrowing will be few. Innovation will generally be frowned upon, and the whole stream of life perpetuated in much its same form from generation to generation. A culture having many contacts with outside cultures, by contrast, tends to borrow new traits and thereby to change rapidly. It profits not only by the experience of the local group in its geographical habitat, not by its cultural history alone, but also by that of others whose cultural building has been along different lines.

The tribe with a dozen contacts with outside cultures, for example, has a dozen times as many chances for picking up a significant new cultural trait which may prove to be basic in its progress and in the development of its own culture. Any one of the dozen tribes may have domesticated some new type of plant for food use or some animal for human use. Any one of them may have invented some new

---

[5] Jules Henry, "Cultural Discontinuity and the Shadow of the Past," *Scientific Monthly*, 66:248–54 (March 1948).

and better device for working the land, for capturing animals, for preventing disease, for dealing with the powers that are conceived to control life and the universe, for handling mothers-in-law, or any one of the other thousands of problems that face man in his life in the natural environment and in the social world.

Contact does not assure that all new traits of neighboring cultures will be borrowed. A people must first find some place for them in the culture which they already possess. Some traits may not be borrowed because they would have a disruptive influence on the culture pattern; others are not borrowed because of fear and psychological resistance of various sorts. But with contact the opportunity for borrowing is there, and borrowing is much more probable. Often traits and complexes which are not actually borrowed have an influence in modifying the culture of the local people, no matter how much they resist the new way of life or the new device. For example, Turkish women and, especially, Turkish men once had little use for Westerners whose women do not wear the veil. But no matter how much they resisted, to the extent that they came to have contact with Western civilization and borrowed its machines and its machine ways of life, to that extent the veil has gradually disappeared along with many of the customs that went with it. So also have been the developments in China. No matter how much China valued the system of beauty that was involved in women's dainty feet, under a system of feet-binding, the custom vanished as women took their places in modern factories and took over Western ways.

Some such basic changes take two or three generations; the first generation may resist change violently, swearing never to have anything to do with the new practice. But as contact persists, the second and third generations will have much less resistance to the new trait than did the generation which was originally shocked by it. As the old become accustomed to it, they become more tolerant and eventually come to use it, or at least permit it to modify their own more sacred ways of doing things.

Throughout history, culture has flowered at the points of greatest contact of peoples. We have already referred to the high development of culture where the land travel routes converged in the Near East in a day of land travel, and then again at the crossroads of the New World, where the diverse cultures that developed in North America converged at the narrow neck of land that joins North and South America. Here culture was *cross fertilized*, as culture borrowing was speeded up by contact and the great civilizations of the New World developed.

CONTACTS BETWEEN MODERN AND PRIMITIVE CULTURES

In the preceding paragraphs the benefits of culture contact have been discussed from the standpoint of speeding up borrowing and hastening change. The general effect is to cross fertilize and enrich the culture and to improve it. This is valid generalization where meeting cultures have comparable strength. But in the modern world, where so often the cultures of advanced nations with machine civilization come in contact with the civilization of primitives, the strength of the two cultures is so different that the outcome may be disastrous to the primitives.

The English anthropologist Pitt-Rivers has indicated different outcomes of culture contact, depending on the culture of the people in contact. He says, in discussing what has come to be called the "native problem," that the following are possible outcomes:

"1. Immigrant and more powerful culture-bearers may so revolutionize the environmental conditions of the native and culturally weaker people that, incapable of readaptation, they become eliminated and die out—examples, Tasmanians, and some Australian, Polynesian and Melanesian tribes; or

"2. The elimination of the people of a weaker culture may be disguised by a blood-dilution which gradually changes the ethos or ethnic continuity of the population, substituting miscegenated stocks, more adaptable to the changed culture conditions, which gradually take the place of a former population—instance, the Maoris of New Zealand.

"3. A people forcibly removed from their own culture environment and transplanted into another, where they are preserved and bred, may become adapted to new cultural conditions, with a minimum of change in ethnic continuity. Example, the Negro population of the United States during the period of slavery.

"4. Gradual culture assimilation and amalgamation of aboriginal people by immigrant people. Example, the Polynesian assimilation of Melanesian or Australoid peoples.

"5. The relative segregation of small cultural pockets maintaining themselves within the sphere of influence of a stronger culture. We might perhaps cite some of the Lolo communities near the Tibeto-Burmese border in Southern China.

"6. Strong immigrant culture-bearers may meet with strong and persistent opposition on the part of the natives who may resist cultural contamination with great determination. I think particularly of the Balinese peaceful, but stubborn, rejection of all European cultural influences, or of the traditional Chinese intolerance of European proselytism, provoking, however, a more emphatic demonstration.

"7. Immigrant culture-bearers may succeed in extinguishing an aboriginal culture, but yet fail either to extinguish or assimilate its bearers, who appear to survive the condition of cultural disequilibrium. May we here not cite some African examples, among, for instance, Basuto or Bantu tribes; and finally—

"8. We may be reminded that the indigenous elements may eventually absorb the immigrants and assimilate them with or without taking over much of the culture of the latter. Here, for instance, we may think of the assimilative tendencies of the Chinese, who appear to have assimilated even the Chinese Jews who in physical features, language, dress, habit and customs, in fact in everything except their religion, appear Chinese."[6]

In our time of world wars which reach even the most isolated island and jungle tribes, the problems primitives face in culture contact are of major importance to them. Can these cultures survive a day of jet aircraft, intercontinental missiles, and atomic submarines, which bring the ways of the industrialized West to the doorstep of primitive cultures everywhere? Culture change will come, but, as in the past, it may be overwhelming to the "natives" because of the vast difference in the two cultural systems.

How far-reaching these changes are can be illustrated by marriage problems in East Africa today. There, where wives have always been purchased by so many cattle or goats, depending on the girl's beauty and physical strength and the father's bargaining power, thousands of Africans have moved to cities to subsist on a wage of $10 to $20 per month. Wives are bought by cash now, but what young man can set aside enough from his meager earnings to buy a wife outright? He gets her on the Western installment plan. Babies come and his economic burdens increase. If he cannot pay, the father has a right to take the wife back and resell her. Even if he is not disposed to do so, strained family relations, such as did not exist in the native culture, develop.

PRESENT IMPETUS TO CULTURE DIFFUSION

Implication of Worldwide Diffusion. With the extensive diffusion of the modern world, is it likely that culture will eventually approach a state of uniformity and similarity throughout the world? This is a logical question, for diversity of culture originated through migration of peoples out from an original culture center and their

[6] G. Pitt-Rivers, "The Effect on Native Races of Contact with European Civilization," *Man*, 27:2–7 (1927).

isolation from the parent culture. It seems logical that the reverse process might be true, that is, that as all peoples of the world come together through new means of contact and communication, which make possible the knitting of the world into one great culture area, a greater culture similarity would eventually come about. This idea is implied in the latter part of the comment of Jules Henry, cited above, as well as in the quotation in the early part of the chapter by Toynbee. Although a logical possibility, one must admit that the time when all cultures will even approach a blending into one great world culture seems beyond realization in the immediate future. It will undoubtedly be nearer Toynbee's A.D. 4047 than A.D. 2047. Diversities of culture are too vast and contacts still far too few for the process of cultural growth toward a uniform cultural pattern to proceed except at a very halting pace.

Another interesting question for speculation in a day of worldwide diffusion is: When will a saturation point be reached with regard to the diffusion of a particular culture trait? This question is an especially pertinent one in the field of business, where increasing markets for the use of goods determine not only the amount a factory can sell but the amount that it can produce and, therefore, the number of people it can employ and the length of time over which it can employ them.

Modern advertising as a propaganda device apparently assumes that the saturation point is flexible: it depends on how badly the advertiser makes the people want the product. If goods are sufficiently advertised, the assumption is that the saturation point will be much further away than if it is poorly advertised. It is also assumed that the saturation point will be reached much more rapidly in the diffusion of a new article, like a vacuum cleaner, if the company insists upon cash rather than credit. The credit contract makes possible a much greater diffusion of an article and, therefore, a greater market.

Even more interesting is the question of how far diffusion, as practiced by modern business through advertising, is practical on a worldwide scale. Is it possible to create markets for many manufactured gadgets of the Western world in other nations which are not now gadget-minded? Or will these nations in the course of time borrow the whole pattern of Western industrial production? These questions are especially pertinent with regard to the future of overpopulated India, China, smaller adjacent Afro-Asian nations, and Latin America. Even more pertinent today are problems of purposeful diffusion on a worldwide scale of ideas and practices in the field of population control. Western methods of life-saving have been diffused widely. This aspect of Western culture appeals to peoples in many lands. But the

West has been less missionary-minded about spreading knowledge of birth control methods than the life-saving techniques of medical science. It remains to be seen whether the prolific masses of India, China, and the Malay Peninsula will borrow Western methods of birth control. A beginning is now being made in India, which in the mid-1950's first sanctioned contraception as a matter of national policy.

It has taken the world thousands of years to reach its present population of two and three-quarter billion. At present rates of growth, however, the world's population will double by the end of this century. In many nations technological development already lags far behind population growth; their populations are far in excess of an adequate food supply, and there seems no likelihood of technology catching up unless birth rates are brought under drastic control.

SUMMARY

In this chapter cultural diffusion has been discussed. It is the major process by which cultural traits tend to move out from the center of their invention and to the extent that they spread, they change the ways of men. As people in one culture area borrow the culture traits and complexes of another, their own culture is modified by the new borrowed elements.

Diffusion is a major process of history; yet the possibility of independent invention must be granted. Rather than spreading concentrically, traits diffuse in the direction of least resistance. Two types of diffusion operate: purposeful, that directed by conscious human effort; and nonpurposeful, that which goes on without conscious human promotion. Both are influential in the modern world, but probably at no other time in history has purposeful diffusion been so possible, because of media for indirect communication, and so much used.

Now as always some traits spread widely; others remain local. Some factors affecting the spread of culture traits are found in the traits themselves—practical appeal, sensory appeal, intellectual appeal, artistic or comic appeal; other factors are in the situations encountered by the diffusing traits—geographical and political barriers, political ideologies, language differences, and differences in general cultural preparedness of the receiving area.

Opportunity for contact and culture borrowing has been a major factor in the destiny of peoples. Civilizations have flowered at the points of greatest contact, where the cross-fertilization of culture was made possible by borrowing. Today in the contact of primitives with machine civilization, the fate of primitives everywhere hangs in the balance. We may actually be approaching a time when a trend toward worldwide cultural uniformity will bring all the diverse cultures of the world that developed through isolation in a day of limited contact toward a common likeness.

DISCUSSION AND REVIEW QUESTIONS

1. Illustrate the spread of culture and discuss the significance of diffusion to human history and to the future.
2. Define the terms "borrowing" and "diffusion."
3. What factors expedite these cultural processes today?
4. Distinguish borrowing between cultural areas and between social classes within a culture area.
5. Discuss briefly the conflict of views between those who believe in diffusion and those who believe in independent invention.
6. Evaluate the concentric theory of diffusion.
7. Define and illustrate purposeful and nonpurposeful diffusion.
8. Do traits in diffusion spread equal distances and at an equal rate? Explain.
9. Discuss and illustrate factors which reside within the culture trait itself that affect rate and distance of diffusion. That are outside the trait itself.
10. Discuss the factor of isolation and contact in borrowing.
11. What are some of the possible implications of the contact of modern and primitive cultures in the world today?
12. Do you think that greater uniformity of culture throughout the world is in prospect?
13. If this should result, what would some of the consequences be?

SOURCEBOOK READINGS

FREEDMAN, RONALD, AMOS H. HAWLEY, WERNER S. LANDECKER, GERHARD E. LENSKI, and HORACE M. MINER. *Principles of Sociology* (rev. ed.). New York: Henry Holt & Co., Inc., 1956.
　　1. REDFIELD, ROBERT, "Culture Changes in Yucatan," pp. 345–51.
GITTLER, JOSEPH B. *Social Dynamics.* New York: McGraw-Hill Book Co., Inc., 1952.
　　2. LINTON, RALPH, "The Role of Diffusion in Cultural Change," pp. 288–89.
O'BRIEN, ROBERT W., CLARENCE C. SCHRAG, and WALTER T. MARTIN. *Readings in General Sociology* (2d ed.). Boston: Houghton Mifflin Co., 1957.
　　3. BARNETT, JAMES H., "The Easter Festival: A Study in Cultural Change," pp. 167–72.
SCHULER, EDGAR A., DUANE L. GIBSON, MAUDE L. FIERO, and WILBUR B. BROOKOVER. *Outside Readings in Sociology.* New York: The Thomas Crowell Co., 1956.
　　4. TOYNBEE, ARNOLD J., "Encounters Between Civilizations," pp. 826–33.
WILSON, LOGAN, and WILLIAM L. KOLB. *Sociological Analysis.* New York: Harcourt, Brace & Co., Inc., 1949.
　　5. LINTON, RALPH, "Diffusion," pp. 93–94.

SELECTED READINGS

ADIR, JOHN, and EVON VOGT. "Navaho and Zuni Veterans: A Study of Contrasting Modes of Cultural Change," *American Anthropologist*, 51:547–61 (1949).
BENEDICT, RUTH. *Patterns of Culture.* Baltimore: Penguin Books, 1946.

COOK, S. F. "Demographic Consequences of European Contact with Primitive Peoples," *Annals of the American Academy of Political and Social Science*, 237: 107–11 (Jan., 1945).

HARDING, D. W. *Social Psychology and Individual Values*. London: Hutchinson & Co., 1953.

JUNGK, ROBERT. Trans. by Marguerite Waldman. *Tomorrow Is Already Here*. New York: Simon & Schuster, Inc., 1954.

KROEBER, A. L. *Configurations of Cultural Growth*. Berkeley: University of California Press, 1944.

MALINOWSKI, BRONISLAW. *The Dynamics of Cultural Change*. New Haven: Yale University Press, 1945.

OGBURN, W. F. (ed.). *Technology and International Relations*. Chicago: University of Chicago Press, 1949.

RUSSELL, BERTRAND. "The Next Eighty Years," *Saturday Review Reader No. 2*. New York: Bantam Books, Inc., 1953, pp. 20–30.

THEODORSON, GEORGE A. "Acceptance of Industrialization and Its Attendant Consequences for the Social Patterns of Non-Western Societies," *American Sociological Review*, 18:277–484 (Oct., 1953).

TOYNBEE, ARNOLD J. *A Study of History* (D. C. Somervell abridgement). New York: Oxford University Press, 1946.

WHYTE, WILLIAM F. (ed.). *Industry and Society*. New York: McGraw-Hill Book Co., Inc., 1946.

WHYTE, WILLIAM H., Jr. *Is Anybody Listening?* New York: Simon & Schuster, Inc., 1952.

Chapter 6

Cultural Inertia

In an earlier chapter the continuity of culture and its tendency to accumulate from age to age was emphasized and its advantages were stressed. That this is a liability at times is illustrated by the two case studies in this chapter. Even though tribes that bear it may perish, most of the traits they develop will be passed on to others. The tendency of culture to persist is so obvious that some cultural anthropologists and sociologists have taken the position that no traits ever disappear. Although historians talk of civilizations rising and falling, these men hold that actually all civilizations go on even though their bearers may disappear in the struggle of races or groups with each other. Even in conquest, the culture of the conquered tends to survive among the conquerors, especially where they take captive men as slaves or women as wives.

Like all extreme positions, it is doubtful that this one can be successfully defended. Certainly some of the early Egyptian arts of embalming have never been rediscovered.[1] The arts of mixing paints of some of the ancients have not been duplicated even in our scientific age. One cannot, however, deny the fact that culture is remarkably persistent.

RESISTANCE TO CULTURAL CHANGE

The resistance of culture to change is known as *cultural inertia*. Because of inertia, both needed and unneeded cultural elements persist. Here we are interested in the undesirable effects of inertia. Many culture traits tend to outlive their period of usefulness and yet continue to be a part of the human baggage that is passed on from generation to generation. Moreover, inertia toward the new often hinders culture change and holds back improvement.

[1] For an interesting discussion of methods of embalming by social class, see Herodotus, *The Histories* (Baltimore: Penguin Books, Inc., 1954), pp. 133 ff.

History is liberally sprinkled with instances of resistance to the new, which is always a threat to certain values and attitudes centering around the old. The problem of cultural inertia is posed clearly in the two historical instances which follow.

Resistance to Innovations in Transportation. One of the striking differences between advanced and backward civilizations is the use of the wheel—one of man's most amazing and useful inventions. Without it, as has been previously stated, burdens are borne on one's head or back, or on the backs of animals. With it, thousands of gadgets for bearing burdens are possible, as well as machines to tell time and measure space. Yet the use of the wheel in ever diverse and more useful ways has met resistance, as is shown in the following discussion:

"It is clearly to man's advantage to be able to traverse distances with facility and in ease, yet innovations permitting more comfortable and more rapid mobility generally have encountered apathy or overt resistance, and their utilization has repeatedly been restricted by vested interests. In the thirteenth century such resistance manifested itself in the case of the use of carriages. Philip the Fair ordered the wives of citizens of Paris not to ride in carriages in order to preserve the prerogatives of the ladies of the court. A law likewise sought to prevent the use of coaches in Hungary in 1523, and the Duke Julius of Brunswick in 1588 made riding in coaches by his vassals a crime punishable as a felony, largely on the grounds that it would interfere with military preparedness, for men would lose their equestrian skill. Philip II, Duke of Pomerania-Stettin, also commanded his vassals in 1608 that they should use horses and not carriages. In England, coaches were not widely used until the time of Elizabeth, who rode only reluctantly in this effeminate conveyance which young men scorned. In Donegal, Ireland, as late as 1821, carts to carry produce, which had previously been carried in creels on ponies' backs, were rejected as useless.

"There were many impediments placed in the way of stagecoaches in all countries. Local authorities often kept the roads in disrepair lest business be diverted elsewhere. Strangers were taxed excessively for horses, repairs, and stoppages. Tolls and passport requirements were onerous. Even at the beginning of the nineteenth century one traveling from Gottingen to Rome had to have his passport visaed about 20 times. Such political interference involved delays and expense, and discouraged travel by stagecoaches long after they were well equipped for distance travel.

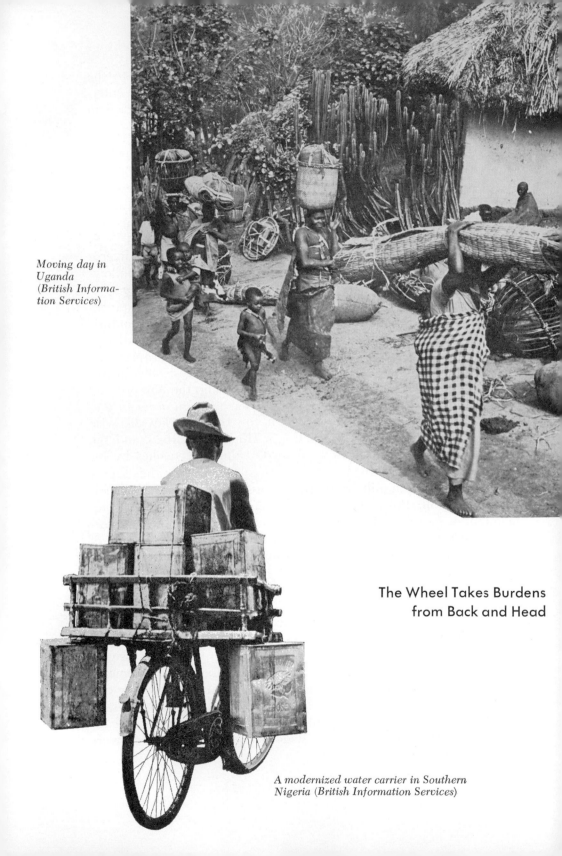

Moving day in Uganda (British Information Services)

The Wheel Takes Burdens from Back and Head

A modernized water carrier in Southern Nigeria (British Information Services)

"Railroads.—Turnpike companies profiting by tolls, and owners of stagecoaches were among the most active opponents of railroads. They were supported by tavernkeepers along the route of the roads, and by farmers who felt that the introduction of the railroad would deprive them of markets for horses and for hay."[2]

Resistance to Anesthesia. Anesthesia is one of man's greatest inventions in the alleviation of suffering. Surely it was welcomed as a new culture trait! The fact is, it was not welcomed.

Various medical men had experimented with pain-killers. Medical students knew how to get an ether "jag" by sniffing a bottle of ether. One doctor had given a demonstration of anesthesia with nitrous oxide (laughing gas), but because of faulty equipment it had failed and he had given up in humiliation. Morton, a young dentist, had been a helper in this demonstration. Rather than giving up, he continued to experiment. After working with ether, trying it on animals, then on himself, he asked to give a demonstration for Dr. John Warren, professor of surgery at Boston's largest hospital. Here is an interesting account of the setting and the sequence of events that followed his successful demonstration:[3]

"The operating amphitheater was directly under the dome and presented a much different appearance than the tiled and aseptic rooms now in use. Around about the old room were large cases containing surgical instruments, while chairs and tables of curious and unusual construction were scattered here and there about the pit. The many hooks, rings, pulleys and other restraining devices that were to be found on the walls all testified to the necessary brutality of surgery of the period. The profound learning of Boston Medical society was shown by the presence of an Egyptian mummy whose lugubrious countenance must have been an ever-inspiring spectacle in this den of horrors. The surgeons themselves were accustomed to come directly from their offices in all the glory of whiskers, stovepipe hats and frock coats, with their spare instruments in their pockets, for sterilization was as yet unknown and patients still died of 'bilious fevers' and 'humours.' There was generally a crowd of medical students on the benches that sloped up in tiers from the pit, and their appearance could not have been very inspiring, for the students of that age were notoriously unkempt.

"Warren had set the date for October 16, 1846, and there was to be a representative gathering of the surgeons of the city. There had al-

[2] Bernhard J. Stern, "Resistances to the Adoption of Technological Innovations," *Technological Trends and National Policy*, National Resources Committee (Washington, D.C.), June 1937, pp. 39–54.

[3] C. A. H. Smith, "The Discovery of Anesthesia," *Scientific Monthly*, 24: 64–70.

ready been much angry discussion as to the possibility of Morton doing what he claimed, and there was a considerable group that did
not like him personally, for his rather shy nature and the fact that he
was only a dentist or at best merely a medical student was not entirely in his favor.

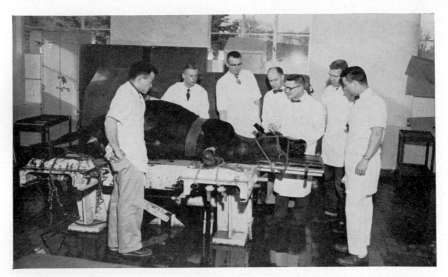

*Resistance to the new—inertia—marks the story of human culture. Today even a
horse is granted the blessings of drug-induced sleep when undergoing surgery;
yet the inventor of anesthesia was hounded by the clergy and by men of his
own profession for betraying man. (Veterinary College, State College of
Washington)*

"There was great difficulty in getting an inhaler suitable for the
occasion. As there was no precedent for this work, Morton was accustomed to administer the ether from a bottle with a long snout that
was inserted in the patient's mouth and on which he sucked rather
than by the administration of the ether with a mask over the mouth
and nostrils as is done today. The instrument maker was not able to
devise an appliance that entirely satisfied Morton and at last he took
a hand and made something up to his own specifications. . . . The
patient was willing to have anything done to alleviate the pain and
with few preliminaries the administration began. The spectators
rather expected a repetition of the Wells fiasco,[4] but nothing unusual

[4] (Author's note.) Dr. Horace Wells had previously attempted a demonstration of
anesthesia which had failed because of poor equipment and haphazard administration.

happened and the patient soon lapsed into a deep slumber. Morton turned to Warren and said, 'Your patient is ready, sir'; and the operation was begun while an astounded silence fell on the room. Accustomed as the surgeons were to the struggles and torture of their patients, this seemed like black magic. Warren finished and broke the silence with, 'Gentlemen, this is no humbug.' Dr. Bigelow chimed in with, 'I have seen something today that will go round the world.' There should have been a prayer of thanksgiving offered up in the old Puritan town on that occasion if ever. . . .

"Unexpected opposition came from some of the clergy, based on the assumption that pain was the direct consequence of original sin and therefore must be endured. Morton was threatened with prosecution and there was general condemnation of this terrible drug that set aside the laws of God and man. Dire pictures were painted of the use of this drug by criminals and all the hysterical fire of misguided religious zeal was brought to bear upon the matter.

"One clergyman wrote of ether as 'a decoy in the hands of Satan, apparently offering itself to bless Woman, but in the end it will harden society and rob God of the deep earnest cries that rise in time of trouble. . . .'

"The opposition grew stronger within the first few months of the new year (1847) and the storm of protest and recrimination aimed at Morton fouled his fame and even today is responsible for the lack of appreciation of his work. The most abominable blow came from the members of his own profession in the form of a manifesto, published in the Boston Daily Advertiser and signed by Dr. J. J. Flagg and most of the leading dentists of Boston, making a formal protest against the use of ether and predicting all sorts of dire calamities from its use. This was to confront Morton at every turn and be used to discredit him when he went to other communities.

"Cheap cynicism and irony were lavished upon the discovery by jealous medical men from less enlightened areas as follows:

"Professor A. Westcott, of Baltimore, remarked that if Morton's sucking bottle would perform all the marvels accredited to it, the proper place for its use would be for squalling infants in the nursery; R. M. Huston, M. D., Philadelphia, 'Quackery'; William C. Roberts, M. D., New York City, 'Humbug and a patented nostrum.'

"The editors of a New Orleans medical journal could not understand why the surgeons of Boston were captivated by such an invention when mesmerism had accomplished a thousand times greater wonders.

"It seemed as if the entire medical profession, outside of a few men in Boston, felt personally insulted that they had not been taken into confidence regarding this invention.

"The efforts to discredit Morton are too loathsome to repeat. He was persecuted unmercifully, his dental practice broken up, his personal morals viciously attacked and every possible effort made to alienate any affection that his friends might have for him. The attacks were carried into his own home and he and his wife suffered endless humiliation. There was not any limit to which his enemies would not go and at times it was actually dangerous for him to appear in public. . . .

"The shoddy methods used to discredit Morton were entirely unjustified. The only considerable honor that he received in his lifetime was a gold medal from the French Academy of Sciences and an honorary medical degree from an American university. There is every reason his name should rank with those of the great Americans, for to him must go the entire credit of risking his life and happiness in order that mankind be freed from pain.

"The epitaph on his tombstone in Mount Auburn Cemetery at Cambridge best describes his lasting claim to fame:

DR. W. T. G. MORTON

BORN AUGUST 19, 1819

DIED JULY 15, 1868

INVENTOR AND REVEALOR OF ANEASTHETIC INHALATION

BEFORE WHOM IN ALL TIMES SURGERY WAS AGONY.

BY WHOM PAIN IN SURGERY WAS AVERTED AND ANNULLED.

SINCE WHOM SCIENCE HAS CONTROL OF PAIN."

CULTURAL LAG

The persistence of old ways often proves a handicap because they condition one's mental set, making it difficult to see situations from new perspectives and to try new approaches. The tendency of non-material culture, especially, is to persist even longer than the material culture with which it originated. This has been made the basis for an important theory in contemporary American sociology developed by William F. Ogburn, leading American student of the process of invention and of cultural growth. By cultural lag he means that *one aspect of culture persists beyond its period of usefulness, lagging behind other elements of culture with which it was originally associated.* Ogburn conceives of cultural lags in our culture as existing primarily in the nonmaterial culture. The old nonmaterial culture traits persist after the technological culture with which they were concurrent moves on and leaves them. For example, machine technology creates new conditions of mass employment with risks to life and limb years before protective legislation for accident compensation is developed. Cultural lag is considered an important aspect of maladjustment in a rapidly changing culture like our own, where the machine tends toward continuous technological improvement and the mores and folkways tend to lag behind in a horse-and-buggy age. Here is Ogburn's own analysis based on his conception of cultural lag:

"Unequal rates of change in economic life, in government, in education, in science and religion, make zones of danger and points of tension. It is almost as if the various functions of the body or the parts of an automobile were operating at unsynchronized speeds. Our capacity to produce goods changes faster than our capacity to purchase: employment does not keep pace with improvement in the machinery of production; interoceanic communication changes more quickly than the reorganization of international relations; the factory takes occupations away from the home before the home can adjust itself to the new conditions. The automobile affects the railroads, the family, size of cities, types of crime, manners and morals.

"Scientific discoveries and inventions instigate changes first in the economic organization and social habits which are most closely associated with them. Thus factories and cities, corporations and labor organizations have grown up in response to technological development.

"The next great set of changes occurs in organizations one step further removed, namely in institutions such as the family, the government, the schools and the churches. Somewhat later, as a rule, come changes in social philosophies and codes of behavior, although at times these may precede the others. Not all changes come in this order but sufficient numbers do occur in modern history to make the sequence of value in charting the strains of our civilization. In reality all these factors act and react upon each other, often in perplexing and unexpected ways.

"Of the great social organizations, two, the economic and the governmental, are growing at a rapid rate, while two other historic organizations, the church and the family, have declined in social significance, although not in human values. Many of the problems of society today occur because of the shifting roles of these four major social institutions. Church and family have lost many of their regu-

Survivals to Another Day

Once a part of practical agrarian culture, domesticated animals are valued today, by an urbane people with a luxury level of cultural development, as objects of affection and recreation companions. In status-giving hobby activities the proper pedigree is required of the beast and the fitting garment of the person. (Northern Pacific Railway and State College of Washington)

latory influences over behavior, while industry and government have assumed a larger degree of control. . . ."[5]

In his *Social Change,* Ogburn spelled out his cultural change thesis, pointing out how various parts of culture change at different rates, often leaving interrelated parts unsynchronized.[6] This is the source of social problems in a technological culture, where the material culture tends to change more rapidly than the nonmaterial culture. For example, industry changes more rapidly than does education, so that education must readjust to catch up with changes in the industrial field. The delay in time required to get education remodeled to fit the new industrial pattern Ogburn called *cultural lag.*

In a rapidly changing technological culture, like that of the Western World, lags in many related fields of life—education, family, church—tend to pile up creating extensive maladjustments. To achieve progress, these lags must be eliminated by making changes to fit the material developments.

While Ogburn's concept of the cultural lag has never been too explicitly defined and has often been challenged on the grounds that he confuses cultural and social factors, the concept has received considerable attention from sociologists.[7] Overenthusiastic disciples have used the concept of cultural lag as an explanation for practically all forms of maladjustment in modern society. Actually the concept, were it explicitly defined to apply to the differential rate of change in the dependent elements of culture, can explain only a small fraction of disorganization, maladjustment, and strain in modern society.

SURVIVALS

A survival is a culture trait which has outlived its usefulness. Many candidates for the Ph.D. degree today are inclined to refer to the requirement of two foreign languages as a survival in the academic realm. The persistence in the curriculum of Greek and Latin years after they have served any useful purpose in American education is another example of a survival in a social institution. The persistence of the smokestack on diesel-powered vessels is still another.

The Roman numeral persists even in our time for certain ornamental purposes such as in giving the date of public buildings, labeling

[5] By permission from *Recent Social Trends in the United States,* pp. xiii–xv. Copyright, 1933, McGraw-Hill Book Co., Inc., New York.

[6] W. F. Ogburn, *Social Change* (rev. ed.; New York: The Viking Press, Inc., 1950).

[7] For a critical appraisal, see Joseph Schneider, "Culture Lag: What Is It?" *American Sociological Review,* 10:786–91 (Dec. 1945).

parts or volumes of books, or adorning the faces of clocks. Certainly the Roman numeral system has nothing to recommend it in the efficient system of American mathematical usage based on the Arabic decimal system. It is awkward, cumbersome, and to many unintelligible—a survival. The continued use of the capital letter in an age of typewriters and linotype machines is a time-wasting and largely senseless practice that might well be classed as a cultural lag.

Why then do these outmoded practices continue? Many traits survive because certain people have vested interest in their continuation; others, simply to satisfy emotional attachments of human beings who have become accustomed to the trait. Certainly the persistence of dead languages in the high-school curriculum was in the past due to the influence of a group of teachers who had built their careers about the teaching of dead languages. Their position was about like that of the blacksmith when the automobile replaced the horse and buggy. Their rationalization, however, was that to see the classical languages go out of the curriculum would be to deny American youth an opportunity for "culture" and for a genuine education. In the case of the smokestack on the diesel-powered ship, people felt so fearful entering a vessel without the customary smokestack that it had to be restored. A ship without a smokestack did not seem safe.

Sometimes traits survive and take on an entirely new meaning, and thus become incorporated as useful devices in the culture. Such persistence of culture traits probably is no great handicap. Take, for example, the tallow candle which once was the standard lighting device of the American family. Long ago it was replaced by the gas light, then by the electric light, and now by the fluorescent light. Today tallow candles are probably as numerous in the average home as they were in colonial times, not as a lighting device, but as an ornament for special occasions.

SOCIAL ATTITUDES TOWARD INNOVATION

A basic factor in invention, borrowing, and change, as far as cultural preparedness is concerned, is the kind of attitudes that exist in the culture area with regard to new culture traits. Man, generally speaking, throughout the ages has been hesitant to accept the new. The old is the familiar; the familiar is comfortable and safe. It requires no new learning; it inspires no fears. In primitive societies danger always lurked in a new experiment. New devices sometimes brought disaster. New ideas might even offend the gods and thereby prove dangerous to man's welfare. Taboos of many sorts have existed to keep man from even trying out new ideas and tinkering with established cultural objects.

Modern society, with its rapid change, has not entirely overcome this notion. When the electric light bulb was invented, it is said that men were afraid to use it for fear it would explode and blow them up. No doubt today the atomic bomb is associated as much with magic as reality in the public mind. And imagined dangers may well be much more numerous than real dangers to the future of society from its other application, as a new source of power.

It must be admitted, however, that modern Western culture, with its emphasis on technology, has given freer play to invention than man has ever done before. Invention is subsidized by the university, by industry, and by government. But even here many a precocious genius has found society unready to accept his invention. Stories are numerous concerning the rejection of significant new inventions by army or navy at the time when they were offered them by the inventor, only to have their value proved later when the crisis was past. No doubt many inventions die thus and the story is never told. And in the field of the creative arts there are countless examples of poets, musicians, artists, and authors dying in poverty, only to become immortal in another generation which recognized their innovations as being worthy of acclaim.

Many a shrewd publisher in our day admits having thrown away an easy fortune by turning down a novel that, when published, immediately became a best seller.

Business has given so much time during the past two generations to promoting new devices and to pointing out their superiority over the old that in the field of gadgets, at least, the American public has actually come to believe that the old can always be improved through the process of invention. This had made the American citizen remarkably receptive to new inventions, so much so that it can be safely said that American culture, perhaps more than most cultures, has a sympathetic attitude toward technological innovations. In fact, it is almost compulsive in American culture to accept the new and to condemn the old.

Yet even here there is less ready acceptance of new ideas, new customs, or new mores. Many fear changes in basic family philosophy. Many fear new ideas in the field of religion. Many do not readily accept new ideas in the field of government. Even a practice like tax-supported medicine, parallel in every way to the present system of public-school education, is condemned by many as being "communistic" or "socialistic."

CULTURAL INERTIA IN INDUSTRIAL AND UNDERDEVELOPED AREAS

The critic can see areas of resistance to desirable change even in rapidly changing America, particularly in certain areas of traditional practice and belief. But America is receptive to change, indeed, compared with many areas of the world. This is such a vital problem in this day of world culture-building, in which the United States is playing the dominant role in history, that it bears further analysis.

As one views the world as a unit, two philosophies of existence dominate the minds of men. The one contends that whatever has been, will always be. This is the static approach to existence. Its acceptance facilitates a resignation to the supposed dictates of fate and promotes a belief that whatever is, is best.

The other philosophy holds that what man has accomplished is only the beginning, the basis of a better and more efficient way of life to be built. This philosophy is dynamic. It looks upon every problem as a challenge, every new change as something which may be turned in the direction of bettering man's life. To accept change as the normal lot of man and to accept the idea that man controls this change is to believe in progress.

The first of these philosophies of life is, of course, as old as history. In fact, it has been only during the last century and a half of Western history that man has been able to read any other lesson into his experience than that man's life is governed by fate. But the last one hundred and fifty years of Western history, and particularly the last fifty years, have demonstrated clearly that man can, by challenging his environment, make of it what he will. And so the Western world has created what is, by any standard of previous history, a Utopia indeed. The material comforts of the average man in the Western world are superior to those of all the monarchs of history.

The two philosophies of life now are face to face and much in conflict. The one now is essentially Eastern; the other, Western. The one is agrarian; the other, urban-industrial. The one has been taught through the centuries by life itself, by nature inexorably cruel and constant. The other lesson is taught by technology, primarily by the annual new model in automobiles and other machinery.

In the Western world, and perhaps in America more than anywhere, even the masses have come to accept the new model as an improvement. No people who have seen the new model appear year after year can retain the typical backward look. They look forward, expect improvement. They expect that tomorrow will bring greater comforts, greater speed, greater longevity, and greater freedom from suffering and disease.

All history has looked back to a "golden age." At some imaginable time, it was thought, there must have been a day when man's miseries were less than in the present. At some time his comforts were greater than now. At some time his stomach was filled more regularly than now. That is the story of civilization.

By the standards of a technological culture, however, there is no "golden age" in history. The finest age that history knew was full of misery, compared with the lot of man today. So, the Western world, and particularly the United States, is now in the process of reversing the philosophy of cultural history. The West now has the difficult task of teaching all men everywhere that there can be a brighter tomorrow. Headway is being made to the extent that demonstrations of reconstructing the environment through the devices of an industrial culture are made.

By the use of skills and materials, the harnessing of water power, the transforming of soils, the West has set out to conquer want, disease, misery, and death. It is trying to promote the philosophy of plenty in a world of want. This is the magic that the Western machine-owning man offers underdeveloped areas everywhere.

But Western man becomes discouraged at times by the skepticism and suspicion he encounters. Yet it is to be expected that cultural inertia will be greatest among peoples who lack the West's years of experience in seeing the old replaced by the new. The idea of betterment shocks the whole conception of existence in much of the world. In many places, religion itself depicts man fatally revolving on the eternal wheel of existence, with his brightest hope that of his transmigrating into a more respectable existence in the next life.

These peoples will learn, as the West has learned, when they see the miracles of science and engineering transform the life about them. This will come about very rapidly during the next fifty years if war can be kept in check, as it must be. No one today can foresee what the world of A.D. 2000 will be like. It is theoretically possible, with the techniques now in hand, to banish poverty and much of sickness, to raise the length of life of peoples everywhere above the 35-year level, where many now are, to the 70-year level of the more privileged peoples. All have been made possible by the knowledge, techniques, and material resources of Western man.

How far these developments will be realized will depend very much on how far the transformation of physical environment and the revision of philosophies of existence can be accomplished. Particularly must the philosophy of family life, in the vast overpopulated areas of the world, be revised. For not only must these peoples come to see that their material existence can be transformed by a voluntary and purposeful attack on the environment itself, but also they must come to see that patterns of family behavior can and must be modified, so that man can make the most of his destiny by choice and planned action.

The most critical revision of philosophy must come in the pattern of reproduction. Peoples accustomed to hunger and famine, to untimely death, cannot conceive that by adjusting their birth rate they can make a high death rate unnecessary. There is scarcely a place on the face of the earth where Western man's ideas of sanitation, medical care, and increased longevity have not been introduced and accepted with great favor. The consequence is that the death rate is falling everywhere and will continue to fall precipitously. This leaves little chance for improvement unless prolific peoples accept Western man's counterpart of increased longevity—a reduced birth rate. This alone will make possible the aspiration of a high level of living and of individual self-development. Birth control technology and philosophy will be most difficult to sell throughout much of the world, and yet it is upon the introduction of change and planning in this area, perhaps more than any other one point, that the reversal of historical population patterns is dependent. The welfare of mankind everywhere, in fact the destiny of man on earth, is vitally involved in this issue.

Cultural inertia is a difficult force to combat, but the Western world of the twentieth century has the tools for combating it in underdeveloped areas, as it has already done at home.

SUMMARY

Change is painful. To discard the old is to discard certain sentiments and values. To live by the new is to challenge old habits, and to learn the new is in itself painful. These are some of the psychological reasons why human beings tend to resist culture change and why culture itself is said to have a static aspect.

Although the Scriptures say the way of the transgressor is hard, the examples in this chapter, like many others that could be taken from history, show quite as clearly that the way of the reformer is also hard, for the reformer speaks of a new day of man's making. Often the introduction of a new cultural trait is costly to the inventor —even though history later pays tribute to him—for the inventor of a new culture trait is one who sees things more wisely than his persecutors.

Even within a rapidly changing culture, where the new is met with little resistance, culture lag is an ever-present factor in the history of culture. Some elements change faster than others, leaving other parts of culture, and consequently, of human life, out of joint.

The Western world today faces the major challenge of combating cultural inertia in underdeveloped areas, where the new is feared and the innovator suspect. If man in the year A.D. 4047 is going to view this age, as Toynbee predicts he will, as one in which Western ways of life revolutionized and unified the life and culture of mankind on the earth, cultural inertia must be overcome by aggressive action and educational programs among these peoples everywhere.

DISCUSSION AND REVIEW QUESTIONS

1. Discuss the proposition that no culture traits are ever lost.
2. Illustrate the working of culture inertia.
3. Discuss the effect of vested interests in retarding culture change by invention and borrowing.
4. Appraise the Ogburn theory of cultural lag.
5. Illustrate survivals in contemporary culture.
6. Show how social attitudes toward innovation affect the rate of culture change.
7. Compare major cultures with reference to their receptivity toward the new.
8. How is the trend of civilization affected by such attitudes?

SOURCEBOOK READINGS

GITTLER, JOSEPH B. *Social Dynamics.* New York: McGraw-Hill Book Co., Inc., 1952.
    1. SMITH, C. A. H., "Resistance to Anesthesia," pp. 265–73.
KOENIG, SAMUEL, REX D. HOPPER, and FELIKS GROSS. *Sociology: A Book of Readings.* Englewood Cliffs, N.J.: Prentice-Hall, Inc., 1956.
    2. STERN, BERNARD J., "Resistance to Technological Progress," pp. 519–27.
    3. HART, HORNELL, "Cultural Lag Problems Solved by Social Science," pp. 527–33.
LEE, ELIZABETH BRYANT, and ALFRED MCCLUNG LEE. *Social Problems in America* (rev. ed.). New York: Henry Holt & Co., Inc., 1955.
    4. OGBURN, WILLIAM FIELDING, "Societal Change and Cultural Lag," pp. 31–32.
    5. BERNARD, LUTHER L., "The Dilemma in Revolution," pp. 452–53.
O'BRIEN, ROBERT W., CLARENCE C. SCHRAG, and WALTER T. MARTIN. *Readings in General Sociology* (2d ed.). Boston: Houghton Mifflin Co., 1957.
    6. MURDOCK, GEORGE PETER, "Uniformities in Culture," pp. 139–42.
    7. BENEDICT, RUTH, "Continuities and Discontinuities in Cultural Conditioning," pp. 204–8.
SCHULER, EDGAR A., DUANE L. GIBSON, MAUDE L. FIERO, and WILBUR B. BROOKOVER. *Outside Readings in Sociology.* New York: The Thomas Crowell Co., 1956.
    8. ROSS, EDWARD A., "Ossification," pp. 268–73.
WILSON, LOGAN, and WILLIAM L. KOLB. *Sociological Analysis.* New York: Harcourt, Brace & Co., Inc., 1949.
    9. OGBURN, WILLIAM FIELD, "The Hypothesis of Cultural Lag," pp. 111–15.

SELECTED READINGS

ADIR, JOHN and EVON VOGT. "Navaho and Zuni Veterans: A Study of Contrasting Modes of Cultural Change," *American Anthropologist,* 51:547–61 (1949).
BENEDICT, RUTH. *Patterns of Culture.* Baltimore: Penguin Books, Inc., 1946.

KROEBER, A. L. *Configurations of Cultural Growth*. Berkeley: University of California Press, 1944.

MALINOWSKI, BRONISLAW. *The Dynamics of Cultural Change*. New Haven: Yale University Press, 1945.

MEAD, MARGARET. *Cultural Patterns and Technical Change*. New York: United Nations Educational, Scientific, and Cultural Organization, 1955.

OGBURN, WILLIAM F. "Cultural Lag as Theory," *Sociology and Social Research*, 41: 167–74 (Jan.–Feb. 1957).

————. *Social Change* (rev. ed.). New York: The Viking Press, Inc., 1950.

SUMNER, WILLIAM GRAHAM. *Folkways*. Boston: Ginn & Co.: 1906.

STYCOS, J. MAYONE, KURT BACK, and REUBEN HILL, "Contraception and Catholicism in Puerto Rico," *Milbank Memorial Fund Quarterly*, 34:1–10 (April 1956).

THEODORSON, GEORGE A. "Acceptance of Industrialization and Its Attendant Consequences for the Social Patterns of Non-Western Societies," *American Sociological Review*, 18:277–484 (Oct. 1953).

TOYNBEE, ARNOLD J. *A Study of History* (D. C. Somervell abridgement). New York: Oxford University Press, 1946.

Chapter 7

Culture and Personality

A cowhand will walk three miles to catch a horse to ride a mile to town.[1] Irrational, you say? Not in the subculture of the cowboy. To go to town without the horse is almost like going undressed.

In India it was long customary for the Hindu wife to cremate herself upon the funeral pyre of her husband. The British stopped this practice, known as *suttee*. But the persistence of custom is strong. As recently as 1956, *Time* reported a widow being successful on her third attempt after neighbors had restrained her on two previous tries.

How one commits suicide anywhere is determined by custom. In Japan, where shame is the main control device rather than guilt, as in our culture, it must be done gloriously. Honor requires that the leader under certain circumstances of failure must commit *hari-kari* by plunging a sword into his entrails. Emperor Hirohito attempted suicide by pistol shot into his intestines after his defeat in World War II.

In some cultures altruistic suicide is favored: under certain circumstances one is expected to commit suicide for the good of his group. This practice is widespread among primitives, and has a long tradition among the Danes. Because food is scarce and the young are more important than the old, it is considered quite in order for the old to do away with themselves. Denmark still has one of the highest suicide rates in the world.

And so it is, even with honor. Think of gentlemen advancing so many paces and shooting point blank at each other. Whatever one may think of the practice, it is commonplace when the dueling code of honor requires it.

[1] This illustration is used by Clyde Kluckhohn.

The intimate village community of South African Zulus—with a cattle pen in the center
(Information Office, Union of South Africa)

Palm leaves, driftwood, and stone are used for El Molo huts, Kenya
(British Information Services)

Personality Is a Product
of the Culture Setting

To know how a man will think, what he will prize most, the goals to which he will aspire, one must know the culture which formed him from infancy. These photographs show the externals of cultural differences, but culture becomes internalized in the experience of every man and every people.

Surviving ways of a primitive culture, Flathead, Montana
(Northern Pacific Railway)

Just how culture shapes the personality, and with what consequences, is the problem of this chapter. Attention is directed, first, to
the molding of personality in a given culture, and second, to the
very complex problem of the effect of transferring from the culture
of one's birth to another.

CULTURE IN PERSONALITY FORMATION

Culture may do everything from the shaping of the body to the
molding of the soul for the world hereafter. If the customs of the
people dictate that the front teeth must be knocked out so that the
soul may escape upon death, the mores of the tribe will dictate that
the front teeth be knocked out. If the culture defines sharpened teeth
as beautiful, the teeth most visible will be sharpened to a canine
tooth shape, as is done in certain African tribes. If it is customary
that the lips be stretched an inch or two, or punctured and a piece of
ivory inserted there or run through the nose or ear lobes, this too will
be done. If the culture requires that the feet of each girl infant be
bound and warped out of shape until she hobbles along more awk-
wardly than a duck on ice, the feet will be bound. If custom dictates
that the Plains Indian youth go out alone in the hills to fast and
struggle with the spirits for days and nights until finally, weakened
by self-inflicted denial and torture, he communes with the spirits and
obtains a vision to guide him throughout his life, he will attempt it.

In Western culture a man who would lie on a bed of spikes as a
gesture of religious penance, or who would hold his arm upright
until it grew into that fixed position, would be lacking something in
the way of common sense. He would no doubt be committed to a
mental institution forthwith. And yet, if such behavior is made a
road to sainthood, as it is in India, holy men will torture the physical
body in order to obtain the favor of the social group and of the gods.

If the culture dictates that a woman be buried alive with her husband's body and all his other possessions, she accedes to the tradition. There is apparently no conflict between this cultural compulsion
and the wish to survive, with which all men are credited in our culture. If culture dictates that in religious worship a man chop off a
finger at the joint to placate the gods, or even kill his own son as a
human sacrifice, he will do so. Abraham would have killed Isaac on
the altar had his hand not been stayed by the angel. That which a
culture cherishes, individuals in the culture will seek, regardless of
what it costs them.

Individuals will play roles defined by the culture, no matter how
ridiculous they may seem to a group with a different cultural history.
The Indian with his war paint and the peculiar gyrations of the war

dance may draw ridicule, or at least an amused smile, from one reared in another culture; but would not the young cheerleader at an athletic game draw the same type of response from one not accustomed to the traditions of American competitive sports? And would not the various images of mayhem and destruction, blood and gore, that appear in front of fraternity and sorority houses before the homecoming game create a peculiar reaction in the minds of people unaccustomed to the weird ways of the modern homecoming ceremonial? Or take the matter of recreation. One can well imagine the scorn which our Puritan forefathers would heap upon us if they saw ten men chasing a ball around a wax-polished basketball court for a period of forty minutes, just to see who could throw it through the hoop most often. And certainly they would be chagrined at the hysterical yelling of the crowd. Their culture was a serious-minded one in which the wilderness was to be conquered, Indians slain, and homes built. Time did not permit leisure nor did the philosophy of the Puritans sanction it.

Culture has been described by anthropologists as a "gigantic molding matrix" in which the personality of the helpless and plastic infant is formed from birth to maturity. It is all of that and even more. It is the supporting framework in which one lives throughout his lifetime. In it his habit system finds free play, since its tools are more or less standardized. In it his attitudes, his etiquette, and his moral values find ready expression since these too are rather well standardized throughout the groups in which his culture pattern is the way of life.

Culture then is, in a very vital sense, the world in which "one lives and moves and has his being" from the time he is born to the time he is ceremoniously laid away.

The early process of cultural acquisition by the child is an unconscious one. He absorbs culture as naturally and as gradually as he matures physically. From the first prattle of words to the acquiring of the subtle attitudes of parents and family members, his personality is taking form within the culture of his social group.

This is all to suggest that from the accent of his *r*'s to the tint of his toenails man is a culture product. From attitudes toward the world to come to attitudes toward propriety and etiquette, all are molded by a culture. Each is, in fact, a product of his own culture. It is for this reason that various peoples throughout the world differ so much in values and attitudes, in habits and life philosophies, in their quest for things that they consider most worthwhile in life and in their thoughts concerning the hereafter. Man's personality is first, last, and always a product of his culture.

Kipsigis dancers, Kenya

CULTURAL TRANSMISSION IN FORMAL EDUCATION

Not all cultural acquisition is so simple as the unconscious absorption described above. Much of it must be acquired by deliberate effort. The Chinese youth who wishes to become a scholar goes through the years of tortuous learning described so well in Richard T. La Piere's novel, *Son of Han.*[2] The American youth who would climb the academic ladder to the highest rung goes through a much less tortuous regime, but nonetheless a long period of self-denial and hard work is necessary in order that he may attain the degree of Ph.D. and thereby obtain the prestige that comes with scholarship

[2] Richard T. La Piere, *Son of Han* (New York: Harper & Brothers, 1937).

106

Nigerian wedding in an American setting

Crowning the dairy queen

Appropriateness
Is a Matter of Culture Patterns

How a man behaves, the values he will approve, are very much a matter of time and place. Anything is tolerated, provided it is within the framework of cultural patterns. As Sumner said, "The mores can make anything wrong and anything right." (British Information Services and WSC Photo, State College of Washington)

and the economic security and social usefulness which have become part of his ideals for his own personality development.

Formal education has an increasingly prominent place in a complex culture, where learning by imitation and by association with others in the play life of childhood and in the work life of the family are insufficient experiences to guarantee that the child will acquire enough of the cultural heritage to function in it. Through education the process of learning is made selective and the stored-up cultural experience is presented in a concentrated form so that the acquisition by the individual of a rich cultural heritage, such as would not be possible through the more informal ways of learning, will be assured.

From six to sixteen years of age, cultural acquisition through the process of formal education has become the business of life. Yet the

107

young person who leaves school at sixteen is rather poorly prepared
to function in many aspects of a complex urban industrial culture.
Better by far if the intelligent young person remains in school until
he is twenty-five. Then he may have enough specialized knowledge
in some field or fields so that he may contribute to the culture by in-
venting new gadgets, discovering new scientific principles, or stating
theoretical, philosophical, or religious principles which may become
a better guide for man.

Certainly enough has been said to suggest that the process of cultural acquisition by the individual is more than an incidental process.
And in its acquisition, whether by informal or formal means, he is being shaped in habit and attitude.

CULTURAL UNIVERSALS AND SPECIALTIES

All cultures are so varied and complex, have so many elements,
that no individual ever participates in all aspects of them. The cultural heritage in advanced cultures, particularly, is so rich that no
one mind can begin to comprehend it all. Some of it is only for individuals who are highly specialized in it, as for example some aspects
of theological learning, and many branches of university learning.

The late Ralph Linton, an anthropologist, classified culture into
three aspects according to the completeness with which persons in a
society are expected to assimilate it: (1) *cultural universals,* (2) *cultural specialties,* and (3) *cultural alternatives.*[3]

Cultural *universals* are those elements of a particular culture which
all adult members of the society acquire as a matter of course. They
must do so to function as normal members of the society. Among the
universals are such matters as language, manners of dress, modes of
housing, and basic moral values.

The *specialties* are those elements of the culture which are shared
by certain groups only. Occupations, representing division of labor,
are of this sort, as are certain roles designated for men and others for
women. Each special profession is also master of an area of cultural
specialties which sets members apart in their own area of proficiency.

The *alternatives* are those aspects of culture which fit neither of
the above groups, such as different schools of art or sculpture. They
represent different techniques known in the culture for attaining the
same goal. In simple cultures there are few alternatives. In an advanced culture there are many. A primitive tribe may have the alternative of travel by canoe or by ox cart. Moderns have the choice of
horse, bicycle, motorcycle, automobile, bus, boat, airplane, train, etc.

[3] Ralph Linton, *The Study of Man* (New York: Appleton-Century-Crofts, Inc.,
1936), chap. 16.

Beyond the area of cultural uniformities, Linton pointed out, is the real one of *individual peculiarities*. The culture does not pass down as a part of the cultural heritage a fear of fire, or of high places, yet some individuals have an uncontrollable fear in these things. Such individual peculiarities disappear with the individual rather than being passed on as a part of the cultural heritage.

CULTURAL STANDARDS AND PERSONALITY TYPE

Living as most other men in the same culture live, few are fully aware of the fact that the type of personality they approve is the product of this particular culture mold into which they have been cast. One's idea of the good person is basically someone who conforms to cultural definitions of goodness in his own society. In other parts of the world many of the traits which he considers proper and good, such as intense business competition, would be condemned.

His ideas of religion are culturally formed. A minister once recognized this when he very fervently stated his reasons for believing the Bible. The first proposition on his list was, "I believe in the Bible because my mother did." In this he was more frank than some exponents of the gospel, for many would argue that they believe the Bible because it is the only rational thing to do. And yet the masses of humanity have never believed the Bible, simply because it has never been a part of their cultural heritage. It is still not a part of the cultural heritage of the dense populations of India, China, and the Malay Archipelago. Such areas make up a majority of the population of the world.

Even one's notions of beauty, not only in matters of dress and ornamentation, but also in matters of head shape, facial forms, and height of forehead, are a product of our culture. In American culture, the college campus standards of beauty call for an architectual model built on vertical lines, fragile, alert, blonde or brunette (according to one's choice), certainly athletic. It is said that in many parts of South American culture, proposals of marriage are dependent upon a woman's girth, those with the plumpest build being preferred.

One may go even further in contrasting styles of beauty and ornamentation. The pictures on page 110 show some of the methods of body scarring, dress, and ornamentation of African chiefs.

While men in American society are inclined to look upon clothing as invention's peculiar gift to women, the facts of the case are that both sexes in practically all cultures have used clothing as a device for improving what nature gave them in the way of appearance. The external ornaments become identified with personal affluence and prestige in the culture.

A Mkamba with his teeth filed to the proper dimensions

Did the Culture Make the Man or the Man Make the Culture?

In a sense it works both ways. Note the distinguishing marks of culture in these members of various tribes of Kenya, East Africa. Men are of one biological heritage, but the culture patterns which form them are many. (British Information Service)

Rank and prestige may be indicated by tricks, such as those of this Kisii elder

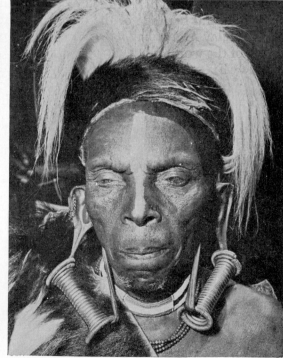

Proper ornaments for the culture setting add to the stature of this man, a Lus elder

REACCULTURATION: ACQUIRING A NEW CULTURE

From the foregoing discussion it is obvious that acquiring one's native culture in the early stages of one's life is a very simple, in fact, an almost unconscious and automatic process. The formal program for acquiring culture is more laborious, especially as one enters upon the higher levels of education. Even more difficult, however, is the process of cultural acquisition by the individual who, after reaching adulthood, shifts from the culture area in which he was born and reared to a new culture area. Such has been the experience of long-distance migrants in all ages. They must become *reacculturated*, that is, they must learn to live in and use a new culture.

The Problem of the Immigrant. Few nations have been built so completely and in so short a time by immigrants as has the United States. It was once called the "melting pot" because of the number of immigrants received each year from foreign shores, most of them coming with the intent of making the United States their permanent home. If one remembers that each of these immigrants had already experienced learning a native culture and yet on arrival was confronted with the necessity of acquiring a foreign culture which differed from his own in practically every respect, from language to the details of customary behavior, he can appreciate the significance of the phrase "melting pot."

The table shows the extent of the American migration since 1910. Observe that for the period 1910 to 1914 an annual average of a million immigrants landed on our shores to be absorbed into American society and to acquire American culture. Most of these immigrants arrived at Ellis Island and made their first contact with the United States in the city of New York, where America offered its greatest contrast to the culture to which they were accustomed, for most of them had come from the peasant classes of Europe. Here they were in a metropolitan culture of the most cosmopolitan, most anonymous, most bewildering city in the world.

HOW REACCULTURATION IS ACHIEVED

The immigrant is likely to be *segregated* because of his culture difference. This springs in part from pressures of the group among whom he settles, but mostly from the fact that those of like backgrounds tend to flock together. Being newcomers in a strange land, they want to hear their native language and to live among their own people. Even those who were strangers to each other in their homeland find a warm and hospitable attitude springing up among them in a new country where they are all strangers.

Admissions and Departures of Aliens in the U.S. 1910–1956:
Indicative of the Problems of Reacculturation

Fiscal Year	Immigrants Admitted	Emigrants Departed	Population Change Due to Migration
1910–1914, total	5,174,701	1,442,892	3,731,809
1915–1919, total	1,172,679	618,223	554,456
1920	430,001	288,315	141,686
1921	805,228	247,718	557,510
1922	309,556	198,712	110,844
1923	522,919	81,450	441,469
1924	706,896	76,789	630,107
1920–1924	2,774,600	892,984	1,881,616
1925	294,314	92,728	201,586
1926	304,488	76,992	227,496
1927	335,175	73,366	261,809
1928	307,255	77,457	229,798
1929	279,678	69,203	210,475
1925–1929	1,520,910	389,746	1,131,164
1930	241,700	50,661	191,039
1931	97,139	61,882	35,257
1932	36,576	103,295	−67,719
1933	23,068	80,081	−57,013
1934	29,470	39,771	−10,301
1930–1934	426,953	335,690	91,263
1935	34,956	38,834	− 3,878
1936	36,329	35,817	512
1937	50,244	26,736	23,508
1938	67,895	25,210	42,685
1939	82,998	26,651	56,347
1935–1939	272,422	153,248	119,174
1940	70,756	21,461	49,295
1941	51,776	17,115	34,661
1942	28,781	7,362	21,419
1943	23,725	5,107	18,618
1944	28,551	5,669	22,882
1940–1944	203,589	56,715	146,874
1945	38,119	7,442	30,677
1946	108,721	18,143	90,578
1947	147,292	22,501	124,791
1948	170,570	20,875	149,695
1949	188,317	24,586	163,731
1945–1949	653,019	93,547	559,472
1950	249,187	27,598	221,589
1951	205,717	26,174	179,543
1952	265,520	21,880	243,640
1953	170,434	24,256	146,178
1954	208,177	30,665	177,512
1950–1954	1,099,035	130,573	968,462
1955	237,790	31,245	206,545
1956	321,625	22,824	298,801

Here is a description of New York written in the mid-twenties, soon after the flood tide of European immigration. It describes the *cultural islands* into which the immigrant population was segregated during America's "melting pot" days.

"New York, like no other city, offers the best study of the nations of the world, samples of each being centered in different sections within easy reach of one another. You can go into the Spanish quarter and forget easily you are in an Anglo-Saxon country. You will be in vaulted, Alhambresque Spain while you are there; listening to songs with guitar accompaniments and feeding on food flavored with condiments imported from Spain. . . .

"You can go into the French district, and live in France while you are there, with Parisians clustering by themselves nearer to where there is light and gaiety, and the Normans further away on the side streets, withdrawing within themselves. The southern Frenchmen from Marseilles and Orleans and Tours gather in their own cafes and restaurants to discuss and talk about their gardens at home across the waters, and to sing their own songs, their own provincial love-songs.

"If you go further, into the Italian colonies, you will see the streets of Naples, the sidewalks littered with fruit- and vegetable-stands of all kinds; and the gay Neapolitan call of the fishermen on Mulberry street is the same gay call of the fishmonger of the Neapolitan Strada. If you walk through Little Italy at night you will hear voices floating through open windows, singing to the accompaniment of guitars the songs of Genoa and Naples, of Rome and Trieste, and never for a moment think that you are elsewhere than in a southern Italian city. And there is the same antagonism between the northern Italian and the southern one. There is the big, bellowing Calabrian who detests his smaller-sized brother from Sicily, and the Roman-born who has contempt for both of them.

"There is the Russian district, with moody Slavs worrying themselves, torturing themselves about this and that and the other eternal question. Big, heavy-boned, broad-shouldered, sunken-eyed Slavs with a mixture of Tartar blood, colorful in their barbaric emotions, powerful in their inert solidarity, more daring because less flighty, more influential because of their resolute steadiness.

"And what is one to say about the Hungarian quarter? Where the children of Attila have kept their own tongue so pure that not a single Anglo-Saxon word has penetrated their speech. You can see them daily. Their homes, in crowded tenement quarters, still retain that individuality which is their own . . .

"Further below them is the Rumanian quarter, a race of men considering themselves superior to all others of the Balkan states because they are the descendants of the old Romans, Trajan's soldiers, who conquered the Dacs of Decebal more than fifteen centuries ago, proud of their tongue because it is still the nearest to Latin of any language; they have their own poets here, their own musicians, uninfluenced by the life and the jazz about them, as if they still lived in Bucharest, which in Europe is known as Little Paris. Their own Gipsies live among them, despised and loved by them; hard-working peasants vainly trying to adapt themselves to a different life, disliking the Hungarians, suspecting the Russians, neighbors here across a dividing sidewalk.

"The great German population of the city, divided and subdivided when there is peace on the other side, is united when its integrity is attacked or endangered. Slow, careful artisans; slow, careful merchants, with the same *Gemütlichkeit* as at home, still reading their home papers to their wives and children, still leaning back in their soft comfortable chairs, in their immaculately clean homes.

"And there are Danish and Finnish, and Norwegian and Serbian, and Slovak and Swedish quarters, each one with its own life, guarding jealously its national characteristics. There is the Syrian district with one principal street and several side streets, one of the oldest in the city, with the houses built a hundred years ago . . .

"And the Chinese quarters, with the picturesque signs and pagoda-style houses, the red-brick walls of streets pasted with announcements and signs and newspapers, on yellow- and green-tinted paper, in that curiously decorative hieroglyphic script in which the laws of Confucius and Lao-tsze are printed.

"A map of Europe superposed upon the map of New York would prove that the different foreign sections of the city live in the same proximity to one another as in Europe; the Spanish near the French, the French near the Germans, the Germans near the Austrians, the Russians and the Rumanians near the Hungarians, and the Greeks behind the Italians. People of western Europe live in the western side of the city. Those who have lived on the other side near the sea or a river have the tendency here to live as near the sea or the river as possible.

"A reformation of the same grouping takes place every time the city expands. If the Italians move further up Harlem, the Greeks follow them, the Spaniards join them, with the French always lagging behind and the Germans expanding eastward . . ."[4]

Studies in urban ecology in Chicago revealed that the slum area

4 Konrad Bercovici, *Around the World in New York* (New York: Appleton-Century-Crofts, Inc., 1924), pp. 14–21.

was the "zone of first settlement," that is, the first residential section to which old-world immigrants naturally gravitated. (See ecological chart on p. 198.) Segregation into colonies of like language and like customs naturally intensified their *isolation* from the American group and hindered their assimilation by it.

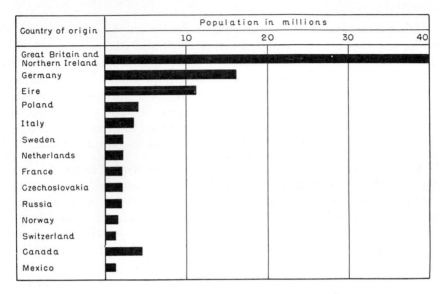

Country of origin	Population in millions			
	10	20	30	40
Great Britain and Northern Ireland				
Germany				
Eire				
Poland				
Italy				
Sweden				
Netherlands				
France				
Czechoslovakia				
Russia				
Norway				
Switzerland				
Canada				
Mexico				

Blended into One People Through Reacculturation and Assimilation

The chart is a summary of the national origins of the white population of the United States as determined by the census of 1920. Of the 100,000,000 whites in the nation, 40,000,000 were descendants of immigrants from Great Britain and Northern Ireland, 16,000,000 of immigrants from Germany, and 11,000,000 of immigrants from Eire. Smaller numbers were descendants of peoples of many other lands.

To speed up reacculturation, Americanization programs were carried out so the new groups could be *assimilated*—become an integral part of the larger social group.

Compulsory Education. The main device used for reacculturation (learning the new culture) and assimilation (being accepted with the group) was compulsory schooling for the immigrant child in the American school system. The child quickly learned the American language and quickly absorbed the American culture in the school and play groups. He found himself embarrassed if he used the parental tongue or reverted to the old-country ways of his parents. He might even be persecuted by American children or ridiculed by them if he showed any evidence of clinging to the old way of life. Every pressure forced the child to break away from a parental family and to push forward as rapidly as possible in learning the American culture.

Adult Education. The second major device employed in America to hasten the processes of reacculturation and assimilation of the immigrant was the adult-education class which sprung up in all major cities where immigrants came in numbers. These classes stressed the learning of the American language and taught the elements of American government and civics, so that the newcomer could learn the steps through which he must go to become a naturalized citizen of the United States and a voter in his adopted land.

Job Pressures. A third major factor was the work life itself. Even the adult of the first generation had to find a place in American industry. In his work life he was forced to learn the American language and certain attitudes of the American working man in order to get along. Because the man was the worker, he frequently assimilated American culture more rapidly than his wife, although most of what he learned he also took home and passed on to her, thereby pushing ahead her learning of American ways and of American philosophy.

The Attitudes of the New Generation. At best the reacculturation process is a three-generation affair. The child of the first generation makes a definite break with his parents. He virtually lives in two distinct cultural worlds. He is an American citizen, is American-educated, and has learned American ways, but the parents still cling to the old culture as the one which is more meaningful to them. They insist on their children learning the parental tongue. They insist on teaching the parental religion and parental philosophy.

Often there is a great contrast between the parents' philosophy and the child's. Take the matter of economic philosophy. In the old-world peasant culture the child's earnings go to the parent. He is supposed to take care of the aged parent. In the individualistic American family the child often saves what money he earns and spends it as he pleases. The two philosophies are bound to clash if the child has learned the one in the American school system among his playmates, and his parents insist on enforcing the other. Hostility may spring up between parent and child, in part because the parents feel inferior at every point and in order to cover it try to force their will upon the child.

The child may be hostile toward any attempt of the parents to teach him the old-world ways of life. His reaction grows out of the fact that any indication of foreign ways is likely to be responsible for his getting snubbed by his own peer group in the American play and school situations. He is interested in forgetting the old culture as fast as he can. This has been one of the major points of clash between the old generation and the new generation in the immigrant home.

Often, because a child has been forced to break away so rapidly and because his parents resisted his doing so, the parent has lost control over him at a very early age. As a consequence, in American cities the children of immigrants have been the most delinquent group in the population.

Gradually, as the immigrant and his family have acquired American culture and gained an economic foothold, they have moved out to the second zone of settlement in the city, that is, to better residential districts (see chart, p. 198). Often this is the area of working men's homes. In many other cases the family has moved out of the city to a farm or smaller community outside the immigrant colony. Here they have blended into American society and been forced to completely adopt American culture.

When the child of the immigrant marries he has usually already resolved that the handicaps he faced as a child will never be the lot of his children. As a consequence he teaches his children only the American language, rather than the old-world language and ways that were forced on him. He is likely to encourage his child to participate fully in the American life and to associate freely with all elements in the American population.

Religious Friction. The last step in acculturation comes in the field of religion. Most often the major conflict between first and third generations centers about the church service, usually hinging on whether or not the service should be continued in the native tongue or given only in English. The grandparent generation feels that the gospel must be in the native tongue or it isn't the gospel at all. The third generation, wanting to lose every semblance of their foreign connection, is insistent, when they come to the age when they have something to say about church affairs, that the services be in English only. The friction between the two generations is first worked out by one church service of the day being in the foreign language and the other in English. Gradually, as the third generation takes over complete control of the church, the old generation's voice is silenced and English becomes the language for all church services.

Intermarriage. In the case of the white-skinned immigrant group, the third generation begins to intermarry with native American stock or with descendants of immigrants from other nations, thus completely losing their identity as a minority group. Intermarriage is the final step in assimilation.

Since the effectiveness of the process of reacculturation is dependent on the interaction between groups, such factors as distinctive race, religion, or language are naturally great hindrances and may extend the process over more than three generations.

THE MARGINAL MAN

The individual who is straddling two cultures, having one foot in each, has been called by sociologists a *marginal man.* As the late University of Chicago professor Robert E. Park defined him, he is "living and sharing intimately in the cultural life and traditions of two distinct peoples, never quite willing to break, even if he were permitted to do so, with his past and his traditions, and not quite accepted, because of racial prejudice, in the new society in which he now seeks to find a place."[5]

Novelist James A. Michener gives a striking picture of a "marginal" man he met in the Orient—a man marginal both in racial and cultural characteristics:

I met Hugh Channing in Singapore and he will haunt my conscience forever. He was taller than me, better looking, better educated and more gifted in the correct use of language. His skin was whiter and his smile was gracious. In fact, there was only one thing wrong with him. His grandmother had been a native woman.

"Therefore I am nothing [Channing explained]. I am not a European. The white people see to that. Nor am I an Asian. Because the white people insist that I never push a rickshaw or clean gutters. I can neither go up nor down. I am the man ordained by God always to be a clerk in some English shop. They don't have to pay me much, for I can't leave. There's no other job I could get. And they don't have to promote me because everybody knows I'm not really to be trusted.

"What am I? I'm a Eurasian. I can never be a European as long as Englishmen despise anyone with even a drop of color. I can never be an Asian as long as my parents bring me up to imitate the white man."[6]

The immigrant and his child, who are facing this terrific problem of reacculturation, are also marginal men in this sense. Because of the marginal position of the immigrant, and the unusual strain which is a consequence to his bridging two cultures, mental disease and suicide

[5] Robert E. Park, "Human Migration and the Marginal Man," *American Journal of Sociology,* 33: 881–93 (1927–1928).

[6] From *The Voice of Asia* by James A. Michener. Copyright, 1951, by James A. Michener. Reprinted by permission of Random House, Inc.

rates have been highest among immigrant groups. As has been pointed out, delinquency rates also have been unusually high among urban children of immigrants. To make concrete the marginal man concept, examine these two excerpts below.

A college student, born in a German-American rural community, describes his marginal experience thus:

"Most of the people had migrated from the old world and had kept some of their customs and folkways. As a consequence, I grew up in a community where the principle language was German, where religion played an important role second only to the home, where the family was the predominating group in molding a child's character, and where sex was treated with a stony cold silence. Surrounding their old culture was the new culture of the modern American community. Theirs was a strict religion and moral code, man was superior to woman (her place was in the home raising children), education meant little, and movies and play were frowned upon. People seldom traveled, but they showed a good deal of hospitality and cooperation with everyone. Everyone was interested in his neighbor and knew his business, as is the rule in a small community.

"Contrasted with this was the American culture stressing education for all, the equality of women, wealth as a means of class status, leisure time and amusements, individual freedom, the automobile complex, and a saner view on the sex problem. As I look back on it now, I can see how the difference between the two cultures made of me a marginal man."

A college youth of Russian-born parents, who grew up under the domineering pattern of the old-world culture of his family, tells of his awakening when he started to school and began to get a picture of the independence of the American child. He then made a rather sudden break away from the authority of his parents. He writes:

"The folks concluded that I had turned bad and would never amount to anything. This only increased my feeling of hostility toward them and multiplied the frictions between me and my parents. What they forbade, I'd do if I possibly could. The situation got so bad I even thought I would have to leave home. I began looking for another place to live in case that happened. I began spending a great deal of my time at one of the neighbors, which hurt my folks very much. He was married but had no children and seemed to take a fatherly interest in me and always welcomed me to his home. We became close friends and I even went so far as to share my grievances against my folks with him and he sympathized with me. He told me the whole neighborhood in which we were living regarded my folks as very old fashioned in their manner of raising their children. This further strengthened my claim against my folks. I gradually became immune to their criticism of me and began staying after school to try out for track and to work on the high-school annual. They were against everything I wanted to do, it seemed."

INTERNAL MIGRATION AND MARGINALITY

The problem of reacculturation and assimilation as experienced by the international migrant and his child has been discussed. Their problems are most imposing, but in a nation like ours, where urban and rural cultures offer such vast differences, ranging from dissimilarities in the work life to those of attitudes and moral patterns, the individual in moving from place to place within the country may experience such striking cultural differences that he faces a problem of reacculturation and assimilation that is quite serious for him—so serious, in fact, that he is for a time actually a marginal man.

This is true of many young people in the United States, especially those who move from the isolated population pockets in mountainous regions like the Ozarks or Appalachian Mountains to metropolitan centers of the United States. In the Ozark culture the large family and close-knit neighborhood have surrounded the individual from birth to maturity. The culture is essentially a hoe culture, as far as the level of agriculture is concerned; it is a self-sufficient, subsistence economy for the most part, with little bought outside, most food being raised on the hill farm.

When young people of this background arrive in the city in quest of work, they find it veritably a new world. Instead of the intimate atmosphere of the home group, anonymity and strangeness characterize the social groups. Instead of the simple handicraft culture of the mountain area, they enter a highly mechanized industrial society. In their work life they must acquire the simple mechanical skills that are demanded in modern industry. Such adjustments bridge a wide gap of cultural difference and place the mountain youth in the position of a marginal man.

Some of the problems of adjustment incident to the transition from Ozark mountain culture to metropolitan culture in St. Louis are described interestingly in the following account of migrant families:

"They said that they were so worried and confused by the pressing need for subsistence that they were numb to other things about them. The tension was released when they were employed and as long as they worked they were quite satisfied. But often 'on the job' it was hard to receive orders and work under 'hard-boiled bosses.'

"The majority of the women described their first weeks in the city as a 'terrible' period during which they almost went mad. Long hours 'cooped up' with a group of children who had been accustomed to spend most of their time outside was far from pleasant. The mothers were too frightened to allow them to leave the crowded rooms. The smoke and dirt were stifling and the noise confusing. Lonesomeness, homesickness, and futile attempts to make friends with the neighbors who lived under the same roof marked the efforts to adjust. The church, which played a big part in country life, failed in the city.

"The men who found work had little trouble 'gettin' along' but leisure time was far from a pleasure. One man spent each Sunday and holiday at the zoo when he could afford carfare. Another family rushed off to the country at every opportunity.

"Some of the children had difficulty when they started to school. Not only were they frightened at seeing so many other children but they were timid and backward in their actions. Their dialect did not contribute to their acceptance among their schoolmates. Some turned belligerent and fought, while others merely withdrew. The children, however, naturally began to make friends and brought them home; they soon went to the public libraries for books; they were invited to the mission Sunday schools and settlement houses, and soon the mothers and fathers were also becoming interested to a limited extent."[7]

So also youth who move from a metropolitan community into a rural area may be in a marginal position temporarily. For example, the young schoolteacher may find herself a marginal person for a time where the culture of the one-room rural school community is unlike anything she has ever experienced before.

The concept of the marginal personality obviously has usefulness in many situations that are characteristic of modern society, where migration from the home environment is the common experience of the masses of mankind.

CULTURAL DIVERSITY AND PERSONAL CONFLICT

In simple societies there tends to be only one pattern of life which is learned by all and accepted by all. *Personality integration* in such a situation is relatively easily attained. The only major conflict is that between personal drives and appetites and cultural restrictions. In the simple rural culture of yesterday and in the culture of primitives everywhere this is the typical situation. Definitions of right and

[7] S. A. Queen and L. F. Thomas, *The City* (New York: McGraw-Hill Book Co., Inc., 1939), p. 412, as quoted in Elsie Huseman, "The Adjustment of Rural Families in St. Louis" (unpublished master's thesis, Washington University, 1932).

wrong, good and bad, are deeply embedded in tradition and become a part of the habit system of each generation. Few decisions are left to the individual. Most of the situations that the young person will face have already been defined by his elders.

Compare this with modern urban society, where social definitions differ from group to group, where ideas as to what is right and what is wrong with regard to certain kinds of behavior are directly contradictory. For example, consider parents' ideas of how one should act on a date and one's own age group's ideas; parents' views of religion and those of the college fraternity or even the college classroom.

In a complex culture numerous patterns of behavior, many of them opposed, are sanctioned by one group or another. The individual who would move in many circles will sooner or later find himself expected to do things in one group that he himself does not believe in and that other groups of which he is a part condemn. He who tries to be all things to all men in modern urbanized culture soon finds himself a bundle of contradictory behavior. Unless he is extremely tough-minded, he may become involved in torturous mental conflicts. In order to avoid psychic pain, either he has to limit his number of group contacts, participating selectively in those groups which represent the values he stands for, or else he must begin to compartmentalize his own personality, shutting off each compartment by a process of rationalization so that the compartments of the self never meet. If he is "the business is business" type, it may take a lot of rationalization to seal this compartment off from his Sunday compartment, provided he is a devout believer in Christianity and a loyal member of the church.

At best we all sense the incompatibilities and contradictions of our complex culture and its rival values. The ideals of Christianity and the intensely competitive ethics of capitalism are miles apart. The passive resistance of the Sermon on the Mount (". . . whosoever shall smite thee on thy right cheek, turn to him the other also. . . . whosoever shall compel thee to go a mile, go with him twain") and more recently that of Gandhi in India are almost beyond the comprehension of one reared in our competitive culture. The Sermon on the Mount with its enunciation of the principle that the meek shall inherit the earth is something very different from the typical competitive behavior of the average American church-goer. An American anthropologist commenting on this scripture said, "The meek will have to inherit it; they can't hope to get it any other way." Even so, Rev. King and the Montgomery, Alabama, Improvement Association used passive resistance and economic boycott to great advantage in their struggle for equal seating on busses in 1956 and 1957.

Few individuals who absorb such dominant, but contradictory, values can escape some sense of contradiction between their own wishes and goals. One even hears ministers try to explain away the literal meaning of turning the other cheek as required by the Sermon on the Mount. There is no question that this was meant to be taken exactly as it was spoken, but it was spoken in an Oriental setting where a philosophy of nonresistance can still make a figure like Gandhi more powerful than the British Empire. The churchmen who try to take away from this scriptural injunction its literal meaning sense the significant fact that in a competitive culture anyone who tried to fight that way would not only be considered a fool, but actually would be one.

In a complex culture, achieving a unified personality is something of a problem. In the United States, where marriages of those of different cultural backgrounds are common, the child may even be subjected to clashes of cultural values in his home. This is suggested by the following account of a college youth who reviews his childhood. He writes:

"The conflict between the idealistic views of my mother and the realistic principles of my father was apparent everywhere in my environmental background. These views between mother and father conflicted most about the part religion should play in the family. My mother firmly believed that the religious influence was the most important in everyday life; therefore, she has never ceased trying to instill her faith in me. Although my father was not an atheist, he was convinced that I should be brought up to face life realistically. Consequently my earlier youth was a period of stress and strain which led to emotional disturbances. I became confused, and nervous tension was high."

SUMMARY

Perhaps there are those who think man can be understood primarily in terms of his hereditary characteristics, his glands, his temperament, his potentialities for growth. The sociologist cannot deny that these things are important. Yet to take man outside his setting of culture is to misinterpret his every act, or to fail to understand what meaning it has to him and to others for whom he performs. Into the structure of personality is woven the cultural fabric of his own people, whoever his people may be and whatever they may stand for in the way of morals, beliefs, etiquettes, and the material traits which constitute the man-made conditions of living.

Personality is so much a product of the culture patterns of the unique time and place that to remove a man from the culture of his birth is to place him in a position of almost intolerable strain, and to require him to learn life anew. And to place an individual where he must straddle two cultures is, in a sense, to almost tear him apart. Certainly it is to face him with a life-long problem of reconciling irreconcilable elements of the two cultures in which he must participate. The marginal man is often one of the tragic characters of history. A part of two cultures, he is no longer completely at home and content in either.

DISCUSSION AND REVIEW QUESTIONS

1. Cite examples to demonstrate the proposition that culture molds personality.
2. Discuss education as an aspect of cultural transmission.
3. Compare cultural universals, specialties, and alternatives.
4. Show how cultural standards become guides to the individual.
5. Why is the process of acquiring a new culture different from that of acquiring the original culture?
6. Discuss the possible effects of segregation, isolation, and competition on the process of acculturation.
7. Distinguish between acculturation and assimilation.
8. Show how education has been used to hasten the acculturation of the immigrants.
9. Compare the acculturation process of the first three generations of immigrants.
10. Show how accommodation between generations is sometimes achieved.
11. What is meant by the term "marginal man"?
12. What are some of the effects of marginality on behavior?
13. Can we say that some internal migrants in America are marginal?
14. Show how diversity of cultural standards may be a factor in personality strain.

SOURCEBOOK READINGS

FREEDMAN, RONALD, AMOS H. HAWLEY, WERNER S. LANDECKER, GERHARD E. LENSKI, and HORACE M. MINER. *Principles of Sociology* (rev. ed.). New York: Henry Holt & Co., Inc., 1956.
    1. HOLMBERG, ALLAN R., "Nomads of the Long Bow," pp. 141–68.
    2. FREEDMAN, RONALD, and DEBORAH FREEDMAN, "Farm Boy in the City," pp. 462–71.
GITTLER, JOSEPH B. *Social Dynamics.* New York: McGraw-Hill Book Co., Inc., 1952.
    4. BARNETT, H. G., "Personal Conflicts and Sociocultural Change," pp. 273–85.
KOENIG, SAMUEL, REX D. HOPPER, and FELIKS GROSS. *Sociology: A Book of Readings.* Englewood Cliffs, N.J.: Prentice-Hall, Inc., 1956.
    5. LABARRE, WESTON, "Wanted: A More Adequate Culture," pp. 55–62.
    6. MORRIS, EDITA, "Acquiring the Cultural Do's and Don'ts," pp. 90–91.
    7. MICHENER, JAMES A., "The Tragedy of the Marginal Man," pp. 510–12.
LEE, RAYMOND L., JAMES A. BURKHART, and VAN B. SHAW. *Contemporary Social Issues.* New York: The Thomas Crowell Co., 1955.
    8. CHASE, STUART, "On Being Culture Bound," pp. 3–14.
    9. LYND, ROBERT S., "Culture and the Individual," pp. 15–20.

LEE, ELIZABETH BRYANT, and ALFRED McCLUNG LEE. *Social Problems in America* (rev. ed.). New York: Henry Holt & Co., Inc., 1955.
  10. ALLPORT, GORDON W., "Is the Urbanite Ego-Involved in His Tasks?" p. 90.
SCHULER, EDGAR A., DUANE L. GIBSON, MAUDE L. FIERO, and WILBUR B. BROOKOVER. *Outside Readings in Sociology.* New York: The Thomas Crowell Co., 1956.
  11. SIMMEL, GEORG, "The Social Role of the Stranger," pp. 142–47.
  12. COTTRELL, W. F., "Of Time and the Railroader," pp. 250–57.
WILSON, LOGAN, and WILLIAM L. KOLB. *Sociological Analysis.* New York: Harcourt, Brace & Co., Inc., 1949.
  13. AGINSKY, B. W., "An Indian's Soliloquy," pp. 129–30.
  14. KLUCKHOHN, CLYDE, and DOROTHEA LEIGHTON, "The Navaho View of Life," pp. 130–41.
  15. COTTRELL, W. F., "Of Time and the Railroader," pp. 579–86.

SELECTED READINGS

ADIR, JOHN, and EVON VOGT. "Navaho and Zuni Veterans: A Study of Contrasting Modes of Cultural Change," *American Anthropologist,* 51:547–61 (1949).

BENEDICT, RUTH. *Patterns of Culture.* New York: Penguin Books, Inc., 1946.

———. *The Chrysanthemum and the Sword.* Boston: Houghton Mifflin Co., 1946.

BOSSARD, JAMES H. S. *The Sociology of Child Development* (rev. ed.); New York: Harper & Brothers, 1956.

COHEN, ALBERT K. *Delinquent Boys: The Culture of the Gang.* Glencoe, Ill.: The Free Press, 1955.

CUBER, JOHN F., ROBERT A. HARPER, and WILLIAM F. KENKEL. *Problems of American Society: Values in Conflict* (3d ed.). New York: Henry Holt & Co., 1956, chap. 23.

DRUCKER, PETER F. *The Future of Industrial Man.* New York: John Day Co., Inc., 1942.

DUBIN, ROBERT. "Industrial Workers' Worlds: A Study of the 'Central Life Interests' of Industrial Workers," *Social Problems,* 3:140, Jan. 1956

FULLER, JOHN F. *Nature and Nurture: A Modern Synthesis.* Doubleday Papers in Psychology, Garden City, N. Y.: Doubleday & Co., Inc., 1954.

GERTH, HANS, and C. WRIGHT MILLS. *Character and Personality.* New York: Harcourt, Brace & Co., 1953.

HALLOWELL, A. IRVING. *Culture and Experience.* Philadelphia: University of Pennsylvania Press, 1955.

HARDING, D. W. *Social Psychology and Individual Values.* London: Hutchinson & Co., Ltd., 1953.

HAVIGHURST, ROBERT J., and HILDA TABA. *Adolescent Character and Personality.* New York: John Wiley & Sons, Inc., 1949.

Journal of Social Issues, Vol. 11, No. 2 (1955). Devoted to aspects of national character of the United States.

KERR, CLARK. "What Became of the Independent Spirit?" *Fortune,* July, 1953, pp. 110 ff.

KLUCKHOHN, CLYDE, and A. H. MURRAY (eds.). *Personality in Nature, Society, and Culture.* New York: Alfred A. Knopf, Inc., 1948.

LINTON, RALPH. *The Cultural Background of Personality.* New York: Appleton-Century-Crofts, Inc., 1945.

———. *The Study of Man.* New York: Appleton-Century-Crofts, Inc., 1936.

MASLOW, A .H. *Motivation and Personality.* New York: Harper & Brothers, 1955.

MEAD, MARGARET. *Sex and Temperament in Three Primitive Societies.* New York: McGraw-Hill Book Co., Inc., 1935.

MURDOCK, GEORGE P. *Social Structure.* New York: The Macmillan Co., 1949.

OGBURN, W. F. *Social Change* (rev. ed.). New York: The Viking Press, Inc., 1950.

PLANT, JAMES S. *Personality and the Cultural Pattern.* New York: The Commonwealth Fund, 1937.

RIESMAN, DAVID (with Reuel Denney and Nathan Glazer). *The Lonely Crowd,* New Haven: Yale University Press, 1950.

——— (with Nathan Glazer). *Faces in the Crowd.* New Haven: Yale University Press, 1953.

RUSSELL, BERTRAND. "The Next Eighty Years," *Saturday Review Reader No. 2.* New York: Bantam Books, Inc., 1953, pp. 20–30.

SEWARD, GEORGENE. *Psychotherapy and Culture Conflict.* New York: The Ronald Press Co., 1956.

SHAPIRO, HARRY L. (ed.). *Man, Culture and Society,* New York: Oxford University Press, Inc., 1956.

THEODORSON, GEORGE A. "Acceptance of Industrialization and Its Attendant Consequences for the Social Patterns of Non-Western Societies," *American Sociological Review,* 18:277–484 (Oct. 1953).

THOMPSON, LAURA, and ALICE JOSEPH. *The Hopi Way.* Chicago: University of Chicago Press, 1944.

WHYTE, WILLIAM F. (ed.). *Industry and Society.* New York: McGraw-Hill Book Co., Inc., 1946.

WRIGHT, QUINCY. *A Study of War.* Chicago: University of Chicago Press, 1942, Vols. I and II.

Part II

SOCIETY

Chapter 8

Society: Groups in Interaction

What is meant by the term "society"? Even the man on the street will answer this one correctly: Groups.

But many beginning sociology students assume that because this and many everyday things are known about groups, there is little to be learned by sociological study. There is, however, much more to formulating a theory of groups and group life than common-sense observation. The following considerations are basic to any proper understanding of group interaction.

1. Society is people in interaction. Its units are the groups into which human beings arrange themselves in interaction. Each person during all or most of his lifetime is a member of many groups. "He who is unable to live in society, or has no need to because he is sufficient unto himself," commented Aristotle, "must be either a wild beast or a god."

2. Communication is the basis of group formation, of social life itself, and of what the sociologist calls "social interaction." Degree of isolation and contact are, therefore, critical to social interaction.

3. The types and scope of communication (direct and indirect) determine the extensiveness of group formation and the size of groups formed.

4. Groups are found not only on the level of human life but throughout nature. Ants and bees are social creatures, never living in isolation from their fellows. Being gregarious in nature, these insects live in colonies, sharing work in a complicated system of division of labor. They may domesticate creatures lower than themselves and carry on organized warfare. Certain types of ants, for example, herd

and milk aphids or plant lice, much as human groups herd and milk cattle. Ants carry on military activity against other groups of ants. Bees carry on systematic robbery against weaker colonies until they take away all their honey and leave them with no food to survive winter.

Monkeys and apes, man's nearest rivals in the animal kingdom, possess many social traits. They get together in groups to chatter—even cooperate to some extent. Some monkeys, in crossing streams, for example, cooperate by making a swinging bridge by holding to each other's hind legs or tails, swinging in a long arc until the lowest monkey grasps the tree beyond.

Although group life is not limited to human beings, the continuity of culture among human groups makes man's group experience unique. His gregariousness is a learned gregariousness, and patterns of group association are legion.

5. A group may be defined as two or more people who carry on social relations. Clearly the number and kinds of groups are so numerous that one has difficulty classifying them all into any satisfactory organizational framework. They differ greatly in their character, the bonds holding them together and the type of consciousness which pervades them. A mob is far different from a family group, a pair of lovers from lawyer partners; yet all are groups.

6. Although no classification of groups is adequate, the following one by Harvard sociologist Pitirim Sorokin is suggestive. He bases his analysis of formation on the kinds of common situations which lead individuals to unite:

   a. Physiological kinship and community of blood or origin from the same physical or mystical (totemic) ancestors
   b. Marriage
   c. Similarity in religious and magical beliefs and rites
   d. Similarity in native language and mores
   e. Common possession and utilization of land
   f. Territorial proximity (neighborliness)
   g. Common responsibility (sometimes imposed by other groups) for the maintenance of order, payment of taxes, etc., and common acquisition of certain privileges
   h. Community of occupational interests
   i. Community of various types of economic interests
   j. Subjection to the same lord
   k. Attachment, either free or compulsory, to the same social institution or agency of social service and social control, such as the same police or political center, school, temple, and church, trade agency, military authority, election bureau, hospital, or any one of the various other agencies
   l. Common defense against a common enemy or common dangers

  m. Mutual aid

  n. General living, experiencing, and acting together[1]

7. Groups employ various devices in adjusting to each other. One common adjustment device is *conflict*. Groups in conflict are determined to destroy each other or drastically reduce the other's power. If the interaction pattern is less militant, they will merely be competitive rivals: instead of trying to destroy each other, they try to outdo each other in achieving their ends or goals. Or, groups often decide to live and let live. This the sociologist calls *accommodation*. They exist side by side and accept the existence of each other as a fact of life. Finally, groups may undergo complete *assimilation;* for example, in the United States white immigrants lose their separate identities and become a part of the American populace.

All of these interaction processes have been evident in the American scene as immigrant groups have come one after the other. With them the pattern of interaction has tended to move from one to the other in the order listed above. At first each was a conflict group, unaccepted because they accepted low wages. Irish, Germans, Chinese, Italians, Hungarians and other Southern Europeans each in their turn were despised. Later they acquired American ways, and the situation was one of competition. Then they were accepted on a live-and-let-live basis, a relationship of accommodation. Finally, by the third generation, those of white skin had intermarried and had completed the "melting pot" cycle of adjustment which has been the history of America. They were assimilated.

These are the kinds of issues, then, that concern the sociologist as he studies society.

Sometimes one can understand the importance of a social phenomenon best by depicting what happens to persons or peoples deprived of it. Thus, this study of the function of communication in group life will begin with examples of social deprivation and its effect, both on the individual personality and on peoples.

FILM LIST FOR PART II

For the Record—19 minutes—sound
  Record of the 1946 strikes of the CIO, the causes and the outcome. *Source:* Brandon Films.

American Anniversary—15 minutes—sound
  Shows the rise of an immigrant to a place of significance in his community. *Source:* National Association of Manufacturers.

[1] Pitirim A. Sorokin, Carle C. Zimmerman, and Charles J. Galpin (eds.), *A Systematic Source Book in Rural Sociology* (Minneapolis: University of Minnesota Press, 1930), I, 307–8.

Story of Communication—22 minutes—sound
> Highlights early developments in communication, writing, and printing and the gradual conquest of time and space. *Source:* Films, Inc.

America and the Immigrant—17 minutes—sound
> Forty million immigrants: where they came from and their contributions to our democracy. *Source:* March of Time Forum Films.

Man—One Family—17 minutes
> Offers a refutation of race inequality. *Source:* British Information Services.

Problem Solving in Monkeys—17 minutes
> Covers behavior of cefus and rhesus monkeys in complex, tool-using tasks. *Source:* International Film Bureau.

Home Town, U. S. A.—20 minutes—sound
> Affords a homey, pleasant picture of life in an American small town. *Source: Look* Magazine.

Maria Chapdelaine—95 minutes—sound
> Deals with life in a primary group in French Canada. *Source:* Brandon Films, Inc.

New York Parade—10 minutes—sound
> Depicts particularly well the relationships of individuals through casual acquaintances in a great metropolis. *Source:* Teaching Film Custodians, Inc.

Arteries of the City—11 minutes—sound
> Illustrates development of a city's transportation facilities. *Source:* Encyclopaedia Britannica Films.

Growth of Cities—10 minutes—sound
> Depicts various types of cities and city plans; clarifies the factors involved in the growth of suburbs. *Source:* Encyclopaedia Britannica Films.

Does It Matter What You Think?—15 minutes
> Treats public opinion, its formation and influence. *Source:* British Information Services.

Gallup Poll—10 minutes
> Shows the Gallup Poll in operation. *Source:* Teaching Film Custodians, Inc.

Public Opinion—11 minutes
> Gives a realistic analysis of public opinion, what it is, how it is formed, and what it can accomplish. *Source:* Encyclopaedia Britannica Films.

Interdependence—30 minutes
> Shows dependence of individuals and communities upon one another, and the relations of cities and country districts. *Source:* Harvard Film Service.

New York—22 minutes—sound
> A colorful film, giving an impression of the crowds of New York City, buildings, markets, playgrounds, etc. *Source:* International Theatrical & Television Corporation.

Life Streams of the City—16 minutes
> Stresses importance of transportation in good city planning. *Source:* General Electric Company.

Dances of the Bees—30 minutes
> Produced by Dr. Karl von Frisch, University of Munich, this film documents his researches into communication between bees—how, through nectar dances a "finder" bee reports to the hive the location, distance, and direction from the hive of a food source. *Source:* Austrian State Office of Education.

Fidelity of a Report—6 minutes
> A film demonstration on accuracy of observation and reports with the story of a man and a woman waiting for a bus: woman opens her purse and reveals her money; man draws revolver and takes the money; another man forces him to pass over the loot, throw away his gun, and lie on the sidewalk. Second man escapes in waiting car. Action time: sixty seconds. Standard set of questions is then answered by

students and there follows a second showing of the dramatic sequence so that answers may be checked. *Source:* Psychological Cinema Register.

Flag Speaks—19 minutes—sound—color
The flag as a symbol. Events in the history of the American flag including unfurling of Revolutionary flag at Fort Stanwix and at the Constitutional Convention. The flag "tells" of abuses of freedom of the press, freedom of religion, freedom of assembly. Gives correct use of flag. *Source:* Teaching Film Custodians.

Story of Communication—22 minutes—sound
Highlights early developments in communication, writing, and printing and the gradual conquest of time and space. *Source:* Films, Inc.

Who Makes Words?—10 minutes—sound
Elementary presentation of means by which language grows; how words are borrowed, invented, or come about through changes in spelling or meaning. *Source:* Coronet Films.

Writing through the Ages—10 minutes—sound
Presents a chronological history of writing as a means of communication. Shows ways in which writing evolved from pictures and signs, and shows how local materials used as writing tools influenced the methods of sign making and writing. Stresses contributions of Phoenicians, Greeks, and Romans to our present alphabet. *Source:* Encyclopaedia Britannica Films.

Experimental Studies in Social Climates of Groups—30 minutes—sound
Part I compares children in autocratic, democratic, and laissez-faire atmospheres. Part II shows the same children in transition from one atmosphere to another. Statistical graphs present quantitative findings. *Source:* University of Iowa.

Propaganda Techniques—10 minutes—sound
Methods of recognizing and evaluating propaganda told through a story of a small-town mayoralty campaign. *Source:* Coronet Films.

Voices of the People—20 minutes—sound
Presents a disagreement between a college professor and a businessman concerning the importance of freedom of speech. Continues with their trip through the Freedom Train, inspection and discussion of the Declaration of Independence and Bill of Rights. *Source:* Office of War Information.

Fury—17 minutes—sound
An excerpt from full-length film. Lynching sequence. Good example of "mob" behavior. *Source:* Teaching Film Custodians, Inc.

Chapter 9

Communication: The Basis for Group Life

An old couple was celebrating their seventieth wedding anniversary. Asked why their marriage had succeeded so well, the wife made this comment: "We never talked much. We mostly just set."

Men of toil, particularly farmers in isolated hill sections, often surprise one by their poverty of conversation when together. Among working men, too, one often notices this characteristic. They live in a world of action and physical performance. The world of exchange of ideas, pleasantries, humor, is not a primary activity. But to many human beings, the art of conversation is highly cultivated. Through the exchange of conversation and ideas, they find the most interesting expressions of their lives.

As one compares man in this respect with other creatures, he cannot help being amazed at how silent most creatures are even when together, at how little actual communication goes on between them. The one exception is certain birds, which during mating season communicate a great deal by song.

COMMUNICATION AND SOCIAL INTERACTION

The contact of person with person and group with group on whatever scale, large or small, leads to an exchange of experience which the sociologist calls *social interaction*. Social interaction is the basic social process of all human life. It takes numerous forms, but the basis of most social interaction is *communication*, that is, the ability of one human being to make himself understood by another. Man's basic social experience consists of contact and social interaction through communication. Social interaction is the essence of all social life, but its primary medium of operation, its tools, are the *symbols* by which man communicates.

But ability to communicate by language is much more than a luxury and an entertainment. Behavioristic psychologists a few years ago proposed the idea that thought was impossible without words. They even went so far as to suggest that in all thinking the individual is manipulating his vocal apparatus, even though he is not conscious of doing so, and his movements may actually be unobservable. That there is something to this theory is suggested by the fact that often people who read comparatively little may move their lips while reading, pronouncing each word silently.

To deny the individual a chance to communicate with his fellows is to deny him social life itself, for if his power to communicate meaning to others is not developed by the group, the individual turns out to be something much less than a human being, as this term is usually conceived. This has been demonstrated on different rare occasions with human beings.

Some years ago Dr. Rene A. Spitz, an American psychiatrist, spent some time in a foundling home for children in South America. He has reported his observations of children denied the most important group experience known to man, the close mother–child relation, with its intimate level of contact and communication.

"Foundling Home was an excellent institution from the standpoint of hygiene. The food was varied, adequate, and carefully prepared; no person whose clothes and hands were not sterilized could approach the babies. A well-trained staff of physicians and many consulting specialists checked daily on the infants' health. This institution harbored babies from birth to the sixth year. Up to the fourth month the infants in this institution developed well, even better than the average of a family child. The average baby up to four months in this institution was a month ahead of its age level.

"From the fourth month on, however, this picture changed radically. The developmental level of these children dropped more and more until at the end of the first year the average child of Foundling Home was alarmingly retarded. A 12-months-old child in Foundling Home showed the picture of an 8-months-old child.

"What happened to bring about this change in the developmental picture of the 69 children in Foundling Home, without any exception? All the conditions of hygiene were identical for younger and older children. There was only one factor which had changed. The presence of the mother. The practice in Foundling Home was that mothers brought in their children at birth and stayed with them until the end of their fifth month. They took care of them and breasted them. After this time the mothers had to leave the institution. Trained nurses took over the care of the children. However, the financial provisions of the institution provided only one nurse for 12–15 children. Therefore infants in Foundling Home from their fifth month on had only a twelfth or a fifteenth part of a mother. Their emotional interchange with human beings was drastically reduced, their response to it was drastic deterioration.

"Unfortunately the limited duration of my stay in the country in which the institution was situated did not permit me to follow these children after their first year. An assistant I trained during my stay was entrusted with the follow-up. Although these data seem superficial they are revealing.

"The most striking result of this study was that 27 children of those observed originally had died. This is really an alarming figure considering the utmost precautions which were taken in regard to hygiene. It seems that in spite of good food and meticulous medical care these children had too little energy left to resist minor and major ailments.

"Besides the 27 children who died, some other children could not be accounted for, as they were adopted, placed in other institutions or simply lost from sight. My assistant had only the opportunity to observe 21 children who ranged from 2½ to 4½ years. These children were all undersized and underweight. Only 3 of these 21 children had the normal weight of a 2-year-old and only 2 attained the length normal at this age. Their mental performance was no better. Of these 21 children, of which the youngest was 2½ years old, only 5 could walk unassisted, only one had a vocabulary of a dozen words and only one, a 4½-year-old, used sentences. On the other hand, 8 of these 21 children could neither stand nor walk, 6 could not talk at all and 11 were limited to the use of 2 words. Even this superficial sketch reveals these children as ranging from mental debility to idiocy.

"Psychotherapeutic intervention was tried in a few cases by other investigators to abolish or at least to mitigate the consequences of such early institutional care. The result was nil. The damage inflicted to the children's systems seems irreversible.

"This tragic consequence of deprivation of the mother represents not only a theoretical challenge to the scientist who investigates the dynamics of early childhood, but also an important challenge to anyone concerned with the future of a nation, with the future of the world. . . .

"Presence or absence of the mother is the 'to be or not to be' for the development of the baby. If a society wants to guarantee the health of its young generation and with that its own survival it has to guarantee an average amount of motherly love to the average child."[1]

This account, and a motion picture produced by Dr. Spitz, presents one of the most stark pictures in scientific literature of the effect of the denial of love, care, and conversation to the young child. It makes clear that socialization is a group task. Denied it, the child fails to develop into a human being capable of group interaction.

EFFECT OF IMPERFECT CONTACT WITH OTHERS

Nothing is more disastrous to the human being than to be isolated from his fellows for long periods of time. In isolation the child fails to acquire language, the basic tool for extensive communication. To be reared without human contact is to become an animal.

A Retarded Child. Here is the case of a normal child reared for six and one-half years under conditions which allowed her few normal social contacts.

". . . Her mother was a deaf-mute, having become so at the age of two, and it appears that she and Isabelle had spent most of their time together in a dark room shut off from the rest of the mother's family. As a result Isabelle had no chance to develop speech; when she communicated with her mother, it was by means of gestures. Lack of sunshine and inadequacy of diet had caused Isabelle to become rachitic. Her legs in particular were affected; they 'were so bowed that as she stood erect, the soles of her shoes came nearly flat together, and she got about with a skittering gait.' Her behavior toward strangers, especially men, was almost that of a wild animal, manifesting much fear and hostility. In lieu of speech she made only a strange croaking sound. In many ways she acted like an infant. 'She was apparently utterly unaware of relationships of any kind. When presented with a ball for the first time, she held it in the palm of her hand, then reached out and stroked my face with it. Such behavior is comparable to that of a child of six months.' At first it was even hard to tell whether or not she could hear, so unused were her senses. Many of her actions resembled those of deaf children.

"It is small wonder that, once it was established that she could hear, specialists working with her believed her to be feebleminded. Even on nonverbal tests her performance was so low as to promise little for the future. Her first score on the Stanford-Binet was 19

[1] Rene A. Spitz, "The Importance of Mother–Child Relationship During the First Year of Life," published by the Washington Society for Mental Hygiene and the Graduate School of Social Work, University of Washington (Seattle, 1947). Based on a series of film lectures presented in Seattle, June 15–17, 1947.

months, practically at the zero point of the scale. On the Vineland social maturity scale her first score was 39, representing the age level of two and a half years! 'The general impression was that she was wholly uneducatable and that any attempt to teach her to speak, after so long a period of silence, would meet with failure.'

"In spite of this interpretation, the individuals in charge of Isabelle launched a systematic and skillful program of training. It seemed hopeless at first. The approach had to be through pantomime and dramatization, suitable to an infant. It required one week of intensive effort before she even made her first attempt at vocalization. Gradually she began to respond, however, and, after the first hurdles had at last been overcome, a curious thing happened. She went through the usual stages of learning characteristics of the years from one to six not only in proper succession, but far more rapidly than normal. In a little over two months after her first vocalization she was putting sentences together. Nine months after that she could identify words and sentences on the printed page, could write well, could add to ten, and could retell a story after hearing it. Seven months beyond this point she had a vocabulary of 1,500–2,000 words and was asking complicated questions. Starting from an educational level of between one and three years (depending on what aspect one considers), she had reached a normal level by the time she was eight and a half years old. In short, she covered in two years the stages of learning that ordinarily require six. Or, to put it another way, her I.Q. trebled in a year and a half. The speed with which she reached the normal level of mental development seems analogous to the recovery of body weight in a growing child after an illness, the recovery being achieved by an extra fast rate of growth for a period after the illness, until normal weight for the given age is again attained."[2]

Feral Children. Even more drastic examples of the effect of isolation from normal social contacts are those of feral (wild) children. One of the most famous cases of feral children, and one extensively studied, is that of Casper Hauser, born in Austria about 1812. Casper was left in early childhood on the doorstep of a Hungarian peasant's hut. The peasant allowed the boy no contact with the outside world, placing him in a dark cellar where he did not see even the person who brought his food. When, after sixteen years of isolation, he was permitted to come in contact with other people, he was hardly able to walk and knew neither language nor social customs.

[2] Marie K. Mason, "Learning To Speak After Six and One-half Years of Silence," *Journal of Speech and Hearing Disorders,* 7:299, 300–304 (1942). By permission of the Editor of the American Speech and Hearing Association.

He was animal-like, stupid, and idle. He burned his hand when he first saw fire and was convulsed with fear at the sound of beating drums. He imagined that bits of paper floating in the air were alive, and could not distinguish between living persons and pictures or statues. He was able to see things very well in the dark and had a wonderful memory for names. When he died, his autopsy showed no abnormalities of the brain.

There are other well-known examples of feral persons. Near Chalons, France, the Girl of Songi was found in a forest in 1731. She caught fish and ate them raw, climbed trees, and uttered wild cries for speech. She had difficulty adapting herself to civilization. However, when she was placed in a convent, she learned to speak, to embroider, and to do housework. There was a Hessian boy, captured in 1341 by hunters, who ran on all fours with a pack of wolves. He never learned to adapt himself to civilized life, was always restless, and died untamed. A Lithuanian boy was found living with bears in 1657. His speech was a growl. His food and sleeping habits were like those of the bears. He was instructed and learned to obey to some extent, but always kept his bear habits. Records also exist of an Irish boy who lived with sheep and consequently bleated like them.

However improbable these examples may seem, records that are considered authentic exist concerning them and a number of similar cases. These clearly indicate that man does not develop a normal personality when isolated from human society. Without the associations of others, the human being grows into a far different creature than we expect a human being to be. The animal is there, with the appetites common to other animals, but the habits, tastes, and restraints that come from human association, and the attitudes and moral values that come from teaching by a group, are all missing. There is even a tendency to acquire the language and ways of behavior of the creatures of instinct if the human being is barred from the companionship of man.

These cases also indicate that even at ten or fifteen years of age the person who has been denied normal contact can acquire many human traits from his new associates. Finally, it is clear from this kind of study that the person's association with other human beings has in reality made him "human," if the term is conceived as descriptive of one possessed of habits, attitudes, values, and philosophies that characterize men in normal society.

Persons with Sensory Defects. Less isolated from social experience than feral children such as those described above are those born with the physical handicap of deafness or blindness. Deafness, especially, is a great limiting factor in social experience, for words are basic to understanding others. The deaf child who hears none of the words which human beings use develops little understanding and intellectual life. As a consequence, modern educational systems have to go to great lengths to develop devices for educating the deaf child.

For the boy, this is the dawn of social contact by sound. Unable to hear normally, he is reached by greatly amplified sound waves. Anyone robbed of either sight or hearing is limited in communication and, therefore, restricted in social interaction. For this reason, continuous research is carried on to develop means, including mechanical devices being used in this photograph, to overcome sensory defects. (Black Star)

This training consists of teaching him to use the same words that other people use, either through some form of tactile sensation such as feeling raised letters or touching the throat of the person speaking, or by watching the lip motions of the person speaking.

Not only does the deaf child have peculiar difficulties in becoming socialized, but the person who develops deafness during any period of his life has to guard himself constantly against becoming suspicious of those about him. He sees them talking and laughing, and naturally wonders if they may not be talking about or making fun of him.

The awakening of the mind is dependent upon the understanding and use of words. This is strikingly illustrated in Helen Keller's remarkable awakening from a world of darkness to one of understanding.[3] Deprived of sight and hearing when very young, she had lost the two means by which normal persons communicate. It was late in her sixth year that an understanding teacher came into her life. Anne Sullivan, her teacher, began associating objects with words by spelling the name of the object into Helen's hand. For example, she handed Helen a doll and then spelled d–o–l–l into her hand, but the finger play made no sense at first, even though Helen imitated the movements.

In this way she learned to spell a number of words, but they were still without meaning to her. It was when her teacher put Helen's hand into water at the pump and then spelled w–a–t–e–r into the other hand that meaning first dawned. "That living word awakened my soul, gave it light, hope, joy, set it free." This she considers the beginning of thought and understanding for her.

Immigrants. The experience of the deaf person is not unlike that of the normal person who finds himself as an immigrant surrounded by those of a foreign tongue. He has a hard time avoiding the feeling that he is being discussed unfavorably and perhaps ridiculed for not being able to use their language. The immigrant in the United States has been an example of social isolation induced by lack of the word tools for communicating with the native population. As a consequence, immigrant groups have tended to flock together during the first generation and form what are known as *social islands,* both in cities and in rural communities. These social islands tend to be shut away from contact with outsiders.

Solitaries. Man is so much a creature of association that when long isolated from his fellows he tends to develop his individualism to the point of eccentricity. The sheepherder is notorious for his peculiar personality traits. He may become so shy that he hides even from the man who brings his weekly or biweekly provisions to camp. Often the sheepherder develops such peculiarities of behavior as to be considered abnormal. So also does the trapper, the prospector, or the mountaineer who lives far away from his fellows much of the time.

[3] For the full account of the training of this remarkable woman read Helen Keller, *The Story of My Life* (New York: Doubleday & Co., Inc., 1903).

One sociologist[4] has made a study of solitaries and solitarization in which he includes solitary geniuses who isolate themselves for the sake of their work, as well as the group we usually consider solitaries. Melancholy, lonesomeness, introversion, sometimes visions and hallucinations, restlessness, thwarted wishes, gradual loss of social sense, and shyness are natural results of long isolation. Life becomes extremely simple for those who live alone.

The most severe form of punishment, used commonly throughout history and still used on occasion as the most rigorous possible form of discipline, is solitary confinement. If long continued, it will break most men. In early prisons mental disease, suicide, or premature death were frequent consequences of such punishment. Today in San Quentin Federal Penitentiary there are for those in condemned row (those sentenced to die) three degrees of punishment for severe infractions of prison discipline. They may be sent to Siberia, the Shelf, or the Hole. Each of these represents a different degree of solitary confinement. In Siberia they are locked up with a cell partner and given a bucket of regular prison food once daily. On the Shelf they are locked up alone with the same food ration. In the Hole, darkness and a bread-and-water diet with a bucket of main-line food only once a week are added to solitary confinement. After a few days or weeks in the Hole, most condemned men lose their balance. They may make night and day hideous by yelling, throw slop buckets, or try to kill any guard who comes near.[5]

For most individuals there can be no greater torture than separation for long periods from their fellow men. Many college students cannot spend an evening alone. They must be either in the library or chatting in some friend's room. Perhaps it is only that they have not yet developed the lonely meditative habits of the creative genius.

Isolated Groups. Isolation affects groups much as it affects individuals. Shut a people away from contact with other peoples, put them on an island in the ocean, in an isolated mountain valley, in a nation that bars its doors to travelers from the outside and forbids travel to its own citizens, and one will find a backward people, suspicious of strangers, resistant to the new, and years behind peoples whose contacts reach out to all the world. In America, "hillbilly" is a term which stands for the person reared in such an isolated social group.

[4] Louis Petroff, *Solitaries and Solitarization* (Los Angeles: University of Southern California Press, 1936).
[5] David Lamson, *We Who Are About To Die* (New York: Charles Scribner's Sons, 1936).

PERSONALITY DEVELOPMENT AND SOCIAL CONTACT

The Child with Social Contacts. Place a child in a normal group environment, and he learns the ways of those whose company he keeps. Long before he reaches adulthood, he evaluates everything he does in terms of what others will think. If when alone he talks to himself aloud, or whistles, or sings, now and then he checks up on himself wondering what others would think if they were there. And if in one of his brief periods of solitude someone says "hello" from behind his back, his mind immediately runs over what he has said or done during the previous few minutes that the visitor might have seen or heard without his knowing it. In every waking thought this society-made person subjects himself to social inspection, not only in the real world, but in imagination as well. He is in and of society. In a real sense, before he is four years old, self and society are already one.

And so it is with the adult. As has been shown, the personality of the solitary is warped by isolation. In utter contrast is the traveling salesman who has a multitude of contacts with different people. He soon learns to talk on any topic, associate with almost any kind of person, and be at home in almost any social climate. Meeting a stranger in a hotel lobby or the smoking car of a train, he will engage him in conversation as though he had known him for years.

Social Contacts of Progressive Nations. Find a people which sits at the crossroads of transportation and travel in any period of history and you will find a people alert, forward-looking, rapid in advancement.

In ancient times, Palestine, the Tigris–Euphrates Valley, and the Nile Valley were on the crossroads between three great continents. There in the Fertile Crescent in the day of river-boat, mule, and camel-back travel, civilization flowered. There were located the ancient wonders of the world—the Pyramids, the Sphinx, the Hanging Gardens of Babylon. There originated two great religions—Christianity and Islam.

When sea-going craft made the Mediterranean the waterway of the world, civilization flowered in turn in Crete, Greece, and Rome. Literature, art, drama, rhetoric, and oratory, even athletics and physical training, reached new heights of attainment. And the Roman Church was to become the great religious institution of the Middle Ages.

Then came Columbus and the conquest of the Atlantic. Large vessels made a waterway of the oceans. The focal point of contact shifted to the coastal ports of Europe and Britain. The civilizations of Western Europe excelled all preceding civilizations of history in mechanical development, in daring, and in doing. These coastal cities of Western Europe became the focal point of activity in the world.

This query might be pushed one step further if we ask ourselves where civilization will again flower, now that air travel is rapidly becoming the key to world contact and world dominion. Certainly it is clear already that the people with the fastest planes and most extensive routes of air transportation will experience the most extensive travel and contact with other peoples of the world. They hold the key to the future.

Wide-awake and progressive nations attempt to extend the range of their social experience through the development of transportation and communication systems which will keep them in contact with peoples over a wide geographical area. In the United States from the earliest times the building of roads and railroads has been a vital concern of government. Although actual construction, especially in the field of railroad development, was done largely by private companies, the federal government granted them large tracts of land and other concessions by way of encouragement. Also the government has subsidized the development of airplane travel and encouraged new developments such as airmail in the mail service. The Post Office system, the largest business organization in the world, is operated by the federal government. It is organized and carried on entirely without profit, in fact, at considerable loss to the taxpayer at times. A progressive government encourages communication and transportation for the sake of cultural unity within the country and for the maintenance of contacts with other parts of the world, not simply for the purpose of exchanging goods, but also for the purpose of exchanging ideas.

In the United States, the main devices for *indirect communication,* radio and newspapers, are relatively free from government ownership. Democratic governments believe that ideas should be freely communicated as long as they do not directly encourage the overthrow of the government. In direct contrast has been the restricting influence of dictators, who have limited communication to the kind of messages the government wishes to release. Whatever the philosophy of the government, the fact remains that communication, the contact of people through words which they can understand, is the basis for the larger social life that has come to be known as the *great society.*

To the extent that all peoples of the world come to understand each other's words, music, art, and all other symbols by which men know and appreciate each other will a world society become a possibility. This is to say that society, like the social nature of the individual, grows by contact. The individual's habits are formed, his life expands, his personality grows in proportion to the meaningful contacts he has with his fellows. A neighborhood, a community, a national society enriches itself, changes, improves its devices for doing things and its ways of doing them, changes its philosophy and ideas in ratio to its contact and communication with other peoples.

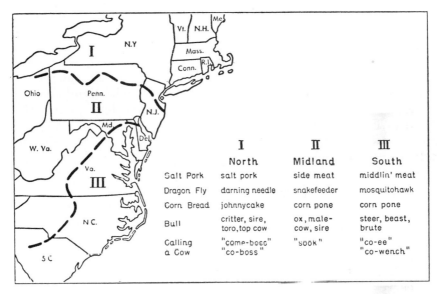

	I North	II Midland	III South
Salt Pork	salt pork	side meat	middlin' meat
Dragon Fly	darning needle	snakefeeder	mosquitohawk
Corn Bread	johnnycake	corn pone	corn pone
Bull	critter, sire, toro, top cow	ox, male-cow, sire	steer, beast, brute
Calling a Cow	"come-boss" "co-boss"	"sook"	"co-ee" "co-wench"

Communication Demands a Common Understanding

This linguistic map of eastern United States shows examples of regional expressions. (Adapted from Hans Kurath, "The American Languages," Scientific American, January, 1950, p. 49.)

Contact and communication are not only the life of the infant, the adult, the nation, but also of all forms of human activity, even of science itself. The following testimony before a House of Representatives subcommittee tellingly presents the case for freedom in scientific communication:

"The problem of dealing with secrets is an old one in government. It existed and had to be dealt with by governments long before we had democracy.

"The concern of governments is with state secrets, which are close to what are really true secrets—the kind of secrets which you won't know unless I tell you. They are concerned with codes, with wave lengths, caliber, horsepower, range, rate, and scale. But the disclosure even of this kind of secret in the contest between states is only a matter of time. Ultimately they become known to the enemy through our use of them and the enemy's interception and capture.

"But these are different from the secrets of nature with which science is concerned. The secrets of nature are open to the discovery by scientists all over the world. As Harold Urey has said, to understand and to originate require approximately the same competence.

"The truth of this statement is sustained by the history of science, where we see time and again the classical situation of simultaneous discovery of fundamental knowledge by scientists working in entire independence of one another, and in ignorance of each other's work.

"The classical story is that of Newton and Leibniz, who simultaneously within the same half decade discovered the calculus; of Priestley, an Englishman, and Scheele, a Swede, who simultaneously made the discovery of oxygen; of Joseph Henry here in America, Michael Faraday in England, and Lenz in Russia, who simultaneously came upon the principle of induction, upon which the dynamo was based, upon which mechanical energy is converted to electrical energy, the event in science in the 19th century which had as large an effect on human affairs as the discovery of the atom.

"This goes on despite all measures that can be taken to maintain secrecy. At the Geneva Conference on the peaceful uses of atomic energy last summer, the scientists of the world who had been working in secrecy and in ignorance of each other's work came together and compared notes. They plotted their figures on curves and put the curves on top of each other, and found that they matched perfectly. The matching curves were the symbol of the common enterprise that science is on both sides of the Iron Curtain and on all sides of national boundaries.

"Again, despite secrecy and censorship, during the Second World War the technology of radar was developed independently by the United States, England, France, Germany, and Japan. Radar functioned on both sides of the fronts.

"More recently, despite the security system under which our atomic technology and research have been conducted for the past decade, we see the story of the development of the synchrotron. This is a nuclear accelerator, an atom smasher. It was invented by an American, McMillan. McMillan's invention was kept secret until quite independently the synchrotron principle was published by Veksler in Russia in 1945. Thereupon the secret on which we had been sitting was released and the synchrotron came into general use in nuclear physics, available to those not working on secret projects.

"It is quite apparent that scientists in every nation working on fundamental research are going to have to agree about nature. Ultimately they are going to make the same discoveries. It is only a matter of time. By concealing what we know we may delay the discovery of new work of others. But they will ultimately discover it no matter what we do. By concealing and frustrating communications within science, however, we will surely slow up ourselves. Not only in the making of discoveries, but in bringing new work into application.

"Communication is a vital part of research. It is inseparable from research. It is not too much to say that research is communication. New scientific work does not have any existence in this world until it has been communicated from one scientist to another. Communication goes on at many levels. It is highly subject to disruption, and to frustration, and to tampering. Among human beings it is a difficult thing to achieve at any time.

"A scientist never publishes until he has argued and discussed and circulated his work among other scientists who work closely with him and threshed out the points with those in his own field that he knows personally. Through publication he undertakes to reach others whom he doesn't know personally, who are outside of his camp. . . .

"Just as scientists cannot tell where to look for work, so we cannot possibly tell to whom it ought to be communicated.

"It is particularly in the realm of cross-fertilization that new work takes place. Progress often comes from the most odd and unpredictable places. Out at Brookhaven, for example, a group of scientists developed a new improvement on the synchrotron, known as the 'strong focussing' principle.

"No sooner had they got the word of their work into print, when one Nicholas Cristofalis turned up as the prior inventor of this development. Cristofalis was not a Doctor of Philosophy. Cristofalis was an electrical engineer. He was engaged in the business of installing elevators, and not in the United States but in Athens. When he originally came up with his idea of the strong focussing principle he sent it in a letter to Berkeley. When Berkeley heard about Nicholas Cristofalis later, they looked up his correspondence, and they found it in the crank file.

"The trouble is that communication in science is all too easy to tamper with. When we tamper with it we tamper with research itself. . . .

"Now we have a new reason to oppose secrecy in the operations of the Government. It is the danger that secrecy lays to the advancement of science, and hence to the general welfare and to national security."[6]

SYMBOLISM, COMMUNICATION, AND SOCIAL LIFE

The Importance of Words. Words are the key to man's social life. There is no better way to illustrate this point than by quoting from the case history of a college man of neurotic temperament who speaks on this matter of communication from the bitter depth of personal experience. A stutterer, he cannot use effectively the common symbols of communication by which most social interaction is carried on within his group. He writes:

> The disability which puts me in the neurotic classification is stuttering. To the layman, stuttering is something of a funny mannerism. It is surefire laugh material for the "ham" comedian, as well as for many boorish people who should know better. To the stutterer, it takes on the form of an obsession. Nothing could be so worthwhile or desirable as good, fluent speech.

Even the absence of a single word in a person's speech habits may affect his adjustment to his group. A youth who had lived in an isolated section of South Dakota before moving to the state of Washington described as a college student his experience upon entering a new and larger high school. One word was a key factor. He says:

> I felt ill at ease among the group and was timid in everything I did. Fully exemplifying this was my encounter with the common greeting "Hi." I had never heard or had I been trained to use it. At first I refused to use it; however, later I resolutely forced myself to say "Hi." Objectively considered, my feelings were highly illogical and ungrounded; however, they persisted and gave me a feeling of insecurity and inferiority in my high-school group.

Because man can use words, he can communicate not only his thoughts but, even more important, describe his external life to his fellows. Because man can use concepts to describe experience, he is a teacher. He can teach animals far more effectively than any animal can teach its offspring, for the higher animals can learn to understand a little of man's language even though they cannot use it. And man, because he speaks, is able to tell his children all that he and his ancestors have learned. As a consequence, his children, by the time they reach the age of youth, step out on the threshold of life already having learned more than any other creature can ever know, and, in fact, what the race took centuries to learn. This human capacity explains why man is a culture-builder, and able to pass culture on as a heritage.

[6] Gerard Piel, president and publisher of *Scientific American,* in testimony before the U.S. House of Representatives, Government Information Subcommittee, March 9, 1956.

Communication and the Primacy of Man. If one were asked, as the sociologist sometimes is, to make a simple statement concerning the one thing that sets man apart from other creatures, he would say, "Man can make himself understood by others through the use of words," or, to state it more theoretically, "He can make symbols of his own invention stand for everything he experiences."

No other creature can. This is conclusively demonstrated by a study of man's nearest rival in communication, the ape. Wolfgang Köhler, German psychologist who found himself marooned on the Canary Islands at the outbreak of World War I, studied the com-

Perception is the basis of communication. What do you see in this picture?*

* *The photograph shows snow and ice fields on one of the sand banks of the Waddenzee near Vleiland, Holland. Is this the scene you perceived? (KLM Royal Dutch Airlines)*

munication system of apes carefully and concluded that although they can make a great variety of sounds, those sounds all have to do with emotions.[7] The great gulf which separates ape and man is the ape's inability to develop any language to describe things external to himself. The ape's language is a language of feeling only.

An ape can learn to put a jointed pole together and reach out through a wire cage and rake in a banana, but he cannot tell his mate or offspring how he does it. Likewise, he can pile up boxes to reach suspended bananas, but he is unable to tell his mate how or why boxes hold him up. A human being can meet the second as well as the first requirement, with the consequence that getting bananas becomes easier for each new generation.

Words, the common symbol of communication, are the foundations of all human social life. Communication by some language is found wherever man is found. The language may be English, Spanish, French, German, Hindustan, or any of some seven thousand other languages and dialects. But within the group there is a common understanding of what others mean, and because there is a common understanding of words, there is a common understanding of what life means.

A little girl visiting Monkey Island in the San Francisco Zoo laughed until her sides ached at their antics and, turning to her mother, said, "No wonder they call them monkeys." The word "monkeys" and "monkeying around" have come to stand for characteristic antics of apes or men only because there is a fairly universal understanding of the way monkeys act. The child had the cart before the horse.

Symbols in Communication. Written language separates primitives from modern peoples. *Primitives,* more properly called preliterates, have language, but it is unwritten. If a people has developed written symbols through which they communicate, they are civilized. The character scrawled on a stone wall with colored stone makes it possible for the savage to communicate a message to another who is absent. The written character in more modern societies has been transferred to the printed page, which makes possible communication through the generations. More recently microfilm has reduced writing symbols to small space, so that much of the experience of one generation can become the property of all generations to come.

A *symbol* is, by definition, *an abbreviated representation used in communication.* Man's ability to develop symbols not only for his

---

[7] Wolfgang Köhler, *The Mentality of Apes* (New York: Harcourt, Brace & Co., Inc., 1925).

Symbols Are Shorthand Representations

These symbols stand for words but symbolize vast systems of iron rails, moving cars, depots, freight stations, factory and repair shops, office buildings, communication systems, personnel, and even intricate patterns of loyalty and unique patterns of competition. (Association of American Railroads)

emotions but for everything that comes in his range of experience is the key to his social experience. Words come to stand for every act, every thought. Words and other symbols even more complicated, such as mathematical symbols, chemical formulas, blueprints, shorthand, and wireless codes, are all devices by which man represents experience to others.

All forms of symbolism, whether gesture, word, writing, musical note, mathematical formula, blueprint, or code, are abbreviated ways of representation. For example, *things* are represented by such words as "trees" or "houses"; *persons* by such symbols as "John Doe" or "Mary Smith"; *situations* by such symbols as "travel" or "flying"; *inner experience* by such words as "happiness" or "fear." In order to be meaningful, such symbols must be understood and have approximately the same meaning to the person who receives them as to the one who employs them.

Coding and decoding messages in secret symbols has become one of the most important aspects of warfare today. To communicate with new symbols which the enemy cannot understand if he intercepts messages is a task of the intelligence service in war. To intercept an enemy message and to be able to reconstruct its meaning is a part of the behind-the-scenes warfare that is never-ending as long as armies are arrayed against one another.

Every vocation has a vocabulary that is unique in some respects. Farmers who use caterpillar tractors have certain words with unique meaning; professional criminals have a vocabulary which carries meaning only to those in the profession; hobos have words belonging to their own group; and so with many specialized occupational groups. Gestures, by contrast, are much more universally understood. All people have to resort to them when they are among foreigners with whom they have no common language. Almost anyone can by gestures show that he is thirsty or hungry, or can indicate the direction he wishes to go and have the roadway pointed out to him. But language, the spoken symbol, is the most reliable vehicle of social life.

Symbols in Social Interaction. Communication through symbols represents tremendous economy in human behavior. For example, the word "religion" to a body of Christian worshipers represents an elaborate system of material things and of beliefs and practices. To express the meaning without some such abbreviated symbol would be complicated and time-consuming indeed. The word "dog" represents the wide range of species of a particular animal with which man has had experience, and needs little elaboration. The word "typewrite" represents a complex form of behavior, but when the boss uses the word in addressing a secretary, she knows exactly what is wanted.

Symbols in Thought. It shocked the scientific world a little when the behavioristic psychologists some twenty-five years ago defended the thesis that man can think only because he can speak. But the notion is not entirely nonsensical. Man has the capacity to think because of innate characteristics that are part of his nervous structure; nature has set him apart from the other higher animals in this regard. But thought is the manipulation of the symbols to which man has reduced his experiences.

Thinking involves actually talking to oneself, manipulating words or other symbols which represent things, behavior, and situations; trying out things mentally on an elaborate scale that one cannot try out in actual experience without years of work; arriving at conclusions through this process of juggling words or other symbols by oneself.

For example, a great structure like the Grand Coulee Dam is all worked out by the juggling of symbols in the process called engineering. Actually, it involves a man working out, through the use of mathematical symbols and the use of numerous concepts reduced to formulas in physics and mathematics, the entire construction process. Thought processes are aided by manipulating these symbols on paper and reducing each major step of constructing the dam to a blueprint, which is another form of symbolism. Before a single shovelful of dirt is moved, the gigantic structure has been worked out through trial and error in men's minds by the use of symbols and reduced to blueprints that describe, in engineers' symbols, every step of the project, the actual construction of which is to require approximately ten years.

Symbols in the engineering field have become so accurate that those trained in their use can try out numerous alternatives on paper and in a short time see whether or not a thing is possible, thereby knowing before the task is undertaken that it will work. Dams such as Grand Coulee would never be attempted if it were not for this exactness in man's thought processes, made possible by his use of symbols. No people could afford to spend the required time, money, and human energy if there were any reasonable doubt that the structure, when finished, would hold back the waters of the river.

Symbols in Learning. In the world today, where symbolism has become so extensive, one could spend all his life trying to master various symbols and still would only have begun. Today most learning is derived not by direct experience with a situation but through symbolism. It begins, now as always, with reading, writing, and arithmetic: reading—learning to recognize the common symbols which all men in the culture use; writing—learning to employ these symbols for indirect communication; arithmetic—learning that other great system of symbols through which is expressed quantity.

By following the process of learning through symbols on to higher levels of university study, the student learns that each field has its distinct vocabulary, concepts, or formulas. With the bachelor's degree today he gets at best but a superficial acquaintance with a few of the symbols of learning. Indeed, the student could spend his lifetime in college and not cover the courses of any large university, with all its highly specialized courses. But as long as he continued his formal education he would be learning through the use of symbols.

Men are learned to the extent that they are able to communicate through a multitude of symbols. The linguist who is at home in seven or more languages has some appreciation of the life and customs of seven peoples, rather than only one.

To be educated is to be able to communicate orally and in writing in one or more languages. To be well educated is to be able to understand the vocabulary of particular sciences, art, literature, and music. Through words, the scientist describes new areas of space and time as he conquers them. Sociology, chemistry, zoology, geology, physics, and other fields of learning have their own unique symbols.

FORMS OF COMMUNICATION IN SOCIAL INTERACTION

Communication is direct and indirect. By *direct communication* is meant *face-to-face communication*. It is by word of mouth. The spoken word is supplemented by the tone of voice, the expression of face, the twinkle of the eye, the smile, the frown, perhaps by gestures of the hand or a nod of the head or a sway of the body.

Direct Communication. Those who are without a written language must depend on direct communication for continuity of acquired knowledge. They develop remarkable memories for history, and evolve methods of imprinting the past on the memory from generation to generation. Those with developed means of indirect communication can store the past in recorded symbols.

A representative of the United States government strikingly illustrates from personal experience the situation of a people without indirect means of communication.[8] During the early part of World War II he was sent into the jungles of Dutch Guiana in South America to arrange for the use of a flat plateau as an American airbase. He had written up the agreement but it was meaningless until he could get the thumbprint of the chief of the jungle tribe. Holding this territory were forty thousand primitive Negroes, descendants of escaped African slaves who were brought into colonial Guiana by slave traders in the eighteenth century. The American representative found that all the Djuka people could repeat word for word a treaty made with the Dutch governor for Guiana in 1762. This memorable peace treaty had been passed on from generation to generation verbatim, simply by memory.

When the American representative concluded his own agreement, he repeated the treaty which he wished to make with the tribe in the presence of twelve old Djuka sub-chiefs. After the representative

[8] William LaVarre, "My Black Friend's Thumbprint," *Reader's Digest*, March, 1948, pp. 83–94.

had read it once, the chief asked the twelve sub-chiefs to repeat it to him so that he would know that they had each word in their minds, no word ever to be forgotten. The old men chanted the words of the treaty as with a single voice and without an error. The American expressed his amazement to the old chief at the performance of this feat. He then remembered a Dutch trader having told him that among the Djuka certain men are trained from childhood to carry long messages in their minds. They can hear a message once, remember it, and repeat it years afterward exactly as originally given. They are the human books to record the important traditions and agreements of the tribe.

Among primitives direct communication is practically the only means of communication. They may use smoke signals or some other simple device of indirect communication, but generally speaking there is little learning except by meeting people. There is no knowledge of other tribes except as members travel and meet others directly, meet them in combat, or steal property or wives from them, and thereby acquire new knowledge that has been developed in other groups.

Indirect Communication. *Indirect communication*, that is, *communication in the absence of personal contact*, has advantages far beyond the appreciation of peoples who live in a world so filled with forms of indirect communication that they are almost a nuisance. But if one has ever been lost in a rugged mountain country with sky overcast and a cold night setting in, he has hoped desperately that someone would understand his plight when, in the early darkness, he fires the distress signal. Just to be answered with a shot, if nothing more, brings a wonderful consolation.

The progress of a society is measured in considerable part by the extent to which it has developed indirect means of communication. Wars are won by speed of message transmission. The signal corps and the "walkie-talkie" are in the forefront of all modern battles. Intercommunication systems are also the key to prompt police action. Trade and commerce are expedited by these devices. Genuine democratic government over large areas of space is dependent upon them. From a simple smoke signal or rhythmic drum beat of the primitive, man has developed numerous means for reaching those at a distance—the personal letter, the printed page, the transmitted message. Our time has developed numerous and complex devices for making indirect communication instantaneous and world-wide —telephone and wireless, radio and television. And to communicate through time we have the printed word and microfilm, mathemati-

From a signal tower the yard-master controls train movements indirectly.

Indirect Communication

A distinct attribute of human behavior is the development of cultural instruments which permit communication over great areas of intervening space. Below the human level communication must be direct rather than symbolic. (Northern Pacific Railways and American Telephone and Telegraph Company)

Telephone switchboard operators at work and (inset) a linesman repairing telephone lines.

cal digits and formulas, mechanical and architectural blueprints, musical notes and art.

The most effective indirect communicative devices for world-wide social interaction now are radio, digest magazines, motion pictures, and newspapers; and television on a world scale is very near. These are the basic implements for achieving world understanding and a world society. However, unless guided by social science research, these devices may create misunderstanding and ill will rather than improving relations. There is evidence that many of the communicative activities of the United States may now be destructive of good will. For example, American movies abroad may portray what other peoples consider vulgarity rather than enlightenment. Digest magazines may be viewed as tools of an imperialistic America. The United States government through "The Voice of America" now carries foreign radio programs for education and information in many foreign languages, but still far too little is known of their effects on peoples with different folkways and mores, who may get far different meaning from our symbolic presentations than we intend.

On the positive side there is much to be said, if the author's observations in world travel are correct. Walt Disney's characters, Donald Duck and Mickey Mouse, are now world characters. Their simple story of the victory of the weak over the powerful appeals to peoples everywhere, particularly in areas where oppression of the masses by the upper classes exists—and this is throughout most of the world.

Coca-Cola is another missionary of the American character. It is found the world over. The European white is known throughout the world for his use of hard liquors, but the American's most popular drink is Coca-Cola and other soft drinks. This appeals to the Middle East and much of Asia and Moslem Africa, for most of these peoples do not sanction the use of alcoholic beverages.

The romantic movie, although its pattern is contradictory to the pattern of mate choice and love-making of most of the world, is destined in time to make individual mate choice universal. The intimate kiss of the movies is responsible in large part for much of the world considering the American woman immoral. The romantic pattern of love-making is considered a form of madness in most cultures and not to be encouraged. Yet these very patterns appeal to young people and are being imitated. In Japan, marriages of choice (love marriages) are increasing and result in a much lower divorce rate than those in which parents make the choice according to ancient custom.

In India, also, a more intimate sharing relationship between husbands and wives is developing as they add love play to sex in imitation of the American movie pattern of romance. Certainly, the old domination of women by men, the degradation of woman nearly to the level of beasts which exists in much of the world, cannot survive a genuine conversion of peoples to the romantic pattern of mate choice and love-making. Just as romance is in the making for people who view the American movie, so also is ultimate sex equality, for they are inseparable patterns.

Finally, America's mass-produced mechanical devices, which have given the world a picture of our great luxury and power, point and will continue to point the way toward liberation from hunger, hardship, and untimely death. The world airlines, with their luxury hotels planted at the crossroads of the world, introduce sanitation and cleanliness. The bulldozer makes the moving of dirt in baskets on the heads of women and other workers obsolete. Western birth-control devices emancipate people from an outmoded slavery to biological forces.

These are the lessons the movies, and even more, the educational projects abroad, the foreign aid programs, and programs for resource development in mechanically "underdeveloped" nations, are teaching. In time these lessons will be learned throughout the world.

SUMMARY

Personality development in isolation and in contact, within and without society, have been brought into contrast. Man, the social creature, is a product of life with people. His socialization consists primarily in his absorbing sufficient language symbols so that he can communicate and thereby share his experiences with the group or groups of which he is a part. Society consists of the social interaction of persons and groups through communication by means of symbols. Symbols are the basis for understanding; they are the short cut to all forms of social experience; they abbreviate human effort by substituting mental trial and error (thought) for physical trial and error. Used in indirect communication, they make possible an expanding world of social interaction sometimes called the great society.

DISCUSSION AND REVIEW QUESTIONS

1. Appraise the Spitz account and point out its significance to sociological study.
2. Show how feral men illustrate the effects of isolation on personality.
3. Discuss this general principle: Isolation hinders personality development.
4. Show how sensory defects may hinder man in his social environment.
5. Discuss the effects of difference in language on social interaction.
6. What are some of the effects of solitarization on personality?

7. Cite effects of isolation from social contact on groups.

8. Defend this proposition: Personality develops through social contact.

9. Discuss the effect of social contact on the destiny of peoples and nations.

10. Indicate why it is important to a government that would be progressive and forward-looking to encourage devices which make for contact and communication.

11. What is a symbol? Discuss its use in social life; its significance to social life.

12. Show the point at which apes fall far short of man in their performance as social creatures.

13. Show by examples how symbols provide for economy in social interaction.

14. Show the importance of symbols to human thought.

15. Defend or criticize this proposition: Learning consists of acquiring symbols.

16. What two types of communication exist in the modern world? Give examples of symbolic devices used in each.

17. Compare the possibilities for contact and communication of peoples with and without written symbols.

18. Show how the use of symbols in indirect communication economizes human effort.

19. Comment on the possible future effects of world-wide communication.

SOURCEBOOK READINGS

GITTLER, JOSEPH B. *Social Dynamics.* New York: McGraw-Hill Book Co., Inc., 1952.
1. DAVIS, KINGSLEY, "The Case of Anna" (extreme isolation of a child), pp. 22–28.
2. GITTLER, JOSEPH, with quotations from Kenneth McGill and George H. Mead, "Symbiosis in Role Taking and Defining the Situation," pp. 7–11.
3. KELLER, HELEN, "My First Word," pp. 5–7.
4. MAXFIELD, FRANCIS N., "The Case of Isabelle" (another case of extreme isolation of a child and the effect on language and personality development), pp. 28–29.

KOENIG, SAMUEL, REX D. HOPPER, and FELIKS GROSS. *Sociology: A Book of Readings.* Englewood Cliffs, N.J.: Prentice-Hall, Inc., 1956.
5. DAVIS, KINGSLEY, "When Culture Is Lacking," pp. 75–81.
6. SINGH, J. A. L., " 'Socialization' in a Non-Human Environment," pp. 82–85.
7. HERZOG, GEORGE, "Words as Social Tools," pp. 420–22.
8. PIERIS, RALPH, "Speech and Society," pp. 422–28.
9. RILEY, FRANK, and JAMES A. PETERSON, "The Social Impact of Television," pp. 429–35.
10. WIRTH, LOUIS, "Consensus and Mass Communication," pp. 436–44.

O'BRIEN, ROBERT W., CLARENCE C. SCHRAG, and WALTER T. MARTIN. *Readings in General Sociology* (2d ed.). Boston: Houghton Mifflin Co., 1957.
11. DAVIS, KINGSLEY, "Final Note on a Case of Extreme Isolation," pp. 189–92.
12. HERZOG, HERTA, "The Daytime Serial Listener," pp. 268–72.
13. RILEY, FRANK, and JAMES A. PETERSON, "The Social Impact of Television," pp. 278–81.

SCHULER, EDGAR A., DUANE L. GIBSON, MAUDE L. FIERO, and WILBUR B. BROOKOVER. *Outside Readings in Sociology.* New York: The Thomas Crowell Co., 1956.
14. LEIGH, ROBERT D., "The Business of Communication," pp. 683–93.
15. Commission on Freedom of the Press, "Freedom of the Press," pp. 694–703.

WILSON, LOGAN, and WILLIAM L. KOLB. *Sociological Analysis.* New York: Harcourt, Brace & Co., Inc., 1949.
16. DAVIS, KINGSLEY, "Final Note on a Case of Extreme Isolation," pp. 173–79.

SELECTED READINGS

CARROLL, JOHN B. *The Study of Language*. Cambridge: Harvard University Press, 1953.

CHASE, STUART. "How Language Shapes Our Thoughts," *Harper's*, April, 1954, pp. 76–82.

——. *The Tyranny of Words*. New York: Harcourt, Brace & Co., Inc., 1938.

COOLEY, CHARLES H. *Human Nature and the Social Order*. New York: Charles Scribner's Sons, 1902.

FARIS, ROBERT E. L. *Social Psychology*. New York: The Ronald Press Co., 1952.

HAYAKAWA, S. I. *Language in Thought and Action*. New York: Harcourt, Brace & Co., Inc., 1949.

HOMANS, GEORGE C. *The Human Group*. New York: Harcourt, Brace & Co., Inc., 1950.

HARDING, D. W. *Social Psychology and Individual Values*. London: Hutchinson & Co., Ltd., 1953.

NEWCOMB, THEODORE M. *Social Psychology*. New York: The Dryden Press, 1950.

OGDEN, C. K., and I. A. RICHARDS. *The Meaning of Meaning*. New York: Harcourt, Brace & Co., Inc., 1938.

SAPIR, EDWARD. *Language*. New York: Harcourt, Brace & Co., Inc., 1921.

Chapter 10

Primary and Secondary Groups

CLASSIFICATION OF GROUPS

The most universally accepted group classification developed by sociologists is that which divides all groups into primary groups and secondary groups. The term *primary group* covers the most intimate groups in which man has experience. Sometimes these groups are so meaningful that one has to say: "The group is all; the person scarcely exists." *Secondary groups,* by contrast, are those which involve only segments of one's personality. In them, one can be an individualist.

Primary Groups. Sociologist Charles H. Cooley defined the primary group and showed its effects on the formation of the personality. By his definition, the primary group is one marked by three characteristics: (1) *intimacy;* (2) *face-to-face association;* (3) *permanence.* Here is his description of primary groups.

"By primary groups I mean those characterized by intimate face-to-face association and cooperation. They are primary in several senses, but chiefly in that they are fundamental in forming the social nature and ideals of the individual. The result of intimate association, psychologically, is a certain fusion of individualities in a common whole, so that one's very self, for many purposes at least, is the common life and purpose of the group. Perhaps the simplest way of describing this wholeness is by saying that it is a "we"; it involves the sort of sympathy and mutual identification for which "we" is the natural expression. One lives in the feeling of the whole and finds the chief aims of his will in that feeling.

161

"It is not to be supposed that the unity of the primary group is one of mere harmony and love. It is always a differentiated and usually a competitive unity, admitting of self-assertion and various appropriative passions; but these passions are socialized by sympathy, and come, or tend to come, under the discipline of a common spirit. The individual will be ambitious, but the chief object of his ambition will be some desired place in the thought of the others, and he will feel allegiance to common standards of service and fair play. So the boy will dispute with his fellows a place on the team, but above such disputes will place the common glory of his class and school.

"The most important spheres of this intimate association and co-operation—though by no means the only ones—are the family, the play-group of children, and the neighborhood or community group of elders. These are practically universal, belonging to all times and all stages of development, and are accordingly a chief basis of what is universal in human nature and human ideals. . . ."[1]

From primary groups the individual acquires basic attitudes toward the world around him, people, and social institutions. From these groups attitudes of tolerance, kindness, love, and generosity are derived, probably more by imitation and absorption of group attitude than by direct teaching, although direct teaching often takes place. Mutual concern and affection are characteristic. Love and consideration for the other person is placed above competition and self-advantage. Mutual help in time of trouble is freely given. Group members gossip about each other, showing an interest in and concern for the absent member. If jealousies or hatred should develop, they are intense and bitter, for betrayal is unforgivable.

Cooley called the primary group the *incubator of human nature,* because he felt that in it were developed those finer traits of human nature which grow from association with warm-hearted interested persons who are more concerned about the child in his earlier years than he can be about them. The helpless infant and dependent child desperately needs such a group; man as an adult needs it much less but is never fully happy without it, although in urban society, adults characteristically spend a great deal of time in groups that are not primary in character. In primary groups people take time to visit and exchange pleasantries. They need not "put on a front" or pretend to be something other than they are. Everyone knows them as they actually are and accepts or rejects them on this basis. In other groups, one may talk about letting his hair down and speaking frankly. In primary groups one's hair is always down.

[1] Charles H. Cooley, *Social Organization* (New York: Charles Scribner's Sons, 1929), pp. 23–24.

Informality characterizes life in primary group settings. (Hutchison Photo Service)

Secondary Groups. Secondary groups represent that "cold world" into which parents in the rural community have always thought of their young people going when they leave home. Secondary groups are those that are relatively casual and impersonal in their relationships. Because secondary groups make only specialized demands on the person, they receive only a segment of his loyalty and usually require little of his time and attention. Relationships in them are usually competitive rather than mutually helpful. Members of secondary groups lack deep underlying loyalties for each other.

Primary and Secondary Groups as Extreme Types.[2] In the use of conceptual symbols, the sociologist must often describe ideal types, which are in reality extremes. In this he is not unique; much communication is so. For example, take the terms "tall" and "short." These are the extreme ranges of height with many intervals in between. So it is in the sociologist's use of primary and secondary.

[2] The German terms *Gemeinschaft* and *Gesellschaft* may well be introduced here if the instructor wishes to go further in contrasting the folk type of society with the "mass" urban–industrial society. The author has felt it best not to complicate the text treatment with these terms.

All groups arranged in order from primary to secondary would look something like that which appears below. At the extreme of the primary groups is the family, which is essential to the rearing of the child and to the shaping of his personality in the days of helpless infancy and dependent childhood. At the opposite extreme is the public, that ill-defined social group which may be the readers of a certain daily paper, viewers of a certain television program, or the population of a nation. The groups shown are only illustrative. Each individual can fit his own groups on the scale.

Family ← Play group ← Neighborhood group ← Sorority ⟷
PRIMARY GROUPS

Community → Civic club → Boy Scout jamboree → Nation
SECONDARY GROUPS

There may be some debate as to where the dividing line between primary and secondary groups ought to be placed. A division in many cases would have to be arbitrary. Actually, of the dozens of additional examples of groups one might add, most would fall somewhat toward the middle. There can, however, be no debate concerning the position of the family. It is recognized as the most important primary group by all sociologists. It is relatively permanent. It is face to face in its relationships and it is by all odds the most intimate social group man knows. Its kinship bonds are supplemented by daily association which assures, in normal cases, a lifelong contact between members, even though long periods of separation may come as children grow older and move away from home. It is the one group in which all human beings expect to spend all or most of their lifetime; the parental family gradually merges into one's own family as he marries, leaves home, and has children. Even after this he still keeps his attachments to the parental family until the death of parents, brothers, and sisters.

Most people would agree that the next most important primary group is the childhood play group. This is especially true for those who live in the same neighborhood over a period of time. In stable communities, likewise, the neighborhood and its various institutions, the neighborhood church and the neighborhood school groups, are primary groups. In metropolitan centers the neighborhood has lost much of its meaning; in fact, for many city dwellers it does not exist at all. The neighbors are more like transients for whom one feels few or no loyalties at all.

Of a primary group character also are college comradeships and fraternity and sorority groups. The army buddy relationship is also a close primary one.

Beyond the neighborhood there are the community groups in the larger geographical area where people carry out certain functions together: fire protection, a consolidated school program, or other joint functions. The community is well over toward the middle of the scale of primary and secondary groups. Somewhere in the middle of the scale the average civic club falls. At the far extreme of secondary groups are the reading public, theater audiences, etc. They are groups in which contacts are casual, superficial, impersonal, and for the most part indirect.

THE SECONDARY GROUP TREND OF MODERN LIFE

Rural civilizations provide an environment in which most social experience is in primary groups. As urban industrial society has grown, and with it the anonymity of large groups, secondary group experience has come to play an increasing part in adult life. The cost of this transition to the individual and to society is great. The following quotation is an appraisal of this trend of history.

". . . A high authority has called Chicago 'an aggregation of separate self-centered units with no common purpose.' 'Chicago,' it has been said, 'doesn't know why it exists; it has no soul.' To quite an extent this is true of all American cities and of all of American society.

"If we had been members of a small New England community 150 years ago we would have been living in a community where religion, neighborliness, and public-mindedness had a working alliance. In this community the farmer, the lawyer, the doctor, merchant, baker, banker, and candlestick-maker would have been carrying on various useful functions in simple, neighborly ways. The farmer refrained from selling too many bad eggs because he expected to see in church the next Sunday the person who bought the eggs. The shoemaker was held back from making a bad pair of shoes because he expected to see on the street the person who was wearing those shoes. Public and social control grew rather naturally out of relationships of this kind. The social imagination by which a man puts himself in the other man's place was easily evoked by the face-to-face contacts of such a community.

"But something happened in American life. The miller left this simple New England community; you will find him in the milling district of Minneapolis. The butcher can now be found running a packing plant in Chicago. The wagonmaker will be found in South Bend, Indiana. The banker is on Wall Street, and the seamstress is in a garment workers' factory. The farmer who left this community and went south became a cotton farmer; if he went to California he became a fruit farmer; and if he went to Iowa he became a corn and hog farmer. Now all these people are engaged in rendering a service to people whom they never expect to see. All the old neighborly control and social imagination which came out of neighborliness has now gone. Men are interested in the success of their business, judged solely on the basis of whether it could show a profit or a loss at the end of the year. A new standard of success has the right of way. The best business was that which made the most money. . . ."[3]

Loss of Primary Group Membership. Homans, studying the historical factors affecting group life, points out how the development of civilization has meant (1) technological change, (2) economic expansion, and (3) warfare, all of which have the effect of breaking up old group units without putting effective forms of social organization in their place.[4] He points to the growth of great cities of the Roman Empire, particularly in the Near East, where peoples uprooted were thrown together without an integrated group life. Here traders, artisans, and slaves from Egypt, Canaan, Gaul, and Spain were gathered without a common tradition.

Comparable today are the great secondary group aggregates of Detroit and Los Angeles.

Moving from these ecological facts to their implications, Homans points out that man is sustained by his experience in integrated groups, where the shocks of life may be in part absorbed by others who care about the individual involved. This is the kind of world that is secure for adults and essential for children. Lacking this primary group security, the person is subject to great stress, and tends to develop disorders of thought, feeling, and behavior.

Because such feelings and behavior are transmitted to children, primary group deprivation in one generation tends to lower the capacity of children to adjust, thus affecting the next generation. "The civilization," Homans says, "that, by its very process of growth shatters small group life, will leave men and women lonely and unhappy."

If new groups of an intimate character can replace the old ones, a cure results, but in a rapidly expanding socio-economic order such replacements come too slowly, and many continue to lack a feeling of belonging.

[3] Arthur E. Holt, "Our Common Perversion," *The Christian Century*, June 26, 1935, p. 850.
[4] George C. Homans, *The Human Group* (New York: Harcourt, Brace & Co., Inc., 1950), pp. 454–68.

The "Publics." Chicago sociologist Louis Wirth stressed another aspect of the growth of secondary group life in our time of mass communication: the "mass" audience (defined in this book as publics).

He described these publics as (1) involving great numbers; (2) consisting of aggregates of men widely dispersed over the face of the earth; (3) having heterogeneous membership, in that it includes people living under widely different conditions, under widely varying cultures, coming from diverse strata of society, engaging in different occupations, hence having different interests, standards of life, degrees of prestige, power, and influence; (4) an aggregate of anonymous individuals who may be and usually are aware of being part of a mass and wonder who the other members are; (5) not involving organized groups; (6) not having common customs or traditions, no institutions, and no rules governing the actions of individuals; and (7) consisting of unattached individuals.[5]

SOCIAL EXPERIENCE IN SECONDARY GROUPS

Secondary groups are for the most part, as has been seen, competitive in nature. Each man is for himself. The protective attitudes which are so prominent in the primary group, the deep concern over weaker members, are absent. In the secondary group, rather than standing on the reputation of friends or relatives, as often occurs in the primary group, a person stands on his own merit. What he does determines his group status.

This is in direct contrast with the primary group, in which the son of respected Mr. Brown gets by with all kinds of pranks—for example, in the small community school. There, one is accepted because of parental reputation as well as for personal character and reputation, for his past follows him. Superficial impressions of the moment are of little value in giving one status. Pretenses are useless. The older members of a primary group have seen him grow up; some of them have even seen his parents grow up. There is a long continuity of experience.

In the secondary group, "front" is an asset. In every contact one may gain an advantage by boldly putting his best foot forward. Dress, manners, connections, publicity, memberships, and badges—all are factors by which status may be gained in the casual contacts of secondary groups. One's past reputation has little place, for no one knows that past. In the secondary group a man may turn over a new leaf, if he chooses, and only he himself will be the wiser. He may also "sow wild oats" without anyone being seriously concerned.

[5] Louis Wirth, "Consensus and Mass Communication," *American Journal of Sociology,* 13:1–15 (Feb. 1949).

The competitive secondary group fails to offer the protection to the *social self* that the usual primary group offers. On the other hand, many people find their greatest opportunity in the secondary group.

First, many young people find their first challenge there. In the primary group, they live in the shadow of a highly respected father or mother and can scarcely expect to rival their parents' reputations.

Widening Group Contacts

First contacts are with those in the intimate, face-to-face primary group, but with increased age and experience come contacts with remote secondary groups.

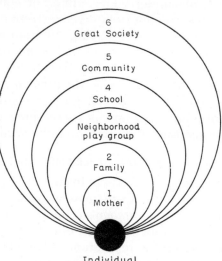

6
Great Society

5
Community

4
School

3
Neighborhood
play group

2
Family

1
Mother

Individual

The secondary group gives them their first chance to be on their own and to make a name for themselves by virtue of their own achievement. A kindly primary group by its very protectiveness may shelter a young person too long. Not until he gets into the secondary group does he have a chance to try his mettle and prove to himself that he can meet the tests of life rather than have others meet them for him.

Second, many young people who grow up in primary groups of underprivileged communities find their first real opportunity in more specialized secondary groups where there is room for the exercise of special talent and where reputation of their underprivileged community does not follow them to threaten their social acceptance.

Third, other young people from families that were of low reputation in their neighborhood group because of family conflict, poverty, drunkenness, or other reasons, find their first real opportunity when they transfer to secondary groups and shed the parental reputation which they would always have inherited through neighborhood gossip had they stayed in the primary group.

Fourth, primary groups are the most effective units of social control, but for many they are too effective. Their definitions of good and bad are often so narrow and restrictive that a young person does not have a chance to develop his worthwhile potentialities. Within the broader moral concepts of secondary groups he often finds opportunity to exercise his special talent and has the moral freedom to do it. Many a young poet, author, or actor, whose rural community condemned his activities as a waste of time or as sinful, would never have achieved success had he remained in the local community and accepted the primary group's definition of the relative importance of, for example, farming and writing. Take the case of the youth who grew up under the dominating influence of a mother whose moral codes were too restrictive compared with outside codes. His freedom could be realized only by leaving the primary group. He writes:

The philosophy of my mother is uniquely her own. Her definition of social strata is her own. It recognizes the highest stratum as those who are "good"— not necessarily clever, powerful, intelligent, wealthy, but "good." This, of course, carries its own concept of "good." There are more negatives than positives to this concept. Having had her share of drunkards in her own family, liquor is the great evil and to drink destroys all "good" in a person. If a person is too vivacious, that person becomes overbearing and is no longer "good." Smoking undermines the health, and consequently lowers the social stature of whoever dares to do so. A person must fulfill all of his potentialities in all fields or is open to censure. A person who is not attentive or observant and fails to tip his hat or nod and speak is liable to find that he has become snobbish and is no longer "good." Nice people don't read any of the recent novels of the type dealing with "oversexed" females, and the existence of a known wanton is not recognized by "good" people—she is considered dead and in Hell.

It is difficult to express this entire philosophy on paper, but it is general enough that these somewhat exaggerated examples should suffice. It is strongly individualistic and unswerving, and judges all else accordingly, avoiding that which disagrees and slowly withdrawing into its own shell. It was this restrictive set of social controls I shed when I left home to enter secondary groups.

Fifth, primary groups stifle individualism. They believe in life going on in its uninterrupted way. As the above quotation suggests, primary groups in their very cohesiveness make life dull for the intelligent man and the innovator.

THE QUEST OF SECONDARY GROUPS FOR PRIMARY GROUP EXPERIENCE

In many secondary groups today there seems to be an attempt to add primary group qualities. The large urban church cannot restore the after-church handshaking gossip sessions that characterize country churches, but it does try to break its congregation down into informal groups like women's societies and young people's groups, and to have dinners and other social evenings. Chambers of Commerce,

Kiwanis, and other civic groups, through team sports activities, pic-
nics, dances, calling each other by their first names, and other such
devices, try to create a primary group atmosphere, artificial though
it may seem at times. The large school system develops clubs, fraternities, and sororities.

Even though the metropolitan newspaper cannot hope to get in
a gossipy little line about everyone in the community once a year, as
does the small town weekly, it publishes lurid accounts of the private
life of actors and actresses, criminals, and famous divorcees so that
its readers will get a close-up intimate view of the primary group life
of these well-known personalities. And the most popular metropolitan comic strips are those which present the never-ending day-after-
day intricacies of life in the primary group, as in Gasoline Alley, with
its commonplace pictures of family and neighborhood life.

The popular radio and television programs also picture these commonplace primary group situations that are a part of all human life—
for example, Gildersleeve and his family and neighborhood in the
small town community with its friendships and its gossip, Lum and
Abner with the crossroads general store gossip, and "I Love Lucy"
with its homely events. One of the most popular novels, plays, and
movies of all time is *Life with Father*.

Primary group experience is the most vital experience of all humanity, as timeless as folk music. Men in the secondary group crave it.

PROBLEMS OF TRANSITION FROM PRIMARY TO SECONDARY GROUP

Lack of Preparedness. In rural societies such as those which have
prevailed throughout most of human history, the average individual
has spent his lifetime in the same primary group. Grandparents, parents, children—all were a part of the great family system; and relatives often made up a substantial part of the neighborhood. Before
one's parents had died, he himself had children growing up around
him, providing a continuous primary group situation within the
family. In most of the contemporary primitive societies of the world,
such as in China, India, and to a lesser extent the isolated districts of
Europe, the entire life cycle of the individual is spent submerged in
primary groups. There is little if any contact with secondary groups
such as now exists in those parts of the world where rapid means of
transportation and communication bring the individual into contact
with persons and places far distant from his original primary group.

In a culture where travel is by foot or by mule and horse, humanity
is relatively immobile. In such a society the personality of the individual is built from the beginning to fit the group of which he will
always be a part. The definitions the individual has been given for

moral situations are adequate for a lifetime. Moral choices are few, for the elders have already defined the situation. The individual is assured a lifelong security in the bosom of his family. He can expect that his children and his grandchildren after him will care for him, even though he may live to be a hundred. In some societies he may even expect that they will respect his opinions after he is gone, perhaps even worship his memory.

In industrial society, secondary groups have encroached on the field once occupied by primary groups, so that the individual today spends an increasing proportion of his time in them. In the city especially, secondary groups have developed to the fullest extent and the daily experience of the individual is in secondary group situations. The work relationships of most people are of a secondary group character—as are their recreation, their travel, their political contacts. Even the education group contacts of a young person today in a large city are likely to be secondary in character, although small primary groups often form within the larger secondary group situations.

Transitional Shock. The transition from primary group to secondary group today is a near universal experience in more advanced societies, and for most young people it comes more or less abruptly and with a certain degree of shock, the extent of the shock depending a great deal on where one grows up. It is one of the major tests of personality adjustment experienced by the average youth today at some time between the ages of sixteen and twenty-five. It is a much more severe test for those who grow up in an isolated world, especially those in mountain sections, where transportation is still more or less primitive, where relatives are numerous in the immediate neighborhood, and where contacts with secondary groups are practically nonexistent until the young person moves out of the mountains to go to work or to school. It is a more severe transition for young farm people who have had strong neighborhood ties and who have gone to one-room schools than for those who have gone to consolidated schools and for town and city young people. It is probably also more severe for the average small-town youth than for the city youth who cannot avoid having had a great deal of contact with secondary groups as a part of his normal experience during childhood.

Take the case of the following college youth who describes his experience as he shifted from the one-room school where he took his first eight grades to a consolidated high school:

My grade school had twenty pupils, distributed throughout all the eight grades. We were all under one teacher and recited in the same room. I had no difficulty in grade school. Most of the children I had known all my life. The big day came when I was to start to high school in town. I shall never forget the first day I took the school bus for the consolidated school or my first day there. I was mystified by the big school rooms and large number of students. I hardly knew how to act and could hardly speak to any of my fellow students. An inferiority complex began at that time which I have never fully gotten over.

ADJUSTMENTS DURING THE TRANSITION PERIOD

The transfer from primary to secondary group has usually been referred to by the older generation as "going out into the cold world." It has been looked upon as a time of danger. Parents have feared it, thinking that their youngsters, who have always been protected, will be subject to the exploitation of the ruthless, that their moral fiber will be tested, that there will be no kindly person at hand to steer them back to the right course if they start out in the wrong direction.

Farm parents have traditionally feared this transition from primary to secondary group, because it has been notable as a time of "sowing wild oats." The primary group is a group of rigorous social control. The all-seeing eye of parents and neighbors is ever-present. The standards which they hold are rigid and demanding. The young person understands them and knows what is expected of him. He knows the penalty that will be paid in terms of gossip and censure from the group if he fails to live up to the standard that his community demands of him.

In the urban society into which he moves, he finds himself suddenly removed from all these common primary group controls. The secondary group world, with its anonymity, seems to be a world without social restraints. Unless he has a strong character, he will find himself throwing off old restraints and trying out a number of new things which he has desired but never dared to try in the primary group. In some cases this may bring him into trouble with the law; in some cases it may be the first step in overthrowing moral standards which the primary group established for him. In all cases, it is a time of experiencing new liberties and trying out new situations, many of which were condemned in the primary group society. Even college students who were well behaved at home have been known to become a problem for the discipline committee as they tasted the freedom of the college campus.

This is a normal and natural transition, and one which, if it does not lead to definite moral or legal delinquency, is a desirable one. Many primary groups are too restrictive in their behavior patterns and demand much more in the way of obedience and submission, much more in the way of restricted behavior, than is necessary or even desirable from the standpoint of the youth's personality growth. The young person must acquire a broader concept of what makes up effective social living—of what makes up proper living, in fact—if he is to function effectively in the larger society he has entered. The transition from primary to secondary group is often a time when the young person increases his tolerance for different groups and different social classes. This is certainly to his benefit.

But for all the advantages to be gained, the transition period is often a time of homesickness. This is especially true during the few months when the young person is casting around in the secondary group to find some small social group or some particular pal or comrade with whom to restore to himself a part of the primary group attachments he has lost.

In the Armed Forces. During the war millions of young men were suddenly uprooted from their primary group and thrown in with large groups of strangers, most of whom had similarly been torn from primary group connections. The natural adjustment was to find a pal or a buddy or a girl friend who could become an intimate, to whom one could confide all of his secrets and tell all of his troubles. Many a G.I. married after an acquaintance of a week or two a girl he met in this period of transition.

On the College Campus. To a less extreme degree, the college student who leaves a small school or community and arrives on the campus of a large university feels lonesome, homesick, alone. If he succeeds in making the adjustment, he soon finds on the college campus or in the college community church a small group that possesses primary group characteristics, or finds in some other young person —a pal or buddy, or a friend of the opposite sex—one who comes to stand for a great deal of what he has lost in moving out of the primary group.

College students in their autobiographies often comment on the shock or adjustment problems they experienced in shifting to a secondary group. A young man from a rural family speaks of the mature attitudes he was forced to develop as he entered the secondary group of a college campus. He writes:

> For the first time in my life, I am away from the influence of my parents and my brother, Louis. I have found that I have to sink or swim, and it is up to me which it shall be. My parents have always showed their appreciation for any work I did, but since I have been "on my own" I have learned that I must do things even if they do not seem to be appreciated.

A girl comments:

When I finally arrived at college, I was rather bewildered. So many situations had to be met by me alone; neither my mother or father could suggest a solution for every little situation. So many things were involved.

This change presented the most severe shock I had yet encountered. For one thing, I was away from home for the first time and had to make my own decisions, something that I had depended too much on others to do for me. Second, the people that I met were very different, and I found it difficult to become acquainted with them. In the small town where I had grown up, nearly all the people had the same habits, ideas, and manners. This was because they have been raised in the same environment. Most important of all, I found the competition even greater than I had anticipated. I had been at the head of the class at home and a leader. I did not expect to become prominent on the campus for I realized that all I had been in my small school meant nothing here. However, I had expected the studying to come nearly as easy as it had before. I soon found that I had never really studied at all. The competition began getting me down and I became discouraged.

Some good high school athletes experience a sudden deflation of the ego when they enter the secondary group climate of a college campus. One honest young man expresses it succinctly:

I came up here with the idea that I was rather a big shot and was soon awakened by the fact that I simply was one cog among 7,000.

A young man still in the bitter struggle of adjustments writes:

I find the secondary group hard to break into and many times get disgusted. I feel like giving up, but I imagine what my family would say of me if I quit, so I stay with it. I haven't time for boxing, my favorite sport. Being a pledge in a fraternity has tended to revive my inferiority complex. I feel I am looked down on by the upperclassmen and not treated their equal. But I have made a vow to see it through.

A girl who fought it through writes:

College proved to be my first real secondary group relationship. I found everything highly competitive and extremely impersonal. There were few intimate, permanent, face-to-face relationships. I did not know my teachers. There were seldom more than one or two of my friends in my classes. I felt lost and alone in a sea of unfamiliarity. Besides, I wasn't just sure of my major, and felt as if I were drifting in no particular direction. I was ready to quit before I really got started, but my own stubborn nature made me stick. Now I am glad, for I have become used to this unfamiliarity.

On Entering the Business World. Most college students could tell of some problems of secondary group initiation that they experienced on entering college, but when a young person moves into a large community to accept his first job he experiences a similar adjustment. Those who fail to make new primary group ties are likely to be miserable, despondent, even in some cases possible suicides. The following represents a normal adjustment situation of a rural girl moving to a city to work.

I was plunged into urban living with practically no idea of what cities were like. The city was so entirely different from the country. The social interaction was more rapid and the urban ways were new and different. The patterns of behavior in the city of Spokane differed considerably from that of my home town. I suffered cultural shock and found it hard to adjust myself. I soon found that urban people are extremely different from those in rural areas. They had broader ideas and more of them. They seemed so sure of themselves. The thing I needed most to help me in this situation was what I had nothing of: self-confidence. Social processes of the metropolitan community are much more complicated. In the city there is a wide range of new habits, attitudes and ideas. I was confused.

Never in history have young people so universally been required to make the difficult transition from primary to secondary groups as today. To get an education, to get a job, to serve one's country requires that youth tear up their roots from the familiar social soil of childhood and become a part of the great society of competitive secondary groups. Fortunately, childhood experience, particularly in city and in rural consolidated schools, helps prepare them for it.

IN-GROUP VERSUS OUT-GROUP

The terms "in-group" and "out-group" were used by William Graham Sumner, the great American sociologist who developed the concepts of folkways and mores, as a means for classifying social groups where inner loyalty was maintained by hostility or opposition to outside groups. The *in-group*, sometimes called the *we-group*, is a closely knit unit which feels itself opposed to all outside groups, for example, Jew against gentile. Throughout history the Jews have maintained a strong in-group attitude, having been suspicious of the gentile out-group. In Old Testament times gentiles were considered vastly inferior. A similar in-group, out-group attitude prevails among Mormons. The Greek-barbarian clash of history represents the same in-group, out-group division of society.

In the same way, many small sectarian religious groups have a strong in-group consciousness, considering all outsiders worldly sinners. In the case of some religious orders, the in-group is identified by peculiar dress which testifies to all the world of their adherence. In some cases, long hair or beards distinguish the righteous in-group from the worldly. Any such device tends to make for in-group solidarity, making in-group members at all times sensitive to the difference between them and the rest of the world.

Many tribes and great family clans throughout history have maintained the in-group, out-group consciousness. "We are the people" or "we are the chosen people," "the rest of the world are stammerers and babblers," has been the prevailing attitude among many local groups which consider themselves uniquely apart from the rest of the society.

In-group loyalties are most characteristic of those who are isolated. Isolation makes for inner loyalty and suspicions of those on the outside. Part of the reason is that there is little change among isolated peoples. They tend to become fixed in the ways of their ancestors, passing them on to their children. Thus personality becomes molded specifically and permanently by the peculiar patterns of life that have developed in the isolated in-group. Other people are not only strangers but subjects of suspicion because they are different. Their ways of life are strange, therefore probably wrong.

On the college campus of today, the social fraternities and the independents represent in a milder way the in-group, out-group conflict. The fraternity members feel that they belong to a unique and distinctive group set apart, by virtue of selection and ritualistic initiation, from the common mass. Each particular Greek house also possesses something of this in-group consciousness. By the use of pins or other identification marks, they testify to the world that they have been initiated into that small inner circle of intimacy from which all others are excluded.

In shifting to new groups, young people often encounter small closely knit in-groups which it is difficult to enter. One writes of his high school experience:

> The first day of high school was the hardest day of school I ever had. I didn't know a single person, and to make matters worse I found that the students at this particular high school were not very friendly. They had an in-group attitude which was hard to break down and if it had not been for other students in a similar position as mine I'm sure the first semester of high school would have been impossible to endure.

In case of war, in-group solidarity is greatly increased as hostility toward the out-group takes possession of a people. Intense patriotism, loyalty, and sacrifice characterize the in-group. The out-group, by contrast, is thought of as possessing beastly qualities.

It is clear that the concepts of in-group and out-group have some meaning even today in cases where a sense of inner loyalty and outer opposition is great.

RENEWED INTEREST IN THE PRIMARY GROUP

Sociologists of recent years have become increasingly aware that, even with the great cities and indirect means of communication to great anonymous publics, many of the intimate ties of folk society remain in various sectors of experience of the urban industrial man. This has led to what LaPiere has described as the "rediscovery of the primary group."[6]

Research reveals that primary group relations are of great importance in the work relationships of big industry, and are one of the main factors in motivating production. During World War II, Stouffer and his colleagues found that a factor of great importance in the soldier's morale and willingness to fight was not ideological orientation, but rather the character and significance to him of his primary group relationship.[7] It was also found that men in the military service were motivated in conduct and in productivity by the primary group influence. This was as true of the German Army as of the American.[8]

The primary group is also becoming an increasingly employed instrument in therapy, as is shown by examples of the following section.

THE PRIMARY GROUP IN THERAPY

Alcoholics Anonymous is the most widely known of the groups which employ the intimacy, helpfulness, and neighborliness of the primary group in rehabilitation. Members gather and testify to their past experience as victims of alcoholism. They pledge to support each other in their weakness, to be on call day or night to help a brother in temptation. They are anonymous only in the sense that the outside world cannot identify them. Within the group there is intimacy, frank exchange of confidences, confession of weakness and failure, and genuine brotherhood.

Through this kind of primary group fraternity, strangers are able to identify themselves with others who have like struggles. Together they gain strength against temptation and many are able to reconstruct their lives.

In the field of children's emotional problems Samuel R. Slavson

[6] Richard T. LaPiere, *A Theory of Social Control* (New York: McGraw-Hill Book Co., Inc., 1954), pp. 23 ff. See also Edward A. Shils, "The Study of the Primary Group," in Daniel Lerner and Harold D. Lasswell (eds.), *The Policy Sciences* (Stanford, Calif.: Stanford University Press, 1951), pp. 44–69.

[7] Samuel A. Stouffer, *et al.*, *Studies in Social Psychology in World War II* (Princeton: Princeton University Press, 1949). 2 vols.

[8] See Edward A. Shils and Morris Janowitz, "Cohesion and Disintegration in the Wehrmacht in World War II," *Public Opinion Quarterly*, Summer, 1948, pp. 280–315.

has probably gone the farthest in employing the primary group in therapy.[9] He proceeds to rehabilitate the emotionally disturbed child by re-educating him in a primary group setting in real-life situations. The child is placed in a group which is analogous to the family: the adult therapist is a parent-substitute and the group members are sibling (brother, sister) substitutes. After the child has learned to perceive the primary group as pleasing and constructive rather than displeasing and destructive, he is gradually led to associate with other groups.

One of the important advantages of the group situation over individual therapy is that the child has to learn to relate himself to the group as well as to the individual therapist. Since the child must have a willingness and desire to be accepted by various groups and to take on their values, this type of a learning situation is all-important to him.

The group atmosphere is permissive. The therapy group is calculated to provide the individual with several activity outlets (physical, emotional, intellectual, social, and aesthetic) and not purely physical activity. It is believed that if activity of all types can be carried on in an attractive primary group setting, a therapeutic adjustment will result.

PRIMARY GROUP EXPERIENCE IN MODERN INDUSTRY

Sociologists studying the psychological world of modern industry have discovered that life within the factory has its informal face-to-face relationships.[10] Social interaction takes the form of pressure of the union local on its members, of face-to-face contact between workers and between foreman and workman, but most of all the informal personal relations within the small work group.

Research in the Bank Wiring Room of the Western Electric Company's Hawthorne Works in Chicago showed workers had, among other things, established rather rigid controls over production.[11] The man who under- or over-produced was punished, often severely, by group opinion and ridicule and even by being hit on the arm. The

[9] Slavson has written several books on group therapy, but presents his *activity* group therapy most completely in *An Introduction to Group Therapy* (New York: The Commonwealth Fund, 1943). See also William U. Snyder, "The Present Status of Psychotherapeutic Counseling," *Psych. Bulletin*, 44:297–386 (1947), for a discussion of Slavson's therapy relative to other group and individual therapy techniques.

[10] E. Mayo, *Human Problems of Industrial Civilization* (New York: The Macmillan Co., 1933); T. N. Whitehead, *The Industrial Worker* (Cambridge: Harvard University Press, 1938); F. J. Roethlisberger and W. J. Dickson, *Management and the Worker* (Cambridge: Harvard University Press, 1939).

[11] Roethlisberger and Dickson, *op. cit.*

group set up a "straight-line" production curve for each worker in spite of the wage incentive scheme. Even though an individual might have desired to produce more, the group tended to hold him to its conception of what represented a fair day's work for a fair day's pay.

This research showed that even inspectors and supervisors were under considerable compulsion to follow the norms of this group. They felt obliged to overlook many work irregularities in the interest of maintaining good relations with workers under them.

Neither manual dexterity nor intelligence increased average hourly output among these workers because of these primary group restraints on output.

Primary group motivations in industry are important to change. When new methods are instituted, production often drops sharply because of worker resistance. However, workers who, as a group, have participated in carrying out a given change make much progress in learning the new methods, and they produce at a higher rate than those who are subjected to changes instituted from above or those who are allowed to participate only partially.[12] In many other aspects of change in social life (work production, alcoholism, criminality, food habits, and leadership), group standards have been found to be all-important. Although it might be expected that an individual would be more susceptible to change when he is without group support than when he is a member of a group, the evidence indicates that it is easier to change individuals who have been formed into a group than it is to change any one of them separately. So long as group norms remain unchanged, the individual remains unchanged; but if group norms are changed, he changes.[13]

In the interaction of the executive with his subexecutives, the friendship and entertainment interaction of the hierarchy are often much more important in determining the outcome of a person's promotion and the success of his work venture than the more formally structured relationships within the business organization.[14]

Research conducted during World War II showed that soldiers developed norms of conduct within small intimate groups, and that these norms were the principal factors in affecting their morale, loyalty, and willingness to fight.[15]

---

[12] L. Coch and J. R. P. French, Jr., "Overcoming Resistance to Change," *Human Relations*, 1:512–32 (1948).

[13] Kurt Lewin, "Studies in Group Decision," in Dorwin Cartwright and Alvin Zander (eds.), *Group Dynamics* (Evanston, Ill.: Row, Peterson & Co., 1953), chap. 21.

[14] William H. Whyte, Jr., "The Wives of Management," *Fortune*, Oct. 1951, pp. 86 ff., and "Corporation and the Wife," *Fortune*, Nov., 1951, pp. 109 ff.

[15] Stouffer, *et al.*, *op. cit.*

PRIMARY GROUP EXPERIENCE IN METROPOLITAN SUBURBS[16]

The most striking change in metropolitan residential development has been the forty-year trend toward the suburbs, a trend which is gathering momentum each decade. The suburbs have brought a new informality and friendliness which is restoring some of the old social controls of primary group life. Here, as within industry, the new primary group is somewhat more segmental in that the individual can readily evade it for much of his recreational life, as he does also in his work life.

Nevertheless, in those areas where group cohesiveness has had a chance to form, the individual feels a sense of belongingness and obligation to his neighborhood group. Nonconformists, although they often desire acceptance by group members, tend to be rejected by them.[17] Thus, there is often a desire not only to develop a reputation and to be a good neighbor, but also a noticeable pressure to conform.

The new neighborhood life demands much less in the way of rigid conformity, and to a point even encourages innovation. Informality of dress (slacks, shorts, and pedal-pushers), speech, and contacts have created in it a freedom which is, in many respects, less compelling compared to the more rigid, tradition-dominated atmosphere of more conservative rural communities and small towns of the pre-automobile period.

In the new suburb, locality groups tend to form in much the same automatic way that they did in rural communities. In the old days a certain valley, a hill, school district, or church area became a neighborhood without any formal plan. Within recognized boundaries mutual interests and mutual aid prevailed. So also today in the suburb the neighborhood seems automatically to develop with a certain street as a boundary, or it may break where there is a person who seems not to fit in.

In the new neighborhood, as in the old, there is mutual interest in children. Children are in fact, the main factor in the newcomer's getting acquainted in the locality. Gossip here, as in the old community, is a powerful force, although perhaps a less powerful one because of the great diversity of interests that the suburban dweller has—with modern magazines, radio, television, and numerous social activities to occupy his attention. There is less need to find one's

16 The next six paragraphs are an adaptation of the author's *Social Control* (rev. ed.; Chicago: J. B. Lippincott Co., 1956). For a fuller treatment, see that volume.

17 L. Festinger, S. Schachter, and K. Back, "The Operation of Group Standards," in Cartwright and Zander (eds.), *Group Dynamics* (Evanston, Ill.: Row, Peterson & Co., 1953), chap. 16.

greatest social satisfaction in neighborhood gossip or in eavesdropping on a party line.

While it is true that these primary group relations, and the effectiveness of their controls, differ in many respects from the primary group relations of rural areas of an earlier day, they nonetheless have many semblances of genuine primary groups. There are person-to-person relationships which are more or less permanent. The degree of intimacy, however, is limited largely to a given sector of life. Rather than the individual being submerged in it in all life activities, he is submerged in it mostly in the segment of life that has to do with his home living. In the primary group of rural society of an earlier day, the influence of the primary group was often too all-intrusive.

SUMMARY

This chapter has presented what is the most significant group classification employed by the sociologist, the classification of groups as primary and secondary. The in-group, out-group classification, which is much less used but which nonetheless has considerable significance, has also been presented. The primary group is one characterized by intimacy, cooperation, permanence, and deep personal loyalties, as contrasted to the essentially competitive spirit of the secondary group. These are in reality two extreme types between which most groups fall. In-groups are characterized by deep internal loyalties which are inspired by the feeling of difference or hostility toward outside groups.

The primary group is the nursery of human nature. It shelters the weak, supports the developing social self, and shelters and protects its members from the cold competitive world of secondary groups. When the youth enters the secondary group, he is, for the first time, on his own. There he matches wits with competitors. There he stands or falls by virtue of his efforts. The transition from primary to secondary group is a common social experience in our mobile society. It is responsible for many of the adjustments which young people of the twentieth century must make in their struggle to attain adulthood.

Even in an age when secondary group life dominates adult experience, sociologists have been finding, as they study industry and the socially maladjusted, that primary group experience is still a part of adult life for many. Those who lack intimate touch with small groups are likely subjects for unendurable personal stress. It is also being found that restoration to a meaningful primary group is often the way back to normality. Primary group therapy is not only used with children, but also with adults in such notable organizations as Alcoholics Anonymous.

DISCUSSION AND REVIEW QUESTIONS

1. What dual classifications does the sociologist use in characterizing groups on the basis of intimacy?

2. Name the author of the concept "primary group" and indicate the three characteristics by which he identified primary groups.

3. Give examples of primary groups and indicate traits that they contribute to personality.

4. Characterize secondary groups and give examples.

5. Show how primary and secondary groups represent extreme types.

6. Give possible implications of the relative decline of neighborhood and small primary group life as it existed in agrarian societies.

7. Compare primary and secondary groups with regard to the protection they give to the social self.

8. Summarize evidence showing that secondary group experience is often an advantage to the young person.

9. Discuss the problems youth often experiences in making the transition from primary to secondary groups.

10. How is modern society unique in this respect?

11. Cite typical experiences of youth in making this transition in our society.

12. Explain the concepts "in-group" and "out-group."

13. Give examples of the way primary group influence is used in modern social therapy; in psychological therapy.

14. Discuss implications of research findings on primary group motivation in work situations. Do you see a new vocation opening here for sociologists?

15. Discuss the emergence of a new type of primary group association in the modern suburbs.

SOURCEBOOK READINGS

FREEDMAN, RONALD, AMOS H. HAWLEY, WERNER S. LANDECKER, GERHARD E. LENSKI, and HORACE M. MINER. *Principles of Sociology* (rev. ed.). New York: Henry Holt & Co., Inc., 1956.
    1. SHILS, EDWARD A., and MORRIS JANOWITZ, "Cohesion and Disintegration in the Wehrmacht in World War II," pp. 96–105.
    2. REDFIELD, ROBERT, "The Folk Society," pp. 262–71.

GITTLER, JOSEPH B. *Social Dynamics.* New York: McGraw-Hill Book Co., Inc., 1952.
    3. HOMANS, GEORGE C., "Western Electric Research in Productivity," pp. 59–74.
    4. MAULDIN, BILL, "Men in an Army Combat Team," pp. 82–83.
    5. SHAW, CLIFFORD, "Boys in a Street-Corner Gang," pp. 83–84.

O'BRIEN, ROBERT W., CLARENCE C. SCHRAG, and WALTER T. MARTIN. *Readings in General Sociology* (2d ed.). Boston: Houghton Mifflin Co., 1957.
    6. HAYNER, NORMAN S., and ELLIS ASH, "Socialization in a Prison Community," pp. 216–19.
    7. BLAU, PETER M., "Cooperation and Competition in Small Groups," pp. 299–305.
    8. SHILS, EDWARD A., "Primary Groups in the American Army," pp. 313–16.

SCHULER, EDGAR A., DUANE L. GIBSON, MAUDE L. FIERO, and WILBUR B. BROOKOVER. *Outside Readings in Sociology.* New York: The Thomas Crowell Co., 1956.
    9. STEINBECK, JOHN, "The Social 'World' of the Transients' Camp," pp. 170–74.
    10. COOLEY, CHARLES HORTON, "Primary Groups," pp. 174–79.

11. THOMAS, W. I., "The Primary Group and the Definition of the Situation," pp. 180–84.
12. HOMANS, GEORGE C., "Groups and Civilization," pp. 193–205.
13. HAYNER, NORMAN S., and ELLIS ASH, "The Prisoner Community as a Social Group," pp. 219–28.
14. WHYTE, WILLIAM FOOTE, "Corner Boys: A Study of Clique Behavior," pp. 228–38.

WILSON, LOGAN, and WILLIAM L. KOLB. *Sociological Analysis.* New York: Harcourt, Brace & Co., Inc., 1949.
15. COOLEY, CHARLES HORTON, "Primary Groups," pp. 287–89.
16. HARTSHORNE, EDWARD Y., "Undergraduate Society and the College Culture," pp. 290–302.
17. REDFIELD, ROBERT, "The Folk Society," pp. 349–66.

SELECTED READINGS

ADAMS, STUART. "Social Climate and Production in Small Military Groups," *American Sociological Review,* 19:401–25 (1954).

BARKER, ROBERT G., and HERBERT F. WRIGHT. *Midwest and Its Children: The Psychological Ecology of an American Town.* Evanston, Ill.: Row, Peterson & Co., 1955.

CARTWRIGHT, DORWIN, and ALVIN ZANDER (eds.). *Group Dynamics: Research and Theory.* Evanston: Row, Peterson, & Co., 1954.

COOLEY, CHARLES H. *Human Nature and the Social Order.* New York: Charles Scribner's Sons, 1902.

GROSS, EDWARD. "Characteristics of Cliques in Office Organization," *Research Studies of the State College of Washington* (Pullman), 19:131–36 (1951).

———. "Some Functional Consequences of Primary Controls in Formal Work Organization," *American Sociological Review,* 18:369–73 (Aug., 1953).

———. "Symbiosis and Consensus as An Integrative Factor in Small Groups," *American Sociological Review,* 21:174–79 (April 1956).

HARE, A. PAUL, EDGAR F. BORGATTA, and ROBERT F. BALES (eds.). *Small Groups: Studies in Social Interaction.* New York: Alfred A. Knopf, Inc., 1955.

LEWIS, SINCLAIR, *Main Street.* New York: Harcourt, Brace & Co., Inc., 1931.

MEAD, GEORGE H. *Mind, Self and Society* (ed. by C. W. Morris). Chicago: University of Chicago Press, 1934.

MILLS, THEODORE. "Power Relation in Three-Person Groups," *American Sociological Review,* 18:351–57 (Aug. 1953).

SHERIF, MUZAFER, and CAROLINE W. SHERIF. *Groups in Harmony and Tension.* New York: Harper & Brothers, 1953.

STONE, ROBERT C. "Factory Organization and Vertical Mobility," *American Sociological Review,* 18:28–35 (1953).

WHYTE, WILLIAM FOOTE. *Street Corner Society.* Chicago: University of Chicago Press, 1943.

Chapter 11

Territorial Groups: Rural, Urban, and Suburban

All human life, like animal life, has its existence in space. Men live on a particular kind of land, in a particular climatic area, in a particular restricted area of space; and they relate themselves to each other in space and to the natural environment about them. To this extent, at least, there is such a thing as *human ecology,* that is, a study of the relationships of human beings within space, just as there is an animal and plant ecology which relates animals and plants to each other in a given type of geographical space.

The great difference is, of course, that animals and plants have little ability to mediate the climatic factor in space and are, therefore, limited in their range. True, they may build a sort of house and protect themselves from the elements, but few animal and plant species are worldwide in their ability to adapt. Human beings provide their own adaptations through cultural invention, and therefore, human beings are not subject in the sense animals are to natural ecology. Irrigation, cloud seeding, air conditioning, drainage, and numerous other controls of man ameliorate his environment.

Something is, however, to be learned about human behavior by studying it in a spatial relationship. Ecological study of human beings has been particularly advantageous in studying people in large metropolitan communities, although rural sociologists were the first to use this method in plotting spatial arrangements of human beings and their institutions in rural communities.

The descriptive accounts which follow take into account some of the social contrasts that exist in given areas of space.

THE IMPORTANCE OF LOCALITY TO GROUPING

The Chicago "Gold Coast"—millionaire residential area—and one of that city's worst slums almost join at their back doors. The two societies, so close geographically, are, figuratively speaking, miles apart socially. Harvey Zorbaugh, sociologist, writing about them some years ago stated:

Back of the ostentatious apartments, hotels and homes of the Lake Shore Drive, and the quiet, shady streets of the Gold Coast lies an area of streets that have a painful sameness, with their old, soot-begrimed stone houses, their none-too-clean alleys, their shabby air of respectability. In the window of house after house along these streets one sees a black and white card with the words "Rooms to Rent." For this is the world of furnished rooms, a world of strangely unconventional customs and people, one of the most characteristic of the worlds that go to make up the life of the great city.

. . . 71 per cent of all the houses in this district keep roomers; and . . . of the people who live in these rooms, 52 per cent are single men, 10 per cent are single women, and 38 per cent are couples, "married," supposedly with "benefit of clergy." The rooming-house area is a childless area. Yet most of its population is in the productive ages of life, between twenty and thirty-five.[1]

Of the Gold Coast he wrote:

The Lake Shore Drive is the Mayfair of the Gold Coast. It runs north and south along Lake Michigan, with a wide parkway, bridle path, and promenade. On its western side rise the imposing stone mansions, with their green lawns and wrought iron-grilled doorways, of Chicago's wealthy aristocracy and her industrial and financial kings. South of these is Streeterville, a "restricted" district of tall apartments and hotels. Here are the Drake Hotel and the Lake Shore Drive Hotel, Chicago's most exclusive. And here apartments rent for from three hundred fifty to a thousand dollars a month. Indeed, the Lake Shore Drive is a street more of wealth than of aristocracy; for in this midwest metropolis money counts for more than does family, and the aristocracy is largely that of the financially successful.

On a warm spring Sunday "Vanity Fair" glides along "the Drive" in motor cars of expensive mark, makes colorful the bridlepaths, or saunters up the promenade between "the Drake" and Lincoln Park. . . .

. . . The Lake Shore Drive is as "foreign" to many a resident of Little Hell as though it were separated from him by the Atlantic Ocean.[2]

Speaking of competitive pressures and status-seeking efforts, Spectorsky[3] points up the importance of locality. He tells of the executive who has failed to move to the exurbs, but who has to hear the big boss say to his rival, "Let's discuss it on the train." The boss promises

[1] Harvey W. Zorbaugh, *The Gold Coast and the Slum* (Chicago: University of Chicago Press, 1929), pp. 69, 71–72.

[2] *Ibid.*

[3] A. C. Spectorsky, *The Exurbanites* (Philadelphia: J. B. Lippincott Co., 1955), pp. 162–63.

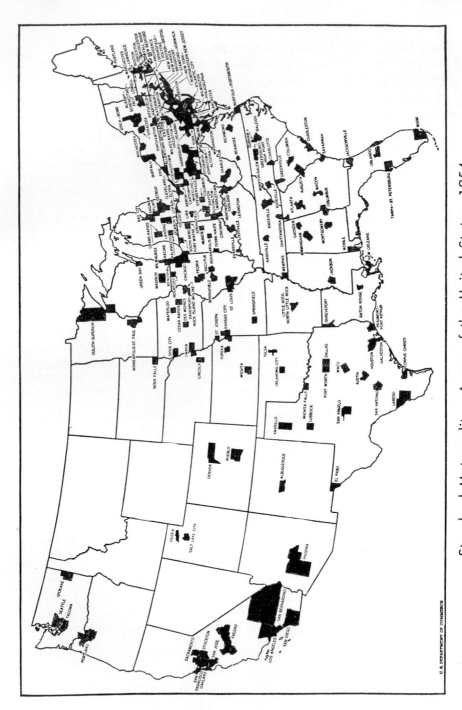

Standard Metropolitan Areas of the United States, 1954

Note the grouping of the metropolitan areas on the coastal fringes of the nation.

the urbanite a memo in the morning. Here his rival has a chance for fence-mending with the top brass which is denied the city resident.

James Bossard, University of Pennsylvania sociologist, in studying Philadelphia marriages found that one out of four couples had lived within two city blocks of each other when they became interested in each other as mates. One third of the couples had lived within five blocks of each other. Dr. Bossard concluded, "Cupid may have wings, but apparently they are not adapted for long flights."[4]

What Bossard found to be true of urban groups is much more true of rural groups, where in stable communities of three or more generations' duration people are often interrelated from both sides of the family. In fact, many such rural communities have practically become clusters of relatives because of the extensive intermarriage within the locality.

These examples are merely to show that living in the same territory affects human grouping even down to the pair relationship of marriage. Attention in this chapter is directed to those groups which are classified by the sociologist on the basis of territory as such.

LOCALITY GROUPS AS COMMUNITIES

The locality group is the basis for that important sociological concept, the community. The community, in its territorial dimensions, is the geographical area in which a social group carries on most of the activities required to meet the more essential needs of life. In its social dimensions, the community is the local group which acting together carries on local functions such as education, religion, local government, recreation, trade, and possibly police and fire protection.

The two main divisions of locality groups based on population, as classified by the United States census, are *rural* (open country and places under 2,500) and *urban* (places of 2,500 people or more). These groupings are used in numerous sociological analyses. Often they may be broken down further, as follows: (1) The *hamlet* is the smallest population unit, usually consisting of little more than a crossroad store with a surrounding population of under 250. (2) The *village*, the next largest unit, is defined differently in various sections of the country. It is often defined as a population unit of from 250 to 999. (3) The *town*, the next largest unit, has between 1,000 and

---

[4] J. H. S. Bossard, *Marriage and the Family* (Philadelphia: University of Pennsylvania Press, 1940), pp. 79–92. For a more recent study see John S. Ellsworthy, Jr., "The Relationship of Population Density to Residential Propinquity as a Factor in Marriage Selection," *American Sociological Review*, 13:444–48 (Aug. 1948).

2,500 population. (Some sociologists consider the town as a place with 1,000 to 10,000 population.) (4) The *city*, if one follows the census definition of urban, is a population center of 2,500 or more persons. Studies which classify places up to 10,000 population as towns begin the city classification at 10,000. (The census once divided rural and urban at this point.) (5) The metropolis is a city falling in the largest population class. A metropolis, as defined by the census prior to 1950, is a population aggregate of 100,000 with not less than 50,000 in the corporate limits of the central city. In 1950 the Census Bureau grouped the central city of 50,000 or more people with the densely surrounding county or counties, calling them *standard metropolitan*

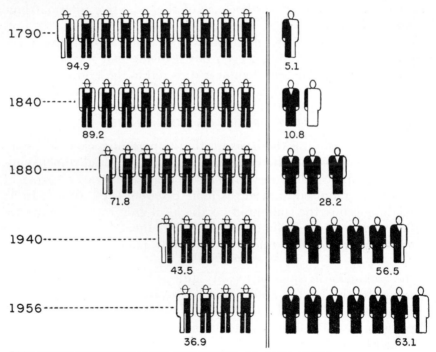

1790--- 94.9 ‖ 5.1

1840------- 89.2 ‖ 10.8

1880------------ 71.8 ‖ 28.2

1940-------------------- 43.5 ‖ 56.5

1956------------------------- 36.9 ‖ 63.1

EACH FIGURE REPRESENTS 10 PER CENT OF TOTAL U.S. POPULATION

Decreasing Proportion of Rural Population in the United States

As the United States has changed from an agricultural nation to a highly industrialized state, the proportion of the population living in rural areas (open country and towns under 2,500) has been steadily declining, while the proportion living in urban communities of more than 2,500 has increased. This change has had important effects on the quality of group life and activities.

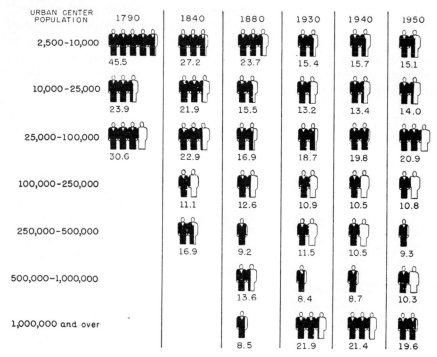

EACH FIGURE REPRESENTS 10 PER CENT OF TOTAL U. S. POPULATION

Proportion of the Population in Urban Centers
of Various Sizes, 1790—1950

In each successive decade the population of the nation is constituted of larger aggregates of people than in the preceding decade.

areas.[5] This is more than a population aggregate; it is a large densely settled community with an integrated economic life.

RURAL COMMUNITIES

Agricultural Village. The most common form of rural grouping and the one that has existed for centuries in most parts of the world is the *agricultural village*. (See pattern *A* of the diagram on page 190.) The agricultural village is a rural town in which both townsmen

---

[5] There are several qualifications to this definition: (1) It does not apply in New England. (2) A county to be called a standard metropolitan area must have 10,000 nonagricultural workers. (3) 10 per cent of the inhabitants must work in the standard metropolitan area. (4) Half of its population must live in areas of 150 persons per square mile density. (5) Nonagricultural workers must constitute at least two-thirds of the workers of the county, etc. (See 1950 Census of Population, vol. II, *Part I: U.S. Summary,* pp. 27–31.)

and farmers live. Farms lie about the village, the farmers going out from the village daily to work them. Land is divided into small plots or strips so that everyone may have land close by. Common pastures are provided for the livestock; common forests provide fuel and building materials. This kind of locality grouping was developed historically for mutual protection and for sociability.

 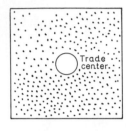 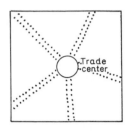

A. Agricultural Village Type   B. Isolated Farm Settlement   C. Line Settlement

Three Major Patterns of Rural Organization

Pattern A, in which farmers live in the village and go out to their fields, characterizes much of rural life throughout the world. In the United States, however, the isolated farm settlement shown in Pattern B, in which farmers live dispersed in unorganized fashion on their farms and use the town as a trade center, is almost universal. The social implications of the pure isolated farm type of rural organization are numerous. Pattern C, the line settlement, is often used as a pattern for development of newly irrigated areas.

Agricultural villages are found today throughout the Orient, in Africa, South America, and many parts of Europe. The New England colonists established this type of community in America, and it is still to be found among the Mormon settlements of Utah.

Isolated Farm Settlement. In direct contrast to the agricultural village is the present-day arrangement of rural life in most parts of the United States. The individualistic American pioneer chose to live on his own farm at a distance from the village. There he erected his dwelling and housed his livestock. The town sprang up, not as an agricultural village made up of the farmers but as a *farm trade center* or *farm service center* to which he went to fill the needs which the farm would not supply. This isolated form of settlement scattered the agricultural population and separated each farmer from his neighbors. It tended to increase his individualism, as it limited the social participation of the farmer and his children in town affairs.

In developing isolated farm settlements as the usual pattern of rural grouping, the American farmer made community services costly and difficult to attain. Every square mile of territory needs its own telephone line and its own electric line if the farmer is to have the conveniences that the town dwellers achieve by living in groups. If he is to have modern sanitation facilities and running water, he must develop his own plant, for the cost of running water mains out from the town and of developing sewage facilities is prohibitive. Little wonder that the American farmer lived in darkness long after his city cousin had electric lights and carried water from the well pump and took his Saturday night bath in the wash tub long after running water and bathrooms were nearly universal in town and city homes.

By isolated settlement, on the other hand, the American farmer gained immeasurably in efficiency of crop production and in the care of livestock. He lives on the farm in the midst of his work; he can give complete attention to it without having to drive back and forth to town morning and night. In fact, it is doubtful that large-scale machine farming would have been developed in the United States had the average community in this nation been laid out on the agricultural village plan, which requires that farms be small in order that all people living in the village will have a piece of land near enough to go out to it daily.

Under the isolated settlement form of rural community development, social conflict between town and country groups in the United States has been traditional, produced in part by the artificial separation of the farm trade center from the open country by means of incorporation. The separate existence of the town tends to exclude the farmer from town affairs and ordinarily from the regulation of town institutions. The open country is under the political supervision of the county—not of the town. The farmer has rarely been included in associations of the townspeople, so that even though he came to the small town frequently on business he was in a real sense an outsider. It has taken years to get consolidated schools on a co-operative basis between country and town. In fact, many states still have hardly begun. The same is true of securing libraries jointly supported by open country and towns. The American farmer until very recently has considered himself something of a stranger in town, a stranger who is not part of its government and social institutions, or, in fact, of its social programs.

Although the younger generation has lost much of its psychological sense of separateness, thanks to consolidated schools, most farm communities are still outside the corporate limits of towns, library districts, and in many states, town school districts.

Line Settlement. A third type of rural social grouping is found in French settlements along the river front in Louisiana. The Mississippi River provided an avenue of transportation, and land was divided into strips running back from the riverfront. Later, when the highway came, it followed the river. Along the highway, churches and stores developed. This arrangement is called the *line settlement pattern.* A minimum of road mileage is required.

A difficulty in Louisiana has been that as the first generation died and land had to be divided among the children, the tendency was to give each child a strip of land running back from the river. Soon the farms were mere ribbons of land which were difficult to farm on an economical basis. In fact, a good part of the farm is needed for roadways to the back part of each piece of land.

PLANNING MODERN RURAL COMMUNITIES

Today, as new lands are developed, such as in the Columbia Basin of Washington where a million acres are being converted from semi-desert or dry wheat farming acreage into land irrigated by water from Grand Coulee Dam, sociologists are naturally concerned with developing the kind of rural communities which will be most useful and most economical for the people living there. Those planning the settlement pattern have considered the advantages and disadvantages of various territorial arrangements in terms of cost, social advantage, and general convenience.

Where topography would permit, the planners decided on line settlement. It was assumed that in an area where there would be a great diversity of settlers lacking the common traditions of religious colonies or long-time neighbors, there would be considerable objection to settling in agricultural villages. Even from a social standpoint, the modern farmer would prefer to be apart from his neighbors and to live on his own farm rather than in town. Therefore the main problem was to figure out the type of settlement that would be of the greatest economic advantage, from the standpoint of public cost as well as cost to the farmer.

It was found that for isolated farm settlement, such as is typical in most parts of America, it would take two and one-half miles of road for each section of land. For line settlement, that is, the arrangement of farmsteads along the end of oblong farms, only one and one-third miles of road would be required. In other words, a saving of almost half the amount of land used in roads and a saving of half the cost of road surfacing would be realized by the line-settlement arrangement. The cost per farm for roads on a scattered settlement basis would be $439; for the line settlement, only $234.

Take farm water supply—a very expensive item under the best of conditions. With scattered settlement, the cost would be $1,385 per farm. For farms clustered in units of four at a crossroads the cost would be $502, since four families could use the same well. Under the line-settlement arrangement, cost could be reduced to $340, as

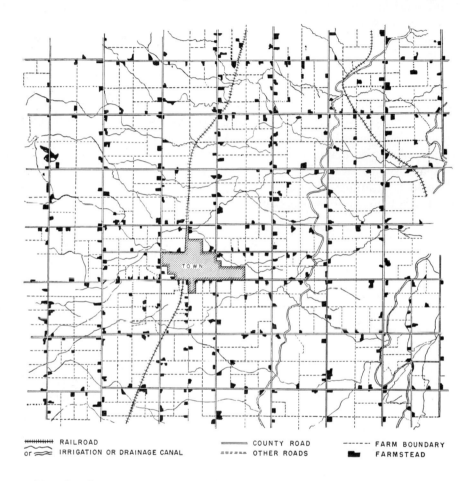

┼┼┼┼┼┼┼ RAILROAD	COUNTY ROAD	FARM BOUNDARY
or 〜〜 IRRIGATION OR DRAINAGE CANAL	╺╺╺╺╺ OTHER ROADS	▬ FARMSTEAD

Line Settlement Pattern in the Twin Falls, Idaho, Irrigated Area

Farm layouts are diagonal, with the narrow ends on the main roadways. This gives a systematic arrangement of residences that produces economies in building roads and providing utilities, and also adds to sociable living. In an automobile age this seems to be a better arrangement than either the unorganized isolated settlement pattern, so characteristic of rural America, or the agricultural village settlement pattern. (Bureau of Reclamation, U. S. Department of the Interior.)

water mains could go down the highway in front of the houses. The cheapest, from the standpoint of water supply, would be, of course, the agricultural village, where all farmers live in the village. The cost there would be only $133.

The map for the Twin Falls, Idaho, irrigated area shows the farm and road layout. Observe that most of the farms are twice as deep as they are wide, thus putting the houses on each road considerably closer together than would be the case if the situation were reversed. Roads go only in front of the farms, making it likely that the farmers will build on these main arteries. It can be seen that the cost of providing electricity for these farms, the cost of telephone service and of school bus service, and the amount of time the family spends in traveling back and forth to town is greatly reduced by this sort of arrangement as compared with the scattered rural type of settlement. This arrangement also makes for greater convenience in living and greater sociability; yet the families still live on their own farms near their livestock, gaining economic advantages over living in town at a distance from their livestock and crops.

THE NEIGHBORHOOD IN RURAL AMERICA

With the isolated settlement of rural America, neighborhood groups became universal except in the Great Plains area of the Far West, where settlement was so sparse that neighborhoods did not develop. Americans lived in intimate neighborhoods where face-to-face contacts and close personal relationships were characteristic. At the heart of the neighborhood was often a rural school or rural church and churchyard, which was the gathering place of neighbors. Often the neighborhood was bounded by recognized geographical features—river flats, rows of hills, a creek bottom, or some other landmark—or by some institution, such as a one-room school house or open-country church. An early pioneer's name sometimes identified the neighborhood.

The American rural neighborhood of earlier days was a genuine primary group, most important of all groups to the individual aside from the family. Much of social life was oriented about neighborhood work. In colonial America the husking bee, house raising, and other such cooperative enterprises were no less social gatherings than they were a system of mutual work exchange. In the rural neighborhood harvest time brought together men, women, and children in a strenuous day of work, but also for a pleasant meal and social visiting. It brought together children in a rich social life such as only those who live isolated from neighbors can appreciate. They remembered for many weeks afterward the play festival with other children.

The spirit of mutual helpfulness predominated in the work exchange of the rural neighborhoods to the extent that an exact accounting of time spent in helping a neighbor was never kept. In fact, such an accounting would have been frowned upon and considered unneighborly, as it was expected that a man would help his neighbor at any time help was needed. He could expect any amount of help in return if misfortune should overtake him. Women likewise came into the home in a time of distress and took over the work as their neighborly responsibility.

With the coming of the automobile, loyalty to the neighborhood has tended to decline and more and more farm people have built their lives about towns and cities, or at least around larger communities where in many parts of the country consolidated grade schools have united several neighborhoods for elementary education. Also, as open-country churches have declined, the neighborhood as a center for religious worship has tended to disappear.

The effect has been, as Kolb and Brunner have pointed out, that rural people now tend to develop *special interest groups,* as town and city people do, for much of their association.[6] It is known that in the city common vocation, common recreational activities, and other factors of common interest determine groupings, rather than living closely within the same territorial space. These same trends are obvious in the rural neighborhoods and communities. Farm people are nonetheless still more conscious, no doubt, of the neighborhood and its importance than are city people generally, and especially more than those living in metropolitan areas.

With the growth of machine agriculture in most parts of the nation, the coming of the automobile, the frequent trips to town, the gradual absorption of urban ideas, and the employment of hired help, the spirit of mutual helpfulness in the farm neighborhood has tended to disappear. In highly mechanized areas the exchange of work is no longer a common practice. One author has written of mechanized American agriculture as *Factories in the Field,* thus taking into account the fact that agrarian culture, with its deep-seated customs, has tended to disappear in the face of the mechanization.[7]

Gradually the larger farm community has become of increasing significance to rural groups. The community usually consists of a group of neighborhoods which recognize themselves as part of the functional unit because they have a common geographical territory and share certain of the larger functions, such as the community

[6] J. H. Kolb and E. deS. Brunner, *A Study of Rural Society* (4th ed.; Boston: Houghton Mifflin Co., 1953).

[7] Carey McWilliams, *Factories in the Field* (Boston: Little, Brown & Co., 1939).

church or community school district which brings together into a consolidated unit several one-room neighborhood school districts. The rural community of today also often unites town and country in joint enterprises.

THE FARM TRADE CENTER IN THE RURAL SPATIAL PATTERN

It has been shown that in the isolated farm settlement patterns of the United States, farm trade centers sprang up, linking isolated farmsteads with the commercial market beyond and at the same time serving as distributing points for goods which farmers needed. These trade centers also became service centers because, generally speaking, professional people and artisans—dentists, doctors, lawyers, teachers, ministers, blacksmiths, and mechanics—lived in the trade center rather than in the countryside.

The open country developed institutions of its own, notably the rural church and the rural school; nevertheless, as means of transportation have facilitated movement, the farm trade center has become a center for most institutional services, including recreation. Thus, the trade center bridges the gap between the rural neighborhood and the commercial, professional, recreational, and institutional organizations of the nation which have their focal points in the metropolis.

Farm trade centers ordinarily have less than 5,000 population, and most of them are much smaller. They are located throughout agricultural districts and range in size from the crossroads store to the larger town which may draw trade from a wide hinterland. There are in the United States over 78,000 places with less than 2,500 population. Of these, approximately 58,800 are places with less than 250 people and 19,200 are places with 250 to 2,500 population. Of all places with less than 2,500 population, 13,288 were incorporated in 1940. In all places with under 2,500 there lived about 17,700,000 people, or approximately 14 per cent of the nation's population. Of this group 4,000,000 lived in places with less than 250 population, and almost 3,700,000 in places with 250 to 2,500 population.[8] The

[8] For the best brief factual summary of data on number of unincorporated and incorporated places, see Kolb and Brunner, op. cit., chap. 13. For original studies of unincorporated places, see C. Luther Fry, American Villagers (Garden City, N.Y.: Doubleday & Co., Inc., 1926); E. deS. Brunner and T. Lynn Smith, "Village Growth and Decline, 1930–1949," Rural Sociology, 9:103–15 (June 1944); Douglas G. Marshall, "Hamlets and Villages in the United States: Their Place in the American Way of Life," American Sociological Review, 11:159–65 (April 1946); Paul H. Landis, "The Number of Unincorporated Places in the United States and Their Estimated Population," Research Studies of the State College of Washington, 6:160–88 (Dec. 1938).

exact proportion of these places and of their resident populations which serve the farm population is not known.

Farm trade centers were originally located within a distance which could be covered by a team and wagon haul. Therefore in more densely populated sections they usually were only eight or ten miles apart, although in more sparsely populated areas they were much more infrequent. As good roads and automobiles have multiplied, the very small hamlets have often disappeared, the farmer now going a greater distance to market his produce and to obtain his merchandise. The small town has lost a number of its functions to the city which could handle them more effectively. The trend of professional service has been the same, highly specialized practitioners locating in the larger community. The farmer today can go greater distances to the metropolis to seek specialized consultation on health, medical, or financial problems.

In all rural areas of the nation are to be found trade centers which vary both in size and in the number and character of their mercantile, artisan, professional, and institutional services. John Kolb, rural sociologist at the University of Wisconsin, has made the following five-fold classification of service centers: (1) the single-service type of center which offers one service, such as the general store, the rural church, or the rural school; (2) the limited or simple service type which has a relatively small service area and offers but a few services; (3) the semicomplete service type which provides almost all the services that farm people need; (4) the complete or partially specialized type which provides the farmer a choice of stores and has most of the social institutions that a community group would desire; (5) the urban or highly specialized type which is prepared to satisfy a great range of interests and desires.[9]

Throughout agricultural areas of the nation, trade centers of the types outlined above are scattered without plan or creative design, their size and frequency depending upon the density of farm population and the prosperity of the region. Since the coming of the automobile, overlapping zones of influence and division of function between small towns and the large towns and cities is characteristic, and most rural areas have within easy driving distance a choice of any one of a number of trade centers. Close at hand may be several small centers and at greater distances one or more large urban centers.

[9] John Kolb, "Service Relations of Town and Country," Wisconsin Agricultural Experiment Station Bulletin No. 58 (Madison, Wisconsin, 1923).

HUMAN ECOLOGY OF URBAN COMMUNITIES

The most comprehensive urban studies of social organization and
group life, from a territorial or spatial viewpoint, have been made by
the *human ecologists*, that is, those sociologists who specialize in a
study of social life in relationship to space or habitat.[10] The term

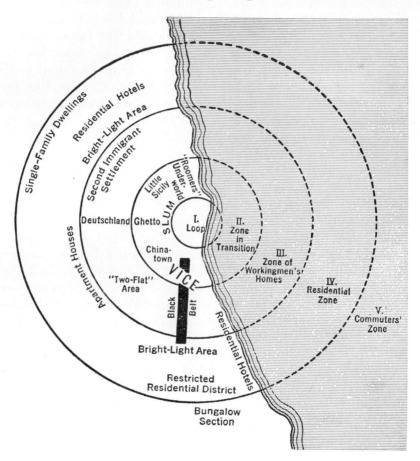

Ecological Scheme of the City of Chicago

This is a classic chart, the result of the first research to give pattern to a great
city. In the shaded area representing Lake Michigan, the concentric zones
typical of the city are broken, shown here by dotted lines. The flow of new
population into Chicago in recent years has changed the specific characteristics
of some of the zones. (Redrawn from The City, *by Park and Burgess, p. 55.*
University of Chicago Press, 1925.)

[10] Pioneers in this field were the late Robert E. Park, and Ernest W. Burgess of the
University of Chicago.

"ecology" has been borrowed from students of plant and animal life, who use it to designate the grouping of interdependent plant and animal life into "communities" in natural environments. The human ecologist, by studying city life from the standpoint of the grouping of different types of social aggregates in space, has discovered many interesting aspects of life in the metropolis. The basic early studies in this field were made in the city of Chicago, depicting group life of that city in terms of spatial or territorial arrangement.

The Concentric Zone Theory. Zone I: The ecologists began their studies by zoning the city of Chicago into what they considered natural areas. These zones began with a central business area, Zone I, known locally as "the Loop." (See chart.) The Loop zone is that in which business activity is greatest. Social groups in this area are mobile and transient. It is an area that is largely vacated at night, although in it or close by is a residential area of cheap hotels and flophouses known as *hobohemia,* the world of homeless men. This is a segregated area within the city. In western cities it is known as "skid row," the term being taken from logging. The men (hobos) who inhabit hobohemias and skid row work seasonally primarily in the logging industry and farming.

Zone II: Around the business area they found Zone II, called an *interstitial* zone or *zone in transition.* It is more commonly called the *slum* because of the unique characteristics of housing that exist there. This area is one of high land values, but the residential properties on it are in a state of deterioration because of the transitional state between residential occupancy and business occupancy. The central business district of Zone I keeps encroaching upon it and forcing land values up. It is only a matter of time until the residences will be entirely vacated and wrecked so the property can be replaced by a business structure.

Because of this situation, landlords have no motive to improve property, and newcomers to the city crowd into it because of the attraction of cheap rents. It is for immigrants a *zone of first settlement.* They crowd into the slum quarters in great numbers, and one newcomer group tends over a period of time to replace another; this process of one group coming in and crowding out another is known, in its first stages, as *invasion.* Its final stage is *succession,* when the process of replacement of one group by the other is complete.

Up until World War I, these slum areas in eastern cities were occupied in turn by the waves of immigrants who came from European countries. At the middle of the last century northern Europeans and Irishmen took over the slum areas until they became established fi-

Skyline of the World

In the central part, where land values are highest, cities pu

nancially and were crowded out toward the latter part of the century by newcomers from southern Europe.

Since World War I the invasion of the slum areas was largely by Negroes moving in great numbers from the rural South. They were replaced by later waves of Negro migrants, as the first waves became established in the city and moved out to more habitable residential districts. Since World War II, New York City, the main entry point for immigrants for well over a century, has been "invaded" by Puerto Ricans. This "invasion" continues as airplanes bring in thousands of Puerto Ricans to find a place in the life of New York City.)

Zone III: Beyond the slum area they found Zone III, *the area of working men's homes.* Considered from the standpoint of succession, it is the *zone of second settlement,* inasmuch as those newcomers who first settled in the slums, having become established economically, move out from the slums to this area—a step up from the standpoint of social status and improved residential quarters. In this area are found the men who carry dinner pails to work rather than eat in the restaurants in the central business district. They live in the zone of working men's homes because it is the closest to the business and factory centers of the downtown area to which they go daily.

argest City—New York

oward, stacking tier upon tier. (Standard Oil Company, N.J.)

Like the slum area, this is an area with a high birth rate, new-comers bring with them from rural areas and from foreign countries the reproductive standards which have been customary in their home communities. The first generation continues to have a high birth rate. Not until the second generation do the immigrant groups adopt fully the restricted birth rate of the native-born Americans.

Zone IV: Beyond the zone of working men's homes they found Zone IV, the *middle-class residential area.* It is a residential area in which democratic family life tends to be characteristic. There is an equal sharing of responsibility by husband and wife in the care of the children, for the father spends his evenings in the home. Usually the dwelling is a single-family dwelling or at most a duplex; there is a small yard, and there is some feeling of neighborliness between people in the same block. The area is a reasonably good place in which to rear children.

Zone V: Beyond this zone, at the outer fringe of the city, was Zone V, called the *commuter zone.* Those who live here usually are the most prosperous classes of the city, those in managerial positions or on the higher professional levels. They commute daily to the city from the outlying areas. In the commuter zone there may be entire towns known as "bedroom towns" to which those who work in the central business district return to sleep. Their families are housed there, often in attractive, sometimes even lavish homes; but the father leaves early in the morning before the young children are up and returns late at night after they have retired. The care of the family is largely the responsibility of the mother, the father scarcely seeing the young children except on weekends. He sacrifices his time at home for the advantage of living away from the noise and dirt of the city.

Within these various zones Park and Burgess found many smaller areas and social groupings that had unique characteristics. The chart (refer again to p. 198) for the city of Chicago shows some of these unique areas that were scattered throughout the city: the underworld, the world of roomers, the various immigrant colonies, remnants of which are still to be found in segregated areas such as are described on this chart—Little Sicily, Deutchland, and others, and the black belt, which is a Negro settlement.

The Sector Theory. Pioneers must always yield to others part of the glory of discovery, particularly in the field of science. Later ecologists have challenged the Park and Burgess theory of ecology and refined it. Some cities do not fit a simple concentric theory. Even Chicago had a "slice" out of one side, made by Lake Michigan, as Park and Burgess recognized. They also recognized zones within zones. Subsequent research shows that the concentric pattern is at best only an illustrative schematic pattern. It is nonetheless useful and has led to a series of significant research, some of which will be cited in later paragraphs of this chapter.

The diagram in the upper right of the accompanying chart presents Homer Hoyt's sector theory. He holds that city growth takes place along the main transportation routes or lines of least resistance, rather than in concentric zones.[11] Growth along a particular axis of transportation, or line of least resistance, almost always consists of similar types of land use. The city is viewed as a circle, and the areas —residential, industrial, business, and so on—are called sectors, which radiate out from the center of the circle. Thus, similar types of land uses begin at the center of the circle and move out toward the periphery or outer edge of the city. A sector of working men's homes would, then, move outward as the city grew, but rather than circling the city as in the concentric zone theory, it would remain in its sector.

[11] Homer Hoyt, *The Structure and Growth of Residential Neighborhoods in American Cities* (Washington, D.C.: Federal Housing Administration, 1939).

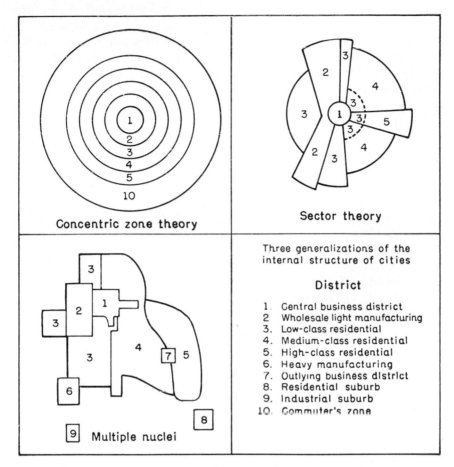

Concentric zone theory

Sector theory

Three generalizations of the internal structure of cities

District

1. Central business district
2. Wholesale light manufacturing
3. Low-class residential
4. Medium-class residential
5. High-class residential
6. Heavy manufacturing
7. Outlying business district
8. Residential suburb
9. Industrial suburb
10. Commuter's zone

Multiple nuclei

Three Theories of the Ecological Structure of Cities

Redrawn from C. D. Harris and E. L. Ullman, "The Nature of Cities," Annals of the American Academy of Political and Social Science, *242:12 (Nov. 1945).*

The Multiple Nuclear Theory. The multiple nuclei theory (lower left diagram of chart) holds that the land-use pattern in many cities is built around several discrete nuclei instead of a single center as in the concentric zone and sector theories. These nuclei in some cities existed from the very beginning of the city's development, and in others they developed as the city grew and migration and specialization were stimulated. Harris and Ullman believe that the development of multiple nuclei is due to a combination of four factors. First is the fact that in cities certain activities must have specialized facilities. For example, the port district must have a sufficient area clear of obstructions to allow the landing and taking off of aircraft; manufacturing districts must have large tracts of land and access to transportation facilities. Second, similar activities group together because they profit from cohesion. It is well known, for example, that retail stores group together because such grouping increases the concentration of potential customers. Third, some unlike activities are detrimental to each other, such as factory districts and residential developments. Fourth, some activities in the city are unable to afford the high rents or the high land prices of the most desirable sites.[12]

There are many varied combinations which the nuclei in different cities may take, but the larger the city the more numerous and specialized are the nuclei. It is probable that in most cities characterized by multiple nuclei there are nuclei which were present from the beginning of the city's history and others which have appeared during the course of time.

NATURAL VS. SOCIOLOGICAL FORCES IN ECOLOGICAL TRENDS

No doubt each of the preceding mechanical theories gives a generalized pattern which many or most cities follow to some extent. But mechanics alone did not satisfy Walter Firey, who felt that psychosocial factors might be as important as so-called "natural trends." Park and Burgess particularly had stressed the fact that the various ecological areas in the city were "natural areas" and that the succession of changes taking place in zones were "natural" cycles in the ecological process. The good housing area in time became the slum, just as a garden neglected became a weed patch; the slum became the business or industrial district, etc., in a more or less inevitable succession.

Walter Firey, in his investigations in Boston, challenged the "natural" ecology theory.[13] He believed that human values were of critical importance in growth trends. "Any aspect of a situation, event, or object that is invested with a preferential interest as being 'good,' 'bad,' 'desirable,' and the like," provides, he felt, at least some of the criteria by which locations for various purposes in cities are chosen.[14] To test this idea Firey studied two areas in Boston, Beacon Hill and the Boston Common.

Beacon Hill is an upper-class residential district which was established around 1800. Over a long period of time residents of Beacon

---

[12] Chauncy D. Harris and Edward L. Ullman, "The Nature of Cities," *Annals of the American Academy of Political and Social Science*, 242:7–17 (Nov. 1945).

[13] Walter Firey, *Land Use in Central Boston* (Cambridge: Harvard University Press, 1947).

[14] Robin M. Williams, Jr., *American Society* (New York: Alfred A. Knopf, Inc., 1955), p. 374.

Hill became characterized by a common unity of sentiment and a feeling of geographic exclusiveness. As Beacon Hill is only five minutes traveling time from the center of the city, its location is very desirable for business uses. However, the residents have several times joined together to resist the encroachment of business establishments and "apartment hotels." Also, the residents cooperated in a program designed to buy old houses on the hill, remodel them, and thus preserve the area's charm and exclusiveness. Thus, where in most cities the people living in residential areas move in the face of pressure of high offers from business establishments, the residents of Beacon Hill have resisted this pressure and kept their area intact.

The Boston Common, taking up some forty-eight acres, is located in the center of the Boston business district. The Common has been of historical importance for three centuries and is now protected by city, state, and even national sentiment, and laws. It is a source of tradition and inspiration to many people. The existence of the Common has, however, resulted in traffic problems, since it is against the law for roads to be built through the Common; the crowding of business establishments, since they cannot expand out to the Common; and various other problems. Yet, in spite of these problems, it can probably be safely predicted that the Boston Common will remain as it is as long as the United States also remains as it is.

This work of Firey's demonstrates that an understanding of the ecological growth of a city requires the consideration of individuals and community value systems in addition to natural factors mentioned in the chapter.

IMPORTANT ASPECTS OF ECOLOGICAL ARRANGEMENT

The Relative Stability of Ecological Areas. While ecological arrangements are never permanent, but always changing, various areas of cities continue to serve the same function for extremely long periods of time. One might wonder, then, about how rapidly ecological patterns, once established, may change their function and character. While there is no direct answer to this question, the cities bombed during World War II provided an opportunity to explore this question.

Fred C. Iklé, in his research in Europe, found that immediately after the war the evacuated inhabitants began to return to the cities whose populations rose to a level only slightly below that of the prewar era.[15] It was discovered that the bombed out population strongly desired to return to their old areas of residence, and in

---

[15] Fred Charles Iklé, "The Effect of War Destruction Upon the Ecology of Cities," *Social Forces,* 29:383–91 (May 1951).

most cases they wanted to live again in the blocks where their former homes were located. It was believed that there were two major factors which accounted for an individual's desire to return to his old place of residence. These were, first, ownership of land, and, second, a wish to reestablish the old social ties which linked a person with his neighborhood.

Evacuated and destroyed business establishments revealed a tendency to return to their old sites. One obvious reason for returning was ownership of the land upon which the business had stood. It was also found that the destroyed and damaged buildings retained some of their value. Another reason for returning could be that the business establishments wished to retain the good will attached to the old location and again serve their former customers.

In Berlin it was found that those partially destroyed blocks which during prewar days had had high delinquency rates continued to have such rates, but blocks and areas which were completely destroyed were likely to lose their former character. In areas in which basic utilities and transportation systems had not been restored, the "cultural component" was not sufficient to result in the rehabilitation of an area. It is possible that an ecological area can, then, be so completely altered that it will not resume its former character. Yet Iklé's research revealed that it is more difficult to change the ecological composition of a city than was once thought.

It must be borne in mind that European cities have many characteristics dissimilar to those of cities in the United States. However, this research too suggests that social and psychological factors, and not merely economic and natural ones, must be taken into account in both the planning of city growth and in the study of social ecology.

Delinquency in Relation to the Ecological Arrangement. Some of the most significant studies of group behavior in urban communities have been those which describe it in relationship to various zones of the city. One of the most striking studies is that of Clifford Shaw and his colleagues who, by studying rates of delinquency in mile-square areas of the city of Chicago, showed that delinquency rates tend to be concentrated near the central business district and in slum areas, gradually declining as one goes from the central part of the city to the periphery, the rates being extremely low at the latter point.[16] In one mile-square area in the slum section, for example, they found that 37 per cent, or one third, of all boys between ten and sixteen

[16] Clifford Shaw and others, *Delinquency Areas* (Chicago: University of Chicago Press, 1929).

years of age were brought to the attention of the police or of the Juvenile Court during a single year.

Assuming that not all of those who were delinquent were caught during any one period, one must accept the fact that delinquency tends to be the usual pattern in such an area. As one goes from this point outward, each mile-square area shows a decline in the rates of juvenile delinquency. At the outer fringe of the city there is scarcely any delinquency at all, indicating that family and community pressures for good behavior are much greater at the periphery, and perhaps also that influential parents offer children considerable immunity from the law when they do indulge in destructive pranks.

In the slum area family and community pressures are too weak to prevent delinquency. Children in this particular ecological area are usually of immigrant parentage and must break away from their families to become Americans. The new ways of America, found in the environment where they grow up, are the ways of gangsters and criminals. The child learns the only patterns of behavior that are available to him, those of the heroes of the world in which he lives. The slum child's games are fighting with the police and with the law, plaguing fruit vendors or merchants, fighting for a place to play ball even though it means breaking a few windows.

Studies by Frederic Thrasher of over 13,000 gangs in the city of Chicago related gang behavior to the particular type of ecological area in which gangs live.[17] He found in areas where the underworld dominates that boy gangs gradually merge into the criminal gang as youngsters get experience in crime and become hardened to the life of the criminal. In some of these areas initiation to the gang requires experience with the police or some deed of daring in defiance of the law. In the better residential areas the gangs graduate from the innocent prankishness of boyhood to the respectability of adulthood when the gangs break up as the young men marry.

These relationships between the behavior of children and ecological location are highly valuable and still constitute a fruitful approach to understanding human behavior. They tell only part of the story however. A more complete analysis must deal with family patterns, individual motivation, etc. For example, Albert K. Cohen has shown more recently that one is dealing not only with ecological area in locating delinquency in a disadvantaged area but with occupational class groups which are differently motivated.[18] In the work-

[17] Frederic Thrasher, *The Gang* (Chicago: University of Chicago Press, 1927).
[18] Albert K. Cohen, "Sociological Research on Juvenile Delinquency," a paper prepared for the meeting of the American Orthopsychiatric Association, March, 1956.

ing class area, boys grow up with a set of values which makes them rough and ready. To fight is part of the pattern of their family and social group; to destroy property is to take vengeance on the social class above them, which measures status and security by property ownership; to be idle is to defy their work values. He feels that one must understand the delinquent boy in terms of "delinquent subculture." In this subculture stealing is not primarily a way of satisfying the need for something to eat, wear, or sell. It is primarily for the glory, prowess, personal satisfaction, and gang respect that accrues. They may go to a store, each pick up a ball, light bulb, or some trinket. They may go to the next store and change the items for like items. They may steal clothes they cannot wear and other items of no value to them. Stealing is a status-gaining game. The delinquent subculture is such that they take delight in making others uncomfortable, in defying the rules, and in flouting authority. In general, this subculture tends to turn the norms of respectable society upside down, to do exactly the opposite of what the general culture expects.

Family Life in Relation to Ecological Areas. Ernest R. Mowrer, a student of the family in the city of Chicago, related family behavior and the type of family to the various ecological areas of the city.[19] The world of hobohemia in the central business district he called a *non-family area.* It is a world of homeless men, many of whom have always been bachelors, but others of whom have forsaken their families by desertion or by divorce and have taken to the road as seasonal workers, spending their periods of unemployment in hobohemia. The few women in the area are usually of questionable character. It is a world without children.

The slum area he found to be an area of large families of newcomer immigrants, or colored groups from the rural south who were trying to get a footing in the competitive life of the city. The family was described as *patriarchal,* that is, father-ruled, since most of the immigrants originated from the peasant cultures of European countries or from rural sections of the United States where father-dominated families are characteristic. The zone of working-men homes, he found, is also a family area, and the family tends to be large and to maintain some of its patriarchal characteristics.

In the slum area he found desertion to be the usual way of breaking up the family grouping. If the burdens get too heavy and the father cannot cope with them any more, he simply runs away. Divorce is a luxury of the man with money; the slum resident cannot

[19] Ernest R. Mowrer, *Family Disorganization* (Chicago: University of Chicago Press, 1927).

afford the cost. He joins up with the men of hobohemia and takes to the road when he wants to be free of the family. In the zone of working men's homes both divorce and desertion are used as methods of breaking the family.

In the middle-class area, Zone III, he found the *"equalitarian family."* In this area the couples shared responsibilities equally, tended to accept a single standard of morality, to have the usual middle-class small family, and to build their joint lives about the home.

In the commuter's zone, Zone V, Mowrer called the family *matriarchal*—mother-centered. This is so because the father is seldom home; he works in the city and naturally has little control over the children because of his long absence from them. They are nearing high school age before he sees much of them except on week ends. The father is the breadwinner; he gives the family status and security; the mother is its emotional and disciplinary center.

The fifth kind of family he found in the city was scattered along the main arteries of transportation, in rooming houses, apartment houses, and residential hotels. Mowrer called it the *"emancipated family."* It is, in reality, not a family at all, if one thinks of a family as husband and wife with children. Many couples live together in the world of furnished rooms without the formality of marriage. They live together in order to have someone to come home to and to whom they can tell their troubles. In this world of anonymity, moral standards tend to break down under the pressure of loneliness.

In the better residential areas of the apartment houses and hotels that lie on the main arteries of transportation, the more prosperous emancipated couples live in apartments that require little care on the part of the wife, in fact little housekeeping at all. In the residential hotel there is no housework beyond preparing an occasional meal when the couple wishes to do so.

In all apartment houses the man is practically freed of duties, since the building is heated and upkeep maintained by janitors or hired custodians. The wife's duties are somewhat greater, but the couple usually take all of their noon meals outside, also often taking their dinner outside and getting their entertainment in the city in the evening. The apartment is a place to sleep and to have breakfast, the morning meal being often a very abbreviated affair which requires little or no cooking. Both members work, and their lives become highly individuated. Sex is the main bond, the couple being emancipated from all the usual obligations and ties of a family with children, with roots in the neighborhood and with a sense of responsibility to the community institutions which family members help support in the normal community.

More recently, Jaco and Belknap have analyzed family life in the urban fringe. They conclude that the "fringe" family has the following characteristics:

(1) Sustained fertility through higher orders of birth; (2) A consequent increase in the size of the fringe family; (3) Marriage rates for males higher in the rural non-farm areas than in both urban and rural farm areas; (4) Decrease in the age at marriage continuing; (5) Employment of both single and married women increasing, particularly for the higher age groups and with mothers of children from 12 to 17 years of age; (6) The historic functions of the family seemingly better retained in the fringe—the economic, with employment of mothers as secondary workers; the educational, in the selection of "better" schools for children; the recreational, in the encouragement of participation of children in selected peer groups and social sets; the religious, in belonging to and supporting the "right" churches, and the protective, in addition to the preceding, in providing the best care and rearing practices of medical and mental science.[20]

Nelson Foote of the Family Research Center at the University of Chicago has called attention to the play nature of the new type of family life developing in the metropolitan suburb. He writes:

"One of the most striking features of our younger suburbs might almost be called the discovery of family living. Almost everyone lives in a family and always has, but the self-conscious recognition of family living as a distinctive and desired activity—quite different from operating a family business, 'raising a family,' or visiting relatives—is uniquely contemporary. . . .

"Family living in the residential suburb has come to consist almost entirely of play. . . . The do-it-yourself movement, for example, is a pleasant simulation of work; it is amateur and unpaid and usually far from efficient, however skillful and productive. Once a family has purchased a home and is thereby licensed to modify its appearance to heart's content, the elaborations which can ensue are limited only by imagination and the need for sleep. The seriousness with which home-making is pursued at its best should not conceal its playful nature, because work and play at their best are indeed indistinguishable. . . .

"The basement or attic which once served as a utilitarian warehouse has now become a museum to display collections dear to the householder—whether trophies, books, machines, pictures, tackle or travel loot. This museum function was often visible in the past, but never quite so self-consciously so. By the accretion of such residues

[20] E. Carly Jaco and Ivan Belknap, "Is a New Family Form Emerging in the Urban Fringe?" *American Sociological Review,* 18:556 (Oct. 1953).

the house, as an old line goes, becomes a home. But more important than defining a home historically or biographically is definition by its users in terms of current activity and current biography. In the acting out of family history as it is lived from day to day, the contemporary home may be most aptly described as a theater.

"By no means is this conception to be reduced to watching television. Another common interpretation of the recent appetite for family living points to the rise in available leisure, but leisure like money can be squandered with little result. The ratio of time spent by family members as an audience for the performance of each other as against time spent in watching commercial portrayals may signify how well the home rates as a theater in their own eyes. . . . The home . . . in its function as a theater awakens aspirations and compassions among family members. . . ."[21]

Human Behavior and Ecological Arrangement. An important study of human behavior in relationship to the ecological setting is that by Dunham and Faris of mental disease in the city of Chicago.[22] They set out to learn whether the peculiar ecological characteristics of an area affect the rate of mental disease. Schizophrenia, a form of mental illness that is considered to be functional (related to experience) rather than being organic (it involves a withdrawal from reality, an introverted escape into a dream world), they found concentrated in the slum areas where social disorganization is characteristic and group controls have largely disappeared—the same areas, in fact, where one finds crime, suicide, and family instability most prevalent. Types of mental disease that are due primarily to organic causes are not concentrated in any one area but are found spread throughout the city.

The study does not show conclusively whether these areas of disorganization tend to draw to them those who are approaching the point of mental breakdown or whether the area itself is responsible for the break. Certainly a sociologist would have to assume that the area itself is in part responsible for the final break that pushes the person beyond the realm of normality.

Suicide rates have also been found to be high in these areas of community disorganization where pressures that hold a man together and make him feel that he has someone to live for have disappeared. Cavan's study of suicide shows this to be true in Chicago,[23]

[21] Nelson Foote, "Family Living as Play," *Marriage and Family Living,* 17:296–301 (Nov. 1955).

[22] Robert E. L. Faris and H. Warren Dunham, *Mental Disorders in Urban Areas* (Chicago: University of Chicago Press, 1939).

[23] Ruth Shonle Cavan, *Suicide* (Chicago: University of Chicago Press, 1928).

Slum Clearance Versus

Stuyvesant Town (left) is the result of a project in which a slum of New York

as do studies by others of other American cities.[24] Census figures also show that suicide tends to be higher in the anonymity and disorganization of the city than in rural communities. Man travels the way of life most safely when he feels that others are interested in the things he does and in him as a person. Rob a man of this feeling, as the anonymous areas of the city have done, throw him into the crowded loneliness of an environment where he sees thousands of people but where they all ignore him and manifest no interest in him, and he finds his hold on life slipping. He may, in times of crisis, find it easier to take his life than to face the loneliness that life brings.

A minister in Philadelphia writing a column for a metropolitan newspaper which brought thousands of letters in response from

[24] Calvin F. Schmid, "Suicides in Minneapolis, Minnesota, 1928–32," *American Journal of Sociology*, 39:30–48 (July 1933). Also his *Suicides in Seattle, 1914–1915: An Ecological and Behavioristic Study* (Seattle: University of Washington Press, 1928).

"Natural" Ecological Trends

(*right*) *was rebuilt.* (*Metropolitan Life Insurance Co.*)

readers, made the significant comment that human beings are never so much alone as in the "crowded cities."[25]

Implications of Ecological Studies. This summary of some important ecological studies is enough to show the significant relationship between particular areas of the city and group life and individual behavior there. They are further evidences supporting the sociologist's view that one's personality is in large part a product of the environment in which he was born, that those in disorganized communities are threatened with disorganized lives, that society has a responsibility, not usually recognized, for the behavior of those who have never had a chance to learn any behavior but that of a disorganized community. Such knowledge as that presented above has great social meaning for programs of slum clearance, in which such

[25] Joseph F. Nelson, "The Minister's Mail," *Reader's Digest,* Oct., 1938, pp. 80–81.

213

Los Angeles Metropolitan Area

The ecologists say that satellite cities tend to group around central cities like planets around the sun. Perhaps no city in the world has spawned so many satellite cities as has Los Angeles, and this trend seems likely to continue. (Fairchild Aerial Surveys, Inc., photo adapted from Newsweek)

areas are destroyed and the process of transition from slum to business occupancy is hastened.

When the public clears a slum, it is usually to replace slum dwellings with large apartment houses which can be rented to workmen desirous of living near the business district. During the Depression of the 1930's considerable activity of this character was carried on. It has been extended since World War II. In New York City, for example, the famous Lung Block, a slum area so named because of the high tuberculosis rate, was destroyed and beautiful apartment houses erected.

RECENT ECOLOGICAL TRENDS

Since the automobile replaced the horse and buggy, each year has seen a merging of life in rural and urban America. Rural life is town- and city-centered. Rural personality is more flexible, life being less isolated; rural personality is less eccentric. Agriculture is oriented toward the commercial market, so the old rural self-sufficiency is gone. Rural people share in the same measures of social security as urban wage workers.

But the city has been moving ruralward, too. For four decades the fringe areas around large cities have grown more rapidly in population than the central city. Satellite towns and cities group around the metropolis, like planets around the sun, as great cities explode outward.

The new city is made by the automobile, and by means of the automobile its workers seek residence at great distance from the city center. The residential suburb, with its combination of primary and secondary group life, has brought family life back in style in the city. The home, with yard and fireplace, has restored home life to urban centers. The new housing project in suburbia has made Americans a nation of home-owners. The young couple purchase their home by a long-term mortgage, and build their life in the new suburban community with its schools, churches, and supermarkets.

And now sociologists are discovering another layer far out in the rural area—*exurbia*. This, according to the author of a popular book titled *The Exurbanites,* is that high-class residential area far out where the elite of communications, entertainment—show, radio, advertising, etc.—business live. It is an area with much "front," and houses a class in which social pressures are intense indeed.

Suburbs have grown not only in numbers but in kinds. There are residential suburbs, educational, mining, resort, governmental, transportation, and wholesale-trade-center suburbs. Generally speaking, the industrial suburbs are centers which employ workers attracted from other parts of the metropolis. They tend to be concentrated in the heavily industrialized areas of the United States and are usually older than other subcenters. As the distance from the central business district increases, the suburbs of the industrial type increase. The industrial centers are most often in low-rent areas. In the residential suburb the retail area is the major economic activity. The residential suburbs are to be found in the metropolitan areas of all regions of the United States. The general tendency has been for the residential suburbs to be found within thirty miles of the central area. The residential suburbs are characterized by high rents and land values.[26]

The above description of the various kinds of suburbs shows that it is incorrect to characterize all suburbs as "dormitory towns" or "bedroom cities," since many suburbs have as their function the manufacturing of goods and the provisions of such services as education and recreation.

The growth of various types of suburbs in the last twenty years cannot be explained primarily by employment opportunities, since rapid transportation makes employment at a great distance possible. Housing in a desirable area seems to be a major motivation.[27] The great housing project, with its low down payment, has lead to the outward expansion of cities. Shopping centers and other essential services follow the residential community. Home ownership in the United States jumped from 41 per cent of families in 1940 to almost 59 per cent in 1957.

In the suburban housing project, "upgrading," or upward mobility, has become evident. The young married couple moves into a one- or two-bedroom home after making a small down payment. They improve it and stay until rising income and a larger family require that they move up into a new project in a higher price class.[28]

William H. Whyte, Jr., sees in these suburbs the new managerial class on the first rung up.[29] "Under the television aerials" in the "Levittown-like" suburbs are the junior executives, industrial civil servants, young corporation lawyers, engineers, and salesmen. He finds they share three things in common: they are between 25 and 35, they are organization men, and all are on the move—whole towns of them. They are the future managers of industry; they are tran-

---

[26] Leo F. Schnore, "The Functions of Metropolitan Suburbs," *American Journal of Sociology*, 61:453–54 (March 1956).

[27] Leo F. Schnore, "The Growth of Metropolitan Suburbs," *American Sociological Review*, 22:165–73 (April 1957).

[28] "Suburbia–Exurbia–Urbia," Part I: "Suburbia," *Newsweek*, April 1, 1957, pp. 36 ff.

[29] William H. Whyte, Jr., "The Transients," *Fortune*, May, 1953, pp. 112–17.

sients moving up vocationally; and they will also move up into new residential communities commensurate with their climb in earnings and status.

Sylvia F. Fava studied the suburbs in an attempt to find out if there was in the residential suburbs a suburban "way of life."[30] The residential suburb was found to have a preponderance of married couples with children, families of middle-class status, privately owned homes, low population density, and a greater availability of open space than was found in the city. The residential suburbs were found to be characterized by a high degree of neighborliness and other informal primary-group contacts. Thus, the residential suburb may be contrasted with the city, which is traditionally viewed as being largely composed of secondary-group-type relationships.

Although the lure of more space, better housing, and greater neighborliness is a basis of the outward expansion, one cannot overlook the fact that it "is the thing to do." Being so, status motivations are very much to be reckoned with. The wealthy obviously select those suburbs which afford privacy and enhance status. The rest share these motives and the rewards of status that accompany the expenditure of less resources in the "right" place.

For four decades the outer fringe of great cities has been growing more rapidly than the central city. Between 1950 and 1956 the suburbs grew six times as fast as the central cities. *Newsweek* has predicted that in the future 80 per cent of the nation's residential growth will be in the suburbs.[31] As a consequence suburban counties have grown more rapidly in population than other areas. The fingers of urban expressways reach further out into the country, and traffic problems increase. More of America's farm land is being absorbed into housing projects and rural tracts for urban residents, some of whom do part-time farming, but many of whom use the rural landscape only for maintaining a horse or dogs or merely to guarantee peace and privacy.

The decentralization of industry and business has not been so extensive as some earlier writers predicted. Certainly the residential community has exploded outward faster than its economic life, extending the distance the city worker must drive to his place of work or business. Yet industry is shifting from the central zone to the outer zone of the large city. For example, one study has found that Chicago, during the 1940–1950 decade, lost 112 industrial plants from its

---

[30] Sylvia Fleis Fava, "Suburbanism As a Way of Life," *American Sociological Review*, 21:34–37 (Feb. 1956).

[31] "Suburbia," *op. cit.*

URBAN GROWTH — IN SUBURBAN AREAS

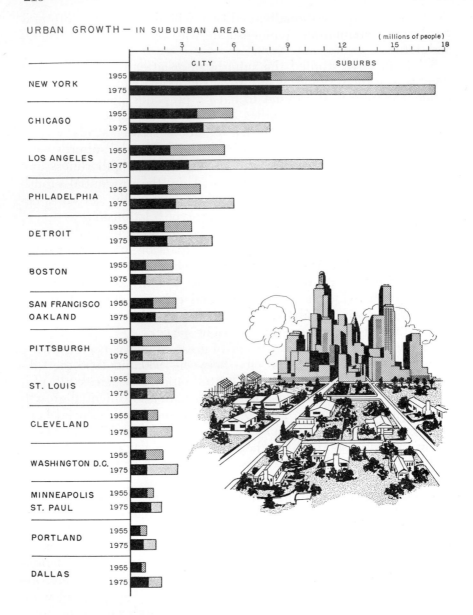

American Suburban Growth Will Continue

Projections for the future indicate that the rapid growth of the years ahead will be in the fringe area of the cities, as it has been for most of the first half of this century. (Based on estimates made by *U.S. News and World Report*) inner zone but gained plants in its outer zone.[32] Such shifts do bring industrial jobs closer to the residents of satellite areas. This trend of urban ecology creates many new problems for the city planner, distorts rural property values, forces farmers on the fringe out of farming, since the urbanite wants roads, central water and sewage systems, dial telephones, and all the conveniences of city living. No farm can carry the cost of such assessments. At the same time, many farmers have profited greatly by the inflation of real estate values.

All of these ecological trends have been greatly accelerated during the postwar period, as prosperity has made people more mobile and more able to afford the kind of living and group relationships they desire.

The outlying farm is still isolated, and with the expansion of the size of farm units in many areas, it is further from neighbors than ever before. Most farmers are still owner-operators, and the farm is still by and large a one-family enterprise, even though corporation farms are on the increase. But the year-round road has made his isolation less real, and his children in most sections no longer attend a one-room rural school, but a town consolidated school. He listens to the same radio and television programs as city dwellers.

SUMMARY

In conclusion, it is clear from this discussion that society has a territorial dimension. Groups tend to be formed on the basis of their occupying a common territory. The spatial structure of groups has a vital bearing on interaction patterns and on personality formation. This has been demonstrated by a brief survey of various classical sociological studies.

The usefulness of locality group classifications for the purposes of population study and for the study and analysis of social organization and interaction patterns of both rural and urban areas has been shown. Typical locality groupings in rural life and in the metropolis have been surveyed.

Changing ecological patterns are modifying rural and urban groups. Interest groups have taken over rural America, although locality as such is still important. Suburban living is creating a new kind of family life, and neighborhood life in metropolitan areas, and now exurbia, is emerging as a locality group of the elite.

[32] Walter T. Martin, "Ecological Change in Rural Areas," *American Sociological Review*, 22:177 ff. (April 1957).

SOURCEBOOK READINGS

FREEDMAN, RONALD, AMOS H. HAWLEY, WERNER S. LANDECKER, GERHARD E. LENSKI, and HORACE M. MINER. *Principles of Sociology* (rev. ed.). New York: Henry Holt & Co., Inc., 1956.
  1. HARRIS, CHAUNCY D., and EDWARD L. ULLMAN, "The Nature of Cities," pp. 374–80.
  2. ZORBAUGH, HARVEY W., "The Dweller in Furnished Rooms: An Urban Type," pp. 471–75.
  3. SHAW, CLIFFORD R., and HENRY D. MCKAY, "Spatial Distribution of Juvenile Delinquency," pp. 482–85.

GITTLER, JOSEPH B. *Social Dynamics*. New York: McGraw-Hill Book Co., Inc., 1952.
  4. BERCOVICI, KONRAD, "Around the World in New York," pp. 135–37.
  5. GILMORE, H. W., "The Old New Orleans and the New," pp. 137–48.

KOENIG, SAMUEL, REX D. HOPPER, and FELIKS GROSS. *Sociology: A Book of Readings*. Englewood Cliffs, N.J.: Prentice-Hall, Inc., 1956.
  6. EDWARDS, ALLEN D., "Types of Rural Communities," pp. 285–91.
  7. DICKINSON, ROBERT E., "What Is a Metropolitan Community?" pp. 292–95.
  8. MUMFORD, LEWIS, "The Evils of the Modern Metropolis," pp. 295–301.
  9. LAAS, WILLIAM, "The Suburb as a City Problem," pp. 306–11.

LEE, ELIZABETH BRYANT, and ALFRED MCCLUNG LEE. *Social Problems in America* (rev. ed.). New York: Henry Holt & Co., Inc., 1955.
  10. RUMNEY, JAY, and SARA SHUMAN, "The Cost of Slums," pp. 91–92.
  11. WHETTEN, NATHAN L., "Suburbanization," pp. 100–05.

O'BRIEN, ROBERT W., CLARENCE C. SCHRAG, and WALTER T. MARTIN. *Readings in General Sociology* (2d ed.). Boston: Houghton Mifflin Co., 1957.
  12. *Fortune*, "Two Billion People," pp. 51–56.
  13. OGBURN, WILLIAM FIELDING, "Air Transportation and the City," pp. 83–86.
  14. MARTIN, WALTER T., "Adjustment to Residence in the Rural-Urban Fringe," pp. 86–91.
  15. FREEDMAN, RONALD, and MORRIS AXELROD, "Who Belongs to What in a Great Metropolis?" pp. 112–18.
  16. WHYTE, WILLIAM H., JR., "How the New Suburbia Socializes," pp. 308–13.

SCHULER, EDGAR A., DUANE L. GIBSON, MAUDE L. FIERO, and WILBUR B. BROOKOVER. *Outside Readings in Sociology*. New York: The Thomas Crowell Co., 1956.
  17. MUMFORD, LEWIS, "The Intolerable City: Must It Keep on Growing?" pp. 612–28.
  18. WIRTH, LOUIS, "Urbanism as a Way of Life," pp. 628–36.
  19. HOYT, HOMER, "The Pattern of Movement of Residential Rental Neighborhoods," pp. 636–46.
  20. MARTIN, JOHN BARTLOW, "The Strangest Place in Chicago," pp. 658–68.

WILSON, LOGAN, and WILLIAM L. KOLB. *Sociological Analysis*. New York: Harcourt, Brace & Co., Inc., 1949.
  21. BURGESS, ERNEST W., "The Growth of the City," pp. 407–14.
  22. GILMORE, HARLAN W., "The Old New Orleans and the New: A Case for Ecology," pp. 414–24.

SELECTED READINGS

ALLEN, FREDERICK LEWIS. "The Big Change in Suburbia." *Harper's*, Part I, June, 1954, pp. 21–28; Part II, July, 1954, pp. 47–53.

BOGUE, DONALD J. *Population Growth in Standard Metropolitan Areas, 1900–1950*. Washington, D. C.: Housing and Home Finance Agency, 1953.

COOK, R. C. *Human Fertility: The Modern Dilemma*. New York: William Sloane Associates, Inc., 1951.

GROSS, EDWARD. *Work and Society: The Sociology of Work Relations.* New York: The Thomas Crowell Co., 1958.

HATT, PAUL, and ALBERT J. REISS. *Reader in Urban Sociology.* Glencoe, Ill.: Free Press, 1951.

HAWLEY, AMOS H. *Human Ecology.* New York: The Ronald Press Co., 1950.

LEE, ROSE HUM. *The City: Urbanism and Urbanization in Major World Regions.* Chicago: J. B. Lippincott Co., 1954.

MARTIN, W. T. "The Structuring of Social Relationships Engendered by Suburban Residence," *American Sociological Review*, 21:446–53 (1956).

QUINN, JAMES A. *Human Ecology.* Englewood Cliffs, N. J.: Prentice-Hall, Inc., 1950.

RIEMER, SVEND. *The Modern City.* Englewood Cliffs, N. J.: Prentice-Hall, Inc., 1952.

RIESMAN, DAVID (in collaboration with Renel Denney and Nathan Clazer). *The Lonely Crowd.* New Haven: Yale University Press, 1950.

SMITH, T. LYNN, and C. A. McMAHAN. *The Sociology of Urban Life.* New York: The Dryden Press, Inc., 1950.

WHYTE, WILLIAM H., JR. "The Transients," *Prize Articles, 1954.* New York: Ballantine Books, Inc., 1954, pp. 39–112.

YOUNGER, J. ARTHUR. "We Need a Department of Urbiculture." *This Week Magazine,* Aug. 9, 1956, pp. 8 ff.

Chapter 12

Casual Groups: Audience, Crowd, and Mob

A teacher of philosophy cautioned his class "Never get lost in a crowd." Watch behavior of people in a crowd, during strikes, athletic contests, in riots—circumstances in which a spirit of excitement grips them—and the statement becomes meaningful. At such times individuals often do things they never intended to do and later regret. During a recent riot following a football game, for example, two neighboring student bodies battled over the goal posts. A young man made this comment about his roommate: "He is a quiet fellow. I didn't know he had it in him, but when I looked up, I saw him socking fellows right and left. He's a short, stocky fellow. They couldn't dent him. But he was socking so hard he literally raised them off their feet and tumbled them."

Likely as not the roommate did not know he had it in him either. Yet in the excitement of a crowd, with the enemy pummeling him, he became exceedingly aggressive. Of course, college students will not ordinarily expose themselves to broken noses, broken ankles, black eyes, and bruises, but gripped by the excitement of this momentary cause, they lose perspective.

This spirit, which captures people in the excitement of crowd situations, is so real that many early sociologists and psychologists talked about crowd mind or mob psychology and visualized a super force taking over a group in physical contact during a period of excitement. Today, sociologists do not explain this behavior in terms of any super mind, but simply in terms of the intensive excitement which seems to be pervasive when large groups of people come together before a common focus of excitement.

GROUP BEHAVIOR ILLUSTRATED

There follows a classic account of a crowd experience—mob violence in an Army situation. In this account there is a basic prejudice already in existence but the excitement carries many far beyond the limits intended. They almost commit murder. Yet, probably not a person in the crowd, acting alone, would have thought of harming the individual concerned.

"We had fallen out and were lounging before our tents when a strange soldier from another regiment passed rapidly down the company streets. 'There'll be some fun at the sutler's[1] shack, just before taps,' he remarked to no one in particular. Twenty paces further on he repeated his statement, mechanically, and we heard him repeat it once more as he passed by the mess tent on his way to another company . . .

" 'What do you think?' murmured my teammate Buck, an eager boy, enlisted under age. 'They've been talking of running the sutler out.' 'Nothing to it,' I asserted. 'They wouldn't dare. Anyway, you and I are going to keep out of it.' 'Well, all right. But damn the sutler.'

" 'Amen,' I agreed. It was two weeks beyond pay day, and not a soul in the company had any money left. The sutler had garnered it all. What could you expect? After two hours' drill on a sweating morning, one had to drink, but not, if he could help it, the tepid water in the company barrel, tasting of vegetable mold and vinegar-soaked wood. At the sutler's were to be had lemonade, passably cool and refreshing, even if it was made without lemons, bottled soft drinks, and a marvelous beverage known as 'blackberry bounce' which made a total abstainer grotesquely gay. Until the pay ran out, the sutler was confronted from morning till night with thirsty and hungry soldiers, sometimes in ranks ten deep. And from morning till night an ugly quarrel was going on over his counter.

" 'Here, you damn dago, I gave you a dollar. Where's my change?' 'No, no, you gave me fi' cents.' 'You're lying. Give my change or I'll knock your damn head off.'

". . . If the trouble maker was very persistent, the sutler would shell out the change with a poisonous gesture. He was an Armenian, and no doubt had learned in the trade with Kurds how far one may defy, how far one must compromise with violence. Current report was that the sutler made a regular practice of short change, but there was a strong minority opinion that this report was eight-tenths pure fabrication and one-tenth founded on mistake. Several men in my

[1] (Author's note) Tradesman near an Army camp.

company boasted of their success in getting drinks for nothing and bullying the sutler out of change besides. Probably someone else suffered for it . . .

"The sutler's shack stood in a clearing about equidistant from the four regimental camps on which he preyed . . . The dusk was growing heavy, I was preparing to turn in when Buck whispered, 'There aren't ten men in D company's tents. Our boys are all gone, too' . . . 'Come on!' cried Buck, tugging at my belt. I blew out my candle and stepped out of the tent. Men from other companies were stealthily slipping through between the tents, headed for the sutler's . . . 'Hello!' sounded a voice in my ear. 'Did he short change you?' 'No,' I replied, 'I never trusted him to make change.' 'You were smart. I don't know another man he hasn't skinned!' . . . 'Gosh! Hear em?'

"I caught a confused wave of sound, shouting interspersed with shrill whistles. We began to run. In the clearing, under the flickering gasoline torch, hundreds of men were packed about the front of the sutler's shack. The Armenian stood in the doorway, pale but imperturbable, his eyes glaring fiercely, his thick lips curving in a nervous smile. The crowd was keeping its distance, as word had passed back from the front that the sutler had his finger on the trigger of a six-shooter. We were after fun, not shooting, and it was enough to hurl imprecations at him. When Buck and I arrived, the spirit of the crowd was good humored, for the most part, but occasionally one could perceive a note of real hatred. What seemed like a deliberate competition in imprecations got in motion, and the more violent curses gained rapidly over the milder ones. The character of the voices too began to change: the currents of deep notes and high would occasionally reinforce each other and make one thrill unaccountably. The crowd was pressing closer. The Armenian kept his nerve, but the movements of his head were becoming spasmodic. It was still fun with us, but the idea that it was serious was visibly gaining on the Armenian.

" 'Poor devil,' I thought, 'this has been carried about far enough.' And then a new baying note rose from the mob, a note I had not supposed to be within the range of the human voice. I shivered and as I glanced again at the Armenian, darting his eyes from one quarter to another in suppressed panic, I felt my pity slip from me. I began to exult, like a hunter who has found a wild animal in a trap, to finish at leisure. 'Kill the damn thief! Kill the damn dago!' the crowd was yelling. It thrilled.

"There was a lull: something was going on that we in the center could only divine. Above the mutterings, subdued for the moment, we heard a sound like the splitting of a timber. Word passed from the flanks of the crowd. 'They've pried out a plank behind.' The Armenian turned to look back into his shack: his jaw dropped; his thin acquisitive profile quivered; the white of his eye seemed to glaze. A sharp pebble hurled from behind him struck him just below the cheek bone; it clung for a second, like a hideous black growth, then dropped, thrust out by a jet of blood. A mantle of frenzy fell upon the mob. An atrocious roar arose, carrying on its waves all the obscenities and blasphemies known to young America.

"'Kill the damn Jew! Kill the God damn Nigger!' The mob surged forward; all around the men wedged between converging lines of force were crying out that they were being crushed. The Armenian darted into his shack, snapping the door to in the face of a dozen men springing for him . . . The shack was rocking on its foundations: another thrust, and over she'd go. Suddenly I became conscious of a weakening of the pressure from behind me; of a subsidence of volume of yells; of a subtle change in the quality of the sound . . .

". . . 'Fix Bayonets!' sounded the command, distinctly. 'The regulars!' murmured voices all around me. In an instant were we rushing across the lighted space, in a panic as infectious and as blind and overpowering as our rage of a moment past . . ."[2]

In October, 1938, Orson Welles decided to dramatize on a nation-wide radio hookup a fictitious invasion from Mars. Starting a regular program, he suddenly broke the sequence with the usual technique of a sudden interruption for a momentous news event. He told, in excited tones, how a mysterious meteorite had fallen at Grover Mills in New Jersey, and reported that the New Jersey police were hurrying to attack the visiting warriors from Mars. As Welles built up dramatic incidents, panic raced through the hearts of a vast audience of American citizens. Here is a description of selected public reactions.

". . . In Newark, New Jersey, in a single block, more than twenty families rushed out of their houses with wet handkerchiefs and towels over their faces. Some began moving household furniture. Police switchboards were flooded with calls inquiring, 'Shall I close my windows?' 'Have the police any extra gas masks?' Police found one family waiting in the yard with wet cloths on faces contorted with hysteria. As one woman reported later:

I was terribly frightened. I wanted to pack and take my child in my arms, gather up my friends and get in the car and just go north as far as we could.

[2] Alvin Johnson, "Short Change," *New Republic,* March 23, 1918, pp. 381–83.

But what I did was just sit by one window, praying, listening, and scared stiff, and my husband by the other sniffing and looking out to see if people were running . . .

"In New York hundreds of people on Riverside Drive left their homes ready for flight. Bus terminals were crowded. A woman calling up the Dixie Bus Terminal for information said impatiently, 'Hurry please, the world is coming to an end and I have a lot to do.'

"In the parlor churches of Harlem evening service became 'end of the world' prayer meetings. Many turned to God in that moment:

I held a crucifix in my hand and prayed while looking out of my open window for falling meteors . . . When the monsters were wading across the Hudson River and coming into New York, I wanted to run up on my roof to see what they looked like, but I couldn't leave my radio while it was telling me of their whereabouts.

Aunt Grace began to pray with Uncle Harry. Lily got sick to her stomach. I don't know what I did exactly but I know I prayed harder and more earnestly than ever before. Just as soon as we were convinced that this thing was real, how petty all things on this earth seemed; how soon we put our trust in God!

"The panic moved upstate. One man called up the Mt. Vernon Police Headquarters to find out 'where the forty policemen were killed.' Another took time out to philosophize:

I thought the whole human race was going to be wiped out—that seemed more important than the fact that we were going to die. It seemed awful that everything that had been worked on for years was going to be lost forever.

"In Rhode Island weeping and hysterical women swamped the switchboard of the Providence Journal for details of the massacre, and officials of the electric light company received a score of calls urging them to turn off all lights so that the city would be safe from the enemy. The Boston Globe received a call from one woman 'who could see the fire.' A man in Pittsburgh hurried home in the midst of the broadcast and found his wife in the bathroom, a bottle of poison in her hand, screaming, 'I'd rather die this way than that.' In Minneapolis a woman ran into church screaming, 'New York destroyed— this is the end of the world. You might as well go home to die. I just heard it on the radio.'

"The Kansas City Bureau of the AP received inquiries about the 'meteors' from Los Angeles; Salt Lake City; Beaumont, Texas; and St. Joseph, Missouri. In San Francisco the general impression of listeners seemed to be that an overwhelming force had invaded the United States from the air—was in process of destroying New York and threatening to move westward. 'My God,' roared an inquirer into a telephone, 'where can I volunteer my services, we've got to stop this awful thing!'

"As far south as Birmingham, Alabama, people gathered in churches and prayed. On the campus of a Southeastern college—

The girls in the sorority houses and dormitories huddled around their radios trembling and weeping in each other's arms. They separated themselves from their friends only to take their turn at the telephone to make long distance calls to their parents, saying goodbye for what they thought might be the last time . . ."[3]

THE NATURE OF CASUAL GROUPS

The two cases presented above portray a quite different type of group relationship in operation than those previously discussed. In the first instance, a crowd of soldiers is transformed into a mob, with the intent of lynching an exploitive tradesman. The second case shows a radio public suddenly converted by fear into a panicking, hysterical frame of mind, many of the public hastening to prepare themselves for the next world, or to protect themselves by police assistance from the threatened danger.

These groups are temporary and transient. In one case they are not even in physical contact, but scattered throughout a nation. They are a group in that for the time interval of a broadcast they have a common focus of interest, a similar response to a situation. They are a listening public.

For want of a better term, all such groups here are termed "casual." They are casual in both the physical and emotional sense. They are at the opposite pole from primary groups, which tend to be enduring in both their emotional bonds and their physical contact.

Casual groups may be broadly classified into *crowds* and *publics*, although within each classification there is great variation in the character of social experience and functions. A crowd, for purposes of this discussion, *includes all casual face-to-face groups. Publics*, by contrast, *include those casual groups based on special interests which never meet except through indirect media of communication.*

A football gathering is a crowd, as was the mob of soldiers. The group is face to face, casual, and extremely temporary. By contrast, radio listeners and stamp collectors are publics. Stamp collectors are a public united by highly specialized hobby interests. The members meet primarily indirectly, through columns of newspapers on stamp collecting, through the catalogues and magazines on stamp collecting, and through personal correspondence.

[3] John Houseman, "The Men from Mars," *Harper's*, Dec., 1948, pp. 74–82.

CROWD BEHAVIOR

Crowd experience, using the term broadly, ranges all the way from the *audience* at the one extreme to the *mob* at the other extreme. It might be represented thus: audience → crowd → mob.

Characteristics of Audiences. An audience is a group met together in a rational frame of mind, with common interests temporarily focused on some line of thought or on some activity. The audience may become a mob if emotion takes over and a high pitch of excitement is reached. If excitement reaches a point where the group gets out of control and violence to persons or destruction of property results, the crowd becomes a mob.

Take the case of Judge Ben Lindsey, who was in his time an advocate of companionate marriage. As a judge in the Juvenile Court of Denver, he had become aware of the problem of sex delinquency among high-school youth. He thought the main cause was delayed marriage and recommended a sort of trial marriage which would let the youthful couple live together in the parental home until schooling was complete, having legitimate sex relations. They would be given information concerning birth control and expected to practice it. In case of conception, the marriage would become permanently binding. Judge Lindsey argued that most such companionate relationships would mature into happy and successful marriages. Those that did not could be terminated without the formalities and embarrassment of divorce.

Clearly such a system, no matter how serious and well-meaning the propagator of it, would raise a storm of protest, as it challenged the very foundations of American marriage and sex mores. Clergy were among the most aggressive in condemning the Judge and his advocated reforms. Bishop Manning of the Cathedral of Saint John the Divine in New York City took it upon himself to preach a special sermon on the Lindsey proposal. On this dignified occasion the Judge, present in the audience, arose when the sermon was finished and demanded that he be permitted to state his side of the question. "He was promptly howled down, ejected from the church, arrested, and charged with disorderly conduct."[4]

Public leaders, particularly when speaking to large groups, must be masters at converting the audience into a crowd, if they desire to secure action. W. D. Scott, in his classic *The Psychology of Public Speaking*, instructed orators in the art of developing crowd-mindedness. He stated as axiomatic that, "The difficult task is not to con-

[4] "Clash in a Cathedral," *Outlook and Independent*, Dec. 17, 1930, p. 604.

vince and sway the crowd, but to create it." He then continued to outline for the student of public speaking standard methods which public speakers use in converting an audience into a crowd. A common device is to get them to sit close together. A packed house is not only easier to speak to but also is easier to unite in a spirit of rapport which fuses the audience and speaker into an emotional unit. The use of ritual, to get all the crowd to act together, is an advantage in creating crowd psychology. Thus the revivalist develops a routine of getting the group to sing together, clap hands together, raise hands together, wave their handkerchiefs together, and go through other such performances of rhythm. The more swing and rhythm the leader can introduce, the more his listeners tend to reach the point where they act in unison.

Cheering together is a common method of crowd leadership in other types of groups, notably the athletic contest, but it is used also in the audience in the form of hand clapping when the speaker appears on the platform, when he finishes speaking, or in the political rally, when he makes a point which is particularly appealing. Clever speakers try to "bring down the house" by applause at regular intervals in order to hold attention and to build group rapport.

Scott instructs the aspiring young orator to weld the audience together into one unit by presenting common ideas, preferably ideas that are associated with feelings that bring a universal response. Such words as freedom, liberty, equality, Christian brotherhood, or such famous names as Washington, Lincoln, Jefferson, and Edison make a common appeal to most audiences and win sympathy for the speaker and for the cause he represents.

Rapport in the Audience. An audience possesses a certain amount of group rapport distinct from that aroused by the speaker; each member of the audience, even though his attention is directed toward the platform, seems to affect the others. Perhaps it is the sense of unity created by many persons assembled for a common purpose.

In all three types of face-to-face casual groups—audience, crowd, and mob—a certain amount of rapport exists; that is, there is a common feeling of participation. This is so strong that early students of society thought of the crowd as representing a type of group-mindedness which was produced almost automatically by leaders. They even used quite literally the phrases, "crowd mind" and "mob mind," implying that crowds are distinct personal entities. They believed that crowds are pervaded by a collective consciousness which temporarily robs the individual of his own self-consciousness, dissociates his mind from reasoning processes, and makes him a victim of the emotions which surge through the crowd. Thus when an audience becomes converted into a highly emotional crowd, with the attendant milling, rhythm, sense of security, and anonymity, the individual member tends to act with the mass, no matter how irrational this action is and no matter how violent it may become.

There is no question about the impelling force of the crowd and mob spirit on the individual. This is evident throughout the account of the soldiers mobbing the sutler. One can feel the spirit of the mob carrying the teller of this tale along. He, his pal, perhaps most of the mob, are being carried along on the emotional swell far beyond anything they intended when they headed for the sutler's cabin. And just as suddenly their irrational hatred, their beastly passion to kill and destroy, vanished when the regulars appeared and they fled in panic.

Everyone who has participated in an excited crowd or in a mob knows how easy it is to get carried away and to do the irrational thing because others are doing it. At the moment it seems appropriate.

So one must grant that the crowd spirit is a powerful motivating force, and the mob spirit even more so. There is such a thing as rapport in the casual group, but to call it mob mind or crowd mind, and to assume that the crowd is a separate entity, is overstating the case.

Research evidence does, however, support the view that crowd rapport affects individual behavior even in ordinary audience situations. Some years ago a psychologist at the University of Illinois studied the effect of seating positions in large lecture rooms on success of performance of members of classes.[5] The experiment was carefully conducted in five large lecture rooms and related midsemester, laboratory, and final grades in the courses to seating positions in the lecture rooms. All students were alphabetically seated and retained the same seats throughout the semester. Courses using the lecture, the quiz, and the laboratory methods were studied.

It was found that an appreciable advantage was gained by students who occupied a central position in the lecture room, where they were completely surrounded by other students, as compared to those who occupied the outer sections of the room. Even aisles down the middle of the room, a group of empty seats, or pillars in the room measurably reduced student performance. The observer concluded that probably the main factor was that persons in the middle of a room who are compacted together in an audience sense greater social

[5] C. R. Griffith, "A Comment Upon the Psychology of the Audience," in M. Bentley (ed.), "Critical Experimental Studies in Psychology from the University of Illinois," *Psychology Monographs*, 20:36–47, No. 136 (1921).

integration with the group than those on the periphery. The integration of even a rational audience is then not only around the speaker, but also within the audience itself.

Suggestion and Crowd Behavior. Most persons have at some time or other felt the impelling force of emotion in crowd situations where rapport is greatest. This is achieved by *suggestion*. Under its stimulus they have done things which they would not have done under any other circumstance. They have booed in a most discourteous manner, have wept almost uncontrollably, and have thrown pop bottles at the umpire. In the intensity of such situations murder has often been committed by mobs, as in lynching and strikes, and often by good Christian people who as individuals would never think of employing violence.

There is the compelling force of suggestibility, rapport, and emotional intensity in a crowd which tends momentarily to reduce to a minimum the individual's power of self-decision. Actually, however, this need not be attributed to any mysterious force. Everyone is highly susceptible to suggestion. From earliest childhood, all learn to follow the suggestions of parents and others in the primary group. All learn to imitate what others do. All habitually respond to group pressures of one sort and another and to group controls. Only in this way can they become socialized human beings adjusted to group life.

It is natural when large groups get together and the atmosphere is one of response to emotional appeal that one should respond to the suggestion, should feel the thrill of emotional excitement that tingles through the crowd, and, unless he actually checks himself by reasoning processes, should find himself participating in what the crowd does.

Excesses in Crowd Behavior. Crowd behavior sometimes takes an extreme form which affects large groups of people, even reaching out to persons not massed together as a face-to-face group. Such contagious psychological sprees have been labeled *mental epidemics*. Such historical cases as the California gold rush, the Florida land boom, or, at an earlier period of history, the Crusades, are illustrative of mental epidemics which seem to seize large segments of the population, involving them in migration or in fantastic quests for sudden wealth.

The following graphic description of the great Florida land boom of the middle 1920's is typical. Although this author did not carry the story to its ultimate conclusion, the outcome is anticipated in the psychology of the situation itself.

"The smell of money in Florida, which attracts men as the smell of blood attracts a wild animal, became ripe and strong last spring. The whole United States began to catch whiffs of it. Pungent tales of immense quick wealth carried far.

" 'Let's drive down this summer when it's quiet,' said canny people to one another in whispers, 'and pick up some land cheap.'

"Concealing their destination from neighbors who might think them crazy, they climbed into the flivver, or big car, or truck, and stole rapidly down to Florida.

"Once there, they found themselves in the midst of the mightiest and swiftest popular migration of history—a migration like the possessive pilgrimage of army ants or the seasonal flight of myriads of blackbirds. From everywhere came the land-seekers, the profit-seekers. Automobiles moved along the eighteen-foot-wide Dixie Highway, the main artery of East Coast traffic, in a dense, struggling stream. Immense buses bearing subdivision names rumbled down loaded with "prospects" from Mobile, Atlanta, Columbia, or from northern steamers discharging at Jacksonville. A broken-down truck one day stopped a friend of mine in a line. The license plates were from eighteen different states, from Massachusetts to Oregon. Most of the cars brimmed over with mother, father, grandmother, several children, and the dog, enticed by three years of insidious publicity about the miracles of Florida land values.

"The first stories of the realty magicians had been disseminated through small city and country newspapers, particularly in the Middle West. Systematic propaganda stressed the undeniable fact that Florida was an unappreciated playground. Yet that was far less effective advertising than the beautiful, costly free balls given by one subdivision in certain cities. Those who attended shortly afterwards received a new invitation, to go without charge and view lots priced from one thousand dollars up.

"Lured by the free trip, many went. Those who bought at the current prices and promptly resold made money. Other subdivisions met the competition, offsetting the overhead by arbitrary periodic raises in all lot prices. Whole states got the Florida habit. The big migration began.

"Millions—variously estimated from three to ten—visited Florida last year, investing three hundred million dollars, and bank deposits swelled till they neared the half-billion mark in July.

"Joining the great migration this summer, I went inclined to scoff. Were the others also confident that they possessed average good sense and were not likely to be fooled much?

"Probably. I was lost, I gambled. I won. I remained to turn land salesman. Not only with no superiority, but with defiant shame rather than triumph, I confess—not brag—that on a piker's purchase I made in a month about $13,000. Not much, perhaps, but a lot to a little buyer on a little bet."[6]

A few years later incomplete houses were burned to avoid paying taxes. Unfinished hotels, acres of unfinished subdivisions, planned towns and cities were as desolate as the ghost towns of exhausted mining camps and cut-over forest areas.

Social Usefulness of Crowds. How are such casual groups as crowds, which represent but a segmentation of the human personality, to be evaluated in modern society, and what functions do they perform?

In a society which is characteristically one of secondary group experience, casual groups play a vital part in carrying out various specialized functions and in meeting specialized needs of mankind. Crowd behavior, with its suggestibility and its emotional tone, provides a way for securing action in large groups ordinarily rather lethargic to numerous public interests. Suggestion is the device used by modern evangelical religious groups in their tabernacle crusades and by community chests in their great rallies with which fund-raising drives are started. It is used by the political organization to rally supporters and to fire them with enthusiasm and zeal so that they will go out and build and keep alive a political organization to support the party candidates. Englishmen viewing the 1956 American political conventions for the first time on television labeled them "organized lunacy." They are, but they fire the spirit of the loyal for the election fight ahead. Even educational institutions, in connection with endowment campaigns, hold great rallies to secure the support of the alumni, public-spirited citizens, students, and teachers. So one might go on listing numerous situations in which crowds are manipulated to inspire action for civic or institutional developments.

Numerous crowd situations provide only a recreational function. Most people cannot participate in competitive athletics, but the masses can be there as rooters to enjoy the thrill of associating with thousands of people in applauding, cheering, and watching the colorful athletic ceremonies. At the more conservative type of crowd gatherings, such as public forums, the give and take of debate and public argument are vital factors in forming group opinions on public issues.

[6] G. M. Shelby, "Florida Frenzy," *Harper's*, 78, 180 (1926).

Even crowd responsiveness to excitement is not necessarily a social liability. It becomes so when exploited by leaders to the point of blindly following a fanatic. It is undesirable when it leads to mob violence. But in many forms of crowd behavior the emotional excitement provides wholesome release from tension. The hilarious indulgence of impulses that are stifled in more formal group situations is a highly desirable and satisfactory experience. Modern man is much restrained in his emotional nature by numerous social control devices. It is a healthy thing to release pent-up tensions in the unrestrained emotion of a baseball or football game or political rally. Our culture approves yelling oneself hoarse on such occasions. He can act without dignity and know that everyone else in the group is doing the same. He need feel no sense of guilt and no sense of social condemnation.

There is much less destructive deviltry in communities with vital athletic contests for youth than in isolated communities where young people have to break up the revival meeting or chase the school teacher out of the neighborhood to have any excitement. A football game is as good as a lynching or a strike to provide excitement and far more accepted as a device for expressing emotion in crowd situations.

Frank Tannenbaum attributes the lynching of earlier days in part to a lack of other emotional outlet in the Cotton South. He says:

"It is this dead monotony which makes the occasional lynching possible. One has seriously to ask why and how a people so generous, kindly, hospitable, free-spirited, and brave as are the people of the South can indulge in a lynching. There is seemingly only one answer. The white people are as much the victims of the lynching—morally, probably more so—as is the poor Negro who is burned. They are starved emotionally. They desperately crave some excitement, some interest, some passionate outburst. People who live a full and varied life do not need such sudden and passionate compensations; but those whose daily round never varies, whose most constant state is boredom, must find some outlet or emotional distortion.

"Something happens; a rumor is spread about town that a crime has been committed. The emotions seize upon this, and the people are in a state of frenzy before they know what has taken possession of them. Their thwarted impulses become the master of the situation. The emotional grip is unrelenting. Men and women are transported from a state of comparative peace into one of intense excitement. The lynching takes place not because the people enjoy it, but because the passions, the shouting, the running, the yelling, all conspire to give the starved emotions a full day of play. What happens is that, instead of planning a lynching for the sake of the excitement, the excitement determines the lynching, and the people who commit it are its victims. It takes place not because they desire the thrill that it brings, but the thrill determines its occurrence. The outburst victimizes the population, and is only a cruel compensation for many months of starved existence.

"After the lynching the community settles back to a state of quiet. One exhausting orgy is enough to last a long while; it provides material for discussion, for argument, for explanation, for reflection. In dull moments the whole thing is lived over again. It helps one to come to grips with the world; it stabilizes the existence of the unfortunate community."[7]

PUBLICS

A public has been defined as a group with special interests held together through indirect means of communication. This does not mean that small sectors of a public may not get together as audiences or crowds or even as mobs; but the group as a whole never meets face to face. Publics in the modern world are numerous—investors, society women, consumers—all are publics. Every magazine has its public, as do actors and television gagsters. They never meet except on pages devoted to special interests in the Sunday paper, in special trade journals which come to these groups, in magazines, on the screen, or through other such means of indirect communication. Advertising and business cater to publics. Publics may have their national, regional, state, and local conventions where selected numbers of them meet as audiences.

The term *general public* is often used; usually meaning the voters or the total body of citizens of the nation, who are conscious of their group ties primarily in times of war or in times of national election. In the field of economics, the term "general public" means the consumers, who in reality include everyone who uses goods produced by the economic system. These numerous publics are responsible for many forms of social interaction which characterize what some sociologists have called the *great society*. By this is meant a society such as exists in and among modern nations which are linked together by press, radio, and other such means of communication, and among which a certain degree of unanimity of opinion prevails, even in the absence of close association.

[7] F. Tannenbaum, "The Ku Klux Klan," *Century,* 105:878–79 (1923). Cf. also his *The Darker Phases of the South* (New York: G. P. Putnam's Sons, 1924), pp. 24–26.

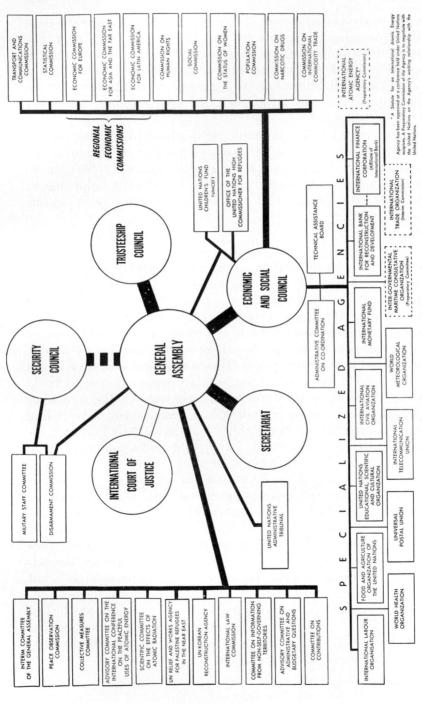

A New Venture in the Great Society

Many branches of the United Nations aim to encourage understanding on a world-wide scale. None is more significant than UNESCO (United Nations Educational, Scientific, and Cultural Organization), for it promotes cultural exchange.

is so accurate that the attitudes and voting behavior of 50,000,000 people can be predicted with a small percentage of error.

DISCUSSION AND REVIEW QUESTIONS

1. What is meant by the concept "casual groups"?
2. Into what two broad classifications are casual groups divided?
3. Distinguish between crowds and publics.
4. Compare three types of crowd situations.
5. Cite an example of a group of people in a short space of time shifting from one extreme to the other of crowd behavior.
6. Mention some of the devices used for converting an audience into a crowd.
7. Present evidence to show that rapport within a group affects individual behavior.
8. Discuss suggestion as a phase of group behavior.
9. Is crowd behavior undesirable? Defend your answer.
10. Characterize the mental epidemic.
11. What do we mean by the term "general public"? "great society"?
12. Show how casual groups are influenced in the great society.
13. Describe tactics of propagandists and pressure groups.
14. What device has been developed for studying public opinion?

SOURCEBOOK READINGS

GITTLER, JOSEPH B. *Social Dynamics.* New York: McGraw-Hill Book Co., Inc., 1952.
  1. DOUGLASS, JOSEPH H., "The Funeral of 'Sister' President: A Case of an Expressive Crowd," pp. 86–88.
  2. RAPER, ARTHUR F., "A Case of a Lynching Mob," pp. 88–91.
KOENIG, SAMUEL, REX D. HOPPER, and FELIKS GROSS. *Sociology: A Book of Readings.* Englewood Cliffs, N.J.: Prentice-Hall, Inc., 1956.
  3. WIRTH, LOUIS, "The Nature of the Mass," pp. 373–74.
  4. *Life* and *Time*, "Types of Mass Behavior," pp. 378–80.
  5. BLUMER, HERBERT, "The Formation of a Crowd," pp. 381–83.
  6. *Life*, "The Cairo Riot," pp. 385–86.
  7. BLUMER, HERBERT, "The Nature of the Public," pp. 387–88.
  8. *Time*, "An Urban Public; Dispute in Dubuque," pp. 388–89.
  9. BARBER, BERNARD, "The Messianic Movement," pp. 415–19.
O'BRIEN, ROBERT W., CLARENCE C. SCHRAG, and WALTER T. MARTIN. *Readings in General Sociology* (2d ed.). Boston: Houghton Mifflin Co., 1957.
  10. BROOM, LEONARD, and PHILIP SELZNICK, "The Jackie Robinson Case," pp. 286–89.
  11. CANTRIL, HADLEY, "The Invasion from Mars," pp. 289–93.
SCHULER, EDGAR A., DUANE L. GIBSON, MAUDE L. FIERO, and WILBUR B. BROOKOVER. *Outside Readings in Sociology.* New York: The Thomas Crowell Co., 1956.
  12. JORDAN, JOE, "Lynchers Don't Like Lead," pp. 274–87.
  13. HOUSEMAN, JOHN, "The Men from Mars," pp. 287–301.
  14. WHITE, E. B., "Camp Meeting," pp. 302–8.
WILSON, LOGAN, and WILLIAM L. KOLB. *Sociological Analysis.* New York: Harcourt, Brace & Co., Inc., 1949.
  15. PRUDEN, DURWARD, "A Sociological Study of a Texas Lynching," pp. 335–43.

SELECTED READINGS

ALBIG, WILLIAM. *Modern Public Opinion.* New York: McGraw-Hill Book Co., Inc., 1956.

ALLPORT, G. W., and L. POSTMAN. *The Psychology of Rumor.* New York: Henry Holt & Co., Inc., 1947.

BOGART, LEO. *The Age of Television.* New York: Frederick Ungar Publishing Co., 1956.

HOVLAND, C. I. and others. *Experiments on Mass Communication. Studies in Social Psychology in World War II,* Vol. 3. Princeton: Princeton University Press, 1949.

KLAPPER, JOSEPH T. *The Effect of Mass Media.* New York: Columbia University Press, 1949.

MERTON, ROBERT K. *Mass Persuasion.* New York: Harper & Brothers, 1946.

SCHRAMM, WILBUR (ed.). *The Process and Effects of Mass Communication.* Urbana: University of Illinois Press, 1954.

SELDES, GILBERT. *The Great Audience.* New York: The Viking Press, Inc., 1950.

WHYTE, WILLIAM H., JR. *Is Anybody Listening?* New York: Simon & Schuster, Inc., 1952.

WOLFENSTEIN, MARTHA, and NATHAN LEITES. *Movies: A Psychological Study.* Glencoe, Ill.: The Free Press, 1950.

Chapter 13

Racial Groups

One cannot travel around the world without being impressed with the different shades of color which peoples in various parts of the world exhibit. And the white man, in traveling, will probably be rather shocked to find that the fair white skin, which he tends to identify with mental and cultural superiority, is scarcely to be found in the vast, densely populated areas where the majority of men live.

The white man is definitely a minority group among human beings. Shades of color from black to white are richly blended among peoples in most parts of the world, some moving toward one extreme and some toward the other. The same is true of other physical characteristics such as thickness of lips, color of hair, hair texture, straightness or kinkiness of hair, shape of the jaw, the head, the height of the forehead, the contour of the face, the length of extremities, the height and weight, and the thickness of the body. In these respects, humanity offers very diverse patterns.

The most significant aspect of race is not any of the physical traits but what peoples choose to make of them in their relationships to each other. It is this aspect of race with which the sociologist is concerned, for it is this which ignores ability, physical energy, longevity, and whatever else may be important biologically and socially.

In the following account a famous American Negro author describes the dawn in his consciousness of a sense of being different because his skin was black.

"Between me and the other world there is ever an unasked question: unasked by some through feelings of delicacy; by others through the difficulty of rightly framing it. All, nevertheless, flutter round it. They approach me in a half-hesitant sort of way, eye me

241

curiously or compassionately, and then, instead of saying directly, How does it feel to be a problem? they say, I know an excellent colored man in my town; or, I fought at Mechanicsville; or, do these Southern outrages make your blood boil? At these I smile, or am interested, or reduce the boiling to a simmer, as the occasion may require. To the real question, How does it feel to be a problem? I answer seldom a word.

"And yet, being a problem is a strange experience—peculiar even for one who has never been anything else, save perhaps in babyhood and in Europe. It is in the early days of rollicking boyhood that the revelation first bursts upon one, all in a day, as it were. I remember well when the shadow swept across me. I was a little thing, away up in the hills of New England, where the dark Housatonic winds between Housac and Taghkanic to the sea. In a wee wooden schoolhouse, something put it into the boys' and girls' heads to buy gorgeous visiting-cards—ten cents a package—and exchange. The exchange was merry, till one girl, a tall newcomer, refused my card—refused it peremptorily, with a glance. Then it dawned upon me with a certain suddenness that I was different from the others; or like, mayhap, in heart and life and longing, but shut out from their world by a vast veil. I had thereafter no desire to tear down that veil, to creep through; I held all beyond it in common contempt, and lived above it in a region of blue sky and great wandering shadows. The sky was bluest when I could beat my mates at examination time, or beat them at a foot-race, or even beat their stringy heads. Alas, with the years all this fine contempt began to fade; for the worlds I longed for, and all their dazzling opportunities, were theirs, not mine. But they should not keep these prizes, I said; some, all, I would wrest from them. Just how I would do it, I could never decide; by reading law, by healing the sick, by telling the wonderful tales that swam in my head—some way. With other black boys, the strife was not so fiercely sunny: their youth shrank into tasteless sycophancy, or into silent hatred of the pale world about them and mocking distrust of everything white; or wasted itself in a bitter cry, Why did God make me an outcast and a stranger in mine own house? The shades of the prison-house closed round about us all: walls strait and stubborn to the whitest, but relentlessly narrow, tall, and unscalable to sons of night who must plod darkly on in resignation, or beat unavailing palms against the stone, or steadily, half hopelessly, watch the streak of blue above."[1]

1 W. E. B. DuBois, *The Souls of Black Folk* (Chicago: A. C. McClurg & Co., 1903).

THE REALITY AND THE FICTION OF RACE

It is generally assumed, both by those who take an evolutionary view and those who take a creation view of origins, that man had a single origin. The most convincing evidence is the fact that the cross between the races is fertile, indicating that they belong to the same biological stock. Blood transfusions may also be given across racial lines.

Anthropologists and historians are inclined to favor some spot in Southwestern Asia or North Africa as the original cradle of man. From that point, members of the race migrated out to various parts of the world. Through the centuries *mutations* developed to start the different races which now characterize mankind. The various peoples of the world became isolated in different environments, and the different racial strains that developed through hereditary mutations were thus perpetuated. It is likely also that climate and other environmental conditions tended to select certain types for particular areas.

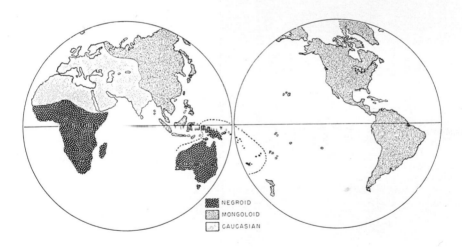

NEGROID
MONGOLOID
CAUCASIAN

Distribution of the Primary Racial Stocks of Man

The maps show the outline distribution of the primary races of man according to the threefold classification. Australians, Ainu, Vedda, Polynesians, and others in that region are included in the stock with which they appear to affiliate most closely. (From Anthropology, *by A. L. Kroeber, p. 133, copyright 1923, 1948 by Harcourt, Brace and Company, Inc., and reproduced with their permission.)*

The Major Races of Man

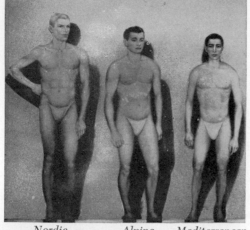

Caucasoid

Nordic   *Alpine*   *Mediterranean*

Mongoloid

Polynesian   *Mongolian*   *American Indian*

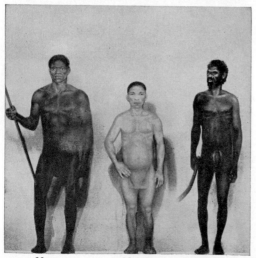

Negroid

Negro   *Negrito*   *Oceanic Negro*
(American Museum of Natural History)

Whatever the reasons for their original differentiation, there are today three major branches of mankind and numerous sub-branches. These race groups are set apart by physiological traits. A race is, in fact, a social group that possesses unique *physiological* characteristics. In making racial classifications, the physical anthropologist considers such measurements as the cephalic index, that is, the ratio of the head length to its width; the nasal index; color, texture, and straightness or kinkiness of hair; body proportions; the projection of the jaw; and color of eyes and skin.

In the classification of races the physical anthropologist is not concerned with their cultural level or their mental traits. He is interested only in physical characteristics as such. It must be kept clearly in mind, therefore, that race from the standpoint of science is purely a physiological fact.

THE THREE MAJOR RACES

There is general agreement among physical anthropologists concerning the three major races of mankind: the *Caucasoid*, or white; the *Negroid*, or black; and the *Mongoloid*, or yellow race. The so-called red and brown races are really hybrids, that is, mixtures of these others. There is some difference of opinion concerning the classifications of sub-branches of the human race; in fact, many sub-branches merge into each other in physical characteristics, so that a classification has to be more or less arbitrary.

The Caucasoid or white race is characterized by light pigmentation, fine silky hair, and a high nose bridge that tends to be narrow to medium. The modern distribution of this race is chiefly in Europe and eastward to the far border of India and in the Americas.

The Negroid group is characterized by dark pigmentation, coarse, wiry black hair, short, broad nose, and thick lips. In addition to the African Negroes, who make up the largest branch of this race, are the Oceanic Negroes found in Melanesia. Their hair is more woolly and their noses more hooked than the typical African Negro. The third branch is comprised of the Negritoes, or pygmies, found in Central Africa, the Malay Peninsula, and the Philippines.

The Mongoloids are characteristically yellow and have slanting eyes, broad faces, and a squat build. The Mongoloids are found primarily in China and Japan, although the American Indian is of Mongoloid derivation. The Indonesians of the Malay Peninsula, the Polynesians, Hawaiians, Samoans, and certain peoples of Southern India seem to be a mixture of the Mongoloid, Caucasoid, and Negroid types.

Branches of the Caucasoid Race. Three major branches of European Caucasoids are recognized by all anthropologists: (1) The *Nordic* branch is characterized by tall stature, fair skin, and long-headedness. It is best represented by peoples in the Scandinavian Peninsula and in the northern countries of Europe. (2) At the southern extreme of the European continent is the *Mediterranean* branch of the white race. This racial subgroup is short, long-headed, and dark-skinned, that is, brunette rather than blonde. Anthropologists believe that this is probably the oldest race in Europe. Greeks, Italians, and other peoples bordering the Mediterranean are most characteristic of this group, but the race is spread eastward to the eastern border of India. (3) In central Europe, between the Nordics and Mediterraneans, is the *Alpine* branch which is, typically, medium in stature, strong and stocky in build, with medium or mixed complexion. This race is broad-headed. Anthropologists classify it as the newest race in Europe.

Outside the European continent there are two main branches of the white race: the *Armanoids,* who are dark, medium-thickset in stature, and found primarily in Armenia, Turkey, Syria, and Persia; and the *Ainu,* an almost extinct branch, of stocky build and hairy body, which is found in Japan.

Today most of the European racial stocks are so badly mixed that detection of pure types is difficult. The population of the British Isles is also a mixture of Caucasoid types, and the population of the United States is an even greater mixture of the European branches of the Caucasoid race.

RACE AND NATIONALITY

Race and nationality are not identical. Although people frequently speak of the French race, the English race, or the German race, this is incorrect. While certain peoples may have lived together in the same nation long enough to build a sort of racial type within the nation, most nations of western Europe are a mixture of races, with one of the subbranches of the white race predominating.

Race is a classification of groups by *physical type;* nationality is a classification of groups based on *political autonomy.* Wars have been fought in Europe between so-called races, the term having been twisted in meaning to suit the purpose of a political leader. Although Hitler built a regime on the theory of the Aryan stock of the German people, the Aryan race as he defined it is largely fictional.

THE FICTION OF RACIAL SUPERIORITY

Although race is a physical distinction, the assumption has often been made that race differences exist in mental traits and general mental ability as well. It is assumed that races might presumably differ in brain structure and nervous system and therefore in the capacity to learn. Much literature in favor of the view that the races do differ in mental ability has been circulated during the last half-century. This literature had as its objective the defense of white superiority. Its authors were propagandistic rather than scientific. For example, Gobineau, a French nobleman, wrote a book called *The Inequality of the Races* (1855) in which he tried to demonstrate the inferiority of the colored races. In the United States, Madison Grant, a retired businessman, took up the race crusade under the title *The Passing of the Great Race* (1916). This was definitely a propaganda book against immigrants; it argued that the immigrants were threatening to pollute the American population stock and reduce the racial quality of the next generation. Lothrup Stoddard wrote *The Rising Tide of Color* (1922), when Orientals were beginning to be discriminated against on the West Coast. He propagandized against the Oriental and made many Americans feel that it was only a matter of time until they would be overwhelmed by the prolific yellow-skinned peoples on the other side of the globe.

These racist propaganda works affected the American people so forcefully at the beginning of the century that the race problem became an important political issue. It was assumed, and propagandists so argued, that the various races in Europe which were entering the United States threatened the superior blood of the American people. Every device of science, therefore, was employed during the early part of the century to search for a scientific answer concerning the relative ability of the various peoples of Europe and the Orient.

It was taken for granted that the Northern Europeans and English had the greatest ability, since these stocks had, during the nineteenth century, populated the United States. The propagandist argued that Southern European stocks, which had begun to enter in great numbers after 1890 and which were coming into the country at a rate of almost a million a year after the turn of the century, were inferior peoples. The Orientals also were supposed to be an inferior race and to threaten the economic welfare of the nation as well as its blood stream.

Scientific research on an extensive scale was initiated to show not only which races but also which nationalities had sufficient native ability to be admitted as immigrants.[2] Over the years since 1900 three general types of evidence have been employed to get at the problem of racial abilities: (1) physiological differences; (2) psychological differences; (3) historical differences.

Physical Differences. The physiological difference of greatest concern in early research into race differences was that of brain size. It was assumed that if differences in brain size could be established, differences in racial ability could be assumed. The skulls of representatives of the various extinct races were filled with millet seed or shot and the size of the brain thereby determined. With living peoples external measures of skull capacity were used. It was found that there are great differences in the brain sizes of various human beings. But much to the surprise of the investigators, certain eminent Europeans had very small brains, and the difference between the size of the brain within the same race was found to be greater than the difference in size between the major races. Women's brains were found to be smaller, on the average, than those of men. The question then began to be raised as to whether or not the size of a brain was after all indicative of its capacity. After some years, investigators concluded that brain size has no real significance as a measure of intelligence.

Another series of studies centered about an attempt to demonstrate the similarity of various branches of the race to the ape. This also proved to be a fruitless hypothesis. One race has greater similarity to the ape than others in some respects but is less like the ape in other respects. For example, the white race has thin lips, as does the ape, and is most like the ape in hairiness of body. The Negro, on the other hand, has dark pigmentation like the ape. Then more scientific-minded investigators raised the question of whether or not ape-likeness in physical traits would prove ape-likeness in mind. It was soon found that such an assumption did not make sense, especially when all evidence pointed to the fact that the adult white male is more like the ape than any other age, sex, or race group. The older he gets, the more like the ape he becomes in hairiness of body and general features.

[2] For example, see such works as Clifford Kirkpatrick, *Intelligence and Immigration* (Baltimore: The Williams & Wilkins Co., 1926); R. M. Bache, "Reaction Time with Reference to Race," *Psychological Review*, 2:475–86 (1895); S. J. Holmes, "Will the Negro Survive in the North," *Science Monthly*, 27:557–61 (1928); R. B. Bean, "Some Racial Peculiarities of the Negro Brain," *American Journal of Anatomy*, 5:352–433 (1906); F. Boas, "Human Faculty as Determined by Race," *Proceedings of the American Association for Advancement of Science*, 43:301–27 (1891); R. S. Woodworth, "Racial Differences in Mental Traits, *Science*, 31:171–86 (1910); Otto Klineberg, *Race Differences* (New York: Harper & Brothers, 1935).

Psychological Differences. Some of the earliest psychological tests of race differences dealt with sensory acuity of the various races—tactual sensation, keenness of eyesight and hearing, and reaction time. Some surprise was registered when it was found that primitives were not as superior to civilized man in the five senses as had often been supposed by anthropologists, explorers, and missionaries. After it was discovered that Negritoes at the St. Louis Exposition in 1904 could not hear as well as American whites, anthropologists suggested, more or less seriously, that maybe the testers should have cleaned out the Negritoes' ears before giving the tests. In general, studies of race differences in sensory perception showed little differences other than what might well be accounted for by difference in interests and training.

Scientific mental testing got under way with psychological examinations, which in their early days were looked upon as definite measures of innate ability. Tests were soon used to demonstrate race differences. It was found, for example, by Army mental tests given soldiers during World War I that the average mental age of the white was 13.1 years, that of the Negro only 10.4 years.

Various examinations were given also to European branches of the white race. It soon appeared that the Southern European was of much lower intelligence, as measured by intelligence tests, than the Northern European. The same tests, however, showed that the American-born Oriental usually tested high. In time more critical scholars began to challenge intelligence tests as a measure of innate ability. They raised the question of whether or not opportunity as well as heredity might not affect intelligence-test scores. Their theory on this point proved to be correct. Actually, certain disadvantaged groups of Southern whites proved to have lower mental ability as measured by intelligence tests than did certain groups of Northern Negroes.

After the arguments subsided to the point where scientific logic ruled, it had to be concluded that the differences revealed by intelligence tests reflected primarily differences in opportunity for learning and for breadth of experience which various members of the race and nationality groups had had, not differences in hereditary factors that were characteristic of the race itself. Most scholars have concluded with regard to difference in mental ability of the races that there may be differences, but certainly there is no conclusive evidence of general inferiority or superiority of any one race over the other.

Differences in Culture History. The argument for historical proof of race differences centers about the culture-building achievements of the races. During the period of known history, various race groups have achieved different levels of culture. At various times in history one race or the other has been at the focal point of cultural achievement, and at any given time one may find branches of certain races that are far below others in civilization. For example, the red man in North America, who stems from the Mongoloid race, was a primitive when the white man came. His civilization was a Stone-Age civilization as ancient as that of the white man in western Europe many centuries earlier. The rural Negro in Africa is a primitive man still today. He is far below the level of civilization of the Negro in the United States who has had opportunity to absorb the white man's civilization in the twentieth century.

Of course the critical scholar must take into account the peculiar accidents of cultural history in order to give race as such a proper evaluation from this perspective. It is true that through much of history the Negroid races have been slave races, although in the Medieval period Negroes of the Western Sudan of Africa had a civilization superior to that of Europe of the time. The University at Timbuctu was one of the greatest of its time. The Mongoloids have built a great civilization in the Far East. The Caucasoids have built a great civilization in the West.

It has been demonstrated again and again that given opportunity for learning, any race is capable of quickly acquiring the civilization of another. Take, for example, primitive aborigines from the bush country of Australia, one of the lowest levels of civilization in the world. Children from this culture, who are accustomed to sleeping naked with only lean-tos for shelter in the worst of weather, and whose culture provides implements more primitive than Stone-Age men, learn American culture in mission schools as readily as white children. The same is true of African natives.[3] The evidence seems to prove that with equal opportunity the historical difference between races can disappear in one generation.

The impartial student of race has to conclude that what the unsuccessful branches of the various races need is not a change in genes but a chance.

RACISM

Social relationships between human groups are not governed by the strict logic of science. In spite of the fact that anthropologists,

[3] Colin Ross, "Primitives and Civilization" (translated from the German), *Living Age,* 143:409–12.

Are Their Architects Inferior To Ours?

Or is the cultural heritage within which they work? The anthropologist says such differences in patterns are due not to race but to culture.

Zulu women building framework of beehive hut (Information Office, Union of South Africa)

Bushman hut in Kalahari Desert, Bechuanaland (British Information Services)

American college dormitory (WSC Photo, State College of Washington)

who know most about race, have for more than a generation held that there is no inferior race in the world, the social system in many parts of the world continues to act as though there were. Our own social system embraces this attitude.

Racism, the expression of this theory, is extant in many parts of the world, especially in the Western world. It is revived again and again to suit the convenience of rulers, or to give one race a competitive advantage over another living in the same environment. "Racism," as Ruth Benedict points out, "is the dogma that one ethnic

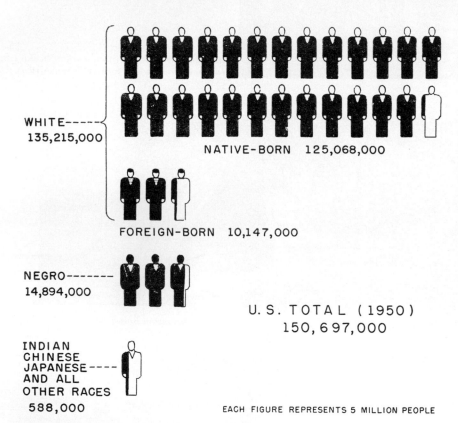

WHITE-----
135,215,000

NATIVE-BORN   125,068,000

FOREIGN-BORN   10,147,000

NEGRO-------
14,894,000

U. S. TOTAL (1950)
150, 697,000

INDIAN
CHINESE
JAPANESE ----
AND ALL
OTHER RACES
588,000

EACH FIGURE REPRESENTS 5 MILLION PEOPLE

A Pictorial Summary of Race Groups in the United States, 1950

Nearly nine out of ten of the people of the United States are white. Of nonwhites, 85 per cent are Negroes. In recent years the nonwhite population has been growing at a higher rate than has the white population; for example, nonwhites increased from 10.4 per cent of the population in 1950 to 10.9 per cent in 1956. In 1956 the total population had increased to 168,091,000. Of this total, 149,824,000 were white and 18,268,000 nonwhite.

group is condemned by nature to congenital inferiority and another group is destined to congenital superiority."[4]

The worst revival of this doctrine in the modern world was under the Hitler regime in Germany where he created the fictitious Aryan race (a language group) in order to revive German pride. On this fiction he built a eugenic program. On this myth he went out to conquer the world. The inferior but fictitious race that was used as a focus for rallying the German people was the Jew (a religious group), who presumably represented the degenerate characteristics of mankind. The Aryan race, of which he set out to build a super-race, expected to defeat the degenerate races of democratic society.

Racism comes to the fore on a less extensive scale wherever prejudice exists against a social group. The Jew is pointed to as a race in many cultures when it suits the convenience of those who wish to persecute him as a minority group. He is, in reality, a blending of many racial types.

Even nationalities are labeled as a distinct race by groups which have prejudice against them. During the history of American immigration, each new nationality group was looked upon as an undesirable race. Each in turn faced the prejudice and discrimination that strangers and newcomers have experienced throughout the centuries: Irish, Swedes, Norwegians before 1860; Germans between 1860 and 1890; Italians and "Bohunks" after 1890; "Chinks" and "Japs" always.

Even in the drought migration of the 1930's from Oklahoma and Arkansas to California in particular but also to the other coast states, the stigma of an inferior group attached to the interregional migrants. Although they were recognized as belonging to the same race, the same kind of prejudices were leveled at them that are leveled at an immigrant group or a distinct racial group. The terms "Arkies" and "Okies" were used to stigmatize these migrants as an inferior and degenerate element of the American population. It was not until the war opportunities opened industrial doors to them that they lost their identity as a separate group and became a part of the social and economic life of the communities in which they settled.

Where nationality is the basis of "race" discrimination, prejudice usually dies down in a relatively short period of time because where there are no marks of race difference, intermarriage and the rapid acquisition of the culture by the immigrant group blends the newcomers in with the older group. They lose their identity and, thereby, the fiction of race inferiority which was once attached to them.

[4] Ruth Benedict, *Race, Science and Politics* (New York: Modern Age Books, 1940).

The real difference between race attitudes and other forms of prejudice against nationality or newcomer groups with a lower standard of living than the prevailing one is that skin color differences are not so easily lost. The identity of the racial group tends to be perpetuated through the generations, and the prejudice, thereby, tends to live rather than to disappear with the absorption of the group. It is for this reason that skin color, the main popular index of race group differences, is such a fundamental factor in social relationships in all societies and particularly in modern society, where worldwide commerce and travel have brought different race groups into closer contact.

THE PROBLEM OF RACE MIXTURE

From a standpoint of social policy, what should be the attitude of a people toward race mixture, scientifically termed *miscegenation* or *amalgamation,* where different racial groups exist in a society? The question is an important one, but cannot be answered in terms of biological laws as such. From a biological standpoint the crossing of pure strains of animals frequently produces hybrid vigor, that is, a much stronger strain than existed before the cross. It is likely that the same law applies to human races, but the difficulty is that we have few pure racial strains left and do not get a real hybrid cross in most cases. Even if hybrid vigor could be demonstrated and we had pure racial stocks to cross, the question of race intermixture could not be answered on that basis. It must be answered in terms of sociological consequences.

Generally speaking, the half-breed is rejected by both major racial groups. He is not accepted fully in either society, although he is forced to find most of his social life in the group with inferior social status. There are, of course, places where race mixture is logical from a sociological standpoint. In Hawaii, for example, race mixture has been characteristic for generations and is accepted in social tradition.

By contrast, in the United States intermixture goes on primarily between the poor elements of both racial stocks, and the race mixture is usually at the expense of the group of inferior status. It often takes the form of exploitation. The half-caste is rejected by white society, although in Negro society he tends to rank higher than the Negro. The social position of the family where marriage is prohibited between racial groups is difficult, since neither person in the marriage is fully accepted in the society of the other race. The situation is difficult for the children of the union, since they belong to neither pure racial group.

Sociologists, therefore, have to conclude that race mixture is socially desirable only in those societies where a certain degree of race equality is recognized and where the offspring can be assured an acceptable place in the society.

RACE IN FUTURE WORLD RELATIONS

In general, the world has, since the days of ocean-going travel, been dominated by the European branches of the white race. Conquest, colonialism, missionary evangelism, and commerce of these nations have placed their stamp on races, nations, and religions of other parts of the world. The dark-skinned races have been under greater or lesser subjugation to the fair-skinned peoples of the West.

Even the great Arab world of the Middle East and the peoples of India, both Caucasoid in race but of darker skin than most of the European branches, have felt the impact of these conquerors and their culture.

The epoch of colonization by Western peoples is drawing to an end. Although Prime Minister Winston Churchill declared early in World War II that he had not come to power to preside over the liquidation of the British Empire, he did just that. Not only the colonial empire of Britain but also those of Holland, Belgium, Germany, Spain, and Portugal have been all but terminated as the world enters upon a new era of global interdependence and a growing spirit of united world action.

The Soviet Union has recently embarked on extensive colonization and is building an imperial regime, but the Western nations have developed a spirit of humanitarianism and voluntarily submitted to the checks and balances of world opinion, which condemns this practice by enlightened peoples as contradictory to the spirit of freedom and self-determination by peoples of all lands.

In our age the great dark-skinned belt (black, brown, and yellow), of the world lies for the most part in what has come to be called "underdeveloped countries." The West has set out to develop these areas by technical assistance and capital expenditure. America is a leader in this movement and is motivated quite largely by humanitarian sentiments. Other Western nations are participating, and even the Soviet Union is to some extent, through the offices of the United Nations.

Yet no movement in international relations is devoid of political implications. In a real sense, the descendants of European whites carry forward into the future the liabilities of their colonial past. Among dark-skinned peoples almost everywhere the European white is suspect because of this past, particularly is this true of the British and the French. The United States is trying to avoid this stigma of a history in which it had little part. Yet the Soviet Union points to the stigma of past European colonialism to detract attention from her own current imperial exploits. It is not an easy past to escape.

Among dark-skinned peoples everywhere there is a growing sense of unity, power, and destiny. They want to shake off the shackles of the past not only politically—they have pretty much done that—but even more important, to shake off the stigma of inferiority which they have always been made to feel in a European-white dominated world.

Perhaps the greatest liability of the United States in facing the racial animosities of the world society in the making is the record of having dropped atomic bombs on a dark-skinned people—the first and only such tragic incident in history. This we try to overshadow by worldwide deeds of mercy, but it takes lots of mercy to correct such a lesson of history among dark-skinned peoples.

These peoples have had to watch the Western nations and the Soviet Union in their vicious struggle to win a race in weapons of increasing destruction. One cannot be surprised if they feel uneasy and somewhat distrustful of this power and how it may be used.

It is certain that the dark-skinned races are dominated by a spirit of ferment and hope and that the racial issue is destined to become a major one in the destiny of many in the years ahead. For capital and industrialization the dark-skinned races are dependent upon the industrialized West, as is the industrialized West dependent on raw materials of native lands, particularly of Africa.[5]

SUMMARY

Race is a physical fact, a group classification based entirely on physical characteristics. Supposed theories of the inferiority of certain racial groups have not stood the test of scientific investigation. This, of course, does not change the attitude of the masses of mankind.

The social significance of race lies in the prejudices and attitudes of such groups toward each other, not in scientific demonstrations of differences; in the way various race groups treat each other when they meet, not in the genes. Too often fictions of inferiority have been applied to minority races. They have been exploited and submerged by the dominant race. Throughout history the minority race often has been subjected to slavery by its conquerors. But wherever men have inhabited the same environment, the races have crossed,

[5] See Franklin Frazier, "Race Relations in World Perspective," *Sociology and Social Research*, 41:331–35 (May–June 1957).

beginning the gradual process of bringing all the human race back to common hereditary characteristics.

Racial groups have often been a critical factor in history. They are destined to be so in the future. In fact, the world has entered a period in history when the racial issue is destined to be a major one in political alignments. The European white has a past of colonization, which although perhaps as humanitarian as any in history, if not more so, seems wrong and unjust in the light of current humanitarian values. Rebellion among the dark-skinned races and a cry for genuine racial equality is heard everywhere. (The status aspect of this problem of race, particularly as manifest in the United States, is the topic of Chapter 19.)

The desirability and the undesirability of race mixture depends on social attitudes rather than upon biological consequences. Where social recognition is given to the half-caste race, no serious problems result. But in most social systems intermarriage between the races leaves the married couple outsiders in both societies and places the child in a social position wherein he is rejected in a measure by both societies.

DISCUSSION AND REVIEW QUESTIONS

1. What is a race as the term is defined anthropologically?
2. What evidence is there to indicate that the races have a single origin?
3. Name the three major races of mankind and give their physical characteristics.
4. Name and locate the three European branches of the white race.
5. Distinguish between race and nationality.
6. Did early theories of race differences emerge from fact or prejudice?
7. What do psychological tests show? How are the results interpreted today?
8. Have measured physiological traits demonstrated the inferiority of any one of the races?
9. What evidence is found in the comparative culture-building achievements of the various races? How is this evidence interpreted today?
10. Discuss racism and evaluate it in terms of scientific research.
11. Why is racism hard to kill, even harder than nationality prejudice?
12. Discuss race mixture, evaluating it both from the biological or hereditary and sociological viewpoints.
13. Discuss the race issue as it has emerged during this century as a major factor in the relationships of major areas of the world.

SOURCEBOOK READINGS

KOENIG, SAMUEL, REX D. HOPPER, and FELIKS GROSS. *Sociology: A Book of Readings.* Englewood Cliffs, N.J.: Prentice-Hall, Inc., 1956.
   1. DUNN, L. C., "What Is Race?" pp. 30–36.
LEE, RAYMOND L., JAMES A. BURKHART, and VAN B. SHAW. *Contemporary Social Issues.* New York: The Thomas Crowell Co., 1955.
   2. MYRDAL, GUNNAR, "An American Dilemma," pp. 466–74.

3. SHAFER, BOYD C., "Men Are More Alike," pp. 458–61.
4. President's Committee on Civil Rights, "To Secure These Rights," pp. 461–66.

LEE, ELIZABETH BRYANT, and ALFRED McCLUNG LEE. *Social Problems in America* (rev. ed.). New York: Henry Holt & Co., Inc., 1955.

5. President's Committee on Civil Rights, "Guilt by Heredity," p. 380.

SELECTED READINGS

ASHLEY-MONTAGU, M. F. *Man's Most Dangerous Myth: The Fallacy of Race.* New York: Columbia University Press, 1942.

ASHMORE, HARRY S. *The Negro and the School.* Chapel Hill: University of North Carolina Press, 1954.

BARRON, MILTON L. *American Minorities: A Textbook of Readings in Intergroup Relations.* New York: Alfred A. Knopf, Inc., 1957.

COX, O. C. *Caste, Class and Race.* Garden City, N.Y.: Doubleday & Co., Inc., 1948.

DUBLIN, LOUIS, A. J. LOTKA, and M. SPIEGELMAN. *Length of Life* (rev. ed.). New York: The Ronald Press Co., 1949.

FAIRCHILD, HENRY PRATT. *Race and Nationality as Factors in American Life.* New York: The Ronald Press Co., 1947.

FRAZIER, E. FRANKLIN. *Race and Culture Contacts in the Modern World.* New York: Alfred A. Knopf, Inc., 1957.

————. *The Negro in the United States* (rev. ed.). New York: The Macmillan Co., 1956.

MYRDAL, GUNNAR. *An American Dilemma: Negro Problem and Modern Democracy.* New York: Harper & Brothers, 1944.

THOMAS, DOROTHY SWAINE, and RICHARD S. NISHIMOTO. *The Spoilage.* Berkeley: University of California Press, 1946. (This is a study of the treatment of the American Japanese population on the West Coast during World War II.)

Chapter 14

Adjustment Processes: Competition, Conflict, Accommodation, and Assimilation

Whenever and wherever human beings come in contact with each other, social adjustment takes place, for men are rarely if ever neutral toward one another. They tend to attract or to repel each other, to associate or to set up bars to hinder social intercourse, to get along together or to fight, to oppose or to cooperate.

This being a basic fact of social life, all sociologists have made some use of these processes of *social adjustment* in analyzing behavior. Some have made "attraction" and "repulsion" the basic processes, but these terms sound so mechanistic that they have little general usage. The terms "association" and "dissociation" are more appropriate. Since, however, they represent the two opposite poles of social adjustment, they are not too useful as analytical tools.

Of wide usage are social adjustment processes employed by Park and Burgess in an early classic work in sociology.[1] They thought of social adjustment as taking place in the following sequences of stages. When social contact takes place between groups, *competition* begins. This form of social interaction is primarily economic. Competition, as it becomes personal, leads to the second stage, *conflict*.

[1] Robert F. Park and Ernest W. Burgess, *Introduction to the Science of Sociology* (Chicago: University of Chicago Press, 1924), chaps. 8–11.

259

Fighting cannot go on forever. Some form of temporary or permanent working relationship must be established. The dissociative
processes—competition and conflict—give way to cooperative processes. A live-and-let-live working relationship gradually emerges in
the third stage and is referred to as *accommodation.* If adjustment
proceeds beyond this stage, *assimilation* is the fourth and final stage
of adjustment wherein the groups become completely merged in
common activity, all sense of difference having disappeared. Thus
accommodation and assimilation are considered associative or cooperative adjustment processes.

Certainly not all contacts between human beings follow through,
uniformly, the four-step sequence of adjustment just described.
This sequence is particularly appropriate for discussing the usual
cycle through which migrant groups pass in their social adjustments
in a new area. The old-world immigrant in America went through
these four steps quite uniformly. First, there was competition with
the American workmen for jobs and housing. The newcomer was
satisfied with a lower wage and poorer living conditions. He was
often the strikebreaker and the victim of resulting conflict. Gradually, various accommodative relationships emerged, and after two
to three generations, he lost his identity as a "foreigner" and became
one of the group (was assimilated). In time, he became as ruthless
in his attitude toward new immigrants as others had been to him.

The Southern Negro in the Northern city tends to pass through a
similar sequence of steps in adjustment, although, because of his
dark skin, he is never fully assimilated. The "Okie" and "Arkie" in
California similarly moved through these four stages of the adjustment cycle.

Outside the traditional Park and Burgess frame of reference for
the study of interaction processes, one may more logically conceive
of social adjustment as a continuum between extreme dissociation
and complete association thus:

Sociation Continuum

Dissociation
                                                                    Association

0
                                                                    100

Opposition processes   Cooperative processes
Conflict   —   Competition   Accommodation   —   Assimilation

While such schematic formulas are helpful, the facts are that the
social processes do not always operate in any order. In the current

case of the Southern Negro the sociation continuum is at least temporarily moving from accommodation to conflict. Both races were accustomed to the caste barriers established by usage until the Supreme Court decision called for a relationship of integration (assimilation). But social processes do not always move smoothly in response to legal edict. In some Southern communities race friction has flared up, and violence and threats of violence have not been unusual. The long-run outcome will undoubtedly be assimilation, but the temporary relationship is at present one of conflict.

COMPETITION AS A BASIC INTERACTION PROCESS

When psychiatrist Alfred Adler applied Freudian psychology to Western society, he found operative a greater urge than the *libido*, which Freud installed in man. He saw the great force to be the competitive one, and man's great suffering, the feeling of inferiority, the self-inflicted torture, come from failure to compete successfully.

W. I. Thomas, early American sociologist, also classed this force among the four great drives ("wishes," he called them) of man. The "wish for recognition" was his designation of man's hunger to satisfy the competitive spirit.

Perhaps sociologists have been too much influenced by the Darwinian concept "survival of the fittest," which assumes that throughout nature there is a constant struggle to obtain space, food supply, shelter, and whatever else is needed for survival in a particular environment. In any case, most of them consider competition a basic, universal, and continuous process. It is hard to find cultures which discourage it.[2]

Impersonal and Personal Aspects of Competition. Men strive for the same goals without any sense of competing. Hog farmers are all competing for the market. Normally if there is a bumper crop, prices drop, and all suffer from their competitive enterprise. Men in rural areas compete with each other for mates, marriageable women being in most farm communities a scarce item. In urban areas, where marriageable men are usually scarce, women compete for mates.

When there is direct personal contact, rather than indirect contact between competitors, the element of personal *rivalry* enters, making the competitive process personal. It is at this point that persons become most conscious of the operation of competition in their experience. Much competition is in the form of personal rivalries for attentions, honors, victories, prizes, goods—such things as cars in a time of production shortage, desirable dates in competition with a

[2] An example is given later in this chapter.

Competition for Free Land—the Cherokee Strip

In Oklahoma on September 16, 1893, all were lined up waiting for the hour when the land was opened up to settlement; then it was the fastest man who won the reward of a homestead. (Oklahoma Historical Society)

fraternity pal, and many other such goals. In this, American society is not unique. Robert H. Lowie, an anthropologist, says, "Primitive man wants, above all, to shine before his fellows; he craves praise and abhors the loss of 'face.' "[3]

Where competition is most intense in American life, a rigorous system of codes comes into effect to regulate behavior and keep competition from getting out of hand. One of the points of greatest competition is at the top of the administrative hierarchy. Here a sort of beginning caste system comes into effect.

Thus in Hollywood there are numerous and subtle patterns of deference for the top executive in the picture industry. And near the top in the military also there is a system of codes and social amenities which set the officers and their wives apart from enlisted men on the basis of rank. And in all big businesses the class code by which conflict is kept at a minimum is recognized by all.

Competition for position in the communications industry has been vividly described by Spectorsky in *The Exurbanites*.[4] This jockeying for position leads to back-stabbing and throat-cutting; yet no person will readily admit that it exists in his own organization or that he personally indulges in it. Yet everyone does it. Everyone acts more important than he is and tries to undercut the rival. All wonder what is going on in the administrative hierarchy that they do not know about and how it may affect them. Thus subexecutives try to get an appointment in the same barbershop as the top executive, to commute on the same train, and to live in the same exurban community.

Competition in Primitive Societies. Presumably the desire to excel or to achieve recognition is to some extent basic in social relationships everywhere. Since individual differences exist as a part of the original nature, it would seem to be a natural thing for those with greater speed, skill, ability, or energy to excel, and for others to look with some degree of respect upon those who do excel. Such seems to be the case in the animal kingdom. In many situations, dominance and submission are characteristic patterns of interpersonal relationships between members of the species. Human cultures may curb these traits, but more often they capitalize on them.

But one can carry that kind of logic too far. Competitive patterns as manifest in any particular society are primarily a reflection of the type of culture pattern which has been developed through the cen-

[3] Robert H. Lowie, *Are We Civilized?* (New York: Harcourt, Brace & Co., 1929), p. 156.

[4] (Philadelphia: J. B. Lippincott Co., 1955), pp. 152–54.

turies by the process of trial and error in working out man's relationship with man in particular natural environments.

Some cultures have been designated by the anthropologist as essentially cooperative; that is, there is a very close working together of the entire group with the mutual interests of all in mind. Individual ascendancy at the expense of others is frowned upon, and in few situations is the individual allowed to get ahead of his fellows. Such a culture was that of the Zuñi of the Southwestern United States. Here is an anthropologist's description of the Zuñi.

"Out of the entire range of human behavior the Zuñi have selected the nonaggressive, sober, cooperative aspects to stress. It is to this norm that the child, if he is to fit into the cultural framework set for him by his parents, must conform. He is not broken or forcibly coerced into this pattern but is gradually fitted into it under the most subtle stress of social sanction. . . .

". . . Zuñi stresses constantly the submergence of the individual in the group, and would frown upon the man who took advantage of his religious position to secure any undue prominence for himself. In his relations to his fellow men he must always cooperate in the work in the fields with the men of his household and with the men of his kiva in the religious performances. Toward all others within the community he may not display any competitiveness. The ideal man in Zuñi is a 'person of dignity and affability who has never tried to lead and who has never called forth comment from his neighbors. Any conflict, even though all right is on his side, is held against him.' He must cooperate readily in both economic and the ritual field."[5]

By contrast, other cultures give the individual a great deal of free play in developing his personality at the expense of others. In these cultures, numerous situations are provided wherein the strongest have a chance to show their strength. Numerous ceremonials and real life situations provide tests for one of ability to show his wealth, physical strength, or artistic talent.

One of the most competitive primitive cultures on the American continent studied by the anthropologists was that of the Kwakiutl of the Pacific Northwest, where the potlatch was the climactic test of ability to outdo a competitor. Here Goldman tells of this major competitive test.

". . . The Kwakiutl are a people of great wealth and they consider it honorable to amass a fortune. But it is not hoarding they are in-

[5] Irving Goldman, in Margaret Mead (ed.), *Cooperation and Competition Among Primitive Peoples* (New York: McGraw-Hill Book Co., Inc., 1937), chap. 10.

terested in. Wealth, such as blankets, boxes, and copper plates, is used in a game of rising in rank, of validating honorific titles and privileges. Upon the occasion of taking on a name a man distributes a considerable quantity of blankets among the men of another numaym in the presence of the entire community. The recipients are obliged to accept the property and must be prepared to repay it at the end of the year with 100 per cent interest. Such men probably have property out at interest, which they call in at the end of the year to meet their payments. Should a man be unable to repay he is "flattened" and falls in social status. The victor, on the other hand, rises another rung in the social ladder. With each successful potlatch a man accumulates more renown as well as more property with which to conduct even greater potlatches. With prestige the driving motive in Kwakiutl society and with the basic intent of the potlatch the crushing of a rival, these property bouts take on a fiercely competitive tone."[6]

American culture too favors strenuous competition between those equally matched. If teams are unequal, the sympathy of the observer is usually with the underdog. This is probably rooted deeply in pioneer tradition and in a democratic philosophy of life. It is well enough for the strong man to win, but it is even better to see a person or team considered weaker come to the top by virtue of strenuous effort and sheer personal merit.

The victory of the weak over the strong is the plot of practically all comic scripts. Not only does this theme appeal to children and adults alike in America; it appeals to peoples everywhere. The amazing success of Disney's Donald Duck and Mickey Mouse throughout the world is no doubt due to the fact that wherever the masses of men are suppressed by the mighty, as is true throughout much of the world, this theme appeals. This is why Disney's characters are more famous and widely known throughout the world today than the political leaders of our time.

CONFLICT AS A TEMPORARY INTERACTION PROCESS

Conflict is a *temporary* form of social interaction. It is personal, and its aim is to destroy the opponent. In business the aim is to drive the competitor to bankruptcy, as in the case of gasoline wars or other cases of severe price-cutting. In war between political groups, the aim is to annihilate the enemy by destroying him as a political entity or at least to bring him into subjection. Conflict in its ideal form always aims at destruction of opponents, but civilization has de-

6 Goldman, in Margaret Mead, *op. cit.*, chap. 6.

Independent speechmaker

Fighting It Out for Campus Office

The conflict here is symbolic. Symbolic conflict is the goal of civilized society. Democratic society substitutes the rebellion of the ballot for that of the battlefield, and this is now the goal of mankind in the international forum. (WSC Photo, State College of Washington)

Political parade

Greek bandwagon

veloped ways of mediating it, refining it to a less violent, animal-like kind of interaction.

Conflict, as an extreme dissociative interaction process, finds a much less prominent place in the American society today than it has in many societies. Good sportsmanship is taught in every aspect of life, even to some extent in war. In the athletic contest a sportsmanship honor award is given to the athlete who follows the highest code of courtesy and fair treatment of opponents and teammates. In business, even, there is a code of ethics, and most states have fair-trade practices which aim at eliminating tactics of conflict which will destroy opponents. Members of professional groups, who are competing with each other for patronage, likewise have strict codes of ethics involving colleagues. Professions, like medicine and law, are forbidden to advertise beyond listing the "professional card." Dueling has been not only outlawed but eliminated from the code of gentlemanly conduct.

War as a Form of Social Conflict. War is by far the most comprehensive of conflict processes in the modern world. Today any war tends to become worldwide and to involve not only the participants but also innocent peoples. War is a type of conflict that aims at the physical and political destruction of the opponent. It sets aside under customary terms the usual mercies and considerations that go with the high standards of ethics and ideals that have developed in the humanitarian sentiments of mankind. It leads to the destruction of untold wealth, to the destruction of millions of lives through the conflict process. When the enemy is annihilated to the point where he admits defeat and surrenders, peace treaties are drawn permitting a system of accommodation to replace conflict. The system of accommodation in international relations is called peace.

Among primitives, war is often much more like a game than a destructive activity. When the going gets too rough, as in most other games, they quit the play. Generally speaking, among primitives the lower the level of civilization, the less man has indulged in warfare; and the higher the level of civilization, the more he has been given to warfare.[7] This generalization does not hold true universally but is characteristic.

Often among primitives war affected their lives comparatively little and brought few readjustments. In modern society war affects the entire population and involves almost every aspect of political, family, and social behavior. It has become a kind of activity which

[7] Wilson D. Wallis, *An Introduction to Sociology* (New York: Alfred A. Knopf, Inc., 1927), chap. 20.

modern man can ill afford. Some day mankind will look back upon our day and describe it as a time when wars were fought.[8] Men then will laugh at the military heroes who were the objects of worship in a time when man was dedicated almost as much to destruction as to creation, almost as much to the useless consumption of wealth as to its accumulation.

The conflict process of war has been so much a part of the social experience of central Europe that some of the sociologists there have made conflict the theme of their sociological writings.[9] This process has seemed to them to be the most important one in social inter-action. The conflict process has been found there in its worst form. Century after century wars have been recurrent. The life of man has been warped by war; his philosophy has been colored by war; his families have been destroyed by war; and his culture has paid a tre-mendous price economically and socially for recurrent catastrophic conflict.

In America, conflict of that character has been much less impor-tant as a social process in molding the life of people. The average mother in this country is less likely to think, when considering hav-ing a child, that he is liable to be cannon fodder for the next war, although after two wars within a span of twenty-five years, this factor may be more prominent in the thoughts of mothers in this nation than it was at one time. But certainly it cannot have the prominent place in the popular mind that it does in most European nations which have actually been the battlefields of war.

France, with her flat terrain and geographical proximity to Britain, has been the center of recurrent wars for centuries. Her soil has often been drenched with the blood of battle. Private investment in hous-ing and even many forms of industry lack incentive, and the homes have iron fences with a locked gate. Even the common man in his household is uneasy about the future and suspicious of his neighbor.

Historically, one of the advantages of major conflicts such as wars was that it increased the range of contact and communication among peoples, thus speeding up cultural change by increasing opportuni-ties for borrowing. In primitive times the capture of women and their introduction into a tribe as wives had much to do with the cross-fertilization of culture. In a similar way today, the contact of major nations in war tends to bring many into close association with people and culture of nations in conflict, or with allied nations,

---

[8] *Ibid.*

[9] Ratzenhofer and Gumplowicz were of this group. For a critical review of works making struggle for survival and war their theme, see Pitirim A. Sorokin, *Con-temporary Sociological Theories* (New York: Harper & Brothers, 1928), chap. 6.

thereby speeding up cultural change and extending the range of communication between peoples. It must be recognized, however, that in the modern world such contacts go on continuously without a worldwide conflict. Nonetheless, there is no time when the world is so much in contact and when the peoples of nations mix so freely and intermarry so much as in time of world war.

Ways of Solving Conflict. Sometimes a smothered conflict is quickly solved by bringing it out into the open. Such a procedure is often recommended as desirable in marriage. The people to fear most are those who nurture grudges and harbor resentments rather than quarreling and getting it over with. The following case is that of a college student who illustrates the advantage of this procedure as it affected a childhood relationship.

During the second year in this town, my cousin came to live with us for a year. He and I did not get along too well. He was getting some of the care that was once mine. We would always argue, but would never come to blows. This kept up until one day my cousin found some of my possessions that I had hid from him. I told my mother, and instead of punishing him, she called both of us in and asked us what it was all about. When she found out that we were hiding things from each other, she became angry. She called in all the neighbor boys, and then put boxing gloves on us and told us to fight until we could learn to get along with each other. We fought until neither of us could lift a glove. Neither of us were hurt, except that our pride suffered before our friends. After that, we got along and shared everything we owned.

Conflict in society, because of its intent to destroy the enemy, is always socially costly. It is costly in war, in labor relations, in the mountain feud, in personal relations. Devices of a social nature have to be established for mediating it and bringing about the termination of hostilities. In the case of war the flag of truce can always be raised when one is ready to say that he has had enough. So, also, in the personal fight. In many cases, a neutral party has to be the arbitrator, bringing the conflict to an end by persuasion or by stepping in at the request of parties in conflict. Thus the mediator or arbitrator tries to bring out of the conflict a situation of accommodation or of cooperation, whichever may be possible.

ACCOMMODATION AS A SOLUTION TO CONFLICT

Accommodation refers to the working out of steps whereby the fight can be called off and new working relationships established.[10] The term is also used to designate a state of temporary peace. If, for example, the conflicting parties are nations, they make a truce and

[10] This is the process of accommodation. One may also speak of a state of accommodation to describe the working relationship achieved.

Approved Outlets
for Competition

William James, in a day of instinct
outlets could replace war and at
the maintenance of the "manly
therapist sees in them a legitimate
and frustration. (WSC Photo, State

later a peace. Still later they may re-establish trade relations and diplomatic relations, thus recognizing each other as nations that have a right to exist on the face of the earth, to claim territory, and to have governments. In the case of a strike the solution is worked out in terms of new working arrangements or by agreement to return to work under the old working conditions.

Among the usual forms of accommodation are: (1) compromise, i.e., both giving ground; (2) domination, as in the case of defeat by conquest; (3) conciliation, in which a common ground for agreement is found; (4) toleration, which is a state of agreeing to live and let live without having anything to do with each other.

In the case of modern nations, peace has proved to be only a temporary form of accommodation, not a permanent one. It exists until rival nations are strong enough or have enough provocations to take up battle again. In industry the relationship between labor and management is usually but an accommodative one, which on very slight provocation again breaks out into conflict. Arbitration boards, medi-

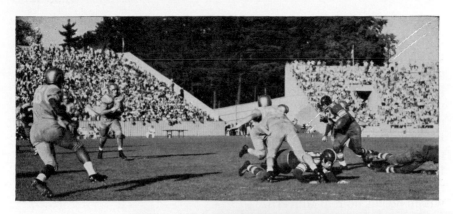

and Conflict

theories, felt that such the same time assure virtues." The modern working-off of hostility College of Washington)

ators, workers' and employers' committees, and numerous other such devices are becoming increasingly useful in maintaining the peace; but, nonetheless, conflict flares frequently in the relationships of most industries with their workers.

In only a few industries which have succeeded in developing a cooperative spirit between management and laborer by profit sharing or other devices is genuine and permanent cooperation realized. One of the notable examples in this country of management cooperation is that of Procter and Gamble which has for years assured the majority of its employees year-round employment. As a consequence of this cooperation, Procter and Gamble has never had any labor trouble. Studebaker, in the automobile field, has a wonderful record of cooperation attained by giving the workers job security, such as few industries have been able to do. The management boasts of the fact that jobs are transmitted from father to son, so that the family is guaranteed a secure place in the industry from generation to generation.

The average worker in America is not interested in owning the industry, but he does want his share of the returns in the form of an adequate wage and good working conditions. His attitude is greatly improved if he can also have some reasonable share of the profits in the form of bonuses, as a reward for conscientious and more than average effort. Thus, industry can give him the same motive for initiative, ingenuity, and creative labor that managers of industry themselves share. In this way, the job becomes much more than a job. It becomes a position in which the worker has a vested interest in doing his best because his best gives something to him and not just to the management and stockholders of the industry, about whom he has no real concern.

In many marriages accommodation, rather than genuine cooperation, characterizes the marriage state. The husband and wife get along together in spite of their perpetual dislikes and antagonism in certain areas. In these families, children, neighbors, and the couple themselves recognize that there is very little real cooperation, but they have declared a sort of truce, mapped out each other's territory for jurisdiction, and managed to get along and to rear their families. Often in the past, because everyone recognized that the relationship was one of accommodation rather than one of romance, they accepted it as such and considered the family successful. And it was, by the standards of the old-fashioned institutional family, which assumed that if a couple maintained their marriage and reared their children to maturity, acquired mutual property, and stuck it out together, they had accomplished about all any human being could accomplish in a marriage relationship.

In most cases of accommodation, conflict flares whenever one party or the other gets off the defined reservation of their relationships to each other.

Accommodation is a natural and necessary psychological process, because conflict becomes exhausting, whether in the war of nations or in the war of couples, whether in mountain feuding, in industrial strikes, or in marriage. Groups usually stop short of complete destruction of one another. It is necessary for them to define the boundary between their places, as in the case of the mountain feud, and to shoot only when one or the other steps over the boundary agreed upon.

ASSIMILATION, THE FINAL STAGE IN COOPERATION

Accommodation is at best a cooperative situation of limited acceptance of the other person or group. The ideal form of cooperation is that realized when groups become so merged (assimilated) that there is no longer a recognition of difference. They work together as one for common ends.

Assimilation on the biological side is complete when intermarriage and the resulting racial crossing (miscegenation) has taken place to the point where race differences are lost. Assimilation on the cultural side is complete when acculturation, that is, the acquiring of the new culture by immigrants, has proceeded to the point where original cultural differences have disappeared. Assimilation on the social side is complete when differences in status are no longer recognized and members of the group associate with no sense of difference and discrimination. Desegregation is a movement aimed at the assimilation of the Negro into present-day American society.

BALANCING COOPERATION AND CONFLICT

In real life the processes of conflict and cooperation gradually merge into each other. In most human relationships, there is some element of both. Even in husband and wife relationships, the most intimate of all human companionships, there is often a delicate balance between conflict and cooperation which gives a marriage zest and interest.

Charles H. Cooley, a shrewd observer of human nature, said: "The best marriage is a kind of strife."[11] He looked upon the sexes as naturally antagonistic as well as complementary, their interests seldom being identical. He believed that out of this complementary antagonism passionate "intimacy" springs. So, also, between the best of friends there is often intense rivalry as they compete in many activities. There may be intense rivalries between groups which often work together. These rivalries may, on sufficient provocation, lead to serious conflict. All human interactional relationships are potentially capable of all degrees of cooperation and all degrees of conflict, even to that of violence which leads to annihilation.

In the area of business competition, an antidote is the Rochdale Cooperative, where all patrons share profits in proportion to the business they contribute to the cooperative during the particular year. As profitable as cooperatives can be to the consumer, the cooperative movement in America has had rough going except in those states which are settled by Danes, Norwegians, Swedes, and other northern Europeans who come out of cultures which are much more cooperative in character. The most successful dairy and consumer cooperatives are in Wisconsin, Minnesota, and other states of that region, settled by people derived from these cultures. In other parts

[11] Charles H. Cooley, *Social Process* (New York: Charles Scribner's Sons, 1922), p. 36.

of the nation private business enterprise, which takes a profit from the consumer, gets most of the patronage of the average American buyer. Buyers are actually willing to give the merchants a reasonable profit if he, in competing with others who are also engaged in business for profit, is able to give them a reasonable product at a fair price.

Cooperation is, however, paid some tribute even in our competitive society. Practically every employer wants to know, when inquiring about a prospective employee, whether or not he can cooperate with his fellows. His ability to cooperate, his ability to get along with his fellows, determines in large measure whether he can have a permanent and useful place in the work organization. This is true in industry and probably even more true in the professions, where ability to cooperate with superiors and with colleagues is considered so important that rarely does any application form for professional position omit it. Cooperation is taught somewhat in schoolrooms. Children are taught that they should get along with each other and play in group games, but even so, the competitive process in most schoolrooms and on most playgrounds is the dominant one, being socially approved and socially encouraged.

In many situations a certain degree of competition, or even conflict, is stimulating and wholesome. It gives zest to human relationships, it forces men at many points to their best efforts. In the field of science, criticism of colleagues is a regularly established part of the folkways, the assumption being that criticism of an objective sort will stimulate productive effort, hold scholars to greater carefulness, and lead to the gradual building of a system of tested knowledge. Science differs from many other systems of knowledge in that it encourages a wholesome conflict in points of view.

The type of social interaction characterizing groups is affected by changes in the population, by the introduction of new cultural elements, by the introduction of new forms of leadership, economic conditions, and numerous other factors. Consider the labor movement in times when jobs are scarce. Competition between workers is at its height, because each worker prizes his job and is willing to exert himself to his utmost in order to guarantee its security. In times of manpower shortage, when labor is scarce in proportion to jobs, cooperation tends to characterize worker relationships. By mutual agreement, and by means of various informal devices of control imposed upon the ambitious worker, trade unions working in the field, say, of building electric motors, agree on the number of pieces of work that are reasonable for the wage they are receiving. Rather than permit the ambitious pace-setter to establish a production level which they will feel obliged to meet, they agree that a certain quota which all can easily meet will be the standard of production. The assumption is that since manpower is scarce and the union is strong, the workers cannot be fired. Even if they were fired, no one else could be hired who would do more. Wages will tend to go up regardless of how much is produced, because of competition between industries for manpower.

The consequence is that labor slows down its production when production is most needed. American industry was full of such cooperative slowdowns during World War II and in the years following, when industry was attempting to produce on a large scale, first to meet war needs and then to meet consumer demands that had been unmet during the war years because of rationing and various other forms of control.

The balance in the labor-management relationship of great industry is always a very delicate one. Both laborers and managers are always competing for a greater share of the returns from the industry, the workers wanting more in the way of wages, the industrialists wanting more in the way of profits to show to stockholders. When this relationship gets out of balance conflict usually results, with labor challenging the terms under which they are employed by industry, or in cases where there are no labor unions, the managers of the industry themselves tending to dictate terms that are more favorable to their interests.

Even social conflict in some of its worst forms may involve some elements of cooperation. There are certain rules of war which both sides agree to regard. They may cooperate in exchanging prisoners, they may keep their pledges not to bomb field hospitals or Red Cross ambulances. One of the disillusioning lessons of World War II was the discovery that Oriental peoples do not practice Western rules of war.

Finally, it should be pointed out that cooperation within a particular group is greatest when there is conflict with outside groups. At no time are the people of a nation so united within as in wartime. Every individual is given a vital place in the social and economic system. He is made to feel that he belongs, that his efforts are indispensable. As a consequence, the average person feels a greater loyalty and selflessness. Often dictators or monarchs who have been uneasy on their thrones, being threatened with internal strife or revolution, have provoked outside war in order to unify their subjects. This was at the heart of fascism.

COMPETITION AND PERSONAL STRESS

The competitive pressures and economic strains are commonplace among professional men. This is well illustrated in the case of the exurbanites. For example, the financial pressures on the top men in the communications industry are intense, where $35,000-a-year men are trying to put on a "front" which only a $65,000 income could support. Debt is heavy and many exurbanites must hope for a continual rise in salary to keep up with committed obligations. From the outside each sees the other as financially independent; yet Spectorsky sees each putting on a front to fool the other, all living in a financially insecure position.[12]

Economically, socially, perhaps even in religion to an extent, keeping ahead of the Joneses is a game which all play more or less unconsciously, although perhaps failing to admit it to themselves. All believe in competition, in a man winning his social position by his own effort and achievement. This competitive philosophy is at the basis of the capitalistic system. A man may even choose a church denomination on the social layer which appeals to him. Protestant denominationalism is in a vital sense competitive.

Competition creates problems of adjustment; in fact, it breeds feelings of inferiority in those who fail to compete successfully. From the grade school on through life, competition is the standard by which success is judged and by which achievement is measured. Those who compete successfully tend to get the positions of status and prestige in the group. Those who fail to compete successfully often feel themselves unfavorably rated and, therefore, feel uncertain of themselves. These are but examples to show how important the process of competition is to social adjustment in a competitive social system.

Because America is a society of open classes which believes in vertical social mobility, it is one of the most competitive societies possible, competition characterizing to a greater or lesser degree most forms of social relationships. We have already indicated that secondary groups provide an increasing amount of the experience for the individual and have defined secondary groups as essentially competitive groups. We have indicated that in an open-class system, no individual and no class is protected from the competitive striving and social climbing of other classes. In a caste system competition may exist only within the particular social stratum in which the individual falls. The ambitious upstart may not threaten the social posi-

[12] A. C. Spectorsky, *The Exurbanites* (Philadelphia: J. B. Lippincott Co., 1955), p. 178.

tion of those in upper classes; thus, a caste system protects those in favored positions and limits the ambitions of those in unfavorable classes.

A college coed describes her strain and growth under the competitive school regime:

I lacked the unbounding supply of energy which many adolescents possess; my energy was used up constantly by trying to meet the demands that I made of myself as well as what others seemed to expect of me. As is so characteristic of our culture, each success and accomplishment leads to the expectations of more and greater achievements, both in the eyes of others and of the individual. Eventually, at least in my case, a feeling of being pushed beyond natural limits of capacity and energy led to a sense of rebellion against each new demand. Nevertheless, rebellion succumbed to the old pattern of working just a little harder and writing both a good history paper and chemistry test on the same day, rather than slighting one for the other out of interest, ability, or the time element. I cannot determine what factors promoted the confidence I felt in my own abilities, but it was probably the fact that I thought I could do successfully what was presented to me to do that accounted for my getting it done that way, mainly as proof to myself that I could do it.

A desire for recognition, to use W. I. Thomas's phraseology, becomes a major motivation in the life of the individual.[13] In a competitive society, recognition is achieved by outdoing one's competitor. So American culture has made of competition, success, and recognition a goal of life which sets for the individual a stiff pace. As a consequence America tends to be a nation of persons strained by the competitive pace, and is sometimes referred to by foreigners as "a nation of neurotics." Certainly, it is one in which the nervous breakdown in one form or another is an experience all too frequent. Competition of a very intense form, and its effect in producing strain and neurotic behavior, is illustrated well by the following account of a young man who describes a part of his training for the Air Corps during World War II. His account reads in part as follows:

I was sent to Yale University for five months of communications training. In fairness to the University, I must make it clear that the school was actually operated by the Army Air Force. The "washout" rate of this school was extremely high. Worst of all, those eliminated appeared to be picked more or less by random selection. It seemed that in this competitive atmosphere ability to pass the examinations depended about as much on luck as on knowledge. Rivalry between each other was replaced in part by bitterness toward those responsible for the training system which prevailed. We were getting so near the goal of cadet training that none of us wanted to fail. It was a situation of desperate strain. Nervous breakdowns were so common that a special ward of the hospital had to be reserved for those who broke mentally. I often feared that I would no longer be able to stand the extreme pressure which I felt and

13 W. I. Thomas, *The Unadjusted Girl* (Boston: Little, Brown & Co., 1923).

often could not retain my food due to nervousness. During one examination I
even urinated in my clothes, a thing I have never done before. I often thought
of resigning as a cadet and probably would have done so if it had not been for
the extreme stigma attached to failure to successfully compete in this situation.

Generally speaking, the further one gets away from primary group
society, such as exists in the rural neighborhood and community, and
the closer he approaches the metropolitan area where secondary
group relationships are the dominant ones, the more intense the
competition becomes and the greater the neurotic strain. It has been
pointed out that in our most urban states, like New Jersey and New
York, the average person of twenty years of age or older has one
chance in twelve of spending a period of time in the psychiatric ward
of a hospital or in a hospital for the mentally diseased. This may be
indicative of the strenuous pace which the competitive metropolis
has brought. It may also be an index of the price the individual pays
for too strenuous striving, a striving which may exhaust him completely, as far as nervous energy is concerned, or at least leave him
so frustrated and feeling so inferior that there seems to be no way
out but temporary or permanent withdrawal from struggle through
a nervous collapse.

SUMMARY

The main difference between competition and conflict is that in
the case of competition *each individual is striving to beat the other
to the achievement of the same ends or to getting the same goods.*
When it takes the form of rivalry, the personal element is introduced. One aims at outdoing another person. In the case of conflict,
outdoing the other person is replaced by a desire to eliminate him
entirely. *Conflict aims at the destruction of the opponent*—in the case
of war, violent physical destruction; in the case of prize fighting,
putting the other person out of the ring, temporarily incapacitating
him for further action. In the case of business, conflict aims at breaking the other person financially, as in the case of the gasoline war or
other types of ruthless business competition; the price-cutting may
reach the point where one person is forced into bankruptcy.

Conflict leads to a third type of adjustment process known as accommodation. *Accommodation is a working relationship between
conflicting groups whose differences are not fully merged.* If a state
of accommodation is reached, groups or persons define their relationships to each other and maintain them; for example, at the close
of a gasoline war the conflicting groups may agree on the price
structure which neither will violate. These agreements come to be
known in business as fair-trade practices. In the case of conflict

between racial groups, accommodation as a form of adjustment usually takes the form of some sort of a caste system in which one group may be recognized as the superior and the other the inferior.

Cooperation is fully realized when all group differences are merged to the extent that they are working together to attain a common end. The groups are then said to be *assimilated.*

Societies with dominantly competitive patterns place great strain on the individual, even though impelling him toward great achievement in the values rated most highly by his group. Those dominantly cooperative are more compatible to the peace of mind of members. All groups, whatever the dominant process the culture approves, stamp it on individual members.

DISCUSSION AND REVIEW QUESTIONS

1. Name and distinguish between the four major adjustment processes as they operate in the association of persons and groups.
2. What do we mean by the term competition? Competitive society?
3. In what sense is an open-class society more competitive than a caste system?
4. Do competitive patterns come primarily from original nature or from culture patterns?
5. Distinguish between competition and conflict.
6. Which process is most highly developed in American society? Illustrate.
7. What is rivalry?
8. Compare societies in terms of their emphasis on competition.
9. What is the ultimate end of unrestrained conflict?
10. Do any benefits derive from the conflict process of war? Explain.
11. Where does accommodation fit into the conflict process?
12. Why is this type of adjustment less satisfactory than assimilation?
13. Discuss various ways of solving conflict.
14. Are cooperation and conflict entirely separate adjustment processes?
15. What are some of the values of competition?
16. Show how miscegenation and acculturation help in assimilation.
17. What do we mean when we say there is often a delicate balance between cooperation and conflict in social relations? Illustrate.
18. Relate competition in our society to personal stress.

SOURCEBOOK READINGS

GITTLER, JOSEPH B. *Social Dynamics.* New York: McGraw-Hill Book Co., Inc., 1952.
1. GITTLER, JOSEPH, "From Conflict to Cooperation in Union-Management Relations," pp. 195–223.
2. GLICK, CLARENCE, "The Processes of Assimilation and Accommodation among the Chinese Immigrants in Hawaii," pp. 189–95.
3. GOLDMAN, IRVING, "A Highly Competitive Society—the Kwakiutl," pp. 170–79; "A Highly Cooperative Society—the Zuñi," pp. 179–89.
KOENIG, SAMUEL, REX D. HOPPER, and FELIKS GROSS. *Sociology: A Book of Readings.* Englewood Cliffs, N.J.: Prentice-Hall, Inc., 1956.
4. SJOBERG, GIDEON, "Is the American Class System Becoming More Rigid?" pp. 316–24.

5. DAVIE, MAURICE R., and SAMUEL KOENIG, "Our Newest Immigrants: The Refugees," pp. 278–84.

SCHULER, EDGAR A., DUANE L. GIBSON, MAUDE L. FIERO, and WILBUR B. BROOKOVER. *Outside Readings in Sociology.* New York: The Thomas Crowell Co., 1956.

6. HUMPHREY, NORMAN D., "The Changing Structure of the Detroit Mexican Family: An Index of Acculturation," pp. 762–69.

SELECTED READINGS

ADAMS, STUART, "Social Climate and Production in Small Military Groups," *American Sociological Review,* 19:401–25 (1954).

CARTWRIGHT, DORWIN, and ALVIN ZANDER (eds.). *Group Dynamics: Research and Theory.* Evanston, Ill.: Row, Peterson & Co., 1953.

Displaced Persons Commission Annual Reports. Washington, D.C.: U. S. Government Printing Office.

DOLLARD, JOHN et al. *Frustration and Aggression.* New Haven: Yale University Press, 1939.

HARE, A. PAUL, EDGAR F. BORGATTA, and ROBERT F. BALES (eds.). *Small Groups: Studies in Social Interaction.* New York: Alfred A. Knopf, Inc., 1955.

GROSS, EDWARD. *Work and Society: The Sociology of Work Relations.* New York: The Thomas Crowell Co., 1958.

MILLS, THEODORE. "Power Relation in Three-Person Groups," *American Sociological Review,* 18:351–57 (Aug. 1953).

QUINN, JAMES A. *Human Ecology.* Englewood Cliffs, N. J.: Prentice-Hall, Inc., 1950.

SHERIF, MUZAFER and CAROLINE W. SHERIF. *Groups in Harmony and Tension,* New York: Harper & Brothers, 1953.

WHYTE, WILLIAM F. *Street Corner Society.* Chicago: University of Chicago Press, 1943.

WHYTE, WILLIAM H., JR. "The Wives of Management," *Fortune,* Oct., 1951, pp. 88 ff., and "The Corporation and the Wife," *Fortune,* Nov., 1951, pp. 109 ff.

Part III

SOCIAL STRUCTURE

Chapter 15

The Structural Framework of Interaction

Generally to treat a woman as if she were a man, a "social superior" as if an equal, a senior as if a contemporary, a guest as if a member of the family, are all serious enough confusions of social distinctions to be called at least bad manners.[1]

In this brief paragraph is a world of meaning. It speaks of people who are different in roles and status; people who, therefore, must be treated differently. This is the subtle but very meaningful world of social relations with which the sociologist is concerned. It is the *social structure*.

The social structure consists of an intangible web of interaction. It can be seen only in its manifestations. Yet, like the framework of a house, it is real. Ask the average person how his house is pieced together, what holds it up, how the framework is braced and joined, and he cannot explain. Yet he lives in it and takes for granted that the foundations will not crumble, the roof cave in, or the walls collapse.

Society is a carefully structured world, long in the making. Each bit of custom, tradition, and etiquette is a part of the structure. Only a Japanese reared in his social system knows what each bow and curtsey means. Only an American knows the subtleties of meaning of our system of rating dates, jobs, religious denominations, men, women, teenagers, Negroes, Democrats, Republicans, bishops and sheepherders.

[1] Elsie Worthington (Clews) Parsons, *Fear and Conventionality* (New York: G. Putnam's Sons, Inc., 1914), p. x.

THE SOCIAL STRUCTURE DEFINED

The following paragraphs set forth the essential features of the social structure.

1. The structural framework of society is *a system of status relationships.* Men, women, children, old, young, and middle-aged, teenagers, debutantes, bankers, farmers, teachers, Christians, Jews, Protestants, Moslems, lower-lower, lower, lower-middle, middle, upper-middle, upper, upper-upper, blacks, whites, browns, reds, coffee-colored—all have a "place," a status rating.

2. These ratings are *generally understood and accepted* through the entire social group, or particular large segments of it, so that all can place themselves and other persons and know the appropriate behavior for each according to the classification in which he falls.

3. In certain instances, the structure is very evident in that *definite barriers are erected* to keep status groups apart in some or all of their social relationships. Here, of course, the structure is most evident, although even these barriers may often be unnoticed by an outsider. They are a part of the understood social rules which members of the groups take for granted, although they may be written nowhere and taught nowhere in a systematic and formal fashion.

4. *Social distance* is a concept used by the sociologist to describe that intangible yet real something which *separates persons and groups of different status rating:* the wealthy from the poor, the dark-skinned from the white, the minority group from the controlling group, the upper classman from the freshman, the "bossman" from the worker. Few if any human groups exist or ever have existed in which all meet on equal terms and in equally close relations. Social distance is a reality of human interrelations.

5. The social structure is in large part evident only on *the psychological and emotional level.* For this very reason, it is one of the most vital aspects of social interrelations in all social systems.

6. *Roles and statuses are closely related.* The role is the part an individual or group of individuals play in society. Statuses are the social recognition of the role in terms of honorific rating.

7. Status classifications *may be based on anything* a group chooses to consider significant: sex, age, color, religion, politics, wealth, work. Because different groups rate these characteristics differently, social structures vary greatly in what is humanly significant in social relations. Whatever trait or traits are "rated" tend to give one his "place," or status.

8. Every man has "his place" in his society. In fact, in any social structure, every human being has not only "his place" but several

places. Not to have some standing in the social structure is to be nondescript, socially lost, less than a person. As an early sociologist put it, *to be a person means to have status or standing* (place).

9. With each status go certain *responsibilities, privileges, im-munities, and obligations*. A mother must, if she meets her social obligations, manifest a different sense of responsibility than a teen-ager. Society holds a judge to a higher standard of accountability than a policeman: for his special honorable position, he carries a much higher than average sense of obligation. The child, by virtue of his age, is granted many immunities to punishment for violating the expectations of others that are not granted an adult. And a man is privileged to indulge in certain vices that are taboo for women. Presumably they are his reward for bearing much responsibility and risk for the welfare of women and children.

10. Societies confer statuses in two ways, by ascribing and assign-ing them: *ascribed statuses* are those *assigned automatically* by the society to all in a particular group, and *achieved statuses* are those *earned* by the individual by virtue of his performance.

As the anthropologist Ralph Linton explains it in *The Study of Man:* "In all societies certain things are selected as reference points for the ascription of status. The things chosen for this purpose are always of such a nature that they are ascertainable at birth, making it possible to begin the training of the individual for his po-tential statuses and roles at once. The simplest and most universally used of these reference points is sex. Age is used with nearly equal frequency, since all individuals pass through the same cycle of growth, maturity, and decline, and the statuses whose occupation will be determined by age can be forecast and trained for with ac-curacy. Family relationships, the simplest and most obvious being that of the child to its mother, are also used in all societies as refer-ence points for the establishment of a whole series of statuses. Lastly, there is a matter of birth into a particular socially established group, such as a class or caste. The use of this type of reference is common but not universal. In all societies the actual ascription of statuses to the individual is controlled by a series of these reference points which together serve to delimit the field of his future participation in the life of the group."[2]

Achieved statuses are granted after the group has had oppor-tunity to observe the performance of the individual, seen him in competition with others, and appraised his competence for the role. For some achieved statuses, such as that of the professional man,

[2] Ralph Linton, *The Study of Man* (New York: Appleton-Century-Crofts, Inc., 1936), pp. 115–16.

this means special training, examinations, certification, etc. For others it means an apprenticeship, or other demonstration of ability to perform the role.

11. Status classifications are constantly undergoing revision. The range in social distance is from *segregation* at the one extreme, which is the maximum social distance, to *integration*, which in the end obliterates all distinctions.

Differentiation is the beginning of the segregation process. It is the process of recognizing and making something of differences. Next comes *stratification*, that is, the psychological setting apart of persons and groups because of these recognized differences. The final step is *segregation*, the setting apart of the group into psychologically walled camps which make the segregated a different order of human beings.

12. The social structure is in essence an up-and-down, over-under affair. At its roots are inferiority and superiority. Status means that. To change status means to move up or down in the social structure's honorific hierarchy. The sociologist has, therefore, coined the term *vertical mobility* to describe changes of position on the social ladder by persons and groups. This is the dynamic aspect of social structures. He defines the *caste* social structure as one in which there is almost no movement, because strata barriers have been fixed through hereditary social transmission. He views the *class* system as one where vertical mobility is approved, accepted, expected.

CONSEQUENCES OF THE SOCIAL STRUCTURE

Place a dozen hens in a henhouse, and before night a pecking order will be established. Each hen will outpeck whomever she can,

Peck Order of Hens

The peck order of hens has been studied by various psychologists. This diagram is based on an experiment by A. M. Guhl, who observed a flock of eight marked Leghorns. In just one hour the superior pecking ability of hen No. 1 was recognized by all the other hens. But it was only after five days of fighting that the rest settled down in the peck order shown here—each hen having feeding and roosting priorities over all hens shown to her right. However, when hen No. 8 was injected with male hormones, she fought her way through the peck order until she had defeated No. 1. (From Life *magazine)*

and find her rank in the henhouse. The hardest pecking hen will have choice place at the feed trough; the weakest pecking one will get what is left after the others have fed. And each by rank takes her choice on the hen roost.

With human beings it isn't all in the pecking, but all social systems have their way of placing people. In fact, placement in the social structure is one of the most basic aspects of social life. The sociologist knows that if you place workers together in a factory, a prestige order will emerge, ranking workers on the basis of skills the job requires, their social traits, leadership ability, etc. He knows that if races are placed together on a continent or in a community, a prestige order is likely to arise on the basis of skin color. He knows that in every community, no matter how democratic, people will tend to place persons, and to associate with them, on the basis of occupation. He knows that wherever several religious, political, or fraternal orders exist, they will not likely be ranked as of equal standing. He knows that even on the college campus there is the eternal struggle between Greeks and independents to establish and destroy the sense of class and quality which the Greek symbols are meant to embody.

The smooth functioning of people in society is due in no small part to the fact that every person has his rank in the social order. This matter of getting individuals and groups into position greatly eases the functioning of group life. It reduces competition and conflict and makes for effective social organization.

In any group, placing persons by status rank limits the roles they can perform and also limits the additional statuses they can acquire by virtue of their performance. For example, to be male or female limits one's performance of social roles and also the types of statuses one may acquire. There are always areas in which women cannot fill the place occupied by a man, because it is taboo for them to do so, and there are still other areas where the man can never play the role of the woman—even areas in which he is physically capable of doing so. In many other ways individuals are given different parts to play, as in the different occupational groups.

The over-all aspect of social status is called *social class*. It is the more generalized aspect of status—the prestige that comes for social performances of a certain rating.

The Problem of Segregation. As has been indicated, these are intangible matters; yet they are among the most important realities of human interaction in all group life. This can be seen clearly today in the program of integration that is now being sponsored on a nation-wide scale with regard to the Negro and the white. Here a type of assignment of place in the social structure is being eradicated by Supreme Court ruling. All of the carefully structured social relationships which have formed the basis of the culture of the Deep South must now be revised and a basic part of the entire social structure of that section of the country abandoned. It cannot be done easily. Negro–white caste is a reality for which some are ready to almost sacrifice life itself. For the dyed-in-the-wool Southerner sees no conflict between this traditional social structure by which the biracial system of the South had been built and the democratic traditions of the American society.

With the possible exceptions of Boston, and perhaps a few other New England communities, the deep South has had a more intricate social structure than any other part of the country. Some years ago three sociologists made a study of class and caste in the Deep South.[3] They found there not only the Negro–white line of stratification, with its caste characteristics, but also many other less fixed but nonetheless real distinctions indicative of rather clear class lines. There were people characterized as the "leading families," "fine old families," "the four hundred," "the society crowd," "plain people," "nice respectable people," "good people, but nobody," "po' whites," "red necks," and other such terms all referring to different status classifications within the white groups. Within the white group too they found that the terms "top," "bottom," "above," and "below" were often used. Among the folk sayings were such phrases as "She isn't our kind," "They are just nobody," "These folk are way-high-up," "Oh, they're nothing but white trash!" "Oh, they're plain people like us."

These researchers found too that not only did people of the Deep South place others in such categories but also that they behaved toward them appropriately to their respective statuses.

Inequities in the Social Structure. In this extreme example depicting aspects of a particular social structure, one gets a vivid picture of the meaning of individual roles and the weight given them by this social group. One sees clearly that not only is one's participation limited by the social structure in which he lives, but also that the kind of rating he can attain for the performance of such roles as he undertakes is also limited by the conceptions of the social group concerning the propriety of the performance. It is also clear that even in

[3] Allison Davis, Burleigh B. Gardner, and Mary R. Gardner, *Deep South: A Social Anthropological Study of Caste and Class* (Chicago: University of Chicago Press, 1941).

a democratic society there are certain limits to social climbing and, consequently, certain protections to those who are fortunate enough to be placed in high positions by virtue of their birth into certain families and in certain communities.

The social structure, as is implied by the above discussions and example, has different rewards for different performances and is often discriminatory in both rewards, privileges, and penalties. Some are immune, by virtue of position, from certain types of criticisms and penalties. Those who are immune may be expected to carry a heavy obligation as compensatory reward to society. Yet they may not. To the extent that they do, social orders tend to be just. If those with great privilege do not carry a heavy load, a social order grants privileges in vain. And the heaping of inferiority on some, limiting their performances, and the failure to reward their activities by recognition are always costly in terms of creative activity, social adjustment, and social progress. Even so, most societies have granted the kind of rewards that make for high motivations very sparingly.

It is for some of these reasons that inequities in the social structure are often at the basis of discontent, rebellion, and at times, violent revolution. Official position, hereditary status, even acquired power are often abused by those granted high statuses by the group. Instead of these persons justifying their privilege by great productivity and great service, they often become the oppressors, abuse their privileges, and exploit those who are assigned menial roles and denied recognition for their essential services. Their immunity to criticism and to punishment, their flaunting of favors, and their display of privilege arouses animosity, and the great submerged masses at the bottom of the social pyramid resort to violence in an attempt to capture the privileges, statuses, and immunities that are always a part of being on top. This is a simple story of revolution.

Inherent in the social structure are some of the most vicious myths that victimize human social orders. Those who acquire high positions and privilege far too often come to rationalize the rightness of their place. They assume that they hold top place because they are in reality superior, that it is their inherent right to rule, to be worshipped, to be praised. And with this attitude goes the notion, so widespread in many social orders, that the masses are possessed of a natural inferiority, that it is the nature of things that they will be at the bottom, that it is inevitable that they can perform only menial tasks, and that it is to be expected that they will receive few rewards, either in the way of recognition or economic substance for such roles as they perform.

Bruno Bettelheim, who spent two years in German concentration camps at Dachau and Buchenwald, where prisoners were deliberately tortured and starved for experimental reasons, reports that prisoners from the upper classes segregated themselves as much as possible from the others and seemed unable to accept what was happening to them. They lived in the conviction that, because of their importance, they would soon be released. They looked down on the other prisoners nearly as much as on the Gestapo. "In order to endure life in the camp they developed such a feeling of superiority that nothing could touch them."[4]

Here we see clearly the psychological fortification, the self-insulating effect of rank on men of upper class. They cling to a deep sense that privilege is their inherent right. Unfortunately for them, their captors held no such conception of social structure as had been internalized in these prisoners from the upper strata.

The great appeal of the Marxian doctrine to the masses of mankind, and even to many intellectuals, has been that it holds out hope that the great masses at the bottom will inevitably replace those at the top. Through revolution they will overthrow the captains of industry, the managers of the big business empires, and acquire the statuses and honors that these leaders have flaunted before them.

It would be difficult, presumably, to find any society in which privilege and responsibility are properly and permanently balanced. To grant high status and privilege to a few, as every society must do to function efficiently, is to risk, unless numerous checks and balances are instituted, that these powers and privileges will be abused. And to say to the masses of men that they can perform only on the lowly level is to fail to inspire them with a creative urge which will bring to the social order the maximum of their talents and inventiveness.

In the following passage, a sociologist develops his ideas on the logical necessity of stratification in the social structure. If this logic is sound, one must expect that some differences in status and privilege will always exist.

". . . The main functional necessity explaining the universal presence of stratification is precisely the requirement faced by any society of placing and motivating individuals in the social structure. As a functioning mechanism a society must somehow distribute its members in social positions and induce them to perform the duties of these positions. It must thus concern itself with motivation at two different levels: to instill in the proper individuals the desire to fill certain positions, and, once in these positions, the desire to perform

---

[4] In Guy E. Swanson, *et al.*, *Readings in Social Psychology* (rev. ed.; New York: Henry Holt & Co., Inc., 1952), pp. 33 ff.

the duties attached to them. Even though the social order may be relatively static in form, there is a continuous process of metabolism as new individuals are born into it, shift with age, and die off. Their absorption into the positional system is competitive or non-competitive. A competitive system gives greater importance to the motivation to achieve positions, whereas a non-competitive system gives perhaps greater importance to the motivation to perform the duties of the positions; but in any system both types of motivation are required.

"If the duties associated with the various positions were all equally pleasant to the human organism, all equally important to societal survival, and all equally in need of the same ability or talent, it would make no difference who got into which positions, and the problem of social placement would be greatly reduced. But actually it does make a great deal of difference who gets into which positions, not only because some positions are inherently more agreeable than others, but also because some require special talents or training and some are functionally more important than others. Also, it is essential that the duties of the positions be performed with the diligence that their importance requires. Inevitably, then, a society must have, first, some kind of rewards that it can use as inducements, and, second, some way of distributing these rewards differentially according to positions. The rewards and their distribution become a part of the social order, and thus give rise to stratification.

"One may ask what kind of rewards a society has at its disposal in distributing its personnel and securing essential services. It has, first of all, the things that contribute to sustenance and comfort. It has, second, the things that contribute to humor and diversion. And it has, finally, the things that contribute to self-respect and ego expansion. The last, because of the peculiarly social character of the self, is largely a function of the opinion of others, but it nonetheless ranks in importance with the first two. In any social system all three kinds of rewards must be dispensed differentially according to positions.

"In a sense the rewards are 'built into' the position. They consist in the 'rights' associated with the position, plus what may be called its accompaniments or perquisites. Often the rights, and sometimes the accompaniments, are functionally related to the duties of the position. (Rights as viewed by the incumbent are usually duties as viewed by other members of the community.) However, there may be a host of subsidiary rights and perquisites that are not essential to the function of the position and have only an indirect and symbolic connection with its duties, but which still may be of considerable importance in inducing people to seek the positions and fulfill the essential duties.

"If the rights and perquisites of different positions in a society must be unequal, then the society must be stratified, because that is precisely what stratification means. Social inequality is thus an unconsciously evolved device by which societies insure that the most important positions are conscientiously filled by the most qualified persons. Hence every society, no matter how simple or complex, must differentiate persons in terms of both prestige and esteem, and must therefore possess a certain amount of institutionalized inequality."[5]

The aim of democratic society is not to eliminate status distinctions but rather to see that high status is accompanied by high responsibility and that even the lowest status is given sufficient recognition so the individual performing his role will feel that his function is useful and important in the social order. It also aims to keep places open at the top. History teaches that a class which fences itself off into permanent caste at the top ultimately dies of stagnation.[6]

Enough has been said to indicate that the social structure is an area of great importance to social understanding. It has so many ramifications that entire books have been written about it, and many more will be. Here it will have to be sufficient to picture briefly the intricacies of the social structure, as they are manifest in the areas of sex relations, age group relationships, race, social classes, occupational and religious groups.

FILM LIST FOR PART III

Americans All—16 minutes—sound
Shows how a community can combat prejudice and deal with the causes of injustice. *Source:* March of Time Film Forum.

Brotherhood for Survival—11 minutes—sound
Illustrates cooperative relationships between various types of organizations including differing religious denominations. *Source:* National Conference of Christians and Jews.

Picture in Your Mind—16 minutes—sound—color
Through the use of symbols the film presents the earlier roots of prejudice and the reasons why any group, tribe, or nation thinks its way of life is superior to any other. *Source:* Association Film.

To Live Together—30 minutes—sound
Describes the experiences of children who took part in an inter-racial camp. *Source:* Anti-Defamation League of B'nai B'rith.

This Is the Bowery—10 minutes—sound
Presents "a story of life along New York's Bowery, a street of despair, peopled by men who have lost their grip." *Source:* Teaching Film Custodians, Inc.

[5] Kingsley Davis and Wilbert E. Moore, "Some Principles of Stratification," *American Sociological Review*, 10:242–49 (April 1945).

[6] A striking description of the "fate of the closed classes" (E. A. Ross) is presented in Chapter 23, pp. 434–35.

Brotherhood of Man—10 minutes—sound—color
> Portrays that differences between the human races are superficial and that differing skins mean nothing. *Source:* Brandon Films, Inc.

Color of a Man—18 minutes
> Provides a story of race discrimination in the South. *Source:* International Film Foundation.

Deadline for Action—40 minutes
> Shows need for political action on the part of the American people to combat the forces seeking to influence Congress. *Source:* United Electrical, Radio and Machine Workers of America.

The House I Live In—10 minutes—sound
> Stars Frank Sinatra; develops the theme of understanding religious and racial problems. *Source:* Young America.

Towards Unity—11 minutes—sound
> Makes a definite plea against racial and national prejudice and for peace. *Source:* Brandon Films, Inc.

Dead End (gangster sequence)—9 minutes—sound
> A gangster risks capture by returning to his old neighborhood to see his mother and his former sweetheart. *Source:* New York University Film Library.

The Good Earth (excerpts)—18 minutes
> Displays the roles and status of women in China. *Source:* Teaching Film Custodians, Inc.

Of Mice and Men—108 minutes—sound
> John Steinbeck's story dramatizing the struggles of migratory farm workers. *Source:* Post Pictures Corporation.

Role Playing in Human Relations Training—25 minutes—sound
> Consists of some half-dozen sequences illustrating various techniques of getting leaders and groups to "role play." *Source:* National Education Association.

Steps of Age—25 minutes—sound
> Story of a woman of sixty-two and the problems engendered by having to retire from one's job and the frustrations of unemployment due to old age. *Source:* Mental Health Film Board.

Chapter 16

Social Class and Caste

The class system tends to measure a man by his performance; the caste system measures him by his ancestry. Where the caste social structure is perpetuated, favorite folk sayings run as follows: "Eagles do not come from crows' nests." "You can't make a silk purse out of a sow's ear." "Blood will tell." Where class principles are emulated the favorite folk sayings run: "You can't keep a good man down." "There's always room at the top." "Bottom to top in one generation." "Log cabin to White House."

The United States, as a frontier nation with its expanding western fringe offering unlimited opportunity for achievement, has built one of the most mobile class structures ever conceived by man. Although most of its immigrants came from countries in which there was considerable rigidity in the social structure, with considerable passing of social status from parent to child, the connection between blood and achievement was forgotten in the rapid climb of men in a land of opportunity—a land where a man's reach determined what he could grasp.

Even so, caste principles die hard and again and again reassert themselves in social relationships. Communities, too, differed greatly in the rigidity of their social classes. Boston and Philadelphia continued to boast Mayflower and pre-Revolutionary War ancestry. An aristocracy developed in Virginia and other states of the cotton South. These areas tried to keep alive the caste principle.

Societies with marked class distinctions make much of family and family lineage. Cleveland Amory, in humorous vein, tells of a Chicago banking house which asked an influential Boston investment firm to recommend a certain young Bostonian whom they were considering for employment. The investment company wrote at great length, giving his pedigree on both sides of the family, tracing his lineage through the Lowells, Cabots, Lodges, Appletons, etc. But the more practical-minded Chicago firm wrote back wanting to know what the young fellow could do, indicating that they had not contemplated using him for "breeding purposes."

Amory goes on to state that the "Proper Bostonian" is not the product of chance; he is planned. He is bred from the right family connections. In Philadephia, it is said, it is sufficient to know about one's parents, but in Boston his grandparents too are important.

A satirical poem of unknown origin expresses the supreme importance of family in old Boston society:

> And this is good old Boston,
>   The home of the bean and the cod,
> Where the Lowells talk to the Cabots
> And the Cabots talk only to God.

While sociologists have worked a great deal in the area of social structure in recent years, classifying many town and city communities into their various social layers, and penetrating the school system, the church, and other social institutions to discover evidence of social class, they have not always equalled the novelist in revealing its intricacies and its delicate meaning to human interaction.

In *Kitty Foyle*, novelist Christopher Morley has drawn a convincing picture of the class system in Philadelphia by presenting characters from two layers of society far apart in the social hierarchy. Wyn is from one of the top families, described here as "Main Line" families. Kitty is from one of the bottom social strata.

Morley has Kitty tell of the first time she met Philadelphia's "Main Line" families, the arrangement having been made by Wyn's mother.

It was a mistake. Of course Wyn had done what any man would, told everybody to be lovely to me, and they were so god damn lovely I could have torn their eyes out. I was the only one that wasn't in the union. That crowd, if they stopped to think about it, would reckon that Ben Franklin was still a boy from the wrong side of the tracks, so what could they think about me. Somebody wanted to know if I was one of the Iglehart Foyles from Baltimore or the Saltonstall Foyles from Pride's Crossing. I said no Pride ever crossed our family except when the old man carried his bat against Merion C. C. That was Wyn's fault, he tried to ease the situation by making everybody drink too many old fashioneds. But it helped because good old Rosey Rittenhouse turned the talk on cricket and said he wished he could get more girls to show some intelligence about it. . . . I knew either I or the rest of them didn't belong, and the embarrassment went around the dinner table all wrapped up in a napkin like that wine bottle the butlers carried.

Even in a Thanksgiving rainstorm, what a lovely lovely place. When I saw Wyn's old faded station wagon out in a hitching shed I asked him to drive me home. Of course he wouldn't and he couldn't. I was supposed to stay the night and I had to go through with it. "I hope you'll rest well," Mrs. Strafford said, "will you want the maid to undress you?" Jesusgod, I blushed like one of those Cornell chrysanthemums. I wanted to say there's only one person here who's good enough to undress me. Wyn saw me turn red, he kept his eyes on me all evening bless him and came across the room to see what was going wrong.[1]

Uncle Kermit, Ken's Quaker Banker Uncle, decides the thing to do is remodel Kitty. Here is Kitty's reaction, as Morley creates it.

"You can tell Uncle Ken he's a white slaver. Listen, Wyn Strafford, I'll be your girl whenever I feel like it because I love you from hell to breakfast. But I wouldn't join the little tin family if every old Quaker with an adding machine begged me to. No, not if they all went back to college and got themselves the idea they'd trim up Kitty so she could go to the Assembly and make Old Philadelphia Family out of her, hey? Cut her out of a copy of Vogue and give her a charge account and make a Main Line doll out of her. They can't do that to Kitty Foyle. Jesusgod, that's what they are themselves, a bunch of paper dolls."

In this final scene Kitty is talking to herself:

Q. Did you make Wyn happy?
A. I think so. Yes, I know so.
Q. Then why did you leave him?
A. If I had done what he wanted, other people would have made him unhappier than I could have made him happy.
Q. What do you mean?
A. He was the product of a system. He was at the mercy of that system.
Q. Is it not your conviction that there are now no systems? That the whole of society is in flux?
A. Not in—I mean, not where Wyn lives.

FIXED AND FLEXIBLE CLASS STATUS GROUPINGS

Favorable status is apparently a quest of men everywhere. The way to win it differs. Robert H. Lowie, University of California anthropologist, in his satire on modern civilization speaks of prestige and etiquette as they minister to man's vanity and pride both in primitive and in modern society. He concludes that "man is a peacock," for man will play the role of the spendthrift or the ascetic, will flirt or smile, wallow in riches or deny himself, strut in pride or act humble, whichever carries prestige in his group.[2]

In some primitive societies a man will put on a big feast at which he gives away princely gifts, kills a slave in cold blood to show that he can afford to dispense with him, pays huge sums for a wife for the purpose of gaining prestige among his fellows. So also the wealthy of American society put on dinners costing $25, $50, even $100 a plate, with all the lavish elegance which money can buy to similarly

---

[1] Christopher Morley, *Kitty Foyle* (Philadelphia: J. B. Lippincott Co., 1939).
[2] Robert H. Lowie, *Are We Civilized?* (New York: Harcourt, Brace & Co., Inc., 1929), p. 58.

display their financial status and thereby gain the prestige with both their social equals and those of more modest means.

Class groups are found in all societies, but the great difference in the character of various status systems lies in the clarity of the lines separating group strata. In some societies the divisions are scarcely distinguishable; in others the lines are heavy and easily recognized.

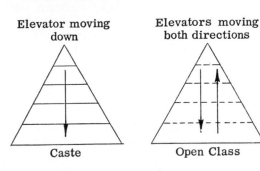

Elevator moving down

Caste

Elevators moving both directions

Open Class

In a caste system one may lose rank, in a class (open-class) system either gain or lose rank. Changing status is called vertical mobility. Vertical mobility is easy in open-class systems because the lines between the classes are indistinct.

Contrasting Social Systems

As a result of this difference in clarity of class lines, some systems are fixed, others flexible. In the fixed social system, crossing class lines is prohibited. One may do it, but only in disgrace; the social elevators move only down. In the flexible social system, with a dim line of division between the social classes, movement across class lines is accepted. The social elevators move both up and down. The accompanying sketch illustrates the two social systems.

The Caste System. *The most fixed social system known* is called a *caste system.* In it the lines between the social classes are drawn by heredity. To be a member of a privileged class one must be born into it. In a caste system social status is passed from one generation to the next. In these societies it is impossible, or nearly so, for one to achieve higher status than that of his parents. He may, by disregarding the traditions which are common to his particular social class, lose caste and fall to a lower rank.

Because the marks and privileges of caste are passed from parent to child, caste systems fix on successive generations their respective places in the social system regardless of their inherent ability. Among the upper castes there is always an assumption of superior ability, and in fact the entire social system may come to accept the philosophy that the privileged castes are privileged because of their superior natural ability. Sometimes, of course, lack of ability becomes obvious. When fools inherit thrones, as they have too often done in the history of hereditary monarchies, the illusion of inherited superiority is dispelled.

The most notable caste system in the world is that of India, weakening, but still today very much a part of the system of social relations. A contemporary describes it as follows:

> The caste system is the classification of all individuals according to the occupation they traditionally follow, the circle within which they must marry, and the group with whom they can mingle socially. Birth lays down the caste to which a Hindu belongs, and there is not any possibility for him to switch to another. In ancient times . . . there were four basic castes—the Brahman, the most revered; the Kshatriyas, the nobles and warriors; the Vaisyas, the traders; and the Sudras, the serfs. Today, however, this fourfold classification has been blurred and complicated by the development of more than three thousand separate caste groups. [3]

In the United States, south of the Mason–Dixon Line, there has been virtually a caste system as far as the Negro is concerned. He has had, because of race, numerous limits beyond which he could not expect to go in the social system regardless of his ability. His "place" has been one of inferior social status in which numerous occupations and opportunities were barred to him, and in which the restrictions of social relationships had been so well defined that they were understood by both Negro and white. (Segregation as a device of caste is discussed in Chapter 19.)

The Class System. By contrast, *the flexible social system* is known as a *class system.* In it an individual may determine his place in the social system by his own efforts. He may climb above the level of his birth, and in the class system of the United States he is expected at least to try to do so. As he does so, he is accepted in social groups on the higher level. Because the United States has such great freedom of movement between classes it is sometimes called an open-class social structure. Sociologists use the terms "class" and "open-class" interchangeably, since the term class means that upward movement is permitted; if such movement is not permitted, the social structure is caste rather than class in structure.

THE EFFECT OF CLASS STATUSES ON THE INDIVIDUAL

Class and Caste Roles Compared. In any social system it comes to be taken for granted that those in the higher classes are destined to play special roles which bring privilege, influence, or wealth. By contrast, those who make up the lower classes play unimportant roles.

[3] T. Walter Wallbank, *India in the New Era* (Chicago: Scott, Foresman & Co., 1951), p. 23.

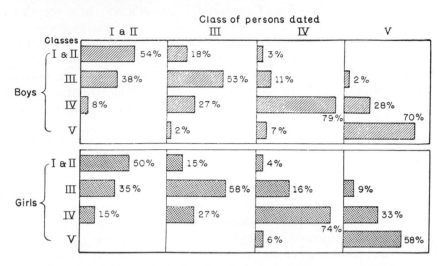

Intra- and Interclass Dating Patterns of Boys and Girls in a Small Community (about 6,000 pop.)

There is evidence here of a very flexible social structure in the United States. (Reprinted, with permission, from A. Hollingshead, Elmtown's Youth, *p. 175. Copyright, 1949, John Wiley and Sons, Inc.)*

Their honors and privileges and responsibilities are few. In a caste system symbols of distinction are used to mark the privileged man. The upper caste may wear a spot on the forehead, as in India. In many societies a distinctive garb is worn to guard the privileged from indignity.

Conformity to role expectations becomes the law of life. Those in the urban register, for example, have to regard with great exactness the peculiar standards of etiquette and conduct which distinguish their strata. So also the Negro in Southern society must carefully conform to the social roles which have been approved for him. To step beyond the bounds defined by the class system has exposed him not only to being snubbed but even to being lynched. In earlier generations such discipline was commonly employed to teach the Negro his "place" within the class structure.

In a caste system ambition is limited by the knowledge that one is confined to a certain area of social space and social endeavor. His roles are defined. Ambitions must be formed within the framework of available privilege. A man knows from the beginning the limitations to his choice of life occupation and range of social participation, and woe to the person with special abilities who cannot be satisfied within the prescribed framework.

Class and Caste Privilege Compared. Caste is a way of protecting and passing on to later generations the privileges of favored groups. The most desirable values of the society are accessible only to the favored few, others being barred by tradition from even striving for them. This reduces competition for the privileged groups and makes more secure their position at the top of the honorific structure. Such a system can exist only where traditions have been made binding through long periods of usage.

By contrast, in class systems where the world is "every man's oyster" there is no limit to ambition. The competitive struggle is likely to be strenuous and lifelong. Increasing nervous strain and tension are common among those who feel that they must attain the highest honorific level of the social system. Moreover, in a class system there are no social definitions by which a man may know when he has enough. The competitive struggle tends to become the life pattern. The general tendency is for a man to become so habituated to competition that when at last he cannot stand the pace and must give up, he is likely to be most unhappy. He may have obtained virtually everything to which he aspired, but the fact that he may no longer compete often robs him of happiness in his later years. Accordingly, men in our culture find it difficult to retire.

On the other hand, a class system tends to make for a progressive, dynamic, forward-moving society. It releases the ambition of the masses and encourages each generation to strive for everything within the horizon of their desires. Such a society is likely to be inventive, energetic, creative, even though the stress of competition may lead to an unnecessary amount of neurotic exhaustion.

CLASS STATUSES IN A DEMOCRATIC SOCIETY

The Middle-Class Norm. Many students of South American countries are impressed with the fact that in most of them there is no real middle class. At the upper extreme is the aristocracy which controls most of the land and industrial wealth. Its members hold the places of social prestige. They are surrounded by privilege in almost every field of social and economic activity. This class is small. The rest of the population, the great masses, are in the lower class. They are plagued with disease, low income, large families, and lack of privilege.

In direct contrast is the population of the United States, which is middle-class conscious. *Fortune* magazine asked representative persons of all social layers in the United States to which class they belonged. Of those polled, 79.2 per cent indicated that they belonged to the middle class. Only 7.6 per cent considered themselves as belonging to the upper class and only 7.9 per cent considered themselves as belonging to the lower class. The remaining 5.3 per cent said they did not know where they should be classified. Even of those with low incomes, 73 per cent considered that they belonged to the middle class. Of the prosperous group, 23.6 per cent placed themselves in the upper class and 74.7 per cent regarded themselves as middle class.[4]

When this study was made, in 1939, 42 per cent of the families of the United States, according to studies of income made by the National Resources Planning Board, received less than $1,000 income per year; 65 per cent received less than $1,500 and 87 per cent received less than $2,500.[5]

Moreover, the study followed ten years of the most severe depression the nation had ever experienced, during which Franklin Delano Roosevelt and others had often referred graphically to a third of a nation ill-clothed, ill-fed, and ill-housed, and when as many as eighteen million workers and their families had been on relief during a single month. Public policy, as it affected both the industrial worker and the farmer, recognized a lower third. Relief and public-works programs had provided for industrial workers, and the Farm Security Administration had been created to help the lower third in agriculture.

Clearly the idea of the middle class being the desirable status in the society of the United States is deeply rooted. This class is identified with democracy itself.

Richard Centers in 1945 made a nation-wide poll with a sample of 1,007 white males, asking them whether they belonged to the upper, middle, lower, or working class. His results showed respondents classified themselves as follows:

	Per Cent
Upper class	3
Middle class	43
Working class	51
Lower class	1
Don't know	1
Don't believe in class	1

Numerous other studies have dealt with the social structure of particular communities or sectors of the nation. Although definitions have differed, as well as interpretations of results, in the United

[4] "The People of the USA," *Fortune*, Feb., 1940, pp. 14, 20, 28 ff.
[5] *Consumer Incomes in the United States* (Washington, D. C.: National Resources Planning Board, 1938), pp. 2–3.

States today the general picture is one of fluid classes, with degree of stratification differing from community to community.[6]

Areas of Class Distinctions. Since World War II a great deal has been said, most of it critically, about class distinctions in the army. Vertical grouping has been worked out more exactly, and the pyramid of status, or rank, built more firmly in the military organization than in most other aspects of American society. From bottom to top the social layers extend from private to commander-in-chief, as shown in the chart. The privilege that goes with high status in the army is the most criticized aspect of the rank system.

Even college campuses have ranks and strata, less well defined, but nonetheless recognizable. Greeks and independents, upper and

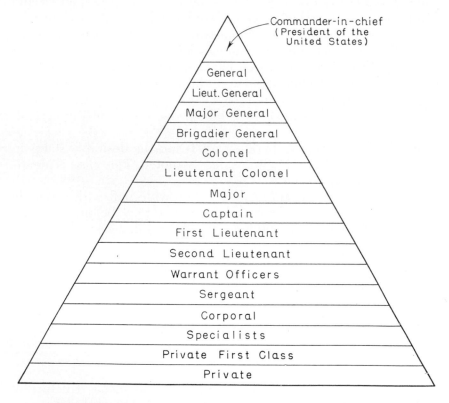

Vertical Dimensions of a Social Organization (U.S. Army)

[6] The list of readings at the end of the chapter includes a great number of these studies of American communities.

lower classmen, class presidents and class members, harvest-ball queens and other girls, all represent differences in social status. A common American saying is "There's always room at the top"—room there for the successful man or the successful few.

All social systems have their hierarchy of responsibility, prestige, and privilege. As a Pullman porter said, when commenting on a serious mistake in designing the Pullman berths for a new streamliner, "When the big feller makes a mistake it kin always be fixed, but when the little feller makes one, there's the devil to pay." He was calling attention to differences in privilege which give one person immunity from punishment for mistakes, the other none.

Multiple Statuses. In a complex society there is no one system of status, but many. One may speak of the upper, middle, and lower classes, thinking in a very general way of groupings based on wealth, social standing, or some other criteria. He may, on the other hand, catalog people into groups on the basis of occupation, and rank them from common laborer up to the professions. Such broad class groupings tend to overshadow all other kinds of groupings in affecting social relationships between persons.

Actually, in any society an individual has many statuses. He may have a status because of his age, sex, or race; because of his educational attainment; because of the wealth that he has inherited or that which he has acquired; because of his occupation, his possession of special deformities, his development of special talents; because of his position in royalty, his place in the church, a secret order, the army, or in any one of many other situations which are used as a basis for sorting individuals into different roles or statuses by the particular culture pattern of the society. His statuses are related to his opportunities in the society. These opportunities, in turn, are limited by the character of the social structure. In class social orders there are many alternatives from which to choose; in caste social orders there are few.

The term "social class" broadly interpreted has to do with the freedom of individual choice in the social system. Class means much choice; caste, little.

ASCRIBED AND ASSIGNED STATUSES IN CLASS AND CASTE SOCIAL STRUCTURES

Class societies trust much more to the current generation in that they permit more social positions to be achieved. Relatively few positions are ascribed as in caste social orders.

A role and status become assigned to an individual because he has earned it, not because his grandfather occupied the position. This was the essential difference in points of view expressed in the anecdote told at the beginning of the chapter. The Chicago banking house wanted a man who had proved his ability. It expected a recommendation which would tell whether the young Bostonian had the qualifications banking requires. Unlike the man who wrote the recommendation, the company did not give a hang about the fellow's family pedigree.

Caste systems trust the current generation very little in placing individuals in work, religion, marriage, or other positions. So, in a caste, a son is automatically in his father's occupation. One must marry a person chosen by his elders, and they always choose within the caste. Thus no risks are taken with positions being left unfilled.

The big risk in caste systems is that high position will be filled by incompetents. Reference has been made to incompetents occupying thrones because their veins carried royal blood. So do lecherous degenerates often rule feudal estates and princes without any sense of social obligation preside over hereditary principalities.

In a class society, there is great risk that many positions may go unfilled. Domestics as a servile class have disappeared from the American scene. Yet they are plentiful in social orders where ascription of status is the basic law of the social order. There is also a shortage of nurses and teachers, positions that promise highest status. But as rewards in money and respect are increased, more young people can be drawn into these high-status callings.

Thus a vital difference in class and caste societies is the very informality which characterizes the filling of all positions. Caste leaves nothing to chance or to individual initiative. The society must function and, therefore, most positions are ascribed for generations ahead. Class societies leave most positions open to individual initiative. Through competitive endeavor, the person seeks his level of performance.

The caste society, therefore, emphasizes traditional placement (ascription of status). The class society emphasizes competitive placement (assignment of status).

STATUS, PRIVILEGE, AND POWER

Those of the greatest prestige and honor tend to acquire the greatest amount of social power. In many societies, official positions are reserved to them. With office comes additional opportunities to acquire even further property, power, and domination. Thus with

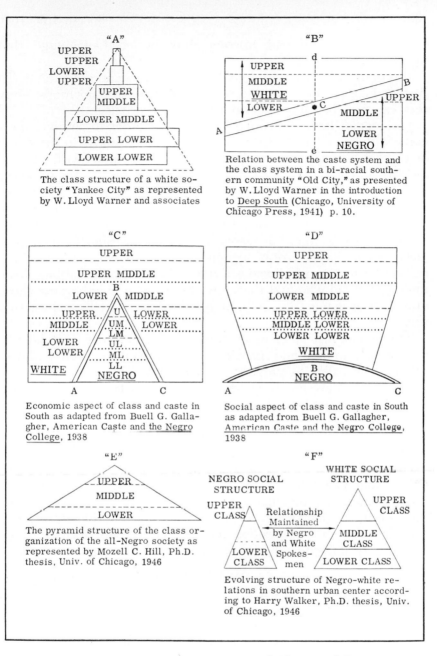

"A"

UPPER UPPER
LOWER UPPER
UPPER MIDDLE
LOWER MIDDLE
UPPER LOWER
LOWER LOWER

The class structure of a white society "Yankee City" as represented by W. Lloyd Warner and associates

"B"

UPPER
MIDDLE
WHITE
LOWER
UPPER
MIDDLE
LOWER
NEGRO

Relation between the caste system and the class system in a bi-racial southern community "Old City," as presented by W. Lloyd Warner in the introduction to Deep South (Chicago, University of Chicago Press, 1941) p. 10.

"C"

UPPER
UPPER MIDDLE
LOWER MIDDLE
UPPER MIDDLE LOWER
LOWER LOWER
WHITE
NEGRO

Economic aspect of class and caste in South as adapted from Buell G. Gallagher, American Caste and the Negro College, 1938

"D"

UPPER
UPPER MIDDLE
LOWER MIDDLE
UPPER LOWER
MIDDLE LOWER
LOWER LOWER
WHITE
NEGRO

Social aspect of class and caste in South as adapted from Buell G. Gallagher, American Caste and the Negro College, 1938

"E"

UPPER
MIDDLE
LOWER

The pyramid structure of the class organization of the all-Negro society as represented by Mozell C. Hill, Ph.D. thesis, Univ. of Chicago, 1946

"F"

NEGRO SOCIAL STRUCTURE
WHITE SOCIAL STRUCTURE
UPPER CLASS
Relationship Maintained by Negro and White Spokesmen
UPPER CLASS
MIDDLE CLASS
LOWER CLASS
LOWER CLASS

Evolving structure of Negro-white relations in southern urban center according to Harry Walker, Ph.D. thesis, Univ. of Chicago, 1946

Diagrammatic Representation of Class and Caste as Revealed by Community Researches

From J. Lloyd Warner, "American Class and Caste," American Journal of Sociology, September, 1936, p. 235. Copyright, 1936, by the University of Chicago.

great privilege there tends to come all of the social advantages that men know.

It is difficult for a society to balance privileges and obligations. To be just, high privilege must carry imposing social obligations. Only then can there be compensation to society for privilege.

Positions of high status and privilege, in order to survive, must carry with them recognized social obligations to those in the lower levels of the social pyramid. When privilege is assumed without compensating obligation, rebellion is in time inevitable, unless all power to rebel is destroyed. And even the most miserable and helpless may rebel if liberty becomes a greater prize than life itself. During the decadent days of the Roman Empire, emperors claimed numerous privileges and powers but recognized few obligations to their subjects. When official position degenerates to this point, the seeds of revolution are sown. Dynasties are overthrown by the rabble of the underprivileged who find their low status intolerable because those granted the immunities of high privilege seem to have forgotten them.

Throughout history there are numerous examples of the tendency of societies to pyramid privilege. Our forefathers, for example, granted the ballot to property owners only. The tradition of the gentleman was prevalent in early American society, and persisted for many years in southern society. In the early days at Harvard, students were rated and seated according to wealth of their families. During the Revolutionary War, a Silk Stocking Company was organized in Philadelphia for a company of gentlemen.[7]

One of the oldest rules of man's social relations is that those of prestige and power tend to multiply protections to their status, fortifying themselves with rules, manners, and etiquette by which they maintain their aloofness from the masses. Their rationalizations of the "rightness" of their position and the "natural" inferiority of those below carry in them seeds of destruction.[8]

SUMMARY

Human beings cannot live together as equals in a psychological and social sense, for they are never equal in their conception of each other. They may be declared equal politically, as in democratic political orders; they may be declared equal in ability and intelligence, as certain groups, for example, the sexes and races, have been by modern intelligence tests; they may be declared equal by numer-

---

[7] This paragraph adapted from the author's *Social Control* (rev. ed.; Chicago: J. B. Lippincott Co., 1956). For a fuller treatment, see that volume.

[8] For a vivid discussion of the "fate of the closed classes" (E. A. Ross), turn to Chapter 23, pp. 434–35.

ous measures. And yet, occupational groups, races, and men and women are never treated as equals. To be a shoemaker is to be considered in some respects a different kind of human being than to be a banker or a college president, and so forth. And every individual within his own group achieves a standing that makes him rate higher or lower than others in certain aspects of his behavior. Status differences are an ever-present social reality.

Social class is an important element in all social structures. Societies differ primarily in the degree to which this intangible matter of class is fixed in the social order. Sociologists conceive of two general types of social structure, as far as class is concerned: the one, the caste system, in which statuses are fixed and inflexible, passed on through social heredity; the other, the class systems, which vary greatly in their degree of elasticity.

In the open-class societies it is possible for the individual to move from one class to another through social climbing. The extent to which upward mobility is encouraged varies greatly, even within open-class societies. In some, the barriers to upward movement are numerous. In others they are almost indistinguishable.

Caste social structures provide continuity through the generations. Most roles can be ascribed, with their accompanying statuses. Much of the competition within the social order is eliminated. Power becomes enthroned through the generations, and often abused. Even so, there is great personal security in knowing one's place and being trained to fit it. This applies to all social layers. Life takes on an automatic quality which greatly reduces the need for personal adjustment.

Open-class structures are by their very nature competitive and place a great deal of strain on the individual in that they offer him great promise as the reward for his effort. In such societies a wide range of roles can be performed and with them goes the accompanying recognition.

Inherent in the open-class systems is the idea of achieved privilege, prestige, and power. The risk of caste structures is that those granted high status will fail to perform the functions that are demanded of those who are given privilege. The risk of open-class structures is that needed positions will go unfilled. The problem of the democratic social orders is not to eliminate social class, but rather to keep it so elastic that those who have arrived at a position of high status can readily be dethroned by those who are willing to give more spirit, energy, and creativeness to the task with which the status is associated.

DISCUSSION AND REVIEW QUESTIONS

1. Define and contrast the workings of class and caste.
2. What is the key factor in distinguishing the two kinds of social structures?
3. Show how the caste principle limits roles open to the individual.
4. How does caste assign privilege?
5. Discuss the significance of the middle-class quality of the social structure of the United States. Compare with the Latin American societies.
6. Which type of social structure grants more assigned statuses?
7. Show how caste privilege becomes social power.
8. Relate doctrines of inferiority and superiority to the social structure.

SOURCEBOOK READINGS

GITTLER, JOSEPH B. *Social Dynamics.* New York: McGraw-Hill Book Co., Inc., 1952.
  1. AMORY, CLEVELAND, "The Proper Bostonian," pp. 151–60.
  2. WARNER and LUNT, "A Case of a Family Whose Members Reside in the Lower and Middle Classes," pp. 160–64.

KOENIG, SAMUEL, REX D. HOPPER, and FELIKS GROSS. *Sociology: A Book of Readings.* Englewood Cliffs, N.J.: Prentice-Hall, Inc., 1956.
  3. COREY, LEWIS, "The Middle Class in Present-Day America," pp. 312–16.
  4. FORM, WILLIAM H., "The Class System in a Planned Community," pp. 324–32.

LEE, ELIZABETH BRYANT, and ALFRED McCLUNG LEE. *Social Problems in America* (rev. ed.). New York: Henry Holt & Co., Inc., 1955.
  5. WARNER, W. LLOYD, LEO SROLE, and PAUL S. LUNT, "Some Characteristics of Yankee City's Social Classes," pp. 348–50.
  6. USEEM, JOHN, PIERRE TANGENT, and RUTH USEEM, "Stratification in a Prairie Town," pp. 350–51.

O'BRIEN, ROBERT W., CLARENCE C. SCHRAG, and WALTER T. MARTIN. *Readings in General Sociology* (2d ed.). Boston: Houghton Mifflin Co., 1957.
  7. HUNTER, FLOYD, "Community Power Structure," pp. 90–103.
  8. O'BRIEN, ROBERT W., "Comment on Class and Caste Diagrams," pp. 334–36.
  9. HILL, MOZELL C., "Class Structure in an All-Negro Society," pp. 336–41.
  10. MILLS, C. WRIGHT, "The Status Panic," pp. 341–45.
  11. KNUPFER, GENEVIEVE, "Portrait of the Underdog," pp. 346–52.
  12. NORTH, CECIL C. and PAUL K. HATT, "Occupational Status and Prestige," pp. 352–60.

SCHULER, EDGAR A., DUANE L. GIBSON, MAUDE L. FIERO, and WILBUR B. BROOKOVER. *Outside Readings in Sociology.* New York: The Thomas Crowell Co., 1956.
  13. BENEDICT, RUTH, "Taking One's Proper Station," pp. 71–77.
  14. LINTON, RALPH, "Status and Role," pp. 118–25.
  15. WARNER, W. LLOYD, MARCHIA MEEKER, and KENNETH EELLS, "What Social Class Is in America," pp. 316–37.
  16. COLE, G. D. H., "The Conception of the Middle Class," pp. 338–51.
  17. MARQUAND, JOHN P., "Portrait of a Striver," pp. 351–59.

WILSON, LOGAN, and WILLIAM L. KOLB. *Sociological Analysis.* New York: Harcourt, Brace & Co., Inc., 1949.
  18. LINTON, RALPH, "Status and Role," pp. 211–23.
  19. MILLS, C. WRIGHT, "The Middle Classes in Middle-Sized Cities," pp. 443–53.

SELECTED READINGS

BENDIX, REINHARD, and S. M. LIPSET (eds.). *Class, Status and Power: A Reader in Social Stratification.* Glencoe, Ill.: The Free Press, 1953.

CENTERS, RICHARD. "Social Class, Occupation and Imputed Belief," *American Journal of Sociology*, 58:543–55 (1953).

————. "The American Class Structure." In Theodore M. Newcomb and Eugene L. Hartley (eds.). *Readings in Social Psychology.* New York: Henry Holt & Co., Inc., 1947, pp. 481–93.

DAVIS, ALLISON. "Socialization and Adolescent Personality." *Adolescence, Forty-Third Yearbook.* Part I. Chicago: National Society for the Study of Education, 1944, chap. 11.

GERTH, HANS, and C. WRIGHT MILLS. *Character and the Social Structure.* New York: Harcourt, Brace & Co., Inc., 1953.

HAVIGHURST, ROBERT J., and ALLISON DAVIS. "A Comparison of the Chicago and Harvard Studies of the Social Class Differences in Child Rearing," *American Sociological Review*, 20:438–42 (Aug., 1955).

HOLLINGSHEAD, A. B. *Elmtown's Youth.* New York: John Wiley & Sons, Inc., 1949.

KAHL, JOSEPH A. *The American Class Structure.* New York: Rinehart & Co., Inc., 1957.

KRONENBERGER, LOUIS. *Company Manners: A Cultural Inquiry into American Life.* Indianapolis: The Bobbs-Merrill Co., Inc., 1954.

LEVY, MARION J., JR. *The Structure of Society.* Princeton: Princeton University Press, 1952.

MILLS, C. WRIGHT. *The Power Elite.* Toronto: Oxford University Press, 1956. See also the review of this book in *Time*, April 30, 1956, p. 116.

PETERSEN, WILLIAM. "Is America Still the Land of Opportunity?" *Commentary*, Nov., 1953, pp. 477–86.

REISSMAN, L. "Levels of Aspiration and Social Class," *American Sociological Review*, 18:233–42 (1953).

SJOBERG, GIDEON. "Are Social Classes in America Becoming More Rigid?" *American Sociological Review*, 16:575–83 (1951).

"The Rich Middle-Income Class," *Fortune*, May, 1954, pp. 94 ff.

WARNER, W. LLOYD. *American Life: Dream and Reality.* Chicago: University of Chicago Press, 1953.

WARNER, W. LLOYD, *et al. Democracy in Jonesville.* New York: Harper & Brothers, 1944.

WARNER, W. LLOYD, *et al. Social Class in America.* Chicago: Science Research Associates, 1949

WARNER, W. LLOYD, and J. C. ABEGGLEN. *Occupational Mobility in American Business and Industry, 1928–1952.* Minneapolis: University of Minnesota Press, 1955.

WARNER, W. LLOYD, and P. S. LUNT. *The Social Life of a Modern Community.* New Haven: Yale University Press, 1941.

Chapter 17

Male and Female Roles and Statuses

In most societies men and women are different orders of human beings. The female is the lower of the species; the male the most desired at birth, the best cared for, and the most honored throughout life. His is the higher status of the species in most societies and, consequently, the roles assigned to him are superior to those assigned to the female. Not all societies by any means assign superior status to any one given role, but whatever the role chosen for a superior rating, it is likely that the male will perform it and the female be given the menial role. Thus, in every culture there is a male subculture and a female subculture, which at many points overlap but still are sufficiently distinct to give men and women a different rating in the social scheme.

Here is a poet's conception of male and female role differences:

> Man's love is of man's life a thing apart,
> 'Tis woman's whole existence; man may range
> The court, camp, church, the vessel, and the mart;
> Sword, gown, gain, glory, offer in exchange
> Pride, fame, ambition, to fill up his heart,
> And few there are whom these cannot estrange;
> Men have all these resources, we but one,
> To love again, and be again undone.[1]

Here Margaret Mead adds the feminine anthropological touch, perhaps with an underlying note of satire. At least it may seem so to the male:

"In every known human society, the male's need for achievement can be recognized. Men may cook, or weave, or dress dolls, or hunt

---

[1] Lord Byron, *Don Juan*, Canto I, stanza cxciv.

hummingbirds, but if such activities are appropriate occupations of men, then the whole society, men and women alike, votes them as important. When the same occupations are performed by women, they are regarded as less important. In a great number of human societies men's sureness of their sex role is tied up with their right, or ability, to practice some activity that women are not allowed to practice. Their maleness, in fact, has to be underwritten by preventing women from entering some field or performing some feat. Here may be found the relationship between maleness and pride . . . There seems no evidence that it is necessary for men to surpass women in any specific way, but rather that men do need to find reassurance in achievement . . . cultures frequently phrase achievement as something that women do not or cannot do, rather than directly as something men do well.

"The recurrent problem of civilization is to define the male role satisfactorily enough . . . so that the male may in the course of his life reach a solid sense of irreversible achievement, of which his childhood knowledge of the satisfactions of childbearing have given him a glimpse. In the case of women, it is only necessary that they be permitted by the given social arrangements to fulfill their biological role to attain this sense of irreversible achievement. If women are to be restless and questioning, even in the face of childbearing, they must have been made so through education . . . If men are ever to be at peace, even certain that their lives have been lived as they were meant to be, they must have, in addition to paternity, culturally elaborated forms of expression that are lasting and sure. Each culture—in its own way—has developed forms that will make men satisfied in their constructive activities without distorting their sure sense of their masculinity. Fewer cultures have yet found ways in which to give women a divine discontent that will demand other satisfactions than those of childbearing."[2]

SEX DIFFERENTIATION IN ROLES AND STATUS

It is to be expected that the biological fact of sex should be a factor in differentiation. Basic biological differences, however, will not explain the marked differences in behavior roles assigned the sexes, for there is no consistency in the social roles the sexes play from culture to culture. During the course of two generations the activity roles assigned to women have greatly changed within American society. This is evidence that the activity role of the sexes is not determined by physiological difference, except within a very narrow biological sphere.

[2] Margaret Mead, *Male and Female* (New York: William Morrow & Co., Inc., 1949).

Patterns of Deference

The Venda girl not only must bring the headman a dipper of water but must also kneel before him as he drinks. The new warrior chief (below) must have his head shaved by his mother before he takes office.

Members of the Venda tribe
(Information Office, Union of South Africa)

Masai of Kenya (British Information Services)

In American culture a large body of folklore has accumulated about the notion of the "weaker sex." This folklore assumes that women should be protected, sheltered, treated courteously and as clinging vines. Women have, by tradition which has only in recent generations begun to weaken, been considered inferior to men, incapable of achieving a higher education and of competing in the business and industrial worlds. It has been assumed that their temperament disqualifies them for making decisions in the economic and political world where the masculine executive's decision has been considered superior. Women are supposed to be by nature gentle, kind, considerate, properly temperate; it is they who are to shield the young and protect the weak and cater to the weaknesses of men.

Men by tradition are supposed to be more strong and sturdy, more independent and self-sufficient, more able to buck the cold, competitive economic structure of the work world. They are less given to chronic complaints of ill health, which are considered women's peculiar right when they must escape from the drudgery of life. In contrast, custom permits the male to escape by way of bottled spirits.

Even in such matters as religion, modern women are supposed to differ distinctly from men. In fact, one wonders if religion in the United States is gradually becoming primarily the province of women, rather than of men, as among primitives. In our social system there is a vast difference in what custom sanctions in the way of emotional display for men and women. From the giggling age of girlhood through old age, women are supposed to be more romantically inclined and more given to the expression of emotions. Their tears are supposed to flow more freely and their love to be more gently and fully expressed.

As for man, his world is more one of work than of emotions. He is supposed to go through a blind state of youthful romance, which lands him in the holy estate of matrimony, but after the initial aura of romance has worn away he is supposed to find his primary satisfaction in work and in the competitive quest for status outside the family.

Today, women are at the social crossroads. Once it was sufficient for a woman to play the role of wife and mother, housekeeper and clinging vine, feeding her husband and helping to build his reputation by her administration of, and entertainment within, the home. But today, due to a new emphasis in the educational system, women also have been taught to be ambitious and have been given the training and skills by which ambition can be realized. In marriage they face a conflict of roles which for many is life-long in duration. Unsatisfied to play the simple, domestic role that satisfied their grandmothers so fully, they want also the role of competitive success, comparable to that of their husbands.

Few women can be happy giving up the domestic role entirely, for they still want romance. It is held up to them in our culture as the highest value obtainable by women. But an increasing proportion find that romance and marriage alone do not satisfy the ambition with which they have been inspired in the school system, where they learned that they can compete as the equal, if not the superior, of man.

Speaking of the college woman, Mirra Komarovsky writes of the contradiction in female roles. She considers the two opposing conceptions of roles in this way:

"One of these roles may be termed the 'feminine' role. While there are a number of permissive variants of the feminine role for women of college age (the 'good sport,' the 'glamour girl,' the 'young lady,' the domestic 'home girl,' etc.), they have a common core of attributes defining the proper attitudes to men, family, work, love, etc., and a set of personality traits often described with reference to the male sex role as 'not as dominant, or aggressive as men' or 'more emotional, sympathetic.'

"The other and more recent role is, in a sense, no sex role at all, because it partly obliterates the differentiation in sex. It demands of the women much the same virtues, patterns of behavior, and attitude that it does of the men of a corresponding age. We shall refer to this as the 'modern' role."[3]

After making this classification the author quotes college girls' reports on their dilemma:

"Girl 1 writes:

How am I to pursue any course single-mindedly when some way along the line a person I respect is sure to say, 'You are on the wrong track and are wasting your time.' Uncle John telephones every Sunday morning. His first question is: 'Did you go out last night?' He would think me a 'grind' if I were to stay home Saturday night and finish a term paper. My father expects me to get an 'A' in every subject and is disappointed by a 'B.' He says I have plenty of time for social life. Mother says, 'That "A" in Philosophy is very nice dear. But please don't become so deep that no man will be good enough for you.' And, finally, Aunt Mary's line is careers for women. 'Prepare yourself for some profession. This is the only way to insure yourself independence and an interesting life. You have plenty of time to marry.'

[3] Mirra Komarovsky, "Cultural Contradictions and Sex Roles," *American Journal of Sociology*, 52:184–89 (Nov. 1946).

"Girl 2 writes:

I get a letter from my mother at least three times a week. One week her letters will say, 'Remember that this is your last year at college. Subordinate everything to your studies. You must have a good record to secure a job.' The next week her letters are full of wedding news. This friend of mine got married; that one is engaged; my young cousin's wedding is only a week off. When, my mother wonders, will I make up my mind? Surely, I wouldn't want to be the only unmarried one in my group. It is high time, she feels, that I give some thought to it.

"Girl 3 writes:

One of my two brothers writes: 'Cover up that high forehead and act a little dumb once in a while'; while the other always urges upon me the importance of rigorous scholarship.

"Girl 4 writes:

One of the nicest techniques is to spell long words incorrectly once in a while. My boy-friend seems to get a great kick out of it and writes back, 'Honey, you certainly don't know how to spell.'

"Girl 5 writes:

On dates I always go through the 'I-don't-care-anything-you-want-to-do' routine. It gets monotonous but boys fear girls who make decisions. They think such girls would make nagging wives."[4]

There is a suggestion in the preceding accounts that women and men act differently, that they differ in roles played and in respect to the way they accept their role assignments in contemporary culture. This is reason for further sociological study of men and women's place in the social structure.

THE BIOLOGICAL AND CULTURAL ELEMENTS IN ROLE DESIGNATIONS[5]

Women and men differ, biologically speaking, primarily in their capacity to bear and nurse children. Beyond the primary sex characteristics are differences in stature, body proportions, muscular development, hair growth, and skin texture. These differences are the organic basis for most rationalized status differences between male and female.

To such biologically differentiating factors are added the customary cultural elaborations, such as those expressed in differences in hairdo, dress, manners, and morals. Cultural conditioning may also explain difference in the development of certain perceptive and sen-

[4] *Ibid.*
[5] This section is an adaptation of the author's *Social Control* (rev. ed.; Chicago: J. B. Lippincott Co., 1950). For a fuller treatment, see that volume.

sory traits. Women, in most cultures, have been considered more gifted in music, color sense, and certain forms of art, just as the male has traditionally manifested greater aptitude for mechanical and mathematical interests.

Some writers believe that alleged differences in personality traits of men and women, even to the extent of assertiveness, submissiveness, dependence, and so on, are not sex-linked, but are rather a matter of conditioning in the culture. They cite the argument that in matriarchies women play the aggressive, dominant, governing roles, just as men do in most cultures. These scholars believe that all such differences are aspects of the social system.[6]

The author of this text leans to a view that male and female, because of sex hormones, do possess certain innate differences with regard to aggressiveness, receptivity, and so on. The fact that most cultures have placed the male in the leading role is probably indicative of the fact that the male is by nature the more aggressive. Exceptions in an occasional culture do not necessarily prove the opposite case. One sees the aggressive male throughout most of the animal kingdom. One also sees the male change to a more docile temperament after castration.

Granting all of this, one must still recognize that cultures may greatly exaggerate the inherited tendencies of both male and female, so that what one sees in the developed personality is far more than rudimentary, innate sex differences. In fact, one often finds elemental traits of male or female elaborated into complex and intricate culture patterns, which, in themselves, become so automatic and so universally established that were it not for one's ability to compare peoples in different cultures, he would have to assume that all human beings shared one common behavior system.

In every culture men and women conform to the cultural norms which are established by their group. They do so automatically and unconsciously, for in each sex is formed from earliest childhood the attitudes and habit patterns which makes it accept and act the role of male or female. Only as the male acts like a male and the female like a female, as defined by a particular culture, are they able to get along in social relations. It is for this reason that adults concentrate on training the child for the particular sex role that he must play in the culture and train him to play it as it must be played.

---

[6] E. T. Hiller, *Social Relations and Social Structures* (New York: Harper & Brothers, 1947), pp. 402 ff., argues for this point of view; and Margaret Mead has described cultures in which sex roles are reversed, the female manifesting the dominant, aggressive traits displayed by the male in most cultures. See her *Sex and Temperament in Three Primitive Societies* (New York: McGraw-Hill Book Co., Inc., 1937).

Masculinity and Femininity. The building of personality for maleness or femaleness is done according to conceptions of what the male and female should be to fit the social structure.

To the extent to which a trait or value is credited to one sex, it must be denied the other, or compensated for by the appearance of the opposite value in the other sex. For example, to the extent that the male is made the strong, domineering, aggressive, warlike creature, the female personality must be made the weak, clinging, gentle, passive, submissive creature. To the extent that the man is made worldly, materialistic, money-minded, and community and politically oriented, the woman must be made moral, religious, virtuous in character, politically innocent, domestic in interests and activities, protective of the weak, and solicitous of the welfare of the child. If the one sex is trained to be demanding, bold, courageous, the other must be trained to compliance and reticence, to hiding in the background and taking second place, the one being the shadow and support of the other, playing an unobtrusive role largely within the confines of the home. To the extent that women are worshipped for their beauty and delicacy, men must be worshipped for their strength and endurance, for their competence and efficiency.

"Beauty," for example, is a delicate product of leisure and cannot be imposed on both sexes alike. Society can never afford such luxury if political and economic life is to continue and society is to be an ongoing affair.

In these various contrasts one sees the usual way in which societies train the personality so that both male and female will play both complementary and supplementary roles in various social structures. It is by being trained in a system of different personal attributes that men find women tolerable, even acceptable and desirable, and it is because of complementary training that women find men desirable and acceptable. In cultures where men are supposed to be strong, women want strong men, just as men want delicate women.

These differences may be carried to an exaggerated extreme, as in China where women bound their feet, and as in early American culture when the beautiful woman was an extremely delicate woman—frail, pale, and almost helpless, encumbered by styles of dress which added even further to this appearance of delicacy and helplessness.

Men likewise try to express their personalities to fit expectations of women. They are trained to do so from earliest infancy. Whatever the masculine role is, most men play it because only by doing so can men win women's hearts and respect. So also, women play up to the role that is typed for them by the culture. They must play up to the expectations of men, whether the expectations are for the passive compliance of a willing servant or for an equal, or even a superior partner. Only by doing so can they attract and hold the interests of men and thus satisfy themselves in the fulfillment of their desires for marriage and family life.

Sex identification is well guaranteed in all societies by differences in dress, hair styles, make-up, manners, and taboos. Any venture of one sex in the direction of closer identification with the other is criticized and suspect. Even though occasionally similarities in certain items of dress are approved, or at least tolerated, like blue jeans for women, most distinctions are preserved.

It is hard to visualize what would happen if all external marks of sex distinction were to be suddenly erased. What would be the implications to morals, manners, etiquette, romance, even sex interest itself? Would romance flourish if it were not for certain external symbols of dress or manner? Would some of the traits of disposition and temperament, which are considered inherent, actually persist from generation to generation were not certain external symbols of male and female character maintained in the culture? Do softness of man-

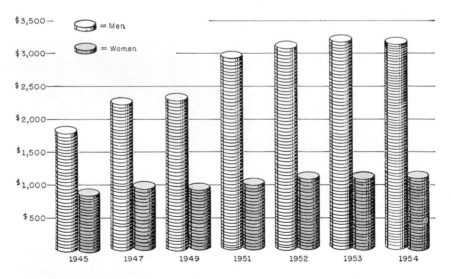

Evidence of Woman's Second-Place Status in the Work World

The low median income of women relative to men reflects in part the greater administrative responsibility men often carry, but part of the picture is discrimination. Women often receive less than men for the same work or even superior work. For further evidence of wage discrimination against women, see the chart on pages 424–25. (*Bureau of the Census*, Current Population Reports, *Series P-60, No. 19, Oct. 1955.*)

ners and voice require silk garments and permanent waves? These are questions to which there is no answer, for no society is likely to do away with masculinity and femininity, with all this implies.

Differences in Work Roles. In the quotation from *Male and Female*, Margaret Mead suggests that men's work must be superior. Yet we know that it is not inherently so. One culture assigns a certain task to men; another may require him to do exactly the opposite. In one culture men carry the loads because "they are strong"; in another the women do "because their heads are so much harder and stronger."[7] In one culture she milks the cows; in another this is man's work. In one culture she may do all the weaving; in another culture the men do it. In one culture she cultivates the fields, while the men are hunters. In another culture her work may be confined almost entirely to the household, with the men doing all of the field work. But certainly baby care is woman's work exclusively! Not necessarily. Among the Marquesas "even cooking, housekeeping, and baby-tending are proper male occupations, and women spend most of their time primping."[8]

Today, in industrial society, one sees the gradual merging of the work roles of men and women. Although still differing greatly, there is much overlapping of roles compared to a few generations ago.

Not only in work roles, but in property systems, sex differentiation has been operative. In many cultures all property rights reside in the male. Often the woman herself is property and has to be purchased. In polygynous cultures, she may actually become a worker for the husband and be regarded largely in terms of her economic value.

Such societies, obviously, have few of the family disputes over economic values, consumption habits, and work roles which are so characteristic of the modern democratic families, particularly those living in states with community property laws in which women have joint property rights.

Differences in Religious Roles. Women are the main custodians of morals and religion.[9] The Bible blames the Fall on the temptations by Eve. During the witchcraft mania, they were usually singled out as mediums and, far more often than men, were accused of sex-commerce with demons, of being conjurers and possessed of power to do evil through allegiance with the spirit world. They were often burned

[7] The latter example is of the Arapesh, cited by Ralph Linton, *The Study of Man* (New York: Appleton-Century-Crofts, Inc., 1936), p. 116.

[8] *Ibid.*, p. 117.

[9] Hiller, *op. cit.*, pp. 420 ff.

at the stake. Most mediums today are women, as are fortune tellers and numerologists.

Women, as protectors of the weak, as the sex most vitally concerned with the matters of birth, life, and death, are supposed in contemporary Western culture not only to need religion as a support more than men, but also to be more interested in it. Theirs is the job of caring for the weak and of giving support and faith to those who depend on them for care.

To the extent that religion is a personal affair in the culture, women are, therefore, generally more interested in it than are men. This is part of the whole complex of cultural values of the Western world which assign to women greater moral and spiritual values than to the male. The male specializes more in economic and materialistic values, which are not always compatible with the moral and spiritual pursuits of the highest order. Achievement, rather than goodness, becomes the goal for the male.

There is, in fact, much evidence that women are more interested in church activities and in religious affairs generally than are men. There has been much evidence in recent history, since women had a chance to influence the social order, of their more aggressive part in various reform movements. They have step by step practically wiped out licensed prostitution and introduced many other moral reforms which are supposed to elevate not only the morals of men but those of women. Yet when it comes to church administration, the ministry, and priesthood, there are few fields equally dominated by male leadership. If women play the role of the consumer of religion in contemporary social structure, as they seem to do, males are the main dispensers.

MALE AND FEMALE PREROGATIVES AND DISABILITIES

One has only to glance at differences in privilege of the sexes to realize that the male has top status in American culture still, as he has had from time immemorial. His status is not so far above women as it has been in most societies, but it is nonetheless superior. Differences in privilege of the two sexes is one of the best measures of real status.

We find that in the home the teen-age boy is much more often given democratic treatment than is the girl. The girl is still protected and shielded by parents and her liberties, consequently, curbed.[10]

10 For a study on this subject of more than 4,000 high school seniors in the state of Washington, see Paul H. Landis and Carol L. Stone, *The Relationship of Parental Authority to Patterns of Teenage Adjustment, Washington Agricultural Experiment Station Bulletin,* No. 538, Pullman, Washington (Sept. 1952); also, Carol L. Stone and Paul H. Landis, "An Approach to Authority Pattern in Parent-Teenage Relationships," *Rural Sociology,* 18:233–42 (Sept. 1953).

Although the female is gaining some rights of sensuous satisfaction, there are still many taboos she must respect, although they have long been the right of the male; tobacco, liquor, even joy in sexual relations are often denied her. And she is held to a much sterner code of manners and morals than is the male.

The double standard of morality still exists, and although many believe that it should no longer be, the fact yet remains that in the average dating relationship the woman is still expected to be the custodian of morals for the pair.

Whether or not she proves equal to the task is her own risk. If she fails, and her moral delinquencies are detected, she suffers disgrace and humiliation. The male is forgiven his ventures in illicit sex relations, even when pregnancy is a result of his activity. The female is less likely to be forgiven. Nonetheless, the moral restraint that society places on one sex acts as a restraint on both.

An age of chivalry denied woman many outlets by defining her role as that of a beautiful and delicate plant. Her dress has often been an impediment to freedom of movement and body grace. Her beauty has often been concealed behind veils and bonnets lest she appear too alluring and tempt man to take advantage of her.

This is not to say that women have never gained anything by the unique roles assigned them in social structures. They have avoided many of the responsibilities and risks of the male. To protect the virtue and good name of women, men have willingly died in duels. So that women may have leisure and enjoyment, many husbands overexert themselves and die prematurely. More than two of every three elderly persons in our nation today are women who have outlived their more active husbands.

But modern women have come to demand a great deal of equality in roles and statuses, and are willing to pay the price in responsibility and risk. This is the character which has come to be called the "new woman." She is a product of the Industrial Revolution, which marked the beginning of work outside the home. She is still in the making. Her every venture outside has been met with criticism and male scorn. The deepest sting has been the male's accusation of immorality which has marked each of these ventures outside.

The latest major venture was her entry into the military services during World War II. Of course, ran the male allegation, only the immoral ones entered the service, those in quest of male companionship and unrestricted sex activity. So ran the absurdity. But it is difficult, in a social structure where masculine values have been dominant, for women to be credited with the same patriotic motives that men have for serving their country.

With all their venturing outside, there are still certain occupations that continue to be characteristically female—nursing, the teaching of small children, library work—work which in some respects carries over elements closely related to home activity.

Enough has been said to prove that men and women have a different place in the social structure; that, in fact, they still play different roles and acquire somewhat different statuses, even though our society has long been moving in the direction of sex equality.

SUMMARY

The American novelist Philip Wylie some years ago pictured two worlds.[11] One was a world in which all women were removed from the scene, and men took over management of life and social relations. In the other, men vanished from the earth, and women ran the family and other social institutions. The picture, of course, is interesting enough to captivate the attention of the reader, for as one can well imagine, the two worlds were operated quite differently. So it would be if that should actually happen, for men and women are each trained for different roles and each is accustomed to different statuses in the social system.

One of the most subtle and far-reaching aspects of any social structure is sex differentiation. It involves almost every aspect of human life, even the matter of social control itself, for women are by custom forbidden in all cultures to do certain things that men do, and vice versa. Male and female are never merely significant biological facts. Social elaborations are built about biological differences and these social elaborations become key factors in the roles and statuses in a social system.

DISCUSSION AND REVIEW QUESTIONS

1. Comment on the phrase "male and female subculture."

2. Would you consider Margaret Mead's appraisal of the relative significance of the male and female roles typical of the view usually held in the United States? Is she correct?

3. What are some of the devices by which different cultures set the sexes apart into status groups?

4. Illustrate contradictions in women's roles in contemporary United States.

5. Try to weigh biological and cultural factors in role designations for men and women in the United States today.

6. Would you say that masculinity and femininity as conceived in the social structure of the United States today are primarily biological or social traits?

7. Illustrate difference in work roles of male and female in different social structures.

11 Philip Wylie, *The Disappearance* (New York: Rinehart & Co., Inc., 1951).

8. Does the male–female structural pattern affect religious participation and practice in the nation today? Explain.

9. Compare male and female in terms of prerogatives and disabilities in our culture at the present time.

SOURCEBOOK READINGS

FREEDMAN, RONALD, AMOS H. HAWLEY, WERNER S. LANDECKER, GERHARD E. LENSKI, and HORACE M. MINER. *Principles of Sociology* (rev. ed.). New York: Henry Holt & Co., Inc., 1956.
  1. HOHMAN, LESLIE B., and BERTRAM SCHAFFNER, "Sex Behavior and Social Status," pp. 247–48.
  2. USEEM, JOHN, PIERRE TANGENT, and RUTH USEEM, "Stratification in a Prairie Town," pp. 249–57.

LANDIS, JUDSON T., and MARY G. LANDIS. *Readings in Marriage and the Family.* Englewood Cliffs, N.J.: Prentice-Hall, Inc., 1952.
  3. KOMAROVSKY, MIRRA, "Cultural Contradictions and Sex Roles," pp. 375–83.
  4. WALLIN, PAUL, "Cultural Contradictions and Sex Roles: A Repeat Study," pp. 384–86.
  5. KIRKPATRICK, CLIFFORD, "Inconsistency in Marriage Roles and Marriage Conflict," pp. 386–92.

LEE, ELIZABETH BRYANT, and ALFRED McCLUNG LEE. *Social Problems in America* (rev. ed.). New York: Henry Holt & Co., Inc., 1955.
  6. KOMAROVSKY, MIRRA, "Contradictions in Middle-class Female Roles," pp. 132–33.
  7. MEAD, MARGARET, "What Women Want," pp. 144–47.
  8. DEUTSCH, ALBERT, "Class Differences in Male Sex Roles," pp. 147–48.
  9. KING, CHARLES E., "The Negro Maternal Family," pp. 153–56.

O'BRIEN, ROBERT W., CLARENCE C. SCHRAG, and WALTER T. MARTIN. *Readings in General Sociology* (2d ed.). Boston: Houghton Mifflin Co., 1957.
  10. KOMAROVSKY, MIRRA, "Cultural Contradictions and Sex Roles," pp. 230–34.

SCHULER, EDGAR A., DUANE L. GIBSON, MAUDE L. FIERO, and WILBUR B. BROOKOVER. *Outside Readings in Sociology.* New York: The Thomas Crowell Co., 1956.
  11. MEAD, MARGARET, "What Women Want," pp. 125–33.
  12. KOMAROVSKY, MIRRA, "Cultural Contradictions and Sex Roles," pp. 133–42.
  13. COTTRELL, LEONARD S., "Roles and Marital Adjustment," pp. 581–91.

SELECTED READINGS

LANDIS, PAUL H. *Making the Most of Marriage.* New York: Appleton-Century-Crofts, Inc., 1955, chaps. 2–5.

———. *Social Control.* Rev. ed.; Chicago: J. P. Lippincott Co., 1956, chap. 9.

LYNES, RUSSELL. "Husbands: The New Servant Class," *Look,* Dec. 14, 1954, pp. 87–92.

MEAD, MARGARET. *Male and Female.* New York: William Morrow & Co., Inc., 1949.

———. *Sex and Temperament in Three Primitive Societies.* New York: McGraw-Hill Book Co., Inc., 1935.

MICHENER, JAMES. *The Voice of Asia.* New York: Random House, Inc., 1951. "The New Japanese Woman," pp. 18–23, and "The New Woman in India," pp. 241–52.

SCHEINFELD, AMRAM. *Men and Women.* New York: Harcourt, Brace & Co., Inc., 1943.

TERMAN, LEWIS M., et al. *Psychological Factors in Marital Happiness.* New York: McGraw-Hill Book Co., Inc., 1936.

WOOD, MARGARET MARY. *Path of Loneliness.* New York: Columbia University Press, 1953.

Chapter 18

Age-Group Status

All the world's a stage,
And all the men and women merely players.
They have their exits and their entrances;
And one man in his time plays many parts,
His acts being seven ages. At first the infant,
Mewling and puking in the nurse's arms.
And then the whining school-boy, with his satchel
And shining morning face, creeping like snail
Unwillingly to school. And then the lover,
Sighing like furnace, with a woeful ballad
Made to his mistress' eyebrow. Then a soldier,
Full of strange oaths, and bearded like the pard;
Jealous in honour, sudden and quick in quarrel,
Seeking the bubble reputation
Even in the cannon's mouth. And then the justice,
In fair round belly with good capon lined,
With eyes severe and beard of formal cut,
Full of wise saws and modern instances;
And so he plays his part. The sixth age shifts
Into the lean and slipper'd pantaloon,
With spectacles on nose and pouch on side;
His youthful hose, well saved, a world too wide
For his shrunk shank; and his big manly voice,
Turning again toward childish treble, pipes
And whistles in his sound. Last scene of all,
That ends this strange eventful history,
Is second childishness, and mere oblivion,
Sans teeth, sans eyes, sans taste, sans everything.

————Shakespeare, *As You Like It*

No society can treat all age groups alike. To be a child is so different from being an adult that the functions of the child, and the rating given the roles of the child, are different from those of the adult. The grandparents are so different in their activities that they are given a different status in the social order than are young mothers and fathers, who must perform quite differently. It is more or less inevitable, therefore, that different age levels will be given not only different role assignments but different statuses which reflect the significance of these roles in the social system. These statuses vary from time to time and from culture to culture.

In all cultures age group differentiations in roles and statuses are key factors in understanding the social behavior of individuals in the particular society. For this reason sociologists are concerned with age-group roles and statuses.

How significant are differences in this area is illustrated by the following example of the grandfather period of life. It describes a man who has gradually cut off one role after another, as energy has waned, and who now sits quietly with dreams of past roles, and resignation concerning the future. In his dreams are vivid memories of more significant roles played in an earlier day, of a time when his social status was far different than that of these last years. Here is David Grayson's Grandpa Summer.

"Uncle Richard Summers' contemporaries have nearly all gone— mostly long ago; one of the last, his old wife. At his home—I have been there often to see his son—he sits in a large rocking chair with a cushion in it, and a comfortable high back to lean upon. No one else ventures to sit in his chair, even when he is not there. It is not far from the window; and when he sits down he can lean his cane against the wall where he can easily reach it again.

"There is a turmoil of youth and life always about him; of fevered incomings and excited outgoings, of work and laughter and tears and joy and anger. He watches it all, for his mind is still clear, but he does not take sides. He accepts everything, refuses nothing; or, if you like, he refuses everything, accepts nothing.

"He once owned the house where he now lives, with the great barns behind it and the fertile acres spreading far on every hand. From his chair he can look out through a small window, and see the sun on the quiet fields. He once went out swiftly and strongly, he worked hotly, he came in wearied to sleep.

"Now he lives in a small room—and that is more than is really necessary—and when he walks out he does not inquire who owns the land where he treads. He lets the hot world go by, and waits with patience the logic of events.

"Often as I have passed him in the road, I have wondered, as I have been wondering today, how he must look out upon us all, upon our excited comings and goings, our immense concern over the immeasurably trivial. I have wondered, not without a pang, and a resolution, whether I shall ever reach the point where I can let this eager and fascinating world go by without taking toll of it."[1]

Many peoples have so differentiated between childhood and adulthood that elaborate rites are entered into at the time when the tribe recognizes the passage of the child from a dependent to a responsible state. These rites of passage usually come around the time of puberty, although the exact time and the nature of the ceremony are matters of custom. Their common feature is that they mark dramatically the entry into adult status. Below are examples of the variety of ceremonials that various peoples employ.

"Adulthood in central North America means warfare. Honour in it is a great goal of all men. The constantly recurring theme of the youth's coming-of-age, as also of preparation for the warpath at any age, is a magic ritual for success in war. They torture not one another, but themselves; they cut strips of skin from their arms and legs, they strike off their fingers, they drag heavy weights pinned to their chest or leg muscles. Their reward is enhanced prowess in deeds of warfare.

"In Australia, on the other hand, adulthood means participation in an exclusively male cult whose fundamental trait is the exclusion of women. Any woman is put to death if she so much as hears the sound of the bull-roarer at the ceremonies, and she must never know of the rites. Puberty ceremonies are elaborate and symbolic repudiations of the bonds with the female sex; the men are symbolically made self-sufficient and the wholly responsible element of the community. To attain this end, they use drastic sexual rites and bestow supernatural guaranties.

". . . In the interior of British Columbia, adolescent rites are magical training for all occupations, girls are included on the same terms as boys. Boys roll stones down mountains and beat them to the bottom to be swift of foot, or throw gambling-sticks to be lucky in gambling; girls carry water from distant springs, or drop stones down inside their dresses that their children may be born as easily as the pebble drops to the ground.

"In such a tribe as the Nandi of the lake region of East Africa, also, girls and boys share an even-handed puberty rite, though, because of the man's dominant role in the culture, his boyhood training period is more stressed than the woman's. Here adolescent rites are an ordeal inflicted by those already admitted to adult status upon those they are now forced to admit. They require of them the most complete stoicism in the face of ingenious tortures associated with circumci-

[1] From *Adventures in Friendship*, by David Grayson, pseud., Ray Stannard Baker. Copyright, 1910, by Doubleday & Company, Inc.

sion. The rites for the two sexes are separate, but they follow the
same pattern. In both the novices wear for the ceremony the clothing
of their sweethearts. During the operation their faces are watched
for any twinge of pain, and the reward of bravery is given with great
rejoicing by the lover, who runs forward to receive back some of his
adornments. For both the girl and the boy the rites mark their entrée
into a new sex status; the boy is now a warrior and may take a sweetheart, the girl is marriageable. The adolescent tests are for both a
premarital ordeal in which the palm is awarded by their lovers.

"Puberty rites may also be built upon the facts of girls' puberty and
admit of no extension to boys. One of the most naïve of these is the
institution of the fattening-house for girls in Central Africa. In the
region where feminine beauty is all but identified with obesity, the
girl at puberty is segregated, sometimes for years, fed with sweet
and fatty foods, allowed no activity, and her body rubbed assidu-
ously with oils. She is taught during this time her future duties, and
her seclusion ends with a parade of her corpulence that is followed
by her marriage to her proud bridegroom. It is not regarded as necessary for the man to achieve pulchritude before marriage in a similar
fashion.

"The usual ideas around which girls' puberty institutions are centered, and which are not readily extended to boys', are those concerned with menstruation. The uncleanness of the menstruating
woman is a very widespread idea, and in a few regions first menstruation has been made the focus of the associated attitudes. Puberty
rites in these cases are of a thoroughly different character from any
of which we have spoken. Among the Carrier Indians of British
Columbia, the fear and horror of a girl's puberty was at its height.
Her three or four years of seclusion was called "the burying alive"
and she lived for all that time alone in the wilderness, in a hut of
branches far from the beaten trails. She was a threat to any person
who might so much as catch a glimpse of her, and her mere footstep
defiled a path or a river. She was covered with a great headdress of
tanned skin that shrouded her face and breasts and fell to the ground
behind. Her arms and legs were loaded with sinew bands to protect
her from the evil spirit with which she was filled. She was herself
in danger and she was a source of danger to everybody else.

"Girls' puberty ceremonies built upon ideas associated with the
menses are readily convertible into what is, from the point of view
of the individual concerned, exactly opposite behaviour. There are
always two possible aspects to the sacred; it may be a source of peril
or it may be a source of blessing. In some tribes the first menses of

girls are a potent supernatural blessing. Among the Apaches I have seen the Priests themselves pass on their knees before the row of solemn little girls to receive from them the blessing of their touch. All the babies and the old people come also of necessity to have illness removed from them. The adolescent girls are not segregated as sources of danger, but court is paid to them as to direct sources of supernatural blessing. Since the ideas that underlie puberty rites for girls, both among the Carrier and among the Apache, are founded on beliefs concerning menstruation, they are not extended to boys, and boys' puberty is marked instead, and lightly, with simple tests and proofs of manhood."[2]

In the preceding examples two biological stages in life are sketched, as are also unique ways of handling them in terms of social meaning given to them.

As the analysis is pursued further with reference to American society and its various age periods, it is important to keep in mind the following propositions:

1. Each age period is unique not only and, in fact, not primarily, in its biological significance but in the meaning a society attaches to the period.

2. Within any social system the status rating given a particular time in the life cycle is an intricate part of the system of social interaction and social control of that society.

3. Individual adjustments, as well as individual hopes and aspirations, are determined in large part by the status ratings given a particular age period in life. For example, if old age is considered the glorious period in life and honors are heaped upon the old, men long to arrive at the upper years. If, as in American society, the period is one of eclipse in social status, men dread it and accept the roles of the age only because they are inevitable.

AGE DIFFERENTIATION

Among the ancient Incas, age differentiation was the basis of the whole structure. The age groups differentiated were:[3]

babe in arms	bread receiver	able-bodied taxpayer
able to stand	one who needs light work	half an old man
fledgling	cacao picker	old man half asleep
	almost a man	

[2] Ruth Benedict, *Patterns of Culture* (Boston: Houghton Mifflin Co., 1934), pp. 19–20.

[3] A. M. Tozzer, *Social Origins and Social Continuities* (New York: The Macmillan Co., 1925), p. 208.

To the extent that there is recognition of age differences as such, social roles are affected. In practically all societies children and young people, up to a certain age, are denied many of the rights and privileges of adult society. They are also shielded from the responsibilities of adult society and from guilt for certain kinds of misbehavior.

In the United States adolescents are barred from many of the privileges that are considered the right of adults. There are many places which they cannot enter; there are certain vices of adulthood in which they cannot participate. But to compensate for this barring of privileges, there are also many responsibilities which adolescents do not share, and there are many acts for which they are not held accountable as an adult would be. And there is greater toleration in the community for their pranks and immature actions than there would be for those of an adult.

In the rural society of yesterday, and still in the backwoods country, there is little differentiation of social life on the basis of age. One finds all age groups participating in the same social functions, from the babe in arms, who is put to sleep on a back seat of the country school or country church, to the young person of marriageable age. All associate with adults in the common social activities of the neighborhood.

In direct contrast, in urban societies there is a social life for children of various ages, for young people of adolescent age, for the youth group who are most interested in pair relationships, and for adults. There is no common life for all age groups in a highly age-stratified urban society. There is scarcely a social institution in the city, even the church, which caters to the entire family as a social unit. The church has had to break down its functions for the various age groups, and, of course, the school program is similarly stratified. Its extracurricular activities cater to those in particular classes or to a narrow age range of classes.

In some societies old age is set far apart from the rest of the age groups of the society and given undue prestige and reverence. Old people are the authorities in the large family systems and wield undue influence throughout the entire social group. In direct contrast is the situation in a scientific culture where youth excel the old by virtue of their more readily acquiring the techniques and attitudes that go with a rapidly changing culture. In American culture the aged tend to be set apart as a group in retirement, and when they go into retirement they lose their prestige and their authority and, in fact, often lose their entire place in the work world as well as in the world of social influence. This creates for the aged unusual problems of adjustment which are not adequately provided for by economic security alone.

The following paragraphs discuss the various age groups in the United States and their roles and statuses.

THE STATUS OF INFANTS AND CHILDREN

Infancy and childhood are periods of dependence. The status of the individual is that of one to be cared for, protected, guided, disciplined, and developed so that he can be made to fit the expectations of the social system of which he is to become a part. He is exempt from requirements of adulthood in that he may fall short of the moral and work obligations that are expected of those of greater maturity and skill and yet be considered a full-fledged and acceptable member of his family and of the social group.

Childhood is a period of receiving rather than of giving, of being supported rather than of supporting others. In American society it is above all a period of learning, of acquiring the cultural heritage, and of training for the days of maturity which lie ahead.

This has been called the "century of the child" in that so much attention has been given to developing the child toward his maximum capacities. Under the regime of the earlier authoritarian family, a child was to be disciplined and shaped to fit the social order of a world oriented to stern work-duty. He was trained in honor and obligation to the parents, and the effectiveness of the parental training program was measured by a well-disciplined and obedient child.

Punishment and the building of a sense of duty were foremost in this age which conceived of the child as a young animal full of potentialities which were to be retrained and disciplined, or in some cases actually destroyed. It was even assumed that a child was not worth much until his will was broken and he was made subservient to the demands of elders and respectful of their authority.

During the last few decades the child has come to be considered as possessing potentialities that are essentially good and that require not frustration or elimination but development. The problem of the parent and of the school is to socialize his natural tendencies, to cultivate and direct his growth, to develop his capabilities and encourage his initiative, to build him toward self-direction and a sense of independence. Then he can move out into the teen world, be capable of choosing right from wrong and of deciding among the very complex values of the teen group of today.

This developmental conception of childhood has led to an entirely new kind of family discipline and school atmosphere. The adult attempts to motivate the child rather than warp him to fit the system. The social institutions are built about his interests and needs rather than the child being shaped to fit the mold of a fixed institutional pattern, as was true in an earlier day. In this regime childhood has a much higher status than ever before in American history.

One of the most significant manifestations of the high status of the child today is found in the democratic family and in the democratic school system where the cooperative relationship between parents and teachers prevails, with the adults treating the child as an equal insofar as his capacities and level of development permit.

Adults, by virtue of their greater experience and learning, do represent authority, but this authority is exercised in an atmosphere of sympathy, understanding, and cooperation rather than in one of dominance and submission, of commands and obedience to demands enforced by punishment. The rod has vanished from both home and school as the principal method of achieving respect and enforcing authority. The more learned adult group has long since learned that to demand obedience in childhood is to lose respect in the adolescent years, and also to lose control.

Another good measure of the high status of the child in contemporary life is the care and support which society lends to his rights as an individual. Under the old regime of the authoritarian family, society rarely interfered with the exercise of authority by the parent, no matter how stern or unjust this authority was. Each man was ruler of his own household, and his demands upon his children were his own concern. Today society is quick to respond to the abuse of a child by a parent and is ready to use legal processes to interfere with any unreasonable demands upon the child or to challenge the parent for evidence of serious neglect.

The society now looks upon the child as a major resource. Increasing amounts of money are spent in training the child and developing his capacities, and society makes an ever increasing demand on the talents of its children, recognizing that through the development of these talents, through the training of the child in initiative and creativity, its future strength and progress depend.

An increasing amount of funds is spent in maintaining and improving the health of children. Population authorities now believe that the way a people treat their children, the way they look after a child's physical needs and protect his health, is one of the best measures of a high civilization.

THE STATUS OF THE ADOLESCENT

Childhood is interrupted by puberty, which brings the beginning of sexual maturation. This general period marks, in American culture, the beginning of what has come to be called the teen years. The teenage group is the younger adolescent group from 12 to 15, which has come to acquire a very unique status in American life because of the universality of the school experience at this age— junior high and the early years of high school. Here is gathered perhaps for the first time in the history of man large aggregates of young people at the age of puberty—in the larger high schools numbering a thousand or more—who create a unique, specialized age strata.

This group has attained high status in the American social system in that it receives a great deal of attention and support from both family and society. Numerous social institutions, most of them grouped around school and church and their extracurricular programs, tend to lengthen the transition to maturity and make the teens a gradual, long-term adjustment to adulthood.

Schooling, itself, at this period, has become specialized and diversified, and increasingly large sums of money and amounts of time are being devoted to developmental activities of an extracurricular nature which will speed up social growth and give outlets for the abundant energy of this group as it struggles with the new forces of maturation. Maturation at this time gives new emphasis both to mental and social growth, and society now capitalizes on it by permitting intense identification with the peer group. The parents and other adults tend to step aside and the teen group is given great freedom in working its way together toward adulthood.

Modern industrial society has become so complex that the transition has been spread, for many, even beyond the teen years. In fact, psychologists recognize three periods of adolescence: (1) early adolescence, the years twelve to fifteen (the teen years); (2) middle adolescence, sixteen to twenty; and (3) later adolescence, twenty to twenty-four, usually called "youth." This whole span is one of gradual, developmental initiation to adulthood. Society recognizes this period as a critical one for the acquisition of adult standards and responsibilities.

In an earlier age childhood tended to merge more or less directly into adulthood. In the American rural economy, as soon as the young man showed signs of physical growth to maturity, he was likely as not put in the field with the plow and team, and thus initiated into a full-time adult work world. The daughter likewise was loaded with responsibilities in the home so that she moved more or less directly from childhood to adulthood.

Primitive societies, too, have usually made the transition rather abruptly from childhood to adulthood. Rites of passage, or initiation ceremonies, have been very extensive. By numerous ceremonials and tests of skill they try out the youth's capacity for suffering by rites of torture, impressing upon the young person that he is now moving from the freedom, independence, and irresponsibility of childhood into the area of adulthood. The initiation ceremonies are often accompanied by brief but intensive periods of teaching which build a realization of the responsibilities of adulthood. Immediately after these initiation ceremonies the adolescent is expected by the tribe and community to assume the responsibilities of adulthood and to live as an adult.

THE HIGH STATUS OF AMERICAN YOUTH

The period in the late teens and early twenties has in many respects become a period of unique roles and statuses in the American social structure. This group now has been removed almost entirely from the labor market, except for part-time and vacation jobs. Schooling and play have for them become the business of life. Much of the play is school organized in the form of music, drama, athletics, folk dancing, dancing, and so forth. This period has become so much a playful one that even adults envy the high-school and college student his freedom, his unbounded joy, his close identification with his peers in both school and extra-school activities.

Members of this age group still feel that they have a right to depend upon the parents for economic support and at the same time use their own earnings to acquire the symbols of success in the peer group—a car for the boy, clothes for the girl, etc. They expect a great deal of independence and freedom in the unique teen world which the modern high school and college have created. They share many immunities from adult responsibilities and are relatively free to follow the values, standards, codes, and practices of the youth group, which to a remarkable extent has been allowed to create its own moral standards and behavior patterns.

This period is now looked upon as a time of preparation for marriage, during which young people indulge in free dating and free sexual contact, intimate but usually short of sexual intercourse, learn the characteristics and potentialities of the opposite sex, and through trial-and-error dating experience develop the capacity for the free and completely independent choice of a mate.

It is considered normal for both boys and girls to experiment in the work world by part-time jobs during summer and during the school year. The main motive of the young person in the part-time job is not to earn and supplement the family income, as was true in an earlier day, but rather to earn spending money, to indulge tastes and habits which are common in the youth group.

The main work motive for the teenage boy is to acquire a jalopy, which may need rebuilding but which at least will give him the freedom to move about in an automobile, use it in dating as well as use its inefficiencies as a practical course in engineering and mechanics.

While the male youth's major interests and major roles are considered to be those having to do with exploits in the field of gadgets and activities, the girl of this period specializes in roles having to do with feminine attractiveness and charm, which are considered essential in the competitive game of winning the attention of the opposite sex.

Dating is still largely a matter of male initiative, which means that the girl must cultivate some traits which will make her the object of male attraction. This calls for a lot of attention to dress, makeup, manners, and etiquette of the type which are in vogue in the youth community.

The older adolescent girl, with her effervescent beauty, her unspoiled spontaneity, her enthusiasm about life, has in many respects become the supreme picture of American womanhood. In fact, an American sociologist has stated that the late teens and early twenties are the period in life when the American woman receives the maximum ego satisfaction.[4] She is the envy of the entire female population, and at this time more attention is showered upon the successful girl, particularly the "beauty queen," than she may ever expect to attain at any other time in life. Most cultures by contrast have made the period of motherhood or the period of grandmotherhood the period of supreme social recognition.

This teenage girl, particularly if she has the resources and family backing to attend college, is able to prolong this period of being the stage-center in the play-world of dating until approximately twenty-two years of age, when marriage becomes a serious concern. Many girls, of course, drop out of school for marriage even prior to completing the college course.

It is after this long period of energetic, enthusiastic following of one's own propensities and interests, as motivated by the peer group,

[4] John Sirjamaki, "Cultural Configurations in the American Family," *American Journal of Sociology*, 53:464–70 (1948).

that the youth of today begins to settle down to the serious business of choosing a life mate for himself and also a vocation, and enters into the adult roles which in most cultures have been thrust upon young people at a much earlier stage in life.

The very high status of the youth group in our culture is partly due to the envy and longing with which all adults look back upon their school years. Never again can they expect the freedom, spontaneity, and close identification with a sympathetic group which the successful unmarried youth has in the American high school and college scheme.

While the adolescent is denied certain of the prerogatives, privileges, and vices of the adult, his general lack of accountability in many areas, his freedom from restraint and inhibition, his right to choose, to experiment, to venture, and even to make mistakes, seem, in the present social system, to far more than offset the disabilities which he faces as a minor.

The high status accorded the youth group today reflects the need for a long period of growth and social maturation for life in a complex society, in which longevity is guaranteed and in which initiative and a high degree of individuation are essential to success. The freedom of the teen years, a freedom such as societies have rarely if ever accorded this age group, gives experience in choice and tests the ability of the maturing person to choose.

During this period of life he will, through a long period of dating experience, make his own choice of a life mate. In other societies this responsibility has, for the most part, rested with adults. During this period he chooses a moral pattern that will be his. A society of democratic freedom has to take the risk that he may choose the immoral rather than the moral. He may emerge from the period a criminal rather than a morally responsible citizen. But a complex society of many codes and patterns must risk it, since the adult world into which he moves can offer no one homogeneous pattern of life. There are no longer sufficient pressures in our world of movement, urbanization, and change to force anyone to be moral if he does not choose to be.

Finally, during this period he must, after trial-and-error experience with part-time work, vocational testing in the school, vocational guidance, and testing his own aptitudes by his success in various types of school subjects and extracurricular performances, arrive at an independent and self-made choice of a life vocation. In our society there are no caste limits to his vocational opportunities.

Thus to prepare the child for life, society must now place trust in the adolescent and youth in the hope of attaining a morally mature, self-sufficient, creative end product. As a consequence, never has a society come so near worshipping the adolescent-youth period as the supreme period of life.

ADULTHOOD

Adulthood is marked, in the American culture as in most cultures, by two distinct characteristics: (1) the assumption of marriage and family responsibilities; and (2) the assumption of the responsibilities of the worker. In addition to these, of course, are many minor responsibilities.

The adult is accountable as a citizen. He must be considered a criminal if he violates the rules, whereas at an earlier date he was immune from this classification. He is a voter. He becomes an officeholder in the community and in its various institutions.

For the woman the status of wife and mother is normal even though this status has less glamour than that of the beauty queen of twenty. Yet wifehood and motherhood do bring their own unique status in family and community, and with them various new roles which involve privileges and obligations.

For the man the new status of adulthood brings him the opportunity to begin building toward the highest status of which man is capable in our culture, that of a successful worker who gradually builds up to a respected position in his chosen field. The man in his thirties or early forties attains what is for the male the highest status rating at any age of life. As a successful young man builds for his family a secure economic foundation, his status rises even above that of the young college blade, with all his freedom and adventure.

We do not know, as yet, very much about the various statuses and roles of adulthood in the complex structure of American life. It is, however, significant that at last sociologists are devoting large volumes of writing to what has come to be called "industrial sociology," or the sociology of the worker. Gradually the intricate picture of the roles and statuses of the American male in the working ages is being portrayed. Even less clear, as yet, is the picture of the woman worker, who is becoming an increasingly prominent person in numerous phases of adult work life in the American culture scheme.

The individual aspect of status in the work world is unique in that an adult worker's prestige is measured by the degree of his success in climbing in his chosen vocational field. Again, each occupation has its own status rating. Bankers rate higher than ordinary merchants, for example. But within each occupational hierarchy a man's own status is dependent upon the success with which he plays his various roles as he gradually moves upward within the occupational scheme.

The American philosophy, in all phases of work, is that there is always room at the top. At the top lies the managerial power of the executive who has proved his competence in manipulating men and situations.

The unique roles of the adult in the American social structure are discussed in detail elsewhere in this text: Chapter 17 differentiates many aspects of adult male and female roles; Chapter 20 deals with adult occupational statuses. To tie the whole together, a few comments are made here in these two areas.

In the area of male-female adult roles the key role of the younger adult woman is that of the wife and mother; her role as a worker is secondary. For the male the key role in the social structure is that of the worker. This status for him is lifelong, or until retirement. His part in the family as husband and father is secondary to that of being a worker.

With the increased length of life, woman's role as mother is not sufficient to keep her occupied and to give her a significant place in the social structure for a lifetime. She too is becoming a worker and often remains one during her period of child-rearing, but even if she drops out, she tends to return to the labor market as soon as the children reach the age of semi-independence. This calls for many adjustments in husband-wife roles and makes the marriage relationship a lifelong adjustment.

Women are now finding in gainful work, as men always have, a part of their feeling of respect and importance in community and society. The modern world has, consequently, increasingly become one in which work roles of women, and the economic rewards and social statuses accorded them, are significant parts of the social structure.

In our society, as in most societies, adults experience such uniform demands that they will be family members and/or workers, that adulthood is not considered a problem period. Family and work responsibilities carry the major burden of social control. In this sense, adulthood is not only freer from problems than are adolescence and youth but also freer from them than is old age.

STATUS OF THE AGED

The aged in American culture is the retired group. Retirement here brings lowered status because the roles in which the old participate are usually considered of little importance to the social system. Therefore, the period of retirement for the American worker is a period of eclipse in status.

This point in the life cycle often brings severe adjustments. There is for the aged male particularly a lack of significance in the roles he is forced to play as he drops out of the actual active vocational routine which has constituted his life pattern. In a society where the inventiveness of youth is rewarded above all other traits, where mechanization requires the quick hand, the quick eye, and the quick reaction, the vigor and agility of young manhood are at a premium, not the slowed reactions, the hesitant step of the aged.

Even the wisdom of the old in a rapidly changing, mechanized, secularized social order is soon outmoded. For the voice of science pays little heed to the voice of experience, and the traditions of yesterday are mocked by the findings of the rapidly changing age which worships no sacred cows and leaves inviolate no sacred precedent if it is contradictory to the findings of the laboratory.

It is for these reasons that a mechanized, urban-industrial society holds age in low status and finds great difficulty in providing a realistic situation in which the aged can find true meaning during the remaining years of their lifetime.

In this respect American culture is far different from that of many Oriental peoples. There, age is held in great reverence. In China one may properly inquire, "What is your glorious age?" considering years the thing of greatest importance about a person. Here also the old may sleep in their coffins looking forward to the day when they will be buried and become the object of ancestor worship in their particular clan or village. By contrast, not only do the aged in America tend to die while yet living, they are soon forgotten when dead.

There are a few marked exceptions to these generalizations. In the judicial and legislative areas, where legal tradition and precedent are valued, a long memory and long experience in manipulating human beings have cumulative value, and the aged still hold power, prestige, and office.

The most notable example in American life is found in the Supreme Court, in Congress, and in certain other aspects of political and legal life. Barring these marked but rather striking examples of retaining status until very old age, commerce and industry in general, and American academic life, terminate a man's employment while he is still in the active years. It is assumed that the man beyond sixty-five is a greater nuisance than an asset.

It is also very difficult now for the old to find a welcome place in the bosom of their family. The gap between the generations today is too great. The individuation of personality in the vast complex structure of American social and economic life often builds a great gap between the parent and the child generations during the course of a lifetime. Even the grandchildren are so individuated and independent in personality development that it is difficult for the grandparent and the child to meet on understanding, cooperative, and acceptable terms. Hence, even the status of the old within their own family is threatened.

This is the sociological situation today. It does not deny that in many families the old are treated with great solicitude, are immune from obligations, are given tender care, and are shown great concern by children and often even by grandchildren.

It must be recognized too that the shelving of the aged is a great social waste. In the field of creativeness, history is sprinkled with men who achieved great things late in life. Musical composition, great books, great philosophical treatises, have often been the product of men past fifty and sometimes even by men past eighty. Hobbes completed his *Leviathan* at sixty-three; Locke, his *Essay On Human Understanding* at fifty-five years of age. Michelangelo painted his famous work "The Last Judgment" when he was sixty-six. Thomas Edison was deeply involved in scientific creativeness at eighty. Titian, after age ninety, painted his famous "Pietá." Verdi wrote "Ave Maria" at eighty-five. Chief Justice Oliver Wendell Holmes was active until ninety.

Many, of course, pass their usefulness long before these ages are reached because of failing physical energy and dementia and become very much dependent upon others.

The Aged in American Society. In the United States the measure of a man's status tends to be success in competition with his fellows. This means that the average male spends his life in striving and in tasting the fruits of recognition that come from superior performance. This measure of status is inappropriate for those in the upper years and in many societies has not been the prime measure of status among the aged. Many European cultures, for example, look upon the time of leisure as one to be sought for and desired. A man may retire fairly early, if he acquires enough of this world's goods to be able to do so. Then, he can spend his time in respectable, creative leisure such as the community respects and honors.

Julietta K. Arthur has drawn up a "Bill of Rights for Older Folks" which would increase their status in our social structure.[5] Here are the rights: (1) right to be treated as a person; (2) right to be treated as a grownup; (3) right to have a say about own life; (4) right to a fair

[5] Julietta K. Arthur, *How To Help Older People: A Guide for You and Your Family* (Philadelphia: J. B. Lippincott Co., 1954).

chance on one's merits; (5) right to a future; (6) right to have fun and companions; (7) right to be romantic; (8) right to help of one's family in becoming interesting to that family; (9) right to professional help when necessary; (10) right to be old. Certainly the observance of such a bill of particulars would do a great deal to give elderly persons a place of greater respect in the social structure of the United States.

SUMMARY

In the field of age statuses, as in other statuses determined by physiological characteristics, the picture worldwide is one of great diversity rather than of uniformity. A culture may select any age period in life and build into it its own unique type of significance. Children may be adored or despised. The old may be worshiped, neglected, or even put to death. The adolescent may be put through rigorous rites of passage to enforce upon him the sudden realization that he is no longer a child but a man, or the puberty period may be ignored altogether.

During the middle period of life, when work is the normal lot of man in all cultures, the highly successful person may be greatly respected because of his accumulation of goods, or, on the other hand, a person may be looked upon with suspicion if he rises above the common lot.

So, to know what roles are to be associated with age and what statuses are to be awarded the performance of a particular role at a particular age in life, one has to know the culture in which the human being functions. The only thing one can be sure of is that age periods are never ignored in the building of a social system. They are an important and clear-cut part of all social structures. The particular period in life that is given prestige differs greatly from culture to culture, as does the amount of emphasis a particular society gives to a particular age period. Moreover, the social institutions, in their catering to the needs of particular age groups, vary greatly from culture to culture, depending on the status which a particular age group has in the social structure. In America, there is a great need for increased prestige and status for the aged and hence for the development of social institutions which will make their life more meaningful and worthwhile.

DISCUSSION AND REVIEW QUESTIONS

1. Show how age plays a part in the social structure.

2. Indicate how the roles of different age groups are related to the framework of a given social structure.

3. What are the main age classifications recognized in our society?

4. How has social change modified roles of different age groups in modern life?

5. Comment on the phrase "the century of the child" and relate it to the changing status of children.

6. Characterize the adolescent period in our society in terms of roles and statuses.

7. What is the peak status period in the life of the female in our society? Of the male? Point out implications here for the personal adjustments of male and female.

8. Discuss the responsibilities heaped upon youth in individualistic society but not in more institutionalized social orders.

9. What are the main roles of the adult in our social structure? Compare male and female roles.

10. Comment on the status of the aged in our time, and trace the influences to be reckoned with in explaining this situation.

SOURCEBOOK READINGS

KOENIG, SAMUEL, REX D. HOPPER, and FELIKS GROSS. *Sociology: A Book of Readings.* Englewood Cliffs, N.J.: Prentice-Hall, Inc., 1956.
  1. GUMPERT, MARTIN, "The Implications of an Aging Population," pp. 266–71.

WILSON, LOGAN, and WILLIAM L. KOLB. *Sociological Analysis.* New York: Harcourt, Brace & Co., Inc., 1949.
  2. PARSONS, TALCOTT, "Age and Sex in the Social Structure of the United States," pp. 592–603.
  3. BEERS, HOWARD W., "A Portrait of the Farm Family in Central New York State," pp. 603–11.

SELECTED READINGS

ALBRECHT, RUTH. "Relationship of Older People with Their Own Parents," *Marriage and Family Living,* 15:296–98 (Nov. 1953).

BUCKLEY, JOSEPH C. *The Retirement Handbook.* New York: Harper & Brothers, 1953.

COTTRELL, LEONARD S. "Adjustment of the Individual to His Age and Sex Roles," *American Sociological Review,* 7:617–20 (Oct. 1942).

COLLINS, THOMAS. *The Golden Years.* New York: John Day Co., Inc., 1956.

COWDRY, E. V. (ed.). *Problems of Aging.* 2d ed.; Baltimore: The Williams & Wilkins Co., 1942, chaps. 26–29.

DAVIS, E. "What Are Man's Best Years?" *New York Times Magazine,* Nov. 10, 1940, p. 18.

DERBER, MILTON (ed.). *The Aged and Society.* Champaign, Ill.: Industrial Relations Research Association, 1950. A symposium on problems of an aging population.

GLICK, PAUL C. "The Family Cycle," *American Sociological Review,* 12:164–74 (April 1947).

HAVERMANN, ERNEST, and PATRICIA SALTER WEST. *They Went to College.* New York: Harcourt, Brace & Co., Inc., 1952.

HAVIGHURST, R. J., and ETHEL SHANAS. "Adjustment to Retirement," *Sociology and Social Research,* 34:169–76 (Jan.–Feb. 1950).

HEWETT, J. E., JR. "The Person's Time Perspective and the Social Role," *Social Forces,* 23:155–59 (Dec. 1944).

LANDIS, JUDSON T. "Hobbies and Happiness in Old Age," *Recreation,* 35:60–67 (1942).

LANDIS, PAUL H. *Making the Most of Marriage,* New York: Appleton-Century-Crofts, Inc., 1955, chap. 30.

LANDIS, PAUL H. *Population Problems*. 2d ed.; New York: American Book Co., 1954, chap. 5.

ROSE, ARNOLD M. "Factors Associated with the Life Satisfaction of Middle-Class, Middle-Aged Persons," *Marriage and Family Living*, 17:15–19 (Feb. 1955).

SIMMONS, LEO W. *The Role of the Aged in Primitive Societies*. New Haven: Yale University Press, 1945.

WALLER, WILLARD. *The Family* (rev. by Reuben Hill). New York: The Dryden Press, Inc., 1951, chap. 22.

WOOD, MARGARET MARY. *Path of Loneliness*. New York: Columbia University Press, 1953.

Chapter 19

Racial Segregation

Throughout human society, like associates with like. This is one of the most universal rules of human association. To be recognized as markedly different is to be set apart from the common life, to be looked at from a distance, and to be associated with only under certain conventional terms.

Whenever a group has been granted markedly different status in human societies, it has been fenced off, or to use the sociological term, segregated; and gradually through the years rigorous customs build up to define the conditions under which the segregated group will or will not be able to associate.

THE NATURE OF SEGREGATION

One of the most common and obvious factors of which human beings have made significant difference is that of skin color. The dominant group in a particular area often picks on this trait of skin color and builds around it numerous myths concerning inferiority and superiority. The group with the different skin color is defined as inferior; the group with the favored skin color is defined as the superior; and numerous rationalizations are built up to explain why the one is inferior and the other superior. It is presumed that the one is more intelligent, more moral, more gifted, and possesses in greater measure all of the traits which make for human progress and achievement. It is logical, therefore, that the superior group will be given the superior roles.

The inferior group, which is alleged to be lacking in the real qualities of humanity, is assigned the undesirable tasks. Its members become the street cleaners and garbage collectors, the doers of the menial task, and the recipients of a status that is appropriate to these "insignificant" roles.

Thus segregation becomes the established law of social life in many societies, and human beings define their whole work, marriage, and interactional philosophies in terms of these segregated patterns. The price is always great to the segregated group. This is seen in the following illustration, which describes segregation as it has long existed in the United States and as it was when the Supreme Court entered the area. Although the account is now, fortunately, largely historical, it nonetheless depicts conditions which still exist in many race relationships.

Segregation in the churches:

"There is no better evidence of our conflicting racial policies than in the churches which have been the champions of Negro education. Certainly what the church has done for Negroes has been largely within the pattern of segregation. This is especialy true of the Protestant churches. It seems to be less true of the Catholic church. The difference is to be found in the fact that, in most cases, a Protestant church is to some extent a social organization as well as a place of worship; the Catholic church, with its emphasis on worship, is more nearly an altar before which all men are equal.

"On many Protestant churches are announcements to the effect that 'all are welcome.' A Negro reading this announcement knows that, in most cases, if he turned up at any of the activities he would not be welcome or the embarrassment on the part of the preacher and the congregation would be such as to destroy any sense of spiritual fellowship. These churches give money for the support of Negro schools, hospitals, and orphanages, but would be embarrassed at accepting Negro Christians into full fellowship in their church activities. In most Southern Protestant churches Negro worshipers would be seated in the gallery or otherwise segregated."

Segregation in everyday life:

"One of the great inconveniences to Negroes is the general denial of service by hotels and public eating places, in violation of the civil-rights laws. The American population is mobile. Our type of life necessitates travel. The result is our remarkable hotel system, upon which large sections of our population depend for comfort and health. In being denied access to this public service, Negroes are greatly handicapped. Anyone who knows the facts wonders how even so distinguished a person as Marian Anderson can stand up under the hardships of travel which she encounters because of lack of hotel service.

"Segregation carried to its logical conclusion is often dramatized by cruel and inhuman aspects. A few years ago, a graduate of Fisk University, Miss Julie Dericott, a young woman of charm and culture, was seriously injured in an automobile accident in North Georgia. She was taken to the near-by hospital, where emergency treatment was requested. She was very fair, but when it was discovered that she was classified as a Negro, she was refused emergency treatment. She died on the long journey to Atlanta attempting to reach the nearest hospital known to give emergency treatment to colored people.

"Recently in Atlanta a Negro girl stepped off a streetcar on one of the wider streets. A speeding driver knocked her down and left her lying unconscious. A crowd gathered, and one white woman who had seen the accident requested that an ambulance be called. The ambulance came, but the driver, seeing that the victim was a Negro girl, said, 'We can't haul a nigger,' and drove away, leaving the victim of the accident by the roadside. Such incidents are not isolated. They happen frequently and seem to be an inevitable consequence of segregation as it works out in practice in many sections of America. Most white people are not aware of them.

"Segregation in the South not only separates the races but symbolizes the idea of the inevitable inferiority of Negroes. It 'keeps the Negro in his place' not only on the streetcars and buses, but in the social and economic system. It is more effective as a symbol than as a means of preventing contact between the races. In fact, racial contacts are more intimate in the South than in any other section of the country. Southerners as a rule do not object to contact with Negroes so long as the idea of Negro inferiority is maintained. Segregation does this. This fact explains why the South has never claimed that under segregation there are equal services for the races."

No separate but equal world is possible:[1]

"As a practical matter, separate but equal service under segregation cannot be rendered. Such service would require, for example, the duplication of the present most expensive phases of transportation and the duplication of the state university systems, already poorly supported. Separate and equal services for the races in the South, or any other section, are a luxury which cannot be afforded."[2]

[1] This "separate but equal" doctrine was the essence of an earlier Supreme Court decision in the famous Plessy ruling. The 1954 ruling reversed this decision, arguing that there is no such thing as "separate and equal" facilities. For a discussion of this issue, see Edward S. Corwin (ed.), *Constitution of the United States of America* (Washington, D. C.: Government Printing Office, 1953), p. 1162.

[2] W. W. Alexander, "Our Conflicting Racial Policies," *Harper's* (Jan., 1945), p. 175.

Further evidence of the cost of a segregated social order is indicated by the prevailing stereotypes concerning the Negro and his qualities as shown in the table, based on researches of Bettalheim and Janowitz. And remember that these stereotypes tend to be universally applied regardless of the personal characteristics of the individual being considered.

Stereotypes Characterizing Negroes
(Based on interviews with 150 veterans of World War II)

Stereotype	Number of Veterans Mentioning Stereotypes
They are sloppy, dirty, filthy	53
They depreciate property	33
They are taking over; they are forcing out the whites	25
They are lazy; they are slackers in work	22
They are ignorant; they have low intelligence	18
They have low character; they are immoral and dishonest	18

Source: Bruno Bettalheim and Morris Janowitz, "Ethnic Tolerance: A Function of Social and Personal Control," *American Journal of Sociology,* 45:137–45 (1949).

The racial barrier has by all odds been the most rigid of all barriers in the American social structure. In this one area alone, particularly in localized areas, social relations have been most rigidly fenced off and rigorously defined. Race has come nearest to being the basis for the only semblance of a caste system in the nation, the disabilities of various racial groups in one or more aspects being passed on to their children through social transmission.

The Oriental in western states may not own land, nor may his American-born children. The Negro until recently in many states not only lived "segregated" but passed on this status to his children. In many states no person of colored race may marry a white person and vice versa, and one with even a small proportion of colored blood is classed with the inferior race. The American Indian has in most states been a second-class citizen, and so is his child if he returned to the reservation, no matter if he achieved a Ph.D. degree.

The Supreme Court in 1954 passed the death sentence on the main symbol of the caste system when it declared segregation unconstitutional in a democratic form of government. Yet segregation has not ended as a status-determining mechanism.

In the discussion that follows, attention will be directed to the Negro, the most conspicuous example of segregation in the American social structure. But as we study the segregation-integration issue it will be well to remember that segregation as a factor in the social structure involves much more; as the following statement makes so clear, the perpetuation of all minority groups depends on it.

"The perpetuation of minorities rests upon the maintenance of segregation. As the physical and social barriers that keep racial and cultural groups apart diminish, the differences between dominant group and minority are minimized, and ultimately their separate identity is lost. In the largest sense, therefore, the very existence of minorities and the personal and social consequences that flow therefrom are part of the cost of segregation.

"Wherever racial and cultural minorities exist in society, some degree of segregation is practiced. Segregation is both public and private, formal and informal, direct and indirect. Its consequences affect not merely the minority, but also the dominant group and the society as a whole. The segregation of the Negro in the U. S. A. illustrates all these forms and effects.

"In the North, segregation is for the most part private, informal, and indirect, whereas in the South it is public, formal, and direct. Although the North generally avoids frank measures designed to prevent or discourage free association between whites and Negroes, the physical and social distances between the races are nevertheless obvious. In contrast, it might be said of the South that, despite ceremonial and legal segregation, there is actually a greater degree of intimacy between Negroes and whites than there is in the North. This is indicated by the clearly demarcated and compact Negro residential ghettos or Black Belts in the northern cities in contrast to the sprawling and more or less random location of Negro dwellings in the South."[3]

THE EMERGENCE OF RACIAL SEGREGATION IN THE UNITED STATES

In the Deep South the Negro, because of "Jim Crow" laws, has not been able to ride in the same railroad coach as a white man, to eat in the same restaurant, sleep in the same hotels, attend the same religious services, or go to the same schools. The worlds of white and black have met only in certain situations which are defined as "proper." These situations by and large are those in which the Negro plays the role of servant, does the menial tasks in the economic order, and plays the submissive role in Negro-white relations.

Prejudice hardly explains this situation. It is much deeper than that in Southern culture. It is, in reality, a system of differentiation which has become one of *stratification* whereby the relationships between the races have been so completely defined that each race accepts the status of the other unquestioningly. Stratification is so fixed that a

[3] Louis Wirth, "The Price of Prejudice," *Survey Graphic*, 36:19–21, No. 9 (1947).

segregated system of social relations has been in vogue. The Southern Negro, who has always had an inferior role in the Southern culture, accepts the domination and the superiority of the white man as a matter of course. He has known no other life and therefore accepts the life he knows. The white man of equal habit accepts the role of the Negro as that of the inferior and expects his Negro helpers to act their part.

Let this system be threatened, let the Negro begin to compete in the white man's world, and immediately competition gets over into the field of conflict. The higher status race fears the encroachment of the lower status race and, by one means or another, tries to force it back into the place which the superior groups have defined for it.

In this drama the Ku Klux Klan, and more recently the White Citizens' Councils, have played their part to try, by fear, to force the Negro back to his accustomed status. The Klan has always been most active after periods of great upheaval, as for example after World Wars I and II and after the desegregation ruling. The Negro, because of war labor shortages, entered many new roles that tended to challenge at many points the old system of stratification which both races had previously accepted without question. After World War II, when numerous Negroes returned to the South after experience in Northern industry or in the army, and when numerous Northern whites had penetrated the South to treat the Negro differently than was customary in the region, the Negro race demanded a larger place in the social system. The system of stratification was threatened, and a certain amount of conflict was inevitable.

One of the best accounts of the history of Negro–white relations, as they have existed and as they exist, is that by C. A. McKnight, eminent North Carolina editor, writing for *Collier's*. Concerning the history of race relations, and the historic segregation solution, he says:

"It is important to remember that the problem of the Negro in the South is an old one. The Negro has been at the very core of most of the South's traditions and institutions, even though few white Southerners pause to think about it. He was the instrument of slavery. He made the plantation system possible. He was the worker whose strong back and arms built up our cash-crop agriculture. Over him a Civil War was fought, and around him swirled the turmoil of Reconstruction. In a negative way, he helped to fashion the one-party political system in the South. Much of our regional literature has been about him. His melodies are found in our music. His economic destitution was a factor in making the South at one time 'the nation's number one economic problem,' and his inability to break into higher-income vocations and carry his share of the tax burden had saddled the also-poor Southern white with a double load of taxation, reflected in higher proportionate state and local taxes for the services received.

"Of late, the Negro has been leaving the South by the hundreds of thousands, migrating to the industrial states of the non-South, where his vote has helped to shape national policies often at variance with the preferences of many white Southerners.

"In sum, the Negro has been a central fact of life in the South for the better part of two centuries, and the major Southern problem has been one of race relations—the business of peoples of different colors and different cultures living peacefully together in a segregated society. The problem, then, is not new. But in the past two years, it has taken on disturbing new proportions and new dimensions.

"During almost all of this long period, the two races have lived in a dual society of the white man's making. And since 1896, the year of the Supreme Court's Plessy *v.* Ferguson decision, the 'separate but equal' doctrine—and the mass of Jim Crow legislation it spawned —had the sanction of constitutionality. It is tragically true that the public services and facilities provided for Negroes, including schools, were more often than not separate but *unequal,* but the legality of the system stood unimpaired until, in the last decade, the Supreme Court began chipping away at it. Then, in 1954, the court flatly declared that 'separate facilities are inherently unequal,' and the legal foundation for a dual society collapsed."[4]

FROM SEGREGATION TOWARD INTEGRATION

As has been seen, the world of race relations in the South has been one of segregation. In the North, segregation was never so pervasive, nor was it so effectively implemented. The Negro has been given much greater opportunity there, but he has never been certain where he would or would not be accepted. Yet although he was more uncertain of his place, he could venture much further.

In many Northern cities segregation has been employed in neighborhood life, primarily to protect property values. Often when Negroes "invade" a community and take over property, property values drop because of prejudice against living near a Negro. This permits the complete *invasion* of the area, and the *succession* of a new race, that is, the replacement of the white race by the Negro.

The segregation technique is always expensive to a minority group even in Northern cities. In its residential areas one finds, gen-

[4] C. A. McKnight, "The Troubled South: Search for a Middle Ground," *Collier's,* June 22, 1956, pp. 25–26.

erally speaking, poor living quarters and high rent for a given amount
of space.

There has been increasing agitation on the part of many white
leaders, and on the part of the National Association for the Advancement of Colored People, to break down racial discrimination at many
points, especially in the use of the ballot, in educational privilege,
and in legal rights. Research of the President's Committee on Education in 1947 and various studies by social scientists have called
attention to discrimination practices against minority groups, particularly Negroes and Jews, in the field of higher education, where
tolerance and equality of privilege should certainly be expected to
appear first in public attitudes. In 1948 seventeen states denied
Negroes admission to their principal institution of higher learning.

*Integration in the schools is one of the vital social problems of modern American
society. The Supreme Court decision of 1954 called for gradual integration
and the eventual end of "separate but equal" segregated classes throughout
the nation. (Wide World)*

The 1954 action of the United States Supreme Court declaring segregation in public schools illegal and calling for a gradual termination of the practice in this one act suddenly terminated a basic part of the framework of the American social structure. The further spelling out of this decision in 1955, applying it to all public facilities, parks, means of public transportation, etc., destroyed the remainder.

The blow fell hardest in those parts of the country where the most social relations had been defined in terms of segregation. In the Deep South particularly, where the system of racial accommodation was founded on an elaborate ritual of segregation, the decision produced the most disruptive effect. Here suddenly all social relationships between the races were to be redefined according to legal edict. Inevitably, conflict and violence threatened as the old system of accommodation crumbled.

Suddenly Negroes demanded new rights: attendance at the universities on an equal basis; first-come, first-served seating in buses rather than assignment of the Negro to the "Jim Crow" seats in the rear; etc. Student riots, protesting Negroes in the universities, the misuses of the law to keep the racial bans in effect, the misuses of the law to penalize Negroes who boycotted bus systems, continuation of the practice of separate seating, and other evidences of conflict emerged. Some Southerners talked of seceding, of abandoning the public schools, of defying the law. Politicians took up the crusade for "white supremacy."

No Northerner, who has not lived under a system of complete segregation, can grasp the deep meaning of this issue in a biracial world, where all the amenities of social tradition have been built about the code of segregation. The believer in white supremacy sees his entire way of life collapsing, the social structure disintegrating. Involved in the rebellion against integration is fear, despair, threat to loss of honor.

McKnight summarizes the situation as of the summer of 1956, when the impacts of desegregation ruling were being felt.

"It would have been easier to write this six months ago. The pattern of desegregation had been clear, and in a sense historic. In general, this was the pattern: desegregation accomplished or in process in the border states where the proportion of Negroes to whites is small and where race had never been a major factor in politics; spot desegregation in three states of the mid-South and a policy of watchful waiting in the others; an ever-stronger determination to preserve segregation in the deep South. A 17-state area had thus been fragmentized, and there no longer was a Solid South but many Souths where the race issue was concerned.

"The border states of Maryland, Delaware, West Virginia and Missouri, plus the District of Columbia, had moved toward prompt compliance after the first court decision. There were a few incidents, but on the whole desegregation proceeded smoothly.

"From the very first, a hard core of deep South states—Georgia, South Carolina, Alabama, Mississippi and Louisiana—had made it clear that they would evade the Supreme Court decision, if possible, and defy it, if necessary.

"By the middle of the 1955–'56 school term, Kentucky, Oklahoma, Arkansas and Texas were well into the initial stages of a desegregation program. Virginia, North Carolina, Florida and Tennessee were still following a wait-and-see policy, with prospects of some spot desegregation, at least, in another year or two.

"Since the turn of the year, this pattern has been sharply altered. The moderate states of Virginia, North Carolina and Florida are now moving rapidly into the resistance camp. Arkansas and Texas, despite successful spot desegregation, seem headed in the same direction. What will happen in Tennessee is anybody's guess.

"The significance of this change is that a minimum of eight states, and perhaps as many as 10, will move into the 1956–'57 school term dedicated to the prevention of any mixing of the races whatsoever in the public schools. Most of them have on the books a variety of statutory and constitutional devices that will have to be tested in the courts, one by one, promising the 'generation of litigation' that the late Justice Robert H. Jackson predicted."[5]

McKnight offers these comments on the Southern white's reasons for resisting integration:

"One is politics. It is good politics in the South today, as it has been many times in the past, to stand publicly and emphatically for separation of the races. Another is the arithmetic of numbers. In the so-called Black Belt counties, Negroes number from 40 to 80 per cent of the population, and the whites have a real fear of political domination. Still another is the sex angle—the fear, irrational though it may be, that school desegregation will lead to intermarriage and racial amalgamation.

"Most important of all, perhaps, is the hard fact that, on the average, there are class, social and cultural differences between Southern whites and Negroes which go beyond skin color. This poses the most cruel dilemma of all for the white Southerner who believes in both the inevitability and the essential rightness of the court decision, and who would like to see ultimate compliance everywhere."[6]

[5] Ibid.
[6] Ibid.

In the following account William Attwood, *Look*'s National Affairs Editor, describes vividly the reaction of the South to integration:

"Fear—a fear so deep-rooted that it sometimes defies rational analysis—is the dominant emotion racking the South today. It is fear that makes innately courteous people rant about the 'nine ninnies' on the Supreme Court; it is fear that incites a howling mob to threaten a lonely girl on an Alabama campus; it is fear—fear of self-appointed vigilantes—that stifles the voices of Southern liberals and drowns out the words of moderates.

"During this year of mounting crisis, I have traveled in a dozen Southern states, talking with both whites and Negroes about a problem that torments them all. As an outsider, I could expect blunt answers to my blunt questions. From the answers, some conclusions gradually began to emerge.

"Whatever they may tell you, white Southerners are afraid of the Negro in their midst. And they are afraid of him today as never before. For the Negro no longer behaves like the amiable 'darky' who knew his place and did not question the white man's right to give the orders. Today's Southern Negro, with the ruling of the Supreme Court on his side, appears to be challenging the justice of a way of life that has traditionally given the white man a privileged status.

"Some whites will tell you, 'We understand the Negroes. Except for a few agitators, they want segregation just as much as we do.' But more of them are beginning to realize that they don't know the Negro any more, that the few with whom they have any social contact tell them only what they want to hear. Incidents like the disciplined and effective Negro boycott of the Montgomery, Ala., bus system . . . have helped shatter the illusion that colored people in the South are docile, indifferent and content.

"So the white man begins to wonder—and to be afraid.

"The fear is partly political. In the Black Belt, white men shudder at the prospect of Negro bloc-voting that might put them under the jurisdiction of colored officials. Still haunted by the nightmare of Reconstruction, they now feel that any concession to Negro demands for equality means another surrender, another Appomattox.

"The fear is also economic. Industrialization has enabled Negroes to earn wages that are making them independent of an economic order based on discrimination. New plants are siphoning off the South's traditional source of cheap labor and domestic servants. A Negro with money in the bank is no longer at the mercy of the dominant race; he becomes a customer to be catered to. So you find white men telling you in the same breath that they want to attract new industry but fear its effect on the 'Nigras.'

"And the fear is social, with profound sexual undertones. To a white Southerner, classroom integration implies a kind of social equality that does not exist even on an assembly line. He will tell you that sooner or later, some Negro boy will be walking his daughter home from school, staying for supper, taking her to the movies . . . and then your Southern friend asks you the inevitable, the clinching question: 'Would *you* want your daughter to marry a Nigra?'

"And there is nothing you can say to quiet his fears. You can reply, 'She can say "no," can't she?' You can point out that integrated schools elsewhere have not led to intermarriage. Your friend only shrugs. The fear is too deeply ingrained. The sexual neurosis makes many whites impervious to logic. They are obsessed by the notion that Negroes, given a chance, will take over their women as well as their golf clubs and legislatures. And the fact that most of America's original mulattoes were sired, in the years of slavery, by Southern white men in a segregated society does not inhibit them from asserting that mixed schools will 'mongrelize' the race.

"All these murky fears were brought to a boil by the Supreme Court ruling against segregation in schools. Faced with 'creeping integration' and egged on by some reckless elements of its own press, the Deep South has decided that the line must be held here at all costs."[7]

Even with all this fear and resistance, remarkable progress has been made toward integration. *Southern School News* was able to report in mid-summer, 1956, that more than 100 tax-supported white colleges and universities (half the total in the South) now accept Negroes. Moreover, some 256,000 southern Negroes (10 per cent of Negro students in the South) are now eligible to attend schools with whites. According to this report desegregation generally proves easiest where the Negro population is smallest. But there are exceptions, for example, the integrated schools of St. Louis, where Negroes comprise 35 per cent of the students—a larger percentage than that of segregated Nashville, Richmond, and Dallas.

"PASSING"—INTEGRATION BY SUBTERFUGE

In a social world where light skin is at a premium, the fair-skinned Negro has many advantages. The light-skinned person is preferred in marriage. Children will then be even lighter. The light-skinned also have superior status in both the white and Negro societies. But one of the big advantages of light skin is that one may "pass" into the white man's society.

[7] "Fear Underlies the Conflict," *Look*, April 3, 1956, p. 27. Copyright, 1956, Cowles Magazines, Inc.

"Passing" is an old phenomenon in American life, and will undoubtedly increase. It is estimated that some 12,000 light-skinned Negroes, dominantly white in blood, permanently cross the color line annually in the United States and marry white. It is a fairly safe procedure, since in the Negro–white cross no child will be born with skin darker than that of the darker parent. And what person of Negro blood would not seek to pass as a member of a dominant group and place his children among the privileged sector?

Passing may be either temporary, to gain a momentary social advantage, or it may be permanent, in order that the individual forever loses his racial identity. This sociological phenomenon, which is in reality integration by subterfuge, can best be understood by reading a few case histories of people who have "passed."

"Passing"—Temporary vs. Permanent. "Actually, probably all Negroes who can pass do so. Their passing is, however, of a segmental and temporary nature. It consists of riding in the less crowded front sections of a bus or on 'white' Pullmans, eating in restricted restaurants, attending picture shows, patronizing drugstore soda fountains, or in other ways making an opportune, but temporary, use of their Caucasoid characteristics to avoid unpleasantness or inconvenience. There usually is no disposition to become permanently identified with the white group. This is true even in the case of Negroes who represent themselves as white in order to secure employment but who associate with Negroes after working hours. This is not to say that light-colored women or couples do not completely sever their relationship with the Negro group and even 'marry white.' This latter seems to be the definitive point as far as other Negroes are concerned. Short of this final step, it usually is assumed that the passing is a matter of more or less temporary expediency. This division of passing into degrees is also seen in the attitude of Negroes toward the phenomenon itself. There seems very little disposition to censure a light Negro for passing as white in order to attain some temporary goal, such as a meal, concert, travel accommodation, or a service. The attitudes toward permanent passing are, however, varied. Some race-proud individuals completely condemn it and willingly inform against the impostor. Others feel it a good joke on the whites and delight in the perpetration of the hoax. Still others defend it on rational grounds, saying those who can are fools not to pass. The remainder, a large percentage, do not feel strongly enough in either direction to take any active interest in an individual case, feeling that it is 'none of their business.' Whites, who sometimes suggest or abet temporary passing, very seldom condone a permanent change of status. It is probable that not more than 10 per cent of those who could pass permanently do so. Of course, such evidence does not offer any count of the number who do pass, but it does lead one to give credence to the smaller, rather than the larger, estimates."[8]

Accidental "Passing." "Speaking of passing—a strange thing happened to me this summer. When I went to visit my father in Kentucky, I had to change trains at a station on the other side of the Mason–Dixon line. The porter took my bags and escorted me to the coach. I wasn't paying any attention to him. I just took it for granted that he was taking me to the correct coach. When I stepped into the coach, I immediately knew that he had made a mistake. All of these white people were seated and there I was! I said, 'Listen, porter—' and that's all the further I got. He said, 'That's all right, miss, the conductor will call your stop.' He passed my bags overhead and tipped his hat and walked away. So I sat down and was so ill at ease.

"I noticed several of the white people glancing at me and then after the second look, they looked off. I had had my hair freshly done, and when it is fresh it looks dark brown and wavy, and I did look decent because I was wearing my best. I took a magazine and began reading. After a bit, the conductor came up and after removing his hat and apologetically clearing his throat said, 'I know this is highly irregular, miss, but—uh—pardon me—may I ask you what nationality you are? Uh—are you Jewish?' I could have kissed the conductor for giving me that lead, because as soon as he started talking, I knew what he was going to say. I knew that if I said I was a Negro and tried to explain that I wasn't trying to pass, he wouldn't believe it. Also, to have to go back into the Negro coach with the conductor leading the way would be quite embarrassing to me. The Negroes would think I was trying to pass and got caught. So I decided to play up the situation, 'After all,' I said, 'this is highly ridiculous. Yes, I am a Jewess, and I consider this a grand insult.' I wore my haughtiest expression, and I was scared to death. By this time several of the white people had turned around and were listening to us.

"The conductor flushed and was very much embarrassed. I just know how he must have felt. He apologized again and then walked away. I was scared. I didn't enjoy the ride at all, and but for the company of a little eight-year-old white child, I talked to no one. It was lucky for me that I hadn't told Father I was coming. Suppose

[8] John H. Burma, "The Measurement of Negro 'Passing,'" *American Journal of Sociology*, 52:18 (1946–1947).

he had been at the station to meet me—then I would have been in a mess. I told Daddy about it and he just laughed. He thought it was a joke! And that's why I couldn't be bothered with trying to pass. I'd rather be colored and not be bothered. That's why I hate the South."[9]

Intentional "Passing." ". . . The other night I was out with Harry —you know he can pass for white—and after we had seen a show in the Loop he said, 'Let's go over to the Pump Room.' We did and had a glorious time and it wasn't any more expensive than the Rhumboogie. No, I wasn't in the least nervous. How could they tell we were colored? There were no colored waiters who might have recognized us. After this I am going to places like that any time I am out with him."[10]

Job "Passing." "In our big department stores in the Loop can be found many sons and daughters who come back 'home' at the close of the day, and by the same token would come back home to stay if their identity was found out. They are not as fair as lilies but the fact that most of the stores are 'manned' by Jewish girls whose complexion and hair is swarthy helps the situation out materially. It is a shame and a disgrace that we must be forced in order to make a livelihood, to live this life each day, but there is not another way. We pour thousands of dollars, hard earned, into the coffers of the storekeepers and yet we are denied recognition or a chance to earn some of it back except when we apply for some menial position like running an elevator or janitorship, and in many places we are even denied this class of employment. That our men and women are superior in every way to the average wage-earner found in these stores is without question, but worth doesn't count when prejudice creeps in, so we must fight fire with fire, and those that are able to 'get by' peace be with them and it is our duty not to hinder them in any way. Last Monday was the Jewish New Year and all of that faith were given a holiday—without pay—by the store managers. This, of course, made a number of our young ladies who were Jewish pro tem take two days off. 'There are tricks to all trades,' said one of them laughingly, 'and we had it to do to allay suspicion.' So even with the serious side of it there comes something in the lighter vein. But it does seem with a concerted effort this situation could in a measure be changed for the better, patronize the store

[9] From *Black Metropolis*, copyright, 1945, by St. Clair Drake and Horace R. Cayton, pp. 160–61. Reprinted by permission of Harcourt, Brace & Co., Inc.

[10] From *Black Metropolis*, copyright, 1945, by St. Clair Drake and Horace R. Cayton, p. 162. Reprinted by permission of Harcourt, Brace & Co., Inc.

that offers the most to you and yours and you will be aiding materially in the movement."[11]

"Passing" in Marriage. A certain number of Negroes who pass marry across the color line and become white in a final sense. This involves so many problems, however, that even such a marriage may not prove to be the final solution for an individual. But even when it does, there are many problems to be faced.

A personal account, by a Negro girl who "married up," shows that the hazards of passing by marriage are very great. Reba Lee, the pseudonym for the real girl, was a light-skinned Negress who ran away from home to New York. She passed successfully and eventually married into white society.

But she was forced to resort to one lie after another to handle numerous dilemmas in which she found herself, as, for example, to explain why none of her relatives came to the wedding. She mailed presents to herself to make it appear that relatives had remembered her. She bought a photograph of a white woman and framed it in an antique frame to hang as the picture of her mother. At a night club, a colored boy in the orchestra recognized her as an old acquaintance and identified her. She worried about her baby being born black.[12] When it was born dead, she thoughtlessly asked if it was black. Her husband's suspicions grew in spite of her manufactured explanations.

The strain, misery, and fear of her deception became too great. She suddenly left her husband, deciding to get a divorce and return to her own people. From the experience she concluded that white "society" is "no better, no, not as good, as the colored folk I had known." She admitted they were more mannerly, but "less genuine, less understanding, less tolerant."[13]

[11] An editorial from the *Chicago Defender*, quoted in *Black Metropolis*, copyright, 1945, by St. Clair Drake and Horace R. Cayton, p. 168. Reprinted by permission of Harcourt, Brace & Co., Inc.

[12] Reba Lee was a victim of the so-called "black-baby" myth. In a marriage where one member has "passed," there is very little probability that the offspring will be black. Here are the facts as the eugenists and anthropologists see them: (1) In the case of two persons both theoretically white but having, whether they know it or not, some Negro blood, an accentuation of some Negro characteristics may occur in their offspring, but in all probability the offspring of such unions will be able to pass for white. (2) It is impossible for the offspring of a recognizable Negro and a pure white person to be any darker than the Negro partner, and in all probability it will be lighter. (3) The offspring of mixed-bloods (e.g., mulattoes or quadroons) may be darker than either, but in all probability would not be black. (From *Black Metropolis*, copyright, 1945, by St. Clair Drake and Horace R. Cayton, p. 172. Reprinted by permission of Harcourt, Brace & Co., Inc.)

[13] Reba Lee, as told to Mary Hastings Bradley, *I Passed for White* (New York: Longmans, Green & Co., 1955).

RACE MIXTURE—THE FINAL STEP IN INTEGRATION

In the integration of the races, the greatest fear of all is that eventually integration will mean *miscegenation* or race mixture—the "mongrelization" of the race, as the Southern politician is likely to put it. Some authorities on the American race problem also have suggested that this is the ultimate solution of the race problem. Franklin Frazier believes that if this is the ultimate solution it is still a long way off.[14] If that should be true, it is not a new thing in the nation, and it will not be the catastrophe that the "white-supremacy" advocates hold. In fact, it was their ancestors who started the process of race blending well on its way. Under the code of the gentlemen in the old South, race mixture was not taboo, provided it was the white man who caused the mixing. The white woman's honor was carefully protected, but the black woman had no honor, according to the white man's code.

Race mixture has, moreover, gone on extensively from the beginning. Slave women were often used by their masters for sexual purposes. Some historians credit even so humane a person as Thomas Jefferson with siring mulatto children on his plantation. Here is a verse in which he was twitted for it:

> The weary statesman for repose hath fled
> From halls of council to his Negro's shed,
> Where blest he woos some black Aspasia's grace
> And dreams of freedom in his slave's embrace . . .

In spite of this background, Swedish sociologist Gunnar Myrdal, after an exhaustive study of the American racial scene, concludes that fear of race mixture is at the basis of Negro caste in the United States—the ultimate reason for segregation. He says:

1. The concern for "race purity" is basic in the whole issue; the primary and essential command is to prevent amalgamation; the whites are determined to utilize every means to this end.
2. Rejection of "social equality" is to be understood as a precaution to hinder miscegenation and particularly intermarriage.
3. The danger of miscegenation is so tremendous that the segregation and discrimination inherent in the refusal of "social equality" must be extended to nearly all spheres of life. There must be segregation and discrimination in recreation, in religious service, in education, before the law, in politics, in housing, in stores and in breadwinning.[15]

[14] Franklin Frazier, "Race Relations in World Perspective," *Sociology and Social Research*, 41:331–35 (May–June 1957).
[15] Gunnar Myrdal, *An American Dilemma* (New York: Harper & Brothers, 1944), p. 58.

THE RESULTS OF SEGREGATION

The tragedy of segregation is denial of privilege. The late Walter White, executive secretary of the National Association for the Advancement of Colored People, described in the following account his awakening to the fact that he was a member of a segregated class upon which a social curse was placed. He wrote:

A voice cried out, the voice of the son of our neighborhood grocer: "Let's burn the house of the nigger mail carrier! It's too nice for a nigger to live in!" In the flickering light the mob swayed, paused, and began to flow toward us. In that instant there opened up within me a great awareness; I knew then who I was. I was colored, a human being with an invisible pigmentation which marked me a person to be hunted, abused, discriminated against, kept in poverty and ignorance, in order that those whose skin was white would have readily at hand a proof of their superiority. It made no difference how intelligent or talented I might be or how virtuously I lived. A curse like that of Judas was upon me.[16]

The far reach of discrimination in the denial of privilege is suggested by Myrdal, who lists discriminations in order of the rank of their importance to the Southern white as follows:

"Rank 1. Highest in this order stands the bar against intermarriage and sexual intercourse involving white women.

"Rank 2. Next come the several etiquettes and discriminations, which specifically concern behavior in personal relations. (These are the barriers against dancing, bathing, eating, and drinking together, and social intercourse generally; peculiar rules as to handshaking, hat lifting, use of titles, house entrance to be used, social forms when meeting on streets and at work, and so forth. These patterns are sometimes referred to as the denial of "social equality" in the narrow meaning of the term.)

"Rank 3. Thereafter follow the segregation and discriminations in use of public facilities such as schools, churches and means of conveyance.

"Rank 4. Next comes political disfranchisement.

"Rank 5. Thereafter come discriminations in law courts, by the police and by other public servants.

"Rank 6. Finally come the discriminations in securing land, credit, jobs, or other means of earning a living, and discriminations in public relief and other social welfare activities."[17]

Myrdal then points out that Negroes would write the list in reverse in terms of the disastrous results to them: they consider eco-

---

[16] Walter White, "Why I Remain a Negro," *Reader's Digest,* Jan., 1948, p. 10.
[17] Myrdal, *op. cit.,* p. 60.

nomic discrimination the worst, etc. For evidence of income discrimination see the chart (page 426) which compares annual and lifetime earnings of nonwhite and white by educational level.

The following hypothetical questions were raised by Walter White, himself a light-skinned Negro. They are significant, for they lay bare the whole fallacy of racial segregation: "Suppose the skin of every Negro in America were suddenly to turn white. What would happen to all the notions about Negroes on which race prejudice is built? What would become of the Negroes' presumed shiftlessness, alleged cowardice, dishonesty, stupidity, and body odor? Would they not then be subject to individual judgment as are whites? How else could they be judged?"[18]

SUMMARY

To segregate is to set apart on the basis of differences which are considered socially significant. Who will be set apart and by whom is a problem of history. The culture may set apart one people or another considering them unfit or unqualified to associate with others. To segregate is to imply inequality. To segregate is to question the rights of certain people to share equally with others. To segregate a race is to declare that that race is for some reason not worthy to associate with the other race and must, therefore, pay the penalty for its lack of worthiness.

The Negro in the United States has paid a heavy penalty of segregation. His penalty has been the menial roles and the lowest status, isolation in social institutions, and denial of privilege. This has been the common rule of his life. The sudden termination of segregation, as a legalized situation in the American social structure, has been almost catastrophic in many parts of the nation where social relations have been built on the assumption of a segregated racial order.

Unfortunately, legal pronouncement does not quickly change the attitudes and practices of human beings, for these are part of the deep, underlying tradition by which man lives. Consequently, the sudden termination of segregation, or the threat of its termination, brings conflict to the surface, as men try to redefine their relationships with each other. It inspires fears; it leads to the development of new and more subtle devices by which the old status differentials may be maintained and the old discriminations perpetuated and justified.

In the United States members of the segregated groups have long tried to pass whenever their skin color permitted them to do so. To cross the line and become white becomes a major aspiration, al-

[18] White, *op. cit.*

though the barriers to doing so are immense. The final acceptance of the races as equal will mean, first, integration and, then, intermarriage. This is what the Southern white has feared most, and yet even this is not a new phenomenon in American society, or anywhere else where races mingle in a common habitat. Lines of segregation have never been rigid enough to hinder the frequent crossing of the line in illicit sex relations. The "mongrelization" of white blood, so feared by the Southern politician, has long been a common practice there, with the politician playing his part.

DISCUSSION AND REVIEW QUESTIONS

1. Discuss racial segregation as an aspect of class structures.
2. Illustrate how racial segregation operates to put the segregated minority group at a disadvantage.
3. Show how stereotypes develop to support the segregated structure.
4. Why is racial segregation harder to eradicate than other such barriers?
5. Trace the history of segregation in the United States.
6. What social factors were tending to break down segregation prior to the Supreme Court decision?
7. Show how different groups have reacted to the integration program.
8. Discuss different forms of "passing." What is the motivation for passing?
9. How does the problem of race mixture affect the integration issue?
10. List various discriminations found by Myrdal and appraise them from the viewpoint of each race.
11. Do you foresee an end to segregation in the United States?

SOURCEBOOK READINGS

GITTLER, JOSEPH B. *Social Dynamics*. New York: McGraw-Hill Book Co., Inc., 1952.
    1. DAVIS and HAVIGHURST, "Class and Color Differences in Child Rearing," pp. 42–46.
    2. GITTLER, with a quotation from PAUL RADIN, "Race Myth," pp. 317–27.
    3. HOOTON, E. A., "Major Facts about Race," pp. 330–33.

KOENIG, SAMUEL, REX D. HOPPER, and FELIKS GROSS. *Sociology: A Book of Readings*. Englewood Cliffs, N.J.: Prentice-Hall, Inc., 1956.
    4. LEYBURN, JAMES G., "The Problem of Minorities," pp. 333–42.
    5. CRISSEY, ELINOR, "Prejudice and Its Causes," pp. 343–46.
    6. DAVIE, MAURICE R., "America Needs Tolerance," pp. 347–49.
    7. LAFARGE, OLIVER, "The Problems of the American Indian," pp. 349–53.
    8. KOENIG, SAMUEL, "The Problem of Anti-Semitism," pp. 359–67.

LEE, RAYMOND L., JAMES A. BURKHART, and VAN B. SHAW. *Contemporary Social Issues*. New York: The Thomas Crowell Co., 1955.
    9. President's Committee on Civil Rights, "To Secure These Rights," pp. 461–66.
    10. MYRDAL, GUNNAR, "An American Dilemma," pp. 466–74.
    11. HUIE, WILLIAM B., "The Ordeal of Roosevelt Wilson," pp. 474–83.
    12. HARTLEY, MARGARET L., "Black Boundaries in Big Texas," pp. 483–87.
    13. ROSTOW, EUGENE V., "Japanese-American Relocation," pp. 489–95.

LEE, ELIZABETH BRYANT, and ALFRED McCLUNG LEE. *Social Problems in America* (rev. ed.). New York: Henry Holt & Co., Inc., 1955.
    14. ALLPORT, GORDON W., "Scapegoating," pp. 365–66.
    15. GORDON, MILTON M., and JOHN P. ROCHE, "The Price of Prejudice," pp. 367–70.

16. COLLIER, JOHN, "Indian Takeaway," pp. 378–79.
17. The President's Committee on Civil Rights, "Guilt by Heredity," p. 380.
18. Civil Rights Department of the American Jewish Committee, " 'Hate Groups,' " pp. 392–95.
19. LEE, ALFRED McCLUNG, "Discrimination in College Fraternities and Sororities," pp. 396–98.
20. GALARZA, ERNESTO, "The Mexican American," pp. 398–99.

SCHULER, EDGAR A., DUANE L. GIBSON, MAUDE L. FIERO, and WILBUR B. BROOKOVER. *Outside Readings in Sociology*. New York: The Thomas Crowell Co., 1956.
21. MYRDAL, GUNNAR, "The White Man's Theory of Color Caste and Rank Order of Discrimination," pp. 366–78.
22. DRAKE, ST. CLAIR, and HORACE R. CAYTON, "Crossing the Color-Line," pp. 378–91.

WILSON, LOGAN, and WILLIAM L. KOLB. *Sociological Analysis*. New York: Harcourt, Brace & Co., Inc., 1949.
23. DAVIS, ALLISON, "Caste, Economy and Violence," pp. 479–88.
24. McWILLIAMS, CAREY, "Does Social Discrimination Really Matter?" pp. 500–509.

SELECTED READINGS

ASHMORE, HARRY S. *The Negro and the School*. Chapel Hill: University of North Carolina Press, 1954.

BERNARD, JESSIE. *American Community Behavior*. New York: The Dryden Press, Inc., 1949, chaps. 16–20.

BERRY, BREWTON. *Race Relations*. Boston: Houghton Mifflin Co., 1951.

BURMA, JOHN A. *The Spanish-Speaking Groups in the United States*. Durham, N. C.: Duke University Press, 1954.

FAULKNER, WILLIAM, BENJAMIN E. MAYS, and CECIL SIMS. *Three Views of the Segregation Issue*. Atlanta: Southern Regional Council, 1956.

FRAZIER, E. FRANKLIN. *Race and Culture Contacts in the Modern World*. New York: Alfred A. Knopf, Inc., 1957.

——. *The Negro in the United States*. Rev. ed.; New York: The Macmillan Co., 1956.

KAHL, JOSEPH A. *The American Class Structure*. New York: Rinehart & Co., Inc., 1957, chap. 8.

McGILL, RALPH. "The Angry South," *The Atlantic Monthly*, April, 1956, pp. 31–34.

MICHENER, JAMES. *The Voice of Asia*. New York: Random House, Inc., 1951, pp. 145–49.

MYRDAL, GUNNAR. *An American Dilemma: Negro Problem and Modern Democracy*. New York: Harper & Brothers, 1944.

NICHOLS, LEE. *Breakthrough on the Color Front*. New York: Random House, Inc., 1954.

ROSE, ARNOLD M. (ed.). *Race Prejudice and Discrimination*. New York: Alfred A. Knopf, Inc., 1951.

ROSE, ARNOLD M., and CAROLINE ROSE. *America Divided*. New York: Alfred A. Knopf, Inc., 1948.

SIMPSON, GEORGE E., and J. MILTON YINGER. *Racial and Cultural Minorities*. New York: Harper & Brothers, 1953.

THOMAS, DOROTHY SWAINE, and RICHARD S. NISHIMOTO. *The Spoilage*. Berkeley: University of California Press, 1946. Treatment of West Coast Japanese during World War II.

WALLACE, ROBERT. "The Background of Segregation," *Life*, Part I, Sept. 3, 1956, pp. 41, 43–64; Part II, Sept. 10, 1956, pp. 41, 96–108.

WHITE, W. F. *Man Called White*. New York: The Viking Press, Inc., 1948.

Chapter 20

Occupational Status

The meaning of work to a man is not in bread alone; compensation is important, but for many, perhaps for most persons, the rank that goes with position is even more important to the satisfaction work brings. Surveys of youth from time to time have led researchers to conclude that the average young person wants a job with a swivel chair and telephone on the desk. In Washington bureaucracy, a man's prestige is measured in part by the size of the office and the desk and by the number of telephones he has.

It is difficult to conceive of situations, at least in the American social structure, where one's work status does not in some way affect his general social status. Even in the world of the criminal, the status hierarchy is evident.

"The professional thief, like any other professional man, has status. The status is based upon his technical skill, financial standing, connections, power, dress, manners, and wide knowledge acquired in his migratory life. His status is seen in the attitudes of other criminals, the police, the court officials, newspapers, and others. The term "thief" is regarded as honorific and is used regularly without qualifying adjectives to refer to the professional thief. It is so defined in a recent dictionary of criminal slang 'Thief, n. A member of the underworld who steals often and successfully. This term is applied with reserve and only to habitual criminals. It is considered a high compliment.'

"Professional thieves are contemptuous of amateur thieves and have many epithets which they apply to the amateurs. These epithets include 'snatch-and-grab thief,' 'boot-and-shoe thief,' and 'best-hold cannon.' Professional thieves may use 'raw-jaw' methods when operating under excellent protection, but they are ashamed of these methods and console themselves with the knowledge that they could do their work in more artistic manner if necessary. They will have no dealings with thieves who are unable to use the correct methods of stealing.

"Professional thieves disagree as to the extent of gradations in the profession. Some thieves divide the profession into 'big-time' and 'small-time' thieves on the basis of the size of the stakes for which they play, on the preparations for a particular stake, and on connections. A confidence man who regarded himself as 'big-time' wrote as follows regarding a shoplifter:

> While he is undoubtedly a professional thief, I should a few years ago (before he was committed to prison) have been ashamed to be seen on the street with him. I say this not out of a spirit of snobbishness but simply because for business reasons I feel that my reputation would have suffered in the eyes of my friends to be seen in the company of a booster (shoplifter).[1]

THE PROBLEM OF WORK STATUSES

As the preceding example shows so well, one's position in the occupational structure has much to do with his general status in society. Since every occupation requires a different degree of specialization and competence, and since some types of occupations represent more important social contributions than others, they carry different prestige ratings. So also the jobs within given occupations carry ratings reflecting the rights and duties imposed upon the person filling the given job. A professional thief does not associate with amateurs any more than does a professional golfer.

A king has a unique status in that the powers, privileges, and honors of his office are hereditary. He may have less power than a president or prime minister, but he may, nonetheless, have greater prestige because of the symbolic character of his office: he represents the perpetual succession of the throne. Even a woman in the office of queen suffers no disabilities of her sex, and did not even prior to this age of relative sex equality. Consider the power of British queens of an earlier day, who suffered nothing in prestige for being women in a day when among the population at large to be a woman was to be much the inferior of man.

In caste systems, occupations are fixed by caste. Where stratification is fairly rigid, ideas of gentility enter into ratings of importance of offices. The concept of the "gentleman" has had a large place in most societies. The gentleman is found in high prestige callings.

But lest we carelessly conclude that the status of office is a trait only of rigid social systems, let us consider an article by William

---

[1] Chic Conwell, *The Professional Thief*, as edited and annotated by Edwin H. Sutherland (Chicago: University of Chicago Press, 1937).

Whyte in *Fortune* magazine, which shows how the prestige, pressures, and statuses of office in modern industry flow over into family
life, deeply affecting the wives of business executives. The following
is a brief summary of the behavior of wives of executives.

The good executive wife is not a fixer, meddler, climber, or one
who pushes a husband around, but rather a stabilizer, who makes
the home a place where the lonely and the overworked executive
may relax. At the same time, she must be a gregarious social operator
and be able to put people at ease. Several unwritten rules apply to
her conduct. She (1) doesn't talk shop gossip with the girls; (2)
doesn't invite superiors in rank until after they have made the first
bid; (3) keeps away from the office; (4) avoids getting chummy with
wives of men her husband may soon pass in the climb; (5) isn't dis-
agreeable to company people she meets—one never knows; (6) is attractive; (7) is a 'phone pal' of husband's secretary; (8) never gets
tight at a company party; (9) isn't too good. She keeps up with the
Joneses, but does not get ahead too obviously. Getting ahead must
be timed exquisitely in connection with her husband's advancement.[2]

It is pointed out that if the husband moves up faster than his age
group, the wife is almost forced to move into a higher class residential community, because he so completely controls the destiny
of the lives and families of her former intimates that she no longer
feels at home with them or they with her. Whyte finds that the corporation does not object to a rising executive getting a divorce,
apparently assuming that he will choose a new wife more sympathetic to his position, work, and new status in the corporation
hierarchy.

Family possessions are a symbol of rank. One does not get a grand
piano until one "is ready for it" in terms of the husband's place in
the managerial hierarchy. Automobiles, particularly, are symbols of
one's place in the system. One moves cautiously from one model
Buick to the next higher, leaving the Cadillac for the president and
members of the board.[3]

Sociologist Edward Gross believes that in the life of modern man,
work status has tended to become the key status in human relationships. Once status and identity were very closely associated with

---

[2] William H. Whyte, Jr., "The Wives of Management," *Fortune,* Oct., 1951, pp.
86 ff., and "Corporation and the Wife," *Fortune,* Nov., 1951, pp. 109 ff.

[3] This study was made before the Continental Mark II was announced by the
Ford Motor Company. After it was announced, a rumor circulated, perhaps started
by a shrewd advertising man, that to get one of these cars, of which only 5,000 were
to be manufactured, one had to be in the social register. *Time* reported that some
businessmen sent in a long list of their qualifications.

family and place of residence. In a mobile urban industrial society these means of identity and status lose their meaning and a person's work tends to be the substitute in the social structure. "What do you do?" becomes the key question. The answer to this question becomes the key to one's income, leisure, level of living, and social status. On the basis of the answer others are able to make a judgment as to how they should behave toward him, whether to accord him respect or to offer him help, whether they want him as a friend or not. It is because place of origin and name are no longer sure indices of status that occupation becomes so important to us.[4]

In such a society, work statuses tend to become the basis for social stratification and also for the formation of interest and association groups outside the work situation. This means that work becomes a key to understanding the social structure itself and how it operates.

Certainly there is a suggestion in these examples from widely differing social systems that a person's work has much to do with his place in the prestige scale of the social system. This explains, in part, why sociology in the last few years has been developing a whole new branch of study—*the sociology of work*. For many years there has been a field of study in rural sociology, which deals particularly with the effect of agriculture on a man's status, attitudes, values, and aspirations. Then industrial sociology was born. Workers in this field were concerned with human relationships and status in the complicated factory and business organizations of the large city. More recently industrial sociology has been moving in the direction of a sociology of work. It is concerned with motivations, interaction patterns, ego satisfaction, rank, and statuses within the world of work.

This field of research and study is in its infancy, but the problem with which it deals is as old as history. Therefore, it may be helpful to make a brief study of work in the social structure to illustrate its vital reality in the life of every person.

HOW DO THE DIFFERENT OCCUPATIONS RATE?

Butcher, baker, candlestick maker—all have ratings. None of them is the best. So do shepherds, cattlemen, and swineherds, and they are not equal. In a cattleman's country, a sheepman is likely to rate somewhat lower than a coyote. And certainly a bartender is not likely to have much prestige in the society of church deacons.

[4] Edward Gross, *Work and Society* (New York: The Thomas Crowell Co., 1958), chap. 1.

If a college class were asked to list occupations on some kind of score card, they would agree fairly closely on their placement, particularly on the top and bottom ranks. In the great middle band members would often be doubtful about which occupation to put above which other.

Most young people are in college in part because they aspire to an occupation which carries high status. It is likely that they are as much concerned about status as about pay, perhaps more concerned. In fact, college students are likely to aspire to some type of professional or business activity. And yet many outlets in these fields promise less reward than the plumber or brick mason gets without college. It is the prestige difference that makes college seem worth while.

A few years ago the National Opinion Research Center took a poll of a cross section of the American public in which they asked persons interviewed to rate occupations in five groups: (1) excellent standing, (2) good standing, (3) average standing, (4) somewhat below average standing, (5) poor standing (and a group, "I don't know where to place that one"). The subjects were cautioned not to judge the occupation by any one person they knew in the occupation. Ninety specific occupations were scored.[5]

At the top, with scores of 96 (100 would have been perfect), were U. S. Supreme Court justices. Next were physicians, with a score of 93. Then followed state governors, cabinet members, diplomats, mayors of large cities, college professors (score of 90), scientists, etc.

The table on page 370 gives a grouping of some other occupations and shows the average score for each classification.

The world over, heredity has often been a factor in placement at the top of the occupational hierarchy. This is often true even in societies which do not automatically place most everyone in his occupation at birth. Kings, nobles, lords, and other hereditary dignitaries owe their office to their fathers, grandfathers, and so on back through generations. So, too, do untouchables owe their status to their genealogy.

In societies where few or no occupations are ascribed to certain classes, high status seems generally to be accorded on the basis of (1) service, (2) income, and (3) power exercised, the particular values used in rating positions being relevant to the particular society in which the person performs. As one rates office in American society, he finds these values being the primary ones in determining position.

[5] Cecil C. North and Paul K. Hatt, "Jobs and Occupations: a Popular Evaluation," *Opinion News,* Sept. 1, 1947, pp. 3–13.

Work status tends to become the basis for social stratification as well as for interest and association groups outside the work situation. The goals and economy of any society determine how the status hierarchy is structured. (Ewing Galloway and Standard Oil Company, N. J.)

Here is a simple classification of occupations which will be used in the analysis which follows, beginning with top status: (1) The professions (including government officials of professional caliber—Supreme Court justices, diplomats, etc.); (2) business and management; (3) white collar; (4) skilled workers and farm owners and operators; (5) unskilled workers, domestics, farm laborers, etc.

Status Ratings of Occupational Fields

(Based on interviews with almost 3000 persons)

Classification	Average score
Government officials*	90.8
Professional and semiprofessional workers	80.6
Proprietors, managers and officials (except farm)	74.9
Clerical, sales, and kindred workers	68.2
Craftsmen, foremen, and kindred workers	68.0
Farmers and farm managers	61.3
Protective service workers	58.0
Operatives and kindred workers	52.8
Farm laborers	50.0
Service workers (except domestic and protective)	46.7
Laborers (except farm workers)	45.8

Source: Cecil C. North and Paul K. Hatt, in *Opinion News*, September 1, 1947, pp. 3–13. Reprinted by permission of National Opinion Research Center.

* The census classifies some of these officials as professional and others as managerial.

The Professions. At the top of positions of office in America's open class society are the professions, with Supreme Court Justices (lawyers) ranking highest, and ministers, doctors, lawyers, professors, and teachers all rating high.

These are all achieved statuses. Why do the professions command unusual prestige among the occupations and those holding a professional job rank at the top in occupational prestige?

A profession may be defined as an occupation which requires so much preparation, such a high degree of skill, learning, and competence, that the client is not competent to judge the merits of the service rendered and must, therefore, place his case on faith in the professional man's hands. Perhaps there is another trait too in the professional position: the client has so much at stake that a lack of competence or an ethical failure on the part of the professional man may be very costly to him.

This distinction can be easily seen by comparing the work of a professional man with that of a skilled mechanic. An automobile mechanic who works on a hydromatic gear may have to have skills, the quality of which the client cannot judge, but the risks, even so, are not great. Only a few dollars are at stake. Automobile mechanics are not, therefore, professional men by social definition. But a doctor is dealing with life and death; a minister with problems of emotion, conscience, even the immortal soul; the lawyer is defending reputation, character, and often fortune; the teacher is dealing with character formation, with building mind and shaping the human conscience. Society cannot take chances where the risks are so great.[6]

In the professions there is the safeguard of a stern code of professional ethics self-imposed by the occupation itself. The physician takes the Hippocratic oath, after having completed a rigorous course of training and apprenticeship in an accredited medical school. He is bound for a lifetime by a stern code of professional ethics which puts service to the needs of the sick above personal comfort. He exposes himself to contagious diseases, risks his own comfort and health very often to save a patient from discomfort or risk. Financial reward is secondary. It is a stern code. Not all live up to this code, but society can afford no more lenient code for those whom it entrusts with matters of health and life.

The nurse likewise is bound by a stern code, and may also have something of the dedication of the minister in her personality, since she often enters the vocation in a spirit of religious giving of herself to alleviate suffering. She takes the same kind of risk the doctor takes and, although subordinate to his, her rank is high in the vocational hierarchy. As Thorner puts it:

"The nurse, like the mother in relation to the infant, caters to the patient's needs and, therefore, presents the most convenient 'object of cathexis' on whom he may discharge his craving for response as well as aggressive impulses. This is the situation which predisposes the patient to the transference phenomenon ('falling in love' with the nurse) and provides not only the condition for willing conformance to the nurse's authority but also the opportunity for exploiting the patient's vulnerability. In this complex situation the interests of all (patient, nurse, physician, and hospital) must be safeguarded so that therapeutic measures may be undertaken with maximum effectiveness. But this could hardly occur if the patient should be exposed to grave threats to his pre-existent ties and obligations, especially the primary relations comprising his families of orientation and procreation.

[6] Isidor Thorner has called attention to the greater professionalization of medicine than of pharmacy and believes it is due to the greater degree of responsibility the doctor assumes for the patient and his life. See his "Pharmacy: The Functional Significance of the Institutional Pattern," *Social Forces*, 20:321–28 (March 1942).

"Hence, it is a functional prerequisite that all concerned take for granted that the exclusive focus of interest is not the unique *person,* but the *patient.* The chief obligation of the nurse, as of all the medical professions, is to facilitate the expeditious transition of the patient to the person. To this end the emotional life is culturally defined (and very largely realized in practice) as belonging to the "private" sphere, stopping short of the sickroom, for both patient and nurse. If the former is a gall bladder "case," the latter is, reciprocally, the uniformed female who attends the case's needs. When the case begins to notice the nurse as a person, he is on the path to recovery. . . ."[7]

Thorner goes on to show that the balance of roles between the mother and the impersonal nurse, the person and the patient, is difficult to maintain. A gall bladder case is the patient conception. But when nurses marry patients, the personal has superseded the case conception of roles. Thorner indicates that when he asks nurses what they think of a nurse marrying a patient, the invariable reply is "It is repulsive!"

Marrying a patient is disapproved by the nursing code, since it is considered taking advantage of the patient's vulnerability, and involves substituting a personal role for a professional one on the part of the nurse.

The code for the other professions is less strict, but in all of them there is an essential code of service which supersedes monetary reward, a feeling of obligation to the client, an obligation to treat his confidences as confidences and not to judge, but to serve. All require the highest level of preparation, which in itself is society's principal safeguard.

In addition, most professions are surrounded by legal safeguards to the public. Boards of examiners certify members for most professions. Periodic review may be necessary for recertification. The teacher, and to some extent other professional persons, are more or less expected to continue formal schooling periodically in the interests of keeping up, or of specialization. All professions have their special journals which disseminate the latest theories, findings, and opinions in their respective professional fields, and all professional groups have their state, regional, and national meetings and conventions where the latest information and practices are presented to colleagues.

The Supreme Court Justice, who ranks the highest of all in status, is selected for his high sense of social responsibility. His is the highest

[7] Isidor Thorner, "Nursing: The Functional Significance of the Institutional Pattern," *American Sociological Review,* 20:531 (Oct. 1955).

type of legal qualification. He is the top scholar of the legal profession and on his decisions hang the destiny of democracy itself. His appointment is for life. Rarely is he appointed to this high honor until he has reached the retirement age of other men. Here is a position in which long experience, much testing in the practical art of administration of justice, and a high sense of social duty must have been demonstrated before one is a safe risk for the position. Society has too much at stake to place an inexperienced amateur in the position, no matter how brilliant he may be or how well trained.

Finally, the professions rate high in status because those who enter them have a career motivation, that is, they look forward to a lifetime spent in the particular occupation and to progressing in reputation as their services merit. In their work income is not the primary motivation as with the job worker, for whom income is more directly the end of effort.

Business and Management. If service is the key to high status in the professions, success in competition is the key to high status in business and management. Success in managing men and markets is rewarded by high income and high prestige in this area of intense activity oriented about the market.

It is said that in Hollywood the pressures for status in the business hierarchy of movie management are greater than elsewhere in America, that a subexecutive even gives up his chair to the top man when the latter enters the barber shop. Spectorsky, in *The Exurbanites*, has described the competitive rat race of the world around New York City out beyond the suburbs in what he calls "exurbia."[8] The typical exurbanite is a man in the advertising, writing, entertainment, radio, or TV business—the creator, the merchandiser, the packager of ideas. It is a high-pressure world in which the spirit of competition is so great that each man is presumably living far beyond his income to keep pace and depending on rising occupationally to catch up.

The author goes on to indicate how the exurbanite learns not only to show proper deference to the man who outranks him, but to be equally careful in the face he turns to inferiors.

When a crisis, such as a major snowfall, comes to a community of exurbanites, they are united against emergency, but as soon as the crisis passes the status barriers reappear.

Not all management men live under the stresses in these special worlds of advertising, writing, and entertainment, but typically the executive is the high pressure type. He is more likely than others to

[8] A. C. Spectorsky, *The Exurbanites* (Philadelphia: J. B. Lippincott Co., 1955), pp. 117–19.

die of apoplexy or some other form of heart disease brought on by high pressure. He is the ulcer type, the "go-getter," for whom tomorrow must be bigger.

There is much in American history to make the masses emulate the values for which those in the business and managerial occupations strive. The nation was built by men who placed courage above culture, achievement above class, and work above the gentility of leisure. The creators of empire and wealth still command respect. They are high up in the social structure. In a sense they are the cornerstone of civic life and progress in almost every community.

The Roosevelt New Deal censured men of wealth and economic power as "economic royalists" and replaced their rule by a "brain trust" of the intellectual elite. But the Eisenhower "people's crusade" restored businessmen to power, appointed a cabinet of millionaires, and made making money respectable again. The new "economic royalists," however, do not hold the reins of power as firmly as did those of a more individualistic age. And their power has increasingly been challenged by the mass power of the giant labor unions. In fact, almost parallel to them in power, wealth, and influence have arisen the labor barons with pension funds and investment capital at their disposal, to say nothing of the vote which they command in all instances where political power is to be exercised. These new labor barons are in control of the wage–price inflation cycle, and can cripple the economy at almost any point. They have even defied the power of government on a few notable occasions, only to learn, at the cost of heavy fines and Congressional reprimand, that there is a supreme law of the land that does not yield to political pressure when authority is openly defied. Fortunately for the future of democracy, the mass of citizens have backed their government with overwhelming support of public opinion as clearly as they did in an earlier age, when the blatant power of industrial magnates was trimmed by governmental action.

White Collar. The white-collar group has been described as the "nondescript class" in American life. So it may be, but it ranks middle to lower middle in the social structure in spite of its poorly defined position and its general lack of class consciousness. And it has become an increasingly large group in urban society. Here is sociologist C. Wright Mills' description of the white-collar group and its social position.

"The lower classes sometimes use the term, 'white-collar,' to refer to everybody above themselves. Their attitude varies from the power-class criterion: they are 'pencil pushers' who 'sit around and don't work and figure out ways of keeping wages cheap,' to the social-pragmatic criterion: 'The clerks are very essential. They are the ones who keep the ball rolling for the other guy. We would be lost if we didn't have the clerks.' This latter attitude may be slightly more frequent among those workers whose children have become clerks.

"The upper classes, on the other hand, never acknowledge the white-collar people as of the top and sometimes place them as laborers. An old upper-class man, for instance, says: 'Next after retailers, I would put the policeman, fireman, the average factory worker, and the white-collar clerks.' Interviewer: 'You would put the white-collar people in with the workers?' 'Well, I think so. I've lived in this town all my life and come to bank every day but Sunday, and I can't name five clerks downtown I know.'

"The white-collar people are split down the middle by income, extraction, intermarriage, job history, and education. Of the men in the higher of the two white-collar income classes, 61% are derived from the upper half of the extraction–income hierarchy, as compared with 49% of the lower white-collar men who are from the upper half by extraction. . . .

"The ideology of the white-collar people rises rather directly out of their occupations and the requirements for them. They are not a well defined group in any other readily apparent sense. . . ."[9]

There are many reasons why the white-collar group lacks clear-cut status, as this status is conceived by themselves and others. Their status is affected by the status of the organization they work for: an exclusive label shop brings greater prestige than a clerk job in some obscure factory on a dingy street. It is an insecure group for the most part, and low-paid, because few sectors of it are unionized. In this lack of united strength, it is a weaker bargaining group than much of the skilled and common labor group.

Its greater prestige comes in part no doubt from the fact that it is "white collar" rather than "blue collar." Although the white collar person may lack considerable in prestige, he is closer in his work life and social life to those who do rate high on the scale than are the skilled and unskilled worker groups.

One reason for the lack of financial success of the white collar group, Mills suggests, is that "their attitude toward their work is seldom material." They enjoy their contact with the public; the reason they most often give for liking their work is this one.

[9] C. Wright Mills, "The Middle Classes in Middle-Sized Cities," *American Sociological Review*, 11:525–27 (Oct. 1946).

Mills finds four factors entering into their ideology concerning their work:

. . . (a) the idea that they are *learning about human nature*, which is mentioned by about one-fourth of them; (b) the feeling that they *borrow prestige* from their customers; sometimes the prestige source includes the merchandise itself or the store, but its center is normally the customer; (c) the opposite of prestige borrowing: the feeling of *power in manipulating the customer's appearance and home;* this is more apparent, of course, among cosmetic and clothing sellers; (d) the idea of *rendering service:* about one-fourth speak explicitly in terms of an ideology of service, which is interwoven in various ways with the other contents.[10]

These ideological compensations are no doubt satisfactions laborers do not experience.

Skilled and Semi-Skilled Workers. This is the layer in the occupational structure where work with one's hands begins, but it is handwork with tools of a specialized nature. Unlike the professional and business man, the skilled worker is not on a salary, ordinarily, but a wage. His security is won by unionization and by seniority rather than by special training and competitive performance.

Today his work may be as highly rewarded as the professional man's—in fact, may be rewarded even more highly—yet his status does not measure up to that of the professional person by any means. One who does skilled manual work primarily, uses tools, and has special mechanical skills is considered of less importance to society than one who manipulates people or ideas or deals with life's greatest issues: health, learning, religion, justice, management of people, management of money, management of manufacture.

One of the most exhaustive studies of a particular skilled group and their way of life is Cottrell's study of the railroader.[11] He shows that the railroader maintains his unique social position chiefly by monopolizing training. Training is by apprenticeship on the job. The only road to advancement is through seniority. Beyond a certain mechanical aptitude no other training is needed, so that by controlling apprenticeship the Railroad Brotherhood protects those already on the ladder above.

Farm owners and operators are a unique group. They have a capital investment, are self-determining in the use of their time, and venture and risk much as those in other businesses. Yet they have

10 *Ibid.*, p. 527.

11 W. Fred Cottrell, *The Railroader* (Stanford, Calif.: Stanford University Press, 1940). The study of the factory as a work organization and of various specialized occupations and work situations is becoming a major interest of applied sociology. For studies, see the selected readings at the end of this chapter.

rarely, in American society, had high status. The most notable exception is the plantation farmer of the Deep South prior to the Civil War. There the concept of "gentleman farmer" carried high status, for the farmer was not a worker, but rather a manager over a slave system of labor.

This same type of operation exists in certain specialized agricultural areas, particularly in the West, but there dominion of managers is over hired labor, often, in fact, over large groups of seasonal workers in specialized crop areas. This type of farming has at times been labeled "factories in the field." The injustices of low wages in this farm economy during the Depression of the 1930's was made the subject of the famous Steinbeck novel *Grapes of Wrath*.

For the most part the farmer rates well down the list in status. He is self-employed, and has a degree of independence which even the skilled worker rarely has. Yet he is in most communities considered somewhat inferior to banker and merchant and considers himself so. There are many exceptions to this statement, for a farmer's status in the community is very much affected by the size of his land holdings, the size of his flocks and herds, and the size of his bank account. In communities where certain farmers have moved into the Cadillac class, they may have a very high rating.

Two government programs have been organized among teenagers which are helping to improve the status of the agricultural occupation: Four-H Clubs, organized by the state–federal Agricultural Extension Service, and Future Farmers of America, organized as a part of the Smith-Hughes training program in the high schools.

Unskilled Workers, Domestics, and Farm Workers. In the large group at the bottom of the occupational structure is the workman who works with his hands. He handles tools primarily, or manipulates machines on routine jobs. His income is in the form of wages. He owns none of the tools of production and ordinarily has no investment in the business. His only strength is in unionization and his primary security is that provided by the Social Security Act. His job may prove to be temporary, since he is rarely indispensable.

The status of this large worker group is low for several reasons. First and foremost, their services can be performed by most anyone. Little training or specialization is required. These workers are easily replaceable. Initiative and leadership is not expected, since these workers are paid for performing tasks directed by others. Bosses, supervisors, and managers do the thinking and planning and direct each task.

Although in American society there is no stigma associated with manual labor as such—even the highest status group works manually at hobby and do-it-yourself tasks—the man who serves only in this capacity fulfills only the minimum requirements of the work world.

In the organized shop, the union may reduce even manual performance to a dead level of mediocrity in order to make the work go as far as possible. Even on piecework the union often sets the pace, and to exceed it is to be disloyal to the group and suffer various kinds of humiliations and penalties. Pay is reward for the time spent on the job, not for the amount or quality of the work done. In this sense the work of the modern factory worker is of less significance than was that of the craftsman in the age of handicraft preceding the factory system. Consequently, his status is also lower.

For all these reasons, the amount of consideration given the worker, his prestige, his respect among his neighbors, in fact, his total place in the social structure, is lower than that of groups which assume more responsibility and perform more significant functions.

SOCIAL POSITION AND OCCUPATIONAL STATUS

Over the years, the bearing of a man takes on the stamp of the importance of his occupational rating. The banker is likely to carry himself with dignity and betray a sense of self-importance in his manner and stride. The domestic and service workers show not only the signs of toil, but may also exhibit the personality traits that go with feelings of unimportance and inferiority.

The man at the bottom cultivates a certain respect for the man at or near the top, and the man at the top is likely to expect the deference and respect due one of influence and power. These things are more true in social structures dominated by nobility, but they tend to be true in some measure even in democratic society.

Here is a description of an older community in the East. During the day, as men meet each other, there is an air of friendliness and equality, but in the evening the formalities of work-status differences emerge.

"The democratic principles laid down by the founders of this country apparently die hard in a Puritan community. When a stranger first comes to Burlington, he may well be impressed by the friendly atmosphere which pervades the business section of the city. During the working day it would seem that Burlington is such a small world that nearly everyone knows everyone else. The cheery greetings on the street corners—'Hello, Charlie,' 'Good morning, Tom'—give the impression that people meet on a friendly basis unaffected by class distinctions. Moreover, the brief conversations over-heard between the man who shines shoes and his customer, the clerk serving behind the counter and the restaurant manager, or the plumber, automobile salesman, newspaper man, and stockbroker who happen to share a table at lunchtime, convince one that these greetings are more than merely 'Hail fellow, well met,' and are in-deed the result of a certain knowledge and some appreciation of the life of each individual in the community.

"With the end of the working day, however, something of this in-formality of acquaintanceship ceases. Some of the same people who greet each other informally in the morning give a more formal nod over their wives' shoulders if by chance they happen to meet in the evening at a movie, town concert, or lecture. This slight increase of formality affords a key to the bases of class distinctions which exist beneath the surface appearance of a fairly unified social world.

"The actual division of Burlington's social life into a maze of classes and cliques is arbitrarily based on three kinds of differences, apart from natural differences of interest. There is, first of all, the division based on differences in economic status which separate the community into two main groups—the working class and the busi-ness and professional class. A second large division is created by dif-ferences in religion which separate the community into the two main camps of Catholicism and Protestantism, each with its own social stratification along economic lines. The third division is based roughly on ethnic differences which serve to enhance the divisions based on religion or economic status and also to create division within the religious worlds or the economic levels."[12]

Not only in the East may such sharp contrasts in social status be found. Here is a college student's account of status difference of a most subtle sort in his Far West town.

"An 'elite' group has been formed in my town which considers it-self very modern and tolerates the liberalism of the workers. But since the members are from the higher income group, they think of themselves as superior, deploring the crudity of the other towns-people, the farmers, and the lumbermen. The professional men and women and some business owners make up this group, but it seems to be maintained by the efforts of the women, who 'ape' the big city and try to pattern themselves and their activities after urban ideals. Pleasure and cultural activities occupy their time, whereas work and institutional interests occupy the other people. This same group has its dancing club and holds dancing parties frequently. Everyone

[12] Elin L. Anderson, *We Americans: A Study of Cleavage in an American City* (Cambridge: Harvard University Press, 1937), p. 489.

dresses as if he were going to the Waldorf-Astoria, and the affairs are very formal for a small town. It is positively social suicide to offend a member of this group and 'reputational' suicide also, as they are the most avid gossipers in town. Most of the women of this group have time to spare and when they are not playing bridge they often go to Seattle or Aberdeen for concerts, lectures, or other social events. They see to it that their husbands find time to go also.

"The middle class, containing the church-going citizens, the 'Babbitts,' and the average inhabitants, is dominated by church leaders. Not all of this class are ardently religious, but they at least profess some faith and are conservative in their ideas. The 'goings on' of the lumberjacks and the worldliness of the elite both meet their disapproval. They are characteristically self-centered and interested in developing their town into a city. In spite of the fact that the farmers and lumberjacks provide the trade, these townsmen continue to regard themselves as superior and 'citified.' However, there are a few prosperous farmers and their wives who are leaders in this group because of their economic standing and because they are college educated. Superior education raises their status, as education is highly regarded in rural areas."

Speaking of "Prairie Town," South Dakota, three sociologists who studied it say that this trade center of some 3,500 people has three distinct strata: (1) the low-status groups consisting of ex-farmers, farm hands, and unskilled laborers; (2) the middle class of storekeepers, craftsmen, retired farmers, and professional people; and (3) the successful entrepreneurs and large land holders who constitute the elite class.[13]

The elite group is known colloquially as the "Tops." They live on the bluff on the east side of town. The lowest status group, known colloquially as the "Bottoms," live in the lower area of the town. The two groups are markedly differentiated in terms of family backgrounds, associations, occupational and residential history, forms of speech, relief history, secularism, family type, educational attainments, and vital statistics, as reflected in length of life, infant mortality, and sickness. Dietary habits differ. The "Tops" are interested in preserving the girlish figure; the "Bottoms" are interested in a full stomach.

These sociologists point out that the two groups have stereotyped attitudes toward themselves and toward the other group. The elite feel that they have arrived by personal merit and by the law of "survival of the fittest." They are sure that the "Bottoms" are ex-

[13] John Useem, Pierre Tangent, and Ruth Useem, "Stratification in a Prairie Town," *American Sociological Review*, 7:331–42 (June 1942).

plained by innate shiftlessness, laziness, and lack of intelligence. The "Bottoms" think that the "Tops" are there because of luck, "pull," inherited wealth, and educational opportunities not available to others. The classes are mutually exclusive; each prefers to associate within its own circle. Class distinction affects community cooperation and civic administration. Different social organizations, including churches, attract different strata.

EDUCATION IN OCCUPATIONAL STATUS

Education is the most significant social elevator in American life. To climb the educational ladder is to climb in occupational status and in income. To go to college, for example, is to nearly double one's lifetime earnings over just completing high school. And the upward climb extends throughout much of the work lifetime. (See the charts on pp. 424–25 and 426, Chapter 23.)

Educational expectations among various occupations have been studied by the Social Research Service at Michigan State College.[14] It found that children of the professional group more or less take for granted college education, about two-thirds planning to go. In the unskilled group at the other extreme, less than a third of the boys expect to attend and only one in five girls.

Sufficient evidence has been presented to suggest that in a vague yet meaningful way, occupational stratification is a part of even our social system, as it has perhaps been of all societies from time immemorial, as, in fact, it always will be. Society, to obtain the efficiency and dependability required for certain types of occupational performance, such as medicine, must grant more than ordinary respect to the occupation. Then men of great talent, energy, and competence will be attracted, absorb its code, and perform heroically.

Were it not for the differential status of office, it would be impossible to fill campus positions. Who would carry the responsibilities of the unpaid student body president were it not for the respect of office. Status is society's most ready and most valuable coin for rewarding superior responsibility and performance.

SUMMARY

To be a warrior, a priest, or a ruler is more important in most societies than to be a farmer, a tinkerer, a hunter, or a herdsman. Recognition of the differential importance of different social tasks is the basis of occupational differentiation.

The rating given a particular occupation in one society may not conform at all to that of another society. In a culture where fishing

[14] *Youth and the World of Work* (East Lansing: Social Research Service, Michigan State College), 1949.

is a life occupation for a great number of people, fishing may have less status significance than it has in a culture which defines the role of the sportsman as a superior one. So one cannot be sure that high ranking of an activity is strictly confined to its utility. The status aspect may be derived from the fact that it is a nonmercenary pursuit of persons who achieve leisure and, therefore, great respect. In the latter case the activity of the fisherman is not really an occupation. It is a hobby, a leisure-time activity, and must, therefore, be rated by other standards.

In a mobile urban industrial society, work statuses tend to become key statuses in that they are an index to leisure, income, and level of living. In this, they have tended to replace place and parenthood as indices of social worth.

Certainly this discussion indicates that the sociologist, in setting forth the concept of occupational differentiation, is dealing with a social reality which must be reckoned with. It has much to do with personal striving.

DISCUSSION AND REVIEW QUESTIONS

1. Show how many differentiations of the social structure are based on the rated social significance of one's work.

2. Illustrate how pressures to climb in work status operate.

3. Show how, in certain circles, the status of a man in the administrative hierarchy may affect his family life.

4. Appraise Gross' position that a man's work status in our society tends to become his key status.

5. What is the highest status position in our work structure as shown by research? the highest status occupational class?

6. What are the main work classes?

7. Define "profession." What are its distinguishing marks? Illustrate from the medical or nursing professions.

8. What are some of the appropriate behavior patterns of the exurbanite, as seen by Spectorsky?

9. To use Mills' phrase, who would you say are the "power elite" in contemporary society?

10. What are the distinguishing marks of the white-collar class? What is your appraisal of the status of this class?

11. What traits separate the skilled class?

12. Why, would you say, does the unskilled group rank lowest in the occupational hierarchy?

13. Show how occupational stratification does in reality tend to divide communities.

SOURCEBOOK READINGS

LANDIS, JUDSON T., and MARY G. LANDIS. *Readings in Marriage and the Family.* Englewood Cliffs, N.J.: Prentice-Hall, Inc., 1952.

  1. NIMKOFF, MEYER F., "Occupational Factors and Marriage," pp. 189–97.

  2. MITRA, D. N., "A Hindu Marriage in Bengal," pp. 139–44.

3. MITRA, D. N., "A Hindu Wife," pp. 144–50.

LEE, ELIZABETH BRYANT, and ALFRED McCLUNG LEE. *Social Problems in America* (rev. ed.). New York: Henry Holt & Co., Inc., 1955.

    4. FLOWERMAN, SAMUEL H., "Should Jews Change Their Occupations?" pp. 209–11.

    5. WHYTE, WILLIAM H., JR., "Management Man: Permanent Transient," pp. 353–56.

    6. WHYTE, WILLIAM H., JR., "Management Man's Wife," pp. 356–59.

O'BRIEN, ROBERT W., CLARENCE C. SCHRAG, and WALTER T. MARTIN. *Readings in General Sociology* (2d ed.). Boston: Houghton Mifflin Co., 1957.

    7. HENRY, WILLIAM A., "The Business Executive," pp. 239–43.

    8. ROETHLISBERGER, F. J., "The Foreman," pp. 243–48.

    9. DUBIN, ROBERT, "Technical Characteristics of a Bureaucracy," pp. 316–19.

    10. ROSE, ARNOLD, "The Social Structure of the Army," pp. 320–23.

    11. SHEPARD, HERBERT A., "Democratic Control in a Labor Union," pp. 323–28.

    12. WHYTE, WILLIAM FOOTE, "The Social Structure of the Restaurant," pp. 328–33.

SCHULER, EDGAR A., DUANE L. GIBSON, MAUDE L. FIERO, and WILBUR B. BROOKOVER. *Outside Readings in Sociology.* New York: The Thomas Crowell Co., 1956.

    13. WALLER, WILLARD W., "The Teacher's Roles," pp. 147–53.

    14. JEFFERSON, THOMAS, "Natural Versus Artificial Aristocracy," pp. 412–14.

SELECTED READINGS

BENDIX, RICHARD. *Work and Authority in Industry: Ideologies of Management in the Course of Industrialization.* New York: John Wiley & Sons, Inc., 1956.

BENDIX, REINHARD, and S. M. LIPSET (eds.). *Class, Status and Power: A Reader in Social Stratification.* Glencoe, Ill.: The Free Press, 1953.

CAPLOW, THEODORE. *The Sociology of Work.* Minneapolis: University of Minnesota Press, 1954.

CARR-SAUNDERS, A. M., and P. A. WILSON. *The Professions.* New York: Oxford University Press, 1933.

CARTWRIGHT, DORWIN, and ALVIN ZANDER (eds.). *Group Dynamics: Research and Theory.* Evanston, Ill.: Row, Peterson & Co., 1953.

CHINOY, E. *Automobile Workers and the American Dream.* Garden City, N.Y.: Doubleday & Co., Inc., 1955.

CLARKE, ALFRED C. "The Use of Leisure and Its Relation to Levels of Occupational Prestige," *American Sociological Review,* 21:301–7. June, 1956.

DAVIS, KEITH. *Human Relations in Business.* New York: McGraw-Hill Book Co., Inc., 1957.

DRUCKER, PETER F. "America: Next Twenty Years," *Harper's.* "I. The Coming Labor Shortage," Nov., 1954, pp. 67–81; "II. The Promise of Automation," April, 1955, pp. 41–47; "III. The New Tycoons," May, 1955, pp. 39–44.

DUBIN, ROBERT. "Industrial Workers' Worlds: A Study of the 'Central Life Interests' of Industrial Workers," *Social Problems,* 3:140 ff. (Jan. 1956).

Editorial Board of Industrial Research Association. *Research in Industrial Human Relations: A Critical Appraisal.* New York: Harper & Brothers, 1957.

GROSS, EDWARD. "Characteristics of Cliques in Office Organization," *Research Studies of the State College of Washington,* 19:131–36 (Pullman, Wash., 1951).

————. "Some Functional Consequences of Primary Controls in Formal Work Organization," *American Sociological Review,* 18:366–73 (Aug. 1953).

————. "Symbiosis and Consensus as an Integrative Factor in Small Groups," *American Sociological Review,* 21:174–79 (April, 1956).

————. *Work and Society: The Sociology of Work Relations.* New York: The Thomas Crowell Co., 1958.

HARE, A. PAUL, EDGAR F. BORGATTA, and ROBERT F. BALES (eds.). *Small Groups: Studies in Social Interaction.* New York: Alfred A. Knopf, Inc., 1955.

MEADOWS, PAUL. *The Culture of Industrial Man.* Lincoln: University of Nebraska Press, 1950.

MERTON, ROBERT K. "Bureaucratic Structure and Personality," *Social Forces,* 18: 560–68 (1940).

MILLER, DELBERT C., and WILLIAM H. FORM. *Industrial Sociology,* New York: Harper & Brothers, 1951.

MILLS, C. WRIGHT. *The New Men of Power.* New York: Harcourt, Brace & Co., Inc., 1948.

SELZNICK, PHILIP. *The Organizational Weapon.* New York: McGraw-Hill Book Co., Inc., 1952.

STONE, ROBERT C. "Factory Organization and Vertical Mobility," *American Sociological Review,* 18:28–35 (1953).

SUTHERLAND, EDWIN H., and DONALD R. CRESSEY. *White Collar Crime.* New York: The Dryden Press, Inc., 1949.

––––––. "White Collar Criminality," *American Sociological Review,* 5:1–12 (Feb. 1940).

THORNER, ISIDOR. "Nursing: The Functional Significance of an Institutional Pattern," *American Sociological Review,* 20:531–38 (Oct. 1955).

VEBLEN, THORSTEIN. *The Theory of the Leisure Class.* New York: Random House, Inc., 1934.

WARNER, W. LLOYD, *et al. Democracy in Jonesville.* New York: Harper & Brothers, 1949.

––––––, and J. C. ABEGGLEN. *Occupational Mobility in American Business and Industry, 1928–1952,* Minneapolis: University of Minnesota Press, 1955.

––––––, R. J. HAVIGHURST, and M. B. LOEW. *Who Shall Be Educated?* New York: Harper & Brothers, 1944.

WHYTE, WILLIAM H., JR. "The Wives of Management," *Fortune,* Oct., 1951, pp. 86 ff.; and "Corporation and the Wife," *Fortune,* Nov., 1951, pp. 109 ff.

Chapter **21**

Religion in the Social Structure

Religion is the area of man's life which deals with his relationship to his maker. As such, it is discussed in Chapter 37 as a major social institution. But religion has profound implications for the social structure, entirely aside from its institutional aspects, in that it very often determines the type of status relationships men have with each other. Throughout much of human history, as well as in much of the world today, a man's standing in his community and his relations with his neighbors are determined by the kind of religious affiliation he holds. Whether he is rated at the top of the social pyramid or at the bottom often depends upon where he fits into the religious hierarchy, or on the type of religious affiliation which he holds, or the particular religious beliefs to which he pledges allegiance.

To be a Catholic may mean to be more or less an outcast. To be a Jew may call for segregation. To be a Brahman may place one on the top layer of the society. It is largely in this sense that religion is approached in the paragraphs that follow. It is in this sense that religion is a basic factor in the social structure, for in this sense it determines not only the roles of individuals but their statuses.

RELIGION IN STRATIFICATION

Author James A. Michener describes a riot in Singapore in which a Eurasian Catholic is attacked by a mob, his car wrecked, and except for the interference of a courageous sikh he would have been killed. Moslem policemen stand by and do not interfere. In this brief passage one senses the deep underlying importance of religion in that social structure.

CHRISTIANS (Euro-American) 804,307,000

CONFUCIANISTS AND TAOISTS (Far East) 350,350,000

HINDUS (India) 316,000,000

MOHAMMEDANS (Near East) 416,570,000

BUDDHISTS (China) 150,310,000

ANIMISTS (everywhere) 135,650,000

JEWS 11,867,000

EACH FIGURE REPRESENTS 50 MILLION PEOPLE

Membership of Principal Religions of the World, 1957

Throughout the world, religion is one of the major factors in the social struc-ture. Often it is a key factor in class and caste, always a factor in social status. Throughout history violence has arisen repeatedly between different religious groups, and even in democratic societies minority religions have rarely been accorded equal and fair treatment.

"At the investigation the Malay police were astonished that anyone had expected them to interfere with the mob. 'They were all Moslems,' the police protested. 'How could we fire upon our own religion?' A newspaper man explained that in New York if there's a riot, Negro cops will fire on Negro criminals or Irish cops upon fellow Catholics. The Malay police thought this very strange and said the Irish cops must not take their religion very seriously.

"I myself am a Catholic, and this has been a great solace to me. This was the only church that really welcomed Eurasians and I have always felt myself a brother with all Catholics across the world.

"But recently I have begun to wonder if I ought not to turn my back upon Christianity, confess my sins, and become a complete Malay Moslem. I believe now that my future lies with the Malays."[1]

Throughout history religion has often been a major part of the framework of the social structure. In Europe and England, religious wars occurred frequently in the seventeenth century. In England, the shift of monarchs from Protestant to Catholic, or Catholic to Protestant, led to eras of bloodshed.

Perhaps the most bloody of these epochs was the reign of Mary Tudor, who attempted to enforce the conversion of the nation to the Catholic church. "Bloody Mary" ordered the execution of some of her noblest subjects. The trials began at Oxford in 1555, and Protestant Bishops Latimer and Ridley were among the victims, as was Archbishop Cranmer. Instead of exterminating Protestantism, the wholesale murders of the day rallied Protestants to display daring loyalty to their faith. As the fagots were being lighted at the stakes, Latimer cried the immortal words: "Be of good comfort, Master Ridley. Play the man. We shall this day light such a candle, by God's grace, in England as I trust shall never be put out."[2] Elizabeth in her day condemned many Catholics to death. It was this religious persecution in England and on the continent that was one of the motives for the founding of a new nation in America.

In contemporary history, the great struggle over religion in India, which led to the division of India and Pakistan in 1947 on the basis of Moslem and Hindu, is a striking example of religion as a barrier in human association. The partition was accompanied by much bloodshed. In some areas whole trainloads of men, women, and

---

[1] From *The Voice of Asia* by James A. Michener, p. 149. Copyright, 1951, by James A. Michener. Reprinted by permission of Random House, Inc.

[2] Foxe's *Book of Martyrs* immortalized the victims of these religious purges and generations of Englishmen in childhood learned the tales of their sacrifices and studied the gruesome illustrations of Protestant churchmen being burned at the stake. This era marked the final step in the eventual victory of Protestantism in England.

children were butchered by the opposing religious group. Almost a million in all died during the ensuing riots.

Pakistan is the new Moslem state, divided by more than a thousand miles of India into East and West Pakistan. India is still a state divided in its religion, for some 45 million Moslems chose to remain among India's 324 million Hindus and were permitted to do so. Riots in October, 1956, broke out over the republication by a Hindu of an American book about religion which the Moslems thought made sacrilegious comments about their faith. The religious issue is likely to remain a major one in the social structure of the subcontinent in the future.

Even within India's caste system itself, religion is one of the key factors in status, the Brahman (priesthood) caste being at the top.

India, like ancient Egypt, is a land saturated with religion; its people are obsessed with the destiny and status of man in the hereafter. Nearly every aspect of life, every thought and action, is conditioned by faith and dogma, whether in business, in politics, or in social behavior . . . Hinduism is impossible to define in a terse and neat statement, for it comprehends a way of life, rather than a narrow, church-going creed, and affects a man's social status, his marriage, the very food he eats, the friends among whom he can mingle, and the occupation he follows.[3]

In such instances as those just cited, religion is conceived not merely as an institution meeting the need for religious expression but as a pattern of life which becomes the key to interrelations between large masses of people. It actually becomes one of the principal barriers of the social structure, and many aspects of human interrelations are governed by it.

In this chapter we shall consider religion as an example of how purely cultural creations of man come to be major factors in the social structure of a society. Politics is a similar factor in the framework of many social structures; in fact, it is a major factor in dividing the world into two great armed camps today.

RELIGION AS SEPARATENESS

Religion is often looked upon as the great unifier of men. Christianity, like Buddhism, has preached universal brotherhood. These are great ideals and may someday be realized on earth. But history tells a quite different story of both past and present. In reality, religion tends to stratify all social structures. Rare indeed is the society which does not rate a man on the basis of his religion.

A basic tenet of Christianity is "Come out from among them and be ye separate." Here is a command to the Christian to be different

[3] T. Walter Wallbank, *India in the New Era* (Chicago: Scott, Foresman & Co., 1951), p. 23.

and stand apart from those around him of different belief or behavior. Even among Christians there is great separateness. One churchman has referred to the Sunday morning hour of worship as "the great and sacred hour of segregation."

In British Columbia, Canada, there exists a unique colony of people, originally from Russia, with beliefs differing from those of the Church of England and of any other sect or denomination. Their beliefs at certain points come into conflict with the laws of the state, particularly on such matters as schooling for their children, taxes, and serving in the armed forces in wartime. The Dukhobors, as these people are called, protest these infringements on their liberties by marching naked into town and getting themselves locked in jail, where they continue their protest by religious singing and prayers.[4] Another means of protest is to dynamite bridges and burn schoolhouses and even their own homes. In 1957 they even petitioned the Canadian government to allow them to return to Russia.

Here is one of the many unique religious colonies that have appeared in various parts of Europe and the New World to declare their separateness and maintain it at all costs. No one can question that such a religion sets people apart in status from others about them.

THE JEWS

The long history of the Jews, who after the birth of Christianity were to become a people without a country for almost 2,000 years and who had been dispossessed temporarily even before that and carried off to Egypt, gives a vivid picture of a people which has been held together by religion alone through centuries of persecution, the victim of extermination campaigns, the ghetto, property confiscation, and countless other hardships.

Throughout history, because of their unique religion, the Jews have remained a separate people wherever they have lived. Divorced from nationality as such, with no common habitat, they have yet been a separate people in all nations, with their own unique status.

This has often brought special taxes and other discriminatory sanctions. In Frankfort and many other medieval cities the Christians paid taxes according to their fortunes, but taxes were fixed once and for all on the Jew.

The Old Testament, a book of Jewish life and custom, reflects the ethnocentrism of the Jew. Gentiles are dogs, looked upon with suspicion. Yet there is a ritual for taking in the stranger and making him an accepted member by going through a ceremonial and purification

[4] For a study of this sect, see Harry B. Hawthorn (ed.), *The Dukhobors of British Columbia* (Vancouver: University of British Columbia, 1955).

ritual. The scriptures admonish again and again against the dangers of mixing with the gentiles and marrying with them, so in every part of the world, the Jews have retained their separateness. They have stood alone and apart, a peculiar people, a minority people in the lands they have lived in, always in some measure suspect and in some measure mistreated, even by the most generous of nations.

There is probably no parallel in history to this story of the persistence of a religious group, and no better example of the force of religion in social structures. Here is a brief account of the Jew in Europe during a thousand years of history:

The Ghetto. "The ghetto has a written history extending over a period of at least one thousand years. Even before the ghetto became the characteristic form of Jewish community life we find a richly documented history of Jewish settlements that takes us back to the days before the opening of the Christian era. . . ."[5]

"The ghetto seems to have been originally a place in Venice, a quarter of the city in which the first Jewish settlement was located. It became, in the course of time, an institution recognized in custom and defined in law. It became, in short, not merely the place in which Jews lived, but the place in which they were compelled to live. The walls of that ghetto have long since crumbled, but the ghost of the ancient institution lingers. It is still a place of refuge for the masses of the Jewish people and still imposes upon them, for good and for ill, something of the ancient isolation. . . .

"The ghetto has been the center of all that may be described as sectarian and provincial of Jewish life. It has put its imprint, not only upon the manners of the Jew, but upon his character. It is the interaction of this culture of the ghetto and that of the larger gentile community outside, involving the more or less complete participation of Jews in both worlds, that is the source of most that is problematic and enigmatic in the situation of the Jew of today, as of yesterday. . . ."[6]

Segregation and Survival. "The Jews owe their survival as a separate and distinct ethnic group to their social isolation. The continuity of their particular social life and their survival as a social type depends primarily upon the continuance of this isolation, just as the distinct character of any people depends upon its exclusion from contacts with other peoples. . . .

"The anomalous status of the Jew is based upon the solidarity of his communal life and his amazing ability to act collectively. It is his

[5] Lewis Wirth, *The Ghetto* (Chicago: University of Chicago Press, 1928), p. 5.
[6] Robert E. Park, in Wirth, *op. cit.*, pp. ix, xi.

historical isolation—it is the ghetto, voluntary or compulsory, medieval or modern—which not only accounts for his character, but for the fantastic conception that others have of him. . . ."[7]

The Ghetto and Social Isolation. "The ghetto is not only a physical fact; it is also a state of mind. The laws that regulated the conduct of Jews and Christians are merely the external forms to which, on the subjective side, there correspond the attitudes of social distance and of self- and group-consciousness. The hostilities and outbreaks of violence with which ghetto history is replete represent the friction and the conflicts to which the living together of diverse cultural groups gives rise. The numerous taboos and restrictions that encumbered the behavior of Jew and Christian toward each other are to be regarded, not merely as the fortuitous and arbitrary decisions of members of either group, but rather as physical expressions of the social distance that was emerging out of a conflict relationship. . . ."[8]

Medical School Quotas. This is history. But what of the contemporary social forces that exclude the Jew from full participation in the life of other peoples? American medical schools, for example, have been discriminatory in the handling of students insofar as the Jew is concerned, indicating the stratifying effect of religion in this instance. It has been pointed out that the "wrong" name, church, or ancestry often cancels a scholarship and denies a highly qualified candidate admittance to a school of medicine.[9] Deans of medical schools often operate their own quota system in discriminating against minority groups by religion or race.

A survey made a few years ago showed that in a total of 6,500 medical students only 500 or 600 were Jews. It is reported that the number of Jewish students in medical schools has greatly declined.[10] Of the 35,000 or so applications received annually a few years ago, some 5,000 to 7,000 were Jewish. This means that about three out of four non-Jewish students are admitted compared to about one in thirteen Jewish students.

Jewish Stereotypes. Finally, there are the common stereotyped attitudes toward the Jew which help explain his unique place in the social structure of American life. Some of these are set forth in the table below. The information is based on interviews with 150 veterans of World War II. Many felt that Jews are clannish, have

[7] Wirth, *op. cit.*, pp. 288, 290–91.
[8] Wirth, *op. cit.*, pp. 8–9.
[9] Frank Kingdon, "Discrimination in Medical Colleges," *American Mercury*, 61:391–99 (1945).
[10] *Ibid.*

too much of the money or power, are underhanded in business and avoid hard work. It is such pictures in the minds of men that affect their behavior toward minority religious groups.

Stereotypes Characterizing Jews
(Based on interviews with 150 veterans of World War II)

Stereotype	Number of Veterans Mentioning Stereotypes
They are clannish; they help one another	37
They have money	26
They control everything (Or have an urge to control everything); they are running the country.........................	24
They use underhanded or sharp business methods	24
They do not work; they do not do manual labor	19

Source: Bruno Bettelheim and Morris Janowitz, "Ethnic Tolerance: A Function of Social and Personal Control," *American Journal of Sociology,* 45:137–45 (1949).

THE CHURCH–STATE ISSUE

Throughout Western history, religion has been such a prominent feature in the structure of social systems that it has often rivaled the state itself in power. In the medieval period, the church tended to dominate the entire life of the people, including the political.

Later the issue of whether state and church should be combined or separate became the paramount issue in many countries. One of the victories won by the French Revolution was the separation of church and state. This duality is still a factor to be reckoned with in many aspects of French public life.

Like England, the Scandinavian countries still maintain a state church. In Sweden, for example, one is born into the state church (Lutheran) just as automatically as he is born to citizenship. He pays a tax to the state church just as to the civil government. The minister is not merely a preacher; he is also a civil servant. He acts as sort of a city or county clerk, selling liquor licenses, marriage licenses, keeping many local records and performing many civil ceremonies.

When Princess Margaret was making her momentous decision in 1955 about whether or not to marry a divorced air force officer she had to reckon not only on the effect such a step would have on the prestige of the throne but also how it would reflect on the Church of England, which condemns marriage to a divorced person. In reaching her decision, she consulted the head of the state church as well as with strictly civil authority.

When the American nation was founded, the principle of the separation of church and state was adopted. Here, more than in the mother countries from which the settlers came, political issues and religious issues were kept apart. Officially they have remained so in most areas and at most times.

Yet, of course, the religious issue often becomes involved in political issues. No Catholic has yet been President of the United States. Catholics have been nominated, but the religious issue has always been a handicap to their chances of victory. There has never been a Jew in the presidential office, or as a presidential nominee. Members of both religions have held other high civil offices, but not this top one. Theoretically, of course they may do so. Perhaps a member of one of these religions will, some day, but he will have to have higher qualifications for office than a Protestant needs to achieve this position.

So even a democracy, which guarantees the right of all to worship as they please, has, no matter how covert, a subtle framework of religious structure—at least concerning major branches of religion.

The Mormon polygamy issue was an important one for a time in American political life. It led to violent persecution of the Mormons and, ultimately, to the founding of a new settlement in the mountains of Utah where, in isolation, they could develop and maintain their religious beliefs without persecution from the out-group. However, even they ultimately had to yield to the law of the land on the monogamy question in order to gain statehood. Today only the so-called fundamentalist branch still practices polygamy in certain very isolated communities.

But throughout Utah and in some parts of Arizona, Nevada, and Idaho a person's status, political success, and opportunity to gain public office is very much determined by his religious standing. Where the Mormon culture is dominant, religious values are basic in almost every aspect of the social structure of state and community.

THE CHURCH–SCHOOL ISSUE

Closely allied to the church–state issue, and in fact the most significant religious issue in the political area in the United States today, is the church–school issue. Its two principal forms in the social structure are: (1) Shall the school teach religion or compel reading in the Bible or other sacred literature? (2) Does the democratic state, to be consistent with the principle of free education for all, have the obligation of supporting the parochial school on the same basis as public education?

The first issue may be raised at any time. Rarely, if ever, may the school teach religion if anyone protests the attempt. The question of reading the Bible or saying a prayer at the opening of the school day has in the past been widely sanctioned and is still sanctioned in many communities. But when the teacher begins interpreting the Bible, trouble often results, for none of our three major religious groups agrees on an interpretation of the Bible. Even denominations within Protestantism differ in interpretation and emphasis on certain parts of the scriptures.

The usual compromise today, if the community wants religion taught, is to give children time off from school to attend classes in their respective churches to receive instruction by their own religious group.

Here we are not interested in appraising various proposals but merely in pointing out that the religious issue is a real part of the social structure in every community and school situation.

The second issue, of tax support of parochial schools, is one that has emerged in recent years in many states and in many communities. The Catholic group is the main promoter of the view that the parochial schools have the same right to free bus transportation for their pupils and to tax support for their school facilities as does the public school. The argument advanced is that the Catholic like the Protestant pays taxes to support education, and since he provides his own schools rather than patronizing public schools, he is entitled to the same use of tax funds for educational purposes. Here again the important thing to us is not the rightness or wrongness of the issue; rather, the situation is mentioned as illustrative of the significance of the religious issue in American society, which is free indeed from stratification on the basis of religion compared to most nations.

To cite a recent example of the church–school controversy, the state of Washington voted in 1954 that pupils of parochial schools were entitled to ride on public school buses. But the vote came only after a bitter political struggle.

Here is a sketch of an even more bitter fight in Ohio in which the religious issue split a community of some 5,000 people into bitter Protestant–Catholic conflict groups.

"A quiet suburb of Cincinnati offers today a preview of what may happen all over America in the not distant future. Outwardly North College Hill is a peaceful community of small homes. Inwardly it is trembling on the verge of an open outbreak of civil strife. Already violence has occurred. Its 5,000 people are savagely divided into two hostile camps. Lifelong neighbors refuse to speak to one another or to permit their children to associate. Property values are falling sharply, although there is no such slump in communities nearby, and real-estate dealers have more houses on their hands than they can sell. People even divide their purchases in accordance with the communal difference which has split the town in two, and several undeclared boycotts are in force. This splitting apart of an American town has resulted from what the National Education Association, after an investigation on the spot, calls 'probably the most serious school situation now current in the nation.' . . .

"The trouble began in 1940 with the incorporation of the St. Mary Margaret parochial school into the educational system of North College Hill. This was done after Roman Catholics secured a majority of one on the local board of education. By the vote of the board the community was obligated to pay salaries to the nuns who operated the parochial school and to pay rental for the schoolrooms in the building. The basement was reserved for the use of the parish, which continued to run highly profitable bingo games there. Within a short time after the original action, the rental and salaries were substantially raised. This overreaching brought a reversal of opinion among the voters of the community. The result was that the Catholics lost the election of 1942. The new school board terminated the arrangement with the parochial school. . . .

"In 1945, however, the normal Protestant majority . . . relaxed its vigilance and lost the election. . . . The main issue in the balloting was again the incorporation of the parochial school into the public system. . . .

"A long series of crises ensued which involved the budget of the school district, the administration of school buildings, relations between the superintendent and the teachers, and the ever present question of teachers' salaries. On the surface the dissension had the appearance of an ordinary row between a conscientious school executive and an ignorant and overbearing school board majority. Underneath everybody knew that it was a struggle between the American and the Roman Catholic conceptions of education. The real question was whether the public schools of the community could maintain their integrity once they had admitted the parochial school into the public system.

"The conflict reached its climax over the issue of who should nominate new teachers for the public schools. If the Catholic board members could get control of this function, which is placed by law in the hands of the superintendent, they could flood the schools with Catholic teachers and so put the entire system into the hands of the church. Realizing this, Superintendent Cook took his stand. He refused repeatedly to turn over to the board his confidential files of teacher applications and the correspondence relating to them. He was threatened with dismissal and with legal proceedings, but he stood his ground. In this action he was supported by almost all the teachers and a majority of the community.

"Thereupon he was charged with 'insubordination' and at the February 1947 meeting of the board the Catholic majority voted not to renew his contract when it . . . [expired] in July. . . .

"With the majority in the community circumvented at every turn, the school board met on April 15 in a highly inflammatory atmosphere. Both the Schools Improvement Association, which supported the Protestant minority on the board, and the Citizens School League, which supported the Catholic majority, had urged citizens to attend. They came, over 1,000 in number, crowding a school gymnasium. First an attempt was made by a member of the [board's] minority to present more petitions in support of the superintendent and to move reconsideration of his dismissal. This failed. Then the secretary of the board read, one by one, letters of resignation from 29 of 33 teachers in the system. . . ."[11]

School youngsters all over the room began to cry, as did adults, because of the loss of these teachers. The atmosphere then became tense and certain persons openly attacked the Catholic members of the board. The meeting broke up in a near riot. Some of those who had caused the disturbance were arrested. As various pressures built up, events followed swiftly. Here is the scene as one observer reported it.

"Before more than 1,000 citizens, the three-man Roman Catholic majority on the school board bowed to the will of the people and handed in their resignations. The Protestant minority, which had twice proposed this solution, also resigned. . . .

"One important factor in bringing about the resignation of the Roman Catholic majority was the action of the National Education Association in blacklisting the school system of North College Hill. This unprecedented action followed a similar move by the Ohio Education Association, which also broke precedent when it declared that the local system was 'an unprofessional place for teachers to work.' . . .

". . . The N.E.A. charged the majority with thwarting community efforts at peaceful solution of the issue, causing wholesale teacher resignations and a strike of 700 pupils. In the final count it was charged that the Catholic majority had conducted 'the affairs of the board in such a way that large sections of the community have been divided on religious grounds.'

[11] Harold E. Fey, "Preview of Divided America," *Christian Century*, May 28, 1947, pp. 682–84. Used by permission of the copyright owner.

"Another factor in producing these resignations was a taxpayer's suit filed in Common Pleas court. It . . . [sought] to enjoin the district from carrying out the contract entered into by the majority to pay Archbishop McNicholas of the Roman Catholic diocese of Cincinnati $6,000 a year rental for the use of the local parochial school, which the church continues to use."[12]

RELIGION AND COMMUNITY STRUCTURE

When a new college president comes to a college town, it is fairly common for certain members of his faculty to switch their church attendance to the president's church to gain whatever advantages this may offer. Like persons who put an antenna on the house before they can afford to acquire a television set so they may not lose prestige, these faculty folk hope to profit by being in a position to capture reflected status. No doubt the church of the President of the United States commands unusual loyalty from its congregation when a president and his family begin attendance.

In certain towns the religious division of the population may be a major factor in almost every aspect of the community structure, and this even where the difference is no more than that between two denominations which may differ on little else than how one is to be baptized.

Some years ago the Institute of Social and Religious Research described how the Baptist–Methodist line of stratification worked out in a southern town.

"Class segregation and social and religious divisions are often sharply defined by the railroad. Thus in one historic county-seat town all the Baptists live on one side of the track and all the Methodists on the other. In a village of the Far West, with a population of 2,000, division has gone further. The poorer people and all employees in the fruit-packing industries of the place live west of the track with their own school and their own churches, such as the Church of God, the Holiness and Pentecostal churches. The older denominations have virtually no members among these people and their buildings are all located on the east side of the track in the wealthier part of the town, which also has its own school. This east versus west division also affects local politics and the social life of the community."[13]

There is a saying in the South: "When you are barefooted, you go to the Baptist church; when you buy shoes, you join the Methodist

[12] Harold E. Fey, "They Stand for Free Schools," *Christian Century*, July 2, 1947, pp. 824–25. Used by permission of the copyright owner.

[13] Edmund DeS. Brunner, Gwendolyn S. Hughes, and Marjorie Patten, *American Agricultural Villages* (Garden City, N.Y.: Doubleday & Co., Inc., 1927), p. 71.

church; when you buy store clothes, you go to the Presbyterian church; and when you buy store liquor, then you are an Episcopalian."[14]

MARRIAGE AND THE RELIGIOUS STRUCTURE

In rigid caste systems, it is determined that one will marry within his class and religion. This is the only proper marriage. How far one may depart from his class in marriage is one of the best measures of the strength or weakness of the class structure.

In India's historic rigid caste structure, which in considerable part was based upon religion, one married only within his caste. Marriages were parent-arranged. Although caste is weakening, the few Indians (those with a college education or with no living parents) who assume responsibility in choosing a mate and advertise in the daily newspapers usually specify their caste. Here is an ad typical of those clipped from the matrimonial section of the classified ads of daily newspapers by the author while traveling in India.

> WANTED: a young man of liberal views and well settled in life for a highly accomplished and cultured girl of 23, B.A. degree (honors); only daughter of Gazetted Officer, belonging to Brahman community, holding high position. Write . . .

Although religion is not, strictly speaking, a part of the class structure in the American social system, religion is a vital factor to be reckoned with in mate choice. Therefore, particularly for the minority religious group—the Jews and Catholics—mate choice in many communities is limited. Moreover, the religious barrier, when ignored, as it often is in our open class society, is often the critical issue of the success or failure of the marriage.

There has been considerable study in this field. Research shows that divorce rates are very high in mixed religious marriages— Protestant–Catholic, Protestant–Jew, etc. (see chart). Conflict issues over how the children shall be raised generally emerge, even in the marriages that last.[15] Other issues of religious difference also often plague the marriage.

SUMMARY

Enough illustrations have been presented to show that religion is usually a vital factor in the social structure. It proves to be an issue in the relationships of people ranging all the way from the most impersonal—those of the state—to the most personal—those of marriage.

[14] Cited in James H. S. Bossard and Eleanor S. Boll, *One Marriage, Two Faiths* (New York: The Ronald Press Co., 1957), pp. 47–48.

[15] For a summary of research in this area of mixed religious marriages, see Paul H. Landis, *Making the Most of Marriage* (New York: Appleton-Century-Crofts, Inc., 1955), chap. 12.

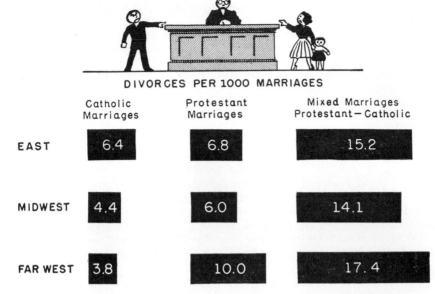

DIVORCES PER 1OOO MARRIAGES

	Catholic Marriages	Protestant Marriages	Mixed Marriages Protestant—Catholic
EAST	6.4	6.8	15.2
MIDWEST	4.4	6.0	14.1
FAR WEST	3.8	10.0	17.4

Divorce Rate in Families of Same and Mixed Religions

Religion is a divisive factor in marriage where the couple are of different religions. (Data from original studies: East, by Howard M. Bell, Youth Tell Their Story, *American Council on Education, 1938; Midwest, by Judson T. Landis, reported in* Building a Successful Marriage, *2d ed., Prentice-Hall, Inc., 1953; West, by Ashley Weeks, "Differential Divorce Rate by Occupation,"* Social Forces, *21:336 ff., March, 1943.)*

Although the ideal of many religions is unity, the drawing of people together into a brotherhood in which all men will be treated as they wish to be treated, in practice religion is very often a divisive factor in the social order. Loyalty and brotherhood are often for the in-group; hostility prevails toward the out-group.

Even so, religion is vital to status relationships and to social interaction. Some social systems, particularly in the Orient, are built entirely about the religious factor. Community conflict and marital conflict, as well as civil wars, have resulted from the stratifying effect of religion. Religion may be the key factor in the social structure, as in India, or only a minor factor, as in the United States.

DISCUSSION AND REVIEW QUESTIONS

1. Distinguish between religion as an institution and religion as a factor in the social structure.

2. Illustrate the working of religion as a factor in social structure in the history of England and of Europe, as well as in the Orient today.

3. Illustrate the factor of religious separateness in the experience of the Jew.

4. Discuss the factor of religious discrimination in various aspects of American life.

5. List some common stereotypes by which gentiles characterize Jews.

6. Review the church–state issue as evidence of religion in the social structure.

7. Show how religion at times emerges as a divisive factor in American community life.

8. Consider the religious factor in marriage, citing examples from different social systems.

9. Would you consider religion more or less important than political affiliation in dividing communities and nations?

SOURCEBOOK READINGS

O'BRIEN, ROBERT W., CLARENCE C. SCHRAG, and WALTER T. MARTIN. *Readings in General Sociology* (2d ed.). Boston: Houghton Mifflin Co., 1957.
1. LENSKI, GERHARD E., "Social Correlates of Religious Interest," pp. 379–85.

SCHULER, EDGAR A., DUANE L. GIBSON, MAUDE L. FIERO, and WILBUR B. BROOKOVER. *Outside Readings in Sociology.* New York: The Thomas Crowell Co., 1956.
2. BOISEN, ANTON T., "Religion and Hard Times: A Study of the Holy Rollers," pp. 430–39.

SELECTED READINGS

BARRON, MILTON L. *American Minorities: A Textbook of Readings in Intergroup Relations.* New York: Alfred A. Knopf, Inc., 1957.

BOSSARD, JAMES H. S., and ELEANOR STOKER BOLL. *One Marriage, Two Faiths.* New York: The Ronald Press Co., 1957.

BRADEN, CHARLES S. *These Also Believe.* New York: The Macmillan Co., 1949.

LANDIS, PAUL H. *Making the Most of Marriage.* New York: Appleton-Century-Crofts, Inc., 1955, chap. 12.

MICHENER, JAMES. *The Voice of Asia.* New York: Random House, Inc., 1951, pp. 145–49.

NIEBUHR, REINHOLD. *Christianity and Power Politics.* New York: Charles Scribner's Sons, 1948.

NICHOLS, JAMES H. "What Disturbs Protestants about Catholics," *Look,* May 18, 1954, pp. 42–49.

NOTTINGHAM, ELIZABETH K. *Religion and Society, Short Studies in Sociology.* Garden City, N.Y.: Doubleday & Co., Inc., 1954.

PFEFFER, LEO. *Church, State and Freedom.* Boston: Beacon Press, 1953.

POPE, LISTON. "Religion and the Class Structure," *The Annals of the American Academy of Political and Social Science,* 256:84–91 (1948).

TAWNEY, R. H. *Religion and the Rise of Capitalism.* Rev. ed.; New York: Harcourt, Brace & Co., Inc., 1947.

WACH, JOACHIM. *Sociology of Religion.* Chicago: University of Chicago Press, 1944.

WARD, H. F. "Organized Religion, the State, and the Economic Order," *Annals of the American Academy of Political and Social Science,* 256:72–83 (March 1948).

WEBER, MAX. *The Protestant Ethic and the Spirit of Capitalism.* Translated by Talcott Parsons. New York: Charles Scribner's Sons, 1930.

YINGER, J. MILTON. *Religion in the Struggle for Power.* Durham, N.C.: Duke University Press, 1946.

Chapter 22

The Process of Status Formation and Revision: Differentiation, Stratification, Integration

Social statuses, which are the brick and mortar of the social structure, are never finally and irrevocably fixed. Even in caste societies, where they may remain fixed throughout generations, they are in time modified.

HOW STATUSES ARE DETERMINED

Since all statuses are based on the concept of social worth, and the social value of a particular trait may change, it is inevitable that statuses will change. To work with one's hands may make one an untouchable, at the very bottom in status. But introduce a factory system, in which working with one's hands produces the abundance of goods that is necessary to a rising standard of living, and the worker may find his position raised in the social hierarchy. This is happening in localities of India where factories have been built.

To have black skin may mean, and often has meant, slave status. But a social order may change and new status values be assigned skin color. Those of black skin can just as easily become Congressmen as those of white skin if the status structure is so constituted that skin color is no longer a measure of social worth.

Differentiation. The sociologist has developed two concepts which deal with the process of status formation and revision: (1) *differen-*

401

tiation and (2) *stratification*. Differentiation is the tendency to base status on a certain kind of trait—physical, social, cultural. Skin color or sex are good examples of differentiation on the basis of physical traits. Differences in social etiquette and manners are examples of differentiation on the basis of social traits. "The 400" in large cities are persons who have arrived at such a level of social competence and distinction as to be recognized as a group apart. Again the Greek houses on many campuses attempt to create a status of separateness because of special competence in manners and etiquette, particularly dating. Differentiation on the basis of the culture is illustrated in such status arrangements as they typically affect the foreigner, the immigrant, the Okie, the Arkie—people who resettle in new cultural settings where they are conspicuous by their cultural differences. Throughout history the stranger has been given a unique status.

Stratification. Differentiation accords importance to unique traits. Stratification is the tendency to perpetuate these status differences through the generations by fixing them in the social structure permanently. Stratification in its fixed form makes statuses hereditary. In this case children of a particular status group will be saddled with the status of their parents.

Differentiation does not always lead to stratification. In fact, certain social forces operate both to fix the status and to eradicate it, to make all persons equal. Which force wins over the long run is dependent on many things of time and chance. Blacks may become equal, or a group rigidly fenced apart. Females may become near equal, or remain a separate status group far different in respect and privilege from the male—in fact, a strata of near slave status in a male world.

In summary, differentiation is society's sorting process by which people are arranged into groups or classes on the basis of roles and statuses. To the extent that differences tend to become fixed in the social system, the society becomes stratified into different social layers or strata. These social strata may be few or many, depending on the particular locality. They may be rather rigid or fairly flexible. Where it is difficult to move from one stratum to another, especially to climb upward, the social system becomes rigid and inflexible. When these lines become extremely distinct, so that it is almost impossible to cross them from generation to generation and social class is passed on by tradition from parents to children, the system of stratification has become so rigid that a *caste system* results.

Social *differentiation* is the process by which status differences come to be recognized; social *stratification* is the process by which they become fixed. This statement is enough to define the two concepts dealt with in this chapter. A further analysis of how they operate follows.

THE TENDENCY TOWARD FIXED STATUSES[1]

America boasts of an open class system in which no statuses are ever to be finally fixed—differentiation, yes, but never irrevocable statuses to be passed from parent to child.

Granted, such a system makes much more concession to special gifts than does a caste system, and therefore has a much greater proportion of achieved statuses; yet as anthropologist Ralph Linton points out, most societies make "only grudging admission" that certain statuses do "require special gifts."[2] Even our society, with its boasted privilege, rigidly cuts down competition for key positions. As he points out, no woman, Negro, or Indian could reach the United States presidency, and a Jew or Catholic would be greatly handicapped. Linton believes that it is only in periods of great social upheaval that individuation gains the upper hand sufficiently for great numbers of positions to be left open for achieved statuses; for example, on the American frontier, the ascribed statuses of European society were found to be inadequate.[3]

He states that established social orders operate on the principle that "individual talent is too sporadic and too unpredictable to be allowed any important part in the organization of society." Social orders tend to be built on the assumption that any average individual can be trained for any given role. Training begins at birth, and society is assured that the position will be filled. If it has many special statuses to be filled and had to wait for people of special gifts, it would risk not having the positions filled at all.

In periods of rapid change and maladjustment, persons with special gifts come to the fore and their gifts are utilized. The area of achieved statuses is temporarily expanded. As new adaptations are realized, the value of initiative decreases and ascribed status roles are again sufficient. Rigidity of social structure again becomes the order of life.

Stratification is particularly effective as a device for maintaining social order because it works largely in terms of attitudes and prerogatives, in terms of ascribed statuses and roles, and because viola-

[1] Parts of this section are an adaptation of the author's *Social Control* (rev. ed.; Chicago: J. B. Lippincott Co., 1956). For a fuller treatment, see that volume.
[2] Ralph Linton, *The Study of Man* (New York: Appleton-Century-Crofts, Inc., 1936), p. 129.
[3] *Ibid.*

tion of ascribed statuses and roles are in the realm of taboo, bringing to bear the strongest emotional forces of the social system against the offender. Stratification is effective, too, because from the beginning a man's aspirations are limited to the possibilities of his particular sector of the social system.

Open class systems lack this effectiveness in regulation, since into every child in the open class system there is whispered the hope of climbing. This hope, of course, makes for discontent at all social levels, for a man's aspirations may far exceed his grasp and, in fact, are likely to. Yet such a system releases much dynamic force in that aspirations can be so high that everyone can struggle upward through a lifetime and feel that there is still room to go. In caste systems, complacency is the general rule. Those at the top are safe from upstarts at the bottom; those at the bottom are well trained in the philosophy that life has no other meaning for them than that which the class assigns to them.

In open class systems, the channels for vertical social mobility are found in every social institution—economic, political, religious, and above all educational. The only limits to human aspirations are those of a man's own energy. Risks are as great as is the promise of reward. Therefore, failure is much more possible and frustration is much stronger in an open class system, and society takes greater risk of rebellion, revolt, and perhaps even of revolution, unless the channels for protest are left free. (The problem of vertical mobility will be dealt with in the next chapter.)

The following excerpts show the limitations at work in a more highly stratified society.

Stratification in Japan. ". . . Every greeting, every contact must indicate the kind and degree of social distance between men. Every time a man says to another 'Eat' or 'Sit down' he uses different words if he is addressing someone familiarly or is speaking to an inferior or to a superior. There is a different 'you' that must be used in each case and the verbs have different stems. The Japanese have, in other words, what is called 'respect language,' as many other peoples do in the Pacific, and they accompany it with proper bows and kneelings. All such behavior is governed by meticulous rules and conventions; it is not merely necessary to know to whom one bows but it is necessary to know how much one bows. A bow that is right and proper to one host would be resented as an insult by another who stood in a slightly different relationship to the bower. And bows range all the way from kneeling with forehead lowered to the hands placed flat upon the floor, to the mere inclination of head and shoulders. One must learn, and learn early, how to suit the obeisance to each particular case.

"It is not merely class differences which must be constantly recognized by appropriate behavior, though these are important. Sex and age, family ties and previous dealings between two persons, all enter into the necessary calculations. Even between the same two persons different degrees of respect will be called for on different occasions; a civilian may be on familiar terms with another and not bow to him at all, but when he wears a military uniform his friend in civilian clothes bows to him. Observance of hierarchy is an art which requires the balancing of innumerable factors, some of which in any particular case may cancel each other out and some of which may be additive. . . .

"Proper station means not only differences of generation but differences of age. When the Japanese want to express utter confusion, they say that something is 'neither elder brother nor young brother.' It is like our saying that something is neither fish nor fowl, for to the Japanese a man should keep his character as elder brother as drastically as a fish should stay in water. The eldest son is the heir. Travelers speak of 'that air of responsibility which the eldest son so early acquires in Japan.' The eldest son shares to a high degree in the prerogatives of the father. In the old days his younger brother would have been inevitably dependent upon him in time; nowadays, especially in towns and villages, it is he who will stay at home in the old rut while his younger brothers will perhaps press forward and get more education and a better income. But old habits of hierarchy are strong.

"Even in political commentary today the traditional prerogatives of elder brothers are vividly stated in discussions of Greater East Asia policy. In the spring of 1942 a Lieutenant Colonel, speaking for the War Office, said on the subject of the Co-prosperity Sphere: 'Japan is their elder brother and they are Japan's younger brothers. This fact must be brought home to the inhabitants of the occupied territories. Too much consideration shown for the inhabitants might engender in their minds the tendency to presume on Japan's kindness with pernicious effects on Japanese rule.' The elder brother, in other words, decides what is good for his younger brother and should not show 'too much consideration' in enforcing it. . . ."

Sex. "Whatever one's age, one's position in the hierarchy depends on whether one is male or female. The Japanese woman walks behind her husband and has a lower status. Even women who on occasions when they wear American clothes walk alongside and precede him through a door again fall to the rear when they have donned their kimonos. The Japanese daughter of the family must get along as best she can while the presents, the attentions, and the money for education go to her brothers. Even when higher schools were established for young women the prescribed courses were heavily loaded with instruction in etiquette and bodily movement. Serious intellectual training was not on a par with boys', and one principal of such a school, advocating for his upper middle class students some instruction in European languages, based his recommendation on the desirability of their being able to put their husband's books back in the bookcase right side up after they had dusted them.

"Nevertheless, the Japanese women have great freedom as compared to most Asiatic countries and this is not just a phase of Westernization. There never was female foot-binding as in the Chinese upper classes, and Indian women today exclaim over Japanese women going in and out of shops, up and down the streets and never secreting themselves. Japanese wives do the family shopping and carry the family purse. If money fails, it is they who must select something from the household and carry it to the pawnshop. A woman runs her servants, has great say in her children's marriages, and when she is a mother-in-law commonly runs her household realm with as firm a hand as if she never had been, for half her life, a nodding violet."[4]

Strata Formation in Small Groups. It is not unusual to find stratification operative in various units of society as well. Consider the following account.

"While men in combat outfits kid each other around, they have a sort of family complex about it. No outsiders may join. Anybody who does a dangerous job in this war has his own particular kind of kidding among his own friends, and sometimes it doesn't even sound like kidding. Bomber crews and paratroopers and infantry squads are about the same in that respect. If a stranger comes up to a group of them when they are bulling, they ignore him. If he takes it upon himself to laugh at something funny they have said, they freeze their expressions, turn slowly around and stare at him until his stature has shrunk to about four inches and he slinks away, and then they go back to their kidding again.

"It's like a group of prosperous business men telling a risque joke and then glaring at the waiter who joins in the guffaws. Combat people are an exclusive set, and if they want it to be that way, it is

---

[4] Ruth Benedict, *The Chrysanthemum and the Sword* (Boston: Houghton Mifflin Co., 1946). These quotations are excerpts from chapter 3, entitled "Taking One's Proper Station."

their privilege. They certainly earn it. New men in outfits have to work their way in slowly, but they are eventually accepted. Sometimes they have to change some of their ways of living. An introvert or a recluse is not going to last long in combat without friends, so he learns to come out of his shell. Once he has 'arrived' he is pretty proud of his clique, and he in turn is chilly toward outsiders.

"That's why, during some of the worst periods in Italy, many guys who had a chance to hang around a town for a few days after being discharged from a hospital where they had recovered from wounds, with nobody the wiser, didn't take advantage of it. They weren't eager to get back up and get in the war, by any means, and many of them did hang around a few days. But those who did hang around didn't feel exactly right about it, and those who went right back did it for a very simple reason—not because they felt their presence was going to make a lot of difference in the big scheme of the war, and not to uphold the traditions of the umpteenth regiment. A lot of guys don't know the name of their regimental commander. They went back because they knew their companies were very shorthanded, and they were sure that if somebody else in their own squad or section were in their own shoes, and the situation were reversed, those friends would come back to make the load lighter on them."[5]

Even on the college campus, informal cliques testify to the presence of strata formation. Here is the picture as drawn by one sociologist.

"Informal clique groups, usually of 3–7 members, structure every large social unit, such as a dormitory, in undergraduate society. In a positive sense the informal, intimate friend-group provides the chief area for individual expression for each member; it satisfies the wishes for response, recognition, security and new experience; it is the closest equivalent to the family in the new strange world away from home. For Freshmen, membership in such a group serves to cushion the traumatic experience of the first prolonged separation from parents. Later on, group membership protects those who 'belong' from the shocks and rebuffs of the impersonal, crowd-like aspects of the larger college community. No one who 'has' such a group need ever fear being a 'wallflower,' a social reject. As one college girl has put it:

Every member is sure of recognition by the group, which will, in turn be recognized by outsiders. We are assured of invitations to visit each others' houses and to dinner parties before dances. We can count on being invited to all the teas, bridge parties, theatre parties, etc., that go on . . . There is no sense of inferiority within the group. There, each individual's talents are recog-

5 Bill Mauldin, *Up Front* (New York: Henry Holt & Co., Inc., 1945), p. 58.

nized; each one is loved for her own sake; genuine friendship is the basis for our solidarity, friendship which may grow over three or four years . . .

"On the negative side, the nucleation of every dormitory society into a multiplicity of such closely-knit cliques inevitably leaves a certain number "outside," more intensely outside, indeed, than they would be in an undifferentiated mass of mutual strangers. At common dormitory activities such as dances, one may check this hypothesis by tabulating the table reservations and comparing the composition of dinner-dance groups with the dormitory clique structure: inevitably the larger parties are dominated or even monopolized by the principal cliques; and while the more sociable rejects band together into unstable associations 'for appearance's sake,' the least sociable ones retreat to the solitude of their rooms or the library, and to comforting rationalizations on the superiority of the studious life."[6]

No society can avoid distinctions, but undergraduate students try to hide their success from their peers. Here are some reasons for this behavior, which goes counter to the status-seeking tendency.

". . . There is pressure for 'success,' but too much success brings with it certain penalties, notably increased social distance between the winner and the losers. Hence the paradox that the most unpopular girl may be the one who has just won a popularity contest. What is gained comes not merely as a reward for the winner but as a rebuff for those who fail to win. Furthermore, the normal distribution curve automatically places those who 'distinguish themselves,' whether by success or by failure, in a minority group. Thus many individual students actually refrain from doing as well as their aptitudes would allow, for the simple reason that they don't wish to put a barrier between themselves and their less able friends. If such an individual does achieve some distinction, then he tends to excuse himself by claiming that the exam was easy, or that he did well by some stroke of luck—never as a result of ability or of hard work. Far from priding himself on having studied for the test, he will deprecatingly remark, 'Why I never even cracked a book!'

"Concealment of honorific symbols occurs with respect to 'social' distinction. Members of exclusive social clubs are often under oath never to tell an outsider that they are club members. If there are insignia of membership, such as watch charms or neck-ties, it is considered bad taste to wear them—although 'social' climbers are expected to display imitations of the real thing! Like football sweaters worn with the letter turned in and Phi Beta Kappa keys kept in

---

[6] Edward Y. Hartshorne, "Undergraduate Society and the College Culture," *American Sociological Review*, 8:325–26 (June 1943).

bureau drawers, even the symbols of 'social' achievement are concealed in order to prevent disruption of other friendship bonds."[7]

THE VEBLEN THEORY OF STRATIFICATION[8]

The Emergence of Social Strata. It was Veblen's belief that at the beginning of time, before the days of known history, primitive men lived together in indolence and good will. Life was essentially noncompetitive. Even when a warrior took a trophy from the fight, it was considered to the glory of the tribe, not of the individual. But as handicraft and agriculture developed, human life took on more drudgery. The captive of war could be put to practical use cultivating food. It was when property acquired productive value and the individual wanted to keep it for himself that distinctions began to grow about property rights.

The institution of marriage began to be established with the male as family head. Possession of a number of wives, obtained through the warrior's prowess, came to be a mark of esteem and inspired envy among one's fellows. Useful work came to be assigned to women. The man soon developed the idea that work was inherently shameful and that no man of prowess and strength would stoop to it. Conspicuous leisure thus began to be a mark of the idler's superiority over those who worked. Invidious distinction also began in the recognized difference between the leisure class and those who were forced to work for a living. It was in this historical setting that the idea of status was born. Social emulation entered the world, and with it a desire to excel one another in social standing.

The leisure class needed something to do, so hunting and warfare became their primary activities. As society developed, government, the priesthood, and sports were added to the list of things one might do without being accused of work. These became honorable activities, distinguished from the work activities of women and slaves. Men of the leisure class made virtues of ferocity, selfishness, trickery, shrewdness, clannishness, and ruthlessness, which eventually helped them to obtain sufficient goods so they could indulge in conspicuous consumption. This involved the use of economic goods in a way that administered not to the physical comforts and fullness of life of the individual or the community, but rather to the gratification of pleasure and to inspiring envy.

[7] *Ibid.*, p. 324.

[8] See Thorstein Veblen, *The Theory of the Leisure Class* (New York: The Viking Press, Inc., 1899). For an excellent recent summary of his views, see "Veblen," *Fortune,* Dec., 1947, pp. 133 ff.

Eventually the ideas and objectives of those in the leisure class became the ideals of what was good, beautiful, and desirable for human beings—not only for the rich themselves, but for all society. The leisure class eventually extended leisure to their women, not for the sake of relieving them of work but for the purpose of enhancing the prestige of the man himself. Thus the tortuous bustle, corset, high heels, and in China the bound feet of women came to bear testimony to man's struggle for conspicuous display. Fashions and standards of beauty of the leisure class came to be the standards of all social classes. "Keeping up with the Joneses" by numerous subtle devices became the standard process of civilized society. These developed man's anxiety about income and the security which income brings. Men really do not fear poverty nearly so much as they fear to lower the level of living to which they are accustomed and thus lose the regard and deference of their fellow men.

The historian may question some of Veblen's facts, but no one can read his analysis of the social processes operating toward stratification without admitting that he shows a great deal of insight into the motives of men.

Wealth and Leisure as Symbols of Social Power. Veblen believed that wealth is a major factor in prestige and considered that people were interested in wealth primarily as a device for displaying their superior social status. Master of satire, he coined a number of highly significant phrases in describing the wealthy class. He called it the "leisure class." By this he did not mean that they were idle, but rather that they participated in activities that did not directly produce wealth. They did not work as the laboring man works, in fact; would not so soil their fingers or their dignity. "Invidious distinctions" developed between the "leisure class" and those who had to work for a living.

In showing how the wealthy try to impress their importance on the public by "conspicuous consumption," Veblen was regarding wealth as social power. By "conspicuous consumption" he meant the lavish use of money for attractive homes, ornamental and highly costly furniture, servants, yachts, jewels, fine horses, pedigreed dogs, and all the other expensive trappings that go with what is considered "good living." The motive behind it all, he believed, is to inspire envy.

He used the term "conspicuous leisure" to describe people's behavior in recreational activities where they show themselves off in fine dress and fine company. The opera, the race track, and other such places have always been favorite spots for conspicuous leisure of the wealthy in this country. Even their charitable activities, "conspicuous giving," are, he felt, in part motivated by a desire to show their importance in the social system. He invented the phrase "conspicuous waste" to describe aspects of the behavior of the railroad kings, merchant princes, banking barons, and their wives as they vied for a place in the social sun by the lavish use of money in wasteful entertainments and gaudy spendthriftness. He referred to them as the "kept classes."

In Veblen's discussion of the "leisure class" he was not thinking of this class alone. He realized that other social classes also try to emulate the so-called leisure class. To the extent that they have funds, they imitate the class above and lord it over the class below them by the use of such money as they have to improve dress and living conditions and to participate in enviable recreational activities.

SOCIAL DISTANCE

Emory S. Bogardus, University of Southern California sociologist, developed an effective scale for measuring the denial of privilege in our social system. His scale is designed to measure social distance, which in reality is a measure of the degree of status differences between racial and ethnic groups. It asks the respondent to check relationships in which he would or would not accept a member of another group.

The following are the items on the Bogardus scale which measure acceptance: (1) to close kinship by marriage; (2) to club as personal chums; (3) to my street as neighbors; (4) to employment in my occupation; (5) to citizenship in my country; (6) as visitors only to my country; (7) would exclude from my country. When the scale was given to 1,725 Americans, 93.7 per cent checked the English favorably on item 1; only 1.4 per cent checked the Negro.[9]

It should not be deduced from the above examples that distinction which carries a penalty is applicable only to race or nationality groups. As has been implied earlier, throughout much of human history discrimination of numerous sorts has been the lot of women. Men have had all the advantages as far as status is concerned. So also the wealthy, who have been successful in accumulating worldly goods, have had advantages which the poor have never dared to claim. Those with political connections have had advantages those without political connections could not claim and have had immunities which those without "pull" have never had.

So one might go on illustrating how marks of distinction carry over into numerous aspects of social relationships.

[9] Emory S. Bogardus, *Immigration and Race Attitudes* (Boston: D. C. Heath & Co., 1928), p. 25. Current revisions of this scale are still in use.

DIFFERENTIATION AND SOCIAL VALUATION

In a stratified society, and all are stratified to some extent, it is assumed that those with like traits are equal, whereas those who do not have like traits fall in the class of unequals. Those above are regarded as having superior qualities to those of the class below.

For example, in the United States it is assumed that the working class is inferior to the business class. This is a traditional notion which has probably grown out of certain logical factors, such as the fact that the business and the managerial classes possess greater initiative, greater wealth, and have power to guide the activities of others. The working class is, by and large, made up of those who are willing to let someone else make most of their decisions for them. They are, as a consequence, paid a wage for doing a task which requires little use of foresight, ambition, and intellectual discipline, and which requires practically no management of the time and energies of others. In fact, on most jobs, little management by the worker of his own time is required, since he is usually under a supervisor or boss who makes all the decisions and who decides how a man's time on a job will be used.

Society, in recognizing a difference between the business and managerial classes and the laboring classes, thus expresses the difference in the values it places on the types of activities which the two groups carry on in the social system. It rates the business and the executive type of activity in the economic structure as being of greater social value than the activities of the working class.

So also, in the differentiating of the professional classes from other classes, it is assumed that the professional group, as we have seen in an earlier chapter, by virtue of special training and a high level of learning, is to be entrusted with a high level of social responsibility. The professional man must render judgments in fields which are beyond the grasp of understanding of the masses. Trust must be placed in the judgments of the professional class because of the exclusive knowledge which they possess.

It must be recognized that status valuations are not always just and equitable. In a free open-class system they tend to be so more than in caste systems, but no society ever achieves complete freedom for moving from one class to another. Lines of stratification tend to form, keeping some groups in an inferior place.

INTEGRATION

When the process of stratification is halted, as it is when men face crises like those of the American frontier or even those catastrophe imposes on local communities, men grow closer together in cooperative effort. Remove the sense of differential status even temporarily and men quickly become integrated. Novelist John Steinbeck, in his description of the drought migration westward during the great depression, has told how a new social world was created each evening as strangers met at camping places which became a community for the overnight stay only, and then at dawn broke up like a circus camp and went their way.[10] There grew up in this world conventions and rules, etiquette and manners, a system of social control for the protection of property and virtue and for dealing with those who broke the rules. "Good people" and "bad people" came to be known very quickly in this temporary social world.

Confusion in the Social Structure as Caste Strata Disintegrate.[11] Few influences are more disruptive to a social order than the disintegration of long-established strata. To a certain extent, this is a world-wide phenomenon in our time, as industrialization makes inroads into the age-old class systems of distant places of the world, with their manners and customs, prerogatives and disabilities. Many social barriers cannot survive industrially organized society. As they are modified, new definitions of social relationships have to be developed.

Take the weakening of the Southern caste system in the United States with the ruling of the Supreme Court against segregation in public schools, in the spring of 1954. This required thousands of communities to redefine race relations in terms of equality rather than of fixed statuses and caste taboos which had persisted from the time of slavery. The real adjustment being made is not merely that of letting people of different skin color use the same schools, parks, swimming pools, street cars, railroad depots, restaurants, and hotels. The real difficulty is that of redefining attitudes rooted in a world of hereditary stratification.

With the removal of barriers of stratification, an entirely new system of social principles must be evolved if the new social equalities are to be carried over into other aspects of racial relationships. In fact, an entirely new problem of social control faces the South with reference to the race problem. In the past there has been a world of meaning in the phrase "in their place," a phrase characteristic of all caste systems.

[10] A reading from Steinbeck appears in E. A. Schuler, *et al.*, *Outside Readings in Sociology* (New York: The Thomas Crowell Co., 1956), pp. 170–74.

[11] This section is an adaptation of the author's *Social Control* (rev. ed.; Chicago: J. B. Lippincott Co., 1956). For a fuller treatment, see that volume.

It is not only in such extreme instances of stratification that the loosening of class bonds and confusion in class status is observed. C. Wright Mills in that stimulating and highly imaginative book, *White Collar*, has described vividly what he conceives to be the "status panic" of the white-collar group, "the new middle class."[12] This panic arises, he feels, from the fact that they do not know where they stand in the prestige scheme. He depicts the attempt of the white-collar workers to acquire prestige from the job, from the customer, from the merchandise. (To work at Macy's carries higher status than to work in some unknown shop; to wait on Park Avenue residents carries higher status than to work with a less distinguished clientele and with lower priced merchandise.) Their main label of distinction is their dress, from which "white collar" derives its name —not too stable a claim to prestige.

Since this group is employed by others, it has no claim to class consciousness, political power, or financial accomplishment. It must depend on "agility rather than ability" for getting along in the context of "associates, superiors, and rules."[13]

Thus it has always been with mankind: there are divisive tendencies which tend to fence men off from each other into tight separate groups, but in crises they are drawn together and, for a time at least, the lines of difference vanish and a more free and equal social order emerges.

SUMMARY

The sociologist views human relations within the social structure as a thing of flux. Certain rigid patterns tend to persist through the centuries, but many of the more superficial aspects of social relations are constantly subject to revision. Certain processes are constantly in operation. *Differentiation* is the process by which social meaning is given to differences which exist, or which appear, in the social order. *Stratification* is the process by which these differences become fixed, and therefore traditional, to be passed on from generation to generation. *Integration* is the process by which differences are obliterated and groups once segregated, or at least differentiated substantially, lose their separateness by being absorbed into the larger group, and thereby disappear as unique social entities.

DISCUSSION AND REVIEW QUESTIONS

1. Distinguish differentiation from stratification.
2. How does differentiation affect social roles of the individual?

[12] C. Wright Mills, *White Collar: The American Middle Class* (New York: Oxford University Press, 1951).
[13] For a more extensive discussion of this group, refer back to Chapter 20.

3. Why do societies tend to move toward fixed social statuses?

4. What factors in the United States have tended to keep classes from becoming fixed and rigid?

5. Compare the United States and Japan in terms of personal statuses.

6. Illustrate marks of status as they appear on the college campus.

7. Is the tendency of your campus to hide or expose marks of high status?

8. Discuss Veblen's theory of the relationship of leisure to prestige.

9. Define "social distance" and show how it has been measured.

10. Show how the process of social valuation enters into differentiation.

11. Discuss integration and illustrate its working.

12. What are some of the problems which arise as old lines of stratification disintegrate?

SOURCEBOOK READINGS

FREEDMAN, RONALD, AMOS H. HAWLEY, WERNER S. LANDECKER, GERHARD E. LENSKI, and HORACE M. MINER. *Principles of Sociology* (rev. ed.) New York: Henry Holt & Co., Inc., 1956.

1. ERICSON, MARTHA C., "Child-Rearing and Social Status," pp. 244–46.

KOENIG, SAMUEL, REX D. HOPPER, and FELIKS GROSS. *Sociology: A Book of Readings.* Englewood Cliffs, N.J.: Prentice-Hall, Inc., 1952.

2. LAPIERRE, RICHARD, "The Nature of Social Interaction," pp. 499–501.

3. BERNARD, JESSIE, "Where Is the Modern Sociology of Conflict?" pp. 501–5.

4. CHASE, STUART, "Paths to Labor Peace," pp. 505–10.

LEE, ELIZABETH BRYANT, and ALFRED McCLUNG LEE. *Social Problems in America* (rev. ed.). New York: Henry Holt & Co., Inc., 1955.

5. FRENCH, JOHN R. P., JR., ARTHUR KORNHAUSER and ALFRED MARROW, "Conflict and Cooperation in Industry," pp. 193–95.

O'BRIEN, ROBERT W., CLARENCE C. SCHRAG, and WALTER T. MARTIN. *Readings in General Sociology* (2d ed.). Boston: Houghton Mifflin Co., 1957.

6. DAVIS, ALLISON, and ROBERT J. HAVIGHURST, "Social Class and Color Differences in Child Rearing," pp. 192–200.

WILSON, LOGAN, and WILLIAM L. KOLB. *Sociological Analysis.* New York: Harcourt, Brace & Co., Inc., 1949.

7. DAVIS, KINGSLEY, and WILBERT E. MOORE, "Some Principles of Stratification," pp. 434–43.

8. USEEM, JOHN, PIERRE TANGENT, and RUTH HILL USEEM, "Stratification in a Prairie Town," pp. 454–64.

9. WILSON, LOGAN, "Prestige and Competition," pp. 716–26.

10. CHAPMAN, DWIGHT W., "Industrial Conflict in Detroit," pp. 727–40.

11. WILLIAMS, ROBIN M., JR., "Propositions on Intergroup Hostility and Conflict," pp. 740–60.

SELECTED READINGS

BALES, R. H. *Interaction Process Analysis.* Reading, Mass.: Addison-Wesley Publishing Co., Inc., 1950.

BENDIX, REINHARD. *Work and Authority in Industry: Ideologies of Management in the Course of Industrialization.* New York: John Wiley & Sons, Inc., 1956.

CHINOY, E. *Automobile Workers and the American Dream.* Garden City, N.Y.: Doubleday, & Co., Inc., 1955.

CLARKE, ALFRED C. "The Use of Leisure and Its Relation to Levels of Occupational Prestige," *American Sociological Review,* 21:301–7 (June 1956).

GERTH, HANS, and C. WRIGHT MILLS. *Character and the Social Structure.* New York: Harcourt, Brace & Co., Inc., 1953.

HAWLEY, AMOS H. *Human Ecology.* New York: The Ronald Press Co., 1950.

HOLLINGSHEAD, A. B. *Elmtown's Youth.* New York: John Wiley & Sons., Inc., 1949.

LEVY, MARION J., JR. *The Structure of Society.* Princeton: Princeton University Press, 1952.

MARTIN, W. T. "The Structuring of Social Relationships Engendered by Suburban Residence," *American Sociological Review,* 21:446–53 (1956).

MERTON, ROBERT K. "Bureaucratic Structure and Personality," *Social Forces,* 18:560–68 (1940).

MILLS, C. WRIGHT. *The New Men of Power.* New York: Harcourt, Brace & Co., Inc., 1948.

MILLS, THEODORE. "Power Relation in Three-Person Groups," *American Sociological Review,* 18:351–57 (Aug. 1953).

SOROKIN, P. A. *Social Mobility.* New York: Harper & Brothers, 1927.

STONE, ROBERT C. "Factory Organization and Vertical Mobility," *American Sociological Review,* 18:28–35 (1953).

WARNER, W. LLOYD. *American Life: Dream and Reality.* Chicago: University of Chicago Press, 1953.

WARNER, W. LLOYD, et al. *Democracy in Jonesville.* New York: Harper & Brothers, 1949.

WARNER, W. LLOYD, and J. C. ABEGGLEN. *Occupational Mobility in American Business and Industry, 1928–1952.* Minneapolis: University of Minnesota Press, 1955.

WARNER, W. LLOYD, and P. S. LUNT. *The Social Life of a Modern Community.* New Haven: Yale University Press, 1941.

WARNER, W. LLOYD, R. J. HAVIGHURST, and M. B. LOEW. *Who Shall Be Educated?* New York: Harper & Brothers, 1944.

WHYTE, WILLIAM FOOTE. *Street Corner Society.* Chicago: University of Chicago Press, 1943.

Chapter 23

Vertical Mobility

The term "vertical mobility" refers to the status changes that occur constantly within a society. The basic difference between class and caste societies lies in this point: the first permits, and may even encourage, movement upward from one social layer to another; the second tries to make class hereditary by hindering movement upward and by using downward movement as a severe penalty for failing to maintain the ceremony required of those of high status.

THE ENTRENCHMENT OF PRIVILEGED CLASSES

Perhaps the process of vertical mobility may best be understood by a brief review of the resistance certain social structures make to it.

"The people who are responsible for the fixing of social relations and institutions, and thus for the blocking of normal social change, are often as helpless as are the people who revolt, when the question of loosening up on the social system is raised. All of their interests and obligations are tied up with the social system as it stands. To promote or to resist change often would be equally destructive to them. The question thus frequently comes to be, 'Shall we perish with the system or shall we be swept away by the flood that is loosed by breaking down the system?' In the French Revolution, for example, that was exactly the problem. A generation before the final debacle came it was clearly understood by the king and the nobles that they were destined to lose, whatever might be the final solution—reform or revolution. Since it is at least as difficult for a class as for an individual to commit suicide of its own free will, they chose revolution in preference to a reform program which would also have destroyed them, and that is the meaning of Louis XV's famous aphorism, 'After me, the deluge.' Even in England, where not infrequently, perhaps usually, reform has been permitted to take the place of revolution, the ruling classes have not willingly surrendered their powers and privileges. Perhaps it is psychically impossible that they should be able to do so. It was a member of the English nobility, Lord Lansdowne, who at the end of the great war of 1914–1918 advised his government to end the war short of complete destruction of German political organization, lest a proletarian revolution should follow and spread to other countries and sweep away all the privileges of the upper classes."[1]

It is a fact of social structures throughout history that those with entrenched status at the top resist any encroachment on their prestige and power. Many a revolution has been fought to dispossess of power and honor those at the top because they forgot their responsibilities to the masses whom they were supposed to serve and lead into a better life. One of the most bloody of these was the French Revolution, which had as its battle cry "Liberty, Equality, Fraternity"—words which are the antithesis of class.

The United States established a different type of social structure— one so fluid that high status would never become entrenched, never hereditary, that vertical mobility would forestall any need for revolution of violence; one in which the ballot would keep alive the spirit of change and provide outlet for rebellion against privilege.

The Depression days of the thirties saw the most violent ferment in the United States since the Civil War, but the revolution nonetheless took the form of a political reform movement, rather than of violent revolution. The New Deal was ushered in. It created welfare measures that made the wealthy and powerful hate Roosevelt and all he stood for. They saw their prestige and power threatened by social welfare measures which dipped fairly deeply into profits and incomes for taxes to carry the Social Security load.

What these somewhat entrenched groups failed to realize then was that had it not been for such measures, which at the time seemed so radical, their heads would have been on the chopping blocks and their wealth dissipated in revolution. It has always been so when those at the top could not be forced to yield by milder pressures.

Social mobility is a fact of history. It may come suddenly and cataclysmically, with the bottom layer replacing the top as an act of desperation, or it may be the gradual systematic process of a democratic social order which makes rebellion respectable and which preaches the doctrine of social climbing as a way of life.

[1] L. L. Bernard, *Social Control in Its Sociological Aspects* (New York: The Macmillan Co., 1939), pp. 340–41.

H. G. Wells some years ago observed the freedom of social climbing in America and expressed astonishment that a place could exist where European immigrants from downtrodden and even suppressed classes could so soon catch the spirit of equality, throw off their sense of inferiority and low-class status, and acquire the feeling that they were as good as anyone else.[2]

If this is a true characteristic of the social structure of the United States, as the citizen also claims it to be, why and how does the machinery operate? And is it still in operation, or is the time approaching, as American society ages, when vertical mobility will slow down, when those at the bottom will become fixed in their lowly status because they have given up hope of climbing?

These are important sociological issues.

THE RELATIONSHIP OF VERTICAL AND HORIZONTAL MOBILITY

Horizontal mobility and vertical mobility have been twin types of social process in the social order of the United States. The nation has prided itself not only on seeing an individual climb the full distance from log cabin to White House, from poverty to the leadership of a great corporation, from a family of unknown and unimportant people to a position of national or international fame—all by virtue of his personal achievements—but also on letting a man move where he might in quest of better opportunity.

The American nation, settled first on the east coast, always has had a frontier to the westward. This frontier called for horizontal movement. "Go West, young man, go West," was a tradition long before Horace Greeley uttered those famous words. West was more than a place where a man might go to escape his past and build his future; the West was presumed to be a world of new opportunities where there were no handicaps of social stratification to keep a man from being whatever he chose to be; a place where he could freely exercise his energy and effort. The West was identified, in the minds of the American public, not only as a place to move to, but also a place to climb in. Again and again men went West and acquired free lands, found gold or other precious metals, exploited timber or some other new resource, or engaged in some new business enterprise, and went back to show the older settled part of the nation that in the West a man could succeed and build for himself a new reputation far exceeding that of his parents.

It is partly because territorial movement and vertical mobility are

[2] H. G. Wells, *Social Forces in England and America* (New York: Harper & Brothers, 1914), pp. 324–40. See also Harry Elmer Barnes, *Society in Transition* (Englewood Cliffs, N.J.: Prentice-Hall, Inc., 1939), pp. 559 ff.

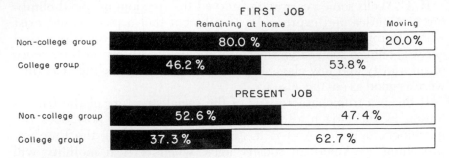

Relation of Education to Horizontal Mobility

Education increases not only vertical mobility but also horizontal mobility. The upper panels of the chart show the proportion of youth whose first jobs on graduation from school or college required moves, as well as the proportion who accepted jobs that allowed them to remain at home. The lower panels show the situation in relation to the jobs the same youths held five years later. (From Paul H. Landis, The Territorial and Occupational Mobility of Washington Youth, *Washington Agricultural Experiment Station Bulletin No. 499, July, 1944. Pullman, Washington.)*

closely related forms of social interaction that rigid class lines which keep a man in his place socially have failed to form. Though a man may have been down and out in his own native land, on the American frontier he might still win fame and high social status. Though he may have failed on a rundown hill farm in New England or on a southern Georgia hillside, he might move further west toward the frontier and, if he succeeded there, have for himself and his children a new place in the social sun. "Okies" and "Arkies" on the West Coast lost their unfavorable status quickly with achievement and become proud, self-confident, socially accepted Californians.

The twin traditions of territorial migration and vertical mobility have been at many points one and the same in America. They still are accepted as a part of the same general social process in the popular mind. Even though at many periods of social crisis migration brings the proverbial consequence of a rolling stone gathering no moss, at other times, such as World War II and the post-war prosperity period, changed locations have usually meant vertical climbing.

Migration as a Hindrance to Stratification. There is little doubt that horizontal mobility has helped keep alive the tradition of social climbing in the American system. Migration helps a man quickly to shed his past; by shedding his past, he is free to start over again.

Where people migrate frequently and divorce themselves from family and neighborhood, reminders of their former situation do not rise up to plague them. They can be what they choose to be and are capable of being. In the new community they establish their status by virtue of the things they can do. It is for this reason that a society that displays horizontal mobility tends to retain vertical mobility.

Where a man must spend his lifetime in a community, he cannot escape the traditions that have been built up about his family, perhaps over two or three or more generations. He must be what his family is, or at least the community will expect him to be this and nothing more. There is no doubt but that the frontier in America was a vital factor in breaking down the last remnants of the caste system of English society. A young man who made good in the frontier community could marry whom he chose; brawn was worth as much as brain, and both worth more than family history had been. As Frederic Jackson Turner, noted American frontier historian, said of the American frontier, "the rifle and the axe made all men equally tall."[3]

Similarly, territorial mobility, as it expanded with the replacement of horse and buggy transportation by automobile transportation, has made it easy today to move from community to community, from country to city, and city to city. It is still easy to shed one's family connections and his past.

It is for this reason, in part, that marriage in America tends to disregard class lines. Marriage is for romance. Young people marry because of personal attraction, largely ignoring family history and family traditions. Taboos against marriage across class lines are the most rigorous ones of caste social order, for this means a mixing of blood. As long as youth in the United States marry across class lines, we know the social structure is fluid.

Through migration many find new opportunities for vertical movement which never would have been theirs had they remained in the restrictive neighborhood community where they were born. Many communities offer few of the occupational opportunities which are necessary to climbing the ladder to success and fame. Many of them offer no work opportunities through which one can exercise special skills, exhibit special kinds of leadership, or display special talent, such as in art or music. Only by migration can those with special interests and talents and those with special leadership qualities find the opportunity that is necessary for vertical mobility.

Through migration also many young women, especially those in

[3] Frederic Jackson Turner, *The Frontier in American History* (New York: Henry Holt & Co., Inc., 1921).

farm communities, expect to be able to achieve the kind of marriage they wish. They hope to marry above the social status of their parents and thereby climb the social ladder, as women often do by marriage. By locating in towns or cities where they can, in secretarial or some special kind of work, associate with those of a different occupational or social level than that in which they were born, they often make those friendships which lead to dating, courting, and eventually marriage. Marriage is thus for them one of the social elevators leading upward in the kind of society which recognizes no fixed barriers between the social classes.

THE SOCIAL ELEVATORS

One may view American society from the standpoint of social mobility as a place in which numerous social elevators move up and down. An individual standing at the bottom viewing the vertical social structure may see, a long way in the distance, opportunities for his special talent or skills. If he can obtain the funds for horizontal migration, he may succeed in getting into the elevator which leads upward.

For example, it is recognized throughout the nation and probably throughout the world that Broadway is the place to conquer if one expects to be an actor or actress. Thousands of young people drift toward Broadway in the hope of mounting the first rung of the ladder which leads up or, to continue the other figure of speech, of entering the elevator which will gradually boost him upward in the acting profession. To succeed on Broadway is almost certain, eventually, to get one favorable attention in Hollywood, which is the acme of professional ambition for most actors. There one can get into elevators which can take him to the very top of prestige and fame in the acting profession, if he has the talent and can make the connections which will give him a chance to display it.

Every social institution in America is a social elevator that moves upward from one rank to another, if a person once gets established. One may climb through the church; he may climb through business; he may climb through the educational system; he may climb through social activities alone, without any reference to special formalized institutional opportunities, by learning to know the right people, making the right contacts at the right clubs, and in many other ways.

In a competitive society the climb up is always a difficult struggle because there are always other people striving for a place at the top of the social pyramid which, as suggested earlier, tends to be pointed at the top with comparatively few opportunities at the very apex. It is usually broad at the bottom, and those who are unwilling or unable to engage in the competitive struggle will find themselves inevitably at the bottom. Those with special skills and talents who are willing to exercise supreme energy will, if they establish connection with the particular institution or social groups that are able to help them move upward, find themselves gradually going upward in the elevator toward the top.

During the Great Depression, opportunities for both territorial and vertical mobility were few. Millions of farm youths had to remain at home in idleness, for the city had no place for them. Urban youth also were idle on the streets and in the pool halls. The traditional opportunities for work and for social climbing were again restored with the coming of the war and with the opening again of the channels for migration that could be followed in the certain hope of finding conditions as good as or better than those left behind.

The School System as a Social Elevator. The public-school system is the most widely used elevator for social climbing that exists in American culture. Through the school system every child is given a certain amount of opportunity. Gradually it selects those of special talent for further training. While lack of wealth is a handicap to achieving the highest level of training, those with ambition often overcome this by working their way through school and thus climb the educational ladder. Climbing the educational ladder is an almost certain way to climb economically and in social status. Educational attainment in itself has prestige. Educational attainment also opens the door to many other opportunities for further social or economic climbing.

Data presented in the charts on pages 424–25 and 426 indicate the relationship between education and income. It will be seen clearly that the more education the person possesses, the higher he can climb the economic ladder. Income is not only an index of economic success but also a partial index of social success and prestige. There is considerable evidence that education is a fairly effective selective factor in American society, actually carrying to the top those of most ability. Psychologist Lewis Terman's famous *Genetic Study of Genius,* which dealt with 580 gifted children, showed that the professional class contributed 1003 per cent of its quota in ratio to its total proportions in the population; the public service group 137 per cent of its quota; the commercial group 128 per cent of its quota; the industrial group only 35 per cent of its quota.[4] Occupational classification was based on father's occupation.

[4] Lewis Terman, *Genetic Study of Genius* (Stanford, Calif.: Stanford University Press, 1926).

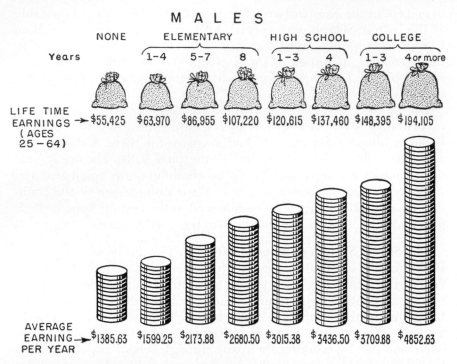

M A L E S

	NONE	ELEMENTARY			HIGH SCHOOL		COLLEGE	
Years		1-4	5-7	8	1-3	4	1-3	4 or more
LIFE TIME EARNINGS (AGES 25-64)	$55,425	$63,970	$86,955	$107,220	$120,615	$137,460	$148,395	$194,105
AVERAGE EARNING PER YEAR	$1385.63	$1599.25	$2173.88	$2680.50	$3015.38	$3436.50	$3709.88	$4852.63

The Relation of Sex and Education to

The higher one climbs on the educational ladder the greater his earnings. These data, for 1949, show that the male college graduate earns almost twice as much in his lifetime as does the grade-school graduate. The college man exceeds the male high school graduate by about $57,000. The college-trained woman also outdistances women of less education, but her earning record is modest indeed compared to that of the male of equal education.

If it is assumed that college education is a way up in our social system, any limitations on the privilege of getting an education is a device for fixing the social classes in their places and is, therefore, undemocratic. The school system, by and large, is the most effective elevator leading up in democratic society. No institutions have been so effective in wiping out class differences and in encouraging marriage across the class line as have the public high school and tax-supported college. In areas where the high school system is open to practically everyone, as in some of the northern and western states, class lines tend to disappear in the association of young people in the school system. Students tend to be rated on the basis of class-

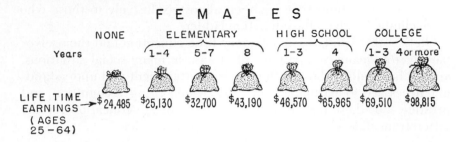

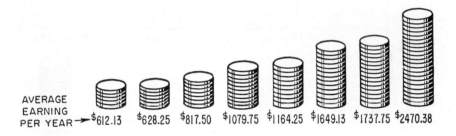

Occupational Success as Measured by Income

Since census data give earnings for age periods only, the life-time earnings shown here are the sum of the average earnings for the various age periods (as of 1949) and necessarily assume the same wage level for the working life-time of the worker. The present wage level is considerably higher, but this study is useful because it contains the most recent available data giving the educational breakdown by sex. (Based on data from U. S. Census of Population: 1950, vol. IV, Special Reports, part 5, chapter 13.)

room achievement and in extracurricular activities. They tend to date and eventually marry without much regard for the social strata of their parental homes.

The college, likewise, is very democratic from the standpoint of encouraging free association, dating, courtship, and marriage between those of various social levels. Many occupations offering greater prestige, security, and opportunities for the kinds of social participation which make for recognition and fame are available only to the college trained. The higher levels of a profession, the pursuit of science in the laboratory, the pursuit of invention as a career, are, save for wealth itself, the surest roads to fame in our culture.

They are occupations that are open almost exclusively to those who have climbed high on the education ladder.

On the other hand, those with very little education find themselves barred from many occupations, ill at ease in many social situations, and, in fact, falling short of the levels of attainment and understanding necessary to participate in roles which bring recognition and prestige. For these reasons the doors to a college education for the gifted from all levels of society must be opened wider.

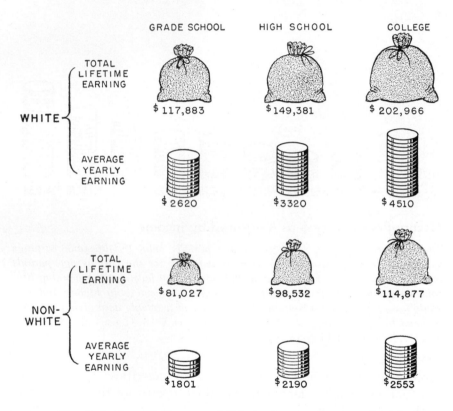

The Relation of Race and Education to Occupational Success as Measured by Income

All earnings increase with education, but the top earnings are far higher for the white person. The greater the education, the greater the difference between whites' and non-whites' occupational success as measured by money income. Earning lifetime here includes ages 25 through 64. The method of calculating lifetime income is the same as that described for the chart on page 425. (Based on data from U. S. Census of Population: 1950, vol. IV, Special Reports, part 5, chapter 13.)

Since World War II, the G.I. Bill of Rights and succeeding legislation have done much to make college training available to all who wish it and have the ability to perform according to required standards. As a consequence, college training has been extended into lower economic and status layers than ever before. It is likely that college training will gradually come to be an aspiration of young people from almost all layers of the population.

As talent becomes scarce and in greater demand in highly specialized urban-industrial society, it seems likely that subsidy of able college students will become a regular practice, motivated by practical social goals and not by ideals of social justice alone.

VERTICAL MOBILITY AS A FACTOR IN SOCIAL ADJUSTMENT

One cannot understand the problems of social adjustment in an open-class society without taking into account the fact that many individuals, in fact most of them, change their place in the vertical social system during their lifetime; some many times during a lifetime. In other words, they find a place in new status groups by playing new social roles. This is essentially what climbing the ladder in the United States means.

Adjustments to Climbing. Now and again Hollywood takes recognition of the difficulty of adjusting to a new class status. A popular motion picture was adapted from *Ruggles of Red Gap*, a book by Harry Leon Wilson which described the life of an English butler born into that rather rigid class society. His father before him had also been a butler. The son had the attitudes of submission and deference toward the master which were characteristics of two generations or more of social tradition. He was won in a card game by an American Westerner, came over to this country, and was given his complete freedom to find a new place for himself through his own initiative. The new master insisted that he associate with him as an equal, drink with him, etc. It took a long period of experience in the West to convince the butler that he actually was as good as other people, to venture out and adopt a pattern of life denied him in English society.

Another interesting film, *Pygmalion*, based on George Bernard Shaw's play, had a similar theme. The main character took a flower girl from the streets of London, cultivated her accent, her dress, and her manners, and introduced her into aristocratic society.

In the American society such rigorous social barriers to climbing of course do not exist, but learning the slightly different manners and customs, etiquette and social forms that one experiences as he climbs

the social ladder even here introduces some strain. Adjustments demanded may be very temporary and for many may not be particularly severe. For others they may become very critical, especially
when a more rigid system of social control pervades the former social
group but not the new group. Often the young person in this situation must compromise standards and, in so doing, sense guilt and a
certain amount of personal stress because his conscience tells him he
is not living up to the best he has been taught.

In a society becoming increasingly complex, and in a world which
has become increasingly mobile, the movements of the average man
in the course of a year bring him in contact with thousands of other
persons to whom he must make some kind of adjustment, either
casual or permanent. Today, also, because of extensive vertical mobility, the person rarely maintains throughout a lifetime all the relationships which he formed at an earlier period. He must, as he climbs
upward or moves outward, come to live in different degrees of intimacy with people who are strangers, people with different pasts,
traditions, moral standards, philosophies of life, vocations, and degrees of wealth, education, and social status.

Strain of Moving Upward. The struggle to obtain a favorable place
in the social structure through vertical mobility places the individual
in a position of competition and strain such as few cultures have
imposed. Although in certain parts of the country the old adage of
an aristocratic tradition is still expressed in "eagles don't come from
crows' nests," or "you can't make a silk purse out of a sow's ear," the
fact yet remains that many young people will successfully learn, as
they climb the social and economic ladder, the manners and customs
of classes with which they have had no experience in their home and
neighborhood upbringing. For those who climb far, life becomes a
series of readjustments to social standards and social expectations
which were foreign to the basic personality patterns acquired in
their primary group. They must become plastic and learn to change
behavior to fit the circumstances of a new social environment.

Such adjustments are not always easy and involve a certain amount
of test and strain for any person. When one adds to social climbing
horizontal movement, which often places the individual in an entirely new community where he has to make all new friends, he begins to appreciate some of the strains that our kind of social system
places upon individuals. They are strains which do not exist at all
in a nation of stable residents, or to the same degree in societies
which set an upward limit to social climbing by drawing rather
rigidly the lines of stratification between social classes.

A single example will help make concrete the problems of social climbing. The author has seen several young women with the Master's degree or even the doctorate, marry considerably below themselves in education and social standing. Their main psychological difficulty seemed to be that they could never feel at home with a young man of their own level of training and sophistication. They felt comfortable and at home, in love situations, with someone who represented the unsophisticated level of their birth and upbringing. After marriage, however, they awakened to the fact that in their present status they were really persons who required sophisticated associations. In almost every instance, in trying to bring the husband up to their level they drove him to drink or neurosis, devices by which he covered his humiliation and inferiority.

Strain of Moving Downward. Adjustment problems of those moving upward, the usual American experience, have been stressed. From the standpoint of personal adjustments, vertical mobility downward probably is the most disastrous in its effects, since it is hard for a person to lose status and maintain his self-respect and the respect of the social groups with which he has formerly been connected. One born to privilege and high society, especially in social systems which are fairly rigid, faces major problems when he must enter a competitive society without the protection and coddling which has formerly been his. If he is a person of high ability and capable of adjustments, he may, in a competitive system, actually achieve high status through his own efforts. If he is one who has used his position of privilege and power without developing his talents, he may find himself about as helpless as a child when facing the competition to which other men of equal ability are subject.

An interesting example is that of Grand Duchess Marie of Russia, who describes in a fascinating autobiography, *The Education of a Princess*,[5] her struggles in a competitive society after her childhood and youth of royalty and privileged status.

Edward VIII may "for the woman I love" sacrifice his throne, but he is not through when he takes that radical step. He must learn to adjust to a life without the homage, verging on worship, paid a monarch, a life without the privileges of a king.

THE OUTLOOK FOR VERTICAL SOCIAL MOBILITY IN THE UNITED STATES

The masses of the population in the United States believe that a democratic way of life forbids the formation of lines of stratification

[5] Marie, Grand Duchess of Russia, *The Education of a Princess* (New York: The Viking Press, Inc., 1931).

such as would seriously hinder vertical social mobility. Yet the process of social stratification is ever going on. Groups in privileged positions never yield their privileges without a struggle, and those who gain new privileges, once they are secure in their new status, begin to search out ways of keeping them for themselves and passing them on to their children. The passing on of private property, of family connection, of political and occupational titles, or of religious and military powers has been achieved in many societies by some system of inheritance designed to insure the perpetuation of statuses through the generations.

No society can ever claim complete immunity to the operation of these social processes, but a democratic society certainly can and must keep them in check. Favorable factors in the United States are: (1) The ambition of most youth to climb higher than their parents, and the willingness of the masses of youth to grant others the same right. (2) The emphasis on scientific achievement and change, which keeps the older and more class-entrenched group from determining the nature of the class structure as they have done in more static societies where the old have been in the saddle, imposing on the young ancestor respect and, in extreme cases, ancestor worship. In such societies it is easy to get the young to accept the system of statuses their fathers developed. In ours it is extremely difficult. (3) Territorial mobility, which frees each generation from the bondage of ancestral status, letting young people build their own status by personal merit.

Sociologists have, nonetheless, expressed great concern about the future freedom of vertical mobility in the United States, and several publications have called attention to the inequities of the class system. (See the selected references at the end of the chapter.)

No more sensible critical appraisal of the American system of vertical mobility has come to the author's attention than that of University of Washington sociologist Robert Faris. Here are some extracts summarizing his conclusions, originally presented in his presidential address before the Pacific Sociological Society.

"It seems to be taken for granted by the public that the view of sociologists is that there is a well-defined class system in this country, consisting of six layer-cake levels with Pullman-berth designations. It is also a popular cliché that class lines are hardening, with the rich becoming richer and the poor getting poorer, so that an 'American Dream' is betrayed. The responsibility for such notions is widely distributed among a range of persons from Marx to Warner. Much of the discussion is clearly politically motivated, bearing little relation to objective knowledge.

"The most extreme emotionalism is apparent in the Marxian fury at the upper and middle classes, and some parallel to this unfortunately remains in contemporary writings in the literature of sociology. . . .

"Other points of view are to be found, of course, including one that classes are open and upward and mobility is easy in this country today.

"The popular notions are not based on research, and are far removed from any reality. In other lands and other times, class lines have been not only precise but official—one could get a list of members of an upper class. But how real is it to refer to an upper class in the United States? Prestige, power, money, value to society, membership in social registers—all correlate only loosely. To refer to the whole body of prominent persons as forming any kind of a class unity is too great a departure from actuality to have any scientific value.

"More persons will admit membership in a middle class than in an upper or lower, but if the designation 'working class' is substituted for 'lower' a much larger number, including many persons of high position and income, will so classify themselves. Any distinction between a middle and a lower class is extremely vague today, as recent research abundantly shows. . . .

"In a class system, there must be boundaries between classes, and the boundaries must in some way operate as artificial barriers to vertical mobility. Many scholars have not only testified to these, but have supported the idea that there is a trend toward increasing rigidity of the barriers, basing the contention on fragile evidence. A considerable amount of recent research bears against any such conception.

"One may point to the increasing cost of professional education, and offer this as evidence of greater difficulty for the low-income candidates. But Adams has recently shown that decade by decade for the half-century from 1870 to 1920 there was a steady increase in the percentage of college and medical training financed by the student himself—the figure reaching 63 per cent in the final decade. Furthermore, the percentage of physicians with physician fathers decreased in the same period from 22 to less than 10. Apparently increasing cost does not make an effectively increasing barrier.

"Hollingshead holds the view that class lines in New Haven are becoming tighter, but his own figures show that between 1910 and 1940 in that city there was an increase in the number of persons in the upper levels and a decrease of those in lower levels. Since the birth rates in upper levels are generally lower, there must have been more vertical mobility than indicated by the expansion of the classes. Mc-

Guire has made computations on the United States population to estimate the amount of such climbing, and states that in a five-level system 'at least 20 per cent of the American population moves upward in social class status each generation.' Similar calculations for the Jonesville of the Warner studies show an even greater average amount; in the upper class of that community over 31 per cent of the members originated in a lower level.

"If we take the more conservative figure of one-fifth of each generation climbing up one step of a five-step ladder, should this be interpreted as an indication of rigid barriers, or of abundant opportunity? It is of course impossible for everyone to be on top at once. Is an 'American Dream' to be satisfied only by a system in which everyone is upper-class, or by a class system in which there is no more than chance continuity between level of fathers and sons? If not, what amount of vertical mobility in the population could satisfy a concept of justice? . . .

"College and professional education is one of the major pathways to a higher occupational level. The opportunity to obtain such education has been immensely increased in the past few decades, and the trend continues. Poverty is not the barrier to this kind of opportunity that it was half a century ago. Contemporary research in the causes of non-attendance at college shows lack of desire to be emerging as one of the major factors. For many youths of lower occupational levels there is a preference not to go to college. This may be a result of such factors as lack of intellectual tradition in the home and consequent handicap in earning school grades, and unwillingness to delay having spending money, getting married, or assuming independent adult status. A number of observations have also shown that to some extent primary groups within the lower levels discourage such ambitions as would tend to remove a member, so that it becomes an unsociable act to plan to desert by moving into a higher occupational classification.

"Some persons stay in their occupational and income levels because they prefer a particular kind of work, or working environment, to any other. Some artists and musicians, who could have done better in the competition for income, simply value their artistic pursuits above money, rank, and position. Some persons want to work outdoors, because they love mountains, horses, or boats, and flatly decline opportunities for advancement that would require them to work indoors. Some academic men have opportunities for jobs paying more than twice their collegiate salaries but stay on the campus by preference. There is no requirement that a system of open opportunities should imply that all must seek the same jobs, or the top levels. If every barrier but personal preference were removed, there would still be a great deal of continuity of occupational classes, and of specific occupations, as many sons acquire their appreciation of a pursuit from the father.

"There are, of course, other kinds of getting ahead than rising through levels of occupational or prestige classes. As Sjoberg recently pointed out, within the same occupation there are great possibilities of progress. A father may be a small-town general medical practitioner and his son a high-priced city surgeon—yet the statistics on class levels would indicate no vertical mobility. Figures on the same occupations over a period of years show spectacular increases in standard of living in practically every case. In the short and atypical period from 1930 to 1947 the standard of living of coal miners almost doubled—to cite an extreme case.

"Incomes afford unreal comparisons of living standards over a period of years. An automobile in 1910 was an expensive machine, and it still is, but a man with a car is now on a vastly higher level of living in respect to transportation—his car is bigger, safer, more comfortable, much more powerful, lasts longer, costs less to keep in repair, and has much better roads to travel. Similar developments have taken place with respect to other spheres of expenditure. The man of 1954 in the same occupational category as the man of 1910 is far above the latter in standard of living; he may have failed to gain relatively to others, but an inquiry into pride of status is a separate matter, and is also subject to the variations in preference mentioned above. It is not an 'American Dream' that everyone can look forward to looking down on everyone else. The fact is that while the rich may have been getting richer, the poor have also been getting richer. The Seattle slums of today are better than the average housing in Texas in the days of our grandparents.

"In the light of modern research knowledge, of which the above is but a small portion, is there any justification for employing such an expression as 'the class system' of this country? And are we justified in stating that the present trends are taking us backward toward a fixed-class arrangement? To such questions we should at last be ready to answer a flat 'no.' It is now time to search for new, objective, accurate terms to describe the ways in which our population varies in terms of money, power, prestige, and occupational way of life."[6]

Certainly this review of the American scene leaves little doubt that vertical mobility is still a reality of the American social structure: class lines are so indistinct as to be almost unrecognizable; moving up

[6] Robert E. L. Faris, "The Alleged Class System of the United States," *Research Studies of the State College of Washington,* 22:77–83 (June 1954).

is a major process of this generation, as it has been of generations since pioneer times.

THE FATE OF CLOSED CLASSES

Revolt is discussed in Chapter 29, but it is important to note here that when fixed classes at the top become unreasonable in their power, they risk uprisings of those in less favored positions. The masses participate, but often the revolt is sparked and led by university students and college professors. The writer, when traveling abroad, particularly in countries where such revolts are common, has been asked why the American university bodies are so peaceful, and never lead major political revolts. The answer is that in a society with free vertical mobility, there is no cause for it. All may seek top honors by their own effort, and face no rigid barriers set up by the privileged to hinder their doing so.

Fixed classes also face the fate of degeneration from within. This tendency toward decay is vividly portrayed in the following quotation of the late Edward A. Ross, giant among the first generation of American sociologists.

". . . it is human nature for those who control a good thing to keep it all for themselves and their children. The greater the luster of a nobility, the more loath are its members to share this luster with outsiders. Hence, unless the iron hand of a monarch holds open the door in order to placate his commoners or to stimulate the zeal of his servants, an upper class closes itself to upstarts and becomes a hereditary caste.

"Thenceforth it moves slowly but fatally toward its doom. As their achieving ancestors recede into the distance the patricians more and more owe their exalted position to privilege rather than to personal worth or conspicuous service. With the aid of the props which an aristocracy well knows how to provide the highborn fool or weakling stays up, while the lowborn man of ability is shut out from wealth and honor. Shielded from that natural elimination of the unfit to which the common people are exposed, a closed upper class loses in the course of four or five generations the virility of its achieving ancestors and becomes an imposture. Nevertheless, thanks to mating continually with the most beautiful women in the population, it gains in good looks and is never so patrician in feature as in the period when it is unable to produce from its loins enough men of brains and force to vindicate its privileges.

"Its tendency to beget handsome fools does not, however, cause an aristocracy to abate by one jot its pretensions to better clay. It nurses carefully its prestige and spares nothing in pose, manner, and surroundings that will keep up the illusion of its superiority. It realizes that entailed estates are not everything, for if their owners miss too many kinds of distinction they will cease to be looked up to. So it not only cherishes and parades its ancestral glories, but, whenever a new source of prestige appears, it promptly gets close to it. Aristocrats take under their patronage such dispensers of glory as minstrels, troubadours, poets, artists, orators, priests, and clerics. If hardihood is admired, their young men will be sportsmen and explorers; if letters are honored, they will play Maecenas; if learning is prized, they will varnish themselves with a thin coating of scholarship. Aristocrats of long lineage dare not let themselves be outshone. They must be the best groomed, the best mannered, the most splendid, must be seen against the richest background or in the brightest limelight. They must be among the first to fly, to navigate under water, to scale a peak, to cross a desert, or to visit a closed land. War with its command of the many by the few gives them their chance, for nobles have a traditional affinity for the martial. Moreover, they exalt themselves by appealing to a theory of heredity that science smiles at, and cry down the role opportunity plays in individual destiny.

"Thus an effete hereditary caste contrives to keep itself at the apex of society until in some crisis it fails to meet the test and its hollowness is plain to all men. Then its privileges are abolished, it collapses like an empty sack, and the way is open for a new and abler group of families to climb into its vacant seats, or else for the social system to be modified in the direction of giving freer play to competition."[7]

SUMMARY

Status differences are eternal in human relationships. Even democracy cannot destroy them completely, although it de-emphasizes them significantly. A democratic society can achieve the goal of movement between classes. A society is democratic, in fact, to the extent that it does achieve this goal of permitting individuals to move from one social layer to a higher one. Sociologists label this process vertical social mobility. The popular term for it is "social climbing" or "climbing the ladder."

Through climbing, the individual may achieve a higher status than that of his birth, by learning to play new roles which bring higher status than his parents' occupation or educational attainments justify. This is the essence of vertical mobility.

Expressed in its most popular form, it means that in a democratic social order, one may move from log cabin to White House, from

[7] Edward Alsworth Ross, *Principles of Sociology* (New York: Appleton-Century-Crofts, Inc., 1923), pp. 368–69.

lowly birth to the most powerful and honored office in the world. This contrasts with fixed social orders, in which to be a monarch one must be born with royal blood. In such orders even to marry a commoner is to sacrifice the prestige of high office inherent in royal blood, and to decline in status.

DISCUSSION AND REVIEW QUESTIONS

1. Show how change of social position is possible in an open-class society.
2. How does vertical mobility relate to social stratification?
3. In what way are vertical and territorial mobility related? Show how the two have been related in the historical development of the United States.
4. What factors today tend to keep the channels of vertical social circulation free?
5. Show how migration brings youth into contact with social elevators leading upward.
6. Discuss the public school as a social elevator in democratic society.
7. Is there evidence that the school helps youth climb to the values that are considered worth seeking in our culture?
8. Show how movement up and down the social ladder intensifies problems of social adjustment for youth.
9. May movement downward also require adjustment? Explain or illustrate.
10. Cite evidence indicating that upward movement is more difficult for the underprivileged than the privileged.
11. Compare opportunities for vertical climbing of youth in times of depression and in times of prosperity.
12. Does it seem likely that the tradition of vertical climbing will be kept alive in the United States?
13. Comment on the dual fates of the closed classes or castes.

SOURCEBOOK READINGS

FREEDMAN, RONALD, AMOS N. HAWLEY, WERNER S. LANDECKER, GERHARD E. LENSKI, and HORACE M. MINER. *Principles of Sociology* (rev. ed.). New York: Henry Holt & Co., Inc., 1956.
  1. ROGOFF, NATALIE, "Class Consciousness and Vertical Mobility in France and the United States," pp. 550–54.
  2. CHINOY, ELI, "Social Mobility Trends in the United States," pp. 555–58.
  3. CENTERS, RICHARD, "Education and Occupational Mobility," pp. 558–61.

SELECTED READINGS

CAPLOW, THEODORE. *The Sociology of Work.* Minneapolis: University of Minnesota Press, 1954.

CHINOY, E. *Automobile Workers and the American Dream.* Garden City, N.Y.: Doubleday & Co., Inc., 1955.

KAHL, JOSEPH A. *The American Class Structure.* New York: Rinehart & Co., Inc., 1957, chap. 23.

MERTON, ROBERT K. "Bureaucratic Structure and Personality," *Social Forces,* 18:560–68 (1940).

MILLS, C. WRIGHT. *The New Men of Power.* New York: Harcourt, Brace & Co., Inc., 1948.

OGBURN, WILLIAM F. "Implications of the Rising Standard of Living in the United States," *American Journal of Sociology,* 60:541–46 (May, 1955).

REISSMAN, L. "Levels of Aspiration and Social Class," *American Sociological Review,* 18:233–42 (1953).

SJOBERG, GIDEON. "Are Social Classes in America Becoming More Rigid?" *American Sociological Review,* 16:775–83 (1951).

SOROKIN, P. A. *Social Mobility.* New York: Harper & Brothers, 1927.

STONE, ROBERT C. "Factory Organization and Vertical Mobility," *American Sociological Review,* 18:28–35 (1953).

"The Rich Middle-Income Class," *Fortune,* May, 1954, pp. 94 ff.

WARNER, W. LLOYD, *et al. Social Class in America.* Chicago: Science Research Associates, 1949.

WARNER, W. LLOYD, R. J. HAVIGHURST, and M. B. LOEW. *Who Shall Be Educated?* New York: Harper & Brothers, 1944.

Part IV

THE SELF IN SOCIETY

Chapter 24

The Social Self

Personality may be viewed from many angles, its development traced from many perspectives. The biologist finds in forces of life and growth itself many clues to personality and its functioning. The psychologist finds in various glandular and maturation factors clues to growth and individual performance. If the sociologist has a contribution to make, it is in viewing personality as a product of a unique culture pattern, its attitudes and values formed by a set of values of a given social structure. The sociologist brings to an understanding of personality an understanding of the group which is its maker, of the culture pattern which is its mold.

Certainly, the student who has followed sociological analysis this far already has a deep appreciation of how fully the structure of the individual personality is formed and misformed to suit the convenience of group life in which it is expected that the individual will live. As a sociologist sees it, to attempt a full, rounded picture of personality without an appreciation of the company the individual keeps is to draw a picture that has little real likeness to reality.

Man is born to be social. To be social, his self must be shaped to fit a particular social scheme. The building of the self from the plastic, unformed mass of human flesh is the task of the social group in which the child is born. In an early chapter a picture of feral man was presented, showing how animal-like the human being develops if denied the shaping influences of social groups, or if rigidly isolated from a social group so that his contacts are limited and he has little opportunity to learn.

Most human beings grow up in the intimate family group, from which their contacts and learning experience is broadened by contacts with the larger group outside. It is through this process of group association that the social self is eventually born. It consists essentially in learning that all life consists of "we" relationships. The individual, formed in the group and learning to identify himself always in a "we" association, comes gradually to fit the norms of the particular society in which he is born.

Charles H. Cooley thought of the social group as a sort of looking glass from which the individual sees himself reflected and thus takes measures of his self:

> Each to each a looking-glass
> Reflects the other that doth pass.[1]

As we see our face, figure, and dress in the glass, and are interested in them because they are ours, and pleased or otherwise with them according to whether they do or do not answer to what we should like them to be; so in imagination we perceive in another's mind some thought of our appearance, manners, aims, deeds, character, friends, and so on, and are variously affected by it.

A self-idea of this sort seems to have three principal elements: the imagination of our appearance to the other person; the imagination of his judgment of that appearance, and some sort of self-feeling, such as pride or mortification. The comparison with a looking-glass hardly suggests the second element, the imagined judgment, which is quite essential. The thing that moves us to pride or shame is not the mere mechanical reflection of ourselves but an imputed sentiment, the imagined effect of this reflection upon another's mind. This is evident from the fact that the character and weight of that other, in whose mind we see ourselves, make all the difference with our feeling. We are ashamed to seem evasive in the presence of a straightforward man, cowardly in the presence of a brave one, gross in the eyes of a refined one, and so on. We always imagine, and in imagining share, the judgments of the other mind. A man will boast to one person of an action—say some sharp transaction in trade—which he would be ashamed to own to another.

The building of the self is a delicate process fraught with grave consequences. Whatever the human self becomes in attitudes, values, and aspirations, it is the reflection of group treatment. The self may be made relatively free of inhibitions, can be taught to accept or condemn itself, depending on the social atmosphere and training program. This self may be crippled by self-condemnation, be loaded with an overwhelming sense of guilt, if the atmosphere is too full of criticism and condemnation, if life is made too humiliating.

---

[1] Charles H. Cooley, *Human Nature and the Social Order* (New York: Charles Scribner's Sons, 1924), pp. 184–85.

So many handicaps to normal expression can be placed in the individual's way, so many blocks to social approval, that the outlets are completely dammed up. He may rebel, lose his sense of direction, and become completely confused.

One sees this most simply in the maze which is constructed by the psychologist for the animal subject: it may be a rat, pig, sheep, or some other creature used for experimental purposes. If the experiment is with the rat, the cheese is placed at the end of a long and complicated runway, where there are many blind alleys down which the rat can go seeking the fragrant cheese. The rat, a fairly intelligent creature, can often learn a complicated maze and eventually find his way to the cheese. But there is a point beyond which the route is so complicated that a particular rat cannot find his way to the cheese. Again and again he goes down a blind alley, only to find himself blocked. Hunger increases, effort increases, he hurries about, down this alley and that, always ending up in defeat. Eventually, emotions are aroused, his mind becomes one of confusion; he struggles in vain. His feelings of frustration increase until eventually he is a confused and defeated individual. If the frustration becomes too great, his normal life organization is destroyed. He becomes a neurotic rat, unable to act at all.

No organism with a nervous system can stand too much frustration without breaking. The human being's life is often complicated by numerous frustrations. His greater intelligence helps him conquer some of them, but his greater sensitivity of nervous system, his greater sense of defeat when social outlets are blocked, make him vulnerable to a keen sense of frustration. He, like the rat, can be driven to neurosis, or even psychosis, by repeated failure to achieve socially defined ends by approved means.

FILM LIST FOR PART IV

Baby Meets His Parents—11 minutes—sound
Points out how the early years in life influence the development of personality differences, with emphasis upon the effect of the parents. *Source:* Encyclopaedia Britannica Films.

Preface to a Life—29 minutes—sound
Shows the importance of parental attitudes in the development of a child's personality. *Source:* Castle Films, Inc.

Growth of Infant Behavior—11 minutes—sound
By Dr. Arnold Gesell. Comparison of growth of behavior patterns at different stages in early infancy. Similar film deals with such growth in later stages of infancy. *Source:* Encyclopaedia Britannica Films.

Feeling of Hostility—27 minutes—sound
Traces the causes of resentment of a child toward others. Trailer to the film has psychiatrist explain the contributing factors and suggest ways parents may avoid such a problem. *Source:* National Film Board of Canada.

Feeling of Rejection—23 minutes—sound
Case history of a young woman who withdraws because of fear of rejection, followed by an analysis of the causes of her personality problem. *Source:* National Film Board of Canada.

Helping the Child Accept the Do's—11 minutes—sound
Portrays the child learning to live in a world defined by do's and shows how personality is influenced by his degree of acceptance of them. *Source:* Encyclopaedia Britannica Films.

Emotional Health—20 minutes—sound
Story of a student who discovers the emotional cause of physical illness. Emphasis on removal of stigma now attached to psychiatric treatment. *Source:* McGraw-Hill Book Company, Inc.

Over-Dependency—32 minutes—sound
Case history of a young man whose life is crippled by a too-dependent childhood. *Source:* National Film Board of Canada.

The Quiet One—67 minutes—sound
Story of a delinquent Negro boy of 10 years who is sent to a school for delinquent boys. There he receives competent help from psychiatrist and counselors and is set on the road to rehabilitation. *Source:* Athena Films.

Unconscious Motivation—38 minutes—sound
Suggests how everyday thoughts, feelings, and actions may be influenced by unconscious motives. *Source:* Association Films.

The Building of the Social Self

To the serious student who has followed sociological study this far, the statement "culture and social groups form personality differently" will seem commonplace. Yet it is such a profound truth that only those who have traveled most widely and observed child training systems most closely can begin to appreciate the far-reaching consequences to human beings.

One training system makes the anxious human being, another the secure one; one a trusting, kindly person, the other a hostile, aggressive one; one training system the high-blood-pressure type, another the placid type; one a people who look upon sex with disgust, as a form of excretion, another a people who treat sex activity as a "light and pleasant dance."

How profoundly the core attitude and value systems of persons in given societies differ, how great the degrees of difference in their self-acceptance and inner security, adjustment and maladjustment can be in various social systems is vividly portrayed by La Barre in the following:

". . . The single most important thing in human cultural behavior is literally and specifically the way we bring up our children. . . .

". . . cultures, so to speak, manufacture their own misfits; societies have the maladjusted they deserve. That is to say, no human being is ever maladjusted to thin air, but only to the specific cultural and moral demands of a given sociey. If cultures corset human beings in differing ways and at different points, then we must expect the bulges to show up in different places. We must expect to find different psychiatric and social maladjustments in different cultures.

This seems to be precisely what, as anthropologists, we do find. . . .

". . . take the case of the Chinese. Psychiatrists have long known that certain cardiac disorders like hypertension were statistical rarities among the Chinese. Recently there has been a suggested therapy for hypertension which to my mind wholly misses the issue: The reasoning is something like this: the major premise, Chinese do not suffer from hypertension to the extent that Occidentals do; minor premise, Chinese eat mostly rice; therefore—conclusion of the syllogism—the cure for hypertension is rice-eating! The point is entirely missed that the Chinese lack of hypertension may be largely owing to a different character structure, culturally different goals, a radically different tempo of life, and pretty completely different modes of socializing and conditioning children. Chinese do not have hypertension because they are not tense, are not compulsive; not because they eat rice. They have different culturally conditioned attitude-stances toward life, and different institutional structures.

"There was an old army man in the 1890's, James Mooney, who was involved in the Sioux wars—the Battle of Wounded Knee and Custer's Last Stand—who from a lifetime of experience with various Indian tribes, came to the kind of understanding that I think is essential to the issue.

" 'The Sioux,' he says, 'are direct and manly, the Cheyenne high-spirited and keenly sensitive, the Arapaho generous and accommodating, the Comanche practical and businesslike.'

"And the reason clearly is that the Sioux, the Cheyenne, the Arapaho, and the Comanche have different ways of bringing up their children. . . .

". . . Through anthropological and psychiatric knowledge and control of the bringing up of our children, we are potentially able to shape almost any kind of human personality that an increasingly integrated world requires. Shall we have a competitive, aggressive Comanche-like personality in our future world citizen, or shall we have an urbane, Hopi-like personality? It is not the knowledge, but the social implementation of it, that is lacking. Will we want the tenseness, the explosiveness, and the compulsive competence of the Japanese; or do we want the security and the aplomb and the realism of the Okinawans? Do we want the Chinese profoundly aesthetic enjoyment of life, or the severe, driving, guilt-ridden morality of Western man? . . .

". . . Is our society loaded with anxious, frustrated, oral-dependent or oral-aggressive individuals, overready at the first breath of cold reality to retreat into dependency or an autistic dream world? Then

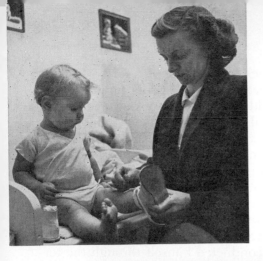

The Secure Person
Is One Who Has Had Close Ties
With Others

*Socialization begins in the
mother–child relationship.*

It develops further in the play group.

*As adulthood approaches, it
takes place in interest groups.
(Standard Oil Company, N.J.)*

let us look at societies in which such individuals are a rarity. In most primitive groups, for example, because of their pediatric backwardness and lack of Frigidaires, a child is ignorantly suckled a minimum of two or three years—and, worst of all, he is fed whenever he is hungry, in a hopelessly unscheduled fashion! (Some American Indians are permitted an occasional visit to the breast even up to the age of five.) Is the dignity, the inexpungeable security, the settled self-judgment and self-possession of such American Indians a surprise to us, then? I have known American Indians whom the threat of the atomic bomb itself would not disorganize; upon knowing the worst of all imaginable situations, they would continue to adjust to them. I know one American Indian who conducted himself through the terrors of a modern war with a really distinguished aplomb. We would mistakenly call it courage—for him it was something to be taken for granted like his own manhood; he simply lacked these reservoirs of neurotic anxiety which flood us in stress situations. He lacked the culturally defined guilts that would lead him irrationally to anticipate punishment; he had not experienced the frustrations and hence did not have the hostilities to project and to be persecuted by as neurotic fears; he had not had his childhood ego systematically attacked and traumatized so that he had any doubt of his ability to cope with any current situation.

". . . the really serious thing is the kinds of human being we make, and the ways in which we go about making them. The child, we say easily, is the father of the individual man. But more than that, in this larger sense, the child is the father of all future mankind."[1]

This account is a realistic sketch of personality formation in its cultural mold. It does not probe man's interior to find what glands are at work or to learn what instincts come to flower. It describes group activities and culture patterns which form of the child the man which he will be.

The sociologist and anthropologist have from the beginning dealt primarily with case-history materials in arriving at their conception of the social self and of personality generally. As the preceding account makes so clear, a social system can make or warp an individual into most any pattern it chooses, within the limits of biological capacity. The individual may be made guilt-ridden or courageous and free from fear. He may be made docile or aggressive. It depends on the group's choice of the patterns it wishes to perpetuate. The group's choice is rooted in their cultural traditions.

[1] Weston La Barre, "Wanted: A Pattern for Modern Man," *Mental Hygiene*, 33:2–8 (April 1949).

THE DEVELOPMENT OF THE SELF

The discovery of the *physical self* is made by the child through tactile sensation as he explores his body and his material environment. He soon learns that when he touches another part of his body he receives two tactile sensations, whereas when he touches the crib or other persons or objects he receives only one sensation. The development of the *psychological self* is a much more complex process. It involves the development of the consciousness that "I," "myself," and "me" is a behavior unit capable of feelings and sensations that are uniquely one's own. The psychological self is really that part of the individual which is reflective. "I have to be myself," is a common expression of it. The person comes to see his individual self as an object of value.

The *social self*, which consists essentially in a consciousness of having a status in groups, is the most complex self conception which the individual develops. It comes from seeing one's self as a unit which reacts to others and to which others react. Charles H. Cooley, inventor of the primary group concept, after studying the development of personality in children, concluded that the social self and society are twin born. One's knowledge of himself as a social being comes from the reactions of others to him in the social groups in which he participates. In various social groups, as in a mirror, one sees his picture reflected differently and thus eventually builds a complex social picture of himself. Eventually one sees himself from so many angles that it is as though he were standing before a multiple mirror reflecting many sides at once. Professor Cooley appropriately called this society-built self the "looking-glass self."

The great psychologist William James had a similar conception of the social self, although he expressed it somewhat differently. He called the different selves developed in groups "club selves," saying that one has as many social selves as he has groups of which he is a vital part. Consider, for example, the town bum at a revival meeting. There he is a lost sinner. When he slips around the corner to the pool hall, where the rest of the bums meet to play poker, he may feel himself to be quite a man, especially on nights when he is lucky.

The *conscience* is a part of the developed social self—the self-critical or self-condemning part. From one's social groups, particularly his primary groups, he acquires standards. When he violates the standards he has been taught, he is punished by parents, and, as he gets older, criticized, condemned, or punished by others. He comes to accept group evaluations of his behavior and, as the social self develops, to condemn himself for violating standards. Thus he feels guilt, even though the groups may not even discover that he has violated the standards.

His conscience, of course, has meaning only in the society of which he has become a vital part as a socialized person. He, like the Apostle Paul before his conversion, might hail Christians to prison and otherwise persecute them in "all good conscience," if his group considered that kind of behavior good, as did Paul's Jewish teachers of the day. Not until after conversion did the apostle become a part of the Christian group and accept its standards as a guide to his conscience.

More recent than the Cooley and James theories of the social self and its development by the group is the Freudian concept employed by the psychiatrist. The social or status-seeking self they call the *ego;* the guilty or self-critical self, the *superego* (censor). The psychiatrist, who specializes in the study and cure of distorted social selves, or egos, believes that the personality of the individual is integrated and unified largely in proportion to the strength of the ego. A strong ego is manifest in self-confidence, a feeling of security, and hopefulness that aspirations can be realized.

The approach of Freud and that of his followers led psychologists quite generally to conceive of the self primarily in terms of frustrated drives, complexes, repressions, "death wishes," and other such pressures. These replaced the animal instincts of the previous generation of educators and psychologists. Only recently has a reaction against this negative approach to human nature become evident. One of the strongest statements for a positive approach to personality is that of A. H. Maslow. In his *Motivation and Personality* he declares that it is time that psychology deals with man's potentialties, his virtues, his achievable aspirations. It is time to understand the normal and to help man attain his full psychological stature.[2]

His research shows that the top one per cent of human beings "feel safe and unanxious, accepted, loved and loving, respect-worthy and respected." He could find no psychology test that would help locate or classify these people, although there are many tests which help diagnose the mentally ill and abnormal.

Maslow believes that discipline, control, suppression—the watchwords of the old regime—must give place to spontaneity, release, naturalness, self-acceptance, impulse-awareness, gratification, permissiveness.

He declares that "the concept of the well-adjusted personality or of good adjustment sets a low ceiling upon the possibility for ad-

[2] A. H. Maslow, *Motivation and Personality* (New York: Harper & Brothers, 1954).

vancement and for growth. The cow, the slave, the robot may all be well adjusted.

"The superego of the child is ordinarily conceived of as introjection of fear, punishment, loss of love, abandonment, etc. The study of children and adults who are safe, loved and respected indicates the possibility of a positive superego built on love identification, the desire to please and to make others happy, as well as on truth, logic, justice, consistency, right and duty.

"The behavior of the healthy person is less determined by anxiety, fear, insecurity, guilt, shame, and more by truth, logic, justice, reality, fairness, fitness, beauty, rightness, etc.

"Where are the researches on unselfishness? Lack of envy? Will power? Strength of character? Optimism? Friendliness? Realism? Self-transcendence? Boldness, courage? Lack of jealousy? Sincerity? Patience?

"Of course the most pertinent and obvious choice of subject for a positive psychology is the study of psychological health (and other kinds of health, aesthetic health, value health, physical health, and the like). But a positive psychology also calls for more study of the good man, of the secure and of the confident, of the democratic character, of the happy man, of the serene, the calm, the peaceful, the compassionate, the generous, the kind, of the creator, of the saint, of the hero, of the strong man, of the genius, and of the other good specimens of humanity.

"What produces the socially desirable characteristics of kindliness, social conscience, helpfulness, neighborliness, identification, tolerance, friendliness, desire for justice, righteous indignation?

"We have a very rich vocabulary for psychopathology but a very meager one for health.

"Deprivation and frustration have some good effects. The study of just as well as of unjust discipline is indicated, as is also study of the self-discipline that comes from being allowed to deal directly with reality, learning from its intrinsic rewards and punishments. . . .

"Child–parent relationships have usually been studied as if they *were* only a set of problems, *only* a chance to make mistakes. They are primarily a pleasure and a delight, and a great opportunity to enjoy. This is true even for adolescence, too often treated as if akin to a plague."[3]

A new approach of therapists has become popular with the gradually changing conception of the self. Unlike the Freudian, who delves deeply to uncover the pain, frustration, aggression, and hate that

[3] *Ibid.*, pp. 376–78.

stem from an emotionally damaged childhood, therapists with the positive approach seek to unleash and develop love, sociability, and goodness in the mental cripple and thus to restore him to the fellowship of man.[4]

THE SOCIAL SELF AND PRIMARY GROUPS

The Adequate Ego Structure. The psychiatrist believes that one of the most important elements in building a strong ego is parental affection, which gives a sense of security, of being wanted, of having a refuge to which one can turn at all times. Nursing and coddling of the child is the beginning. The author of the account at the opening of the chapter relates the security of the American Indian to the long nursing period. The account of children in the South American foundling home, given in Chapter 9, is an even more striking example of the tragic effects of denying the child a warm and intimate primary group experience.

In the normal family group, the building of the self or ego is well begun and then extended outside as the child performs in other group situations with widening contacts. In the neighborhood he performs in an environment of friendliness where success is assured, initiative rewarded, and a sense of power and strength permitted. In a sympathetic family group this kind of situation is provided to give him a chance to show that he can do superior things. Parents and family friends make him feel that his first step is a tremendous achievement; and so it is with his first word, his first accomplishment of any new task. In this atmosphere of appreciation and love, the child develops confidence, self-assurance, courage, and the other traits that enable him to face life boldly.

Parents protect the youngest or the weakest child from exploitation by the older brothers and sisters, take his part, and protect him from too frequent defeat. Most members of the primary group try to shield the weakest member, rather than criticizing him because he cannot do as well as the stronger ones. They praise him for the things he does accomplish and give him an advantage in competitive situations, as

[4] The following are books by some of the leaders in a positive approach to therapy: Ian Suttee, *Origins of Love and Hate* (New York: The Julian Press, Inc., 1935); Karen Horney, *Neurosis and Human Growth: The Struggle toward Self-Realization* (New York: W. W. Norton & Co., Inc., 1956); Smiley Blanton, *Love or Perish* (New York: Simon & Schuster, Inc., 1956); M. F. Ashley Montagu, *The Direction of Human Development* (New York: Harper & Brothers, 1955), and Ashley Montagu (ed.) *The Meaning of Love* (New York: The Julian Press, Inc., 1953); Clark E. Moustakas (ed.), *The Self: Explorations of Human Growth* (New York: Harper & Brothers, 1956); Eric Fromm, *Man for Himself* (New York: Rinehart & Co., Inc., 1947); P. A. Sorokin, *The Ways and Power of Love* (Boston: Beacon Press, Inc., 1954); Rollo May, *Man's Search for Himself* (New York: W. W. Norton & Co., Inc., 1953).

when older brothers or sisters give little Johnny a head start in a foot-race and usually manage to let him win. The play group often gives the younger member special opportunities to achieve success, and there is usually a sympathetic member who will try to smooth over defeat and help the younger child understand it.

The protective primary group provides a situation in which the child's social self (ego) will have a chance to develop. Without this consideration the younger child, because of his lack of physical strength and mental development, would be continuously outdone in every role undertaken. In situations where this does happen, over-whelming inferiority results.

The Inadequate Ego Structure. It is just as possible, however, for a primary group to build a social self (an ego structure) which is com-pletely inadequate for facing the realities of life. Parents can begin by *rejecting* the child emotionally, making him feel that he is un-wanted; they can criticize, depreciate, humiliate him by comparison with others who are able to do better, until they destroy his sense of security. They can make him fearful, self-depreciative, void of initia-tive, anxious concerning life in all its aspects. In fact, they can lay the foundation for a neurotic personality, a personality which has such a weak ego structure that the individual cannot face life's responsi-bilities.

The *underprotected* child, who is so much criticized by parents and older brothers and sisters in every role he undertakes that he fails to develop self-confidence through normal achievements, may suffer complete defeat. The social self, or ego, reflecting this primary group attitude becomes self-critical and self-derogatory. The child feels a sense of guilt and self-condemnation that relates to no specific viola-tion of conscience on his part; he is sensitive and afraid to try new things for fear his efforts will bring further rebuff. He becomes anx-ious and fearful of life. Failing to find ego support in primary groups, it is unlikely that he will find it outside, because secondary groups are essentially competitive and impersonal. A child with this kind of background is likely to become a neurotic adult who fails in meeting the crises, or even the normal adjustments, that life in a complex so-ciety requires of all.

Take the case of a boy whose parents from his early childhood continuously compared him unfavorably with an older sister; criti-cized, dominated, and browbeat him; found fault with him and his companions; made him feel guilty and sinful; restricted and ham-pered all his activities. At twelve years of age he was so fearful of life he could scarcely be made to go upstairs alone at night. He wanted the register open in the ceiling of the living room so the light could shine up in his bedroom and so he could hear his parents talking below. He failed in school, even though he had a brilliant mind. He felt ill at ease with his playmates and had a generally anxious and fearful attitude. He feared to attempt new roles for in all roles attempted he had been rated a failure by members of his primary group. He lacked initiative, for to try was to risk another failure. He tended to over-respond to any show of kindness or friendliness and would become devoted to anyone who gave him affection and kindness.

Here we have the picture of the building of a social self which had no foundation of security, a neurotic personality built by a well-intentioned but unwise primary group, one which blighted the child's ego by criticism.

The building of an ego structure in a sympathetic and understanding primary group is an easy and normal process, but unless the ego is built strongly there, it is unlikely that the child will find an atmosphere where it can be built. In the more highly competitive relationships of school and community, ruthless competitive patterns of secondary groups prevail, leaving little room for the protection of a weak ego.

Continued sociological study is revealing the long-term effects of insecurity on personality and its lifelong adjustments. For example, studies of marriage show that the child who comes from an unhappy home, where a sense of security has been denied him, most often fails in marriage.[5] He tends to use love and affection as a device for restoring everything he has lost. His courtship may be extremely demanding; his marriage may also be much more demanding of affection and attention than it is possible for any individual to give another. On the negative side, such an individual usually employs aggressive tactics as defense reactions and may often manifest hostility, suspicion, and jealousy. In contrast, those who come from happy homes where a strong sense of security has been built usually make successful marriages.

The Balanced Ego Structure. Although the importance of affection and of being wanted by his primary group have been stressed as essential factors in the integrated personality, as has the tragic effect of primary group rejection in creating the disintegrated personality, *overprotection* of the growing ego is possible. The primary group, particularly parents, grandparents, or brothers and sisters, may shield the child too completely from competition. Too much shield-

---

[5] For a brief summary of researches on this subject, see Paul H. Landis, *Making the Most of Marriage* (New York: Appleton-Century-Crofts, Inc., 1955), chap. 11.

ing leaves him unprepared for the setbacks that will naturally occur when he shifts to competitive secondary groups outside of the family. Inasmuch as he has never had an opportunity to develop the toughness that life requires, his self-assurance may prove to be illusory.

The proper balance of success and failure, of warm affectionate responses in the primary group world and correction by it, is not precisely known. It most certainly differs with the hereditary temperament qualities of the person, particularly as they affect sensitivity, and with the patterns of the culture, which provide the individual and the group with their standards of competency.

THE SOCIAL SELF AND SOCIAL ROLES

The personality of the socialized individual, in its patterning of behavior, is a developed series of group-accepted routine habits and a more elaborate framework of group-conforming roles. These roles are defined by the particular group and the individual's behavior is in turn designed to measure up to group expectations.

To illustrate this theoretical conception, the following example from the autobiography of a sociology student is presented. It clearly outlines the expectations of the high-school clique for its members, expectations which had to be the guide to the behavior of any member who aspired to an acceptable status in the group.

This social group that I associated with throughout my school days in the community had its own standards by which to judge its members. In order for a member of the group to be held in highest esteem he must: (1) Be free from parent control, that is, be able to go when and where he pleased and do as he liked. (2) He must be a poor, or at the most an average, student. If he excelled in school work he was ousted and ridiculed by the group. (3) He had to take some part or be associated with one of the various athletic sports of the school. (4) He must not associate with girls as anyone who liked the company of girls or had a girl friend was ridiculed by the group. (5) He had to take part in all of the group's functions whether they were mischievous or not. (6) He had to be able to use tobacco and to have at one time or another drunk some form of hard liquor. (7) He had to have, at one time or another, caused one of the faculty members trouble and to have been kicked out of class at least once.

In the group described, each of the seven roles outlined were clearly identified with attaining or maintaining a desirable status or rank in the group. A person plays different parts in all such groups, whether family, the play group, the school group, and his action in any particular group is determined by the standards, practices, and expectations of that group. He shifts from role to role as the group situation demands.

He comes to appraise his status largely in terms of these various roles; in fact he is, as a person, largely a bundle of habits and atti-

tudes which are related to the particular roles he has had an opportunity to play in various social groups.

Self-estimates shift with role changes. In the family group one's
role may have been that of a big brother, little sister, mama's little
man. If in a play group, he becomes the hero, or is looked up to as
one who is superior in athletic prowess, he gains standing not only in
the group, but in his own eyes.

One tends to develop estimates of his social self that reflect the
attitudes of different groups in which he participates toward the roles
he plays. One's self-evaluation, therefore, often changes as he shifts
from group to group. Many a small-town star of the high-school football team, who has accepted the small-town evaluation at face value,
has had to recast his notions of his athletic role when he first tries out
with the college team. His old social self is badly deflated until he
develops a new scale of measurement. In time he rates himself by
new standards and derives a new conception of self with reference
to the athletic role or any other roles which the new group, because
of its more rigid standards of competition, rates differently.

Statuses attained in the various groups by a person as he plays the
respective social roles expected of him are a vital part in personality
formation. Those who play distinctive roles and achieve high status
tend to trust themselves and to respect themselves. They achieve self-
confidence that makes it possible for them to put themselves to
greater tests. This is essentially what is meant by the old proverb
"nothing succeeds like success."

SELF-CONCEPTION OF STATUS AND PERSONALITY PATTERNS

The broad statement made in the preceding paragraph must be
qualified in some measure. While the person's conception of himself
is a direct reflection of group evaluations of his roles, the individual
may not regard his achievement in any given situation as the group
does. He may be inclined to discount or to overrate his status.

Famed psychiatrist Karl A. Menninger in *The Human Mind* tells
of Herman Schmidt, who before psychiatric treatment felt himself to
be a complete failure.[6] He was elected repeatedly to positions of
highest responsibility and honor by his class, yet still felt he was des-
picable, the "lowest of the low," unworthy of trust and confidence.

Here obviously was a person whose conception of the importance
of his roles in the group was entirely out of line with the status the
group accorded him. He had high status among his peers, yet sensed

---

[6] Karl A. Menninger, *The Human Mind* (New York: Alfred A. Knopf, Inc., 1930),
pp. 61–62.

the guilt and uncertainty that usually goes with lack of success in playing social roles. Why?

If we were to bring all the Herman Schmidt types together, we would find much similarity in their backgrounds. Somewhere along the line they were the victim of severe group rejections; most likely it was their mother or father to begin with, and later playmates. At some painful time, their roles in social groups compared unfavorably with group expectations for them. An unfavorable conception of their rating by others became so overwhelmingly painful that it has stayed with them. Repeated success has not yet wiped it out, if indeed it can ever be completely erased.

They carry forward with them a social self guilt-ridden and tortured. Their personalities are torn by doubt and uncertainty even in the face of success in the new groups in which high status has been accorded them. In this they manifest neurotic tendencies. Their social self is not a unified whole, but a divided entity, with segments pulling in different directions. They are always tired, even though in perfect physical health.

They carry over from the past, in what Freud called the unconscious mind, a conception of a rejected and defeated social self, a conception in direct contrast to the actual status accorded them in new groups. In curative work, the psychoanalysts and psychiatrists try to probe back into the buried past of the tortured individual and bring these painful conflicts to the surface and free him from guilt and anxiety that resulted from his early defeat in making group adjustments.

In the case of the Herman Schmidt in Dr. Menninger's account, the father had been confined to a state mental hospital for a time during Herman's childhood. The mother stayed away from social functions and from other people and kept the child from associating with those of his own age for fear they would tease or mistreat him. The fear of group rejection on account of this past was still overwhelming, even though Herman was succeeding in his current school adjustments.

Temperament and Self-evaluation. It must be recognized that persons of different temperament react in different ways to the success or failure in playing various group roles. Some individuals of sensitive temperament who have suffered little defeat develop painful feelings of social inadequacy. Others of tougher temperament who have been defeated frequently in their attempts to find an important place in some group or groups may suffer less intensely. Those individuals who become habituated to feeling inferior in various group roles in time become victims of an inferiority complex.

An inferiority complex is a set of emotionally toned attitudes developed through experiences which give one a sense of failure in every undertaking. Certainly Herman had an inferiority complex.

It must be concluded from this study that it is important to recognize not only the actual status one has in his group, but also his own evaluation of that status. They are likely to be similar, but not necessarily identical. In some cases an individual may have suffered from unfavorable social status in so many situations as a child that he has developed a habitual attitude of self-criticism and devaluation. Later, even when he encounters favorable reactions from the group, he is still self-derogatory and cannot accept the status given him. Others more tough in temperament *compensate* and refuse to recognize unfavorable group opinions, strengthening their ego by braggadocio behavior or cold, self-sufficient aloofness.

THE SOCIAL SELF AND PERSONALITY INTEGRATION

The preceding discussion has illustrated a characteristic of personality which has key meaning in any analysis: *integration.* By *personality integration* the sociologist means *the coordination of the various social selves in such a way that the person can make an effective response to the social environment.* If the selves are not integrated, the person is torn by internal tensions and conflicts. The internal tensions become obvious to others in social maladjustment, that is, in the inability of the person to function effectively in the group.

Herman Schmidt's internal tensions reflected the conflict between the social self he had developed in the past, when as a recluse he was fearful lest the school groups or playmates know his disgrace, and the present one of a respected leader of the group. The conflict became so overwhelming that he dropped out of school. He could not face group adjustments any longer; in other words, his lack of personality integration expressed itself in social maladjustment. It was at this point that the case was brought to the psychiatrist, who helped to restore harmony between his inner social selves. This done, he was able to function in the group as a reasonably well-adjusted person.

In a complex society, in which all have played roles in many social groups, all carry forward many social selves, some of which, when brought together by new group situations, cause a great deal of strain. Whether the strain is sufficient to make one ineffective as a social participant depends upon the violence of the internal conflict that results.

For example, in the period of youthful conquests, some young men and young women overstep the boundaries of chastity, maybe even becoming temporarily quite promiscuous in sexual relationships. Such a role in some youth groups is an accepted one in spite of the mores of the larger society. The real difficulty is likely to come when the young person involved begins to face the problem of marriage, where virginity, chastity, loyalty to one member of the opposite sex, and parenthood are all in the pattern of adult group expectancy. Many are involved in such painful conflicts that their normal social participation may become very difficult. Particularly for the girl is the reconciling of the two roles often a major crisis, both in personality integration and in social adjustment. In her case, the expectations of the group make the reconciling of the two roles much more difficult than for the boy, for the very reason that the social group, because of a dual standard, holds that the two roles are, in part at least, acceptable for men. Leaving the community of one's acquaintance removes group pressures, and for some the mental conflicts. Others of more sensitive temperament carry the internal conflict with them in spite of anonymity.

BUILDING THE SOCIAL SELF IN GROUPS—CASE HISTORIES

It has been shown that the social self, the status-seeking aspect of personality—or ego, to use Freudian terminology—is developed through group experience. The part of the primary group in building the social self, and the roles the individual has played in his groups from childhood up—all are vital. Statuses gained in these group situations determine one's evaluation of himself. To summarize the theory concerning the effect of group experience on personality and to make it more concrete, three case histories of college youths are presented. The first is that of a college girl whose various roles, as reflected in the "looking glass" of social groups, made of her several different personalities during her transition from childhood to maturity. She was a robust tomboy until suddenly stricken and taken to the hospital for a serious operation, after which she became an invalid for six months. There she had at her beck and call her mother. As the girl herself expresses it, "I was the owner of a woman who would come at my slightest yell, the baby darling of the sisters, and the recipient of constant gifts from friends of the family."

After six months in the hospital the rude awakening came, "No one told me that I was no longer the pretty little girl I had been when

I came—and the first sight I caught of myself was an awful blow. With a shaved head and only half my previous weight I looked like a starving child. I found the security I had built up in the affection showered on me in the hospital rudely shattered."

Finding herself unable to adjust to the school group when she returned to school, she became involved emotionally in her family. The family, sensing this, thought it necessary to transplant her to a new environment where she could find a satisfactory new role for herself. She was sent to boarding school. On this experience she comments:

The next few months were, as I remember them, nothing but torture. We lived by bells, were disciplined severely, and spent so much time on our knees praying that my knees soon developed "prayer bones"—calluses of a most sturdy sort. My reaction to this forced absorption of the standards of a different group was most violent and the pains of loneliness made me antagonistic. I pleaded with my mother to allow me to come home, but without effect. Never I hope, will I be in an environment which will frustrate me so completely as that environment did. Life would have been unbearable but for a Sister who looked like my aunt and who also bore a resemblance to my mother. Soon I drew close to her and through her built up a new feeling of security. Before long I was planning to seek security throughout my whole life in the order of the Holy Names.

She then describes her experience on transferring to an outside school group and the long and painful process of learning to adjust herself to an out-group. She and another girl who was similarly maladjusted decided to take the bold step of becoming junior hostesses during the war at the officers' club in a nearby community. She comments on this, "We were both scared stiff. I came to think of us as sufferers together. We moped around feeling lonesome."

Then she describes the final experience which helped her to develop a strong social self. She says:

At last an incident came which shaped me into the person I am today. It was the crisis that came with my father's death. To remove suddenly the person who for years has been one's bulwark against the world was a blow to the whole family, especially to my mother. Suddenly I found myself becoming maternal toward my own mother. She was in such a desperate frame of mind she wouldn't eat or sleep except by the determination of our doctor. She would have soon joined Dad if it hadn't been for our doctor's persistence. Meanwhile I tried to help her as much as I could. In this experience I grew up to the extent that even now when I come home from college on vacation she talks to me as she used to talk to Dad, telling me her plans, worries, and funny stories. Now I am treated as an adult in the family. This change in my mother's eyes has given me a new sense of my own status and a new respect for myself. Yes, I finally became aware that there is someone else outside myself and in making this discovery after Daddy's death I found also the key to bring me all the things I've wanted. My status, as reflected by family and friends, is such that my social self is sufficiently satisfied to keep me a happy and adjusted person.

To illustrate further the building of the self in social group, con-sider the case history of a college youth who compares his roles and statuses throughout childhood and youth with those of his older brothers, and particularly one older brother under whose shadow he lived until adulthood. The case is convincing evidence that heredity is not the only variable with which one must reckon in the family; the environmental forces often affect children within the same fam-ily differently. Seldom do two children in the same family grow up subject to the same social influences.

The case is that of a youth of Russian descent who grew up on a North Dakota farm, isolated three miles from neighbors, with only his older brothers for playmates. He was teased and pestered by them, never able to keep up with them in their group games, always considered the little boy who was not able to do the things they were doing. Even when he started to school he was expected to tell his parents the meanness the older boys got into, which tended to further exclude him from the brothers' inner circle. As a conse-quence, he developed feelings of inferiority and frustration which, he indicated at the time of writing his autobiography in college, were still with him.

In school he was unable to equal the performance of one brother in particular, the one just above him in age. He always felt inferior. In each new school situation from grade school through high school into college, his parents and teachers expected him to play the exact role of his next older brother, who was an outstanding success in scholastic activities, school leadership, and football.

Later when the older boy enlisted in the army the younger boy could find no peace until he entered the army also, but even there the older boy's record at first exceeded his own. Finally the older brother was captured in Germany. The younger brother working up in the Air Corps eventually equalled his position, but even then the old inferiority complex tended to plague him and he found himself daydreaming of flying to Germany and somehow rescuing his older brother and bringing him back safe and sound, thereby making him-self the hero of the family.

It was not until the older brother was finally released from the German prison camp and on returning home stopped to visit the younger one that a comradeship and sense of equality developed. At last they seemed to be equals and to treat each other as such. It was not until that point that the feeling of inferiority that the younger brother had harbored for years gradually began to disappear.

But he was not yet through. When he returned to college he was pushed by the students into being a candidate for the student body presidency, the same job his brother had filled while in college. He reports that he actually experienced elation when he was defeated for the office, feeling that at last a chain of events which had bound him to follow in his brother's footsteps had been broken and that he was an individual on his own.

The final case is that of a mobile youth, too foot-loose to find a stable group in which to achieve a certain place. Born in Switzerland, he came with his parents to the East and then to the West Coast where they followed the crops as farm laborers.

I have glided down the stream of life too fast to lodge long enough to grow roots. I have not stayed in one place the proper length of time to associate myself closely with any one environment. "Where's he gone?" and "Where're you from?" have been asked altogether too often in my life. I have drifted by and watched the scenes on the bank reel past. This has led me to be a spectator, not an actor. This hesitancy about jumping into the activities of men is one of my most serious deficiencies. Even now I cannot take an interest in the playworld activities of campus life. It remains to be seen whether I can apply myself in my chosen field and assume my share of the burden of the community.

As an introvert in a transient life I learned to know myself only too well, but the view was too close up and the image blurred and distorted. I saw fears that had no substance. I imagined peculiar and base attributes which I thought no one else had. The knowledge that others experienced similar fears and saw similar flaws in their make-up has taken the novelty of looking only at myself away. I have since learned that one's personality is mirrored in the faces and attributes we see in others. Lately I have not been seeing as many nightmares as formerly and I am somewhat more self-assured.

DISCUSSION AND REVIEW QUESTIONS

1. What did La Barre mean in saying societies "manufacture their own misfits"?

2. Distinguish between the psychical and psychological selves. Trace their development.

3. What did Cooley mean when he said "self and society are twin born"?

4. Show how the physical self differs from the looking-glass picture one sees reflected in social groups.

5. What does the psychiatrist mean by the ego? The conscience?

6. Compare the newer positive psychology of human nature with the former negative approach.

7. What values and attitudes does Maslow feel need to be stressed in child training?

8. Show how the primary group builds a weak or strong social self in the child.

9. Explain the concepts of rejection and underprotection.

10. Relate childhood security to marriage success and failure.

11. Describe the neurotic symptoms of the underprotected child.

12. Discuss the problem of overprotection.

13. Show how social roles in a particular group affect the development of the social self.

14. Show how a person's conception of his role may affect his social adjustment.

15. What do we mean by personality integration, or the integration of the social self?

16. Cite case history evidence that personality is a product of group experience.

SOURCEBOOK READINGS

GITTLER, JOSEPH B. *Social Dynamics.* New York: McGraw-Hill Book Co., Inc., 1952.
  1. GITTLER, with a quotation from Cooley, "The Genesis of the Self," pp. 46–53.

KOENIG, SAMUEL, REX D. HOPPER, and FELIKS GROSS. *Sociology: A Book of Readings.* Englewood Cliffs, N.J.: Prentice-Hall, Inc., 1956.
  2. LA BARRE, WESTON, "Wanted: A More Adequate Culture," pp. 55–62.
  3. HORNEY, KAREN, "The Neo-Freudian View: Man for Himself," pp. 65–67.
  4. MASLOW, A. H., "The 'Good Savage' View: A Modern Version," pp. 68–72.
  5. BROWN, L. GUY, "The 'Emergent' View: Man a Candidate for Personality," pp. 72–74.
  6. LANGER, IRVING, "What Is Normal Behavior?" pp. 112–15.

O'BRIEN, ROBERT W., CLARENCE C. SCHRAG, and WALTER T. MARTIN. *Readings in General Sociology* (2d ed.). Boston: Houghton Mifflin Co., 1957.
  7. LINDESMITH, ALFRED R., and ANSELM L. STRAUSS, "The Social Self," pp. 186–89.

SELECTED READINGS

BAIN, READ. "Making Normal People," *Marriage and Family Living,* 16:27–31 (Feb., 1954).

COOLEY, CHARLES H. *Human Nature and the Social Order.* New York: Charles Scribner's Sons, 1902.

FARIS, ROBERT E. L. *Social Psychology.* New York: The Ronald Press Co., 1952.

FULLER, JOHN F. *Nature and Nurture: A Modern Synthesis.* Doubleday Papers in Psychology. Garden City, N.Y.: Doubleday & Co., Inc., 1954.

GERTH, HANS, and C. WRIGHT MILLS. *Character and Personality.* New York: Harcourt, Brace & Co., Inc., 1953.

GESELL, ARNOLD, *et al. The First Five Years of Life.* New York: Harper & Brothers, 1940.

GUTHRIE, E. R. *The Psychology of Learning.* Rev. ed.; New York: Harper & Brothers, 1952.

HARDING, D. W. *Social Psychology and Individual Values.* London: Hutchinson & Co., 1953.

KARDINER, ABRAM. *The Psychological Frontiers of Society.* New York: Columbia University Press, 1945.

KLUCKHOHN, CLYDE, and A. H. MURRAY (eds.). *Personality in Nature, Society and Culture.* New York: Alfred A. Knopf, Inc., 1948.

LANDIS, PAUL H. *Making the Most of Marriage.* New York: Appleton-Century-Crofts, Inc., 1955, chaps. 11, 26–28.

MEAD, GEORGE H. *Mind, Self and Society.* (Edited by C. W. Morris.) Chicago: University of Chicago Press, 1934.

MOUSTAKAS, CLARK E. (ed.). *The Self: Explorations in Personal Growth.* New York: Harper & Brothers, 1956.

NEWCOMB, THEODORE M. *Social Psychology.* New York: The Dryden Press, Inc., 1950.

SCHWEITZER, ALBERT. *Out of My Life and Thought.* New York: Henry Holt & Co., Inc., 1949.

Chapter **26**

The Frustration of the Social Self

The preceding chapter has shown that every society, for that matter every family, manufactures the kind of people it contains. Human beings must be shaped. Shaping can be along the lines of the individual's own growth toward self-realization and self-acceptance or it can be such as to multiply frustrations to the point where he has a basic anxiety about life. The self may be cultivated, nourished, expanded, made independent and free. Or it may be denied, criticized, and thwarted until fear and uncertainty become the pattern of life.

The account which follows is the autobiography, presented in a letter to a psychiatrist, of a woman who begins to find her "real self" after 38 hours of psychoanalysis. It is the story of a once frustrated and defeated individual. The frustration built up was not that of a maze of physical obstacles; it was a maze of social taboos, of "Thou shalt nots," of negatives in the training patterns which eventually instilled in her an overwhelming sense of the futility of life. She shows herself first as a completely frustrated individual and, later, as one who achieves social expression as normal human beings do.

Dear Dr. X:

. . . Until now I have known nothing, understood nothing, and perforce could love nothing, and for the simple, unbelievable reason that I wasn't here! For over forty years I have been exiled from myself without even suspecting it.

Merely to understand this, now, is tremendous. It is not only the end of all that dying, it is to begin life.

The story begins with your friendship, your generosity—when I was almost too sick to receive it. In the deepest sense that *was* my sickness. I couldn't be friends; I had never been free, humanly, nor ever wanted to be. And you did

464

somehow get through in spite of me, although two years more were to pass before this final chapter. The end, now, the opening of the door, belongs to my present analyst, Dr. Y . . .

The first thing she tackled was that which was readiest at hand: my cast-iron "should system." My complete armor of "shoulds": duty, ideals, pride, guilt. This rigid and compulsive perfectionism was all that held me up; outside it and all around lay chaos . . . She let me talk, fumble, stop, turn, begin again, always going in circles until at last, little by little even *I* could begin to see what sort of strait jacket held me: I existed only because I *should!* I began to mention "spontaneity"—to dare think of it, and at last to realize how I longed for it—I who had always deliberately fought it, even in childhood! And Dr. Y pointed out that there is an inverse ratio between genuine, spontaneous feelings and the "should system."

Then . . . she played a trump card—daring to play it so early in the game. Just four words! An apparently innocent, even naive question; but it was loaded. As she put it: "Perhaps there isn't even an answer to this as yet . . . but what *do* you want, really?"

I tried to keep it from striking home and retreated any way I could to defend what was still my sole *raison d'etre*, but within hours the medicine began to work way down inside me. For the first time in my life I saw that I was quite simply unable to *want* anything, not even death! And certainly not "life." Until now I had thought my trouble was just that I was unable to *do* things: unable to give up my dream, unable to gather up my own things, unable to accept or control my irritability, unable to make myself more human, whether by sheer will power, patience, or grief.

Now, for the first time I saw it—I was literally unable to *feel* anything. (Yes, for all my famous super-sensitivity!) How well I knew pain—every pore of me clogged with inward rage, self-pity, self-contempt, and despair for the last six years over and over again and again! Yet, I saw it now—all was negative, reactive, compulsive, *all imposed from without; inside* there was absolutely nothing of mine! There just was nothing. Had I been a little less numb I suppose I'd at last have cut my throat. And Dr. Y knew it.

This was it. the crisis, the turning point.

I went home and began once more to think down to the bottom of my rootlessness. Perhaps a week or two passed.

There is only one way out of chaos; and now that I knew all the other doors were locked, I made the tremendous discovery . . . I had discovered the very core and essence of neurosis—my neurosis and perhaps every neurosis. The secret of wretchedness was SELFLESSNESS! Deep and hidden, the fact and the fear of not having a self. Not being a self. Not-being. And at the end—actual chaos . . .

I saw now all the way down, how and why, and how completely neurotic *needs* come to replace desires . . . until you are canceled out. One couldn't ask a starved man, a dead man, if he would *prefer* oysters to caviar; cut off from desires the very concept of *choice* cannot exist. Here at the end of this thought I had seen how neurosis happens and what it's all about. Selflessness! (The lack of self, of selfhood, of entity, of integrity.)

How is it possible to lose a self? The treachery, unknown and unthinkable, begins with our secret psychic death in childhood—if and when we are not loved and are cut off from our spontaneous wishes. (Think: What is left?) But wait—it is not just this simple murder of a psyche. That might be written off, the tiny victim might even "outgrow" it—but it is a perfect double crime in which he himself also gradually and unwittingly takes part. He has not been accepted for himself, *as he is*.

Oh, they "love" him, but they want him or force him or expect him to be different! Therefore *he must be unacceptable*. He himself learns to believe it and at last even takes it for granted. He has truly given himself up. No matter now whether he obeys them, whether he clings, rebels or withdraws—his behavior, his performance is all that matters. His center of gravity is in "them," not in himself—yet if he so much as noticed it he'd think it natural enough. And the whole thing is entirely plausible; all invisible, automatic, and anonymous!

This is the perfect paradox. Everything looks normal; no crime was intended; there is no corpse, no guilt. All we can see is the sun rising and setting as usual. But what has happened? He has been rejected, not only by them, but by himself. (He is actually without a self.) What has he lost? Just the one true and vital part of himself: his own yes-feeling, which is his very capacity for growth, his root system. But alas, he is not dead. "Life" goes on, and so must he. From the moment he gives himself up, and to the extent that he does so, all unknowingly he sets about to create and maintain a pseudo-self. But this is an expediency—a "self" without wishes. This one shall be loved (or feared) where he is despised, strong where he is weak; it shall go through the motions . . . not for fun or joy but for survival; not simply because it wants to move but because it has to obey. This necessity is not life—not his life—it is a defense mechanism against death. It is also the machine of death. From now on he will be torn apart by compulsive (unconscious) *needs* or ground by (unconscious) conflicts into paralysis, every motion and every instant canceling out his being, his integrity; and all the while he is disguised as a normal person and expected to behave like one!

In a word, I saw that we *become* neurotic seeking or defending a pseudo-self, a self-system; and we *are* neurotic to the extent that we are self-less . . .

The clue is that word *want*—to wish, not to need. You know, as I do, that the neurotic, so far as he is neurotic, is no longer able simply to want or wish anything but is driven right, left, and around in circles by his compulsive needs, which can never be less than absolute starvation. He really does need everything, desperately, and therefore *cannot* give up anything; and there is no solution. He *has* no choice; alternatives he has (many, and all bad), but *who is there* to do the choosing? . . .

He cannot will because he cannot even wish! Almost literally he is not there. He may strive desperately toward his goal and never make it (or at what a cost!), because *it isn't he* that is doing the striving. His real self is stifled by the neurosis . . .

If our human purpose is to live and grow and express ourselves, then the *chance to grow* is everything—for it takes years, even with incalculable love or luck, to walk and wind our own willingness through the whole structure of things. Yet it is this willingness we can't afford to give up. It is our sole strength, our wish to live! Who gives it up, from fear or force, has to that extent lost himself; he is emasculated . . . and sold into slavery and compulsion . . . You cannot will yourself to *want* a thing! I know. I've tried for years.

One thing only separates "I should," or "I need," from the simplest "I do want"—and that is not *choice* but the *freedom to choose*. . . .

Personality development is deeply influenced by childhood experiences. Will this child become a secure, well-integrated person? On what will the answer depend? (Standard Oil Company, N. J.)

Who . . . would not rather *be himself*, affectionate and free, if he could afford it? No other self is free to feel, to express our nature, to know another and be known. This alone is the human self, that can go out; that can love, and endure, and be loved—because it wants to live.[1]

It is clear that the crux of this woman's difficulty was the frustrating of normal wishes until neurotic symptoms made her unable to function at all. Consumed by her anxieties, she sought psychiatric help. Relief came when she was freed from the restrictive inhibitions raised by normal wishes and began to express them as individuals with a positive orientation to life and society do.

Sociologists have long recognized wishes as a normal and inherent part of the socialized personality and have concluded that they must be expressed if the individual is to function as a human being.

THOMAS' FOUR WISHES THEORY

The most famous list of wishes by a sociologist is that developed by W. I. Thomas, who concluded that human beings have four basic wishes.[2] Whether his list of four is adequate or not, whether the wishes he names have an organic basis or reflect only values of our culture need not concern us here. His list is illustrative of the kind of striving which all do in an attempt to fulfill their social needs.

The wish for *new experience* leads one to seek variety in life. Some express this wish by travel, some by reading about the imaginary or fantastic, many by venturing into new social situations, slumming, or trying out new types of creative activity. Man is much a creature of habit, but living entirely on one habit level can become boring. New experience relieves monotony and gives zest to life.

Almost directly in contrast is the wish for *security*. Individuals want a safe haven to which they can flee in trouble. They want the assurance that they can always drop back into the primary group where they will be welcome, given affection, and made to feel their worth-whileness. Everyone needs someone to come home to. In the family group this security is given children by affectionate parents, husband and wife by each other. Those who lack a family group may find it in a comrade, a pal, or a buddy.

Thomas was thinking of security not primarily in the economic sense, as it is being used so often today, but in the psychological sense, the sense of knowing that one is wanted, that he means a

---

[1] "Finding the Real Self," a letter by a person who, during psychoanalytic treatment, found her real self. Published by psychoanalyst Karen Horney in *The American Journal of Psychoanalysis*, 9:3–8 (1949).

[2] For the best brief statement of Thomas' theory, see his *The Unadjusted Girl* (Boston: Little, Brown & Co., 1923).

great deal to someone. It is a sense of belonging such as the great French sociologist Émile Durkheim felt was indispensable to man. In Durkheim's theory of suicide, he stated the view that suicide is primarily the result of feeling that one has been entirely forsaken by others, left alone and unwanted, completely isolated from mankind.[3] Both Thomas and Durkheim concluded that he who travels in an intimate group travels life's highway most safely.

The third wish discerned by Thomas is the wish for *response*. In this wish is expressed man's longing for friendship and love. Men need to love and to be loved. This was dramatically illustrated in the case of infants denied love in the South American foundling home (see p. 135). Response finds its most intimate expression in the sex experience of married life.

The fourth wish is that for *recognition*. The individual wishes to be appreciated by his fellows, or in other words to have status in various social groups. Status is so closely associated with one's social self that man requires an expression of recognition from the group to bolster his self-respect and make him feel that he is useful and important.

Like Thomas, Alfred Adler, the psychiatrist who formulated the theory of the *inferiority complex*, made a great deal of this desire for recognition; in fact, he made it the basis for his psychological theories.[4] He believed that the individual, failing to achieve recognition from his fellows, strives more desperately to attain it through *compensation*, that is, overreacting.

VALUES TOWARD WHICH WISHES ARE DIRECTED

Thomas' wishes are highly suggestive of forces in human behavior, but one must recognize in approaching them from a sociological viewpoint that the particular methods of their expression, the values toward which they are directed, are determined by the society in which the individual lives. The culture of one people makes eternal life the supreme value of human striving; that of another, material success. The channels that new experience will seek out differ vastly for those who have a world-wide view of geography and those who have never been outside their isolated mountain valley. The kind of parental treatment that builds security in the child differs immensely in a Polish immigrant home, where the tradition of beating children and shaping them to parental authority is accepted by parent and child alike, and in a democratic American family, where

[3] Émile Durkheim, *Le Suicide* (Paris, 1887). English edition published by The Free Press, Glencoe, Illinois, 1951.

[4] Alfred Adler, *The Patterns of Life* (New York: Cosmopolitan Book Co., 1930).

affection is expected by the child and where its denial leaves him insecure and anxious.[5]

The kind of response expected in marriage is far different among various peoples. In modern marriages youth expect to find supreme happiness, to merge all major problems and anxieties in a wedding ceremony. Our ancestors expected marriage to be the beginning of a life of work, child-rearing, mutual economic struggle. They took seriously that part of the ceremony which said "in sickness and in health."

The amount of recognition demanded and the way it may be obtained differ vastly from culture to culture. In one social group prestige is obtained by giving away everything one has; in ours, by the accumulation of wealth and the display of economic goods. In some societies intense competition, always trying to get ahead of the other fellow, is frowned upon. In ours, most recognition from childhood up comes from successful competition. The desire for social approval, recognition, is always present in any group and the values which the group holds uppermost determine the channels of activity through which the individual will strive to attain it.

The blocking of channels of expression by the social group leads to a thwarting of the wishes or learned drives. One with thwarted wishes is said to be *frustrated*.

FRUSTRATION

Failure to satisfy wishes through achieving those values which have become most meaningful to the individual dams up energy and leads to what is called in psychological language frustration, or what sociologist Graham Wallas called "balked dispositions." Frustrated wishes are the principal causes of personal hostility and aggression, for one who is not able to satisfy his wishes in social groups fights others.

Causes of Frustration. One common source of frustration is the conflict of organic drives with social codes. The animal in man is always present. Over animal nature has been imposed the habit and attitude structure which keeps it well under control in most situations, yet the animal must at times be reckoned with. In much of popular literature, as well as psychological and sociological thought, attention has been directed toward this basic conflict between man's original nature and society's restrictions. It is the fascinating theme of much of modern fiction.

[5] For evidence see Arnold W. Green, "The Middle Class Male Child and Neurosis," *American Sociological Review*, 11:31–41 (1946).

Sigmund Freud built a whole system of psychology around the view that certain cultures suppress the libido, or sex urge, so completely that neurotic behavior tends to be characteristic. He developed the thesis that man has an unconscious mind level in which unpleasant and frustrating experiences are submerged. If too many submerged conflicts accumulate, they completely disrupt the normal functioning of the conscious mind. Psychoanalytical treatment in which the analyst, by questioning, brings to the surface of consciousness the submerged experiences is required to help the individual recognize his conflict and resolve it.

We are not so much concerned here with particular theories but with the important fact that organic drives, natural urges, and appetites at many points run counter to social codes. This is a source of mental conflict and creates a situation calling for adjustment.

Most frustrations of man in society have to do with *interpersonal relations*. Failure to achieve the favorable recognition of groups which are meaningful to one is the cause of serious frustration. So, also, failure to achieve response in romantic love often leads to violent emotional upset and calls for readjustment of one's world. Failure to realize a single ambition may frustrate a basic wish. For example, many a girl when she failed during pledge week to get into a college sorority has felt as though her whole future was darkened, her way forward blocked. She had expected through the sorority to climb the social ladder to new heights, to gain a new level of recognition. Likely as not even her parents also expected to obtain favorable recognition from this achievement of their daughter.

Serious frustration, such as that caused by the loss of security through marriage conflict and divorce, through failure to achieve membership in the sorority or fraternity, failure to obtain a college degree and the recognition which goes with the sheepskin, leaves the individual defeated or else faced with the requirement of reordering his world so that his wishes may be achieved through some other means. He may submerge his defeat in the unconscious. This device, as we have seen, is considered a dangerous procedure. Freud's psychological theories hold that the unconscious must always be reckoned with. Repressed frustration continues in the subconscious. In case of extreme suppression, it may lead to neurotic behavior or more serious mental difficulties.

Adjustment Mechanisms. Adjustment to frustration may be made by the substitution of one goal for another or one value for another. *Escape* is another type of adjustment. It may be into the world of fantasy through daydreaming or the reading of fiction. It may be

through drink or, in the case of woman, the socially sanctioned avenues of imaginary sickness. It may be through a life of hermitage or
by way of a nervous breakdown.

A young man frustrated in social response by his stuttering describes his escape in daydreaming and neurotic behavior, when after
joining a club to relieve his desire for group recognition he fails to
attain it. He writes:

After going through the arduous initiation period and becoming a member
of the club, I suppose that I thought that my social adjustment was complete.
To be sure, this was not the case. As a matter of fact, it seemed to me that I
was now more maladjusted than ever. Upon joining the club, I was in contact
and also in competition with people who were, for the most part, very gregarious and socially inclined. For a person who was often ill at ease, as I certainly
was, this was rather one-sided competition. Quite naturally my part was not one
of leadership, but one of following, if I were to be one of the group. This concept was wholly unacceptable to me and I fought it for quite a time. Then
slowly it was that I lapsed into one of the worst pitfalls that a neurotic encounters—the daydreaming vice. If my thwarted ego could not be saved in the
everyday world, I certainly could protect it in a world of my own making. This
is precisely what I did, unconsciously, of course. In due time, my daydreams
had become so dear to me that I had little desire to strive for actual recognition
of attainment in the outside world. Why should I? In my world I was the central figure of every situation—the perfect leader and never a follower. The theme
of my thinking, and it soon became an obsession, was that if only I had fluent
speech, these dreams of mine would not be dreams but would be in fact a
reality.

This affliction of mine became my excuse for every failure. Did I have a poor
grade in my history class? Only because I couldn't (or wouldn't) recite in class.
Did I fail to make a terrific impression on that new girl that I had just met? If
only I hadn't stuttered to her on the telephone, she would surely be more
friendly toward me by now.

In the following case, a young man frustrated in love resorted to
drink. It is an account by a college youth, returned from service as
an ensign in the South Pacific.

Within a year after leaving the States, I received my "Dear John" letter. It
was like millions that were sent out to servicemen overseas in which the wife or
fiancee states that she still thinks a lot of him and wants him to keep writing,
but that his best friend has been taking her out and they are engaged now.

All interest in my work, which up to now had been of high caliber, was gone,
and my only aim in life was to stay drunk enough not to be able to remember,
but sober enough to be able to sign my name to the work which now was dele-
gated to others to prepare.

The unpleasant event of the letter was followed by a year of intensive and
dangerous drunkenness during which my overseas time expired and I was sent
home for an honorable discharge. My arrival home was chaotic. I sincerely
wished to avoid hurting either of my parents by my misconduct, but was unable to avoid their becoming aware of the extent of my maladjustment and of
their being caused considerable discomfort thereby. A good many of my closest

friends were beset by the same difficulties, and fortunately civilians had been well warned to expect it of us. Fortunately, my parents were very understanding, and although not reconciled to the circumstances, made no issue of it. Slowly their understanding began to sink in and I began to search within myself for an answer to my problem. The full answer has not yet been found—adjustment is not complete even now—but what remains to be answered is negligible, improvement has been so great. It has been such a short time ago—only two years since the peak of maladjustment and less time since drunkenness began to lose its dangerous aspects—that it is very difficult to discover just how my readjustment came about.

Another common mechanism of adjustment is *compensation,* that is, overreacting in an attempt to gain desired recognition. A fellow who wants to get into a fraternity but is not selected may strive desperately in athletics or scholarship to achieve recognition in his group even above that which might have come from fraternity membership.

Another device is that of *regression,* which is resorting to a more infantile level of behavior. Adolescents in some of their adjustment struggles revert to baby talk.

A person may also resort to *projection.* This, in a case of serious frustration, usually takes the form of attributing one's failures to others; in fact, attributing to others faults he himself has. It is a good deal like the primitive practice of burning an enemy in effigy.

Or one may find vicarious satisfaction in becoming identified with some great hero of literature, fiction, or screen. This is known as *identification.*

Finally, one may attempt to justify himself by devising good reasons for his failure rather than facing the real cause. This common mental practice, of which all are guilty to some extent, is known as *rationalization.* It is a way of excusing social failure to oneselves or others. The youth with the stutter, in the first case above, used this device as well as escape, as was suggested in the last paragraph of his account.

The extent to which one uses these various adjustment mechanisms probably depends upon the extent to which his basic wishes are frustrated or fulfilled. Those who are often frustrated resort to many adjustment mechanisms and use them often in self-defense. Those who usually realize the fulfillment of their wishes find comparatively little need for protective devices and the occasional frustration may be so well balanced by repeated success that it requires little effort for satisfactory adjustment.

FRUSTRATION AND AGGRESSION

In a competitive society, where all characteristically look ahead toward goals to be achieved and resent deeply any interference with them, the natural reaction of the human being to extreme frustration is aggression. He is militant and hostile toward the person or group that frustrates him.

In a competitive society, from childhood all are taught to use subtle forms of behavior rather than overt aggression, yet from childhood onward smothered tendencies are there. Take, for example, the first-born child. When he sees the new baby beginning to get most of the attention of parents, and a great deal of their affection, his own social self is frustrated and aggressive behavior is the natural result. He may feel like picking the baby's eyes out, but after a few assaults on the new baby the parents are likely to impose such a severe penalty that he has to work out his frustration in some other way or submerge it. Of course, the wise parent tries to create an attitude on the part of the first-born which will give him a sense of responsibility and pride in the new brother or sister. Thus the situation is changed from one of frustration for him to one which will minister to his feelings of status and security.

Perhaps there is no better way to clarify and summarize the frustration–aggression theory than to present an actual case of a college girl who is setting forth her account at a stage in life when she is just beginning to escape frustration. She writes:

My name is Carol. Although I am in college, I still feel like a little girl on tiptoe looking into a warm room of companionship through a cold window of loneliness. If people knew I felt that way, they would say it was impossible for a child in a family of seven to feel alone, but I can assure them that it is only too real. I was born on a farm near Kansas City, Missouri, in a very close-knit family group. Every Sunday I was queen of a large gathering of relatives, since I was the only small child in the group, but this high status was soon shattered as the family increased in size. When we moved from Kansas to a Western state, my real loneliness began. There we had no relatives and there were no friends. My father had a low-paying job. The family steadily increased in size. With each new arrival there was a tightening of the family budget and new responsibility was placed on me.

For as long as I can remember, I have been given the responsibility of all my younger brothers and sisters. I have never been a child playing with them. I have always been a small and efficient overseer. My brothers and sisters soon regarded me as someone to hide from because they couldn't have fun when I was around. When the family went to town on Saturday, I was hardly ever allowed to go along. My parents didn't want to be bothered with all of the children so left some behind for Carol to take care of. They always assumed that Carol could not only take care of herself but also of the younger ones. "Leave Carol" is a phrase I learned to hate. I became indifferent to my parents and was unable to play with children my own age. I simply did not know how to get along with them. More and more I withdrew within myself. For the lack of affection of my parents and lack of association with others, I compensated in daydreams and by stroking the more sensitive parts of my body. As I grew older, I retired further and further within myself and played fascinating games in my imagination.

Later as Carol went away to school she freed herself from the family and gradually began to form friendships and to gain some new sense of freedom from parental authority and from burdensome responsibility. Once when she returned home for a vacation, another child had been born to the family. She expresses her extreme resentment at having this new child in the family. "I felt hostile toward him and refused to pick him up for any cause. The new baby symbolized all my frustration and defeat of the year." It was not until she got completely away to college that she lost this feeling of hostility (aggression) toward the new baby.

SOCIAL ROLES IN WISH FULFILLMENT

The various roles society defines for different age and sex groups vitally affect the extent to which it is possible for them, through the normal channels of activity, to satisfy their wishes through the realization of values sought. Consequently the amount of wish fulfillment experienced differs a great deal from individual to individual and group to group.

Racial Roles. What opportunity does an educated Negro trained to seek the values of the white man's world have of realizing his wishes? His is likely to be a life of repeated frustration, if he ever dares dream of participating fully in the security, recognition, and status which an educated man has a right to expect in America.

The gradual awakening of a Negro youth to his social limitations has been described by a sociologist who takes the case of a Negro boy born in the Northeast, where as a child he participated as an equal in a school which accepted members of both races.[6] His family was respected in the community, his parents being old settlers. In this community there was practically no stratification. His family had been skilled workers or public servants and enjoyed the high level of social acceptance which these occupations bring in any community. Throughout most of his childhood and grade-school experience, there was little occasion to be reminded that his skin color was different from that of his playmates. Upon reaching high-school age, where dancing and the mixing of the sexes begin, discrimination became evident. Gradually he adjusted himself to the role of not participating in dances and other intimate associations which might prove to be socially awkward. He still enjoyed great success in sports, however, so felt no particular discrimination or unjust treatment.

[6] Arden R. King, "Status Personality Changes in Northern Negroes in Southern United States," *Social Forces,* 26:153–66 (Dec. 1947).

In college social separation became even more severe, although there was no race discrimination as such. He got a major rebuff in traveling with the football team. He and another Negro were refused admittance to the student-union building of a college. Later, when he returned with white friends, he was, however, admitted. Another shock came when he was not elected to Phi Beta Kappa, even though some white individuals who ranked lower were chosen.

It was not until he moved to the South after completing his college degree that he came into contact with the real caste system which separates the races in the United States. He had been warned by his family and friends what he must do in order to get along peacefully with the Southern white. His first shock upon arriving in the South came upon alighting from the train. He found that no white taxi would carry him to his destination. He found segregation facing him in public conveyances and theaters. He had already been made aware that such discrimination existed, but still it was a shock to actually face it. It was also a shock to find that the Negro had a subordinate position in all contacts with the whites. Gradually, the consciousness that he was of a different social world became a part of him.

Occupational Roles. Not all occupations give an equal chance for wish fulfillment. One often hears the modern assembly line job criticized on the ground that it makes an automaton of the worker, that it robs him of a chance for creative expression. To offset this possible source of frustration the working day has been shortened and numerous leisure-time activities created through which this man–machine may achieve wish fulfillment.

A craftsman expressed in common-sense terms the essential frustration of many today whose work is directed by others. A skilled carpenter on a college maintenance staff was put to work at masonry repairing an underground steam tunnel. After a half day of his work, he told the foreman he would do no more work on that job. The foreman, knowing him to be a reliable workman, instead of firing him sent him to the superintendent of the maintenance department. This man asked him why he had quit the assigned job. The answer was, "I'm a carpenter. All the pleasure I git out'a life is in doin' the work I want to do. If a man can't have that, what's the use of workin'!" He was put back on carpenter work.

The Female Role. Sex roles are defined by society. (Refer again to Chapter 17.) Modern woman faces this almost impossible dilemma: she must marry to satisfy the most basic wishes a human being possesses, those for response and security which come in love, sex, and child-rearing. But at the same time she pays the price of sacrificing all of the competitive achievement values about which her recognition wishes have been oriented during a long period of schooling and often during a period of work after finishing school. Few women can achieve both ends; therefore they must choose between these vital wishes.

The average educated woman is apt to suffer a great deal of frustration compared to the educated man. Her training in the school system is directed toward the same social goals as that of men. She comes to experience the same thrill in competitive success that the man experiences in obtaining grades, achieving success in athletic participation, achieving the goal of economic independence and all of the freedom that goes with it. Later she marries, finds herself suddenly pulled out of this world of values for which she has been trained. She drops into that insignificant role of housewife. Her career is gone, many of the old social contacts are gone, the thrill of competitive success is no longer obtainable. She finds herself bored with the chatter of women's clubs, robbed of new experiences, and soon is so frustrated she is on the verge of becoming neurotic. All of the props that once bolstered her self-confidence and sense of importance have been removed.

She is an unusual person indeed if she does not begin expressing her frustration in conflicts with her husband or children as a means of expressing her aggression. To avoid this reaction many able and ambitious wives have to get back into the work world on a part- or full-time basis and again sense the thrill of status won in competitive endeavor and in earning. This, together with the emotional security of marriage and family, makes life complete.

Little wonder that Adler built his system of psychology in part about the idea of masculine self-assertion. He felt that manliness and the recognition it brings was the quest of both man and woman.[7] Failure to achieve recognition for manliness brought feelings of inferiority.

The social roles defined for women by the great-grandparent generation placed them in no such dilemma concerning which wishes to realize and which to frustrate. They expected to marry; they were trained for it; their wishes from infancy up were oriented toward this goal. Only modern woman has experienced the position of being in that no man's land halfway between the male and female worlds.

---

[7] Adler, *op. cit.* Margaret Mead has a contrary view. She sees all men envying the mother role. See *Male and Female* (New York: William Morrow & Co., Inc., 1949); also published by Mentor Books, 1955.

Mothers of 1900 may have died early from too frequent child-bearing or from carrying too many buckets of water from the spring in the hollow, but they didn't find their way by the thousands to psychiatrists, psychopathic wards of hospitals, and institutions for the mentally diseased. This is a phenomenon of the transitional period. Universal education promises equality to women, but society has denied many women most of the things that education promises them.

GROUP SHIFTING AND PERSONAL STRESS

One of the significant adjustments of a person in modern society is that brought about by the vast difference of the warm protective atmosphere of the primary group, in which human nature is nurtured, from the cold competitive casualness of the secondary group with its virtual anonymity, in which the adult is forced by virtue of urban industrial society to spend much of his life.

Protective Nature of Primary Groups. The radical transition from the one kind of group to the other is especially difficult for those reared in more isolated rural communities. Sociologists have given far too little attention to relating personality breakdown, neurotic behavior, and mental disease to the shock of group transition. The primary group, if the individual remains in it for his lifetime, is protective; it throws about him a shield in times of crisis, helps carry his burdens from birth to funeral. He is not alone. By contrast, as a person moves into the secondary group he too often feels that he is entirely dependent upon himself. Crisis finds him with no intimate group on which he can depend. His own resources at times become exhausted by the nervous tensions, the uncertainties, the fluctuating circumstances, that life in a secondary group brings. These prove to be overwhelming for him. In a primary group, where others help shoulder the catastrophe, the individual could face similar crises without suffering complete nervous exhaustion.

Take the instance of death in the family. In the rural primary group of an earlier day, neighbors and family members shared the loss. They were there to console and help the bereaved both before and after the funeral. The funeral in the family home was a social occasion in a vital and meaningful sense. All wept together at the service and at the graveside, and then shared in carrying on life together afterward. The burial may have been in a simple pine box carried to a hilltop by neighbors, but the bereaved knew they were not alone.

Compare this with the modern funeral in urban life. The undertaker is well groomed, the hearse immaculate, the chapel in the funeral parlor modern, but the immediate family group sits apart behind a screen to bear their sorrow alone. They return home afterward to rebuild their life without the support of neighbors.

Impersonal Nature of Secondary Groups. No amount of economic security through a Social Security Act or through other protective devices that secondary groups have developed gives the same sense of emotional security and certainty in life that the primary group, historically, has been able to give to the individual, especially the primary group which extended beyond one's own relatives to include neighbors or perhaps the great family of aunts, uncles, and cousins who made up the neighborhood or community in which one lived.

The impersonal nature of secondary groups is typified in this scene of G.I.'s being processed on entering an army camp. (U.S. Army)

It is true that as every individual shifts from the primary group he tries to make new primary group attachments, but it is hard in a secondary group society, especially for people who move after they reach maturity, to ever establish close intimate ties such as they had within their own family. The individual in marriage, of course, reestablishes a primary group, but for many in our time, when so many marriages end in catastrophe, even this is no guarantee that the individual will have a warm intimate primary group throughout his lifetime.

The extreme strain that shifts from primary to secondary groups put on personality as the individual attempts to re-establish himself in primary group relations is well illustrated by the experience of millions of young men and some young women during wartime. Suddenly, without choice, young people in their late teens or early twenties are torn away from the primary group in which they have lived since childhood. They find themselves naked in a line of strangers, stripped of all their attachments to civilian life, being examined physically for entry into the Army. With a new uniform and in a group of strangers they begin a new life deprived of all the warmth and intimacy of the primary group.

Student autobiographies written since World War II often describe the stress of army adjustments. One youth writes:

> At San Diego I felt as if all the world, my world at least, had toppled. I felt hopelessly lost. True, war was imminent, but it hadn't arrived yet. It all seemed so damnably useless. I missed those intimate face-to-face contacts always so necessary a part of my life; here everyone was a stranger, a very indifferent stranger I thought. Seemingly our only trait in common was those damned navy-blue uniforms. We shared a common destiny, we were all lonely, and somehow felt we no longer mattered much in the everyday operation of the world. Imprisoned at a naval base in California, we were indeed but the infinitesimally small cogs of a vast rapidly growing military machine. (My mother fortunately saved the letters I wrote home during this period; they now provide a source of tender amusement.) In a very few days, we began to know each other well enough to make buddy associations. Our wall of security built up as we realized the importance of having a few intimate friends. When you had a buddy, life assumed somewhat more significance; it became more meaningful when after an exhausting day of drilling you sat in the semidarkness of the patios and smoked each other's cigarettes, talking of home, the girls, or the folks. A great thing this smoking with someone. As the acquaintanceships progressed, the more you cherished those intimate moments with Eddie and Pete. What a monster this navy was to take you so far from home, but since Eddie and Pete had to submit to the same torture, it was tolerable, if loathed.

Another youth writes:

> With a year and one half of college under my belt, my next move was into the army. This was my first experience of having to look out for myself. The shifting from the primary to the secondary group was really a personality strain. Like most of my fellow soldiers, I immediately tried to make acquaintances and attempted to find some sort of security. Each time I changed stations the same process had to begin again. With so much moving around and all of the uncertainty the letters I got from home were the stabilizing influence that kept me going until I was discharged.

As is seen from these cases, to weather the shock the soldier immediately begins to cast around for new primary group attachments. Soon the buddy associations begin to form. A comradeship is likely to result. This buddy attachment becomes the standard pattern of primary association in war. This attachment, of course, is often shattered by the buddy being killed, or separation by other means.

Neurotic behavior is especially prominent in wartime, not simply because of anxieties growing out of the extreme risks that men face, but also in part, and perhaps much more largely than is recognized, from the rather abrupt tearing of the young person away from his primary group and the shelter it offers. His being thrown into a secondary group, where he may or may not be successful in establishing buddy relationships that are satisfactory, where even though he does establish these buddy relationships the hazards of war may destroy them, adds to the strain. A letter from home or a sweetheart may be the only bond he maintains with the primary group. If this is removed, even greater strain takes place, for in no situation in life is the letter so meaningful as among those who have been separated from primary groups involuntarily and drawn into the armed forces.

Never in the history of mankind has the shifting of group roles been so much a universal experience as in urban industrial society, where practically every young person leaves the family nest and the home community to make himself a place in other groups. This requires that he struggle to re-establish himself in a position of prestige and recognition in the new social groups with which he is thrown.

It is partly for this reason that modern society is so highly competitive and that each individual has to exert his best effort to try always to make an impression. In primary groups, one is known for what he is and for the reputation he has established. In secondary groups, the tendency is to put the best foot foremost, to dress well, and to make a good impression, for one is usually conscious that he will be insignificant unless he creates a place for himself by some form of successful gesture.

The necessity of shifting from group to group and of establishing new group statuses requires flexibility. Even the flexible person's capacity to adjust may be taxed and the inflexible are likely to break altogether under the stress of fitting themselves to the new group situations which are an inevitable part of life in a complex society.

SUMMARY

The discussion here and in the preceding chapter dealing with personality formation and personality frustration as functions of group experience, can be reduced to a concrete, even if somewhat oversimplified, formula: To understand any person, (1) know his attitudes toward himself; (2) know his attitudes toward others.

If one were to classify personalities by types under this formula, he would elaborate it thus:

1. Attitudes toward self
   a. Feels sure of himself, is emotionally secure, senses a unity within himself (is integrated).
   b. Feels unsure of himself, is emotionally anxious, often has an unprovoked sense of guilt, senses strain and tension within himself (lacks integration).
2. Attitudes toward others
   a. Friendly and sociable, is in harmony with his social groups (is adjusted).
   b. Hostile and aggressive (in the militant sense). Feels out of harmony with his social groups (is maladjusted).

Attitudes both toward self and toward others, outlined above, are explained by the same factor in the person's experience. All his attitudes reflect the way other people have treated him since earliest infancy. Both types are extremes. Most people fall somewhere between the extreme adjusted and malajusted types shown.

Even though the formula is oversimplified, the group's part in determining the structure of personality is not. In a very true sense, long before one has reached maturity the social self and his society are one.

And therapy for those whose selves are inadequate must come from their reinstatement in the group. As Maslow phrases it so well:

A good marriage, success in a suitable job, developing good friendships, having children, facing emergencies, and overcoming difficulties—I have occasionally seen all of these produce deep character changes, get rid of symptoms, etc., without the help of a technical therapist.[8]

He believes that "good life circumstances are among the *ultimate* therapeutic agents and that technical psychotherapy often has the tasks only of enabling the individual to take advantage of them."

DISCUSSION AND REVIEW QUESTIONS

1. Analyze the factors in neurosis as presented in the case history at the beginning of the chapter.
2. What factors entered into the treatment? How was this person different before and after treatment?
3. Discuss Thomas' Four Wishes theory.
4. What are social values and how are wishes related to them?
5. What natural reactions follow the blocking of wishes?
6. Cite common cases of frustration. Show how the group has a part in the frustration of the social self.

[8] A. H. Maslow, *Motivation and Personality* (New York: Harper & Brothers, 1954), p. 378.

7. Cite examples of adjustments thwarted individuals make to frustration.

8. Name the various mechanisms of adjustment employed by the frustrated person.

9. Explain aggression as a natural reaction to frustration.

10. Show how social roles as defined by culture for certain social groups or individuals almost inevitably lead to frustration.

11. Discuss social forces that tend to frustrate the educated woman in our society.

12. Discuss how a radical shifting of group roles may lead to personality stress and neurotic breakdown.

13. Discuss the necessity for selective participation in order to realize personality integration in a complex society.

14. Summarize briefly the things one needs to know about a personality to understand it.

SOURCEBOOK READINGS

KOENIG, SAMUEL, REX D. HOPPER, and FELIKS GROSS. *Sociology: A Book of Readings.* Englewood Cliffs, N.J.: Prentice-Hall, Inc., 1956.

1. GOUGH, HARRISON, "Social Factors in Personality Disorganization," pp. 116–19.

SCHULER, EDGAR A., DUANE L. GIBSON, MAUDE L. FIERO, and WILBUR B. BROOKOVER. *Outside Readings in Sociology.* New York: The Thomas Crowell Co., 1956.

2. GREEN, ARNOLD W., "The Middle-Class Male Child and Neurosis," pp. 104–11.

WILSON, LOGAN, and WILLIAM L. KOLB. *Sociological Analysis.* New York: Harcourt, Brace & Co., Inc., 1949.

3. GREEN, ARNOLD W., "The Middle-Class Male Child and Neurosis," pp. 236–47.

4. FARIS, ROBERT E. L., and H. WARREN DUNHAM, "The Concentration of the Alcoholic Psychoses and Drug Addicts in the Zone of Transition," pp. 252–60.

SELECTED READINGS

ALVAREZ, WALTER C. *Nervousness, Indigestion and Pain.* New York: Paul B. Hoeber, Inc., 1943.

BEERS, CLIFFORD. *A Mind That Found Itself.* Garden City, N.Y.: Doubleday & Co., Inc., 1935.

BOWMAN, K. M., and E. M. JELLINEK. "Alcohol and Mental Disorders," *Quarterly Journal of Studies on Alcohol,* 2:378 ff. (Sept., 1941).

BURROW, TRIGANT. *The Neurosis of Man.* New York: Harcourt, Brace & Co., Inc., 1949.

CAMERON, NORMAN. *The Psychology of Behavior Disorders.* Boston: Houghton Mifflin Co., Inc., 1947.

CLAUSON, JOHN A., MARIAN RADKE YARROW, LELIA CALHOUN DEASY, and CHARLOTTE GREEN SCHWARTZ. "The Impact of Mental Illness: Research Formulations," *Journal of Social Issues,* 11:6–11 (1955).

DEASY, LELIA CALHOUN, and OLIVE WESTBROOKE QUINN. "The Wife of the Mental Patient and the Hospital Psychiatrist," *Journal of Social Issues,* 11:49–60 (1955).

DEUTSCH, ALBERT. *The Mentally Ill in America.* 2d ed.; New York: Columbia University Press, 1949.

DEXTER, LEWIS A. "Towards a Sociology of the Mentally Defective," *American Journal of Mental Deficiency,* 61:10–16 (July, 1956).

DUNBAR, FLANDERS. *Mind and Body: Psychosomatic Medicine.* New York: Random House, Inc., 1947.

DUNHAM, H. WARREN. "Social Psychiatry," *American Sociological Review,* 13:183–97 (April, 1948).

FARIS, ROBERT E. L. *Social Disorganization.* 2d ed.; New York: The Ronald Press Co., 1955, chap. 9.

FARIS, ROBERT E. L., and H. WARREN DUNHAM. *Mental Disorders in Urban Areas.* Chicago: University of Chicago Press, 1939.

FRUMKIN, ROBERT M. "Social Factors in Schizophrenia," *Sociology and Social Research,* 38:383–86 (July–Aug., 1954).

HORNEY, KAREN. *Neurosis and Human Growth.* New York: W. W. Norton & Co., Inc., 1950, pp. 17, 19, 37, 38, 157–58.

HUNT, MORTON M. "They Go Home Again in Kansas," *American Mercury,* 79:25–30 (Sept., 1954).

JELLINEK, E. M. "Phases in the Drinking History of Alcoholics," *Memoirs of the Section on Alcohol Studies,* No. 5, Yale University, 1947.

Journal of Social Issues, vol. 11, no. 4 (1955). Issue devoted to "The Impact of Mental Illness on the Family."

LINDESMITH, ALFRED R. *Opiate Addiction.* Bloomington, Ind.: The Principia Press, Inc., 1947.

MARTIN, JOHN BARTLOW. "The Struggle to Heal," *Saturday Evening Post,* Nov. 10, 1956, pp. 36 ff.

———. "We'll Never Make Her Well," *Saturday Evening Post,* Oct. 20, 1956, pp. 42 ff.

MASLOW, A. H. *Motivation and Personality.* New York: Harper & Brothers, 1954.

MOUSTAKAS, CLARK E. (ed.). *The Self: Explorations in Personal Growth.* New York: Harper & Brothers, 1956.

ROSE, ARNOLD M. "Neuropsychiatric Breakdown in the Army," *American Sociological Review,* 21:480–88 (Aug., 1956).

SEWARD, GEORGENE. *Psychotherapy and Culture Conflict.* New York: The Ronald Press Co., 1956.

SHORT, JAMES F. "Psychosomatic Complaints, Institutionalization and Delinquency," *Research Studies of the State College of Washington,* 24:150–59 (June, 1956).

Social Problems, vol. 4, July, 1956. Issue devoted to medical sociology, with particular emphasis on problems of mental disease.

"The Outlook for Mental Patients," *Statistical Bulletin,* 36:1–3 (April, 1955).

WARD, MARY JANE. *The Snake Pit* (a novel). New York: Random House, Inc., 1946. Condensed in *Reader's Digest,* 48:129–68 (May, 1946).

WEINBERG, S. KIRSON. "The Combat Neuroses," *American Journal of Sociology,* 51:465–78 (March, 1946).

WRIGHT, QUINCY. *A Study of War.* Chicago: University of Chicago Press, 1942, vols. I and II.

YARROW, MARIAN RADKE, and R. ROBBINS. "The Social Meaning of Mental Illness," *Journal of Social Issues,* 11:33–48 (1955).

Part V

SOCIAL CONTROL

Chapter 27

Social Organization and Disorganization Processes

The freedom to do as one pleases is never granted to man. To live as a socialized human being, to be a member of the group, subjects one to restrictions of an elaborate and constant sort. This is the area of *social control*, with which sociology must concern itself. How society achieves control over the individual, makes him a conforming creature, but leaves him with sufficient individuality and initiative to be creative and useful is a problem of all societies and of every family and other social group.

There is the problem of controlling his almost overwhelming biological desire with which the group must cope. If there is to be a stable family life, for example, the control of the sex impulse is essential. If property rights are to exist, as they must in society, hunger must be socialized by etiquette, and respect for the possessions of others must be instilled. And there must be some kind of elaborate training system by which the individual is taught the patterns that are required of him if he is to fit his group—patterns which might make him a misfit anywhere else on earth, but which will make him what he must be in the local group. This calls for a complicated educational program to shape the impulses of the child from the very beginning to fit a given social order. Social standards must be internalized in the individual and the majority of men become self-regulated if the society is to be safe and orderly.

Society must reconcile itself to the fact that there will be a certain amount of failure, some rebellion, and considerable frustration on the part of large numbers of individuals. There must, therefore, be some form of correction and discipline which is designed to teach individuals that failure to conform is costly.

Systems of social control operate by such subtle and extensive devices that only a casual analysis is possible in this book, but such an analysis will be sufficient to increase the students' awareness of the ever-present nature of the regulative system in human society.[1]

When social control fails, a certain amount of social disorganization is inevitable; in fact, sociologists use the term social disorganization to describe the breakdown of social control. When the individual for some reason evades the controls of the social group, he exposes himself to personal disorganization. Many a man on the frontier, where there was ineffective social control, literally drank himself to death. In an area where social controls were in the direction of sobriety, these men might have survived. On the frontier, where normal family life does not exist and social controls against prostitution are lacking, many a man indulges in illicit sex relations who in a community where different standards of social respect were current would have remained chaste. Many an individual in the disorganized areas of large cities, where there are few social pressures toward conformity to the code of behavior which exists for the large society outside, become involved in petty crime or in immoral behavior, because there are no strong social controls in the community.

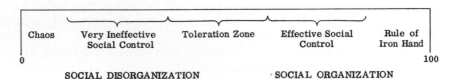

Social Organization Is a Continuum

Social organization extends from the chaos of revolutionary disorder on the one hand to extreme and intolerable social regimentation on the other. The problem of every society is to maintain effective social control without suppressing the individual to the point where he will revolt. Over the long span of history a society may move from one position on the continuum to another. This movement may be gradual or violent, depending upon the nature of the social control in use in a particular instance and on the nature of the individuals in the society.

When a society temporarily overthrows the political and economic controls by which it has been maintained and revolution erupts, the society is said to be disorganized. But social control in most societies throughout history has been so rigid, so permanent, so unchang-

---

[1] The author has devoted a book to this subject. See his *Social Control* (2d ed.; Chicago: J. B. Lippincott Co., 1956).

ing, that even long-range planning and policy-making have been unnecessary. The old ways of life persist in their routine, with only an occasional change taking place, and it being so minor as not to disrupt the normal trend of events.

Change has become the order of the day in modern life, when new inventions are sponsored and new social and political movements appear almost annually. Such societies must plan their way ahead, or be subjected to temporary chaos followed by costly reform. And since social planning and policy-making are far less costly than reform and reconstruction, they have become a part of the normal procedure of urban industrial society. By looking ahead, change can be directed and controlled, at least in a measure, and a great deal of its disorganizing effects avoided. Remodeling and reform become less frequent as plans and policies become more wise in anticipating needs of the future.

FILM LIST FOR PART V

Helping the Child Face the Don't's—11 minutes—sound
Portrays the child learning to live in a world defined by don'ts and shows how personality is influenced by his degree of acceptance of them. *Source:* Encyclopaedia Britannica Films.

One World—or None—9 minutes—sound
On atomic power, with vividly graphic animated drawings and live-action scenes. Good as a discussion starter. *Source:* Association Films.

Man in the 20th Century—17 minutes—sound
Present-day man's groping toward the means which will ensure peace and happiness. *Source:* March of Time Forum Films.

Grapes of Wrath—120 minutes—sound
The much-discussed Steinbeck film based on the book of the same title, which deals with the migration of "Okies" to California as farm laborers. *Source:* Films, Inc.

A Criminal Is Born—20 minutes—sound
Four boys, whose parents show insufficient interest in them, turn to crime and pay the price. *Source:* Teaching Film Custodians, Inc.

Devil Is a Sissy (gang sequence)—13 minutes—sound
Deals with boys' gangs. *Source:* New York University Film Library.

Levittown, Pennsylvania—26 minutes—sound
The development of a completely planned city of 60,000 population. *Source:* March of Time Forum Films.

Law and Social Controls—10 minutes—sound
Three broad areas of social control are discussed: customs, moral codes, laws. Local, state, and national levels of law are explained. *Source:* Coronet Films.

Unconscious Motivation—38 minutes—sound
Suggests how everyday thoughts, feelings, and actions may be influenced by unconscious motives. *Source:* Association Films.

A Story of Teen-age Drug Addict—20 minutes—sound
Young high-school boy first encounters narcotics with a fellow student, is led into their use, becomes an addict, and finally begins the cure for his addiction. *Source:* Young America Films.

And So They Live—25 minutes—sound

Study of rural school and community under poverty conditions. Poor housing, sanitation, diet, and schooling affect the whole community. *Source:* New York University Film Library.

Nation's Mental Health—18 minutes—sound

A survey of the mental health problem. Describes training procedures and various treatments and methods of therapy. *Source:* March of Time Forum Film.

Problem Drinkers—20 minutes—sound

An account of studies to control alcoholism and to have it recognized as a disease. Traces the development of an alcoholic through his ultimate recovery. *Source:* March of Time Forum Films.

Right or Wrong?—10 minutes—sound

A gang of high-school boys break a warehouse window; one of them is caught. The moral decisions of the watchman, the boy's mother, the property owner, the police sergeant, a social worker, and the boy are discussed. *Source:* Coronet Films.

Chapter 28

The Process of Social Control

Social control is the process by which order is (1) *established and* (2) *maintained in society.* It is not only the ever-vigilant policeman that jogs the traffic along, but also the ever-alert teacher who shapes the young by seeing that they absorb patterns for living acceptably in the social group of their birth.

No society can exist without a system of social control. It may be a subtle one of gossip and the pressure of local opinion, or it may be one of force, where dictators backed by a Gestapo or powerful armies enforce their will by imprisonment or death. The sociologist must always, in analyzing a society, consider the process of social control and how it operates to keep the society interacting with a reasonable degree of order and efficiency. He must always be interested in those processes by which the individual is kept in line with the desires, interests, and objectives of the social group.

Social control says not only "thou shalt not," but also "thou shalt," for both obligation and restraint are a part of human life in the group; in fact, without both no society could long endure nor could any individual long remain social. Social control, therefore, not only guarantees the social group a certain orderliness in its manner of life, but also protects the individual from his own worst self, his laziness, and his vices, by enforcing upon him numerous restraints.

A society may control many things in the person's physical and social behavior, or few. C. S. Ford, in an investigation of behavior control, studied twenty-five different cultures and found that in every one of them the following behavior was controlled, although not always in the same way: eating, vocalizing, talking, coitus, incest, giving, marriage, being formal, naming of people, mourning, harming others, and harming self. In most all the cultures (96 per cent) there was some control on how one may enter another's dwelling, how he may clothe himself, and on stealing, self-mutilation, and murder. Ninety-two per cent of the cultures had regulations regarding adultery, in-law incest, body cleanliness, and work.[1]

Ford found a great number of traits which few societies control. For example, the matter of eating condiments, sneezing, laughing, kissing, whispering, homosexuality, greeting others, and asking permission for atonement of crime he found controlled in only 12 per cent of the cultures studied. The following were found not to be regulated by any of the twenty-five societies studied: belching, coughing, yawning, shivering, menstruation, blinking.

When it comes to nonbiological factors, societies differ vastly in the number of things they control and in the nature of the controls applied. They vary also in the nature of the punishment used for the violator, but wherever man is found, social control is a major process of the society and the cultural heritage is rather specific with regard to how a person will live and act, and also about what will happen if he fails to live and act according to the standards set by his group.

But society's great job of social control goes on not in disciplinary action but in the teaching, formal and informal, by which the personality is shaped to fit the social order. No amount of discipline could handle the situation were it not that every man of a given group has within himself the guides and standards, values and aspirations, that for the most part conform to social expectations. These have been internalized by the group which has custody over his upbringing.

SOCIAL CONTROL IN FAMILY AND SOCIETY

Ordering and Forbidding. For the child social control begins in the primary group in the ordering and forbidding by parents. This process of ordering and forbidding is begun even before the child learns to speak—it is begun, in fact, as soon as he can understand the language of his parents. It continues until he leaves the family roof and goes out to establish a new family of his own. It may not cease even then if the person remains in the community of his parental home. It takes the form of simple direct lessons such as this one, vivid still in the mind of a college girl when she wrote her autobiography:

[1] C. S. Ford, "Society, Culture and the Human Organism," *Journal of General Psychology*, 20:167–68 (Jan. 1939).

One day I decided that I wanted to eat some brown sugar. I was afraid Mother wouldn't let me have it, so I asked her if I could have some raisins, as an excuse for opening the cupboard doors. Just by pure chance, she asked me how many I had (she was in the other room) and I said I didn't know. I was acting so funny, that she asked me to open my hand and show her, and for this deceit I had to sit in the corner. From that incident on, I could never lie convincingly, and so I very seldom attempt it.

In ordering and forbidding there are present the two elements of all social control: (1) the direction of the individual to get him to habitually perform in harmony with the standards of his group; and (2) the forbidding element which stakes out territory on which he is not supposed to trespass.

Pattern of Authority. In the family primary group also one sees another element that enters into all social regulation: conception of authority, which for the child resides in the parents. The nature of this authority and the way it is exercised determines the pattern that social control will take. Whether it will be the kind of authority that is intelligently administered, primarily in the direction of guiding the child and helping him understand how he must behave until gradually, with increasing maturity, he becomes self-disciplined, or whether it will be an authority of arbitrary command, enforced by the parent's superior physical strength, depends on a parent's conception of his role as disciplinarian. But, however administered, in every home situation there is some form of authority pattern. So also in all social life there must be, if men are to be regulated, some conception of authority.

In an earlier age the conception of authority was that of divine authority which ruled over man. It found expression not only in the belief that an all-seeing eye of providence was forever watching one and keeping an account of his good deeds and his misdeeds, but also in a belief that earthly rulers were representatives of God. The theory of the divine right of kings, even in the history of Western society, long prevailed as the conception of authority. It was powerful in regulating larger social groups and nations. This conception has passed from the Western world and in its place the authority of the people has been substituted through the ideals of democratic government. In the Orient, the conception of divine authority of rulers dies hard even today.

Individual Versus Group. Turning to another aspect of social control, there is, even in the family situation, a conception that an individual cannot be a group member without sacrificing some of his personal liberties so that all members of the group may have greater

The town meeting is an integral part of democratic social control in parts of New England. (Standard Oil Company, N.J.)

freedom in their living together. If the family is to function effectively a child cannot be a tyrant, having his own way in everything. He must sacrifice liberties in the interest of other members, thus learning that group living has its obligations as well as its privileges. Establishing this notion in the child is essential if he is to fit into the family and later into the larger society outside. This element of individual restraint within boundaries established by the group is a basic element in every aspect of social control.

The degree of individual liberty which is tolerated varies from group to group, and from one historical epoch to another, but no society has ever existed in which a certain amount of curbing of personal freedom was not a requirement of social order. It can be stated as axiomatic that the more dense the population group, the more complicated its functions; the closer people live together in the mass, the greater must be the restraint on individual freedom and the more complicated the framework of regulation and authority. For example, the only child in the family need be less restricted than the sibling in a family of ten. Large families tend to be authoritarian; small ones, democratic.[2] In the past the only child tended to be a "problem child." He had to learn the rigorous lessons of discipline and sacrifice of self-interest outside the family rather than within the family while a small child. Now that the democratic family is in style, he is no longer so.[3]

Carry this principle over to other groups. On an isolated hill farm in the mountains, one can dump his garbage in the garden, have an unsanitary water supply, no toilet facilities at all, and even let his children grow up in relative ignorance, and no one will be too seriously concerned. The mountaineer's world can be one of few regulations. There is the gossip of neighbors to keep one in line, but group expectations may be very low. The overpowering reach of law is scarcely present at all. Transfer the mountaineer to the city and he is immediately made conscious of the more complicated and formal framework of regulation. If he throws his garbage in the back yard, the city health authorities call him to account at once. His water supply had already been inspected before it was released in the water main. Rigid standards of sanitation concerning toilet facilities are enforced where the risk of disease is not a family risk alone but the risk of the neighborhood, the larger community, and perhaps of the entire city.

In all aspects of large-scale living together, social regulations established by kinsfolk and neighbors in the smaller community have to be supplemented by impersonal authority and professional supervisors. So the "great society" has social-welfare workers, police, courts, judges and lawyers, and zoning ordinances.

Gradually, through experience in the family and then through experience in outside groups, the child becomes socialized and learns to do what is expected of him in whatever group he is a participant. One may state it as a general rule for a complex society that where groups have so many standards, every individual must choose whether he will conform or not conform to group patterns, but by and large he conforms to those which are in harmony with the ideals established in the family and in his early play group and neighborhood. He tends to reject the ideals and standards of groups that come in conflict with the codes and principles which his primary group has succeeded in establishing for him.

[2] Paul H. Landis, *Teenage Adjustments in Large and Small Families*, Washington Agricultural Experiment Station Bulletin 549 (Pullman, Wash., 1954); also Paul H. Landis and Carol L. Stone, *The Relationship of Parental Authority Patterns to Teenage Adjustments*, Washington Agricultural Experiment Station Bulletin 538 (Pullman, Wash., 1952).

[3] *Ibid.*

In analyzing behavior of the person as it relates to his functioning in the group at a given time, the sociologist uses two concepts: the *reference group* and the *membership group*. One is a member of many membership groups from which he takes few behavior cues, and by which he is little controlled. But that all have a "tendency to behave in terms of a group not physically present, but psychologically important, is perceptible at all levels of social functioning."[4] This psychologically important group, the one the individual identifies himself with most closely, is his reference group.

Generally speaking, the group that dominates in controlling one's behavior is the one which holds greatest promise of support and status. This is the key reference group, and often determines how he will act when a member of other groups with different standards and behavior codes.

SOCIAL CONTROL IN RURAL AND URBAN AMERICA

Historically, and to a considerable extent even today, rural social interaction has been geared to face-to-face dealings with those one knows and trusts. In many sections still a man's word is as good as his bond. The oral contract is sufficient to bind a bargain between members of the neighborhood primary group. As late as 1938 the Farm Security Administration (now Farmers' Home Administration) in a study of farm-leasing arrangements, found that 80 per cent were by word of mouth only.[5]

In the rural primary group, custom has been an adequate basis for settling disputes, resort to law being the exception rather than the rule. Problems of juvenile delinquency have been worked out among neighbors, with resort to the law being the last step taken and that only after all measures of persuasion by parents and neighbors have failed. Many pranks of the teenager that would have led to the juvenile court in the city have been overlooked in the rural community, it being assumed that the youth with good parents would outgrow his meanness if given a fair chance.

The city is a man-made world in a more subtle sense than that of being a geographical environment transformed by man-made structures. It is a man-made world in that an intangible framework of law and regulation governs almost every act of man, his comings and goings, his building and his business. It is a world of zoning, of traffic regulations, of building permits, and of parking meters. Little wonder

---

[4] Eugene L. Hartley and Ruth E. Hartley, *Fundamentals of Social Psychology* (New York: Alfred A. Knopf, Inc., 1952), chap. 5; see also Muzafer Sherif, *An Outline of Social Psychology* (New York: Harper & Brothers, 1948).

[5] *The Flexible Farm Lease*, U. S. Department of Agriculture, Washington, D.C.

that the country man, living near nature in a world of little law, finds himself hemmed in and frustrated by the city. Little wonder that it seems a cold and unattractive world. It is not only that he likes the sunset and the sunrise, the freedom of open fields, work with plants and animals, but also the close-up feeling of man to man and the freedom from restraint that are his in the sparsely settled rural area.

The city is the world of written contracts. There are honest people in the city but one less often knows when he has met an honest man in the anonymity of the metropolis. He takes no chances; he has the lawyer draw up a foolproof contract, and if the terms are not lived up to, he resorts to the courts in quest of justice. Thus man's dealing with man is far different in a man-made world than in a rural environment where the neighborhood with its age-long rule of custom survives.

Where people are few and customs seriously regarded, one can leave his cabin unlocked and stocked with canned goods for the wayfarer who happens by; but where people are more numerous and customs taken lightly, one must lock the door and leave the cupboard bare. A Montana cattle rancher, commenting on the change he sees coming in rural areas, said to the strangers sitting opposite him in the train diner: "You can't trust people any more. Why in my country, a salesman comes around every week trying to sell us insurance to protect us against liability suits brought by our hired help. When I hire my men, I tell them they're responsible for their own accidents. It makes them more careful."

The lady opposite, a state leader of home demonstration agents for the Agricultural Extension Service, said, "I had a bad accident in Los Angeles many years ago; was hit by a car. I was a complete stranger but the item got in the paper. I had lots of callers—all people who had had accidents—there is sort of an informal fraternity among people who have been in accidents. One young man visited me whom I shall never forget. He was badly scarred and crippled but his story was the most interesting of all those who came during the months I was there.

"He had been hired on a big cattle ranch in Wyoming and was thrown from a horse and badly trampled during the first roundup. The other cowboys carried him out of the corral and put a blanket over him, sure he was dead, he was so badly mangled. The boss happened around and learned of it. He raised the blanket and saw there was some life in him. He put him in his big car and rushed him to a hospital, insisted that everything possible be done, and stayed around anxiously to see that it was done. He visited the hospital daily and saw that the youth got every care. When the youth got out after many months, the boss paid the bill in full.

"When the young man visited me, he was trying to think of a present to give this former boss for Christmas. The previous Christmas he had given him a beautifully finished saddle."

The rancher at the table observed, "It used to be that way. You took the cowboy in and treated him as one of the family. You can't do that any more. If one goes to the hospital, some lawyer follows him in and wants to sue."

SECULARIZATION AND SOCIAL CONTROL

In the regime of absolute authority, the moral system is rigid. It is characteristic of absolute views of morality and conduct that any violation is considered wrong, that the system itself is perfect, and that the human being who errs is to be condemned.

In a secular society all codes are tentative, all morals are a matter of time, place, and history. An individual appraises his own conduct and that of others by these relative standards. It is assumed that there must be exceptions to all rules, that all human beings frequently fall short of measuring up to the moral and legal standards that exist in the world about them. There are always certain kinds of crisis or supposed crisis when certain influential persons, those who seem important to meeting the crisis, openly violate the rules of the games and are granted immunity for doing so. In a secular society it is assumed that to expose and punish one of influence who has violated the rules is to do greater social damage than to ignore his delinquency. This person has proved himself to be a safe human being. There is no social risk in his violation of certain standards. The weaker individuals with a less widely established reputation would be considered a risk and be apprehended, however.

In a secular society the scales of justice are rarely justly balanced. This tends to make cynics of those who are tender-minded, and provide rationalizations by which the uncalloused salve their consciences. By contrast, in a sacred order justice is always done, if one considers justice as the enforcing of the rules uniformly, without question and without weighing the human motives and circumstances of the act.

A secular society, of course, believes that justice consists in weighing the circumstances and motivations, taking into account how the person in question has been shaped by the social system itself. A secular society believes the only true justice is found in differential treatment of individuals. One does not punish acts, be they crimes or moral violations. He analyzes circumstances, considers the developmental influences that have surrounded the individual and the environmental forces that have impinged upon him, and after having made an appraisal of these facts, considers action. Often as not no penalty is given. Therapy is considered more proper to the case.

Obviously this approach to problems of social regulation is much more flexible and much more difficult to enforce than the more simple approach of an absolute authoritarian regime. This conclusion applies to every institution: religion, education, the home, government, all of which may approach their problem from either a sacred or secular viewpoint, from an absolutist or an experimental, developmental approach.

INFORMAL DEVICES FOR SOCIAL CONTROL

Gossip. Gossip is often condemned by the minister in the pulpit, by the educator in the classroom, and by the gossip himself. Yet almost everyone gossips, even college professors who call it analyzing their friends. In spite of its condemnation, in groups where people know each other well gossip is probably one of the most effective of all devices of social control. Fear of what people will say, or fear of being talked about, makes people in primary groups constantly aware that they are being watched and that what they do will draw approval or disapproval. Man is always aware of his fellows, at least as long as he lives in friendly groups. "What will the neighbors say?" is a query which pops into the consciousness of any individual used to living in a neighborhood group the minute he thinks of stepping off the beaten path. It is gossip, in part, that helps the person in the primary group to live up to his highest ideals and to behave consistently with his reputation. It is really a desire to keep from being gossiped about unfavorably that keeps the person in line.

Some time ago *Harper's* magazine published an account of Kitty Smith, a graduate of the University of Michigan, who arrived in Caribou, Nebraska, to teach the fifth grade of Henry Wadsworth Longfellow School.[6] Probably the names are all fictitious, but the situation is characteristic. On a Sunday morning soon after her arrival in the small community, she took a sun bath in her bathing suit on the front lawn of her roominghouse. Her superintendent, in deference to community opinion, felt obliged to reprove her and to suggest that she should be in church on Sunday morning. Kitty's failure to conform to the accepted codes of the community on one thing after another led to so much community gossip that her superintendent felt it necessary to dismiss her at the end of the school year. She was not sufficiently aware of the effect of her behavior, perfectly proper by standards of other communities, on gossip in the community of Caribou, Nebraska.

[6] Bernard DeVoto, "Tyranny at Longfellow School," *Harper's*, Jan., 1937, pp. 22 ff.

One may well ask, if he is inclined to be sympathetic toward the young teacher and to condemn Caribou, why the community acted as it did? What did they have at stake in the nonconforming behavior of this school teacher? Obviously, as they saw it, the standards of the good and right, on which the moral upbringing of their children depended, were at stake. Compared to these values, Kitty Smith's tenure was of little importance.

Disapproval, Laughter, and Ridicule. A primitive man will give away half his property lest he be considered a miser, if the codes of his tribe require it. If jealousy is taboo in a tribe, a man will yield his favorite wife to a guest in order to avoid the charge of being jealous. But it is not only the primitive who will torture himself or make great sacrifice in order to avoid the mockery of his group. Human beings in all societies are cautiously aware of approved styles and manners lest they should suffer the sting of scorn. It is all right to wear freak dress for a day in a fraternity or sorority initiation, but the college man or woman otherwise toes the mark.

There are, no doubt, still country schoolrooms where a small boy who misbehaves is set up in a corner and has a dunce cap put on his head so that he can be laughed at by the rest of the pupils. In earlier colonial times the stocks and pillory were a common type of punishment for the man who beat his wife or who got drunk. He was placed conspicuously on main street where small boys could throw stones at him or sick their dogs on him. He was made the public example of a fool, which the community considered him to be. Such ridicule is considered too severe a form of discipline today, for society recognizes that there are few worse tortures for the human being than to be laughed at.

The device of ridicule can often be used very effectively in the larger society, however, and accomplish the ends sought. For example toward the close of the Depression decade members of Congress were in session debating whether or not to raise their salaries. There seemed to be considerable likelihood of the measure passing, when a campaign labeled "Bundles for Congress" was launched in Spokane, Washington. Soon the campaign was going full tilt in the press throughout the nation. Congress quietly tabled the proposal to raise the salaries of its members.

Here is another instance, reported by the *Associated Press,* where ridicule was used in an attempt to curb legislation, although in this instance it didn't succeed.

Representatives in the South Dakota legislature had their fun yesterday at the expense of their colleagues who are of Norwegian descent.

When a senate bill designating October 9 of each year as Leif Erikson day was brought up for final passage, a flood of amendments were rushed to the chief clerk's desk. Proposals were made to set aside a Peter Norbeck day, a Peter Sorenson day, a St. Patrick's day and a Leon Trotsky day. Others wanted Erikson named McErikson and Relcif Erikson.

After the levity had subsided, the house voted down a motion to indefinitely postpone the measure and passed it 88 to 9.

Gossip, laughter, and ridicule are informal devices of social control. Many more might be listed. Among common ones used in daily life are *flattery* and *praise*, both of which are highly effective in getting what one wants from others. The secret of Dale Carnegie's famous book, *How To Win Friends and Influence People,* lies essentially in his telling one how to flatter and praise the other fellow without being too obvious in doing so.[7] No human being ever gets enough of either, so one wins him by being generous with flattery and praise. Flattery is undeserved praise, whereas praise is an expression of appreciation of genuine merit in the other person.

Satire, name-calling, rewards, and other such devices should also be listed among devices that are essentially informal in character. And always present as a framework of social control is the residue of the past in the form of *ancestors' wishes, customs,* and *traditions.*

FORMAL DEVICES FOR SOCIAL CONTROL

In many aspects of human behavior, social control is fairly well formalized. Much of it resides in institutional systems. The educational system is primarily a formal machine for social control that achieves its end through teaching and directing the young and also through disciplining them. So, also, a military organization is an elaborate device for social control, insofar as its members are concerned.

Military organizations depend primarily on rules, statuses, and ranks to maintain control. Rules without adequate motivation here, as in all institutions, tend to lack something in effectiveness, as the following account from a student autobiography suggests.

In the army, we developed a whole new set of attitudes with respect to petty regulations. It became a great game to see how much we could get away with. There was no respect for the rules as such. Each disobedience was weighed against the punishment which might result. Quite often the punishment was found to be less distasteful than compliance with the rule. As we gained more knowledge of the army system our skill in escaping the consequences of our disobedience increased and disobedience became the rule rather than the exception. Lying, cheating, and even stealing became sanctioned as acceptable

[7] Dale Carnegie, *How To Win Friends and Influence People* (New York: Simon & Schuster, Inc., 1937).

behavior in this great game with the authority as long as it did not injure another of our own group. In some cases compliance with orders was considered detrimental to the welfare of the group and therefore was frowned upon.

Religion, also, is, among other things, a vast system of social control in which codes and ritual, doctrines and creeds, traditions and precepts provide a gigantic molding mechanism wherein the individual is shaped for the particular religious system. Involved in religious controls also are a series of penalties. They are visited on a person, either in this life or in the life hereafter, for his failure to live up to these codes and creeds as defined by the particular denomination or religious body. Certainly one must recognize that, historically, religious institutions have provided a major bulwark of social control in societies where they have been effective. Religious systems, even in our society, still provide a powerful force in social regulation for conscientious adherents, even though the mass of people have lost some sense of the authority of religion over their own personal lives.

In the modern world of secondary groups, by far the most important institutions for formal social control are government and law, with all their devices for administering social regulation. Law is extremely formal in that there is a codified and published definition so that all may know what is expected. Not only does the law define specifically the kind of behavior that is forbidden, and in some cases the kind of behavior that is obligatory as, for example, in marriage or other contractual relations, but also law carries with it certain penalties and punishments which are rather rigidly prescribed and known in advance, not only to the lawmaker and the law enforcement agency, but also to the citizen.

The framework of law in modern society has become increasingly vast at every level of public administration. There is not only the law of the local community (county, town, and city), but also that of the state and of the nation. The great society depends more and more on this vast framework of codified law and its penalties to maintain social regulation. This is primarily because group controls of an informal sort tend to become less important as people live in larger aggregates and care less about the gossip of their fellows; in fact, as they come to live in anonymous situations, they are not sufficiently concerned about each other to gossip.

This formal framework of legal regulation, it must be recognized, is far less effective than the informal control devices previously discussed. The major problem of the great society is to develop effective *public opinion* which will inspire in people a regard for law and the obligations it imposes. Only as people are affected by such opinion can law ever become anything more than skin-deep. Otherwise the typical attitude of the citizen is that of the lawbreaker: the law is something to obey only if you cannot get by with disobedience.

It has been pointed out repeatedly by students of social science that regard for law in democratic society is weak indeed, that it lacks a framework of public opinion which makes people want to do what the law expects. Part of this may be rooted in the fact that there are so many laws that a conscientious citizen could scarcely keep track of them, much less obey them scrupulously. It is due in part to the fact that harried legislatures, faced with the immense complexities of modern society, resort to lawmaking too frequently in trying to cope with situations which probably can be met only by more subtle means of social control. Moreover, we probably have not given enough attention to using propaganda as such to develop public attitudes which will be favorable to behavior which we now try in vain to achieve by lawmaking. Propaganda is much less formal than law and can, through its numerous subtle devices of operation, often be used to form public attitudes in large secondary groups much as gossip does in primary groups.

As to the devices of punishment used with lawbreakers, contemporary society still has not arrived at the most effective means of correction. With the minor offenses, the fine and publicity in the press are probably fairly effective control devices. But for major offenses, imprisonment is still used, on the assumption that houses of correction actually will make the person a law-abiding citizen. All evidence indicates that the opposite is the case, and that until we classify, study, understand, and re-educate the lawbreaker, using every device of psychological and social science, we will have used punishment in vain as a device for correction. Our schools of juvenile correction, as well as our prisons, are known to be our higher institutions in crime. Punishing a man does not reform him.

It would appear that urban society will continue to depend increasingly on governmental administrative measures in the field of law. In wartime in this country as never before restrictions were placed on numerous personal liberties by a new framework of law. Price control, rent control, gasoline control, control over all strategic materials, control of agriculture through numerous agricultural policies—such regulation became the order of the day. One might go on at length describing the vast new field of formal social regulation that came into being during the course of World War II, not only in dictator nations but also in democratic societies.

The United States has been drifting for at least two generations toward more and bigger governmental administration, which has become increasingly centralized and increasingly powerful. This is probably an inevitable trend where machine civilization and great aggregates of people have created such a complex civilization that local governmental units can no longer cope with major problems of formal social control. To the extent that this trend continues, the citizen is subject to new forms of governmental regulation as the nations wrestle with problems of economic control and human welfare. The government will also increasingly enter into regulating the relationships between large interest groups of the population, such as between labor and management, and between producer and consumer.

SUMMARY

Social control is the process by which society establishes and maintains order. Through social control society protects itself and often shields the individual from his worst self. Social control is maintained by many devices, ranging from gossip to law, the most effective being informal rather than formal. The amount of formal regulation required depends on the size and complexity of the group. The modern world has had to rely increasingly upon the formal control device of law to keep the social traffic moving with regularity and order.

DISCUSSION AND REVIEW QUESTIONS

1. Define social control, mentioning its two broad functions.
2. Cite examples of particular aspects of behavior that a society may or may not control.
3. Discuss ordering and forbidding as they are used by the family to establish control over children.
4. Show how the authority pattern of a group affects its approach to social control.
5. Discuss the conflict of individual and group interests, as it enters into the problem of social control.
6. Cite examples which demonstrate the differences in social-control processes operative in rural and urban America.
7. List some informal social-control devices and show how they operate.
8. Cite examples of formal social control, showing how it operates.

SOURCEBOOK READINGS

For Sourcebook and Selected Readings, see Chapter 29, pages 516–17.

Social Control and Social Revolt

W. I. Thomas, great American sociologist of the past generation, felt that social control originated out of the dual interests of the individual and society. The individual seeks self-expression; society is concerned with the security of the group. The individual says pleasure first; society says safety first. Society, therefore, finds it necessary to suppress the individual up to a point that the security of the group may be assured. There must exist, therefore, in any society a commonly accepted system of behavior patterns which indicate what is expected of group members. These common patterns of behavior Thomas appropriately named *group definitions*. This is how he viewed the subject.

"Preliminary to any self-determined act of behavior there is always a stage of examination and deliberation which we may call the definition of the situation. . . .

"But the child is always born into a group of people among whom all the general types of situation which may arise have already been defined and corresponding rules of conduct developed, and where he has not the slightest chance of making his definitions and following his wishes without interference. . . .

"There is therefore always a rivalry between the spontaneous definitions of the situation made by the member of an organized society and the definitions which his society has provided for him. The individual tends to a hedonistic selection of activity, pleasure first; and society to a utilitarian selection, safety first. Society wishes its member to be laborious, dependable, regular, sober, orderly, self-sacrificing; while the individual wishes less of this and more of new experience. . . .

505

"It is in this connection that a moral code arises, which is a set of rules or behavior norms, regulating the expression of the wishes, and which is built up by successive definitions of the situation. In practice the abuse arises first and the rule is made to prevent its recurrence. Morality is thus the generally accepted definition of the situation, whether expressed in public opinion and the unwritten law, in the formal legal code, or in religious commandments and prohibitions.

"The family is the smallest social unit and the primary defining agency. As soon as the child has free motion and begins to pull, tear, pry, meddle, and prowl, the parents begin to define the situation through speech and other signs and pressures: 'Be quiet,' 'Sit up straight,' 'Blow your nose,' 'Wash your face,' 'Mind your mother,' 'Be kind to sister,' etc. . . . His wishes and activities begin to be inhibited, and gradually, by definitions within the family, by playmates in the school, in the Sunday school, in the community, through reading, by formal instruction, by informal signs of approval and disapproval, the growing member learns the code of his society."[1]

SOCIAL CONTROL AND ACCEPTED GROUP PATTERNS

In the foregoing account Thomas showed how the helpless infant is born into the world with relatively few behavior patterns, and how in this world he will face numerous problems of choice. Each of these choices would involve him in a great deal of deliberation were he to make them for himself, but in any society there has accumulated through the centuries group definitions which are in reality a part of the cultural framework of patterns that define the situation for the individual. The social group, by making the individual aware of these definitions, gradually forms his behavior and provides for him a system of habits and attitudes by which he, in large measure, controls himself.

Rather than deliberating at every crossroad, he tends to make the choice which the society has already indicated is the acceptable one. Whom he shall marry, when he shall marry, how many wives he will have, when it is proper to have children, general relationships of husband and wife to each other, relationships to relatives, the use and responsibilities of money in connection with the family, all of these vital issues which every man as an individual has to meet in life have been defined for him by the social group so that, generally speaking, he lives within this framework of definitions rather than starting out on new paths for himself.

[1] W. I. Thomas, *The Unadjusted Girl* (Boston: Little, Brown & Co., 1923), pp. 41–44.

In the training of the child, especially in the primary group, any variation from the patterns that are accepted as proper in the group are frowned upon. He is ordered and forbidden, punished or censured if he strays from the path, and is pointed back to the acceptable course if he would live within the framework of accepted social definitions. This greatly simplifies life for the individual and also makes the problem of regulating him a relatively simple one for the group.

To illustrate by a homely example, in any social group there are numerous situations which demand a choice of alternatives, such as where travel goes in both directions on a highway. If travelers' passing is to be systematic and orderly when they meet, some accepted definition as to which way one shall turn when he meets a traveler going in the opposite direction must have been established. If there were not such commonly accepted group definitions, collisions would be commonplace in an age of speed. The group definition in America is turn to the right; in British society it is the opposite, but serves the same purpose since all know the group definition. The extent to which society moves in an orderly fashion, in other words the effectiveness of social control, depends upon the extent to which society has defined situations and made them acceptable to its members.

Many group definitions have such antiquity that no one ever stops to question them, for example, taboos against marrying relatives, regard for human life, regard for property of others. One could go on cataloging the commonly accepted definitions until his list totaled thousands of items. These commonly accepted definitions of behavior are the underlying foundations of social order.

In addition to the social definitions, there are, of course, various penalties for those who violate accepted definitions. These coercive or corrective elements are never absent from any society. They, too, are most effective when subtle and informal rather than when obvious and formalized. Fear of gossip in primary group situations is a stronger force than law, so and so's wagging tongue than the policeman's bullet. Regard for one's own reputation will cause him to toe the mark among those for whom he has high regard when no amount of law could do so. No threat of dictators or tyrants could be so strong in keeping a righteous man true to character as his regard for men's good opinions of him.

If what has been said is true about effective group definitions compared to formal control devices such as law and law enforcement agencies, and if it is true that the subtle corrective pressures of a social group are more effective than the procedure of courts, why do the latter come into existence?

The answer is simple. There are many primitive social groups, historical and contemporary, where the informal methods of control are adequate to guarantee that social definitions well established in the group by custom will be followed. There are numerous rural communities in which no law would ever be required, except as some transient from another group, who does not understand accepted local definitions or who does not yield to local pressure, comes in. But in a complex society of mobility and of rapid change, group definitions are never fully adequate and the subtle pressures of enforcement fall short of meeting the demands of the situation, for mobile people have little knowledge of or regard for them.

THE WEAKENING OF PRIMARY GROUP CONTROLS

The late L. L. Bernard, sociologist and social psychologist, contrasted the workings of social control in primary and secondary groups with an interesting example.[2] He takes the case of a man who is on trial for having won his seat in the Senate by buying votes. His priest appears at the trial and testifies that the man is a good father, an ideal church member, a respected citizen in his neighborhood. Bernard points out that a man can be all of these, that is he can measure up to primary group morality in every respect, and yet be a criminal from the standpoint of civic morality in secondary group situations.

The shift from primary to secondary group control not only affects behavior in general, but also the adjustments of the individual person. American society has only so recently become dominated by large secondary groups that these groups lack the more subtle devices of social control that are most effective in regulating human behavior. Hence, those who migrate from the primary group to the secondary group often feel a sudden release of the effective social-control devices of the primary group. If they do not indulge in a period of sowing wild oats, they at least are tempted and have the opportunity to do so. Many, of course, carry over primary group controls into secondary group situations, and others who try to shed them end up by becoming neurotic from the strain of an unsuccessful attempt.

Others in shifting to a secondary group situation in a real sense lose themselves, or to use a common expression of folklore, "go to the dogs." A college young man writes:

[2] L. L. Bernard, "Conflict Between Primary Group Attitudes and Derivative Group Ideals in Modern Society," *American Journal of Sociology*, 41:611–23 (March 1936).

Going away to college completed my transition from primary to secondary group relationships. In this transition, I took advantage of the opportunity to make a few "improvements" in my personality and sow a few wild oats at the same time. Whereas I had formerly been rather reserved and shy, I now became the loud-mouthed extrovert; where before I had been moderate in my habits, I now became a nervous chain-smoker and boisterous drinker. I also made up my mind that I was going to go to dances and go out with girls until I overcame my shyness. This was not too difficult to do as most men were still in the service, and there were four times as many women as men. As a result of the aforementioned "improvements" in my personality, a few weeks after the beginning of the semester, I was going with three girls, averaging two dances a weekend, and drinking a little too heartily for my own good.

With the growth of secondary group society, the family also has lost many of the pressures that hold it together as an institution. The neighborhood pressures of a small community help hold man and wife together, and remind a son and daughter of their obligations and responsibilities as members of a family. There are many areas in the large city today where neighborhood pressures are entirely absent and a family may disintegrate without a single pressure from the social environment to hinder the process.

GROUP COMPLEXITY AND SOCIAL CONTROL

As has been implied in the preceding discussion, it is when groups become complex and the individual extremely mobile in shifting from group to group during his daily experience and during his lifetime that problems of control are multiplied and problems of choice for the individual become more numerous. The young person in a complex society like our own, with its many secondary group contacts, has great difficulty finding in the primary group a set of social definitions that is adequate for all the experiences he will meet in life. He, therefore, must constantly relearn in many new situations and must often find it necessary to cast aside definitions of propriety learned in the primary group.

Take for example the experience of the adolescent girl in American society; she has numerous choices never faced by girls in simpler cultures. This is strikingly brought out in a study of the adolescent girl in New Guinea, who grows up in a stable society with primary group experience.[3] There the tribe has long ago decided how she must act in almost every situation with regard to courtship and marriage. The simplicity of social definition is in direct contrast to the complex social experience of the adolescent girl in our society. The

[3] Margaret Mead, "Adolescence in Primitive and Modern Society," in V. F. Calverton and Samuel D. Schmalhausen (eds.), *The New Generation* (New York: The Macaulay Co., 1930), pp. 183–84.

American girl faces many conflicting standards of morals. In her in-experience, she is expected to decide for herself whether she will marry and when, and whom, and whether she will or will not have children. "She can choose not only whom she will love but whether she will love in or out of wedlock, one or many."[4]

The above analysis explains in large part why the young woman of today suffers a good many tensions and emotional conflicts in her adjustment which were not present in the experience of young women in earlier society. The average woman of today, with her free choice of dates, her dating without chaperonage, her numerous decisions to make as to how she will conduct her dating and her romantic experiences, her choice of standards between the parent and the peer group (her own age group), between her own past and her lover's past, has numerous decisions to make. It seems likely that the average young woman of today, before she is twenty, has made more moral decisions than her great-grandmother, who lived in the simple primary group surrounded by the simple control devices of that primary group, made during her entire lifetime. Morality for young people today is a matter of choice, because most young people have a chance to be immoral. Society has increasingly left the problem of social control to their own individual decision. Group definitions are not adequate in an individualistic society for all situations the individual faces.

Changes in American society come so fast that the definitions of one generation may be seriously challenged by the next generation. Definitions of the adult generation and of the youth's own peers are, figuratively speaking, often miles apart.

SOCIAL CONTROL AND THE COMMUNITY

A great number of studies have been made showing how problems of social control are related to ineffective community organization. In the city of Chicago, in particular, sociologists have related juvenile delinquency, mental disease, gangsterism, divorce, desertion, suicide, and other such personal breakdowns and personal failures to the disorganized community.[5] Near the Loop district in the slum areas, where community controls are ineffective, where families are weak, where neighborhoods are also weak, these patterns of personal breakdown are most frequently found. At the outer fringe of the city where communities are intact, where the neighborhood is strong, where families are well integrated, such failures on the part of the

---

[4] *Ibid.*
[5] For brief summaries of these studies refer again to Chapter 9.

individual are rarely found. These studies show rather clearly the importance of an effective system of neighborhood and community control over family and personal life if the individual is to be protected against his own failure.

More recently, certain studies, however, have raised the question of whether or not part of the failure in these areas may not be due to the fact that in better communities the individual with a respectable family and with a respectable neighborhood is given a certain immunity to punishment for crime which those in the decadent area do not have.[6] For example, a questionnaire study of a large group that had never served any time as delinquents or criminals showed that most of them confessed to having committed, one or many times during their youth or adulthood, acts that were under laws of the state defined as serious crimes. The authors of this study themselves raised the question of whether or not having respectable parents and living in a respectable neighborhood does not protect a person from being apprehended for crime, and from being punished if apprehended. Parents and neighbors in good family sections are able to exercise influence which the parents of children living in the slums do not possess.

Certainly both factors are influential. Society is discriminating in the exercise of social control. Gladstone is reputed to have said, "If a man steals a loaf of bread, we put him in prison; if he steals a railroad we send him to parliament." He was, no doubt, implying by this that there are certain types of socially harmful acts which, though often within the law, still actually constitute a crime against the welfare of man. But if a man succeeds in making himself wealthy by them, he is likely to receive the prestige and power that goes with wealth and success.

Sociologist Edwin H. Sutherland has pointed out that certain social groups have great immunity to punishment for crime because they are in professional fields where they are given a certain immunity from the law, for example, the fee-splitting between doctors and the specialists, and the cutback to the prescribing eye specialist of perhaps five out of the fifteen dollars charged for the glasses by the optical company.[7]

---

[6] James S. Wallerstein and Clement J. Wyle, "Our Law-Abiding Lawbreakers," reprint from *Probation*, April, 1947 (New York: National Probation Association). See also James F. Short, Jr., "A Report on the Incidence of Criminal Behavior, Arrests and Convictions in Selected Groups," Proceedings of the Pacific Sociological Society, *Research Studies of the State College of Washington*, 22:110–18 (June 1954).

[7] Edwin H. Sutherland, "White-Collar Criminality," *American Sociological Review*, February, 1946, V, 1–12.

Fraud, embezzlement, the sale of fraudulent securities, misrepresentation of assets of corporations, graft, bribery, and other such forms of "white-collar" crime cost the public millions. Much of this crime goes unapprehended. Sutherland points out that whereas lower-class crime originates from disorganized communities, in slum areas, in broken homes, and other disadvantaged social conditions, the other kind of crime is learned in the best of environments, where ruthless competition in financial circles provides a setting for the game. Many of these white-collar criminals are college graduates, and may even have graduated with considerable idealism, but got into business situations where criminality is in reality a folkway of the business practice.

Clearly certain groups have too great an immunity to social control.

SOCIAL CONTROL IN HISTORICAL PERSPECTIVE

David Riesman, analyzing American character in historical perspective, believes that personality throughout the world may be analyzed into three types: (1) tradition-directed, (2) inner-directed, and (3) other-directed.[8]

The tradition-directed personality is found in areas of the world where technology and rapid population change are unknown. There are few disturbing influences from without. The pattern established in childhood is good for a lifetime. This type of personality development was characteristic of all human society prior to the Renaissance, Reformation, and Industrial Revolution, and still exists in more backward areas of the world.

After these movements, the inner-directed personality developed in Western society. Instead of tradition being passed on from parent to son and being considered adequate as a guide for life, in the new changing and mobile society the elders satisfied themselves with implanting a deep sense of direction toward lifelong goals to be achieved, but had some realization that the means of their achievement could not be by the tradition of the ancestors. This is likened to providing the individual with a gyroscope by which he can find his way toward goals in a rapidly shifting social scene.

Riesman believes that on the American scene the philosophy of Calvin on the religious side and that of Adam Smith on the material side provided basic gyroscopes for the American personality; that it

[8] For a summary of Riesman's views, see *Time*, Sept. 27, 1954, pp. 22–25. His books are *The Lonely Crowd* (New Haven: Yale University Press, 1950), *Faces in the Crowd* (New Haven: Yale University Press, 1953), and *Individualism Reconsidered* (Glencoe, Ill.: The Free Press, 1954).

was on these forces that was built the American personality of the epic era of invention, striving, pioneering, and material achievement.

Since 1920, however, Riesman believes, the American personality, particularly in certain sectors of society, has been shifting from the inner-directed personality toward other-directed personality.

The other-directed personality becomes like one equipped with built-in radar equipment which enables it to take its cues from the social environment. It is a personality directed by others rather than by fixed goals. Its radarlike equipment is constantly on the alert for direction and hints from others, and the personality takes its direction from these soundings. These numerous soundings become internalized, so that the individual eventually achieves a sort of inner sense of guidance that has not been implanted by parental teaching.

In this new culture setting, personality formation has none of the elements of the tradition-directed personality building process. It is rather the internalization and organization of numerous external signals as to what others expect.

In appraising American society, Riesman feels that except for Southern Negroes and a few unassimilated immigrant groups, few tradition-directed persons remain. He feels that most Americans are inner-directed. The working class has gradually shifted from its tradition-directed orientation to an inner-directed one. The middle class, he believes, is still inner-directed, although this group is badly split between the inner-directed and other-directed. He feels that the old middle class—the farmers, small businessmen, technicians, engineers, and bankers—is still largely inner-directed, whereas the new middle class—bureaucrats and salaried business employees— is largely other-directed. He also believes that other-directed people are on the increase and are concentrated in cities, the larger the city the more of them.

SOCIAL REVOLT

Social revolt is the process of temporarily or permanently throwing over restraints which formerly were accepted by the group. The most obvious case of social revolt is that of political revolution. Regulation often becomes so intolerable that citizens find their only escape in defying authority and throwing it aside.

But revolt may take place in any situation where authority is exercised over a person. It was very common in the old-fashioned family, where the young person, under the domination of his elders, found no release from authority as he approached maturity except through defying parents by virtue of his greater physical strength or running away from home. The following account by a college youth is illustrative of a natural revolt against patriarchal parental authority. He begins:

> It seems I've lived two complete and unattached lives. One was under a strict family discipline, the other an all-out fight against a normal good society. During the first stage my personality was integrated. During the second, distorted and disorganized. During the first my behavior was conventional, during the second stage it was unconventional.

He describes the discipline of work in the farm home; the absolute obedience expected by his father. He was taught to be seen and not heard, was brought up with strict religious teachings which tended to enforce respect for authority. His attitude toward responsibility led to his election as president of his class in high school and to many other responsibilities characteristic of a leader in the youth group. Because he had been conditioned to accept authority unquestioningly, he followed training rules in athletics with almost a religious conviction.

Upon graduation from high school at nineteen he joined the Navy. Free at last from all the rigid restrictions of too imposing duty, which had been enforced upon him from early childhood, he tore away from the old mores. He says:

> I started drinking and smoking, things that were rigidly condemned in my earlier primary group. My whole moral system seemed to break down. I started running around with the tough crowd and going with women of questionable character. I neglected study, lost interest in sports, and got a great thrill out of defying all my previously accepted home standards and moral codes. It seemed that all the old influences of home were easily cast away and I became a changed man. Bars in taverns, where a man was judged by the amount of liquor he could hold, were my hangout.

He describes then the experiences of war; the tragedy of seeing friends and buddies killed, the sobering effect of seeing life in its more costly aspects, and then, finally, the discharge from the Navy and the long way back home to civilian life. He gradually resumed his old life and found himself quite happy in accepting many of the regulations which he had formerly cast away.

The tragedy of the old-fashioned stern discipline of the family was that it provided for no gradual transition to maturity, wherein a young person could make his own decisions and thereby experience adulthood gradually, rather than in one big step. Today the wise parent lets the child make decisions for himself, insofar as his physical growth and understanding justify, so that by the time he is through high school he has learned to be largely self-regulating. The parent gradually releases his authority as the child proves capable of making his own decisions and of regulating his own life. No period of rebellion is then necessary in order for the youth to become free.

In the case of individuals, as of nations, revolt is usually temporary. No society can continue as a revolutionary society. It must afterward establish other restraints and control devices to replace the liberty, equality, and fraternity which sweeps over a nation as an epidemic for a period. So also with the individual; no individual can continue sowing wild oats for a lifetime without his life being short and useless. He must, after revolt has run its course and he has declared his freedom, again submit to regulations, perhaps broader in character and permitting more liberty; but he must submit if he is to be a useful member of society and to be at peace with himself. It is a rare person indeed who spends his lifetime in rebellion against the major control devices of a society.

It has already been indicated that our society provides rather standard devices for revolt. The crowd and the mob were discussed, especially the athletic crowd, as providing situations for revolt against the restraints all feel in life. One can yell as loud as he wants to, even cry for murder of the referee or the opposing team. In addition, this country has a party political system, which stages a paper revolution every four years, pitting candidate against candidate, each group boosting its candidate with bands and banners, political rallies and hilarity. The citizen of a democratic government expresses his revolt, not in the violence of revolution, but by the peaceful means of the ballot, whereby he himself decides who will rule.

Such regularized channels for revolt would seem to help people let off steam, hinder the accumulation of a spirit of rebellion that may break out in more violent forms of conflict, temporarily overthrowing the means of social control and producing social disorder.

SUMMARY

Society develops definitions which restrain the individual in his quest for pleasure at the risk of social safety. The individual is born in this world of social definition which provides the individual readymade decisions. To the extent that social control is well established, life moves in orderly fashion. Where the social definitions are unquestioned and where man lives in the gossipy primary group, society keeps a strong hold over the individual. As primary group controls become weakened in secondary group social relations, the problem of controlling the individual by standards that meet the test of civic morality has become an increasingly difficult one. The individual is placed under greater strain since there are fewer protective devices of social regulation about him.

There is much evidence that in communities where effective social control has broken down there is great strain on the individual. It is evidenced by his pathological behavior. It is also evident that in these disorganized communities, where the individual often lacks the protection of an influential primary group, he often pays for delinquencies which would be overlooked in more established communities.

Social revolt is a reaction of the person to social control where restraints become too rigid. It is a wise social order that knows when to be firm and when to relax authority. This is as true of the family as of the state. Revolt must be considered a temporary state since no society can get along without an established and accepted set of principles by which men are guided.

DISCUSSION AND REVIEW QUESTIONS

1. What did W. I. Thomas mean by "group definitions"? Show how group definitions enter into social control.

2. What are the implications to social control of the individual's emphasis on pleasure first?

3. Discuss the effect of the weakening primary group controls.

4. Can the old primary group controls be made to work in secondary groups?

5. Compare the problem of social control in simple and complex societies.

6. Compare standards of successive generations in the United States and show how social control is affected.

7. Show how problems of social control differ in different kinds of communities.

8. How are individuals affected by the prevailing system of social control?

9. Discuss Riesman's view of personal motivation in social control as viewed broadly.

10. Discuss social revolt. Show how it relates to problems of social control.

SOURCEBOOK READINGS

KOENIG, SAMUEL, REX D. HOPPER, and FELIKS GROSS. *Sociology: A Book of Readings.* Englewood Cliffs, N.J.: Prentice-Hall, Inc., 1956.
1. BREARLEY, H. C., "The Nature of Social Control," pp. 481–85.
2. LASSWELL, HAROLD D., "Social Control by Terror: The Garrison State," pp. 486–92.
3. MARCSON, SIMON, "Social Control through Education," pp. 492–95.

O'BRIEN, ROBERT W., CLARENCE C. SCHRAG, and WALTER T. MARTIN. *Readings in General Sociology* (2d ed.). Boston: Houghton Mifflin Co., 1957.
4. WESTLEY, WILLIAM A., "Violence and the Police," pp. 414–19.

WILSON, LOGAN, and WILLIAM L. KOLB. *Sociological Analysis.* New York: Harcourt, Brace & Co., Inc., 1949.
5. THOMAS, WILLIAM I., "The Regulation of the Wishes," pp. 185–86.

6. MEAD, GEORGE HERBERT, "Play, the Game and the Generalized Other," pp. 187–94.
7. PIAGET, JEAN, "The Rules of the Game," pp. 194–207.

SELECTED READINGS

BARUCH, DOROTHY WALTER. *New Ways of Discipline.* New York: McGraw-Hill Book Co., Inc., 1949.

BIERSTEDT, ROBERT. "The Discipline of Free Man," chap. 3, *Freedom and Control in Modern Society,* edited by Monroe Berger, *et al.* Princton: D. Van Nostrand Co., Inc., 1954.

BLOOD, ROBERT O., JR. "Consequences of Permissiveness for Parents of Young Children," *Marriage and Family Living,* 15:209–12. Aug., 1953.

FARIS, ELLSWORTH. *Discipline without Punishment.* Salt Lake City: University of Utah Press, 1952.

FUESS, CLAUDE M. "The Perils of Conformity," *Saturday Review Reader No. 2.* New York: Bantam Books, Inc., 1953, pp. 41–48.

HOVLAND, C. I., *et al. Experiments on Mass Communication.* Volume 3 of *Studies in Social Psychology in World War II.* Princeton: Princeton University Press, 1949.

KAHL, JOSEPH A. *The American Class Structure.* New York: Rinehart & Company, Inc., 1957.

KLAPPER, JOSEPH T. *The Effect of Mass Media.* New York: Columbia University Press, 1949.

LANDIS, PAUL H. *Social Control: Social Organization and Disorganization in Process.* Rev. ed.; Chicago: J. B. Lippincott Company, 1956.

MacIVER, ROBERT M. *Social Causation.* Boston: Ginn and Co., 1942.

RICH, GILBERT J. "The Tradition of Force and Punishment," *The Nervous Child,* 5:222–25, 1956.

SELDES, GILBERT. *The Great Audience.* New York: The Viking Press, Inc., 1950.

STONE, CAROL L., and PAUL H. LANDIS. "An Approach to Authority Patterns in Parent-Teenage Relationships," *Rural Sociology,* 18.233–42. Sept., 1953.

VALENTINE, ALAN. *The Age of Conformity.* Chicago: Henry Regnery Co., 1954.

Chapter 30

Social Disorganization

In Chapters 28 and 29 social control was discussed as the process by which order is established and maintained. While this process is always operating in society, there is a counter process which also operates: the process of social disorganization.

Social disorganization consists essentially of a breakdown of social control so that disorder and confusion rather than orderliness prevail. Group functions cannot be carried out effectively, or at least their carrying out is impaired.[1] Social organization and disorganization are both matters of degree (refer again to the chart on page 488). Both processes are operative in a society at all times, and neither process is ever fully operative in ideal form. Norms are relative. Moreover, attempts at reorganization in one field are seldom made without disrupting other aspects of social organization in some measure.

Personal disorganization characterizes the individual when he is no longer susceptible to the pressures of others and to the conventions of society. He is disorganized when his life pattern temporarily or permanently becomes one of mental breakdown where he escapes from the ordinary control devices with regard to property rights, life, and welfare of others. He is disorganized when he becomes a victim of poverty to the extent that he is no longer willing to try to maintain a respectable self-sustaining existence but becomes an object of constant charity. He becomes disorganized when he becomes a victim of physical defects, such as the loss of the senses, and becomes a dependent member of society discouraged with trying to keep the pace of a competitive social order and with attempts made by others for his rehabilitation.

[1] Robert E. L. Faris, "Contemporary and Prospective Social Disorganization," *Sociology and Social Research,* 32:679–84 (Jan.-Feb. 1948).

A *family* is disorganized when the functions of child care are not carried out and the mutual responsibility of husband and wife are not met, whether or not the family is actually broken by death, divorce, or separation.

A *community* may be said to be disorganized when the normal restraints and social-control devices of the larger community of which it is a part are no longer regarded with respect and obedience. Police protection breaks down in the face of organized rackets and blackmail. Such communities may develop crime and gangsterism as a traditional pattern of life, or they may become accommodated to a life of poverty and degradation, immorality or loose living.

If *government* in a nation becomes disorganized, revolutionary forces take over and bloodshed and violence rather than law and order prevail.

Social unrest is one of the best indexes of social disorganization in a political regime. In a community poverty, dependency, vice, crime, and suicide are often taken as indexes. Community deterioration such as slum dwellings and unkempt areas, poor sanitation, and lack of community pride are indicative. And in the field of interpersonal relations conflict is indicative of disorganization, as in the family, where it is the forerunner of desertion and divorce.

CHANGE AS A FACTOR

Social disorganization in the broadest sense is due to change—change in any aspect of man's environment, social or cultural, or even radical change in the natural environment such as that produced by catastrophe. Were there no change, life would tend to become perpetuated in the old routine and as such would experience no disorganization. This does not mean that life would be perfect by any standard; it might be miserably degraded from the standpoint of social advantages or from the standpoint of making a living, but there would be no disruptive forces to challenge the existing system of social control or to challenge the integration of the social system as such. Therefore, the society would not be disorganized in the sense in which this word has come to be used in sociology. Disorganization implies change which has produced problems of which people are conscious. In static societies people are not conscious of what are considered problems by other people or groups because they have had no different past with which to compare the present. Things have been the same for so long that they tend to be taken as the inevitable state of affairs.

Social disorganization in its worst forms comes about, not through

the deliberate intent of any person or group, but as a consequence
of various social forces which operate quite impersonally. Social
disorganization is, for the most part, a by-product rather than a
deliberate social creation, an aftermath of changes which were not
intended to disrupt the social order.

Social disorganization, by and large, is a stage of transition between an old system of social control and a new system yet to be
developed. It may be a temporary period; it may be a long period
in which society through trial and error tries again to establish
efficient regulation over the individual and the group to protect man
from his worst vices and to protect society from the depredation of
vicious individuals and groups which ignore social pressure and become a hazard to the welfare of the larger groups.

Social disorganization is rarely complete; that is, social regulation seldom completely disappears. There are stages in political
revolution when it is fairly complete, as most of the normal restraints
to which men are subject tend to disappear. The restraints that make
men work for a living, that make them regard marriage vows, that
make them regard their obligations as citizens, that make them regard the lives of their fellow men, may temporarily disappear and
licentiousness and terror reign among great numbers of people. Then
people again seek leadership and control in order to re-establish the
normal processes of life.[2]

One may also observe the temporary breakdown of social control
and the appearance of disorder and confusion in times of crisis,
such as flood, earthquake, or other natural catastrophe. Emergency
workers have to take charge to prevent looting, to help the distressed,
and to save the situation from complete confusion. A complex society
must always have its riot squads, militia, police, firemen, Army, National Guard, Red Cross, or other such groups trained to establish an
emergency system of order in such crises. The breakdown of order
during a strike may also occasion the use of the National Guard.

The above examples refer to the excesses of social disorder when
practically all social control breaks down. But how does social disorganization in its milder forms, as it develops in various phases of
normal society, manifest itself? What are the forces that tend to disrupt the system of social control and to weaken its hold over the individual and over large groups of people? What are the consequences

[2] For a study of civil revolution in Russia, see Pitirim A. Sorokin, *Sociology of
Revolution* (Chicago: J. B. Lippincott Co., 1925). Sorokin is now an American, but
he was a participant in the Russian revolution and wrote his account of it as an eye-
witness. See also Rex D. Hopper, "The Revolutionary Process," *Social Forces*, 28:270–
79 (March 1950).

of the milder form of social disorganization that have affected many aspects of American life?

SOME DISRUPTIVE CHANGES

For purposes of this discussion, five major forces that have tended to undermine the process of social control and to weaken social order in American society are considered. They are: (1) population movement and social climbing; (2) rapid cultural change; (3) urbanization; (4) the transition from primary to secondary group experience; (5) secularization.

Each of these forces is taken up briefly to show its effect in breaking down the established system of social control, thereby freeing man from numerous social regulations that have been inherent in the society throughout past decades.

Population Movement and Vertical Mobility. In a stable society where people remain anchored in the same community for a lifetime, there is little chance to evade the social-control devices that become established in such communities and are passed through generations as part of the cultural heritage. The strong hand of the aged and tradition rule. Young people grow up under the tutelage of the older generation and remain under its supervision during their lifetime. They gradually take on the responsibilities of the work world and assimilate the traditions and moral standards of their elders. In such stable societies problems of social control scarcely exist, since the influence of the group is so overpowering.

By contrast, one of the most significant forces in breaking down social control in contemporary society is the movement of population. Those who move frequently lose contact with the intimate local group—the strongest force of social control in the experience of any person. With mobility comes anonymity, and with it an easy evasion of the restrictions of one's past, the shedding of one's reputation, a chance to turn over a new leaf not only for better but also for worse.

Migration is also frequently a time of stress and readjustment for the person so that he is inclined to throw off certain old restraints and to experiment with new ventures which may previously have been taboo for him. Mobility, especially in wartime, often brings separation from family because of housing shortages and conditions of crowding. In boom communities where neighbors are also footloose, some of them perhaps having engaged in many migrations, there are few restraints. Add to this the fact that in America there is a large "floating" population that follows jobs in industry and agriculture, having no permanent place of abode. The migration factor must be recognized as a disorganizing factor in American society. (One must recognize also that it is often also a constructive force providing opportunity for some to better themselves economically and socially.)

Migration generally produces an unbalanced sex ratio because different communities offer work primarily for one sex or the other, not both. As a consequence, such communities become disorganized from the standpoint of normal patterns of association between the sexes. This, to an extent, affects marriage stability and family life of the community.

In addition to migration of population, which has always been a disturbing source of social change in the United States, is the factor of vertical mobility. As has been shown, movement up and down the social ladder is a type of social change that calls for much adjustment. Certainly the strain incident to vertical mobility must be mentioned as a source of stress and strain in our society and, consequently, as a factor in personal disorganization.

Rapid Cultural Change. The problem of the marginal man who suffers tensions in bridging two cultures, the one of his birth, the other of his adoption, has been discussed. To a lesser extent any rapid cycle of cultural change produces varying degrees of maladjustment in persons and in social groups.

Take, for example, the acceptance of the theory of evolution by scientific thinkers after the development of the Darwinian thesis and its presentation in the *Origin of Species*. For generations afterward orthodox religious groups suffered a certain amount of disorganization in trying to reconcile their belief regarding creation to this evolutionary hypothesis. For many young people, reared in the strict tradition of the orthodox doctrine of creation, this new idea presented in the classroom proved to be a disruptive one which caused them deep emotional concern. For many it meant a loss of faith which was never regained; for others it meant a reconstruction, which was achieved by a reinterpretation of their orthodox religion in terms of scientific concepts, with some compromise, of course, of old beliefs. In an earlier age the theories of geology regarding the antiquity of the world as evidenced in rock formations caused similar disorganization in the religious faith of peoples.

In the field of mechanical devices the disorganization of life habits, occupation, even to some extent moral standards, is such a common experience as to almost require no demonstration. The automobile ruined the livery-stable business, the blacksmith's trade, the harnessmaker's occupation, the carriage-making industry, and many other related aspects of the transportation complex which had been oriented around horse and carriage. The automobile even caused a certain amount of disorganization in the agricultural occupation throughout the nation. Huge surpluses of feed grains and cereal grains accumulated during the 1920's after the automobile had become a near universal means of transportation and after the tractor had come into extensive use, causing the disappearance of millions of grain-eating horses from the American farm and from the streets of towns and cities. Greatly magnified by subsequent events, the problem of farm surpluses has not yet been solved, even though the United States Department of Agriculture has spent billions in the attempt.

The automobile also brought extensive moral changes. Farm parents could no longer keep close checks on their children. New problems of parent–teenage relationships developed with the consolidated school and the teenager's use of the automobile. So one might go on listing the rather sudden changes produced by the automobile, all of which were temporarily disorganizing in their effect on some phase of American folkways and which even at points challenged existing moral standards.

When one adds to this single invention the thousands of others that appear constantly in the American culture pattern, and the new ideas that are constantly emerging and being propagated by one group or another, he begins to appreciate the tremendously dynamic effect of culture change in challenging at many points old folkways and mores, forcing people out of their accustomed channels of thinking and doing.

The modern industrialized world has come to take a certain amount of cultural disorganization for granted, even to the extent that one of the aims of the secondary school has become that of preparing youth for a world of change, or, as it is sometimes stated, to teach young people to be adjustable rather than to be merely creatures of habit.

The borrowing or invention of new culture traits often produces maladjustments between related elements of culture which are also a source of disorganization. This aspect of culture change has been referred to as *culture lag*. To illustrate, the advent of our machine-age civilization, with its inevitable unemployment and economic fluctuations, came years before social security in the form of unemployment insurance. And again, in most countries families were on salaries and wages long before family allowance plans were developed to protect children in such income groups from the hazards of cutting the family's income into too thin slices. In fact, the United States stands almost alone among industrial nations in not having any family allowance system.[3]

To cite other cases of cultural lag, a cotton picker was invented to replace the Negro worker long before social policies were developed to assure the Negro an income by some other means. Courses to fulfill college entrance requirements, compulsory for all, continue to dominate in the high-school curriculum long after the demands of urban society clearly indicate a need for youth trained in home administration and family living, training which half must receive in high school or not at all, as they do not go on to college.

Urbanization. Urbanization has been one of the most significant changes in the history of mankind. From time immemorial the race has lived in rural environments and in small groups where face-to-face relationships were characteristic. The struggle through the ages was with natural environment. While fairly large cities have existed over a period of several centuries, it remained for the machine age and the industrial revolution to convert the masses from a life in rural areas and small towns to life in the great metropolitan centers. Even though this process has been under way at a rapid rate for a hundred years, it remained for the last few decades to see the concentration of the increasing numbers of people in the great metropolises and their satellite cities where industry, trade, commerce, and communication all meet.

In less than a century and a half the old folk culture of rural society in the United States has gradually been replaced, or at least modified extensively, by the processes of urbanization. This has led to various interactive forces which have been disruptive and disorganizing in effect, even though many of them have been responsible for some of the most far-reaching attainments in the economic sphere, the rising standard of living, and the growing objectivity of modern man.

In the rural community the person keeps his eyes on his neighbors. Their comings and goings are known to all. Problems of social control are relatively simple. The community has one standard of conduct which is expected of all. The reprobate as well as the respected citizen knows what the codes are. The reprobate who chooses to disobey them at least knows the penalty he will pay, for he knows what is expected of him. Children and youth grow to maturity under the simple framework of standards and beliefs of the neighborhood

---

[3] In Canada, for example, all mothers get money from the government for each child from birth to age sixteen. Allowances begin at $6.00 per month and increase up to $9.00 as the child gets older.

Slums are a manifestation of social disorganization in many urban communities. They are often found in areas occupied by underprivileged ethnic minority groups. This photograph shows Mexican quarters in a Texas city. (Ewing Calloway.)

and community. Not so in the great city, where peoples of numerous standards congregate, where "birds of a feather may flock together" and develop patterns of behavior that are different from those generally accepted. In densely settled areas a human being loses interest in what the other person does. His conduct comes to be his own business; the neighborhood loses supervision over him, and the community relaxes its controls. Each person is allowed to go his own way as long as he does not commit a major infraction against the rights and privileges of other persons.

In the concentrated population areas of the city one finds the greatest anonymity, the greatest freedom from social control. The slums of the city, the roominghouse areas, and the hobohemias are areas where one may be alone in the midst of dense concentration of population. He may die and no one is particularly concerned. He may be in the deepest trouble, but each man has his own troubles and ignores his neighbor. Even the refugee from justice can hide better there than almost anywhere else, certainly far more easily than in the average rural community. The city from one standpoint is the most highly organized form of life known to man, yet many of its aspects are most highly disorganized.

Our great cities have seen the terror of gangsters, have been victimized by racketeers, and the police and public have often been powerless to cope with them. Far too often the law itself has been ineffective because the policeman has joined forces with the underworld. Even government in the city has tended to become polluted. On the surface there has been evidence of democratic control but underneath there has often been the machinations of those who lived by graft and patronage, blackmail and crime. Urban political machines have far too often been identified with the underworld, and paid it tribute in return for political favors and for political power.

Of a Chicago slum some years ago, Zorbaugh said:

"There is tolerance of 'foreign' customs and ideas not to be found without the slum. Groups in accommodating themselves to one another assimilate one another's folkways and mores. Cultures lose much of their identity. The mores tend to lose their sanctions. And in this cosmopolitan world, by virtue of this tolerance of the 'foreign' and interpenetration of customs, traditional social definitions lose their meaning, and traditional controls break down. Groups tend to lose their identity, and the social patterns of these groups tend to merge into a hybrid something that is neither Sicilian nor Persian nor Polish, but of the slum. This is particularly true of the smaller groups, like the North Side Jew, Pole, and Greek, who do not live in colonies but are scattered throughout the slum.

"The life of the slum is lived almost entirely without the conventional world. Practically its only contacts with the conventional world are through the social agency and the law. The social agency is looked upon as a sort of legitimate graft whereby small incomes may be considerably supplemented; and the law, symbolized by the 'copper,' the 'bull,' the 'flivver,' and the 'wagon,' is to the dweller in the slum a source of interference and oppression, a cause of interrupted incomes, a natural enemy. The Lake Shore Drive is as 'foreign' to many a resident of Little Hell as though it were separated from him by the Atlantic Ocean."[4]

Depicting the world of furnished rooms, Zorbaugh wrote:

"The constant comings and goings of its inhabitants is the most striking and significant characteristic of this world of furnished rooms. This whole population turns over every four months. There are always cards in the windows, advertising the fact that rooms are vacant, but these cards rarely have to stay up over a day, as people are constantly walking the streets looking for rooms. The keepers of the rooming-houses change almost as rapidly as the roomers them-

[4] Harvey W. Zorbaugh, *The Gold Coast and the Slum* (Chicago: University of Chicago Press, 1929), pp. 151–53.

selves. At least half of the keepers of these houses have been at their present addresses six months or less.

"The conditions of life in the world of furnished rooms are the direct antithesis of all we are accustomed to think of as normal in society. The exaggerated mobility and astonishing anonymity of this world have significant implications for the life of the community. Where people are constantly coming and going; where they live at best but a few months in a given place; where no one knows anyone else in his own house, to say nothing of his own block (children are the real neighbors, and it is a childless world); where there are no groups of any sort—where all these things are true it is obvious that there can be no community tradition or common definition of situations, no public opinion, no informal social control. As a result, the rooming-house world is a world of political indifference, of laxity of conventional standards, of personal and social disorganization.

"The rooming-house world is in no sense a social world, a set of group relationships through which the person's wishes are realized. In this situation of mobility and anonymity, rather, social distances are set up, and the person is isolated. His social contacts are more or less completely cut off. His wishes are thwarted; he finds in the rooming-house neither security, response, nor recognition. His physical impulses are curbed. He is restless, and he is lonely."[5]

Again the disorganization of the slum is contrasted with the normal community:

"The 'normal' community tends to meet crisis situations for its members. The 'normal' family does the same thing. But the slum community and the slum family fail in this respect. Over a large area of the slum, the area of cheap lodging-houses, there is nothing of the nature of a community. And the persons and families who live in these lodging houses are segregated there because they have failed, for one reason or another, to adjust elsewhere. Many of these are merely ineffective. Moreover, the very physical conditions of lodging-house life, particularly its mobility, make impossible that constellation of attitudes about a home, with its significant ritual, which affords the basis for that emotional interdependence which is the sociologically significant fact of family life. As a result, the person who dwells in the lodging-house of the slum has to meet his problems alone. This is peculiarly significant in the behavior patterns of the child."[6]

Zorbaugh found that more than a third of slum boys ten to sixteen years of age had been apprehended by police or other law enforce-

5 *Ibid.*, p. 153.
6 *Ibid.*, p. 155.

ment agencies in the course of a year, as was shown in a previous citation to a study of delinquency in Chicago (Chapter 11).[7] Mental disease, suicide, and other evidences of human wreckage have also been found to be concentrated in disorganized areas of the great city.[8]

By and large one must conclude that urbanization has been one of the major factors in producing social disorganization in the modern world. Effective devices for social control, that is, for maintaining order in all areas of the city, have yet to be developed. For this the city pays a heavy toll to those forces which prey upon society.

Among the important reorganizing factors is the new city suburb with its emphasis on family living, neighborliness, and community institutions. Here a more effective social control is being established. It lacks the rigorousness of the small-town primary group, yet is effective in maintaining reasonable restraint over the individual.

Increasing Influence of Secondary Group Experience. Another major force of personal disorganization especially, but also of social disorganization, is the rapid and continuous growth of secondary group relationships with the consequent decline of primary group relationships. It has been indicated that the primary group is protective. Mutual interest tends to be its characteristic trait. *Secondary groups are naturally disorganizing to the person in that they give him an immense amount of freedom to follow out his own selfish wishes but also impose great strains upon him.* In times of crisis he may break because no intimate group is near by to share his burdens. Then psychiatrists and social workers try to take over part of the load of the overburdened individual.

The strain of urban secondary group experience has become so great that in highly urbanized states about one in every dozen adults spends a longer or shorter period in a hospital psychiatric ward or in an institution for the mentally ill.

Secularization. By *secularization* is meant *the gradual tendency to interpret all of life by purely naturalistic explanations as compared to the mythical and theological explanations of sacred cultures.* Certainly this century has seen a gradual shift in man's thinking away from theological interpretations of the universe to purely scientific and rational ones. As this trend in thinking has come about, many of the old traditions and controls that centered about religion and the church have been weakened.

[7] So studies of the Chicago slum by Clifford Shaw and his colleagues show. See their *Delinquency Areas* (Chicago: University of Chicago Press, 1928).

[8] Refer again to the section on urban ecology in Chapter 11, pp. 198–215, for a summary of some of these studies.

Men once lived in fear of an all-seeing God, and felt themselves subjected to his rule and to his providences. In a purely naturalistic world man chooses his own way, works out his own destiny, and takes the consequences of his behavior. Once religious attitudes were major factors in social control; they tended to make men self-regulated under the guidance of their religious ideals and scruples. As great numbers have questioned the authority of religion, challenged the divine inspiration of the Bible, and rejected it as a guide, they have questioned the precepts of the church and its doctrines and creeds.

American culture has been moving rapidly in the direction of the venturesome, experimental secular culture, away from the security of the old and tried ways of religious tradition. One of the major consequences has been that religion has declined as an influence in regulating human beings. It has lost much of its controlling force because it is no longer accepted by great numbers as an infallible guide to what is good and right in human relationships. As yet no force of equal strength in maintaining authority over the individual has been developed.

Secularization has brought new liberty to mankind, but there has not as yet been developed with it a high sense of man's obligation to his fellow men. The development of an objective morality that will be as powerful in regulating human affairs as religion of an in-group character once was remains for the future. Secularization must, therefore, be listed as one of the major forces in the breakdown of social control, personality strain, and a certain amount of personal and social disorganization.

SUMMARY

Social disorganization has been defined as the breakdown of social control to the extent that disorder rather than order prevails in the aspect of group life under consideration. The social norm is organization; disorganization is a variation from it to a degree that a society is aware of a problem in social control. Forces of change in modern society and in contemporary culture are basic in contemporary social disorganization. Leading aspects of disruptive change are urbanization, population movement, the growth of large secondary groups, rapid cultural change, and secularization.

DISCUSSION AND REVIEW QUESTIONS

1. Discuss factors involved in social disorganization.
2. Cite examples of social disorganization.
3. Discuss change as a factor in social disorganization.

4. List five major forces of change that are prominent in social disorganization in contemporary society.

5. Show how population movement and vertical mobility are factors in social disorganization. Explain how standards become confused in such a world.

6. Show how material and nonmaterial culture change are forces.

7. Discuss urbanization as a factor in the shift toward secondary group experience.

8. Define secularization and show how it is a disruptive force in social control.

9. Do you feel that the recent interest in revivalistic religion of the Billy Graham type may indicate a return to a more sacred approach to life in the Western world?

SOURCEBOOK READINGS

GITTLER, JOSEPH B. *Social Dynamics.* New York: McGraw-Hill Book Co., Inc., 1952.
  1. SHAW, CLIFFORD, "The Life History of a Delinquent," pp. 292–317.

KOENIG, SAMUEL, REX D. HOPPER, and FELIKS GROSS. *Sociology: A Book of Readings.* Englewood Cliffs, N.J.: Prentice-Hall, Inc., 1956.
  2. FULLER, RICHARD C., and RICHARD R. MYERS, "The Natural History of a Social Problem," pp. 550–56.

LEE, RAYMOND L., JAMES A. BURKHART, and VAN B. SHAW. *Contemporary Social Issues.* New York: The Thomas Crowell Co., 1955.
  3. FRANK, LAWRENCE K., "Society as the Patient," pp. 281–84.

LEE, ELIZABETH BRYANT, and ALFRED McCLUNG LEE. *Social Problems in America* (rev. ed.). New York: Henry Holt & Co., Inc., 1955.
  4. FRANK, LAWRENCE K., "The Character of Social Problems," pp. 4–7.
  5. FULLER, RICHARD C., and RICHARD R. MYERS, "Social Problems in Relation to Values," pp. 9–11.
  6. FULLER, RICHARD C., and RICHARD R. MYERS, "The Natural History of a Social Problem," pp. 11–13.
  7. THOMAS, WILLIAM I., and FLORIAN ZNANIECKI, "The Concept of Social Disorganization," pp. 17–18.
  8. MERTON, ROBERT K., "Social Structure and Anomie," p. 20.
  9. MILLS, C. WRIGHT, "An Attack on Disorganization Theorists," pp. 25–26.
  10. FRANK, LAWRENCE K., "Society as the Patient," pp. 36–38.

WILSON, LOGAN, and WILLIAM L. KOLB. *Sociological Analysis.* New York: Harcourt, Brace & Co., Inc., 1949.
  11. MERTON, ROBERT K., "Social Structure and Anomie," pp. 771–80.
  12. FULLER, RICHARD C., and RICHARD R. MYERS, "The Natural History of a Social Problem," pp. 780–88.

SELECTED READINGS

BLOCK, HERBERT A. *Disorganization, Personal and Social.* New York: Alfred A. Knopf, Inc., 1952.

BOWMAN, K. M., and E. M. JELLINEK. "Alcohol and Mental Disorders," *Quarterly Journal of Studies on Alcohol,* 2:378 ff. (Sept., 1941).

CLINARD, MARSHALL B. *Sociology of Deviant Behavior.* New York: Rinehart & Co., Inc., 1957.

DURKHEIM, EMILE. *Suicide.* (Translated by John A. Spaulding and George Simpson.) Glencoe, Ill.: The Free Press, 1951.

FARIS, ROBERT E. L. *Social Disorganization.* 2d ed.; New York: The Ronald Press Co., 1955.

FARIS, ROBERT E. L., and H. WARREN DUNHAM. *Mental Disorders in Urban Areas.* Chicago: University of Chicago Press, 1939.

FRUMKIN, ROBERT M. "Social Factors in Schizophrenia," *Sociology and Social Research*, 38:383–86 (July–Aug., 1954).

HORTON, PAUL B., and GERALD R. LESLIE. *The Sociology of Social Problems.* New York: Appleton-Century-Crofts, Inc., 1955, pp. 390–420.

JELLINEK, E. M. "Phases in the Drinking History of Alcoholics," *Memoirs of the Section on Alcohol Studies*, No. 5, Yale University, 1947.

JENKINS, RICHARD L. "Adaptive and Maladaptive Delinquency," *The Nervous Child*, 11:9–11 (Oct., 1955).

KEFAUVER, ESTES. *Crime in America.* Garden City, N.Y.: Doubleday & Co., Inc., 1951.

LANDIS, PAUL H. *Social Control: Social Organization and Disorganization in Process.* Chicago: J. B. Lippincott Co., 1956, chaps. 23–26.

MERRILL, FRANCIS E., H. W. DUNHAM, A. M. ROSE and P. W. TAPPAN. *Social Problems.* New York: Alfred A. Knopf, Inc., 1950, chap. 5.

MERTON, ROBERT K. "Social Control and Anomie," *American Sociological Review*, 3:672–82; also *Social Theory and Social Structure.* Glencoe, Ill.: The Free Press, 1949, chap. 4.

NISBET, ROBERT T. *The Quest for Community: A Study in Ethics of Freedom and Order.* New York: Oxford University Press, 1953.

OGBURN, WILLIAM F. "Cultural Lag as Theory," *Sociology and Social Research*, 41: 167–74 (Jan.–Feb., 1957).

———. *Social Change.* Rev. ed.; New York: The Viking Press, Inc., 1950.

——— (ed.). *Technology and International Relations.* Chicago: University of Chicago Press, 1949.

RECKLESS, WALTER C. *The Crime Problem.* 2d ed.; New York: Appleton-Century-Crofts, Inc., 1955.

SHAW, CLIFFORD R., *et al. Delinquency Areas.* Chicago: University of Chicago Press, 1929.

SHORT, JAMES F. "Psychosomatic Complaints, Institutionalization and Delinquency," *Research Studies of the State College of Washington*, 24:150–59 (June, 1956).

SUTHERLAND, EDWIN H., and DONALD R. CRESSEY. *Principles of Criminology.* 4th ed.; Philadelphia: J. B. Lippincott Co., 1955.

WRIGHT, QUINCY. *A Study of War.* 2 vols. Chicago: University of Chicago Press, 1942.

Chapter 31

Social Planning and Social Policies

In the preceding chapter discussion was focused on the process of social disorganization and its result in weakened social controls. This leaves society exposed to predatory groups and removes from the individual many of the protections which keep him a regulated and orderly creature, as well as protecting him from his own vices.

When a particular problem reaches crisis proportions and society becomes acutely aware of its existence, social movements develop to cope with the situation and to restore order. In a revolution, of course, order has to be restored to counteract famine which comes from people's refusal to work. In time of widespread strikes which threaten public disaster, the government has to step in to keep the public from suffering for want of fuel, transportation, etc. When unbelief and skepticism prevail, conscientious religious leaders start their revivalistic movements to win man back to religious faiths and to righteous living.

When political corruption and racketeering take over the city government and citizens become sufficiently alarmed, citizen committees are formed and public opinion is crystallized through propaganda to vote in a reform government. Gradually the constructive forces of the community begin to take over, to clean out racketeering, and to reconstruct political control of an acceptable sort, control that is motivated by public interest rather than private profit.

When waste and exploitation of natural resources threaten the welfare of future generations, social movements are started by conservationists to institute political and legal reforms. They may employ every device of propaganda known in a world of secondary groups—radios, newspapers, magazines, and television—for teaching methods of conservation, making people aware of the dangers of waste, prejudicing them against the exploiter. This may create a widespread public consciousness of the existing social problem and its solution.

These examples are enough to show that the forces working for social reorganization and social reform are operative. These forces, for the most part, are consciously directed. Social disorganization, as has been seen, usually comes about as a by-product of widespread social changes, without anyone intending that disorganization should be the result. Social progress comes primarily by man's striving to initiate social movements to bring about reform. Social improvement comes by the conscious direction of change toward desired goals.

SOCIAL REORGANIZATION

One of the classics of American sociology is *Folkways*, Sumner's famous study of folkways and mores.[1] In this analysis the author stressed the resistance which all cultures offer to change. In his description of the persistence of folkways and mores through the centuries, he gave the impression that man is in the grasp of the inertia of his own ways of life, that man can scarcely change anything at all by his own choice, planning, and deliberate volition. He was accused of propagating an enervating fatalism, and to some extent this charge was justified.

It must be admitted that culture is never entirely logical; in fact, it can never stand a rigid pragmatic test. All cultures are built more or less blindly through trial and error. The useful and cumbersome both tend to survive and to be passed on from generation to generation. One anthropologist has called civilization a thing of shreds and patches.[2] In using this description he was referring to all civilization, ours included. Another has commented that all civilizations need revision; no one of them is perfect as it stands and never will be.[3] Some serve the needs of the individual better than others; some serve the needs of the race better than others; but many patterns of civilization have been developed with sufficient usefulness to man that he has been able to survive in them.

Through the ages man goes on tinkering with his cultural environment, always with the idea that he is improving it. Some things he does actually do improve it; other phases of his tinkering add greater

[1] William Graham Sumner, *Folkways* (Boston: Ginn & Co., 1906).
[2] Robert H. Lowie, *Are We Civilized?* (New York: Harcourt, Brace & Co., Inc., 1929).
[3] Ruth Benedict, "The Science of Custom," *Century*, April, 1929, pp. 641–49.

burdens. Humanity seems to have been capable of shouldering much needless cultural baggage, and still survives in spite of it. For example, custom in some cultures requires that much of an individual's property acquired during his lifetime be destroyed in his funeral fire. Many items of style add a needless burden to human life and human inconvenience, and yet humanity survives in spite of these various burdens which the culture keeps adding.

Consider the tremendous burden that war loads upon mankind. If humanity were not tough, it certainly could not carry this burden, which has been civilization's greatest one over many centuries. In spite of all its costs, it would be hard to show that man has gained anything in the way of improving his life on earth for war's vast expenditures of blood and treasure. If man cannot improve his way of life by rational planning and policy-making, he has no choice but to continue to carry many such needless burdens.

But there is every evidence that modern man is, in part at least, the master of his fate. There is little doubt that Sumner's theory of the folkways took too little account of the dynamic forces of invention. Actually modern man has in this century developed what may be appropriately called *technicways*, that is, ways of doing things that are adjusted to a machine age. These ways have to change as man's inventive technology changes, for to use new machines, man must develop new folkways and make numerous readjustments.

Moreover, in this age, deliberate planning, backed by scientific inquiry and objectivity, is a major culture complex. Such planning and objectivity were not a part of the life of early man, nor is it a prominent part of primitive culture anywhere today. In the machine world man is constantly challenging traditions. He is secular minded, as has been pointed out. As a consequence, social reforms, social movements, evangelistic crusades of one sort or another, even violent political revolutions are characteristic of the experience of modern man.

He has become a long-range planner, using the laboratory as a device for improving his knowledge and his material civilization. He has introduced trial and error in the laboratory on the experimental scale; he has developed the pilot plant; he has developed mathematics so he can test projects of gigantic proportions, and know the outcome before he ever begins construction. To a lesser extent he formulates policies toward which to work in the realization of better social relations and better social conditions. As a consequence, modern man has the capacity to reorganize and reshape society and does it to a greater extent than men in history have ever done.

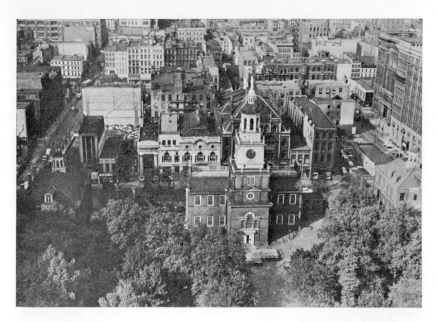

Social Planning Can Preserve the Nation's Cultural Heritage

In 1949 the state of Pennsylvania and the federal government began a multimillion-dollar development program to save Independence Hall and other colonial buildings in Old Philadelphia from the inroads of industry and slums. The Independence Hall area is shown (top) before the project was begun and (bottom) after much of the work was completed. (Wide World)

In saying this, of course, one must recognize that at many points he falls short of taking care of problems that arise before they become critical. At many points his hindsight is much better than his foresight and much of social planning falls short of realizing the high goals for which it was intended. On the other hand, modern man is becoming increasingly effective in introducing counterforces to correct social disorganization or to check the process of disorganization before conditions reach a critical stage. It is possible that as he has more experience with urban living and with a rapidly changing industrial civilization, he will become much more efficient in planning his destiny and in controlling the trend of culture-building.

In a real sense, planning and policy-making must become world-wide in many of their aspects. One of the vital problems of the Western world, particularly of the United States, in an age when development of "under-developed countries" has become a recognized responsibility, is that many nations have no conception of planning, policy-making, or of progress through directed change. Deep-seated customs, family systems, caste in social and work relations, and fatalistic religious philosophies are the antithesis of change, improvement, and planned development. To sell these social systems on the view that the golden age is of man's making is difficult indeed, but necessary and in time possible.

ATTITUDES TOWARD PLANNING

Even in the Western world reform is usually more popular than planning, yet much less sound. Reform is remedial, correcting errors of the past. Planning is constructive and preventive, laying the groundwork to keep problems from developing. Yet planning is often condemned by those who believe in *laissez faire,* or any who like to think that the affairs of the world will run themselves. Modern society has become so complex that life on a large scale is impossible without a great deal of planning. The greater the population aggregate, the greater the degree of planning and systematic direction required for social traffic. One need not talk about social planning if he lives in an isolated region in the Ozark Mountains and depends largely on the foodstuffs which he himself raises for a living, but the commercial farmer must plan if he is to succeed. The businessman must plan. Industry is constantly planning for the future; in fact, models of next year and for five or ten years hence in automobiles and aircraft are already being designed in the great laboratories where research and planning are as continuous as is the production line itself. If this were not so the production line would soon stop.

So, also, the city must plan if it is to have any order and arrangement. If there is to be any beauty, it must be zoned, scenic spots protected, residential areas shielded from the incursion of industry, pedestrians protected against traffic hazard. If the city is to handle the transportation and communication that is necessary to keep the urban lifelines open, it must plan on an extensive scale and look years ahead. If it fails to plan adequately, it must in the future rectify its error at a terrific cost, as many cities increasingly have had to do in widening streets, digging tunnels under streets or rivers, or in making other adjustments to facilitate the daily movement into and out of the central part of the business district.

On a national scale, planning is required if a nation is to make the best use of its resources today and to assure their conservation for future generations. Scenic beauty must be protected if it is to be preserved for posterity to see and to use for recreational purposes. So also must plans be formulated for the development of waterways, of highways, and of airways. In 1956 the United States, long aware that the high death toll of the highways was in part due to overcrowding on outmoded highways, projected a ten-year plan for the construction of superhighways across the nation.

On a world-wide scale also man must plan increasingly in order to regulate the commerce and trade, the development, exploitation, and conservation of resources, and to regulate population numbers in relation to potential food supply.

The real objection to planning, as usually expressed, is a fear that planning may regulate liberties. And yet it is obvious that there is no way in which man can live in great aggregates without a great deal of regulation. The more dense life becomes, the thicker the social traffic, the greater the amount of planned development required.

Another objection to planning grows out of the conception that all planning smacks of communism, since the Soviet Union's five-year plans for industrial development have been so well publicized. Fears have been aroused, also, because the modern world saw much planning in the dictator nations prior to World War II—planning which was motivated not by the common welfare but by the ideal of a planned superstate to minister to the selfish interest of demagogues who sought unlimited political power. Planning in such nations was so highly efficient and so comprehensive that the public had no way of protecting itself from the arm of the Gestapo or from the rigorous holds which the political regime had upon the economy. Thus lessons of totalitarian regimes make many fear planning and policy-making. Yet abuses of a system do not necessarily prove that it cannot be reasonably used. Misuse of these devices by totalitarian dictator regimes brings the destruction of the regime and the dictators with it, as recent history has so often shown.

In a democratic society planning must always be motivated by the ideal of the greatest good for the greatest number. It is true that in time of war, to compete with the rigidly controlled societies of dictator nations, democracies have had to centralize control on a scale never before experienced. Food, natural resources, and industrial production were government-controlled. Even the citizen's comings and goings were regulated by restrictions on motor fuel. Such restrictions cannot, however, be the characteristic philosophy of life in a democratic society except in times of crisis.

SOCIAL PLANNING AND SOCIAL POLICY DEFINED

Social planning and social policy both have to do with deliberate conscious processes of setting goals for realization through social action. The term *social planning* refers to *goals for action in the field of improving material aspects of culture and arrangements of it in space*. The term *social policy* is used to refer to *goals for action in the field of improving social relations or social conditions*. Such a clear-cut distinction is not always followed in common usage, nor can all types of social action in the direction of realizing socially established goals be put into one category or the other, yet the distinction is about as good as can be made.

In the field of social planning, city planning is an example. It has to do with the arrangement of thoroughfares, parks, playgrounds; the zoning of land use to provide for a systematic, logical, convenient, sanitary, and attractive arrangement of structures that make up the material pattern of the city; the projection of city growth on a tentative basis, so that present developments will permit an orderly and convenient pattern of material expansion, and so forth.

In the field of social policy, an example is the restriction of immigration, the group allowed to enter to be rigidly selected on the basis of nationality, health, mental fitness, and so on. Here the concern is with the effect of immigration on the health and welfare, standard of living, and wage scale of the citizens of the nation.

Planning and policy-making may well be considered social processes in that they involve setting goals for action. These goals are always tentative and are modified often as they are approached by action programs. Social planning and social policy, then, are a setting of tentative goals to be reached by successive series of action programs. No sooner does social policy, in the field of welfare for example, realize its goals in a social security program than new and higher welfare goals emerge for attainment. Unemployment insurance is good, but why not a year-round job for every man? Medical care and rehabilitation programs for the crippled are good, but why not adequate medical care and preventive health care for the sound also? And so policy-making stakes out new goals.

Planning and policy-making are also social processes in another vital sense: there are always alternative policies. Public discussion, leadership, and various other forms of interaction enter into the formulation of the plan or policy ultimately made the basis for action.[4]

In the broadest use of the terms, planning and policy-making include all the activities by which modern society attempts to correct social disorganization, strengthen social control, and establish a more effective system of social organization and social relationships.

SOME NEEDED SOCIAL POLICIES FOR THE UNITED STATES

Social policies, that is, those more specific measures, often of a legislative nature, which aim to cure specific problems in social relations or social conditions, are always in the making in an inventive society which is receptive to change. Intelligent social policy works not simply with the symptoms of social disorganization, trying to cure particular problems themselves, but also, insofar as it is possible, with modifying the social forces that produce the maladjustments.

Delinquency and Crime. In areas where social disorganization is so great that juvenile delinquency tends to be the rather universal pattern of life, the proper approach is not to attack delinquency by greater and more effective police methods, but to introduce playgrounds with constructive programs of recreation, to provide clubs staffed with wise leaders, to clear slums, and through other such devices to provide constructive activities in place of the socially destructive ones which characterize life in the area.

In handling the criminal, society must not resort to further punishment because he has failed to conform to the regulations of society; it must provide, as has been done increasingly, for his constructive learning and personal development while he is in the custody of the state. The prevailing philosophy of prison treatment has been changing over the period of a generation, but penology is still far from

[4] For a penetrating analysis of policy-making in the field of government, see Robert M. MacIver, *The Web of Government* (New York: The Macmillan Co., 1947), pp. 9–12. Also see Joseph S. Himes, *Social Planning in America: A Dynamic Interpretation*, Doubleday Short Studies in Sociology (Garden City, N.Y.: Doubleday & Co., Inc., 1954).

applying most effectively the devices for reconstructing personality which are now known. Every prisoner when he enters a prison should be given a complete series of tests and classified according to his abilities and aptitudes. His problem should be analyzed and a definite program of instruction instituted for him. The aim should be his early return to society as a fit member of that society. If such a program were instituted, especially for youthful offenders, many of the problems of punishing and housing criminals would disappear. Leaders in penal theory even look forward to a time when the majority of criminals will not be placed in prison at all, but placed in training situations, where their custody would be directed at reform rather than at punishment. Certainly such an approach must, at an early date, become the one used with all delinquent children, not just with those few who are lucky enough to fall into the hands of a wise and far-seeing judge or probation officer when they commit their first serious offense and come to the attention of public agencies.

Social Security. Not until the year 1935 did the United States recognize on a national scale that economic disorganization was an inevitable counterpart of the business cycle in a highly competitive industrial society. Not until then was it recognized on a national scale that man is a victim of these forces when he finds himself in poverty. Until that time the old idea persisted that a man is responsibile for his own economic misfortune, and that if society helps him, it should be on a charity basis, as though they were helping someone who was incapable of helping himself because of moral or mental deficiency. Now society guarantees food, clothing, and the minimum of shelter to all industrial workers. It recognizes that all people are exposed to economic hazards. Moreover, there must be continuous policy-making in this area as economic conditions and new conceptions of welfare make citizen needs here apparent. (A study of welfare institutions is made in Chapter 39.)

Health. It would seem that a democratic society must also extend help and protection to all of its citizens through an adequate system of medical care, either by a health insurance scheme similar to current unemployment insurance, through the Social Security Act, or through tax-supported medicine (socialized medicine) on a basis comparable to public education. Certainly the health of a nation's people is as important as their universal enlightenment through education. The United States has reached the time when the best medical science has to offer is inaccessible to the masses on a fee basis. Over a period of a few years medical costs have more than trebled.

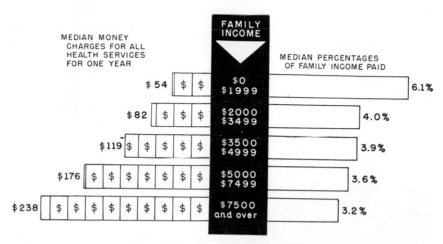

MEDIAN MONEY
CHARGES FOR ALL
HEALTH SERVICES
FOR ONE YEAR

FAMILY
INCOME

MEDIAN PERCENTAGES
OF FAMILY INCOME PAID

$54 $ $ | $0 $1999 | 6.1%

$82 $ $ $ | $2000 $3499 | 4.0%

$119 $ $ $ $ | $3500 $4999 | 3.9%

$176 $ $ $ $ $ $ | $5000 $7499 | 3.6%

$238 $ $ $ $ $ $ $ $ | $7500 and over | 3.2%

A Weak Area in Social Policy

In the United States the privilege of schooling at the level of basic training has long been separated from ability to pay. Should democratic society similarly remove the privilege of good health and long life from ability to pay? This question has involved much debate and political controversy in the past two decades.

The average individual cannot afford the specialist; in fact, many of the largest families cannot even afford the attentions of the general practitioner. One of the revealing discoveries of the Depression era was that those who had the greatest responsibilities for the health and welfare of children, that is, the heads of very large families, were most often on relief. Certainly society must protect its children if it has a proper regard for the welfare of the next generation.

Some of the most progressive reforms made in the last two decades have been in the field of human welfare through Social Security. The development of a program to insure medical care to all would seem to be the logical next step forward.

With the fantastic rise in cost of surgery and hospital care, voluntary health insurance plans have gained millions of subscribers, and many industries and institutions share the cost of such plans in order to protect their employees from bankruptcy by a surgical emergency. Yet many do not and cannot afford to subscribe, and few plans are adequate to cover the most serious health risks of the middle-class and below middle-class income family.

Previous Congresses have considered bills providing for compulsory health insurance as a part of the Social Security program, but none of these has withstood the attack of the American Medical Association, which assessed each member doctor $25 to provide a fund for defeating the Congressional proposal. (The health problem is discussed more fully in Chapter 39.)

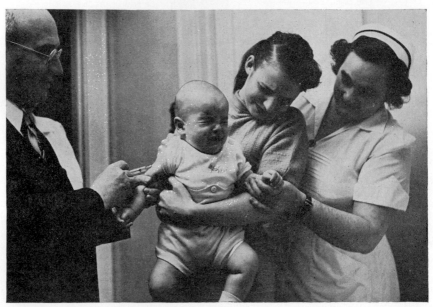

Public health is a vital area of policy-making. Here a toddler receives (reluctantly) an inoculation at a well baby clinic. (Standard Oil Company, N.J.)

Education. The privilege of education must also be increased. For many years the nation has had a rather completely socialized system of public education. The general tendency has been to decrease the cost of schooling to the individual family, not only by making grade schools and high schools tuition-free, but also by providing free school lunches and school books. Further developments in this line will do more to equalize educational opportunity. Unfortunately, in many states the rural young person still must pay tuition in order to go to a high school. This tends to bar many young people in rural areas from high school attendance. In other states high schools are so far away that attendance means moving to town and paying board and room. Federal aid to education so that such rural areas may have bus service and all schools may become tuition-free, even to those pupils that are not in the immediate district, would seem to be steps forward in equalizing opportunity for all groups in American society.

The privilege of college attendance must also be extended. Tuition fees, the cost of books and of board and room have risen. Future leadership comes from the college classrooms. This will be true tomorrow in an even greater sense than it is today. Providing jobs through some kind of a national youth organization so that those who cannot afford to attend college may do so; providing loans for worthy college students at low-interest rates, with a long period of repayment; perhaps even providing subsidies for a large group that should be offered scholarships and fellowships are devices that could be used to open the doors of institutions of higher learning to a larger group of young people with talent and ability. Many of this group now, because of the economic circumstances of their families, are unable to attend college. A democratic society cannot afford to lose any of its best leadership, and certainly in the lower economic classes will be found many of its future leaders if they are given a chance to climb the educational ladder and acquire the qualifications necessary to leadership in the modern world.

The G. I. Bill opened the doors of colleges to many thousands of capable youths who would never have been able to go to college otherwise. This was an investment in the future. During the first twelve years of its operation, the subsidy of veteran's education saw 8,000,000 ex-servicemen receive training, much of it in college courses. This program turned out 238,000 teachers, 450,000 engineers, 180,000 doctors and nurses, 112,000 scientists and 36,000 clergymen.[5] How much greater the nation's shortage of trained personnel would have been without this subsidy of college education!

During the 1950's (up to 1956) the average income of those trained under the G. I. program has climbed 51 per cent, compared to an increase of only 19 per cent for non-veterans of the same age.[6]

But the most significant aspect of this program is that a substantial portion of these persons could not have gone to college without the subsidy. Might it not be sound social policy to invest in the nation's future by comparable subsidy for all youths of demonstrated competence and ambition? As the shortage of scientists, teachers, engineers, and other professional personnel increases this may well become necessary. The Ford Foundation has recently created a group of scholarships for brilliant students and the Congress has considered various bills for making loans or scholarship grants to qualified young people needing assistance with their college training.

[5] *Time*, August 6, 1956, p. 44.
[6] *Ibid.*

The Aged. Throughout America, and especially in American cities, the aged feel their lives disorganized when they are compelled to leave the work world when they reach sixty-five. It is society's responsibility to provide constructive programs of social life, recreation, and part-time work so that these people may learn the creative

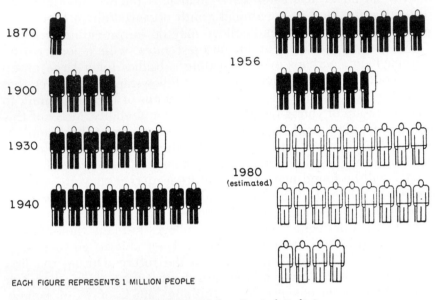

EACH FIGURE REPRESENTS 1 MILLION PEOPLE

Growing Need for Social Policies
Providing for the Aged

Crowded out of most parts of the labor market, those over 65 have often found themselves without resources. And advances in medicine and a rising standard of living have greatly increased the numbers of the aged in American society. Already many new social policies have been formulated to meet the needs of this group, and more will be necessary as the number of aged climbs to a projected 22 million in 1980.

use of leisure and not spend their last years in loneliness, isolation, and idleness, the victims often of imaginary sickness, boredom, and senility. Attention must also be given to housing for older persons.

SOCIAL SCIENCE IN PLANNING AND POLICY-MAKING

Man must direct social change toward desirable goals if he is to realize better conditions. In order to know what the better goals are and how to obtain them, he must depend increasingly upon research in the fields of social sciences, especially in sociology. Too much planning and policy-making have been guided by folklore and common sense, too little by an actual understanding of the forces at work in man's group life. Too often a thing is assumed to be true without being known to be true. Plans and policies built on erroneous conceptions accomplish results opposite to those intended. Man has the capacity to control and direct in a measure the forces of cultural and social change as he does the cultural forces of borrowing and diffusion.

The phrase "in a measure" is used advisedly. It is recognized that man cannot always, even with the best scientific insight, foresee all the consequences of a new invention or of a new trait borrowed from other cultures. If he cannot foresee its complications, he cannot, of course, know the direction in which he wants to have change move or know how to bring progress about. But with greater open-mindedness he can, where serious errors have been made, get at the seat of the difficulty through research and attempt to redirect change toward desirable goals.

There will always be trial and error in man's adjustment to his environment. He will continue to make mistakes in handling the natural environment, in making adjustments in the social environment, and in directing the course of cultural change and growth. Social science research, as it improves its tools and techniques and comes to obtain and handle sociological data more effectively, offers the most powerful device available to man for understanding problems of adjustment in the relations of man with man and of group with group.

On every level of society from the local neighborhood to the international area, social science research can get at the motives of human behavior which are in reality the driving force that determines behavior; it can provide the information necessary to change human motives and redirect human energy; it can prove a powerful force in teaching how to manipulate group behavior more effectively and make it conform to desirable social ends; it can provide the information necessary to guide the individual in his own adjustments to various social groups; it can provide information to help in the intimate adjustments of day-to-day living in marriage; it can provide information for a more effective administration of government and for the more effective organization and control of international relations.

The findings of social science cannot create Utopia, but it is the best tool man has at his disposal for bringing about change in the direction of desired goals and helping man understand what desired goals are. A better society must reckon with the forces inherent in man and in his experiences in group life. The social scientist is at home in dealing with these forces. The following passage will illustrate this point.

Traffic congestion in urban areas is an important problem of social planners. Modern cloverleaf highways and bypasses are being built to solve transportation problems. (Standard Oil Company, N.J.)

"In effect social science is a new instrument, not only for the getting of certain specific things done in the management of society, but for the clarification and development of our more ultimate values. The social uses of social science are not exhausted when we have said that social science can improve the efficiency of industrial production or test the aptitudes of young people for one kind of occupation rather than another. Social science is one of the ways to form our convictions as to the good life. This it does not as preaching does it, by telling us what the good is and what our duty is. It does not do it as ethics does it, by examining central questions as to the nature of conduct and by criticizing and formulating systematic rules of conduct. It does it by remaining science. It does it by making clear to us where our choices lead us and what means must be employed to reach what ends. It does it by extending our understanding of where our ideals are in conflict with our practices, and where our ideals are in conflict with each other. And it does this through those intensive studies of particular societies and particular men which are not ordinarily carried on in ethics and which are outside the powers and the responsibilities of the preacher. . . .

"There never was a time when social science was more needed than it is today. The extreme peril in which we live arises from the small political and social wisdom we have in the face of our immensely dangerous material strength. We should have more control over the physical world, yes, surely; but it is far more necessary that we learn to control the relations among men. We know now that we can destroy one another and the fruits of civilization, and we are far from sure that we can prevent ourselves from doing so. If social science could effect an improvement of our chances of preventing it of no more than one per cent, a great expenditure in social science would be justified.

"In explaining social science it needs to be said that social science is not only a box of tools. It is also a light. The social scientist is not only a sort of plumber to the circulatory and other ills of society; he is also, at his best, a source of understanding and enrichment. It should be pointed out that the test of good social science is not only: Will it work? There is another test: Does it make sense? For social science also justifies itself to the extent to which it makes life comprehensible and significant."[7]

THE ROLE OF THE SOCIAL SCIENTIST[8]

F. Stuart Chapin, one of the most objective of American social scientists, has pointed out that the resistance to social science knowledge is directly proportional to its validity. For the more valid the social scientists' analysis of crime, sex, politics, wealth, and vested interests, the more it is likely to challenge values and judgments currently held, thus arousing emotion and courting opposition. By exposing things as they are, it often disturbs vested interests.[9]

This comment implies that no matter how neutral and objective social science research may be, its findings are never neutral in their effect. The more sound, the more challenging to change and social action they are likely to be.

[7] Robert Redfield, "The Social Uses of Social Science," an address first published in *University of Colorado Bulletin*, May 27, 1947. Also in *University of Chicago Round Table*, No. 510 (Dec. 1947).

[8] The first seven paragraphs of this section are an adaptation of the author's *Social Control* (2d ed.; Chicago; J. B. Lippincott Co., 1956). For a fuller treatment, see that volume.

[9] F. Stuart Chapin, "Social Obstacles to the Acceptance of Existing Social Science Knowledge," *Social Forces*, 26:7 ff (Oct. 1947).

Shils feels that adequate science requires more than just an ability to manipulate data; there must be a sense of what is important. An adequate sociologist is one who is motivated by a broad curiosity about human affairs and a sense of responsibility to his fellow men. He is concerned about the clarification and improvement of moral rules and has a practical desire to perceive the conditions which have to do with their preservation or improvement.[10]

As eminent an authority as Robert S. Lynd maintains that the sociologist who refuses to express any opinion about values tacitly accepts the current values of the day. "There would be no social sciences," he says, "if there were not perplexities in living in culture that call for solution." Therefore, if the scientist does not interpret the implications of his findings, he leaves it to be interpreted by someone who is likely less qualified and more biased than he. He should not attempt to be a soothsayer, but at the same time he cannot drift in a disorganized culture without paying some attention to it.[11]

Lynd does not question the indispensability of detachment in weighing and evaluating data but he says that many social scientists are not as "pure" or as "neutral" as they pretend to be. There is such a thing, he says, as "idle" and "focused" curiosity but no such thing as "pure" curiosity. "Scientists are trained not to count the bricks in a building, but to be sensitive to problems which occur and which are significant."[12]

Somewhat opposed to those views just expressed, John F. Cuber and Robert A. Harper maintain that a sociologist should be an interpreter of values rather than an advocate of them. His job is to be an expert on the sociology of social problems, and not an expert on social problems. Therefore, before he studies any given area as a problem area it should already be so defined by the culture in which he lives.[13] Had Edwin H. Sutherland followed this formula, his notable presidential address in which he defined white collar crime as real criminality would never have been given.[14]

Most sociologists would agree that the primary role of the soci-

[10] Edward A. Shils, *The Present State of American Sociology* (Glencoe, Ill.: The Free Press, 1948); see especially p. 64.

[11] Robert S. Lynd, *Knowledge for What?* (Princeton: Princeton University Press, 1939), chap. 5.

[12] *Ibid.*

[13] John F. Cuber and Robert A. Harper, *Problems of American Society: Values in Conflict* (New York: Henry Holt & Co., Inc., 1948), pp. xi–xviii.

[14] For the full address, see "White Collar Criminality," *American Sociological Review,* 5:1–12 (Feb. 1940).

ologist is to treat values as data rather than advocating a value position. But, as Lynd points out, culture is not neutral. It involves people and emotions, and where these are, neutrality departs. Therefore, it is doubtful that the sociologist, in his interpretation of values, can appear to the various vested interests to be so neutral as not to appear to espouse some value position.

The sociologist, by being an objective analyst of culture, often strips the folkways and folklore down to their very essentials, and when they are so presented, the public immediately sees that better conditions could and should be created. Sociologists may even at many points see and compare the better and the worse in terms of human welfare.

For example, one of the strongest arguments the student of population has for better medical care, especially better medical administration, is that the death rate in the United States is still much higher than in many other nations with more efficient medical programs. He cannot but prod public conscience by making comparisons between our death rate and, for example, that of New Zealand or Australia. The maternal death rate, especially in this country, is a disgrace compared to the maternal death rate of nearly a dozen other nations. By such scientific comparisons he awakens the public to greater interest in improving the existing system of medical administration.

The sociologist, in analyzing various aspects of behavior, often calls attention to behavior which is not generally recognized as crime but which actually creates great social damage and should be defined as crime, as Sutherland's presidential address concerning white collar criminality showed so clearly.

To the extent that social science comes to understand all aspects of behavior man will learn to control, regulate, and direct behavior toward happier and more effective living. Social science knowledge is being used increasingly even in the field of international relations. During World War II, studies of morale, both in the native country and in conquered and enemy countries, were conducted regularly. In peacetime the opinion poll is becoming the standardized device for measuring opinions of population on particular issues, testing them out with regard to new reform measures and new political devices. Such scientific measurement is a valuable guide to political administration.

One might go on at great length to show that the social scientist can be a scientist and, by so being, have a large part in directing the course of reform and human improvement. In fact, for too long social improvements have been guided by the hunches and pressures of folklore thinking. Only by a scientific approach is a people able to rise above and evaluate many of the folkways and traditions that have been accepted as being in the best interests of mankind, even though they may not have been so. As Robert Redfield has so clearly pointed out, "social science is not morally indifferent. It is morally significant." It deals with the values of which human society consists. It is motivated by "objectivity, honesty, accuracy, and humility before the facts."[15] No group of people can work with this kind of aims without actually, at many points, lifting society above the current ethical level to a new level of human relationships.

Redfield further calls attention to the fact that society has become so complex that its future development can be trusted less and less to the informal processes of folklore. Its direction must become a conscious effort in the management of human affairs. To the extent that this is true, social science will come to be depended upon as a guide.

SUMMARY

There is a better guide to the future than folklore and the blind course of chance. Planning and policy-making, backed by social science findings, can save much needless trial and error, can help set and achieve goals in both the material (planning) and nonmaterial (policy-making) spheres. Some of the goals that might well be set by a democratic society are to create adequate conditions of nutrition, health, recreation, and education for the young; a reasonable and useful retirement for the old; a better system of penal treatment; an adequate system of medical administration; and an extension of Social Security provisions to new groups.

The research scientist is not a planner, but he can provide a sound research foundation on which the social engineer and social reformer can build. Again and again his findings challenge the status quo, and call for social action.

DISCUSSION AND REVIEW QUESTIONS

1. Discuss philosophies concerning man's capability of improving social conditions. What is your view?

2. Would you say that social events and cultural developments in the past have developed according to a set of plans and policies?

3. What conditions in the world have made planning and policy-making more imperative?

[15] Robert Redfield, "Prospects for the Scientific Study of Human Relations," *University of Chicago Round Table*, December 28, 1947, p. 13.

4. Distinguish between planning and policy-making.

5. Compare the place of planning in totalitarian and democratic regimes.

6. Why do many citizens of the United States fear planning?

7. What are some planning goals you would establish for the nation? for the world?

8. What kind of a health plan do you feel would come nearest meeting the needs of all the population?

9. What are the main needs of the college age group in the field of education which should be met if the nation were to adopt a policy calling for the maximum development of the nation's talent?

10. Appraise social science and social scientists in their role in the area of planning and policy making. Could they be made a substitute for politicians and legislators?

11. Do you feel a sociologist is out of his proper role when he engages in planning and policy-making? Discuss.

SOURCEBOOK READINGS

FREEDMAN, RONALD, AMOS H. HAWLEY, WERNER S. LANDECKER, GERHARD E. LENSKI, and HORACE M. MINER. *Principles of Sociology* (rev. ed.). New York: Henry Holt & Co., Inc., 1956.
1. NELSON, DONALD M., "Planning for Modern Warfare," pp. 572–82.
2. LILIENTHAL, DAVID, "Planning in the Tennessee Valley," pp. 583–88.

KOENIG, SAMUEL, REX D. HOPPER, and FELIKS GROSS. *Sociology: A Book of Readings.* Englewood Cliffs, N.J.: Prentice-Hall, Inc., 1956.
3. CRESSEY, PAUL F., "Social Disorganization and Reorganization in Harlan County, Kentucky," pp. 576–81.
4. LERNER, ABBA P., "Does Planning Mean Loss of Freedom?" pp. 582–89.
5. BRITISH INFORMATION SERVICE, "Britain's Planning Machinery," pp. 589–93.
6. GROSS, FELIKS, "Uniformity and Pluralism," pp. 593–97.
7. MCCRACKEN, ROBERT, "Why Can't We Learn to Live Together?" pp. 597–601.

LEE, ELIZABETH BRYANT, and ALFRED MCCLUNG LEE. *Social Problems in America* (rev. ed.). New York: Henry Holt & Co., Inc., 1955.
8. SUMNER, WILLIAM GRAHAM, "A Tough Old World," pp. 440–41.
9. PRAY, KENNETH L. M., "The Social Worker in Social Action," pp. 441–42.
10. WATSON, GOODWIN, "Social Action to Improve Intergroup Relations," pp. 442–45.
11. COHEN, OSCAR, "Social Research and Intergroup Relations," pp. 445–48.
12. BERNARD, LUTHER L., "The Dilemma in Revolution," pp. 452–53.
13. SUMNER, WILLIAM GRAHAM, "The Solution of One Problem Leads to Another," pp. 457–58.
14. CLINARD, MARSHALL B., "The Group Approach to Social Reintegration," pp. 465–70.

O'BRIEN, ROBERT W., CLARENCE C. SCHRAG, and WALTER T. MARTIN. *Readings in General Sociology* (2d ed.). Boston: Houghton Mifflin Co., 1957.
15. HIMES, JOSEPH S., "Social Change: The Context of Social Planning," pp. 424–32.

WILSON, LOGAN, and WILLIAM L. KOLB. *Sociological Analysis.* New York: Harcourt, Brace & Co., Inc., 1949.
16. SUTHERLAND, EDWIN H., "White-Collar Criminality," pp. 788–97.
17. LEE, ALFRED MCCLUNG, "Techniques of Social Reform: An Analysis of the New Prohibition Drive," pp. 812–27.
18. ABEL, THEODORE, "The Pattern of a Successful Political Movement," pp. 827–31.
19. HOOK, SIDNEY, "Law, Freedom and Human Action," pp. 831–40.

SELECTED READINGS

ALLEN, FREDERICK LEWIS. "The Big Change in Suburbia," *Harper's Magazine.* Part I, June, 1954, pp. 21–28; Part II, July, 1954, pp. 47–53.

BARNES, HARRY ELMER, and NEGLEY K. TEETERS. *New Horizons in Criminology.* 2d ed.; Englewood Cliffs, N.J.: Prentice-Hall, Inc., 1951.

BROWN, HARRISON. *The Challenge of Man's Future.* New York: The Viking Press, Inc., 1954.

BURCK, GILBERT. "The American Genius for Productivity," *Fortune,* July, 1955, pp. 86 ff.

CHAPIN, F. STUART. "Some Obstacles to the Acceptance of Existing Social Science Knowledge," *Social Forces,* 26:7–12 (Oct., 1947).

CHASE, STUART. *The Proper Study of Mankind.* Rev. ed.; New York: Harper & Brothers, 1956, chap. 28.

COOK, R. C. *Human Fertility: The Modern Dilemma.* New York: William Sloan Associates, Inc., 1951.

COWLES, GARDNER. "What the Public Thinks about Big Business," *Look,* Feb. 8, 1955, pp. 19–21.

CUBER, JOHN F., ROBERT A. HARPER, and WILLIAM F. KENKEL. *Problems of American Society: Values in Conflict.* 3d ed.; New York: Henry Holt & Co., Inc., 1956, chap. 23.

FARIS, ROBERT E. L. *Social Disorganization.* 2d ed.; New York: The Ronald Press Co., 1955, chap. 15.

HATT, PAUL, and ALBERT J. REISS. *Reader in Urban Sociology.* Glencoe, Ill.: The Free Press, 1951.

HIMES, JOSEPH S. *Social Planning in America: A Dynamic Interpretation.* Doubleday Short Studies in Sociology. Garden City, N.Y.: Doubleday & Co., Inc., 1954.

HORTON, PAUL B., and GERALD R. LESLIE. *The Sociology of Social Problems.* New York: Appleton-Century-Crofts, Inc., 1955, part III.

KROEBER, A. L. *Configurations of Cultural Growth.* Berkeley: University of California Press, 1944.

LANDIS, PAUL H. *Population Problems: A Cultural Interpretation.* Rev. ed.; New York: American Book Co., 1954, chap. 26.

————. *Social Control.* Rev. ed.; Chicago: J. B. Lippincott Co., 1956, chap. 28.

LUNDBERG, GEORGE A. *Can Science Save Us?* New York: Longmans, Green & Co., Inc., 1947.

LYND, ROBERT S. *Knowledge for What?* Princeton: Princeton University Press, 1939.

MALINOWSKI, BRONISLAW. *The Dynamics of Cultural Change.* New Haven: Yale University Press, 1945.

MCCLENAHAN, BESSIE AVERNE. "Social Problems and Social Planning," *Sociology and Social Research,* 39:151–57 (Jan.–Feb., 1955).

MYRDAL, EVA A. *Nation and Family.* New York: Harper & Brothers, 1941.

OGBURN, W. F., and MEYER F. NIMKOFF. *Technology and the Changing Family.* Boston: Houghton, Mifflin Co., 1955.

POTTER, DAVID M. *People of Plenty.* Chicago: University of Chicago Press, 1954.

RUSSELL, B. "Science to Save Us from Science," *New York Times Magazine,* March 19, 1950, p. 9.

RUSSELL, BERTRAND. "The Next Eighty Years," *Saturday Review Reader No. 2.* New York: Bantam Books, 1953, pp. 20–30.

SOROKIN, P. A. *Man and Society in Calamity.* New York: E. P. Dutton & Co., Inc., 1946.

SPENGLER, OSWALD. *The Decline of the West.* New York: Alfred A. Knopf, Inc., 1926.

Part VI

SOCIAL INSTITUTIONS

Chapter 32

Institutions: Major Cultural Structures

Humanity is careless about many things, but the basic issues re-lated to survival are never left to chance. They are provided for by great formal cultural structures known as *institutions*. Sex is animal; alone it would provide for procreation. But what of the survival of the helpless child? Only marriage and family institutions can guaran-tee that. And how does a creature which senses destiny in his make-up cope with fear? Religious institutions are built to rescue man from the peril he sees lurking in the shadows of the unknown.

Hunger will drive man to seek food; cold will drive him to seek shelter and a covering for his body. But haphazard methods are not sufficient to guarantee the survival of all. Institutions having to do with food-getting and food-using, with property rights, and, much later in history, with welfare take over the custody of man's eco-nomic life.

In the disputes, conflicts, and delinquencies that are ever a part of man's social interaction, there must be a court of final appeal, an over-all authority which all recognize as having the last word. Gov-ernment has been man's answer to this need. The young must be taught the skills, the symbols of communication, the attitudes, and the history of the social group. For the purpose of cultural transmis-sion, educational institutions have emerged.

Out of man's long past of trial and error all his social institutions have been built. In defining *social institutions* as *formal cultural structures devised to meet basic social needs*, the sociologist is merely taking account of the fact that the fulfillment of the most essential human needs is most fully guaranteed by organized cul-tural systems man has carried forward from his past.

555

Of what do institutions consist and how do they function to meet social needs? The answer is the essence of the sociological problem.

1. Institutions are made up of cultural objects of a material nature. Some of them are merely symbolic (like the flag as a symbol of state), but some also embody ritualistic patterns of behavior and defined roles for individual participants. They also involve a set of attitudes and of social expectations.

2. Institutions are the main vehicles through which society carries on its activities. They define roles for individuals and train them to perform routinely; they form attitudes and character to meet institutional expectations; they formulate both method of procedure and goal to be achieved.

3. Institutions achieve for man the realization of some basic need. In the family the most basic is child care; in economic institutions, food-getting; in religion, reconciliation with the powers that control life; in government, recognition of a final authority above all other human authorities; in welfare, security against economic catastrophe.

4. Institutions are, in one aspect of their operation, gigantic mechanisms of social control, shaping the individual to their pattern and keeping him in conformity. They overshadow the individual and in the end win over his own "pleasure first" impulses. In the end he conforms or is broken by their imperative demands.

5. Institutions are the better-organized and more stable aspects of the culture. Since they emerge to meet basic human needs and these needs are in some sense constant, institutions become in time gigantic culture complexes. Although they are the most stable aspect of culture, institutions do, nonetheless, change. It is only that institutionalized aspects of the culture change less rapidly than some of the less basic phases. Styles in dress, for example, change more frequently than styles in weddings. Moreover, certain core traits of basic institutions change much less rapidly than fringe traits. Attitudes toward monogamy, incest, and chastity—core traits in our marriage–family system—are much less subject to the whims of culture change than are attitudes toward size of family or style of architecture of the family dwelling. The marriage ritual changes less frequently than the bridal costume.

6. Because they are change-resistant, institutions have continuity beyond the life of generations, giving assurance that the basic needs of life will always be met.

7. In their very resistance to change, social institutions give life stability and order and give an individual's life meaning and form, even a great measure of security. Herein lies one of their greatest

weaknesses, too. Many institutional values have their roots in antiquity. They do not change to meet the new conditions of the world in which they exist today. American legal machinery was adequate for George Washington's time, but today the courts are crowded and justice is so long delayed that often there is no justice. Some sociologists feel that the lag in institutional change is the major weakness of the social order, that much of the thinking carried on in the institutional framework today is still geared to the stage-coach era.

8. There is an overlapping and interrelation between all the major social institutions. For purposes of convenience, however, the sociologist takes the various institutional structures and studies each as though it were a distinct and complete cultural entity in and of itself. The family is an institution and so is government. But the government is intertwined at many points in the family institution. The school is the teaching institution, but the church has a teaching function also. Welfare institutions have become great cultural structures today, but their operation is primarily by government and their emergence is attributable in considerable part to the failure of economic institutions to provide economic security for the individual as they once did.

9. Finally, as just suggested, when one institution fails to meet a basic human need adequately, another takes over the burden. Once most education was in the family. As the transmission of culture became a greater burden for humanity, special teaching institutions had to be developed. The school began to emerge as a special teaching institution and has been taking to itself an increasing burden of carrying the load of cultural transmission since. Now it takes the load of teaching off the family, in some instances as early as nursery-school age. So also, as the family and economic institutions have denied the child an apprenticeship to work life, the school has had to make vocational guidance and training a part of its teaching programs.

So we return to the statement made at the beginning of this introduction. The major needs of the race cannot be left to chance. Great cultural structures are built to see that they are met according to the standards which a people have evolved through ages of experience. So men come and go as the generations succeed each other, but social institutions live through the ages.

Chapter 33

Marriage and the Family

All recognize the family as the basic social institution, but its significance is much greater in some societies than others. The quotation below is a simple statement of a primitive American Indian contrasting two vastly different family institutions—his and that of the American white man around him. In the tribal world he knows best, the family institution is much of an individual's total world. In the more individualistic culture of the white, the family is a more fractional part of the person's institutional experience because of the many supplemental institutions that help channel, direct, and provide for his wants and needs.

. . . What is a man? A man is nothing. Without his family he is of less importance than that bug crossing the trail, of less importance than the sputum or exuviae . . . A man must be with his family to amount to anything with us. If he had nobody else to help him, the first trouble he got into he would be killed by his enemies because there would be no relatives to help him fight the poison of the other group. No woman would marry him because her family would not let her marry a man with no family. He would be poorer than a newborn child; he would be poorer than a worm, and the family would not consider him worth anything. He would not bring renown or glory with him. He would not bring support of other relatives either. The family is important. If a man has a large family and a profession and upbringing by a family that is known to produce good children, then he is somebody and every family is willing to have him marry a woman of their group. It is the family that is important. In the white ways of doing things the family is not so important. The police and soldiers take care of protecting you, the courts give you justice, the post office carries messages for you, the school teaches you. Everything is taken care of, even your children, if you die; but with us the family must do all of that.[1]

Although the family institution springs everywhere out of the sex needs of male and female and the needs of the helpless human infant

[1] B. W. Aginsky, "An Indian's Soliloquy," *American Journal of Sociology*, July, 1940, pp. 43–44.

for physical and emotional nurture, it is highly variable in its socio-logical characteristics from culture to culture. Nonetheless, the soci-ologist tries to classify family institutional types that characterize peoples the world around and throughout human history. Before analyzing the elements in the American family institution, a review of family systems in general is in order.

THE BROAD PERSPECTIVE OF THE FAMILY INSTITUTION

Marriage Systems. The two main types of marriage systems are monogamy (pair marriage) and polygamy (plural marriage). *Polygamy* has been the most common throughout history. It takes two forms: *polyandry,* in which a wife has two or more husbands; and *polygyny,* in which a man has two or more wives. This second form of plural marriage has been much more common, historically, than the first, and still is, although polyandry still exists in parts of India, on the high plateau of Tibet, and in other scattered localities. Here is an account of polyandry in India today.

"In the high Himalayas polyandry has the sanction of immemorial legend . . . in the upland valleys, existence depends upon a limited number of tiny terraced fields and the careful balancing of popula-tion against food reserves. Each family avoids dividing its meager tillage in ever-diminishing lots among its progeny by having the younger sons share the wife of the eldest son. Not only does this prac-tice reduce the number of children in each generation, and keep each property permanently within the family, but it has some other curious results. Polyandry, for some reason not wholly accounted for by anthropologists, reduces the fertility of wives, and produces an abnormal ratio of male to female births. In Jaunswar Bawar, where men outnumber women four to one and more than 60,000 people practice polyandry, only one birth was reported last year.

"Jaunswar women who live with their several husbands are called *rantys.* Custom obliges them to treat each husband with equal favor, but it often happens that a *ranty* will prefer one brother to all the others. It also happens that a *ranty* will reject the whole pack of brothers for an outsider. After a trial by the entire village, an adulter-ous *ranty* is fined the cost of a community dinner (paid for by her parents), after which her husbands may have her back, readily for-giving and forgetting because women are so scarce.

"But a *ranty* may also divorce her husbands and return to her parents' house. She is then called a *dhyanty* and has a good deal of latitude about her choice of lovers. Should she elect to remarry, however, her new set of husbands must pay the first set of husbands a sum which is fixed by the village council. Since an individual suitor is rarely able to afford paying off several husbands, a *dhyanty* usually has to marry another group of brothers.

"Despite the freedom they enjoy, Jaunswar women are in revolt against polyandry. More and more are preferring a plethora of lovers to a profusion of husbands, and the number of *dhyantys* is increasing. A certain sophistication has been brought to Jaunswar Bawar by the invasion of immigrant laborers, mostly tree cutters from the plains, who have a knowing way of asking a girl whether she is a *ranty* or a *dhyanty*. But, although some *dhyantys* in some villages have become little better than prostitutes, the real basis of the revolt is an embarrassment many Jaunswar women have recently discovered in being married to more than one man. A Jaunswar girl who admitted to two husbands quickly added, 'But I live with only one. The other is now living with my sister.' Jaunswar mothers who have been sending their children out of Jaunswar Bawar for modern schooling have been pained to see them weep when the plains children jeer: 'How many fathers have you got?'

"The government of India would like the Jaunswaris to adopt monogamy. But teams of social workers who have gone up into the hills have been driven out by village elders. Said one elder indignantly: 'They asked us indecent questions.' Among the Jaunswaris themselves a reform movement, with all members taking the vow of monogamy has been organized by a college graduate named Surat Singh. Although his movement is enthusiastically supported by the women, the menfolk are threatening to drive Surat Singh and all his followers into the plains. Now the Indian government has a new idea. Provincial Social Welfare Minister Acharya Jugal proposes to halt immigrant labor, seal off Jaunswar Bawar from outside influences, and to send in a new group of social workers, who, this time, will all be women.

"But last week Jaunswar women seemed to be doing pretty well on their own account. Against a backdrop of Himalayan mountains, a pretty, 16-year-old girl was busily spinning wool while her five husbands and the village headman pleaded with her not to become a *dhyanty*. Said she: 'I married only Gulab Singh. I will have nothing to do with his four brothers.' Said the headman: 'My child, you know that by our custom, when you marry one man, you marry his brothers also.' Retorted the 16-year old: 'Gulab Singh or none. If I cannot have only one husband, I will divorce all five.'

"Said an Indian government official: 'The men who defend polyandry are fighting a hopeless battle. Women always have the last word everywhere.' "[2]

While plural marriage is still the approved marriage form in most of the densely populated areas of the world, and is today the dominant type, as cultures and peoples go, most couples remain monogamous even within polygamous societies. Most marriages in the world are, therefore, pair marriages.

The Moslem religion sanctions polygyny, four wives being permitted the male, according to the religious creed. China has always had its system of concubinage. Much of Africa practices polygyny. Historically, most peoples practiced polygyny with concubinage as an integral part of the marriage–family system. (A concubine is a sort of wife with inferior status.)

Polygamy is accompanied by a series of attitudes, roles, and statuses making it socially possible and appropriate, just as is monogamy. In East Africa the wife of a prosperous man will insist that her husband buy a young wife (cattle and goats are the coin used) to help her with the farm work. If he fails to increase his wives as his cattle increase, existing wives feel mistreated. More wives mean more rest for the older wife, as the younger ones can grub the brush, plant the corn and tend it against jungle beasts.

Place the attitudes of the monogamous American wife in this setting, and they will not fit at all. She sees in such an arrangement only jealousy between women, quarreling, and perhaps a little hair pulling. But wives fit into polygamous settings, just as do husbands into polyandrous settings, if the institutional forms demand it. Here is the account of a Chinese concubine that reveals attitudes of that family system. She was married to a man as his concubine and bore him a child. On conversion to Christianity she learned of its monogamous requirements. Her story reflects not only attitudes, but what for her is a serious dilemma as she finds little place for herself outside the marriage she has:

But, oh Worthy One, there is a problem daily before me, and what must I do? The Christian Way of Life does not allow a man to have several wives; neither should a Christian woman be a concubine, yet here I am, a lowly sinner, concubine number four. It frightens me and often in prayer my heart falls to pieces. This lowly one knows her fault, but I have gone into a blind alley and do not see a clear way out, neither a path to continue on. I am of one heart with our household and our master looks upon all of us with favor and kindness. Willingly he uses silver high and low for me and the others. Every day the maidservants enter our women's quarters carrying in their hands plates of good meat, dishes of fish fried with sweet-sour sauce, bowls of rice and platters of warm steamed bread. It is not as if I am afraid to eat coarse food, work hard, and wear a coat of common cloth, but from childhood I never was taught to provide for my own living and earn pieces of money.

I am but a feeble woman and my learning is little. I know only what is connected with the duties of a wife and mother. Our ways in China are not the bold ways of Western lands where a woman is taught to stand by herself and, yea, even compete with a man for a living. If I should leave the lord of our household, another man would put forth his hand before the next moon could shine and would place me in his house. Clearly I could not stand out against my father and uncles in such a thing, and they surely would want to put me into another home.

You, Shepherd Teacher, are greatly learned about the way of life, the will of God, and the teaching of Christ, therefore tell this lowly one what to do. I will let it be as you decree, and will then make my bow of farewell and depart. It will be to me as if Heaven sent me the message through your lips.[3]

As the Western pattern becomes known to women in polygynous cultures, there is increasing revolt. Take Pakistan, which is rapidly borrowing Western education and other Western practices. The feminist movement calls for the cessation of polygamy. Here is a recent popular account of the controversy over polygyny in the Moslem state:

" 'Marry such women as seem good to you, two, three or four,' the Holy Koran exhorts the faithful, 'but if you fear you will not be equitable, then only one, or what your right hands own, so it is likelier you will not be partial.' Through 13 centuries, Moslem males have enjoyed polygamy and insisted that they have avoided partiality. But the truth is quite otherwise, to hear the 20,000 members of the All-Pakistan Women's Association tell it. 'If any man is honest with himself and understands human nature,' argued one passionate Pakistani feminist, 'he will realize that he cannot treat four wives equally.'

"The feminists found something to focus their anger on last April, when then Prime Minister Mohammed Ali made his pretty young social secretary his second wife. In response to the outcry, the government assigned an advisory Commission on Marriage and Family Laws (four men and three women) to chart out the dangerous ground between the feminists and the powerful polygamy lobby—Moslem mullahs who seek a theocratic state, and would, according to their critics, confine Pakistan to a 9th-century Arab feudal pattern.

"The commission sent out thousands of questionnaires in Urdu, English and Bengali, last week reported six to one for reform. Henceforth, it recommended, Pakistani males should get permission for sec-

[3] James P. Leynse, "A Chinese Concubine Tells Her Story," *Review of the World,* April, 1937, pp. 191–92.

ond marriages from special new courts of matrimony; they should prove themselves able to support two families; they should not marry again 'merely . . . to marry a prettier or younger woman.' The commission added that child marriages and the sale of brides should be outlawed, and that women and men should have equal rights of divorce. As of now, Pakistanis can divorce their wives in Islamic fashion by saying 'I divorce thee' three times in their presence.

" 'Polygamy,' said the commission, 'is prompted by the lower self of men who are devoid of refined sentiments.' Anticipating objections from the mullahs, the commission insisted that it was not amending the Koran—only reading it right. The commission then went on to grapple with the touchy and important problem of reconciling progress with religion in a nation whose principal basis for being was its Moslem faith. The commission appealed to the right of *ijtihad,* or exercise of individual judgment within the broad framework of the revealed word. Moslem law, said the commission, holds that in the Koran 'what is not definitely prohibited is permissible,' and the failure of Moslems to exercise this right of individual judgment is the reason for the 'universal backwardness' of the Moslem peoples in the past three centuries. 'No nation can stand aside as an idle or wondering onlooker while the world progresses rapidly.' "[4]

Authority Patterns. Historically, the patriarchal family has been the most common, that is, the family in which the father's authority was dominant, although in some cultures *matriarchal authority,* the dominance of the mother, has been the traditional method of family administration.

Polygyny is almost inherently patriarchal, which means that most marriage systems the world around have been father-ruled, or at least ruled by male elders. Often maternal uncles, the oldest son, and other male figures have had great authority over a woman. In cases of the father's death, a girl's life might be ruled by the elder brother. Polyandry is likely to be matriarchal. The pair marriage arrangement may readily be either. Historically, as it evolved in the West under the impact of Christianity, pair marriage was patriarchal. It has been gradually shifting toward a democratic arrangement, with the survival of a substantial element of the patriarchal, since men yield their traditional authority reluctantly.

In its ideal form the democratic family involves a cooperative decision-making arrangement in which husband, wife, and even children, to the extent of their age and maturity, have a part in making

[4] "Polygamy Reviewed," *Time,* July 16, 1956, pp. 25–26. Courtesy *Time;* copyright Time, Inc., 1956.

decisions. Rather than discipline or making the children "mind" being the goal of the family, the goal of child training is growth toward individual self-sufficiency. Rather than human nature being looked upon as inherently bad, something to be curbed and reformed, it is seen as something to be conserved and developed in infants and children. As a noted child authority put it, "The intrinsic charm and goodness of childhood still constitutes the best guarantee of the perfectibility of mankind."[5]

Residence and Descent. Family cultures differ in methods of fixing residence, tracing descent, and naming offspring.

In *patrilocal* societies custom dictates that the couple go to live in the husband's home; in the *matrilocal,* in the wife's tribe or family. In individualistic societies separate residence is established by the new couple.

India is one of the most striking examples of patrilocal societies in the world today, although much of the Moslem world is similar. Not only do the children reside with the parents after marriage, but they are subservient to the parental and family wishes where major decisions are concerned.

The author encountered a clash between this system and the Western type of individual residence under most unique circumstances. We were hunting elephants in Kenya, East Africa, when my hunting guide, a man belonging to a cultured professional family from India settled in East Africa, told me his story. He had contracted tuberculosis and badly needed an operation, which the family felt could be performed properly in Sweden. Not wanting to use up the family's joint resources in such a manner, this son held out against the plan until finally the father said, "We have decided that you are going, son," meaning that he and the two brothers, who made up the male side of the household had decided. "Either you go or you leave this family never to come back," was the father's final ultimation.

"I couldn't leave my family and be cut off," he told me. "I wouldn't think of doing such a thing."

At the family's expense he went to Sweden, had the operation, and convalesced for a full year. While there he fell in love with a Swedish girl, who returned with him to Kenya and lived as a guest of the family for six months. The couple planned to be married, but just prior to the marriage the girl told her Indian lover, "There is one condition. I must have a house of my own. We must live separate from your family."

[5] Arnold Gesell and Frances L. Ilg, *The Child From Five to Ten* (New York: Harper & Brothers, 1946).

Two years had passed since then, but there was still deep resentment, mingled with a sense of amazement, in his tone as this man told me how he had reacted: "You expect me to leave my family! You want a home of your own! Why, my family have given you a home and shared food with you for six months. They have treated you like one of us. You expect me to leave them to live with you! How unappreciative can a person be!"

The girl's ultimatum ended the marriage plans abruptly. This Swedish girl could not accept, as a part of the bargain for marriage, living with the parents, two brothers, and their wives and children; yet to the Indian this is the way family life must be.

As Western ideas spread, the joint family system in India itself is being challenged. Suicides are high among Indian women, and social workers there find that the main cause is persecution by the husband and members of his family, particularly the wife's mother-in-law. It is no doubt because of this joint family, joint residence arrangement that the mother-in-law is proverbially considered a "devil" throughout India. An ex-governor of Bombay suggested recently that the law provide punishment for mothers-in-law and sisters-in-law to protect the wife living in the husband's household.[6]

Marriage–family systems also differ in method of tracing descent. In general there are three types of descent tracing: (1) the *matrilineal* method, under which custom dictates that ancestry be traced through the mother's family; (2) The *patrilineal*, under which ancestry is traced through the father; (3) the *bilineal*, under which ancestry is traced through both lines.

Actually, institutional systems are much more complicated than this classification implies. Anthropologists have written volumes on methods of tracing descent in tribal life of various peoples, for descent is not traced strictly by blood lines as it is in the Western world. *Clans* are elaborate social systems in which descent is traced through long periods of time and to all clansmen. *Gens* are tribal systems in which descent is traced through a male line only. In tribal life these family social systems include blood brothers who may not be any blood kin at all, but only fellow clansmen.

Clans survive today in the Scottish highlands and are still common among American Indians.

A teacher in the Navaho reservation, in a seminar paper in one of the author's classes, described some of the complications of school administration among teenagers there. At dances teachers expected certain young people to dance with others of the opposite sex. But

[6] N. P. N. Pillai in *Journal of Family Welfare* (Bombay), March, 1956.

the youngsters explained that they could not do so. Any form of physical contact with a clan member of the opposite sex is strictly taboo. For a boy to dance with a clan sister would be considered a form of incest.

Finally, naming is another marriage–family variable which can take any one of several forms, or some variation of them. In *patrinominal* societies the father's name is taken; in *matrinominal*, the mother's. American society is patrinominal in that the couple uses the husband's name, but is *bilineal* in that descent is traced through both lines of ancestry.

A variation in the Western naming custom is the practice of many women who substitute their family name for their given middle name after marriage in order to retain name identity with their family. A few professional women who have made a career prior to marriage retain their maiden name for business purposes after marriage. Still another method of perpetuating the woman's family name is to use it as the given name of one or more of the children.

FAMILY CULTURE IN THE UNITED STATES

There are in the United States two basic kinds of family systems, with many variations between the extreme types. One, the institutional type, is rooted in tradition which strongly emphasizes the customary aspects of family life; the other arises from contemporary individualism which emphasizes individual benefits derived from marriage and family. The first is often called the *institutional* family system, the other the *individualistic, companionship,* or *romantic* type.

The basic cultural structure of the two family systems is markedly different and leads to different types of family–social systems. To find the institutional family today requires a search in the isolated mountainous sections where pioneer philosophy still dominates. To find the extreme individualistic-companionship family, one must go to the apartment house of the large city where the couple, both of whom are working, share little of each other's lives except in companionship and sex.

The two families vary markedly in: (1) attitudes and values; (2) roles and expectations; (3) symbolic culture traits; (4) utilitarian culture traits; and (5) codes and ceremonies.[7]

Attitudes and Values. In the traditional institutional family the basic family attitude is one of *duty and obligation*. The marriage

---

[7] Four of these type parts of culture in the family institution are listed in F. S. Chapin, *Contemporary American Institutions* (New York: Harper & Brothers, 1935), chap. 2.

ceremony stresses the duties of husbands to wives and wives to husbands "to care for each other in sickness and health," and so forth. Social pressure supported this code. The social system also placed great stress on the obligations of children to parents. They were expected to honor and obey.

In direct contrast is the emerging value of the new marriage–family system which places romance uppermost. Love of mates for each other is the first consideration. If this is absent, the sense of obligation is weak indeed; in fact, unless the demands of the *romantic love* are met, the family has no excuse for existence even though there may be children. Divorces are granted, even where children are involved, if couples can prove that they no longer love each other. This lack of love must be phrased legally, of course, as "mental cruelty."

Most American families today, especially in the middle classes, have a mixture of the attitudes of the institutional and the romantic. Against values of duty, loyalty, and faithfulness are projected the newer ones of affection, supreme love, mutual physical and psychological satisfaction in each other. One cannot understand modern marriage and the modern family without understanding the conflict between these two systems of attitudes and expectations. In the parental family, many young people are taught the traditional loyalties, but on the screen, in fiction, in magazine stories, and in conversation with peers, the romantic conception of marriage is presented.

Too many youths, therefore, seek a love that will surpass all other experience. They expect a marriage that will bring supreme happiness—a happiness that will override all the practical considerations that face every man on the hazardous road of life. After marriage unrealistic expectations are blighted. As a consequence, the stark realities of daily adjustments to married life—facing trouble and sickness, economic hardships, and other trials that marriage brings—prove more than they can adjust to in the light of their previous attitudes concerning what marriage should produce in the way of happiness.

It is, in part, the conflict between the two systems of attitudes, especially as they are realized in marriage, that makes divorce in the modern companionship family such a commonplace affair.

One of the main objectives of teaching in the marriage field in both high school and college today is to discount romantic expectations and build realistic attitudes toward marriage and family. Marriage is presented as life's major ongoing adjustment—a life-long one—the outcome of which depends in considerable part on the stability of purpose and seriousness of intent the couple bring to the relationship. It is hoped by this approach to improve the outcome of the marriage

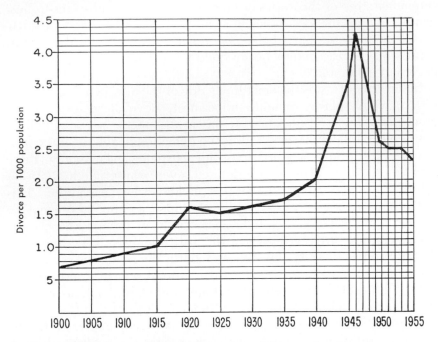

The Divorce Rate in the United States During the Twentieth Century

In many marriages today, divorce rather than death ultimately terminates the union. The highest divorce rate came in 1946; there has since been some decline. This graph shows divorces and reported annulments per 1000 population. (Rates, which are estimated for most years, from Statistical Abstract of the United States, 1957.)

venture, rather than to return to the duty-bound institutional system, which no longer fits an individualistic urban society.

In the area of child training, attitudes and values have changed markedly with the shift to the individualistic family pattern. The old regime made the child a worker, a useful member of the family. As soon as his strength and intelligence permitted, he was loaded with simple chores, and the work burden was increased as he grew older. Concepts of duty and industry were deeply instilled. To be idle was almost equivalent to sin.

This regime not only required obedience, but also extolled honor and obedience as the cardinal virtues in child character. Children graduated into a stern world of rural work and duty, a world which expected the child to carry a life-long sense of responsibility for parents and their welfare. In a real sense, the training of the child was so shaped as to give the parent maximum benefit and security.

The individualistic family system sees the child as a potential creative individualist, who will go out from the family after a long period of school training and make a rather complete break with the parental home. Parents shape the child for choice by permitting him to grow in a democratic environment, in which he makes his own decisions from the beginning as his capabilities and physical and moral safety permit. They increase his freedom with the years, knowing that by the time he enters the teen group at the high-school age he must be nearly morally self-sufficient or fail.

Parents pour their best effort, and their resources, into the child and teenager's development, expecting nothing in return in the way of work or income, or even of security in their old age. Their satisfaction comes in seeing him graduate to moral adulthood, to a marriage of his own choice, and to a vocation which fits his temperament and interests rather than their projected ambitions for him.

At almost every point the two family systems are at odds in values, methods, and goals. Little wonder then that there has been, over the period of two or three generations, much tension between parents and teenagers, and that parents who today cling to the old values find themselves at a loss to know how to deal with or understand their teenage sons and daughters.

Role Expectations.

What I don't understand is he said he was a Christian, but when I got to Baghdad, I found he was no Christian. He was an Arab. When an Arab marries, he doesn't want a wife or a companion; he just wants a slave. They treat their women like dirt—worse than dirt. They slug them and spit in their faces and then go off and leave them at home while they go sit in these coffee houses . . . His parents expected me to sit on the floor and do the baby's washing by hand, but he didn't seem to care. I begged him to get us a house by ourselves, but he wouldn't do it . . .[8]

This is the story of an American girl who met and married a student from Iraq at an American college. When she moved to Baghdad with her Arab husband she found that their respective conceptions of the female role differed substantially. She finally managed, through the American Consulate, to flee the country with her infant son.

Institutional relationships are smooth to the extent that roles of individual members are typed and specific so that members function reciprocally rather than in conflict or competition. In the institutional

[8] "Baghdad Honeymoon," *Time*, August 13, 1956, p. 23. Courtesy *Time*; copyright Time, Inc., 1956.

family system, roles of men and women, and of children, too, are definitely typed. The Iraqi wife would not have rebelled against the role which the American wife found incompatible.

The place of each sex and of all age levels were specifically defined by the family culture in the United States in an earlier day. There was little need for adjustment. Marriage was considered a *state*, which meant a fixed relationship for male and female in which they played supplementary parts with little risk of overlapping or conflict.

First, the woman's place was in the home. That part was settled; both men and women understood it. Second, her station was subservient to that of the husband. The strong man and the yielding, passive woman was the culturally sanctioned relationship. The whole social structure rated woman in second place in capacities, judgment, and most of all, in authority.

Here is a recent autobiographical account of a woman teacher of sixty. It reflects the characteristic role of woman in a by-gone day: "My father's word was law in our house. I never resented this, but rather felt that whatever he said was all right. I believed that men were wiser than women or children, that they really knew what was best. I wanted him to make decisions on everything. When my husband asked me to marry him, I went to my father to have him make my decision. After I was married I expected my husband to make all my decisions. Now that he has gone, I am having an awful time trying to make decisions for myself."

This subservience of women meant many things: lack of legal status in money matters, particularly with regard to equal rights of inheritance; lack of initiative in mate choice and divorce matters (this is still true of patriarchal marriage systems most everywhere); lack of equal rights to participate in the sex act (her sex life was to cater to male vulgarity, she was to be a passive participant). Prostitution was considered a male necessity, and is still in male-dominated cultures the world around. Presumably it protects the virtue of good women. Her subservience also meant lack of vocational opportunity, and in general, denial of creativity except in the area of domestic arts and skills. This is still true in institutional family systems throughout Latin America, the Middle East and Asia where women are neither in the labor market nor active in areas of artistic creativity.

These are but a few of the many areas in which the traditional institutional marriage system relegated the female to second place, and often a place far below the male indeed.

In this marriage–family system men and women did little quarreling; quarreling assumes equality and this did not exist in philosophy or practice. Quarreling and tension indicate areas where adjustments must be worked out. In the institutional marriage system it was a matter of taking what life brought rather than working for a better relationship. Even divorce was rarely used as a solution for a disastrous personal relationship in marriage. "What God hath joined together let no man put asunder."

Certain aspects of this older system have carried over into the newer individualistic pattern. For example, the marriage pledge has been modified very little to fit the new individualistic marriage–family system, yet role conceptions of men and women are almost directly opposite to those outlined above. Male and female roles are no longer definitely typed. Either or both may be the breadwinner. Woman's place is no longer in the home, unless that is where she wishes to be. Male and female roles overlap at many points, and the possibilities of conflict and competition are therefore great.

Women are not subservient, yet a good many husbands would like them to be, and in most marriages they must still do more adjusting than the husband. There is great likelihood that they will do the yielding in a more rebellious spirit than did their great-grandmothers.

Cultural expectations as to the appropriate role for women in many of these areas lack consistency, so that the typical female attitude, particularly before marriage but often afterward, is one of confusion. They cannot fully accept the traditional role, yet have many reservations concerning certain of the newer female ventures in freedom.

Every marriage relationship, particularly during the first years, is a series of adjustments in which two people struggle to define their roles in such a way that they will be supplementary and yet avoid either party's feeling greatly frustrated in finding outlets for personal drives and in realizing personal ambitions. In some areas they are almost certain to come into role conflict or role competition. Thus they will have to try to work out a rational adjustment by give and take; the alternative is to subject the marriage to increasing strain and eventually, perhaps, to abandon the idea that they are people who can function together as husband and wife and as parents.

The marriage of individuals who assume role equality is a courageous, even though risky venture. Its rewards are great for those who are mature enough to meet its demands. So far it appears that men have had greater difficulty in making the transition between family systems than have women. Most research in this area clearly shows that women are more ready and willing for the new roles than are men to accept women in them.[9] Women have suffered most in the transition, but men have stubbornly held out for the values of the old system and made it hard for both sexes to function in the new system.

As equality is approached in man–wife relations, husbands have become a more integral part of the family system. Many young people are looking upon marriage and family life as fun, are building their lives about their suburban home and entering into childbearing and childrearing in the spirit of adventure. The marriage becomes a real joint enterprise.

When Oregon Senator Richard Neuberger was a member of the state legislature, his wife was elected to the same legislative body. He has told how it was at this time that he first accepted her as an equal and came to respect her as a person of real competence, rather than as "just" a wife, a companion, and the mother of his children. An important bill was before the house and Mrs. Neuberger was to speak on it. Her husband took her aside and coached her carefully in what to say. She was new in the legislature; he, in the typical masculine manner, knew all the ropes, or so he thought. His wife thanked him generously, but having a mind of her own, and ideas of her own, she went ahead and prepared her own talk. It was much more effective than the attack he had planned and he had to admit this, even to himself. Mr. Neuberger no longer regarded his wife with condescending tolerance, but respected her as an equal.

In this new family regime the status of the child, too, has increased immeasurably. The ideal of the individualistic family system is to make him a full and equal participant, insofar as his growth permits. No longer is the motto "children are to be seen and not heard." Junior not only expects to be heard, but his parents train him in initiative and assertiveness so that his voice will make sense in the real world of decision-making. His contemporary role is not that of a choreboy, but of a school child who needs, in addition to formal learning, the jest and growth of play. This conception of the child's role has been pushed up further into the mature years until now, not only the high school student, but also the college student may legitimately engage in play during most of his spare time without compunctions of conscience. Much play, in fact, is structured and guided by church, school, and community, and is considered as real and important a role as work.

[9] For a more comprehensive discussion of this subject, and data, see Paul H. Landis, *Making the Most of Marriage* (New York: Appleton-Century-Crofts, Inc., 1955), chaps. 3 and 4.

When the young person does choose to work, it is not generally at the parents' command, as under the institutional family regime, or in order to share income with parents as formerly, but rather to have spending money with which to increase personal freedom and meet personal desires.

Rather than the child being an earner for the family, the family now, in lieu of work and earned income, substitutes the allowance, acting on the assumption that learning to spend money is an important aspect of growth toward economic maturity.

THE MODERN FAMILY IN TRANSITION

This brief survey of old and new role conceptions in the area both of male–female activities and of children is illustrative of the profound changes taking place in the marriage–family institution of a transitional culture. Although role changes are peculiarly Western, they are appearing in many parts of the world with some striking effects. There was recently an account in *Time* of an Indian father, a Moslem who resided with his family in Durban, South Africa, where thousands of Indian settlers rub shoulders with the West and where young people like the roles of Western youth, both the methods of mate choice and the freedom within the family authority pattern.

Being a strict Moslem, Father Moonsammy, a farmer, kept his wife and five daughters—ages fourteen to twenty-six—under the veil in the "second-rate status of purdah," according to the strict Moslem culture. Around them many Indian girls were being permitted to dance and date, but not Moonsammy's daughters. They worked in the fields all day, and in the evening waited patiently, as is the traditional Indian custom, for the menfolk to eat. After the men had eaten, the girls were allowed to squat on the floor with their mother and eat what was left.

The girls asked permission of their father to visit a brother a few miles away. The request was denied. Here is the sequel:

> The girls went to their beds. Eight hours later, when their mother looked in on their room which they shared together, all five were gone. Calling on his neighbors for help, Father Moonsammy frantically searched the darkness for the missing girls. At dawn he found them. Silhouetted by the eerie morning light their five young bodies hung lifeless from the branches of two wild fig trees just 100 yards from their father's house. Amid the wailing of friends and neighbors, the police announced the cause of death: suicide.[10]

[10] "Five Daughters," *Time,* August 1, 1955, p. 25. Courtesy *Time;* copyright Time, Inc., 1955.

Symbolic Culture Traits. By far the most widely recognized symbol of the marriage system is the wedding ring, which is nearly universal as a symbol of the bond between man and wife. It is especially a symbol of the wife's bond to her husband, although an increasing proportion of husbands in the romantic type of marriage are also wearing wedding rings as a symbol of their loyalty to their wives.

Historically, leading families have had coats of arms, have passed on various heirlooms from parents to children and children to grandchildren, or have had other such symbols representing the loyalty and continuity of the family. In the highly mobile individualistic family of today, such symbolic culture traits tend to be lost with the migration of young people. Often they are not present at the funerals of their elders to claim heirlooms. Even when present at the funeral, they may have lived so far apart that the heirlooms of parents and grandparents have no sentimental meaning. They may not be taken away simply because of the inconvenience of moving them about, especially where the sentiments of close living together are absent.

Genealogies have been important symbolic traits in many historic families, too, but are becoming more rare today as evidences of class and caste are vanishing. Pride in genealogy flourishes in social structures which place great emphasis on proper breeding, which assume that aristocracy is in the blood stream. With the greater freedom of interclass marriages in the American population, with its blending of many peoples into a middle-class society, few can claim aristocratic parentage, and those who do gain little in the way of social eminence by doing so. They are likely to be looked upon as first-class liars rather than worshipped as descendants of the gods.

The individualistic marriage system stresses personal mate choice, rather than the institutional practice of mate choice by parents or other elders. Where parents choose, genealogical and property matters are given weight in mate choice. Where youth make the choice, there is often little emphasis on genealogical pride.

Finally, a social structure which has so long placed supreme value on vertical mobility, so long preached that there is room at the top for any man who can make the climb, as American society has done, is short on family ceremony and family pride in the usual sense. This is in a way a weakness insofar as the individual family is concerned. A genealogical bond, a pride in ancestors, can be a strong bond in stabilizing marriage and in causing a couple to strive to make the best of even a poor marriage arrangement. But the individualistic type of marriage system emerging from the urban-industrial society is not likely to find a large place for such a bond. Tracing the growth of children in the marriage by tape recorder and movie camera is enough continuity for most couples, for they are likely to feel they can do a better job in every way than their parents did and, therefore, feel no great allegiance to parental blood or tradition.

Utilitarian Culture Traits. The most important aspect of utilitarian culture of the modern family is the home itself, which is symbolic of the unity of the family members, and which gives them a common

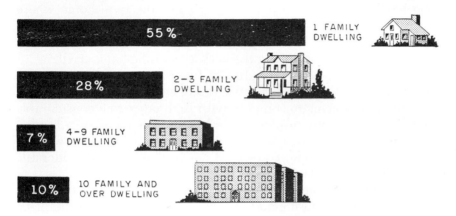

Types of Family Dwellings in Metropolitan Areas, 1950

The family is affected by its setting. Most Americans consider the ideal home the single-family residence with its own yard and play space; yet in great cities families often live in multiple dwellings with little private space. How may this affect the character of family life itself?

meeting place even though modern life takes them in different directions during the working hours and often also for recreation.

Even in this field of culture there is a vast difference between the traditional American family and the modern family of the metropolitan community. Once the single-family dwelling, located on the family farm or in the small community, was the typical dwelling. With the growth of urban civilization, and especially of the large metropolis, an increasing proportion of couples and of families are living in multiple dwellings where very few of the functions of the traditional family are carried out under the family roof. Over the years there has been a continuous increase in permits granted for multiple dwellings—duplexes, four-plexes, and apartment houses (see chart). Over the years all families, and especially companionship families, have shown a marked decrease in the number of functions performed within the family itself.

W. F. Ogburn, one of the leading American students of the family, showed in *Recent Social Trends*, a report of a study made during the late 1920's, that even in that period there had been a marked increase in the consumption of canned and packaged goods within the home and in the use of bakery-prepared foods. He observed a marked decline in the amount of clothing made within the home, a marked increase in restaurants, laundries, and other such establishments, which indicated a decreasing amount of domestic activity. A similar trend has been noted by rural sociologists in the farm home where the increase in the use of bakery-made bread, ready-to-wear clothing, canned goods, and many other such items of domestic consumption indicate a marked shift in the activities of the home itself.[11]

On the other hand, in the matter of furnishings and general ornamentation of the home there is little doubt that modern individualistic families have come to compete with each other to a considerable extent in conspicuous display. This has put an increasing burden upon the wife by making housekeeping and cleanliness somewhat of a fetish, although the effort involved has been offset in considerable part by labor-saving devices.

Perhaps the most significant aspect of this new trend is the effect of the new type of housing and of home ornamentation on the place of the home in child rearing. Apartment houses are not made to accommodate children. One can readily correlate the declining birthrate trend with the type of family dwelling that has developed in the United States.

Of course, the dwelling is not the cause, but it is, in part, a symbol of many other forces that impinge upon the family. In central metropolitan areas where multiple dwellings have become the dominant type of housing, children are scarce; the larger the metropolis, the less attention to dwellings which will house children. Consequently, large metropolitan centers have generally fallen far below the level of births required to reproduce themselves in the next generation. The rural farm and rural non-farm population produces a surplus to replenish the urban deficit.[12] (See the charts in Chapter 11.)

In general this is and has been the picture of the effect of urban-industrial civilization on family living. In the United States, however, there has been an important counter trend that has gained momentum very rapidly during the postwar years, namely, the great

[11] See Paul H. Landis, *Rural Life in Process* (2d ed.; New York: McGraw-Hill Book Co., Inc., 1948), chap. 25.

[12] For data see Paul H. Landis, *Population Problems* (2d ed.; New York: American Book Co., 1952).

expansion of residential suburbs on the fringe of the metropolis. This is the most effective adaptation of the family to the metropolis so far, and holds great promise. It has been made possible by the commuter automobile, the high level of urban income, mass housing developments, local supermarkets, and the low down payment and easy credit made available for home purchases.

It has led to a revived interest in family life among young people in metropolitan communities, has increased the birth rate and led to the building of life about the home and family yard in a more vital sense than was previously possible. Home ownership, on contract of course, has become the pattern in these areas, and throughout the nation generally there has been a sharp upswing in home ownership.

Finally, the modern home differs from the traditional one in that it has become a strictly family household. No longer is the great family a part of the American tradition. The young couple, after having made an independent mate choice, want to get away from relatives, to be on their own economically and to manage their own lives. Parents and grandparents and joint households are not a part of the family institution in industrial society.

Social security cares for the old and the broken family. The old have to plan to live alone or seek an institutional attachment in a society of individualistic families.

Codes and Ceremonies. Another area of family culture is that of codes and ceremonies centering about marriage and family. The marriage system is initiated by the marriage license and the marriage ceremony. The ceremony may be religious or civil. If religious, it seems more binding and impressive. Some religious bodies hold the marriage ceremony itself to be a sacrament. It is so with the Catholic. He must, therefore, be married by the priest in the church. The devout Mormon must marry in the temple, for such a marriage is binding for both this life and the life to come.

Also, in the codes of family behavior everywhere is some system of inheritance which determines in what way the accumulated property of the parent generation will be passed on to offspring. In many cultures, *primogeniture*, inheritance of all property and authority by the oldest son, has been the customary code with regard to the passing on of property and authority to administer it, as well as authority to supervise the lives of the younger children.

American family culture is democratic in that property is divided equally among the children, both boys and girls. A will may dispose of it in some other way, but generally speaking it is expected that all children will share and share alike, regardless of sex and order of birth. The companionship family of urban life often has little property of a tangible character to pass on and tends to be a one-child or two-child family. Problems of inheritance, therefore, are rather simple compared to those of the traditional American family where land had to be passed on and divided among four, five, six, or even a dozen children.

All family social systems have a series of codes, written or unwritten, with regard to sex behavior, for no society has ever left the sex impulse unbridled. Most societies have some kind of code with regard to extramarital conduct. In this area cultures are generally strict. A study of 250 cultures showed that only 2 per cent sanction adulterous relationships.[12] There are also codes having to do with premarital sex relations. These also differ in various cultural settings and are subject to change even within our own culture. In comparing the mores of 250 societies on the matter of premarital chastity, it was found that 70 per cent permit experimentation; 30 per cent make it taboo for girls. This study concluded that most taboos are really strictures against prepubertal intercourse by girls.

There are, also, very rigid codes in many societies with regard to expressions of the sex impulse which are considered unnatural, such as homosexuality, and all societies have incest taboos. These may apply to only the closest blood relatives, to distant cousins, or, as has been seen, in tribal life to entire clan groups.

Another set of codes and standardized attitudes have to do with the treatment of the child born out of wedlock. Since the child is born helpless and is dependent upon parents for a name as well as for support, an illegitimate child usually creates a serious problem. Rather strict codes govern the problem of illegitimacy.

DISCUSSION AND REVIEW QUESTIONS

1. Compare our kind of family life with that described by the American Indian in terms of protection to the individual; his security; his freedom; his personality integration.

2. Compare family systems in terms of marriage types, and appraise from the standpoint of male and female roles and problems. Would you say adjustment is likely to be the perspective of the polygamous family, for example?

3. As world cultures approach similarity, with modern contact and the speed of indirect means of communication, which marriage system is most likely to survive, as you view the situation? Do you think yours is an ethnocentric point of view?

4. Describe typical systems of family authority. By whom are they administered, with what results to children, etc?

[12] George P. Murdock, "Sexual Behavior: What is Acceptable," *Journal of Social Hygiene,* 36:1–31 (1950).

5. Compare matrilocal and patrilocal systems with the family system in which young people establish independent households. Illustrate.

6. Indicate how the tracing of descent may extend far beyond true blood lines in tribal society.

7. What is the most important symbolic culture trait in modern marriage?

8. What are some of the utilitarian culture traits of the modern family? How have they changed in recent decades?

9. Discuss codes as an aspect of family culture.

SOURCEBOOK READINGS

KOENIG, SAMUEL, REX D. HOPPER, and FELIKS GROSS. *Sociology: A Book of Readings.* Englewood Cliffs, N.J.: Prentice-Hall, Inc., 1950.
1. LEVY, JOHN, and RUTH MUNROE, "Why People Marry," pp. 131–35.
2. LEVY, JOHN, and RUTH MUNROE, "How We Select Our Mates," pp. 136–38.

LANDIS, JUDSON T., and MARY G. LANDIS. *Readings in Marriage and the Family.* Englewood Cliffs, N.J.: Prentice-Hall, Inc., 1952.
3. KIRKPATRICK, CLIFFORD, and THEODORE CAPLOW, "Courtship in a Group of Minnesota Students," pp. 79–90.
4. LANDIS, JUDSON T., "Time Required to Achieve Marriage Adjustment," pp. 169–80.
5. LANDIS, JUDSON T., "Marriages of Mixed and Non-Mixed Religious Faith," pp. 203–10.
6. SIRJAMAKI, JOHN, "Cultural Configurations in the American Family," pp. 9–17.

SELECTED READINGS

For Selected Readings and Film List, see Chapter 34, pages 592–93.

The Modern Family

The ancient institution of marriage and family has been greatly modified in urban-industrial civilization, for the footloose human being is relatively free from age-old controls on the marriage relationship. Not only has mate choice taken on an individualistic aspect in cultures within the urban-industrial sphere, but the duration of the marriage itself is also a matter of personal choice. True, the restrictions on divorce are there, but both the vow and the law are taken lightly by persons who live under the individualistic marriage–family pattern.

The ideals and aspirations of this marriage are the satisfaction of personal wishes for the achievement of happiness and the realization of a mutual satisfaction in the marriage bond. If the marriage fails to produce this result it is subject to criticism and doubt, and often to dissolution.

It is doubtful that any marriage system ever sought so much, or that man ever needed so much in marriage as he does in the relatively anonymous society of the modern world, where many live without close contact with neighbors and large family groups.

The nature of these new ideals bring to marriage the highest type of happiness and the worst of all misery. It is for this reason that marriage today is fraught with such great consequences. Those who have great expectations may also suffer great disappointments.

Those who work in the field of marriage and family relations realize that there is no returning to the stern institutional values of an earlier age. History does not move backward. The values of that system do not fit into urban-industrial society. They never will. The researcher and teacher today look forward to a time when individual mate choice will be more wisely guided. Research indicates clearly that more effective and objective sex education, training for marriage and parenthood, and a more realistic appreciation on the part of youth of the qualities that are required for successful marriage seem to point toward the goal of better marriage and family life.

The tools of science must come into play in order for marriage to realize its high goal in this kind of marriage system. This calls for extensive research into marriage and child-training problems, for the development of scales and measurements which will help direct young people in mate choice, as well as for the further elaboration of counseling facilities to guide young people prior to marriage, and to help those whose marriage is headed for the rocks.

THE AMERICAN FAMILY IN RECENT HISTORICAL PERSPECTIVE

Toward the Companionship Marriage. In this review of the general cultural framework of the marriage–family institution, attention has been directed to the radical way in which the American family is changing from the traditional institutional pattern toward the modern companionship emphasis, which is variously designated as the *individualistic family*, the *democratic family*, the *romantic family*, or the *modern family*.

It has been indicated that this new family has become unstable because it seeks romance rather than accepting a pattern of duty and responsibility. As a consequence, an increasing proportion of marriages end in divorce, even those marriages where there are children. If parents fail to realize romantic satisfaction in each other, they seem to be willing to sacrifice the interests and welfare of the children for their own personal happiness. These are the negative aspects of the new trend in culture-building in the family institutions. But the new marriage system is not to be condemned without a hearing. Does it root in some new kind of social reality?

The Basic Causes of the Changing Marriage–Family Pattern. As one reviews social experience in a highly mobile society, he must conclude that man is essentially lonely when dissociated from intimate primary groups of fellows. In the anonymity and strangeness that comes with mobility, the individual tends to seek in a mate all of the qualities of intimacy, friendship, and security that earlier societies gave him through these other primary groups. For this reason the individual in a mobile society of today makes much greater demands of marriage and the marriage partner than did his ancestors. Man, now as always, longs for love, intimacy, and emotional security, but finds increasingly only the pair-relationship outlet for it. If he fails to find all of this in marriage, he feels that his marriage is a failure.

The subsidized veteran marriage brought a new student pattern to the college campus—and with it, problems of college housing. This cultural innovation proved so popular that now both family and educational institutions are changing, and further innovations are inevitable. The married student today is no longer subsidized by the G. I. Bill, in most instances. Will this lead to subsidy of the married student by parents? to government loans? What is the college marriage doing to role and status positions of male and female—are distinctive male roles and perogatives vanishing? What is it doing to child-rearing practice and theory? (WSC Photo, State College of Washington.)

Romantic expectations today often far exceed the capacity of the mate to fulfill them. Even those marriages which succeed require a tempering of romantic expectations based on a more realistic conception of what human beings can be to each other through mutual dependence and mutual trust, rather than merely as objects of romantic inspiration.

The individualistic marriage does place pleasure above responsibility and duty. It aims at the satisfaction of the individual rather than at the perpetuation of the race or of the family institution as such. This philosophy of individualistic marriage has its natural counterpart in freedom of divorce. It is assumed that if the marriage is not satisfactory, divorce is a natural and necessary solution. Increasingly, courts are permitting divorce whenever couples claim that they have no affection for each other, or even when one member of the marriage claims that he has no affection for his mate.

These claims may be expressed in such terms of mental cruelty and mental torture.

That happiness has become the prime aim of marriage is in itself highly significant. Under the institutional family, marriage was not measured primarily in terms of producing happiness. In fact, this was not its main task. Marriage was successful if it produced children and provided sufficient economic security for their support and rearing. The great problem of life historically was survival—having sufficient food, shelter, and clothing to live. It is still so in the densely populated areas of much of the world. Man and woman were joined together for life. They accepted their marriage vows with all seriousness. Regardless of whether they found their marriage satisfactory from the standpoint of their personal relations, they maintained it. This attitude toward marriage is still the prevailing one in many cultures throughout the world today.

Contrast this with the modern American marriage system which assumes that if the person does not find supreme romantic love and personal happiness, he is free to dissolve the marriage and try to find it in some other marriage. This has led to what some call *sequential marriage*. By a series of divorces and legally sanctioned monogamous marriages, the individual realizes some of the variety of polygamous marriage.

Is anything, then, to be said on the positive side? Indeed, much!

Positive Values in the Companionship Ideal. Never in history was the child so well treated as in the modern family. Never was his right as an individual to develop to the fullest extent of his capacity so well recognized. The pattern of child discipline is not authoritarian; it reflects the democratic philosophy which assumes that the child's personality should have room for expansion and that he should be developed and trained so that he can take his place as a member of an individualistic society in which creativeness and individual freedom are assumed to be the right of every man.

Never before has the level of living of the American family been so high, or the standard of health and general welfare. Never have parents had more freedom from the responsibilities of child care, from the risks of the child being maimed, or from the risk of his untimely death. Never have parents been able to produce so few children and have so many survive. The infant death rate is at the lowest point in history. Half as many births as exist in many parts of the globe where half the increase is cut off in the first year by an excessive death rate maintains our population growth.

Never have couples realized so much in each other as they do to-day, if the ideals of the romantic marriage are even approximated. This new form of marriage assumes equality of husband and wife. It assumes their mutual sharing of responsibility as well as their mutual enjoyment of each other in a physical and psychological sense. Such freedom and unity of personality was not conceived of in the old patriarchal family where the obligations of wife to husband were stressed rather than their mutual realization in each other. Even the divorce rate must be taken as an index of the freedom of a person in modern society to make his decisions and to free himself from a bargain which has proved to be unsatisfactory. Many marriages in the old institutional scheme of family life continued for the lifetime even though the couple was continuously at odds.

Never has the lot of woman been as desirable as her place in the companionship marriage. Throughout history she has been more nearly a slave of man than his equal. She is so today throughout much of the world. She is the burden bearer, the hoer of corn, carrier of water, and worker in the field with buffalo or oxen. Take the proverbial attitude of the Orthodox Church in Russia: "A hen is not a bird, neither is a woman a human being"; or "Woman (says the manuscript of a religious sectarian) is the weakest creature, the receptacle of all woes, the red-hot coal of dissensions, the baneful toy, the enemy of the angels, an insatiable animal, an abyss of credulity, a bunch of obstinacy, vanity of vanities, an attraction in the distance, an angel in the street, a devil at home, a magpie at the gate, a she-goat in the garden."[1] Compare such attitudes with the comparative equality of woman today in American marriage.

In the companionship family system, individualism has come to be a right of woman and child as well as father. Democracy, as it gradually spreads throughout the family, admits woman to educational privileges, income, and other rights once reserved for the male. She has equal rights in mate choice but, of course, man is still the aggressor. She does have rather complete freedom of choice as to persons with whom she will associate. Growing economic independence of women gives them a chance to actually exercise their freedom as no other generation of women has been able to do.

And let those who challenge the values of happiness and companionship, stressed today as supreme values of marriage, remind themselves that no aspect of life has the stern visage of an age of struggle for survival. The American standard of living makes all

---

[1] E. J. Dillon, *Russia Today and Yesterday* (Garden City, N.Y.: Doubleday & Co., Inc., 1930), p. 218.

stress happiness as a supreme life value. Why should they not expect marriage to be the supreme happiness value? And can one call companionship a spurious value in an age of leisure and loneliness when so many are deprived of the intimate ties of long-time neighbors and close relatives and must have someone to talk to and share with. Life in a mobile society is bankrupt without these values.

THE DEMOCRATIC CHILDREARING PATTERN

There are always critics of the new order of child training in home and school. There are those who cry for the return to the rod. But there is no way back even if we chose to return. Throughout industrial society life moves toward greater individuation of personality. The individuated personality grows only in an atmosphere of freedom, not one of repression and stern discipline.

To be authoritarian today means losing the child's respect, love, and loyalty. To send him into the world after a successful use of authoritarian training methods is to send him out a cripple or a rebel who must defy parents to be free.

BIRTHS DURING FIVE-YEAR PERIODS

PERIODS	TOTAL BIRTHS
1910–1914	13,250,000
1915–1919	13,750,000
1920–1924	14,375,000
1925–1929	13,375,000
1930–1934	12,125,000
1935–1939	11,250,000
1940–1944	13,750,000
1945–1949	17,000,000
1950–1954	19,000,000
1955–1959 (estimated)	20,000,000

The Birth-rate Trend Is Upward in the United States

Family mores change, but the desire for children seems to be greater now than two decades ago. And the near-universal adoption of birth-control methods has not led to race extinction as some pessimists of earlier years predicted.

There is a spurious type of family democracy which identifies freedom with the child's right to do anything he pleases, and there are always those who at each stage of his growth overemphasize the strength of the child and expect decisions of him they should make themselves. Democracy does not mean letting the child make choices in areas where he is not yet physically or mentally prepared to act. But no other method works like the democratic method, if used intelligently and with love and understanding.

DIVORCE IN FAMILY PATTERNS

Although no society encourages divorce or approves it, all permit it. Some who are joined together must be allowed to separate because they find their marriage and family relationships intolerable.

The universal restriction on divorce is logical, for no society dares take the risk involved in loose family ties. Marriage must be a permanent and lifelong bond to carry out the purposes for which it is designed: the care of helpless children, the care of the aged, the protection of morals, the transmission of property. Divorce threatens the security of children, the security of dependent members of the family, the sex code, and the inheritance system. Consider the economic aspects of marriage alone. From time immemorial a stable marriage has been the only protection afforded children during their dependent years, and the only safeguard for aged parents when they reached the point of dependency. It is such considerations as these that require all societies, if they would survive, to treat the matter of family relationships as something more than a casual one. The permanence of the man and wife relationship cannot be left to the whims of romance or to changes in tempers of individuals. Social pressures of an imposing character must be built around this relationship, and its permanence guaranteed.

Generally speaking, societies taboo the kinds of activities which threaten the pair relationship. As we have seen, only 2 per cent sanctioned adulterous relations.[2] Societies generally consider adulterous relations a serious threat to the stability of the married pair. It is, of course, also assumed that such sex experience, since it involves the risk of pregnancy, threatens the security of the child, since not all men are willing to assume responsibility for a child sired by another.

Societies also have many taboos in regard to the mother-in-law relationship. This relationship has proved in most societies to be a difficult one—one threatening to successful marriage. Consequently, many primitives forbid a son-in-law to look into his mother-in-law's

[2] George P. Murdock, "Sexual Behavior: What Is Acceptable?" *Journal of Social Hygiene,* 36:1–31 (1950).

eye or to speak to her. In some tribes he may not enter a room where she is present.

Similarly, incest taboos are universal among mankind. This is probably not entirely a matter of genetics; probably, in fact, it is not a matter of genetics at all in its origin. In reality, incest taboos cut down the risks of jealousy, bitterness, and conflict within the family group and its close kin, thus lending greater stability to the marriage.

HOW SOCIAL SCIENCE SERVES THE FAMILY

It is clear from the preceding discussion that the companionship, or the so-called individualistic, family is much less stable, psychologically speaking, than the institutional patriarchal family of the grandparent generation, which still survives in isolated rural sections. It is also clear that a part of this instability is inherent in the companionship family itself, which is much less given to childrearing and economic survival and much more given to seeking personal satisfactions in the mate.

If one admits that the new kind of family is desirable and that it often leads to supreme happiness, he must, rather than envisioning a return to the institutional family, seek to strengthen the companionship family by helping it realize the goals for which it is intended. This would seem to be a logical approach since history rarely moves backward. Under modern conditions, the institutional family no longer fits and never can again.

Science as a Guide in Mate Selection. Since the companionship family holds the ideal of achieving maximum personal satisfaction in a relationship with a person of the opposite sex, one of the main problems is to see that only those people marry who are capable of functioning satisfactorily within the intimate relationships of marriage. It is also important that various devices be developed for helping those who marry to select the right mate. Such an approach to problems of the modern family may at first seem fantastic in a society where so many are accustomed to the idea that love is all that matters. On the other hand, for more than twenty-five years an increasing amount of effort has been directed to research which aims to develop various devices for measuring personality traits and acquisitions. The validity of such tests is beyond question.

Today, for example, few colleges admit a new student until they have given him a thorough going over as far as his emotional tendencies, educational preparation, innate abilities, aptitudes, and interests are concerned. On the basis of such an evaluation, institutions try to guide him into the fields for which he seems to be most adapted by temperament and interests, or, if he seems not to have the capacities to do the thing he wants to do, to steer him away from that field. It is often necessary to tell the young person that he does not possess the capabilities that are required for college entrance. As a consequence, he may be advised that he should enter immediately into the work world or into some kind of vocational training or apprenticeship where he will be able to develop his special talents. Such testing was long ago removed from the realm of mere chance. It is known that guidance based on thorough testing is in the person's best interest.

For many years sociologists and psychologists have been making a similar approach to the problems of mate selection in marriage. Paul Popenoe has for some years used emotional maturity tests in connection with his clinic on marriage and family life in Los Angeles.[3] These, together with tests of physical fitness, are used as a basis for guiding the individual in determining his own capacities for a successful marriage.

Burgess and Cottrell, after a study of over five hundred marriages, developed an elaborate scale based on the characteristics which were found to be associated with successful and permanent marriage.[4] They also learned the traits associated with difficulty in marital adjustment. By checking this scale, the young person can find whether he has traits that are usually associated with successful adjustment in marriage or whether he has many traits which go with unsuccessful marriage.

Clifford Adams, psychologist at Pennsylvania State College, has developed a series of ten simplified tests based on the above research and others of less extensive scope by which a young man or woman can measure his or her fitness for marriage on many personality traits.[5] These tests are easily administered and easily scored. Adams has also developed tests by which two young people who think they are "made for each other" can actually test themselves and match their personality traits to see whether or not they are headed for success in marriage.

Even popular magazines are carrying an increasing number of articles and simple tests which at least give some index to a person's probable success in marriage. No present test is adequate, for in-

[3] Paul Popenoe, *Marriage, Before and After* (New York: W. Wilfred Funk, Inc., 1943).

[4] E. W. Burgess and Leonard S. Cottrell, *Predicting Success or Failure in Marriage* (Englewood Cliffs, N.J.: Prentice-Hall, Inc., 1938).

[5] Clifford Adams and Vance O. Packard, *How to Pick a Mate* (New York: E. P. Dutton & Co., Inc., 1946).

sufficient data have been used in establishing norms. They are useful, and serve as another guide by which the intelligent young person who wants to know as much as he can about his fitness for marriage, or that of someone he plans to marry, can have a better foundation on which to make a final decision.[6]

Premarital Advice. Another modern device which is being used to insure an enduring marriage is the marriage clinic, which is capable of giving to the couple advice as well as tests such as have been described. These clinics also provide for complete physical examinations and answer young people's questions fully and frankly in the areas of sex, childbearing, and other such aspects of physical and psychological adjustment.

Marriage Courses. An increasing proportion of college students take courses in which almost every aspect of marriage and child-rearing is discussed. Such courses have been fairly widely established in high school. The public is becoming more tolerant toward the idea of young people of high school and college ages being given full and frank information on matters of sex adjustment, marriage, and childrearing. Even the general public is beginning to suspect that the old wives' tales, folklore, and the movies, which have been the only guide of young people for marriage in the past, are inadequate.

Marriage courses have an important psychological advantage in that they help young people to recognize that a successful marriage is rarely achieved by chance. All such courses stress the fact that marriage is an adjustment—a whole series of adjustments, in fact— in which young people with different social and economic backgrounds and different role conceptions try to work out a social and economic relationship which will affect every aspect of their living, their earning, and their spending; in which two people with different biological drives and motivations will work out a sexual adjustment after a period of trial and error and patience; in which two families of relatives will be merged in a new working relationship; in which the couple will make an adjustment in the field of religious views as they affect their own religious life and that of their children; in

[6] For a good summary of personality traits as they affect marriage success, and for a view of the important research findings that underlie all reliable tests developed to date in the field of mate selection, see Judson T. Landis and Mary G. Landis, *Building a Successful Marriage* (2d ed.; Englewood Cliffs, N.J.: Prentice-Hall, Inc., 1953), chap. 5, or their *A Marriage Handbook* (Englewood Cliffs, N.J.: Prentice-Hall, Inc., 1949), chap. 5. The appendixes to these books also lists marriage counseling agencies. See also Paul H. Landis, *Making the Most of Marriage* (New York: Appleton-Century-Crofts, Inc., 1955), chap. 6.

which an adjustment will be made to the friends every young person brings to his marriage; in which a whole series of adjustments will be made in the field of recreation and leisure-time activities.

Today youth is being taught that these adjustments to differences in backgrounds, interests, points of view, and social roles require tolerance and understanding, a willingness to let the other person live his own life as well as share one's own. They are made to see that when children are born, a new series of adjustments begin. Discipline, religious training, educational training for the child, the problem of how many children to have, how they will be spaced, and other such problems come as the marriage proceeds from its early stages to its established phases.

Marriage necessitates continual adjustment, even as the couple advance in years. What will the wife's life be when she reaches the empty-nest stage of marriage when the children have left home and married? Will she be content to remain at home and simply participate vicariously in her husband's life, or will she try to renew her interest in the work world? If she finds this necessary in order to fill her empty years after the children are gone, will her husband be tolerant of her interests and understand them and be willing to sacrifice some of his own interests to let her develop ambitions which she has smothered through the long years of caring for children?

No young person can take a course in marriage and family life without understanding how extensive are the adjustments in the life of every couple. From the day the marriage ceremony is completed until the time in life when their paths are parted by death, adjustments are required in every marriage. Then come the adjustments of bereavement and widowhood.

Certainly it is desirable that young people be given a realistic perspective of the life cycle of the family.

Marital Advice. Another device for trying to help marriages today reach a better level of adjustment is the marriage clinic and counseling center, where married couples may go to seek help from expert counselors who are accustomed to dealing with marriage and family problems. Counselors analyze difficulties and help couples work out solutions where they themselves have not been able to see a way out of their problems.

Unfortunately, clinics for premarital advice and testing and clinics for giving help to married couples are available only in a few large cities and on a few college campuses. There is, however, an increasing interest in studying the family, and as more personnel is trained, clinics will become more widespread. And the public, as they become more informed on matters of sex education, marriage, family, and childrearing, will come to use these devices for adjustment and to gain confidence in them.

SUMMARY

The family is everywhere. But what it means to an individual and to a people depends on the place it has within their culture. The helpless young require care. In their early years, this care must be continuous. Even through the years of childhood, the protection and care of adults is essential. This is the basic reason for the long-time marriage tie between man and woman. This is the biological reason for the elaborate human institutions of marriage and family which all societies have developed.

Throughout the world marriage has an enduring quality that no other personal relationship has. It is institutionalized, and numerous social obligations are built up about it. Marriage and family become not merely personal institutions, but vehicles by which society transmits the most essential element, the cultural heritage, and through which its transmits economic goods through systems of inheritance.

Much of the moral system of a society also is built about the personal relationships of men and women, for here is the one sexual bond which societies recognize and try to make enduring.

The American family has been going through a transition from an institutionally oriented arrangement to an individualistically oriented one. Greater sex equality, freedom of women to pursue their interests in vocations and avocations outside the home, the democratic treatment of children with stress on development rather than discipline are new trends. With the greater individuation of husband and wife, and their greater stress on the interpersonal relationship of marriage, to the neglect of the institutional, has also come a higher divorce rate.

DISCUSSION AND REVIEW QUESTIONS

1. Compare the institutional and companionship marriage–family systems in terms of attitudes, values, goals, and sex roles.

2. What social forces have been responsible for the trend toward the companionship type of marriage?

3. What are the inherent risks of the romantic marriage conception? the positive values to be realized?

4. What are the relative merits of the developmental system of child training compared to the historic authoritarian pattern?

5. Why has the companionship type of marriage posed an unusual threat to the universal goal of permanence in the marriage tie?

6. Outline ways in which social science serves the needs of the modern marriage and family.

7. Do you believe that science can ever act as a safe guide in mate choice? Do you think it can do so at the present state of research knowledge?

8. Do you see hope in premarital counseling? in education for marriage in the high school and college classroom? in marriage counseling for married couples in trouble?

SOURCEBOOK READINGS

LANDIS, JUDSON T., and MARY G. LANDIS. *Readings in Marriage and the Family.* Englewood Cliffs, N.J.: Prentice-Hall, Inc., 1952.
1. SIRJAMAKI, JOHN, "Cultural Configurations in the American Family," pp. 9–17.
2. BURGESS, ERNEST W., "The Family in a Changing Society," pp. 21–27.
3. LANDIS, PAUL H., "The Changing Family," pp. 27–31.
4. NYE, IVAN, "Adolescent-Parent Adjustment," pp. 274–76.
5. DAVIS, KINGSLEY, "Statistical Perspective on Divorce," pp. 333–38.
6. ———, "Children of Divorce," pp. 351–60.
7. ALEXANDER, PAUL W., "A Therapeutic Approach to the Problem of Divorce," pp. 360–74.

LEE, RAYMOND L., JAMES A. BURKHART, and VAN B. SHAW. *Contemporary Social Issues.* New York: The Thomas Crowell Co., 1955.
8. ALEXANDER, PAUL W., "Our Legal Horror: Divorce," pp. 441–50.

LEE, ELIZABETH BRYANT, and ALFRED McCLUNG LEE. *Social Problems in America* (rev. ed.). New York: Henry Holt & Co., Inc., 1955.
9. DAVIS, KINGSLEY, "Parent-Youth Conflict," pp. 127–30.

SELECTED READINGS

BERNARD, JESSIE. *American Family Behavior.* New York: Harper & Brothers, 1942.

BOSSARD, JAMES H. S. *The Sociology of Child Development.* Rev. ed.; New York: Harper & Brothers, 1956.

BURGESS, ERNEST W., and HARVEY J. LOCKE. *The Family.* 2d ed.; New York: American Book Co., 1953.

CAVAN, RUTH SHONLE. *The American Family.* New York: The Thomas Crowell Co., 1953, Part II.

FOLSOM, J. K. *The Family and Democratic Society.* New York: John Wiley & Sons, Inc., 1948, chap. 16.

GESELL, ARNOLD, *et al. The First Five Years of Life.* New York: Harper & Brothers, 1940.

GLICK, PAUL C. "The Family Cycle," *American Sociological Review,* 12:164–74 (April, 1947).

HAVIGHURST, ROBERT J., and HILDA TABA. *Adolescent Character and Personality.* New York: John Wiley & Sons, Inc., 1949.

KIRKPATRICK, CLIFFORD. *The Family: As Process and Institution.* New York: The Ronald Press Co., 1955.

LANDIS, JUDSON T., and MARY G. LANDIS. *Building a Successful Marriage.* 3d ed.; Englewood Cliffs, N.J.: Prentice-Hall, Inc., 1958.

LANDIS, PAUL H. *Adolescence and Youth: The Process of Maturing.* 2d ed.; New York: McGraw-Hill Book Co., Inc., 1952.

———. *For Husbands and Wives: A Plan for Happy Marriage.* New York: Appleton-Century-Crofts, Inc., 1956.

———. *Making the Most of Marriage.* New York: Appleton-Century-Crofts, Inc., 1955.

———. *Understanding Teenagers.* New York: Appleton-Century-Crofts, Inc., 1955.

Marriage and Family Living, Vol. 16, No. 4 (Nov., 1954), is a study of family life in various nations.

NYE, F. IVAN. "The Rejected Parent and Delinquency," *Marriage and Family Living,* 18:291–97 (Nov., 1956).

OGBURN, WILLIAM F., and MEYER F. NIMKOFF. *Technology and the Changing Family.* Boston: Houghton Mifflin Co., 1955.

QUEEN, STUART A., and JOHN B. ADAMS. *The Family in Various Cultures.* Chicago: J. B. Lippincott Co., 1952.

WALLER, WILLARD. *The Family: A Dynamic Interpretation.* (Revised by Reuben Hill.) New York: The Dryden Press, Inc., 1951, Part V.

FILM LIST

The Boss Didn't Say Good Morning—1 reel—sound
Demonstrates the psychological effect a boss's failure to say good morning has on an employee; "recommended for use in connection with parent-child relationships." *Source:* Teaching Film Custodians, Inc.

Wednesday's Child—9 minutes—sound
Evidences the problems of a child involved in the dissolution of his parents' marriage and the events which lead up to the divorce. *Source:* New York University Film Library.

Wife, Doctor, and Nurse—21 minutes—sound
Deals with marital relations in general and with jealousy in particular. *Source:* New York University Film Library.

Men in White (excerpt)—15 minutes
Deals with problems of choice between marriage and professional training; whether or not a wife should aid her husband's support while he studies; and whether or not people with widely differing backgrounds should marry. *Source:* Teaching Film Custodians, Inc.

Courtship to Courthouse—15 minutes
Analyzes the marriage and divorce problem. *Source:* RKO Radio Pictures, Inc.

Marriage for Moderns—average about 15 minutes—sound
Set of five films to be used in conjunction with Henry Bowman's book *Marriage for Moderns.* Each film can be used effectively alone. Titles are: This Charming Couple; Marriage Today; Choosing for Happiness; It Takes All Kinds; Who's Boss. Intended to educate young people to an awareness of the problems of courtship and marriage. *Source:* McGraw-Hill Book Co., Inc.

Chapter 35

Educational Institutions

The passing on of a select part of the cultural heritage is the function of educational institutions. In an earlier day, and in primitive societies still, education is scarcely differentiated from family and tribal life. The child learns as he grows up, serving a natural apprenticeship in the simple household tasks and in the hunting or agricultural folkways of the tribe. There is little formal education, except at the time of puberty when boys and girls must begin to think of taking over the responsibilities of adulthood.

Education is so completely missing as a separate cultural complex among many peoples that Clark Wissler did not even show it separately in the universal cultural scheme presented in Chapter 2. Today, however, the task of passing on the cultural heritage to the young, of teaching them the things they must know to function in the social system, has far exceeded the ability of the family and of the neighborhood to handle. With the increasing complexity of the cultural heritage, its transmission to the young has become such a major task that education has emerged as one of the great institutions of our time. And the end is not yet. Each year an increasing demand is made upon state and federal governments for financial support of education. Each year an increasing proportion of the population spends an increasing proportion of time in school and school-sponsored activities. Schooling occupies a large part of the time of the normal-minded able-bodied of the age group six to sixteen. With the development of kindergarten and nursery schools, the lower age levels are reached, and with increased high school, college, and university attendance, the upper age levels. In a complex culture, the education of the adult has also become accepted, so that educational institutions not only reach those in the formative years of life but, through extension programs, adult education reaches all classes.

The demand for this kind of education seems to be on the increase, not only among town and city people but also among farmers, whose adult-education program finds its main expression in the Agricultural Extension Service, sponsored jointly by the various states and the United States Department of Agriculture.

Not only has education come to include these more formal ways of passing on the cultural heritage through the process of teaching and demonstration in classroom and laboratory, but it has also been expanded in the form of great libraries in cities, and more modest libraries in almost every type of community center. Some would include as educational institutions those less formal devices for the transmission of knowledge such as the newspaper, the national magazine, and radio and television, through which the American public can increase its knowledge as well as entertain itself.

This description is enough to show the vast reach of educational influences in the modern world. Attention has previously been called to the fact that a person can spend his entire lifetime taking courses in any large university and still at the close of a long life be relatively ignorant in many fields of knowledge. This is indicative of the tremendous load of the cultural heritage that is to be passed on to the young in an age when cheap printing makes possible storage of not only the experience but the techniques and skills and scientific methodologies that have become a rich heritage in our time.

In the transmission of the cultural heritage, educational institutions have come to have such a key place that it is now believed that universal education is essential, not only to political intelligence, but also to economic self-sufficiency. In former times the "three R's" were enough preparation for successful living, but today much more is expected. Moreover the height of a man's climb on the educational ladder is one of the best indexes of his preparation for a successful climb in the economic and honorific structure of our open-class system. Education is also to an extent a measure of one's potential usefulness as a contributor to the cultural heritage which will be passed on to posterity.

THREE LEVELS OF CULTURAL TRANSMISSION

F. S. Chapin, leading American sociological student of institutions, has indicated that elementary schools concern themselves primarily with the acquisition of language and number symbols.[1] These are used in daily communication and are the basis for drill and

[1] F. S. Chapin, *Contemporary American Institutions* (New York: Harper & Brothers, 1935), chap. 8.

memory work by which the child acquires the skills of the race. This level of cultural transmission is, of course, as old as humanity.

The second level of cultural transmission, the high-school level, introduces the student to technical vocabularies and places emphasis on the acquisition of tested knowledge, that is, knowledge derived from scientific experimentation. This phase of cultural transmission is given vocational orientation and places considerable emphasis on self-improvement.

The third level of cultural transmission is the university level, where the student is expected not only to acquire further scientific knowledge but where he is supposed to learn to use abstract symbols. He progresses further in self-development and in the increase of knowledge until he has sufficient training to discover new knowledge. This latter goal is the particular aim of the higher levels of graduate work, especially on the Ph. D. level, which sets as its requirement for graduation a contribution to knowledge by the candidate.

At the higher levels of learning a good teacher raises more questions than he can answer, the aim being to challenge students to question all knowledge, to criticize all research procedures, and thus prepare themselves to seek better answers. To the extent that these ideals are attained, the higher levels of education have to do with more than cultural transmission; they lead the student through an apprenticeship in the development of scientific knowledge so that he will make a creative contribution to the culture base of the current generation.

THE INCREASING BURDEN OF THE SCHOOL

Supplementing the Home. Each generation places an increasing burden on the school, not only from the standpoint of passing on a greater volume of the general cultural heritage, but also from the standpoint of helping carry the burden of other social institutions. To the extent that the family has been made increasingly unstable by mobility, divorce, and increased job opportunities for women outside the home, educational institutions have had to take over burdens once carried by the family.

The school is the one institution which can be depended upon to pass on essential parts of the cultural heritage. Does the home fail in giving adequate sex education? Then the school must do it. Does the home fail in developing morals and ideals? Then the school must do it, for what other agency except the school reaches everyone, and no generation dare be allowed to grow up without having been given the essential ideals and standards of the social group. Is the home failing in giving an adequate diet? Then the school must do it by the school lunch, which ideally serves as a teaching device in the field of nutrition and also improves the child's diet by seeing that he gets at least one properly balanced meal per day. Has the home of today failed to give an apprenticeship to vocation? Then the school must bridge the gap, for every youth, as he approaches maturity, must know something about the work world which he must enter. Adulthood consists first of all in earning one's own way in the world. Every youth must someday fall into the role of breadwinner, so that he will be able to support not only himself but, as he reaches the full stage of maturity, support others also. Is the family failing to pass on the domestic art which every girl must have to function as a homemaker? Then, the school must pass them on, so home economics with all its diversified curriculums comes in to replace with scientific training in these fields the traditions and folklore once passed on from mother to daughter.

So one might go on elaborating the new tasks the school is undertaking in response to the new type of family system.

Handicraft had its apprenticeship system. Industry never has had a program of training new workers that is systematic and comprehensive. Vocational attitudes, vocational training, and to quite an extent vocational placement have become responsibilities of the school in urban-industrial society.

In metropolitan areas special trade schools at the secondary school level are a part of the vocational program, and even the small school has its commercial training program, shop courses for farm youth, and so forth.

The college is the training school of those moving toward the profession, the diploma being the prerequisite to work in the various professional fields.

Supplementing Government Institutions. Respect for law and governmental authority might be expected to derive from these authorities themselves. But too often law-making bodies and law-enforcing officials, from police to judiciary, have failed to inspire confidence, trust, and respect for law. The school must therefore teach regard for law and officialdom as part of the training for loyal citizenship. Unable through law to reach the goal of safety with the automobile, the school takes on the job of driver training.

Strengthening the Community. The school has also had to compensate for inadequacies of neighborhood and community environment. In almost every community throughout the nation, no matter how degraded the neighborhood or community or how low the level of living of its families, the school is the best-equipped and the best-looking structure in the area. It gives underprivileged youth their first glimpse into a higher standard of living than that to which they are accustomed. It helps them rise above the level of the immediate environment into a cleaner and better one, as well as giving them a glimpse of horizons of ambition beyond the immediate locality. (This obviously does not apply to some of the one-room rural schools, but is generally true of town and city schools, for in urban areas most communities put their best efforts into at least the material aspects of the educational institution.)

THE FUNCTION OF THE SCHOOL IN DEMOCRATIC SOCIETY

Interestingly enough, the school now holds a position in relation to government not far different from that held by the Church during the Middle Ages. Then, church and state were joint public institutions. Today, in most modern states, church and state are separate. Education, on the other hand, has become a socialized state function. It is publicly supported and used as a tool of government. As such it enjoys unusual prestige and also is in a position to act as a powerful agent of control, shaping the individual for the political order. In democratic societies, the function of control is broadly conceived, and the individual is shaped for an individualistic social order. He is trained to consider alternatives and to exercise choice and initiative. In autocratic societies, education becomes narrow-gauged, and is used as an instrument of indoctrination.

As an agency of democracy, universal education originated in part to prepare the citizen for the intelligent use of the ballot. Today its scope is far greater. It has become the open door to numerous opportunities, and therefore is the one institution which does most to equalize privilege among the various social classes. It is for this reason in part that democratic society has tried to remove step by step all handicaps to equality of education. This ideal is far from being realized in that there are still economic handicaps to pursuing education to the higher levels. But even these are being removed, as the need for parity of educational opportunity for all economic classes is being recognized.

The high school, in that it deals with a large youth group on the threshold of maturity, has probably been the most leveling influence in American democracy. It throws together youth of all classes and lets them compete on the basis of ability. For this reason, it tends to erase class lines and to encourage participation as equals on the basis of intelligence. Extracurricular activities and social life also erase class barriers, paving the way for marriage across class lines.

The high school is having, and will continue to have, similar effects in erasing lines of stratification as racial integration becomes a universal reality in school programs throughout the nation. Intelligence and ability know no racial limits and as the races mingle in the classroom this will become evident to all. Further removal of economic and racial handicaps to college training, so that a greater proportion can continue their training to the highest level which their ability justifies, will further tend to break down class lines and to equalize privilege.

SCHOOLING IN THE UNITED STATES

Enrollment Trends. School attendance in the lower grades has been universal for several decades, except in the most backward communities. The approach toward universal high-school attendance is a recent development. At the turn of the century less than one youth in ten of high-school age was in school; by 1955 nearly nine in ten were. There has been a rapid climb in the curve of high-school attendance since 1910.

SCHOOL ENROLLMENT TRENDS SINCE 1870

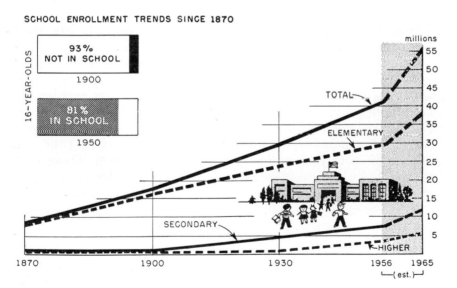

Education Progress Since 1870

In 1956, college enrollment was equal to the high school enrollment of 1920. In 1900 only 7 per cent of 16-year-olds were in school; by 1950 the proportion was 81 per cent. Education has become a matter of national concern.

The growth of college enrollments as measured by the proportion of those aged eighteen to twenty-four in school shows a similar upward trend. In 1900 only 4 per cent of youth in this age group were enrolled in institutions of higher learning. Even as late as 1910 only about 4.5 per cent were enrolled. Since that time the increase has been very rapid. By 1930 more than 12 per cent were enrolled, by 1940 almost 16 per cent; by 1955 enrollments of the eighteen- to twenty-four-year age group had risen to over 21 per cent, with almost a third enrolled in the seventeen- to nineteen-year age group.

School Enrollment in the United States, 1955

Age Group	Per Cent Enrolled	Per Cent Enrolled		
		Rural Farm	Rural Nonfarm	Urban
10–13	99.2	98.6	99.0	99.4
14–17	86.9	82.8	88.1	87.9
18–19	31.5	26.7	29.5	33.5
20–24	11.1	4.5	6.8	13.7

Source: U. S. Department of Commerce, "School Enrollment: October 1955," *Current Population Reports*, Series P-20, No. 66 (April 6, 1956), p. 8.

The mass movement toward college of young people in late teens and early twenties creates a new challenge to educational institutions themselves.[2] Overwhelmed at the close of World War II by enrollments exceeding their facilities, all colleges have expanded greatly since the war and have faced the challenging problem of adapting their education program to mass attendance. The exact solution has not yet been developed, but probably one eventual solution will be termination of education for a great number at the end of the sophomore year, as in the junior-college system. Those who have the desire and the ability to progress to higher levels of education will continue through four years of college. In many special fields, five or more years will be required to acquire competence.

Social Adjustment as a New Goal. Because of the increasing complexity of modern life, education has recently had to adopt as its goal the social adjustment of the masses of youth, in addition to transmitting the cultural heritage and even preparing some to be creators of new culture. This is leading education into new experimental realms in an attempt to meet the need of the new generations. During this century, testing and measurement have been de-

[2] L. J. Elias, "Democracy Hands the College a Dilemma," *Association of American Colleges Bulletin*, 34:486–92 (Dec. 1948).

veloped in an attempt to understand the human personality—its capacities, its emotional traits, and its adjustment possibilities.

It is being realized increasingly that the interrelationship of persons and the status of the individual in his group are vital things of lifelong importance. As a consequence, guidance and personnel work are becoming one of the major functions of the school. Proceeding by tests and measurements to learn what the individual's capacities are, the guidance expert works from this information to help the individual achieve satisfactory relationships with his peers, his elders, and with the environment generally. Few fields hold such great promise as this one.

Man in our complex culture is suffering from an increasing load of nervous strain and its counterparts—crime, delinquency, mental disease, vice, and personal demoralization. The school, by detecting maladjustments early, can help the individual learn to live in harmony with his group; it can save him from lifelong suffering, and can reduce the overwhelming burden society now carries in the institutionalization of those who have failed to make satisfactory adjustments for functioning in normal society.

The objectives of the social adjustment effort of the school, usually referred to in high school as the "guidance" program and in the college called counseling or personnel work, may be summarized as follows: (1) to help young people understand and make the most of their present educational opportunities; (2) to aid them in their adjustment in the education system and to give them while in school an appreciation of the future application of their present educational and social activities; and (3) to prepare them for and assist them in making the transition from school to society.

These programs, although comparatively in their infancy, are based on the case method of approach to problems of the individual pupil. The emphasis is in the direction of orienting the school about the pupil rather than about the curriculum.

The table on page 602 summarizes the characteristic anxieties of young people of high-school age, as revealed by a study of some 4,500 seniors. These problem areas, particularly those being checked by a substantial proportion of young people, indicate the direction which must be taken in preparing young people for social competence.

An Experimental Laboratory. From the standpoint of the person playing the role of the pupil in the modern school system, the school offers the best apprenticeship available today for the vocations he may choose and the multiple roles he must play in adult life. The

Personal Problems Checked by 4,500 Seniors in
Washington High Schools, 1947

Problem		Per Cent Checking				
		Rural	Town	Suburban	City	Total
Being able to	Girls	34.8	32.6	31.0	31.4	33.1
talk to people	Boys	29.3	25.4	28.8	26.2	27.7
Making some-	Girls	31.6	30.6	37.4	34.3	32.9
thing of myself	Boys	28.3	30.4	31.2	24.2	27.2
Developing	Girls	35.2	29.5	30.3	34.7	34.1
self confidence	Boys	14.8	20.5	22.4	22.4	18.7
Can't seem to	Girls	26.8	24.8	27.7	27.2	26.8
concentrate	Boys	27.9	25.4	29.6	27.0	27.4
Having a good	Girls	26.4	29.5	24.5	23.6	25.5
personality	Boys	22.9	24.6	29.6	23.2	23.6
What makes a	Girls	35.1	33.7	41.3	28.7	32.9
good marriage?	Boys	15.3	13.4	15.2	11.6	13.8
Hurting people's	Girls	27.3	26.7	28.4	23.6	25.9
feelings	Boys	23.1	22.3	20.8	21.4	22.2
Wanting people	Girls	24.8	29.5	24.5	25.4	25.5
to like me	Boys	16.2	20.1	17.6	16.1	16.7
Worrying too	Girls	22.1	27.5	22.6	24.1	23.4
much	Boys	12.1	19.2	17.6	15.9	14.6
Don't know what	Girls	27.4	26.0	24.5	19.6	24.1
I really want	Boys	25.8	16.1	28.0	20.3	22.8
Mistakes I have	Girls	25.9	25.2	20.6	20.6	23.5
made	Boys	15.9	14.7	16.0	12.4	14.5
How to do my	Girls	21.4	11.6	16.8	16.2	18.1
best	Boys	12.6	14.3	8.8	11.0	12.0
Whether to go	Girls	16.6	15.1	25.2	16.9	17.1
to college	Boys	25.6	22.3	23.2	18.9	22.6
Can't take the	Girls	14.0	11.2	14.2	7.0	11.1
subjects I want	Boys	16.0	12.5	20.0	8.7	13.2
Worry about my	Girls	19.4	18.6	16.8	20.8	19.7
grades	Boys	12.3	14.3	20.8	17.5	14.9
Have no regular	Girls	15.7	11.2	12.9	11.6	13.5
allowance	Boys	9.6	8.5	8.0	8.0	8.8
Have to work	Girls	13.1	9.7	14.2	12.3	12.5
to buy things	Boys	21.4	17.9	10.4	17.1	18.8
Getting along with	Girls	20.4	17.4	16.1	14.0	17.4
brothers and sisters	Boys	14.8	12.1	8.8	10.8	12.7

Source: L. J. Elias, *High School Youth Look at Their Problems* (Pullman, Wash.:
Division of Rural Sociology, Washington Agricultural Experiment Stations. 1949).

school is an enriching social experience, teaching the young person to adjust to varied standards and ideals. The school is a testing laboratory where the individual may try out his talents, develop them, and most of all learn what his special interests are. These interests, to the extent that the curriculum is adequate, he may compare with opportunities available. The school offers a much less costly field of trial and error than the real world and, to the extent that teachers are competent, one in which error may rather quickly be corrected and the individual directed toward the fulfillment of his talents and the realization of his interests. For many rural youths, particularly, high school is a broadening experience bridging the gap between the narrow paternalistic world of their homes and the broader world of secondary group experience.

Even more, the college is a testing ground challenging the individual's interests and abilities, placing him in situations of increasing complexity and demanding of him an increased insight into his own abilities and into the profession toward which he aspires.

The Poor Student. From the standpoint of the pupil, the most tragic situation is that of the numerous youths who lack the high level of intellectual ability required to pursue the usual high-school or college curriculum, but who are given no opportunity to pursue a program of education that is adapted to their particular talents and interests. As a consequence, those least competent to compete economically and socially in a complex society are forced out into the world of ruthless secondary group competition at an earlier age than are those of greater competency. There is need for the development of more practical terminal education for those who have no mind for the traditional high-school and college curriculum.

Many feel that the school is doing just as poorly with the very bright youth, who in a system of mass education can excel with no serious effort on his part. But this at least can be said: he can continue to compete in school situations until he matures to the point where he can of his own initiative pursue new paths of learning.

THE EDUCATIONAL CHALLENGE OF THE FUTURE

Although the school is one of the most significant institutions in the personality development of youth today, the fact still remains that it has not adequately met its full social responsibility. The New York Regents' Inquiry concluded after a survey of high schools in the state:

Although these pupils had been members of the school group for years, teachers and principals were unable to identify any special abilities for the great

majority of them . . . little attention has been given to the discovery of unusual strengths and weaknesses . . . boys and girls have gained from school
experiences only the most casual appreciation of their own peculiar talents and
skills. Even more serious is the school's inability to recommend at least a
fourth of all leaving pupils as ready to take a constructive part in the activities
of the factory, office, or farm, and in the broader social relationships of home,
community, and state.[3]

Equality of Opportunity. The problem of parity of educational opportunity is always one of major concern in democratic society, because the school is the principal elevator for social mobility. To deny
large groups educational opportunity is to deny them the chance to
climb both in status and in income.

Large groups have been at a disadvantage in educational opportunity, even under America's system of free public education.

1. The Negro. Under the scheme of "separate but equal" facilities
operative throughout the South and in many border states, there has
been no equality. Objective students of the race problem have declared that separate schools are not equal. Those of the Negro are
vastly inferior. Both white and Negro systems are inferior to what
one unified program would be, for most of the area in which desegregation has been practiced lacks resources for one first-class school
system, and certainly cannot afford to support two.

2. Rural Children. Particularly in states which continue to support a one-room school program, rural schools provide inadequate
basic schooling. There is also the problem of lack of facilities for
high-school training for farm youth in many areas. Many states have
resisted consolidation and the expanded educational opportunity
which it brings to rural youth. This has been in part due to rural resistance to education at the higher levels as such, but in part to fear
of putting the school program under town control.

3. Economically Handicapped Groups. Finances are one of the
reasons why young people drop out of high school. Financial limitations are even more important in keeping many qualified young
people from attending college. During the Depression various government work programs helped many young people attend high
school and college. Today there are many scholarships and fellowships, but they are far short of the goal of assuring all capable youths
the privilege of a college education.

We know from experience under the G. I. Bill and subsequent
veterans' training programs that, given the opportunity, many from

[3] Ruth E. Eckert and Thomas O. Marshall, *When Youth Leaves School* (New
York: McGraw-Hill Book Co., Inc., 1938), p. 119.

the lower economic classes will go to college and profit by it if the economic handicap is removed. (Refer again to Chapter 31, p. 543, for a summary of the numbers of students trained under the G. I. Bill. Many of these students were from economic groups in which the college tradition had not previously been a part of family expectations.)

Shortage of College-trained Personnel. Occasionally a critic raises doubt as to merits of college training for the masses, and some fear that there will be too few opportunities for the college-trained.

As a matter of fact, a society with the high level of professional competence reached by the American nation needs far more trained and highly skilled persons than it is training. This will be true into the foreseeable future.

One only has to review casually the current demand to know how great the shortage of college-trained people and of those trained beyond the college level:

1. *Nurses.* For years there has been a shortage in spite of repeated recruitment campaigns and national publicity. Hospitals are short of nursing help; the armed forces are short of help.

2. *Engineers.* Again and again the call goes out for more men trained in engineering and other highly technical skills. The hunger for talent is evidenced by the army of recruiters from business and government who raid the college graduating classes each spring. It is almost impossible to save enough graduates to maintain the staff of professors to train the new crop.

3. *Scientists.* The shortage of scientists, particularly in chemistry and physics, is often cited as a national calamity, as statesmen compare our scientist-training programs with those in the Soviet Union. Scientific men are identified with national survival in a day of war and preparations for war. In this area, too, industry outbids the colleges and universities for talent so that only those who love teaching stay on to teach. The financial rewards in industry are double what they are in teaching.

4. *Teachers.* The teacher shortage is nation wide. Teachers' aids have been hired in many places to handle routine so teachers can carry a bigger classroom load. Housewives have been drawn into part-time teaching, and a campaign to recruit teachers has been carried out on a nationwide scale. Yet there are not enough teachers. The baby crop rose from about a million and a half in 1932 to three million in the early 1940's, and then increased to almost four million annually by the mid-1950's. The schoolrooms are full and building programs are the order of the day in every community. Furthermore, the teacher shortage is here to stay for many years.

The Phenomenal Increase in School Enrollments Has Put Great Strain
on the Educational Facilities of the Nation

School Year	Teachers	Enrollment
1945/46	831,000	23,299,900
1949/50	914,000	25,111,500
1951/52	963,000	26,706,700
1953/54	1,042,000	28,836,000
1954/55	1,080,000*	30,673,800*
1955/56	1,127,000*	31,448,000*
1956/57	1,178,000*	32,159,000*

SOURCE: National Education Association and Office of Education, U.S. Department of Health, Education, and Welfare. Data are for public elementary and secondary schools.

* Estimated.

College Education and Democracy's Future. Entirely aside from the practical aspects of an educated generation are the cultural aspects. College education brings prestige. After World War II college attendance reached about the point in social acceptance which high school training reached after World War I.

College education is hereafter for the masses. It is becoming a part of the cultural tradition. Once a woman was suspect if she went to college and then got married. Now young women go to college to find a more suitable mate than they have been able to find at home. College is looked upon by both young men and young women as a way to develop talent and social competence and to make friends. It is part of growing up for life in a complex society.

Finally, education is the great hope of democracy, as Harry Elmer Barnes states so emphatically in the following quotation.

"The world finds itself today in a serious social, economic, and political crisis. We must go ahead or backward. All sane persons want civilization to move ahead rather than collapse. Education can provide the only safe and assured leadership toward progress and prosperity.

"If we are going to move ahead we have a clear choice—and only this choice—between orderly progress under intelligent guidance, or revolution, violence, and a gambling chance with the future. If we choose orderly social advance, we must rely more and more upon the educational direction of the social process. The problems of today have become so complicated and technical that only well-educated public servants can hope to deal with them effectively.

"If education is going to assume a more important role in public affairs, it must set its own house in order and prepare itself for realistic instruction in terms of contemporary facts. The present system of education is inadequate to supply the type of leadership which is necessary in the current world crisis. It failed to live up to the responsibilities of the last generation. It did not save the world from war or depression.

"We must eliminate useless antiquities from the curriculum, stress the realities of the twentieth century, and offer protection to members of the teaching profession who expound courageously and honestly the facts as they see them.

"The social studies present the only cogent information that can enable us to bridge the gulf between machines and institutions. More time should be given to the social studies; also, their content must be made more vital and be linked up with the immediate problems of our day. We must provide security for the teachers of the social studies, for it is here that most of the heresy-hunts are waged. No teacher is in much danger analyzing the binomial theorem, but the teacher who resolutely describes our economic and political system is constantly flirting with dismissal.

"Education is our best safeguard—almost our only safeguard—against Fascism and Communism, and the foremost bulwark of democracy. The more courageous and realistic it is, the better will it serve such purposes. If it is cowardly, evasive, and time-serving, it cannot aspire to vigorous leadership. Indeed, it will only contribute to the inevitability of general misery and chaos. If the latter comes, education will share in it to a particularly disastrous degree. In an era of social decline and barbarism, there is little place for education. Let those who are sceptical about this statement study the history of the Dark Ages. And let those who are sceptical about the return of another Dark Age study world events of the last fifteen years."[4]

SUMMARY

Educational institutions originated to transmit the cultural heritage. To this function has now been added many more, particularly those of giving an apprenticeship to vocational life and of training the individual to make adjustment in a complex society. Cultural transmission now operates on three levels: the elementary, which is the level of transmitting skills and symbols of communication; the

[4] Harry Elmer Barnes, *Social Institutions*, pp. 727–28. Copyright, 1942, by Prentice-Hall, Inc., Englewood Cliffs, N.J. Reprinted by permission of the publisher.

high school, where acquiring knowledge and insight into scientific method is begun; and college, where more questions are raised than answered, at least at the higher levels of training. The school has had to shoulder an increasing load with the failure of other institutions to meet specific needs of the individual.

As an instrument of democracy the school trains for intelligent citizenship through the use of the ballot, rather than indoctrinating. In the opportunity it offers for contact on the basis of equality within the school, the modern high school has become a great leveler. Still educational opportunity needs to be extended so that all those whose needs are not met by the standard curricula may find things of interest and importance to them in the school. Since the school is the principal social elevator upward, it must be made more accessible to all in democratic society. This is not merely in the interest of social justice. A complex society has created more demand for those trained in college or university than can be met.

DISCUSSION AND REVIEW QUESTIONS

1. Discuss educational institutions as transmitters of the cultural heritage.
2. Why has education become a greater necessity than formerly?
3. Compare three levels of cultural transmission.
4. Illustrate how the school has had to assume burdens formerly carried by other social institutions.
5. What functions does education perform in democratic society?
6. Are we near the ideal of giving every youth an opportunity for a high-school education? Give facts to support your answer.
7. What factors determine the ability of states to provide adequate educational opportunity?
8. What do we mean by equalizing educational opportunity and how might it be realized?
9. Outline the goals of guidance and counseling in the school.
10. What is meant by the case-method approach?
11. Discuss the need for college-trained people.

SOURCEBOOK READINGS

KOENIG, SAMUEL, REX D. HOPPER, and FELIKS GROSS. *Sociology: A Book of Readings.* Englewood Cliffs, N.J.: Prentice-Hall, Inc., 1956.
    1. BENJAMIN, HAROLD, "Education in a Democracy," pp. 238–45.
    2. HUTCHINS, ROBERT M., "The Meaning of Academic Freedom," pp. 245–48.
    3. GIDEONSE, HARRY D., "The Moral Prerequisites of Academic Freedom," pp. 248–62.
LEE, ELIZABETH BRYANT, and ALFRED MCCLUNG LEE. *Social Problems in America* (rev. ed.). New York: Henry Holt & Co., Inc., 1955.
    4. BENEDICT, RUTH, "Transmitting Our Democratic Heritage in the Schools," pp. 177–82.
    5. KONVITZ, MILTON R., "The Churches and Education," pp. 182–84.
    6. "The United States Supreme Court Speaks on Separation of Church and Education," pp. 184–85.
    7. "The Plight of the Schools," pp. 187–90.

O'BRIEN, ROBERT W., CLARENCE C. SCHRAG, and WALTER T. MARTIN. *Readings in General Sociology* (2d ed.). Boston: Houghton Mifflin Co., 1957.
    8. GLICK, PAUL C., and HERMAN MILLER, "Educational Level and Potential Income," pp. 419–24.

SCHULER, EDGAR A., DUANE L. GIBSON, MAUDE L. FIERO, and WILBUR B. BROOK-OVER. *Outside Readings in Sociology.* New York: The Thomas Crowell Co., 1956.
    9. SIEPMANN, CHARLES A., "A Perspective on American Education," pp. 533–39.
    10. BROOKOVER, WILBUR B., "Education in American Culture," pp. 540–51.

SELECTED READINGS

BUTTS, R. FREEMAN, and LAWRENCE C. CREMIN. *A History of Education in American Culture.* New York: Henry Holt & Co., Inc., 1953.

COOK, LLOYD A., and ELAINE F. COOK. *A Sociological Approach to Education.* New York: McGraw-Hill Book Co., Inc., 1950.

HAY, CLYDE L. *The Blind Spot in American Public Education.* New York: The Macmillan Co., 1950.

LANDIS, PAUL H. *Adolescence and Youth: The Process of Maturing.* 2d ed.; New York: McGraw-Hill Book Co., Inc., 1952, Part V.

RUGG, HAROLD, and WILLIAM WITHERS. *Social Foundations of Education.* Englewood Cliffs, N.J.: Prentice-Hall, Inc., 1955.

SCOTT, C. WINFIELD, and CLYDE M. HILL. *Public Education Under Criticism.* Englewood Cliffs, N.J.: Prentice-Hall, Inc., 1954.

VALENTINE, P. F. (ed.). *The American College.* New York: Philosophical Library, 1949.

VEBLEN, THORSTEIN. *The Higher Learning.* New York: B. W. Hubsch, 1919.

WARNER, W. LLOYD, R. J. HAVIGHURST, and M. B. LOEW. *Who Shall Be Educated?* New York: Harper & Brothers, 1944.

WILLIAMS, ROBIN M., JR., and MARGARET W. RYAN (eds.). *Schools in Transition.* Chapel Hill: University of North Carolina Press, 1954.

FILM LIST

Schools March On—18 minutes—sound
    Emphasizes that a vital factor in America's development has been public education, although in rural schools many inadequacies may exist. Shows how one county solved school problems. *Source:* McGraw-Hill Book Company.

School and the Community—14 minutes—black and white or color—sound
    Stresses need for all members of a community to cooperate to better their schools. *Source:* McGraw-Hill Book Company.

Design of American Public Education—16 minutes—sound
    Organizational structure of public education in America as it might be if under central control and as it actually is under decentralized state and local control. *Source:* McGraw-Hill Book Company.

Campus Frontiers—28 minutes—sound
    Portrays life at Antioch College. *Source:* Antioch College.

Design for Education—25 minutes
    Delineates life at Sarah Lawrence College. *Source:* Sarah Lawrence College.

New Schools for Old—10 minutes—sound
    Contrasts the little red schoolhouse, its methods and results, with the modern classroom. *Source:* Museum of Modern Art Film Library.

What Can Be Done about Juvenile Delinquency?—19 minutes—color—sound
    Condenses the practical suggestions of recognized authorities on delinquency in a colorful, action-stimulating film. *Source:* Chicago Board of Educational Film Council.

Chapter 36

Government

There must be an over-all authority in the life of man, whether it be, as with primitive peoples, a chief or tribal council which rules in favor of one or the other in case of dispute, or the body of law and tradition of the modern state. Be the society simple or complex, there must exist in its framework of institutions one vested with final authority to which the group makes its final appeal, an authority which by its decision ends all disputes. This is government.

In the final analysis, *government is a system of social control which is above all others in the secular experience of man.* In a modern nation, of course, government is a multi-armed octopus that reaches out in numerous directions, not only as an agency of control, but also as an agency for promoting and protecting the welfare of the people. It becomes in a democratic nation, particularly, not only a framework of authority and regulation but also a system of services and protective covenants by which men govern themselves.

Government is one of the most basic of all institutions, defining for the individual his role as citizen or alien, taxpayer or dependent, voter or nonvoter, as well as carrying out those broader powers of making peace or waging war and making trade agreements or erecting tariff boundaries for the organized national group as a body.

Government begins in tribal life, evolves eventually through feudalism, in which personal allegiance is the basis for loyalty, and finally emerges into the territorial state, with its civil society in which loyalty is to territory. The most advanced development of civil society is the nation-state, with common territory and common political tradition.

ATTITUDES TOWARD GOVERNMENT

Among the attitudes which characterize governmental institutions are respect for authority (and in a democratic government, respect for majority opinion) and patriotism and loyalty to the territorial unit (the state) which the government represents. In times of crisis government is more demanding of the loyalty of the individual than any other institution. Willingness of the citizen to lay down his life to defend his nation against aggressors is expected. No other institution expects so much. Similarly, in times of crisis government loyalty must supersede all other loyalties. Religious creed must be forsaken (if it is pacifistic) and job and family left behind when government calls for service in arms.

Because government has power to enforce its will on subjects, fear of punishment in case of violation of law is an important attitude of the citizen. Punishments range from death for treason down to fines or imprisonment for lesser violations of governmental regulation.

Attitudes toward government are represented by such symbols as the flag, the seal, the emblem, and the national anthem. The ritual and the tradition that center about these symbolic culture traits are important in intensifying and keeping alive attitudes of loyalty and devotion.

In the field of governmental codes, at the national level and at the state level, are constitutions; at the local level, charters and ordinances. At the national level also, treaties symbolize relations with other nations. Throughout all levels of government, a body of law defines the activities of the citizen and limits his prerogatives, specifying what he may not do and also specifying the punishment that will be meted out if he violates the law.

THE FUNCTIONS OF GOVERNMENT

Prohibitive Functions. Government enforces the mores and establishes other restrictions which are conceived to be in the interest of all. It prohibits the destruction of property, the taking of life or property, and similar actions. This field of social control is primarily negative and restrictive.

In the more vital aspect of man's conduct, law is an effective control device to the extent that it has sanction of the mores. Laws enacted in violation of deep-seated customs are difficult and often impossible to enforce, for the law operates externally and the mores operate from the attitude system within the person.

In an earlier day of "white supremacy" anti-lynching laws were not effective controls if the Negro in the South crossed the line with regard to respect for the white woman. Nor is a United States Supreme Court decision on desegregation enough to assure that a dual system of educational institutions will quickly vanish from all communities.

The late Howard W. Odum, distinguished Southern sociologist, discussed the report of a Southern commission on the study of lynching. In rating the strength of the stateways and folkways he concluded:

> "*Every time,* the folkways will defeat the stateways if they are against the stateways." The special report on lynching says: "The lynching method is a recognized custom in many communities. Hence, church members and civic leaders, instead of taking a determined stand against mob violence, often yield to it either by silence or by apology." What the outside observer does not see is that the folkways are so strong that the enforcement of law by local or State forces would mean literally civil war in the community. The folkways have ruled continuously since the days of reconstruction. Progress is being made, but it is in proportion as the folkways are being changed by education, publicity, civic appeal, and courageous leadership. . . .[1]

Regulative Functions. Also in the field of restrictive controls are the innumerable regulative functions of government, such as tariffs and trade restrictions, the restriction of immigration, the regulation of currency, the supervision of national property, particularly the public domain, and of natural resources. In addition to this, of course, are the regulative functions of the numerous units of civil government—restrictions with regard to traffic, marriage, divorce, education, recreation, in fact, any one of the thousands of activities of man in his group relationships. The legal code of the average state fills volumes and the traffic code of any large city is a lengthy booklet. The more dense the population, the more man must be hemmed in by the regulative force of government. Zoning regulations have become one of the main devices for social planning. They have a legal nature and violations are backed by the penalty of law.

Promotive Functions. In the modern world, government far exceeds the mere matter of social control by negation and regulation. It exercises social control along positive lines. Through land grants, education and railroad development were promoted in pioneer times. Through grants of funds today, the federal government and the respective state governments promote education by setting standards which must be met if the grant is to be given the school district. Numerous activities of welfare have been promoted in modern times by government as will be seen later in studying Social Security. The welfare aspect of government has become a great supplemental social institution which protects the citizen against the tragedies of unemployment, old age, loss of the breadwinner, or incapacity because of physical handicap.

[1] Howard W. Odum, "Lynching, Fears and Folkways," *The Nation,* Dec. 30, 1931, p. 720.

Modern government, in fact, both develops and affects social policy through social legislation. Beginning with the New Deal, social legislation has marked one of the major phases of government expansion, first at the federal level and then with matching legislation in the various states.

THE RANGE OF GOVERNMENT ACTIVITIES

New Services. It is implied in the preceding discussion that the more complex living becomes and the greater the aggregate of people who are brought together, the more imposing must become the framework of government. A mountaineer who is relatively propertyless and who seldom sees another human being can get along with little law. But let him discover precious metal, and so begin a gold rush, and law must quickly be established or men will struggle to death over property rights alone. Multiply the contact of the few struggling for property rights in a mountain area by the thousands in modern city life, who have not only property rights but rights of safety, and of peace, sanitation, and quiet, and one begins to see how complex the web of government must become.

Restrictive laws have multiplied, from the township through the national government, and mankind looks forward to a time when a real world government, under which law and justice rather than violence will prevail, will be a reality.

As much as the American criticizes and condemns the extension of government in almost every aspect of private life, it is doubtful that the trend will be reversed as long as the tendency toward greater concentrations of people continues. Not only must the restrictive aspects of government continue in effect, as they manifest themselves in numerous and complex forms of social control, but government services and welfare programs will also be multiplied. The hazards which an individual faces in a highly complex industrial order, and in an urban society of secondary groups, require the over-all protecting hand of government, not only in the sense of shielding the individual from dangers that are inherent in crime, fraud, embezzlement, and other such risks, but also to protect him from the uncertainties that threaten his very existence as an economic unit. The primary group is no longer present to meet the individual's need in times of want or crisis and lift him above the daily anxieties of common woes to which all citizens are subject.

Even while making demands for security, the average citizen is inclined to bemoan the tremendous tax burden which government welfare measures entail. Even though economies in government certainly are to be desired and can be realized by more efficient administration, the fact remains that the citizen apparently feels that he gets more through government for his money than he can get by handling many affairs on his own. Increasingly he expects the government, with funds from taxes, to provide recreation through local parks, playgrounds, national forests, and national parks, for he assumes that he can enjoy more in this way than through providing his own recreation or paying for it from commercial sources. He expects the government to expand further in the field of education and to tax him for it. As will be seen in Chapter 39, there is an increasing demand for the expansion of health services, either on a tax-supported or an insurance basis, which will be supervised by the government.

Add to this all the numerous government services which have emerged for extending credit, providing housing, and placing a price floor under agricultural products, to mention a few current programs. There is expansion not only in the direct field of welfare and credit but also in the field of developing natural resources through such activities as building dams for great irrigational projects for flood control and for the development of public power. Tennessee Valley dams, Bonneville Dam, Grand Coulee Dam, and Hoover Dam represent vast expenditures of tax moneys for developments which stagger the imagination, developments which no private business enterprise would have the resources to undertake. These are all sponsored expenses of the tax-payer, even though many of them in the long run pay a substantial part back into the public treasury. They represent a type of development which the federal government has always had to undertake as a service to its citizens, the beneficiaries of which will be primarily the next generation rather than the generation now living.

Where government service and government business should end is a question of perpetual debate in American politics. The public interest versus private enterprise issue is one of the challenging political issues of many an interparty battle.

Future Trends. One of the most prominent trends of the modern state is to use political institutions for manipulating economic institutions. Fascism and communism exemplified this tendency from the beginning, but even democracy has come to recognize that economic conditions are readily converted into social conditions. Full employment or lack of it is not merely a theoretical economic problem; it is also a stern social reality concerned with the individual's welfare and even his survival. So, also, questions of wages are no longer considered theoretical; they are the vital concern of a democratic government which has come to recognize that they have a direct bearing on the worker's level of living and set limits to his participation not only in economic life but in social, educational, and other privileges.

Kimball Young, in his presidential address before the 1945 American Sociological Society, summarized this trend of federal government as follows:

"Perhaps the greatest and most basic change in the relation of the state to the nongovernmental aspects of national society has to do with the economic order. We certainly have moved a long way from the position of the late eighteenth and early nineteenth centuries which held that the chief function of government was to provide protection to person, property, and contract at home, and to defend the country against its enemies abroad. The state has come increasingly to regulate the economic processes in the name of the general welfare or to aid some special interest group or other in their struggle for a larger share of national income. For decades business secured support through high tariffs, rationalized in the name of weak 'infant industries' which could not stand competition in the world markets. More recently farm groups and labor organizations have had the help of government in the name of equalizing their competitive strength in the struggle for a share in the nation's wealth. So, too, controls have been introduced to maintain the competitive system in the face of monopolies.

"In our country these and other controls have been introduced in piecemeal and even haphazard fashion. They have often been improvised on the spot in the face of some immediate crisis. . . ."[2]

THE STRUCTURE OF GOVERNMENTAL ADMINISTRATION

There are in the United States over 100,000 units of government. All have the power to regulate spheres of human behavior and the power to tax. These units have been classified from the national government at the top down to townships and school districts, and the "special districts" such as park districts, road-building districts, sanitary districts. In 1957 the classification was as follows:[3]

The Nation	1
The States	48
Counties	3,047
Municipalities	17,167
Townships and Towns	17,214
School Districts	50,453
Special Districts	14,423
	102,353

[2] Kimball Young, "Society and the State," *American Sociological Review*, 11:137–146 (April 1946).

[3] *Governments in the United States in 1957*, U.S. Census release for May 9, 1957, G-CGA-No. 2.

There is little question that many of these small governmental units are unnecessary from the viewpoint of logic and that they are needlessly expensive. Small governmental units are often inefficient and burdensome, and yet people fight for them if their existence is challenged. There has been much propaganda in favor of county consolidation, now that the automobile has removed the necessity of having a county seat within a day's horse-and-buggy drive of all rural dwellers, but only five counties (three in Georgia and two in Tennessee) of more than three thousand have ever been consolidated. School-district reorganization has been a little less difficult, but even today few local districts ever give up their autonomy to the more efficient consolidated school district without a struggle. Government experts have long believed that township units of government should be abolished, but they persist.

As to newer forms of governmental administration, such as the rural municipality which would combine town and countryside in one administration, it is difficult to sell the citizen on their merit. As a consequence of resistance to change, the town and country remain separated, with the country in many states having no access to the town library or other services and protections.

Behind the tenacious persistence of local governmental institutions is a deep American tradition, that of local autonomy. The individualistic American prefers to be governed not only by his peers, but by his neighbors. He can watch local government and know what is going on, and have his say-so if he does not approve. He has always been a little suspicious of what goes on in the greater units of government removed a distance from him. The farmer has often even distrusted the consolidated school on the ground that the town would dominate the district and assess taxes on his land without his having a representative voice. Taxation without representation still stirs deep emotions in the heart of any American.

It is perhaps paradoxical that even though the citizen fights for local autonomy and suspects bureaucracy, nowhere in government does nepotism and other questionable practices exist to the extent it does in local government. And in many counties, elections continually place in office one or two local families through generations without reference to their competence or qualifications other than that they are citizens of the required age of eligibility for office.

GOVERNMENT IN ACTION

Threefold Pattern of Government. The more formal structure and functions of the institution of government have been outlined. In democratic society, government is carried out by political parties. At

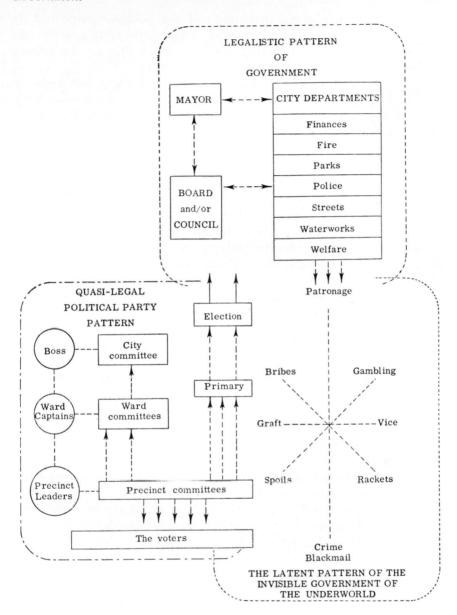

The Legal and Illegal Fabric of Political Institutions

The formal pattern of legal government is one thing, the political party system quite another. And in many large city governments there is a third layer—illegal, antisocial, often brutal, and always costly to the citizen. (Redrawn from F. S. Chapin, Contemporary American Institutions, *p. 39, Harper & Brothers, 1935.)*

many points the informal machinery of the political party and its supporters ties in so closely with the formal aspects of government that the party system in reality controls the destiny of the citizen and has custody of his interests.

Again we draw on Chapin for a realistic analysis, in this instance for his threefold classification of government as it operates in large cities. Taking a typical city government (see the chart on page 617), he shows that underneath the legalistic pattern of government, that is, the formal government provided for by constitutions, charters, and laws, is the quasi-legal government, represented by the political party with its organization for getting votes. Closely tied to the political party and the legalistic government itself is the invisible government of the underworld. This close tie-in has often been exposed in American history. Two generations ago Lincoln Steffens and other "muckrakers" exposed the underlayer of government in America's leading cities, and reform administrations were ushered in.[4]

Then, as always, the underworld soon took over again, for the vested interests of many of those who actually operate government and of other influential citizens are threatened by such exposures. Moreover, the average citizen is not sufficiently vigilant to inconvenience himself to protect his own interests. Strange as it may seem, many administrations which have been most guilty of graft or corruption have contributed most to a city's growth. Motivated by a desire for personal gain, they have gone in for expansion programs, which in many instances have cost the public twice as much as they were worth, but in feathering their own nests crafty administrations have often expanded civic improvements, even if at an excessive cost.[5] Unfortunately, the public is not sufficiently conscious of its own interests to use the more economical way of achieving civic development in many instances.

To offset spoils and to give government employment some semblance of professional status, Civil Service has been developed on an extensive scale in the federal government and on a smaller scale in the state and local governments. It tries to replace patronage with merit by making a requisite for office the passing of a qualifying examination and by guaranteeing tenure for competent performance of duties.

Even this has not raised government service to the high level of professional competence which might be desired. There is need for

[4] *The Autobiography of Lincoln Steffens* (New York: Harcourt, Brace & Co., Inc., 1931).

[5] The author discusses this in his study *Three Iron Mining Towns—A Study in Cultural Change* (Ann Arbor, Mich.: Edwards & Brothers, 1938).

the development of a profession of government and for the creation of positions and salaries which will attract men of competence who are willing to make public service their career. Only in such a way can we bring to it the same administrative talent that is found in the higher levels of business administration and the same mental caliber that is found in some of the professions where high levels of mental ability are rewarded by recognition in the field of science or invention.

The Role of the Politician. A politician has been defined by political scientist Milton Merrill as a professional appeaser, who spends his time trying to reconcile conflicting interest groups—agricultural, industrial, financial, proletarian—so that he can win office and then hold it by re-election.[6] Politicians are important administrative functionaries in government, in fact, indispensable, for within a society of free and independent interest groups compromise is the key to successful government. Only dictators can ignore compromise as a basic process of governing.

Thus, in a democratic government the political way, the way of compromise, is the "right" way of governing, or as Merrill puts it, "compromise within the limit of principles, or at least compromise." He also sees many pitfalls in compromise, but still views it as the prime necessity of political administration. He contends that although politicians do not establish virtue, politics does establish "freedom in which men can become good."

Merrill goes on to point out how the "adamant man" tends to be a dangerous man in politics, that a man with faith founded on a rock is all right provided he does not try to impress his faith on another. Roosevelt, he feels, was a great compromiser—and a great political leader because of it. In his opinion, the American people were ready for anything in the early 1930's. Hence it is fortunate there was no radical in the White House then, but rather a great compromiser. "What might have been the case," he asks, "had a Hitler or a McCarthy, adamant men, prophets, demagogues, been in the White House then?"

Democratic governments have and must have rival political parties to state issues and debate them, and thus stage periodic rebellion against the status quo in government. Through the rivalry of political parties and their perennial struggle for office the actions of government are reviewed, criticized, and laid open for public inspection. Even third parties, or for that matter other splinter parties, may arise

[6] Milton R. Merrill, Dean, School of Commerce, Utah State Agricultural College, in an address before the 1956 Summer Session convocation. Published by the Faculty Association of Utah State Agricultural College, 1956.

to sponsor reforms or the fight for social politics. They may not win, and rarely do, but their freedom to present issues is a social gain in that should they represent an issue vital enough to the majority, major parties will adopt their crusade.

Taxation. Government has the power to tax its citizens. Today taxation has become the main device of government through which essential services and protection are provided all citizens regardless of their ability to pay. The graduated income tax, particularly, serves to equalize privileges in a democratic way, and has been used increasingly by democratic governments in extending their protective and promotive functions.

The revenue from the federal income tax is shown in the accompanying chart for various income levels. It will be seen that when a

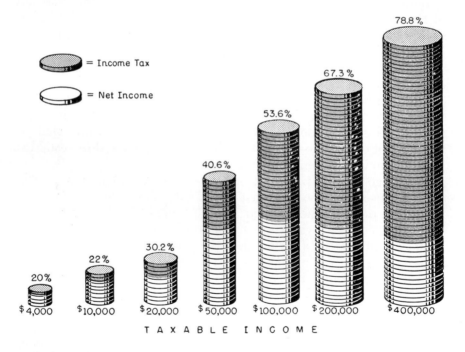

The Graduated Income Tax

This comparison of taxes by income levels is based on taxable income—that is, income after legitimate deductions have been taken. Of course, those with high incomes often own real property which permits non-taxable depreciation to be deducted from gross income. Even so, the income tax is an equalizing factor in a democratic society. Some states also impose their own graduated income tax, thus further cutting into large taxable incomes.

Expenditures of the Federal Government, 1789-1956

Year	Expenditure ($)
1789	5,776,000
1850	34,097,000
1900	457,451,000
1910	693,617,000
1919	18,522,894,705
1920	6,482,090,191
1930	3,994,152,487
1940	9,434,327,930
1945	100,397,472,705*
1956	66,386,338,250

* In 1945 expenditures reached $719.07 per capita, the all-time peak.

person receives above $100,000, a very large proportion of his entire income goes into tax. It must be remembered, too, that this is only the federal income tax. There are other taxes of many sorts—property, luxury, sales, excise, etc.—levied before the income tax. And in addition to the federal income tax here discussed, many states also have graduated income taxes.

Western society has shifted further toward the social philosophy that the minimum essentials of health, shelter, recreation, and education must be guaranteed to every man. The only way to accomplish this welfare goal is to tax heavily those who have a large income. Taxation has thus come to replace in large measure the traditional tithe which supported the charity of the church. At least it has come to carry the load that was carried much less successfully by such charitable organizations as the church and private welfare agencies.

With the development of the welfare state the standard of what constitutes an adequate living has constantly been rising. Once enough food to keep a man alive was the level of necessity. Now it is assumed that every person—man, woman, and child—has the right to an adequate diet, with the protective and health foods included. Standards of adequate housing, adequate dress, and adequate recreational opportunities for a community and for the individual living therein have also been raised substantially. Values of what constitutes an adequate education have also changed and found expression in public facilities to extend educational opportunity through high school and for many through college. Only through the efforts of a welfare-oriented government possible through taxation can such goals be realized and such a level of living for all be achieved.

Unfortunately, during recent decades the cost of war has added a tremendous burden to the normal costs of government services, denying the citizen many of the benefits that might come in the way of a higher standard of living were the same amount of funds spent improving the general welfare within the nation.

The late Nicholas Murray Butler, famed president of Columbia University, estimated that the money spent on World War I alone could have built houses valued at $2,500 each, furnished them with $1,000 worth of furniture and placed them on five acres of land valued at $100 an acre—one for every family in the United States, Canada, Australia, England, Wales, Ireland, Scotland, France, Belgium, Germany, and Russia. Every city of over 20,000 inhabitants in these countries could have been given a $5,000,000 library and a $10,000,000 university. Out of what was left, a sum could have been set aside to draw interest at 5 per cent that would have provided a $1,000 yearly salary for an army of 125,000 teachers and 125,000 nurses.[7]

If this were true of World War I, what might have been done with the vast waste of World War II and the subsequent billions that have gone into armaments? But in a world without an effective world government, no nation dares neglect its preparation to wage a war, for this will continue to be one of its functions until nations believe in law as the device for regulating their affairs and relationships to each other.

SUMMARY

Government is the over-all agency of social control, the final arbitrator of disputes between men. It exists in all societies, in the more primitive only in the form of custom, in the feudal in the form of personal allegiance. In modern society, the gigantic web of government reaches from the locality to the nation, and must ultimately include the world. Government prohibits, restricts, promotes. In all these fields it is acting as an agency of social control in the interest of the citizen. Our age has seen the expansion of government as the complexities of modern living have made greater demands on regulative authority. It has also witnessed a great expansion of welfare services in response to demands of the citizen, who is likely to criticize the cost of government at the same time that he demands increasing services of it.

But the web of government is more complex than necessary, and many small units of government could well be abandoned in the interest of economy and efficiency. Government operates through the

[7] Reported by George Wilson, *Why Wars Are Declared* (New York: Basic Books, 1935), p. 23.

political party which is so closely tied into the underworld at many points that too often the legal government is but the front for the underworld machine of patronage, bribery, and graft. Civil Service has been developed to improve the profession of government and make it serve the citizen better, but government as a competent profession is still an ideal for the future. Yet the political way is the only practical way to preserve freedom of choice for the governed, inasmuch as only through free participation in politics is choice offered the governed.

And finally, the modern device for extending welfare services and equalizing privilege in democratic society is the income tax which equalizes the benefits of wealth by seeking funds from those who have much and spending them for services and benefits for all.

DISCUSSION AND REVIEW QUESTIONS

1. How does government rank among other institutions in regard to authority? in demands it can make on the person?
2. What are some of the symbolic culture traits of government? some codes?
3. What role for the individual does government define?
4. List three broad fields of governmental function.
5. Distinguish between prohibitive and regulative functions.
6. Give an example of promotion by government.
7. Discuss trends that have lead to the expansion of government.
8. Explain why the citizen is largely responsible for the expansion of government. Cite data to prove your point.
9. What is the modern function of government in the economic order?
10. Give data that indicate the complex layers of government in our culture.
11. What basic American tradition helps perpetuate small units of public administration?
12. Discuss the three layers of government as described by Chapin.
13. Point out some implications of the latent government.
14. Give data to indicate the way income tax is graduated.
15. Show how taxation can be used by democratic government to help equalize privilege.
16. To what must the major burden of taxation be attributed?
17. Point out benefits that might be derived from present tax revenues if they could all be devoted to human welfare and general improvement.

SOURCEBOOK READINGS

KOENIG, SAMUEL, REX D. HOPPER, and FELIKS GROSS. *Sociology: A Book of Readings.* Englewood Cliffs, N.J.: Prentice-Hall, Inc., 1956.
1. TANNENBAUM, FRANK, "Characteristics of American Democracy," pp. 181–86.
2. DEMADARIAGA, SALVADOR, "What's Wrong with Democracy?" pp. 186–90.
3. MEYER, CORD, JR., "World Government Is Possible," pp. 200–208.

LEE, RAYMOND L., JAMES A. BURKHART, and VAN B. SHAW. *Contemporary Social Issues.* New York: The Thomas Crowell Co., 1955.
4. BUNCHE, RALPH J., "The United Nations: Pathway to a Peaceful World," pp. 836–44.

LEE, ELIZABETH BRYANT, and ALFRED McCLUNG LEE. *Social Problems in America* (rev. ed.). New York: Henry Holt & Co., Inc., 1955.
   5. CLEVELAND, HARLAN, "Loyalty, Security and the 'Tolerant Center,'" pp. 231–36.

O'BRIEN, ROBERT W., CLARENCE C. SCHRAG, and WALTER T. MARTIN. *Readings in General Sociology* (2d ed.). Boston: Houghton Mifflin Co., 1957.
   6. LAZARSFELD, PAUL F., BERNARD BERELSON, and HAZEL GAUDET, "The People's Choice," pp. 394–405.
   7. MATTHEWS, DONALD R., "Social Background of Political Decision-Makers," pp. 405–9.
   8. CLARK, J. M., "The Interplay of Politics and Economics," pp. 409–14.

SCHULER, EDGAR A., DUANE L. GIBSON, MAUDE L. FIERO, and WILBUR B. BROOKOVER. *Outside Readings in Sociology.* New York: The Thomas Crowell Co., 1956.
   9. WEBER, MAX, "Bureaucracy," pp. 402–12.

SELECTED READINGS

ALBIG, WILLIAM. *Modern Public Opinion.* New York: McGraw-Hill Book Co., Inc., 1956.

BOORSTIN, DANIEL J. *The Genius of American Politics.* Chicago: University of Chicago Press, 1953.

HALE, ROBERT L. *Freedom through Law: Public Control of Private Governing Power.* New York: Columbia University Press, 1952.

HATT, PAUL, and ALBERT J. REISS. *Reader in Urban Sociology.* Glencoe, Ill.: The Free Press, 1951.

KERR, CLARK. "What Became of the Independent Spirit?" *Fortune,* July, 1953, pp. 110 ff.

KEY, VLADIMIR ORLANDO. *Politics, Parties and Pressure Groups.* 3d ed.; New York: The Thomas Crowell Co., 1952.

KNEBEL, FLETCHER. *"The Welfare State Is Here to Stay,"* Look, Jan. 25, 1955, pp. 81–84.

LIEBERMAN, ELIAS. *Unions before the Bar.* New York: Harper & Brothers, 1950.

LUBELL, SAMUEL. *The Future of American Politics.* New York: Harper & Brothers, 1952.

MERTON, ROBERT K. "Bureaucratic Structures and Personality," *Social Forces,* 18: 560–68 (1940).

ORWELL, GEORGE. *Nineteen Eighty-Four.* New York: American Library of World Literature, 1950.

PFEFFER, LEO. *Church, State and Freedom.* Boston: Beacon Press, Inc., 1953.

SCHRIFTGEISSER, KARL. *The Lobbyist.* Boston: Little, Brown & Co., 1951.

VALENTINE, ALAN. *The Age of Conformity.* Chicago: Henry Regnery Co., 1954.

FILM LIST

Political Parties—20 minutes—sound
   Explains the operation of political parties, and emphasizes that parties can exist only if citizens are free to state opinions and take action on them. *Source:* Encyclopaedia Britannica Films.

Democracy—11 minutes—sound
   Defines the requisites of democracy in a modern society. Illustrates the concept of "shared respect and shared power." *Source:* Encyclopaedia Britannica Films.

Despotism—11 minutes—sound
   Presents basic social concepts of despotism. Analysis is made in terms of respect scale and power scale, these in turn related to economic distribution and information or enlightenment. *Source:* Encyclopaedia Britannica Films.

The People's Charter—17 minutes—sound
>   Documentary on the birth of the idea of the United Nations, its organization and first meeting. *Source:* Films of the Nations, Inc.

Two Views on Socialism—16 minutes—sound
>   Designed to stimulate discussion on the differences between socialism and capitalism. *Source:* Coronet Films.

Where Will You Hide?—20 minutes—sound—color
>   Dramatizes with realistic narration the fact that peace is everybody's business. *Source:* Encyclopaedia Britannica Films.

Chapter 37

Religious Institutions

THE SPHERE OF RELIGION

Man has always found it necessary to come to terms, by some means, with the powers that he conceives as controlling human life and human destiny. This is the realm of religion. Because of man's imagination and intelligence, he has always felt it necessary to tread softly in the universe lest he disturb or anger powers which his mind tells him must have made it and him. Unlike the beasts, which seem to go their way without fear of the supernatural, man cowers before it and imagines he sees its power manifest in the world about him. Indeed, religion consists of the attitudes and beliefs concerning the nature of these powers that are presumed to control man's destiny and of methods employed in the culture in coping with them.

In the following accounts the problem which religion meets for man is clearly suggested.

Life is one big puzzle. You bend every effort on the hunt and fail, while some lazy good-for-nothing brings home plenty of food. Your comrades on a war-party are killed, but *you* escape. Neighbor X looked hale and hearty when he suddenly fell dead. Why does cousin Y always win at button, button, who's got the button? Why did his wife bear twins? What's the meaning of that owl hooting outside the lodge night after night? All this is strange, some of it uncanny. There is supernatural power floating about; the universe teems with it. By hook or crook you had better get some if you want to live safely, gain social position, win at gambling, or prevent your wife from bearing twins. You have to solve an equation with an infinite number of unknown quantities, and unfortunately your happiness, your life and death, depend on finding the right answers. So tread softly in the universe. . . .[1]

In the face of the luck-element, men had to act. What to do right away, rather than what to think, was the pressing matter. Through what gropings mankind went before hitting upon religious rites as the answer to the inex-

[1] Robert H. Lowie, *Are We Civilized?* (New York: Harcourt, Brace & Co., Inc., 1929), chap. 20.

626

plicable, cannot be known, for the world's peoples, as they enter history, are already practising the rites. In their prehistoric castings-about, they seem to have found the spirit-world opportunely present, ready to explain the inexplicable, and to have developed ways of dealing with the supernatural that seemed to them to work. . . .[2]

BASIC ELEMENTS IN PRIMITIVE RELIGIONS

Until science was developed, most of the mysterious occurrences in the natural environment were attributed to supernatural forces with which man was to reckon and make himself friendly. Trees, rocks, mountains, and clouds were vested with spirit life. One saw these powers manifest not only in nature about him, but in the events which befell man himself. Because sickness or innumerable other catastrophes might overtake him on the road of life, he developed techniques for dealing with forces that seemed to control the events of man's own life, as well as those that seemed to control nature.

Some ventures in life were lucky, others unlucky; some brought great happiness and success, others heaped failure upon failure. Certainly such outcomes were without rhyme or reason unless unseen forces were at work.

Animism. The belief in *animism* is widespread throughout primitive cultures. It is an attitude which holds that all inanimate objects are possessed of spirit powers. Every rock, every tree, the mountains, the clouds are vested with spirits with which man must reckon. An East African Negro will revere the tip of an antelope horn crammed with clay and herbs. A Plains Indian brought anthropologist Robert Lowie a little bundle and told him it contained the greatest thing on earth. The anthropologist watched while the man untied the bundle, pulled off one covering after another, and in the end displayed a bunch of feathers.[3]

Such behavior seems strange indeed, and yet it is not so strange if one understands the logic of people living under the religious system of animism. The Plains Indian who prized his bunch of feathers had had a vision in his youth. An apparition appeared to him wearing feathers like those the Indian carried in the package. He was told to wear like feathers in time of battle, in which case he would escape wounds and death. The African Negro with the antelope horn worshiped it because of an in-dwelling god. As Lowie points out, what the savages prize is the supernatural power linked with the inanimate object. They are not worshiping the dead thing, but the power which it possesses to bring them good or evil.

[2] Albert G. Keller, *Man's Rough Road* (New Haven: Yale University Press, 1932), p. 198.

[3] Lowie, *op. cit.*, chap. 20.

Mana. Closely allied to the idea of animism is the idea of *mana*. Our closest equivalent for it is good luck. This good-luck element is sought after in charms and fetishes, by ritual and placation of the spirits. By these devices and activities primitive man strives to get the luck element on his side. Before going out in quest of a wife, on a hunt for wild beasts, or to plant his crops, he uses his charms and seeks omens of good luck. If he can but win the spirits to his side, things will turn out the way he wishes. If he fails in this, his quest for a wife may be a failure, the hunt may end in disaster, his crops may fail to grow.

Even in such matters as conception, human beings have always had to reckon with chance. If births were too frequent, various magical devices were employed by women to forestall pregnancy. Throwing apples or stones, kernels of grain, wooden pegs, or nails into neighborhood wells, springs, or rivers are typical of magical rites supposed to guarantee that a woman does not become pregnant.[4]

The Evil Eye. Opposed to mana is the *evil eye*, or the ill-luck element of life. Those who fail to placate the spirits and to deal with them properly are subject to it. It is likely to plague them at every step.

Numerous devices are employed to aid one in escaping the consequences of the evil eye. For example, the *couvade* is a wide-spread custom among primitives: the husband goes to bed and plays sick at the birth of his child, the logic of this being that the evil eye will attack the weakest member of the family. The infant being extremely weak probably cannot weather an attack by the evil eye; therefore, the father pretends to be desperately sick so that the ill-luck element will think that he is the weakest one and attack him. He will wrestle with the evil spirit and defeat him, thus protecting the infant until it gains enough strength to match the evil one.

Magic. In primitive religion, magic is the device employed in dealing with the luck element. It may take several forms. A very common type is *imitative magic*. By means of it one can accomplish wonderful things. For example, if he wants to destroy an enemy, he will make a figure of the enemy and burn it, or stick a spear through it. This is not unlike burning an effigy today, although the modern has less faith in its ultimate destruction of the enemy than does the primitive.

Another device frequently employed by primitives is *contagious magic*. It is based on the assumption that things which logically be-

[4] Norman E. Himes, *Medical History of Contraception* (Baltimore: The Williams & Wilkins Co., 1936), pp. 64 ff.

long together cannot be separated. By obtaining a part of the body of an enemy, for example, one can, if he knows the proper words, cast a spell over it and gain control of the person in that way. Thus he may perform magic rites with a hair or tooth or nail paring of an enemy, which will lead to the enemy's destruction. Likewise, if he can get the hair of a lover and by incantations cast the love spell over it, he can win the evasive sweetheart.

Repetitive magic is also believed to be effective. It is based on the superstition that things that happened in sequence once will happen so again. Many luck superstitions are of that character, for example, weather superstitions and bad omens. The idea that a black cat may bring bad luck if it crosses one's path probably originated in bad luck once following the crossing of someone's path by a cat. Gradually such superstitions become ingrained in a culture, until it comes to be accepted as inevitable that when a black cat crosses a path, ill luck will follow.

SURVIVALS OF PRIMITIVE RELIGION

Science has pushed back for modern man the mysterious curtain of natural forces. This has left much less to imaginative mythology than in earlier ages. Yet modern man, unless he is gripped by a deep faith in Christian doctrines, still reverts frequently to devices presumed to be helpful in meeting the luck element. This is especially true in the gaming aspects of life—in gambling, love, war, or athletic contests. He is as likely as not to employ fetishes, charms, ritual, or other devices with which to win the favor of the luck element. Numerous superstitions center about the athletic uniform, the rabbit's foot, the good luck piece, the lucky pencil or fountain pen. Thousands, even millions, consult fortune tellers, numerologists, and other quacks, paying them millions of dollars annually. Other large sums are spent for astrological magazines and other such fakery, which is supposed to give some clue to what luck tomorrow holds.

In times of crisis, those with religious faith turn to it for solace; those without religious faith resort to superstition or tremble helplessly in fear. Approaching more nearly the accepted expression of orthodox religion is the attendance of millions at the motion picture *Song of Bernadette,* during World War II. In wartime the story seemed to offer solace and hope to millions who, in times when the chance element was less prominent in life, would have been as likely to ridicule as to accept the logically fantastic miracle portrayed. But in wartime, when many women have sons or husbands in battle, even the irreligious cling to faith and to superstition to solace fears, having no other way of coming directly to terms with the luck element.

It was a common saying, during World War II, that "there are no atheists in fox holes." It is doubtful that much "foxhole Christianity" survived the wartime experience. Rather it was something akin to primitive magic which men clung to in their desperate struggle with chance. In any case, it is a fact that throughout human experience, institutionalized religion or institutionalized magic in some form has helped man to conquer his fears of the mysterious and of the unknown events of the future.

BASIC ATTITUDES OF CHRISTIANITY

In contrast to the attitudes of the primitive toward religion are the attitudes of the modern Christian who, although he generally acknowledges a strong mystical element in his religious belief, nonetheless conceives of an increasing number of realms as being entirely in the sphere of natural law. God dwells in his heaven and rules the earth by natural law so that modern man does not need to people inanimate objects with spirits.

Today, one may believe that a stone can be turned into bread, but if so, it will be by God's setting aside a natural law in a particular instance and performing a miracle. Coming to terms with God is not done by use of magic, which would be automatically forcing God to do what one wants, but by prayer and intercession, worship and adoration, whereby the worshiper seeks God's favor and thereby receives acts of goodness from Him.

Some modern men, like some primitives, believe in immortality, but whereas most primitives identify the soul with the breath, and in many cultures make provisions for the breath to escape from the body upon death by knocking out the front teeth, modern man conceives of the soul as a sort of indefinable essence which is the person himself formed in the likeness of the supernatural creator. The soul departs from the body at death and goes to the destination designed for it. This destination is determined in large part by the kind of life the person has lived while upon earth. The afterlife of the Christian is considered a reward for behavior in this life. Those who have lived righteously get the reward of the righteous; those who sin and defy God throughout their lifetimes are consigned to a life of damnation.

Religion in modern life is that sphere of man's activities wherein he deals with supernatural powers he conceives to be in control of life and the universe. *Morals* is the field of man's right relationships with man. *Ethics* is the study or science of morals.

THE CHRISTIAN CHURCH

The church is the social institution through which the religious needs of Christians are met. It is the systematized cultural structure for religious expression. The basic attitudes provided for in the culture pattern are love, reverence, devotion, and to some extent fear. Historically, the fear element was an attitude encouraged by the church more fully than today; the newer emphasis represents a shift toward love and devotion, minimizing fear.

In a day when fear was one of the basic attitudes implanted by the church, the emphasis of religion was otherworldly. Preparing oneself to escape the torments of the future life and garnering the reward of the righteous was the major goal. While this element is still prominent in the religious revival of the more evangelical sects, it has practically disappeared from the more liberal church body, which is much more concerned with man's attitudes toward man and God than with preparation for the future life as such.

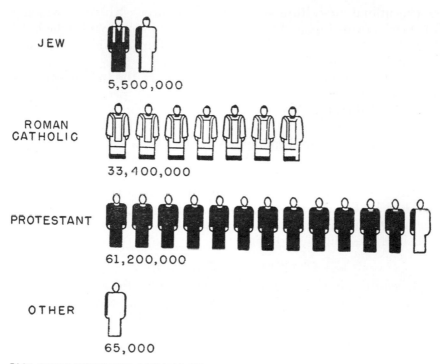

JEW

5,500,000

ROMAN
CATHOLIC

33,100,000

PROTESTANT

61,200,000

OTHER

65,000

EACH FIGURE REPRESENTS 5 MILLION PEOPLE

Religious Affiliation in the United States

In the United States religion is purely voluntary in that the principle of the separation of church and state has always been accepted. In this voluntary system all the major Western religions and numerous denominations and sects find a following.

The most significant symbolic culture trait of the Christian church is the cross, which varies in meaning between Catholics and Protestants and among the various denominations, but which in all Christian groups has considerable symbolic significance. There is also the altar and among the more formal groups the icon, shrines, relics, statues of the Virgin and of the saints, and other such material objects which are given spiritual significance in the ritual of worship. Even the church architecture, for many denominations, has symbolic significance, especially the stained glass window and the religious art. The more secularized Protestant denominations, however, are shifting to the plain glass window, and abandoning most symbols of traditional Christianity. Religion becomes very much a person's own direct relationship with his Maker, and the church a strictly utilitarian structure rather than a symbolic one.

The utilitarian culture traits are the church structure, which is the place of worship, and the useful material objects with which it is furnished. It may be a tent, a simple frame building, a great temple, or a multimillion-dollar cathedral.

The codes and tenets of faith are the core of the institution of religion. Creeds and doctrines, and among literate peoples holy books and sacred literature, have a vital place in religious worship. It has been so with Christianity. The Bible has been the code of religious worship and the moral guidebook. It has been considered by the conservative religious denominations the inspired word of God, and its tenets, therefore, have been beyond question. Various creeds and doctrines have been formulated and the proper course of conduct outlined by the various religious denominations. In the hymns and the altar ritual are expressed in greater detail the faith, hope, and beliefs of the religious doctrine.

RELIGION IN SOCIAL CONTROL

Religious values and goals have been powerful factors in social control in Christendom. The Puritan tradition has been at the roots of the entire American value system, which has been essentially religious. Here one finds the sex-centered moral system that is uniquely American. Here one finds the beginnings of the supreme value, chastity, and the control devices which have enforced it from the days of *The Scarlet Letter* to the present time. (Hawthorne chose the chastity theme as the best example he could find of consuming personal guilt—a guilt which literally destroyed the offending Reverend Dimsdale.)

A culture which implants a deep sense of guilt in the individual has already won the battle of effective social control.

Recent research by the late Dr. Kinsey and his colleagues has shown that moral objections are the main ones in the control of sexual behavior of the human female in the United States.[5] One can be sure that the moral objections are in most cases fortified by deep religious objections. And among those who have premarital intercourse, the more devoutly religious, he finds, most often suffer regret.

In all fields religion is a potent force in social control in that, as presented by Christianity, it deals with man's inner life, and in so doing internalizes social controls. To the extent that religious teachings are effective, social controls are thus internalized and the person becomes self-controlled.

THE CULT OF REASSURANCE

A new set of attitudes and values have become prominent in the church in the United States since World War II. Religion has come to play a vital part in giving man reassurance in the face of threats of annihilation. This value has great meaning in a world shaken by fear and anxiety, plagued by threat of war and the destruction of civilians on a vast scale.

The revival of religion has not been confined to the lower classes, but embraces all levels. "High-brows" and "low-brows" alike have flocked to the "cult of reassurance," whose current spokesmen are such authors of religio-psychological books as Bishop Fulton Sheen, Norman Vincent Peale, and Joshua Liebman.[6] In this new approach man is offered the hope of lifting himself partly by his own psychological bootstraps and partly by divine help.

Quite different is the gospel of Billy Graham, who also sends moderns flocking to the churches by thousands. He offers the old-fashioned personal redeemer, but employs in doing so every device of modern communication, organizational planning, and mass salesmanship.

THE SOCIAL GOSPEL

One of the marked trends in Christian thought during this century has been the shift away from a religion oriented about fear and otherworldliness toward what has been termed "the social gospel." The old orientation was evangelical and eternity-centered, basing its system of social control on man's eternal rewards which were vividly pictured from the pulpit. The new orientation is edu-

[5] Alfred Kinsey, *et al.*, *Sexual Behavior in the Human Female* (Philadelphia: W. B. Saunders Co., 1953).

[6] *Life Is Worth Living, The Power of Positive Thinking*, and *Peace of Mind*, respectively, are typical works of these writers.

cational, and aims at building character. Eternal rewards are seldom mentioned.

This shift in philosophy and goals has modified church programs greatly. The social gospel is not promoted by revivalistic evangelism, but rather by greater emphasis on Sunday school and daily vacation Bible schools, summer youth camps and special young people's programs. As a result of its emphasis on the social gospel, the church has entered the field of recreation and entertainment, of drama and art. It tries to help build the well-rounded person.

It should not be implied that the trend toward a social gospel has entirely superseded the militant evangelism of the church. Rather, the two gospels exist together in various degrees of purity, and have come to represent class approaches to Christian living. The social gospel is primarily for the upper and middle classes; the evangelical gospel for the masses of the socially dispossessed.

DENOMINATIONALISM

Denominationalism is the breaking down of the Christian religious body into numerous sub-bodies, each of which claims to be Christian but each of which differs from the others in some detail of doctrine or belief. That denominationalism has been carried to extremes in the United States is shown by the fact that in 1956 there were 256 Protestant religious bodies in the nation.[7] Even this number included some grouping together of minor sects.

The essential difference in the various denominations is the creed or doctrine. Each holds for man a slightly different standard of religious behavior, although they all point to the goal of Christian character. These denominations range, in their expression of religion, from the extremely conservative fundamentalist emphasis to the extremely humanistic and nonmystical emphasis. At the one extreme are groups interested primarily in the afterlife and in preparing man for it. At the other extreme are those who scarcely believe in the afterlife at all and are essentially interested in what man can accomplish in this world. At the one extreme is the sect, the aggressive, proselyting religious "in-group," to which all "out-group" persons are lost souls. At the other extreme is the tolerant, nonproselyting denomination that has lost the evangelistic urge. The *sect* is the militant conflict group. The *denomination* is the more staid, established institution that recognizes the equal merit of other religious denominations.

Denominationalism has been widely condemned, and its weaknesses are sometimes very apparent, especially when many denomina-

[7] *Yearbook of American Churches,* Federal Council of Churches.

tions are located in a small community and because of this competition for members are unable to support their ministers in a reasonable standard of living. Yet something is to be said for denominationalism in a democratic society, with its open-class social system. Many denominations, and especially many sectarian groups, cater primarily to the culturally dispossessed, the poor and downtrodden. Their emotional religious message, their emphasis on the world to come, makes a vital appeal to those who have about given up hope of attaining anything in this life. This kind of appeal has no meaning for the well-fed, well-clothed, and generally well-off members of society. This social class finds the present world generally satisfactory and prefers to be consoled in its present ways, instead of being told that the present world is in a state of decay and man must wait until the afterlife to find all wrongs righted.

Denominationalism is in reality an expression of American open-class individualism. Personality is developed in different people to various levels of education, aesthetic appreciation, and scientific-mindedness. Churches are in reality stratified, adapting Christian doctrines to various social, aesthetic, economic, and educational levels in the population. It is probable that no church would claim to be an exclusive upper-class church and that no church would claim to be an exclusive lower-class church, yet the membership of many church denominations is drawn predominantly from one stratum or another.

One might argue that half a dozen Protestant denominations could as well meet the needs of the various strata of the American population. This no doubt is true, but with individualism in religion, which permits any leader to start a new church if he can get a following, denominationalism will not so easily submit to a rigid course of logic or economy. It has become an inherent part of the American religious tradition. It permits the development of creeds and of various levels of rationality and emotionality; thereby it serves quite well the religious needs of a highly diversified population.

The trend toward reducing denominationalism by merging denominations of slightly differing faiths probably will continue, but the emergence of additional sectarian groups as new and vitalized revivalistic religious movements probably will also continue. In a society of stratified religious bodies, the sectarian group of previous generations gradually takes on conservative characteristics, attracts a more prosperous and educated clientele, loses its revivalistic spirit, and gradually becomes one of the staid old denominations, as hundreds of other sectarian groups before it have done. For example, Methodism, in the days of John and Charles Wesley and George

Whitfield, was a revivalistic movement as radical and sectarian as the great tabernacle movements of today. It catered in those days to the dispossessed of the coal fields and industrial sections of England. Today Methodism has moved uptown, built its brick and stone temples, and become a nonrevivalistic middle- to upper-class denomination.

We may conclude, then, that the various denominations and religious sects are methods by which a social system of many indefinite classes meets the religious needs of all social levels. Anyone can find a religious institution that conforms to his temperament, aesthetic sense, and level of educational and emotional development.[8]

One may carry the implications of denominationalism a step further by considering its significance as a factor in the adjustments of youth as they engage in social climbing, accepted behavior in our society. It seems likely that the various religious denominations offer the young person a chance as he outgrows the faith of his childhood, especially if he is reared in a sectarian group of a revivalistic character, to move up to a more conservative denomination which more nearly expresses his belief as his education and critical-mindedness increase.[9]

SUMMARY

Man is an imaginative creature, with a sense of time and destiny. His mind conjures up not only images of the past, but dreams of the future. He must concern himself with the powers which he conceives as controlling life and the universe about him. Only as he develops means for reckoning with these powers, controlling them, and making them serve his purpose, only as he learns to propitiate them, so that they will not bring him ill, does he feel safe. This is the area of religion. Practically all peoples have developed formal cultural systems which deal with these powers beyond man's immediate material experience.

The primitive sees spirit life in all objects—he believes in animism. Mana is the good element in life, the evil eye the bad-luck element. Through various forms of magic, the primitive man tries to compel the good element to favor him, the evil eye to avoid him. It works automatically if the correct trick of magic is known. While many such primitive conceptions survive today, the basic attitudes of Christianity are those of worship and intercession, rather than of magic

[8] For support of this point, see Andrew G. Truxall and Francis E. Merrill, *The Family in American Culture* (Englewood Cliffs, N.J.: Prentice-Hall, Inc., 1947), p. 53.

[9] A study by Marvin J. Taves, *Factors Influencing Personal Religion of Adults*, Washington Agricultural Experiment Station Bulletin No. 544 (Pullman, Wash., 1953), lends support to this view.

compulsion. The religious system becomes closely allied with the prevailing system of morals, that is, the realm of man's relationships with man. The church in its various cultural aspects, material and nonmaterial, has become the channel for religious expression in the United States, and by means of denominationalism reaches the various class strata at the level of their intellectual and aesthetic development.

DISCUSSION AND REVIEW QUESTIONS

1. With what realm does religion deal?
2. What is meant by animism? mana? the evil eye?
3. Discuss three forms of magic.
4. Has the luck element disappeared from modern thinking?
5. What are some of the basic attitudes of Christianity?
6. Define the spheres of religion, morals, and ethics.
7. What basic change has come in attitudes of the Christian church in recent decades? Give the elements of the new "cult of reassurance."
8. What are some of the basic culture traits, both material and nonmaterial, of the Christian church?
9. Discuss denominationalism as it has developed in America.
10. What is a sect?
11. Do you think that denominationalism is a natural counterpart of an open-class society? Explain.

SOURCEBOOK READINGS

KOENIG, SAMUEL, REX D. HOPPER, and FELIKS GROSS. *Sociology: A Book of Readings.* Englewood Cliffs, N.J.: Prentice-Hall, Inc., 1956.
1. HERTZLER, JOYCE O., "What Religion Is and How It Functions," pp. 209–20.
2. OXNAM, G. BROMLEY, "Religion and Science in Accord," pp. 221–28.
3. REISER, OLIVER L., and BLODWEN DAVIES, "Religion and Science in Conflict," pp. 228–37.

LEE, RAYMOND L., JAMES A. BURKHART, and VAN B. SHAW. *Contemporary Social Issues.* New York: The Thomas Crowell Co., 1955.
4. KRISTOL, IRVING, "Civil Liberties Today: A Study in Confusion," pp. 130–44.

LEE, ELIZABETH BRYANT, and ALFRED McCLUNG LEE. *Social Problems in America* (rev. ed.). New York: Henry Holt & Co., Inc., 1955.
5. FOLSOM, JOSEPH K., "Kinsey's Challenge to Ethics and Religion," pp. 136–39.

O'BRIEN, ROBERT W., CLARENCE C. SCHRAG, and WALTER T. MARTIN. *Readings in General Sociology* (2d ed.). Boston: Houghton Mifflin Co., 1957.
6. FICHTER, JOSEPH H., "The Marginal Catholic: An Institutional Approach," pp. 386–91.
7. YINGER, MILTON, "Religion and Social Change," pp. 391–94.

SCHULER, EDGAR A., DUANE L. GIBSON, MAUDE L. FIERO, and WILBUR B. BROOKOVER. *Outside Readings in Sociology.* New York: The Thomas Crowell Co., 1956.
8. BARBER, HOLLIS W., "Religious Liberty v. Police Power: Jehovah's Witnesses," pp. 439–42.

WILSON, LOGAN, and WILLIAM L. KOLB. *Sociological Analysis.* New York: Harcourt, Brace & Co., Inc., 1949.
9. BECKER, HOWARD, "Four Types of Religious Organization," pp. 655–58.
10. POPE, LISTON, "Patterns of Denominational Development: Churches and Sects," pp. 658–74.

SELECTED READINGS

BOSSARD, JAMES H. S., and ELEANOR S. BOLL. *One Marriage, Two Faiths*. New York: The Ronald Press Co., 1957.

BRADEN, CHARLES S. *These Also Believe*. New York: The Macmillan Co., 1949.

HUTCHINSON, PAUL. "Have We a New Religion?" *Life*, April 11, 1955, pp. 138–58.

LANDIS, PAUL H. *Social Control*. Rev. ed.; Chicago: J. B. Lippincott Co., 1956, chaps. 2 and 14.

LEIBMAN, JOSHUA L. *Peace of Mind*. New York: Simon & Schuster, Inc., 1946.

NANNES, CASPAR. "Will All Protestants Unite in One Church?" *Collier's*, Aug. 20, 1954, pp. 17–22.

NIEBUHR, REINHOLD. *Christianity and Power Politics*. New York: Charles Scribners' Sons, 1948.

NOTTINGHAM, ELIZABETH K. *Religion and Society*. Doubleday Short Studies in Sociology. Garden City, N.Y.: Doubleday & Co., Inc., 1954.

PFEFFER, LEO. *Church, State and Freedom*. Boston: Beacon Press, Inc., 1953.

SMITH, WILLIAM C. "Sociology and the Social Gospel," *Sociology and Social Research*, 32:609–15 (Nov.–Dec. 1947).

STACE, WALTER T. *Religion and the Modern Mind*. Philadelphia: J. B. Lippincott Co., 1952.

TILLICH, P. "Religion and Secular Culture," *Journal of Religion*, 26:79–86 (April 1946).

WACH, JOACHIM. *Sociology of Religion*. Chicago: University of Chicago Press, 1944.

WARD, H. F. "Organized Religion, the State, and the Economic Order," *Annals of the American Academy of Political and Social Science*, 256:72–83 (March 1948).

FILM LIST

Three Great Religions—15 minutes
  Taoism, Buddhism, and Confucianism. *Source:* China Film Enterprises of America, Inc.

Indian Temples—11 minutes—sound—color
  Description of Hindu religion, temples, rites, gods, etc. *Source:* Teaching Film Custodians, Inc.

Brotherhood for Survival—11 minutes—sound
  Program of the National Conference of Christians and Jews explained. Illustrates cooperative relationships between various types of religious organizations and denominations. *Source:* National Conference of Christians and Jews.

Church in the Atomic Age—19 minutes—sound
  Development and use of the atomic bomb raises questions regarding moral justification of atomic warfare. *Source:* Film Forum Foundation.

Jerusalem—The Holy City—11 minutes—sound—color
  The pageantry of Jerusalem and of the historical shrines sacred to three religious traditions—Jewish, Christian, and Mohammedan. *Source:* Encyclopaedia Britannica Films.

Primitive Religions—15 minutes
  An interpretation of various primitive religions showing basic religious attitudes of man toward the forces of nature. *Source:* Religious Film Association, Inc.

Totems—10 minutes—sound—color
  With background of tribal chants this film presents historical and interpretative facts concerning totem poles of coastal British Columbia tribes. *Source:* National Film Board of Canada.

The Nuremberg Trials, the Churches, and International Justice—29½ minutes
  Shows pictures of the atrocities presented as evidence at the trials and raises questions regarding the moral foundation of international justice. *Source:* Films Forum Foundations.

Chapter 38

Economic Institutions

In the American social system the conquest of leisure has become a major individual and social concern. But this is not the story of history; in fact, it is not the story of most of the world today. The conquest of want has been, and is, man's major struggle. This is the area of economic institutions.

THE NATURE OF ECONOMIC WANTS

But the conquest of want is not enough. Once the basic necessities are acquired, and often even before, man uses economic goods for show (conspicuous consumption); and they are in most cultures a means to high status. So even economic values are not merely utilitarian in the material sense as some superficially conclude but are highly symbolic of other values which humans prize highly. From time immemorial a man's prestige and power, his affluence and influence, have been predicated on the size of his flocks and herds, his fields, and his dwelling places.

The key to acquisition of goods is work, and for this reason work is avoided in most parts of the world by those who have already acquired sufficient goods to live without resort to work. Thus they show to their fellows that they are aloof from the menial requirements of human existence.

Showing off in all the ways that enhance a man in the eyes of his fellows becomes the great game of economic life for those who dare reach beyond subsistence values to psychological ones. No sooner does man satisfy hunger than he adds foods and utensils to minister to his vanity. One can live on the simple foods, but pea-fowl tongues, or the breast of guinea hen or pheasant, have to be prepared on occasion to do justice to a man's social position. Again, crude shelters without art or design are but the beginning. Give man sufficient resources and sufficient freedom from want, and he displays his creative skill and inspires the admiration of his fellows by building a better dwelling than his neighbors. In time this requires the skill of architects and the lavish expenditure of funds.

Or consider clothing. It originated not in modesty but in man's pride. Clothing is used, even by those who live in warm climates, as a method of ornamentation. Clothing is one of the frills of the decorative art that comes to be associated with high status. Ornamentation may range all the way from precious stones that adorn the fingers to heavy rings of iron that hang from the lobes of the ears or from the septum in the nose. Far from always being items of convenience or need, clothing and other ornamentation may load a man down heavily, yet he will carry pounds of iron bands around his ankles, his wrists, or even around his neck if his culture considers these things to be marks of distinction. To the external ornaments attached to the body must be added the numerous decorative touches achieved by scarring, and by paints, powders, and perfumes, with which man improves the appearance or appeal he is endowed with by nature.

This brief discussion is enough to indicate that economic culture soon develops beyond its original purpose of meeting basic organic needs of the human being. If it did no more than that, man would never rise much above the level of animals in food-getting and food-using. But even the savage far exceeded this point in economic achievement.

Some of the major competitive processes in society operate in the field of economic life, for economic goods are a common measure of status. Many societies use the terms lower, middle, and upper class as a classification based entirely upon possessions held by the individual—cattle and flocks, houses and land, stocks and bonds, money, or any one of numerous forms of property that exist in a complex society. No society is free from distinction based on economic goods possessed by its members.

PROPERTY

At the basis of economic life is the concept of ownership. No society exists in which a sense of ownership is not found. This sense of ownership, however, may be radically different from the concept that prevails in Western society. Among most primitive peoples, communal ownership of the land and other natural resources, such as fishing places and hunting areas, is characteristic. Private property consists of personal belongings, clothing, and often also such things as livestock and household utensils.

In direct contrast to this is the system of private property in a complex society, where not only personal belongings but vast natural resources such as land, minerals, water rights, and even a certain domain in the air above is considered personal property. Thus, where the concept of personal property develops there also develops a vast complex of ideas and patterns having to do with returns from use of property by others: rents, interests, leases, insurance, contracts, etc. And with the private property system there must develop elaborate codes for inheritance, which decide what happens to a man's possessions after his death. Custom may require that his possessions be buried with him. If his wife is considered a possession, she may be included with his other possessions or perhaps burned on a funeral pyre.

Custom may decree that possessions go to the eldest son (primogeniture), who becomes the authority of the household at the decease of his father. Codes may develop for the passing on of property on some kind of a shared basis, the major share going to the wife for her lifetime, after which children share and share alike; however this customary practice, to be carried out, requires elaborate legal procedure involving the probating of an estate.

The use of the will to transmit property much as desired by the person who accumulates it permits its transmission to charity, its use to finance some structure as a memorial to the donor's name, or its transfer to others entirely outside the circle of close family relatives.

Property may, through certain social inventions, become a highly complex possession, as in the case of the modern corporation, with its stocks and bonds which divide ownership of vast multimillion-dollar enterprises among millions of people, each of whom own a fraction of it according to their investment and have rights of control of the property only to the extent of this ownership.

Work is the means to a livelihood of man; by work he wins his keep from the natural environment. But in time he feels safe enough to use economic goods for other purposes than meeting economic needs. Here is Thorstein Veblen's classic picture of members of the "leisure class" who have attained a position where they can engage primarily in spending.

"The . . . gentleman of leisure, then, not only consumes of the staff of life beyond the minimum required for subsistence and physical efficiency, but his consumption also undergoes a specialisation as regards the quality of the goods consumed. He consumes freely and of the best, in food, drink, narcotics, shelter, services, ornaments, apparel, weapons and accoutrements, amusements, amulets, and idols or divinities. In the process of gradual amelioration which takes place in the articles of his consumption, the motive principle and the proximate aim of innovation is no doubt the higher efficiency of the improved and more elaborate products for personal comfort and well-being. But that does not remain the sole purpose of their consumption. The canon of reputability is at hand and seizes upon such innovations as are, according to its standard, fit to survive. Since the consumption of these more excellent goods is an evidence of wealth, it becomes honorific; and conversely, the failure to consume in due quantity and quality becomes a mark of inferiority and demerit.

"This growth of punctilious discrimination as to qualitative excellence in eating, drinking, etc., presently affects not only the manner of life, but also the training and intellectual activity of the gentleman of leisure. He is no longer simply the successful, aggressive male—the man of strength, resource, and intrepidity. In order to avoid stultification he must also cultivate his tastes, for it now becomes incumbent on him to discriminate with some nicety between the noble and the ignoble in consumable goods. He becomes a connoisseur in creditable viands of various degrees of merit, in manly beverages and trinkets, in seemly apparel and architecture, in weapons, games, dancers, and the narcotics. This cultivation of the aesthetic faculty requires time and application, and the demands made upon the gentleman in this direction therefore tend to change his life of leisure into a more or less arduous application to the business of learning how to live a life of ostensible leisure in a becoming way . . . Hence arise good manners . . . High-bred manners and ways of living are items of conformity to the norm of conspicuous leisure and conspicuous consumption.

"Conspicuous consumption of valuable goods is a means of reputability to the gentleman of leisure. . . ."[1]

Not all people accept property values as the measure of a man, although it is doubtful that they are ever fully ignored. Here is Theodore Rooevelt's comment on the subject.

I am simply unable to make myself take the attitude of respect toward the very wealthy men which such an enormous multitude of people evidently really feel. I am delighted to show my courtesy to Pierpont Morgan or Andrew Carnegie or James J. Hill, but as for regarding any one of them as, for instance, I regard Professor Bury, or Peary, the Arctic explorer, or Rhodes, the historian, why, I could not force myself to do it even if I wanted to, which I don't.[2]

[1] Thorstein Veblen, *The Theory of the Leisure Class* (New York: The Macmillan Co., 1912), pp. 73–75.
[2] Theodore Roosevelt, quoted in Matthew Josephson, *The Robber Barons* (New York: Harcourt, Brace & Co., Inc., 1934), p. 337.

After this review of some of the basic values of economic life, attention may now be turned to a consideration of the elements in the institutional structure of contemporary industrial culture.

UTILITARIAN CULTURE TRAITS

The Factory Production System. In the growth of the modern economic system, the most significant single forward step has been the development of the factory system, which uses machine power, labor, management, and capital more efficiently than any economic system in the history of mankind. The great factory system of today is able to employ many shortcuts in the use of all of these aspects of modern technology and administration to the greatest possible advantage. The corporation is able to accumulate, through the sale of stocks and bonds, capital resources for assembling a plant which can use highly specialized labor; it can employ every device or means of mechanical efficiency known to man; it can, through its capital structure, extend its advertising throughout the nation or even throughout large parts of the world, creating a mass market. It can even use a part of its capital for the hiring of research specialists to forward the inventive process.

In the factory system there has been developed the piece-work method of using labor so that each individual can become a highly trained specialist in performing a single act or single phase of the manufacturing process. This is combined with the conveyor-belt system for assembling the standardized parts of complex machines. Modern machines, such as automobiles, roll off the conveyor belt at the rate of hundreds per day. The standardization of all parts of particular machines makes not only the conveyor-belt and piecework systems possible, but also the quick repair of any machine in operation, since any part for a given model is interchangeable.

It is in the field of factory production that the genius of the American economic system has been unrivaled. This is sometimes referred to as "know-how" in the modern industrial system. This "know-how" in American industry has saved the nation from catastrophe in two great world wars.

It is the factory system of production with its accompanying capital structure that has for the first time in human history permitted building a society in which want has been virtually banished and in which abundant leisure is the birthright of the common man as well as of the rich. In other ages, leisure and plenty were won for the few by the long hours of toil by slaves, serfs, peons, or poorly paid workers who struggled long hours and lived on the bare necessities. Leisure and plenty are still so won in what the West calls the "underdeveloped areas"—areas without machine production and machine power.

The Distribution System. The corporate-factory system of American industry is probably the most complicated financial arrangement ever developed for the production and distribution of goods. It has become so vast that it involves financial structures which have become not only national in scope but also international, and a factory system which may have branches throughout a nation and even in different nations. Combined with this, there is often a system of distribution which is as nearly world-wide as is the particular culture which employs the manufactured article. Compared to the primitive barter system that has characterized rural societies throughout antiquity, this type of economic organization seems something entirely different. Yet in a modern world, with transportation and communication on an international scale, it serves the same function that barter serves in a primitive economy.

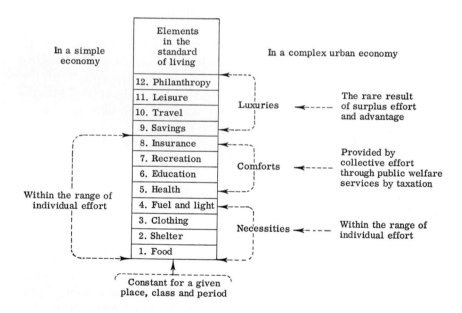

Living Standards in Two Types of Economies

The twelve elements of the highest standard of living are constant for any given place, social class, and period of time. But more elements are within the range of individual effort in a simple economy. (Redrawn from F. S. Chapin, Contemporary American Institutions, p. 11, Harper & Brothers, 1935.)

In the accompanying chart, developed by sociologist F. S. Chapin, the center column lists services and goods ranging from the most simple to the most elaborate. Chapin shows here the various things which are available through effort in an economic system of two levels. The values realized through economic effort range all the way from the necessities at the bottom, the most important necessity being food, to philanthropy at the top. At the left side of the column, he shows that only eight of these items are available to the individual through his efforts in a simple village economy. He shows by contrast the number of items that are available through individual and collective effort in a complex economy.[3]

The Value System. Of the utilitarian culture traits of the modern economic system, none is more significant than money, which actually is largely symbolic. It is used as the medium of exchange, standing for all values that are represented in the economic system. Through the simple device of money, trade and commerce can be carried on with ease. Money, to be most useful, has to have certain characteristics. It must be highly *malleable, divisible, permanent,* and have *intrinsic value.* Gold and silver have become the principal materials used in economic exchange in the modern world.

Even the use of these media of exchange has been simplified by the use of credit instruments such as the bank check, note, and other paper documents which facilitate the exchange and yet do not necessitate transporting bullion. Paper money, symbolic of precious metal on deposit, is lighter, and even though easily destructible is used because it is much easier to transport and exchange than the heavier precious metals. The bank check or draft is still more convenient, as there is no limit to the amount of money which one piece of paper can represent, except the limit set by credit in the account of the person or corporation signing it.

Many other utilitarian culture traits make up the very complex modern economic system, which reaches from mine, forest, and farm to the highly complex industrial structure, and from there reaches out to retail distribution through business or merchandising.

CODES AND SYMBOLIC CULTURE TRAITS

In the codes of modern economic culture are the written contract, licenses to operate particular kinds of business in particular places, and franchises which grant the right to operate a utility within a municipality or some other civil area. Articles of incorporation for large

[3] F. S. Chapin, *Contemporary American Institutions* (New York: Harper & Brothers, 1935), p. 11.

corporate structures which must meet the requirements of federal or state statutes in order to operate, sell stocks and bonds, and in other ways conduct a business enterprise are also a part of the intangible legal structure.

In the field of symbolic culture traits, one of the significant items of today is the trademark, which may be accompanied also by slogans to be used in advertising. To protect ownership of the rights to manufacture a particular product, the patent, or, in the case of a literary production, the copyright, has also been developed, which assigns this right to a particular individual, usually the inventor or author, or the corporation which has purchased the right from the inventor or author.

WORK WORLD ROLES AND VALUES—THE SELF-EMPLOYED

The Philosophy of Self-Employment. From time immemorial the masses of mankind have been self-employed. They planned their own work and carried it out on their own schedule. This is in marked contrast to our time when, with factory production and large-scale business organizations, the masses of mankind are employed by others. Many of them, employed in organizations like General Motors or Bell Telephone, supervise the work-life of hundreds of thousands. Under self-employment, the person gets the return which his energy produces; in employment by others, he gets the wage which the employer sets.

Self-employment survives today among the farm population, small storekeepers, and businessmen who own and operate their own enterprise, and in a few other such economic activities. The self-employed man has little regard for hours of work. He tends to work long hours and is not much concerned about a vacation. The typical philosophy of the American farmer has been to work from sun-up to sun-down, and sometimes much longer hours than this, to go year in and year out with little or no vacation, and to expect the entire family to work on the farm and contribute their labor to it. It has been assumed in a rural economy of self-employment that a man's success is achieved by getting up early in the morning, working long hours, being thrifty, and being a good manager of crops and livestock. This philosophy of self-employment went much further. It was assumed that if a man had not made good economically, it was direct evidence that he was lazy. The blame fell upon his own shoulders. If he were poor, it was because he lay in bed in the morning while his neighbors worked, or because he spent his time loafing in town, spent his money on drink, or was trifling and wasteful.

Apprenticeship of Children Under Self-Employment. The philosophy of the self-employed man carried over to the training of his children. From their early years, farm children did chores, the number of their chores being increased as they increased in age and in physical strength. Before they were ten years old they were expected to spend their mornings and evenings and their school vacation helping on the farm. By the time they were in high school they would spend evenings after school with the heavier chores about the place and Saturdays and vacations doing a man's work about the farm, handling machinery and livestock as unpaid family laborers. Farming was, in other words, a way of life that involved the activities of the entire family, binding it together as a work unit, building attitudes about habits of work and duty. The life of the small storekeeper was not much different from that of the farmer, except that it was oriented about the store. The same was true of the craftsman of an earlier day.

The idea of a short work day and an annual vacation of leisure and recreation was not a part of the folkways and mores of the culture. In fact, these things were condemned. Young people gradually grew into the work world and had a natural apprenticeship to it long before they were expected to take on a full-time work life of their own. But at a relatively early age they went out on their own farm or set up their own business with whatever assistance the parents could give them. Entering the work world for the young person created no particular problem. It was largely a matter of attacking the local environment, staking out a new farm or business enterprise, or working along with the parent in his. Even today many of the above values survive among the self-employed, although modified somewhat by urban industrial influences and by the increase in high-school attendance of rural youth.

WORKERS EMPLOYED BY OTHERS

Contrast this world of self-employment with the typical present-day work world in which the father, and in many cases the mother, is a wage worker in a large industry. Work is entirely separated from the home. Individuals go out in the morning and by some means of transportation travel several blocks, or even miles, to their place of employment. The new economic structure has created a vastly different situation as far as the work world is concerned. Workmen own no tools. Both tools and place of work are provided by the employer. The conditions of work, the hours of work, the nature of the tasks are determined by the employer. The work is supervised by foremen. The finished product is checked by an inspector. Likely as not, the

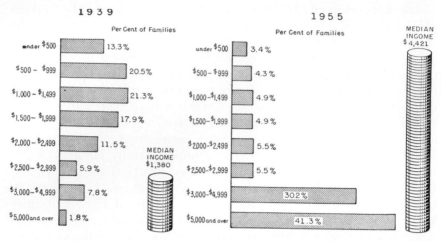

Median Income in the United States, 1939 and 1955

Inflation accounted for part of the increase shown, of course, for the dollar of the mid-1950's was worth less than half that of the late 1930's. And part of the increase reflects the fact that a greater number of wives are gainfully employed. Even so, the consumer made a real gain; his income was multiplied by more than three. These income differences help explain the remarkable improvement in the level of living of the average American family during the past two decades.

individual will do only a simple routine task in the manufacture of a particular article—and do this repeatedly throughout the work day.

In this work situation the philosophy of the worker is far different from that of the self-employed person. The worker is interested in good working conditions, short hours of work, and high wage rates. He is interested in steady employment. All he has to sell is his time and skill, and the rate at which he sells them determines the amount of his income. Under these circumstances the worker is not interested necessarily in producing the most goods for the least money. Many unions feel that it is to the worker's interest to get the highest possible wage for the least production. As a consequence, in most factory situations work output is definitely limited by the work group to what the workers themselves consider a reasonable output. The extent to which the work output is large or small depends on the bargaining power of the workers. In times when workers are scarce, the output tends to decline because, with a scarcity of workers, there is little danger of being fired. In times when workers are abundant and jobs are scarce, output tends to rise because workers can readily be replaced, although in strongly unionized industries even in slack periods the worker is protected against dismissal even when not producing at a high level.

Leisure in the New Work World. Recreation and leisure-time activities have become a major part of a well-rounded life, for under a corporate system of industry workers do routine jobs in which they fail to find the satisfaction in work that craftsmen of other days found. The earlier craftsman was a creator. The modern workman is not a creator, but an automaton. The workman of today may step on a foot pedal which clamps on the heels of shoes in rapid succession. He may put on thousands of heels during the day, but he never makes a pair of shoes, and he has little pride in the shoes that come off the end of the assembly line. His creative energies, his desire for personal expression must be satisfied, if at all, outside the work day. Leisure-time activities of a recreative nature have been developed to compensate in part for the monotonous hours of work, as have the abbreviated work day, the abbreviated work week, and the annual

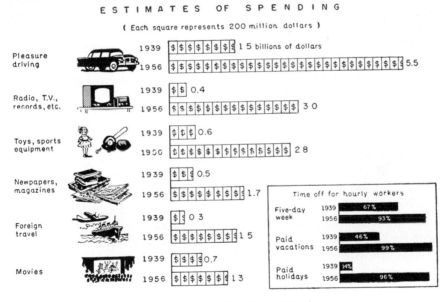

ESTIMATES OF SPENDING

(Each square represents 200 million dollars)

		1939	
Pleasure driving		1939	$ $ $ $ $ $ $ $ 1 5 billions of dollars
		1956	$ $ $ ... 5.5
Radio, T.V., records, etc.		1939	$ $ 0.4
		1956	$ $ ... 3 0
Toys, sports equipment		1939	$ $ $ 0.6
		1956	$ $ ... 2 8
Newpapers, magazines		1939	$ $ $ 0.5
		1956	$ $ ... 1.7
Foreign travel		1939	$ $ 0 3
		1956	$ $ ... 1 5
Movies		1939	$ $ $ $ 0.7
		1956	$ $ ... 1 3

Time off for hourly workers		
Five-day week	1939	67%
	1956	93%
Paid vacations	1939	46%
	1956	99%
Paid holidays	1939	14%
	1956	96%

More Luxury for Less Work

Comparison of the luxury expenditures and leisure time of the American public in 1939 with those of 1956 tells the success story of the American capitalistic economy, with its assembly-line methods of mass production. President Franklin D. Roosevelt is reputed to have said that the thing that would ultimately defeat Communism was the Sears, Roebuck catalog, meaning that it served as a display of the fruits of capitalistic enterprise.

vacation to give the worker a chance for leisure-time activities, avocations, and hobbies—a chance to indulge those vital interests which make a man feel that he is creative, that he is expressing himself.

The short work day has given the workman a chance for this leisure. If he has money, he can enjoy many of the privileges and opportunities that are made possible through free time. His automobile makes him mobile. Under the regime of employment by others, the annual vacation has become an accepted part of the American folkways.

Little Apprenticeship in New Work World. The new work situation has vitally affected the home, since work is now outside the home. The worker, once he leaves the family fireside, divorces his family situation from that of the work world. The members of the family have little contact with the father's work and little understanding of it. The children, rather than getting a natural apprenticeship to the work of the parents, as they do on the farm or in a small business owned and operated by the family, get no apprenticeship to the occupational world at all. In the home of the average worker of today there are practically no chores. There is no way that children can learn directly the various skills and attitudes involved in the work-world situation. Children must, therefore, in vocational curriculums of the school program or through trial and error after graduation make their first contacts with the work world and acquire the attitudes and habits that go with the regular work life of the adult.

The shift away from self-employment has, therefore, created a rather abrupt break from dependent childhood and adolescence to self-supporting youth of today. Rather than gradually growing into work as he matures, today's youth comes up against the stern realities of a routinized work day and work week after years of schooling and of living in a relatively free play world of childhood and adolescence.

In times of abundant employment opportunity the modern teen-ager seeks his own work experience in such part-time and summer jobs as are available to him. His motive usually is to get spending money rather than to learn a vocation of his choice. Nonetheless, such experience does build attitudes, skills, and confidence in the area of work.

Over more than two decades there has been some effort to revive the apprenticeship system in certain industries. The United States Department of Labor has a Bureau of Apprenticeship. Employer and employee groups set up apprenticeship committees. Today apprentices are being trained in some 300 skilled occupations under 90 trade classifications. Some 150,000 employers take part in this training program. Such training involves a minimum of 144 hours of organized instruction in technical subjects, and job experience in various work processes, for which the worker receives pay. In-service training and adult education are also widespread.

The New Philosophy of Welfare. With the shift away from self-employment, the employment of any person, young or old, is dependent upon opportunities available in industry at a given time. Prior to Social Security, youth found it increasingly difficult at times to find employment, and adults with developed skills and years of experience often found themselves temporarily excluded from the work world. Consequently, the old philosophy of poverty is no longer accepted. It is now recognized that unemployment is not necessarily a product of laziness, personal shiftlessness, or vice, but rather that today the masses of workers are cogs in an economic order which periodically fails to provide a place for them. Therefore, a new philosophy of welfare has emerged. This new philosophy and the welfare programs themselves are discussed in the following chapter.

From this brief outline it should be clear that the shift from self-employment to employment by others represents a marked change in the character of the American economic system.

THE INDUSTRIAL SYSTEM OF THE UNITED STATES

The Organization of Industry. Under a regime of self-employment, the worker owns not only his tools but usually his place of work too. If he is engaged in agriculture, he owns his tools and his land. This is in marked contrast to the modern economic system in which ownership is diversified among numerous investors through the sale of stocks and bonds, and in which management is controlled by a board of directors, members of which often hold large blocks of stocks and bonds in the company.

Much of American production is concentrated in the hands of large corporations which are organized in this manner. In fact, large-scale production, almost of necessity, is so organized. A few such large corporations as General Motors have millions of dollars of capital available for the building of plants, for the purchase of tools, and for manufacturing and distribution. Great laboratories for research are built; millions are spent in engineering plans. The management is vested in a board of directors, and the ownership is scattered widely among those who hold the securities of the General Motors organization. The members of the board of directors receive a salary, bondholders receive interest on their bonds, and stockholders receive dividends on their stock when operations show a profit.

Most workers do not have capital to invest, so they are not as a class bondholders or stockholders. Their main contribution is their labor; their return from their work is their wage. They are, of course, a part of the public which may buy the finished product—in the case of General Motors, the automobile—but they pay the same for it as any other person, regardless of the fact that they work for the company.

The corporation system pyramids wealth used in production and concentrates management. A few great banking institutions of the

Contrasting Economics

Item	Minutes Required for a Worker to Produce	
	U. S. S. R.	U. S.
Rye bread (one pound)	31	7
Wheat bread (one pound)	70	7 ½
Veal (one pound)	315	34 ½
Butter (one pound)	642	48 ½
Beer (one bottle)	171	6 ¼
Cotton dress	1,911	142
Woolen suit (man's)	34,815	1,684

Source: Time, Dec. 29, 1947, p. 25. From the New York Times.

nation finance much of American industry and its transportation and communication systems. This has led to the interlocking directorates which are so common in the nation's centers of wealth and finance. By virtue of these interlocking directorates, the administration of these great financial structures—the major corporations that control much of the wealth, production, transportation, and communication in this country—is centralized in overlapping boards of directors.

Such centralization is not to be condemned in a capitalistic system. It explains in large part many of the economies of the American system of production and the abundance of goods which America has. When control tends to become monopolistic, the government takes a hand and institutes antitrust suits which break down centralized control.

The "heartless corporation" is sometimes condemned; yet large-scale industry can seldom operate except on a corporation basis. General Motors, for example, represents a type of industrial organization that is highly efficient in its use of capital, of labor, and of machinery. Self-employment of a handicraft character could never have produced the automobile or other complex machines and gadgets which are commonplace in most American households. If an automobile were to be produced by handicraft it would cost many thousands of dollars, and few would own one.

The Organization of Labor. At the beginning of the factory system, those who worked for others worked under the supervision of the owner and manager. Personal relationships were some guarantee that conditions of work and employment would be satisfactory. Of course, this was not always the case, but if the employee was loyal to the employer as a person, relationships between the two could be worked out on a man-to-man basis. By contrast, the modern economic system has divorced management from ownership. The corporation has hired managers; its owners are its numerous security holders.

With the growth of the large industrial structure of America and the organization of the capitalistic corporation as the major employer of millions, the workers' only defense against unreasonable conditions of work, unreasonable pay, unreasonable hours of labor, and unreasonable dismissals was to unite so they could bargain in their interests with the industry which controlled their destiny as workers. Thus there has gradually developed in the nation the labor union,

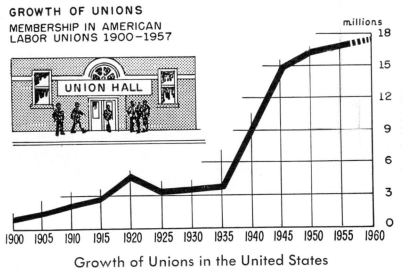

GROWTH OF UNIONS
MEMBERSHIP IN AMERICAN
LABOR UNIONS 1900-1957

Growth of Unions in the United States

The American labor movement has grown more rapidly since the New Deal era. Legislation enacted during the Depression Decade provided a legal atmosphere favorable to organized labor. Today labor faces quite different problems—particularly the task of consolidating the merged AFL-CIO and the handling of corruption and mismanagement in certain unions.

which bands workers together for the purpose of bargaining for the best possible job conditions.

Although it is a logical outcome of the kind of economic system which developed in the United States and, in fact, throughout the industrialized world, the labor movement has a long history of struggle and violence. Laborers have been victimized by employers, and employers victimized by radical labor movements. In the early days, before labor unions were so well recognized by law as currently, many industries engaged in vicious practices such as hiring strikebreakers, which often resulted in pitched battles between workers and the "scabs" who were brought in to take over their jobs, thus forcing the strike to a conclusion. Strikebreaking, until a few years ago, was a regular profession, with certain strikebreaking organizations hiring thugs and shipping them in to the factory where the strike was in progress, putting them on the job, and thus threatening to take away the worker's livelihood. Often, strikers were killed in trying to drive the strikebreakers from the job.

By and large the labor movement has been responsible for the progress of American workers toward a better standard of living and better conditions on the job. It has thereby also placed a greater portion of the returns of industry in the hands of the masses who purchase industry goods.

Gradually public tolerance of the labor union has increased. Only recently, when unions began to be so strong that they threatened to abuse their privileges, as the vested interests of capital once did and still would do if they had the opportunity, Congress passed legislation to protect the public against the unreasonable wielding of power by the labor unions and from the use of the strike when it jeopardizes the health and welfare of a large number of people.

The Taft-Hartley Labor Law, passed by Congress in 1946, was a major step in making labor unions as responsible as employers to the public, which is always the ultimate victim of the inefficient use of capital or labor that is reflected immediately in shortages, in higher prices, and in inferior goods.

Capitalism, Communism, and the Labor Movement. The ideology of capitalism justifies profit by the use of opportunities for the exchange of goods. The capitalistic philosophy is dominated by the motives of acquisition, competition, risk-taking, and profit-making. It is, essentially, individualism applied to the economic system.

In direct contrast to the basic attitude patterns of capitalism are those of communism, the other great economic ideology of the world. *Communism,* following the Marxian doctrine, assumes that there is an irreconcilable conflict between capital and labor and that there can be no real industrial peace until capitalistic civilization, by virtue of its exploitative tendencies, disintegrates and the means of production become the possession of the worker. It assumes that this must happen throughout the industrialized world in due course. The communist employs disorganization and revolution as steps toward this goal.

The American labor movement generally has been little motivated by communist ideology. Except for small radical sectors of it, the American labor movement leadership has been as capitalistic as the captains of industry themselves. The average American laborer expects to climb the economic ladder and someday be a foreman or a boss. He expects to exercise his freedom to shift from one occupation to another at will. He often hopes to own his own business some day. This is not the philosophy of a communistic economic order.

The American laborer, in striking against the employer, has had no intention of taking over the industry; he neither expects nor wants to. Even when the "sit-down strike" has been practiced, it has been employed only to protect the job, to improve conditions of work, and to improve his wages. Basically he respects the man who has initiative and enterprise to own and operate industry. He expects to be given the privilege of owning one himself if and when he obtains the capital and wishes to exercise the initiative. His philosophy is as capitalistic, therefore, as that of the man who employs him.

RATIONALITY OF AMERICAN ECONOMIC INSTITUTIONS

Economic institutions are probably among the most rational of any institutions in modern society. While family, church, and government are deeply embedded in tradition, traditions tend to pass quickly in the field of economics. This field, invaded so rapidly by technology, is probably the most highly competitive of any aspect of modern culture. For this reason the attempt to adopt the new, more efficient, and more economical devices is an eternal game between competing economic institutions, since by these means greater profits are insured. Old traditions therefore tend to hold little sway, and new devices find a ready welcome. Millions are spent in research by modern industries in an attempt to improve manufacturing processes, and speed up invention itself and thereby to outdo competitors.

Science and research have found a large place in our economic institutions simply because they have been found to be profitable. The more efficient and scientific an industry, the more likely it is to succeed in manufacture and sales competition. Even economic activities which are not scientifically founded claim the backing of

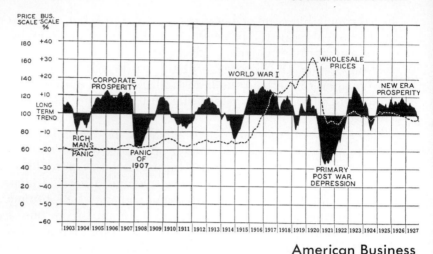

American Business

The ups and downs of a capitalistic economy are shown here by the fluctuations computed on the basis of the growth of population and the long-term trend of measures will save the nation from the recurrence of severe depression. (The

science in their advertising. Cigarettes, soaps, tooth paste, cosmetics, and many other devices of modern culture claim to have medical or scientific opinion back of them. This indicates clearly that science has prestige which aids in the marketing process.

Fluctuations in an Industrial Economy. The capitalistic economic system, by its efficient production, tends periodically to outrun the amount of goods that can be used by the public. At such times the market becomes glutted with factory products. Inventories pile up on the shelves of retail merchants, in wholesale warehouses, and in the factories. Industry must slow down or shut down. This means that the workers are unemployed, and, therefore, have no income. So far, no means have been devised for keeping the American productive system on an even keel. After periods of greatly increased production, there comes the damming up of large excess supplies of goods, shut-downs, and unemployment.

Various measures of social security, however, tend to keep a minimum income flowing into the hands of the unemployed. Some economists believe that this has so evened out the business cycle that there will never be a great depression comparable to that of the 1930's. This opinion may or may not be too optimistic. No one knows. During all the years since World War II vast supplies of manufactured goods have been produced for purposes of war. To employ the

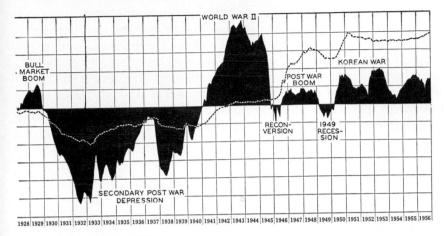

WORLD WAR II

BULL MARKET BOOM

KOREAN WAR

POST WAR BOOM

RECON- VERSION

1949 RECES- SION

SECONDARY POST WAR DEPRESSION

1928|1929|1930|1931|1932|1933|1934|1935|1936|1937|1938|1939|1940|1941|1942|1943|1944|1945|1946|1947|1948|1949|1950|1951|1952|1953|1954|1955|1956

Activity, 1903–1957

in the physical volume of industrial production above and below a normal level, production. Some economists believe that social security legislation and fiscal Cleveland Trust Company.)

more than 60 million men and women currently working, and to do so solely in production of peacetime goods would require a much higher level of living and use of goods and services than now exists.

PERSONALITY IN A COMPLEX ECONOMIC SYSTEM

A complex economic order has many sociological implications for workers and for people generally, only a few of which can be mentioned for illustrative purposes. The high degree of job specialization is a key factor in shaping aspects of personality in the modern industrial order. It has been indicated in an earlier discussion of the social structure that occupation is one of the main factors in determining social class. It is also one of the main factors in determining a man's values, attitudes, and habit patterns. In the American social system a man's whole life organization is built around the job, much more than is often realized, from the time he gets up in the morning to the time he returns home at night. The amount of time he spends away from home, where he will eat his lunch and what he will eat, the time he returns at night, and the time he will spend with his family are all influenced vitally by his job.

This was brought out clearly by Robert and Helen Lynd's study, *Middletown*, made thirty years ago.[4] They indicated that various

[4] Robert Lynd and Helen Lynd, *Middletown* (New York: Harcourt, Brace & Co., Inc., 1929).

occupational classes go to work at different times in the morning, work at different kinds of work, eat from dinner pails or in different types of restaurants. Even the hour of eating lunch is affected to some extent by the particular occupation, as is the amount of time taken for lunch. These are but samples of the pervasive effect of the American economic system on the habit patterns and attitudes of the individual. Recreational activities and one's associations outside work life are also in considerable part determined by one's work.

SUMMARY

Economic institutions are concerned with getting and using material goods to meet man's basic needs and to satisfy his vanity. For these purposes the factory system, which uses with great efficiency machine power, labor, management, and capital, has been developed in the Western world, and with particular efficiency in the United States. Goods are produced in abundance and distributed widely, both geographically and throughout the different social strata. A counterpart of this efficient system is the gradual shift from self-employment to corporate employment, which has modified the philosophy of the worker, developed a new philosophy of leisure, and led to the organization of labor to protect the job, thus matching the power of the corporate industrial organization in control of capital and management.

This type of economic organization in the Western world has at last freed man from the bondage of want. But it has also sharpened the contrast between the economic value systems and techniques of the West and the great "underdeveloped" areas of the world in which most peoples still live on a subsistence level.

DISCUSSION AND REVIEW QUESTIONS

1. What is the sphere of economic institutions? Relate leisure to economic life.
2. Do economic goods serve only to meet basic needs of life?
3. What are the main culture traits of the modern economic system?
4. Explain the importance of a medium of exchange for goods.
5. Show how the shift from self-employment to employment by others has affected (a) work philosophy, (b) attitudes toward leisure time, (c) the problem of the child receiving an apprenticeship to the parent's occupation, (d) the attitude of workers toward unionization, (e) the problem of youth entering the work world.
6. What do we mean when we say that the worker has lost his tools in the modern industrial system?
7. Show how corporate development has increased American productivity.
8. Why have workers in an age of corporate employment found unionization necessary?

9. Discuss the basic philosophy of American labor as it bears on capitalistic and communistic objectives.

10. What do we mean when we say that economic institutions are among the most rational aspects of human culture?

11. Discuss the business cycle. Why does it exist?

12. Mention some effects of the modern economic system on personality.

13. Discuss abundance as a new problem of economic life.

SOURCEBOOK READINGS

FREEDMAN, RONALD, AMOS H. HAWLEY, WERNER S. LANDECKER, GERHARD E. LENSKI, and HORACE M. MINER. *Principles of Sociology* (rev. ed.). New York: Henry Holt & Co., Inc., 1956.
  1. BERLE, ADOLPH A., and GARDINER C. MEANS, "The Appearance of the Corporate System," pp. 439–43.

KOENIG, SAMUEL, REX D. HOPPER, and FELIKS GROSS. *Sociology: A Book of Readings.* Englewood Cliffs, N.J.: Prentice-Hall, Inc., 1956.
  2. JOHNSTON, ERIC, "Not a Monopolistic but a People's Capitalism," pp. 158–65.

LEE, RAYMOND L., JAMES A. BURKHART, and VAN B. SHAW. *Contemporary Social Issues.* New York: The Thomas Crowell Co., 1955.
  3. HARRIS, EDWARD A., "The Growing Concentration of Economic Power," pp. 634–38.
  4. LILIENTHAL, DAVID E., "Big Business for a Big Country," pp. 638–47.
  5. CHASE, STUART, "Paths to Labor Peace," pp. 677–82.

LEE, ELIZABETH BRYANT, and ALFRED McCLUNG LEE. *Social Problems in America* (rev. ed.). New York: Henry Holt & Co., Inc., 1955.
  6. BELL, DANIEL, "Management vs. Worker," pp. 195–97.

SCHULER, EDGAR A., DUANE L. GIBSON, MAUDE L. FIERO, and WILBUR B. BROOKOVER. *Outside Readings in Sociology.* New York: The Thomas Crowell Co., 1956.
  7. DURKHEIM, EMILE, "The Division of Labor in Society," pp. 443–53.
  8. ORTON, WILLIAM A., "Business and Ethics," pp. 453–60.
  9. "Veblen," pp. 461–74.

WILSON, LOGAN, and WILLIAM L. KOLB. *Sociological Analysis.* New York: Harcourt, Brace & Co., Inc., 1949.
  10. DRUCKER, PETER F., "The Industrial Reality of the Twentieth Century," pp. 567–75.

SELECTED READINGS

BENDIX, REINHARD. *Work and Authority in Industry: Ideologies of Management in the Course of Industrialization.* New York: John Wiley & Sons, Inc., 1956.

BERLE, ADOLPH A., JR. *The Twentieth Century Capitalistic Revolution.* New York: Harcourt, Brace & Co., Inc., 1954.

BURCK, GILBERT. "The American Genius for Productivity," *Fortune,* July, 1955, pp. 86 ff.

CAPLOW, THEODORE. *The Sociology of Work.* Minneapolis: University of Minnesota Press, 1954.

CHASE, STUART. *The Proper Study of Mankind.* Rev. ed.; New York: Harper & Brothers, 1956, chaps. 24 and 26.

COWLES, GARDNER. "What the Public Thinks about Big Business," *Look,* Feb. 8, 1955, pp. 19–21.

DAVIS, KEITH. *Human Relations in Business.* New York: McGraw-Hill Book Co., Inc., 1957.

DRUCKER, PETER F. *The Future of Industrial Man.* New York: John Day Co., Inc., 1942.

Editorial Board, Industrial Research Association. *Research in Industrial Human Relations: A Critical Appraisal.* New York: Harper & Brothers, 1957.

GROSS, EDWARD. *Work and Society.* New York: The Thomas Crowell Co., 1958.

HUGH-JONES, E. M. (ed.). *The Push-Button World: Automation Today.* Norman: University of Oklahoma Press, 1956.

KERR, CLARK. "What Became of the Independent Spirit?" *Fortune,* July, 1953, pp. 110 ff.

LIEBERMAN, ELIAS. *Unions before the Bar.* New York: Harper & Brothers, 1950.

MAYO, ELTON. *The Social Problems of an Industrial Civilization.* Cambridge: Harvard University Press, 1945.

MILLER, DELBERT C., and WILLIAM H. FORM. *Industrial Sociology.* New York: Harper & Brothers, 1951.

MILLS, C. S., and HELEN SCHNEIDER. *The New Men of Power: America's Labor Leaders.* New York: Harcourt, Brace & Co., Inc., 1948.

MOORE, WILBERT E. *Industrial Relations and the Social Order.* Rev. ed.; New York: The Macmillan Co., 1951.

MORSE, NANCY C., and ROBERT S. WEISS. "The Function and Meaning of Work and the Job," *American Sociological Review,* 20:191–98 (April 1955).

POTTER, DAVID M. *People of Plenty: Economic Abundance and the American Character.* Chicago: University of Chicago Press, 1954.

ROSS, ARTHUR M. *Industrial Conflict.* New York: McGraw-Hill Book Co., Inc., 1954.

SELZNICK, PHILIP. *The Organizational Weapon.* New York: McGraw-Hill Book Co., Inc., 1952.

SHULTZ, GEORGE P., and JOHN R. COLEMAN. *Labor Problems.* New York: McGraw-Hill Book Co., Inc., 1954.

STALEY, EUGENE A. *Creating an Industrial Civilization.* New York: Harper & Brothers, 1952.

"The Rich Middle-Income Class," *Fortune,* May, 1954, pp. 94 ff.

VEBLEN, THORSTEIN. *The Theory of the Leisure Class.* New York: Modern Library, Inc., 1934.

WHYTE, WILLIAM F. (ed.). *Industry and Society.* New York: McGraw-Hill Book Co., Inc., 1946.

Youth and the Work World. Science Research Services, Michigan State College, East Lansing, 1949.

FILM LIST

What Is a Farm Worth?—12 minutes—sound
There are many factors to consider in the evaluation of a farm: soil, drainage, pasture, extent of erosion, water supply, buildings, and location in terms of schools, stores, and other community facilities. *Source:* U.S. Department of Agriculture.

Educating Father—5 minutes—sound
Deals with the choosing of a vocation. *Source:* New York University Film Library.

Man and His Job—18 minutes—sound
Treats the problem of unemployment and the rise and functioning of Unemployment Insurance. *Source:* Brandon Films, Inc.

The Work of the Stock Exchange—15 minutes—sound
"Shows not only the detailed operation of the Stock Exchange but gives a background of information about the part the Stock Exchange plays in our entire economic structure." *Source:* Coronet Films.

Chapter 39

Health and Welfare Institutions

The institutions covered in the preceding chapters deal with standardized ways of meeting group needs that have existed for centuries; some, for example, the family, go back to the very earliest experience of man. In discussing welfare institutions, we are dealing with institutions most of which have emerged in their present form during the last half-century. Welfare institutions have come into being because of new developments in society which have threatened every individual with want.

INSECURITY AND WELFARE INSTITUTIONS

The degree of care given the unfortunate member of the group varies from people to people and time to time. Most societies have been content to leave this problem to the large family of kin or to the tribal group. In many tribes it has been customary for all to share adversity. In times of shortage all go hungry, rather than the more ambitious or lucky living well while others die.

The modern state extended its conception of welfare to include the needs of the citizens. For centuries England had its Poor Laws which guaranteed a certain subsistence to the pauper. America developed a similar conception of poor relief. With little modification, the belief that the poor could be cared for adequately by county poor relief or city poor relief, or by the church charities, remained in vogue until the Depression of the 1930's. Then the United States followed the pattern set earlier by other industrial societies and established a Social Security program.

Security in the Old Rural-Agrarian Economy. In a society of primary groups where the problem of one was the problem of all, where there was sharing among relatives, children felt responsibility for parents and parents for children throughout each others' lifetime. Families were large and scarcely anyone lived any part of his lifetime without relatives. Most neighborhoods and communities were thickly sprinkled with related families, and the slow means of transportation were assurance that most relatives would not be far away. Children and parents alike found their security in the work life of the family. Each felt mutually dependent, and even after the children established homes of their own, family members could depend upon each other for assistance. The child was expected to help the parent in old age just as the parent was expected to help the child get on his feet economically at the time of his marriage or during a crisis.

The culture of the rural neighborhood contributed to this general philosophy of helpfulness and security. There was a great deal of exchange of work and in time of crisis neighbors were always on hand to help, without compensation. When both parents died, leaving orphaned children, relatives took over, but if there were no relatives, friendly neighbors reared the orphaned children to maturity. Add to this the fact that the majority of persons lived directly from natural resources: agriculture, forestry, fishing, and mining. Being thus self-employed and largely self-sufficient, there was small danger of want. It can readily be seen why welfare institutions in the modern sense were not considered necessary.

Security in an Urban-Industrial Economy. Contrast with this picture of a rural economy the modern economy where only about one in fifteen workers draws his livelihood directly from agriculture and where even those few are dependent on a world market for the sale of their products, rather than living directly from them. Consider this in an economy in which a very small proportion of the working population is self-employed, in which the masses are dependent upon the paycheck given them periodically by an employer as a reward for their work. The masses of workers own no tools, work in some other person's or corporation's establishment, have little to say about their conditions of employment and wages, and nothing to say as to whether they will be employed at all.

In the highly complex corporate system of today, the decision of whether a factory will or will not work depends upon the decision of the board of directors. But the directors, even though they may control the destiny of thousands of workers, are not masters of the fate of their particular industry. Their business sagacity and the extent to which they have provided the factory with competent administration and successful sales personnel have a bearing, but even more responsible for the success of the industry are the economic forces of a particular period in history. There are times when the most astute

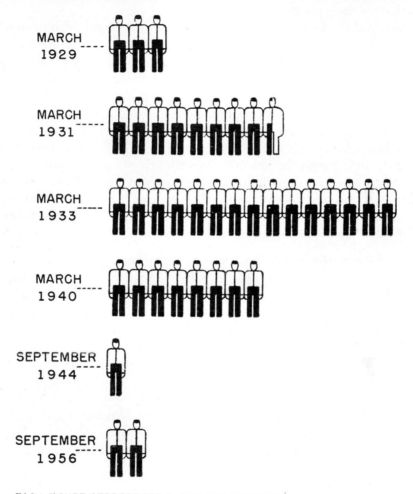

EACH FIGURE REPRESENTS 1 MILLION WORKERS

The Unemployed During the Fat and the Lean Years

Prosperity and depression are reflected in employment. In prosperous years there are few unemployed; in depression years there are many. The depression years of the 1930's saw 15,000,000 unemployed. The prosperous war years, when manpower was scarce, saw fewer than 1,000,000. Unemployment insurance now bridges periods of unemployment for many workers.

industrialists are unable to find a market for their products. Public buying power has dried up. Even though they have normally succeeded well in competition, many great industries have in the past shut down periodically during conditions of general business depression. They have periodically laid off workers because there was no market for their goods.

Not until the Depression of the 1930's was it recognized how much the masses of American wage workers depended upon employment by others. Even salary workers face the risk of losing their jobs with the fluctuation of the business cycle. And those who had secured themselves against economic adversity also, through losses of various sorts, found themselves without an income in old age.

Add to these hazards of the economic order the hazards and costs of sickness in a society where the cost of medical care is extremely high. Consider also the hazards of death of a wage or salary worker in homes where mother and small children are dependent. A review of these elements of insecurity make one appreciate somewhat why an individualistic society has had to think in terms of new institutions to underwrite the economic risks of the masses of its citizens.

Security in Modern Agriculture. In an earlier day agriculture and rural life generally were almost self-sufficient, in that the country man lived from what he produced. His sense of deep security rested in his land. Come what may, as long as he could work he would eat. As American rural life has been geared to the industrial market, the self-sufficiency of the farm has weakened. Those who buy manufactured goods must pay cash for them. This requires selling that which is raised on the farm or ranch for cash to buy manufactured goods. And even in the production of agricultural products there has been a marked shift toward mechanization, which requires a cash outlay for farm operation unknown to pioneer forebears, who with horse, oxen, and plow could make the earth yield food for the family.

THE ECONOMIC LESSON OF THE DEPRESSION DECADE

As a consequence of the Depression, there had to be devised a system of protection which would be nationwide and would provide for the insecurities inherent in the American economic order. The old philosophy of self-sufficiency and the assumption that a man's unemployment and poverty were due to his laziness and thriftlessness could no longer prevail. When the Great Depression struck the nation, many of the most industrious and energetic persons were un-

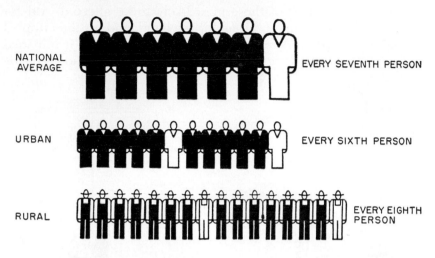

Workers on Relief in the United States, May, 1935

Modern welfare institutions were developed to meet the needs of workers in our industrial society.

employed. Some had been faithful employees for twenty years or more. They had been thrifty. But their jobs folded up and their savings were soon gone.

Even the farmer, who with his extensive mechanization was required to buy gasoline to operate his tractor and to expend a lot of cash over a period of months before his harvest, found himself unable to meet the demands of his farm operation. He found also, during 1932, that it cost him more to operate his machinery than the wheat crop brought on the market. As an outgrowth of that great crisis, the Social Security Act was developed and with it an entirely new philosophy of individual responsibility in the field of poverty and unemployment came into being. For the first time it was recognized that poverty is not always a man's fault, that for many unemployment is beyond their control. Welfare institutions, which would help those in need, regardless of the reason for their need, were the result.

THE SOCIAL SECURITY ACT

Gradually, as the initial effects of the Depression wore off and it was recognized that such periods had been recurrent in industrial orders, there evolved the institutionalized Social Security Act, passed in May, 1935, to provide a regular and dignified method of meeting

such crises in the lives of those most likely to be affected. Aid for
mothers with dependent children, for the blind, and for the crippled
are vital parts of this Social Security program. Insurance is provided
for periods of unemployment and reserve funds are laid aside by

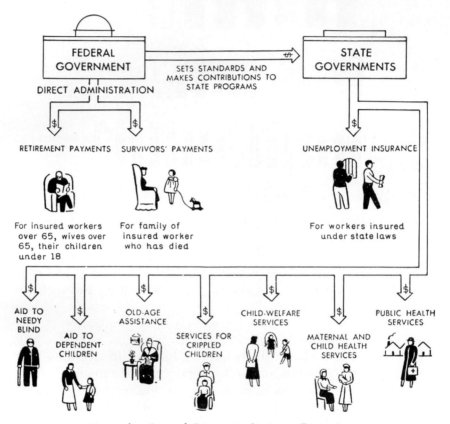

How the Social Security System Functions

*The state and the worker share the risk of want in industrial society. The joint
family and tribal systems provide security in nonindustrial society.*

compulsory savings deducted from payrolls. The Social Security Act
also provides for the aged through pensions and annuities. By payroll
deductions funds are saved for those who reach retirement.

In addition to the Social Security Act, which is a monumental
piece of legislation in the field of welfare, the nation came to accept
the philosophy that, when the wheels of industry bog down so that
employment cannot be provided by private industry, public works
should be expanded to provide employment. The building of public

buildings such as post offices, and of streets, roadways, and waterways, the improvement of parks and forests, and even international projects such as the construction of a Panama Canal are illustrative of activities and plans in the field of public works.

Through such programs the government can, in times of unemployment, preserve for the individual the opportunity to work at dignified employment and improve the resources and facilities of the nation. In the future, if great depressions come, the public will assume a substantial part of the employment load. Presumably advance planning will have made possible the efficient utilization of skills and materials in public works.

What was, during the 1930's, a revolutionary doctrine of the New Deal Democrats has now become the accepted welfare policy of the nation, added to and expanded by both political parties and supported by an overwhelming public opinion.

PERSONALITY AND WELFARE INSTITUTIONS

To many persons a discussion of welfare institutions sounds abstract and impersonal. Accounts of college youth who look back on their childhood days spent in families victimized by the Depression will bring the problem closer home.

The first is the account of a girl from a farm family which moved to a city.

I was born as the fourth and last child after a girl and two boys, and just sixteen months after the second boy. The year of my birth, 1927, also brought the last good wheat crop which we had on the farm, so when I was four, we moved to Spokane, ninety miles away. This put us in a completely new place at the beginning of the depression when it was difficult to keep a job, let alone get a new one. I suppose our family was among the millions of victims of circumstances, but my attitude toward my father has stemmed from that. I have never been able to rationalize the fact that a college graduate could not keep his family off the relief rolls. If he had been more of a family man and closer to us children, I think my ideas of him would have been softened considerably, but Mother was *the* parent in everything we did—telling us "yes" or "no," administering punishment, organizing games, etc.

The second is also the account of a girl from a once well-to-do family.

Until the depression of 1929, my family was considered well-to-do. My father had prestige and a very honorable place in his class of society, which in turn put my sister and myself in a very promising and pleasant position. However, as many others, when the crash came we lost nearly all that we possessed. It was a great blow to eventually find ourselves in an entirely new financial and social status.

First, our family joined the family of an aunt and uncle in order to share costs of the household. My uncle was a pharmacist and owned a drug store. It seemed that no matter how bad times were, he was always able to have some kind of an income. My father was a general contractor and had built a considerable number of large buildings. When the crash came, as there was no construction going on whatsoever, he took whatever work he could find. Consequently, his income, after what money could be salvaged from his investments, was inconsequential. This, as time led on, caused friction within the household. For me, this was the greatest period of frustration. My grades in school lagged; I was unhappy over the many arguments between my parents. The happy relationship in our own home was gone and the confidence I had placed in my parents was weakened.

A young man reared in New York City writes of his days in a "relief" family.

Out of this series of situations must have started the real chain of my inferiority feelings. The knowledge at last that I was one of the poorest class, that I was dependent on the financial aid of relatives, coupled with the various little things that I had to do as a result of our poverty, really weighed heavily on my young mind. To collect wood because we could not afford coal, not to have new clothes when they were really needed, to have to purchase liver or other cheap meats ostensibly for pets, which strangely enough, we still had, to walk miles to a strange neighborhood to pawn some treasured article so as not to be recognized, just to maintain false pride. Yes! Here was food for an inferiority complex and mine must surely have grown by leaps and bounds during those years. Perhaps things were a bit more difficult for me, having been relatively spoiled throughout my previous life. These things have left their mark on my personality.

In the fourth case, the youth felt little stigma as relief experience was near universal in his community.

During the depression and drouth of 1930–36 and the economic failure of these once rich Dakota farms, the government stepped in and provided relief work and surplus commodities for everyone. I don't recall any loss of social status because of being on relief since everyone was doing the same thing in order to subsist. Now that I am older I can see how it would affect one's social standing in a community if relief measures had to be accepted to gain subsistence, but since I was just a little fellow then it didn't worry me in the least. I can't remember ever going hungry or not having clothes and shoes to wear. My parents hated to accept relief but it was about the only way to gain a living at the time. My mother in particular was against the idea and even to this day tries to avoid talking or thinking about it.

The final case illustrates the piling up of economic difficulty to the extent of eventually breaking the courage of a once highly prosperous and self-confident fruit rancher. The account is by his son.

I felt exceptionally secure; my mother and father enjoyed considerable status as a prosperous farm couple, and through my role as the son of a successful farmer, I too derived more than a little status among my intimate school and neighborhood friends. However, in 1933 conditions changed rapidly, the environment changing overnight from one of security to one of relative insecurity. For the following six years I did little other than work on the farm throughout the long summer months, go to school in the fall, winter, and spring, working every spare moment trying to keep the ranches. There was no time for play. Like all good farm communities, ours overlooked poverty if one were industrious. Each year saw us farther in debt, finally the wheat warehouse closed, and one by one my father began to close his holdings. Your operations simply can't pay when it costs $1.17 per box to produce apples that sold on the eastern markets for $.90. Dad finally accepted public charity as a W. P. A. worker; lost forever was the position he once occupied in the community, and unfortunately, he has never to this day fully recovered from this admission of failure.

No matter how severe economic conditions may become in future downturns of the business cycle, these experiences of the individuals will not be repeated. The main psychological and social value of the Social Security program is that it makes security a matter of right and not of charity.

Another benefit of the Social Security program is that the very measures of protection extended the citizen act as a hedge against violent downturns in the business cycle. The unemployed worker has some money to spend, as does the injured worker, the survivor of a worker killed by an accident, etc. These expenditures help keep the lines of production in operation, making public employment or other remedial measures less necessary.

CHILDREN AND WELFARE PROGRAMS

The crux of a nation's welfare problem is the next generation. The most important consideration of a democratic society should be to guarantee that its children have adequate housing and proper nutrition in order to insure the fullest development of their physical potentialities. Unfortunately, American society has fallen far short of this ideal and still has not discovered effective measures to guarantee it. The Depression Decade of the thirties was tragic from the standpoint of childhood, for by and large families on relief were families with children. Generally speaking, the larger the number of children in the family, the greater the likelihood of its being on relief. This fact was demonstrated by a great number of studies in both rural and urban areas. The young couple who start out having children have little chance of saving, compared to the couple without children, for each child requires three years of a father's working lifetime for its rearing.

The Midcentury White House Conference on Children and Youth, called by the President of the United States in 1950, showed that the larger the number of children, the smaller the pieces into which the family's economic pie is cut. This is illustrated by the more recent data in the following table.

Median Family Income in Terms of Number of Children in Family, 1957 (U. S. Census)

Children in Family	Median Family Income	Income per Person
1	$4,335	$1,445
2	4,506	1,130
3	4,335	870
4	3,949	660
5	3,155	450
6 or more	3,252	410 or less

Allowance Schemes. A competitive economic order places those with children in a very disadvantageous position from the standpoint of being able to provide health, nutrition, housing, and educational facilities at personal expense. Population policy in several countries and welfare policies in still other nations have been used to insure an income to families with children in a competitive society.[1] One of the best plans in operation of those in effect in more than 30 nations and among the simplest to administer, is that of Canada. Under this plan, adopted in 1945, each family with children gets an average allowance of seven to nine dollars per child per month, depending on the child's age, until the child is sixteen years of age, unless he drops out of school prior to that age. The family allowance is provided through taxation to all families regardless of need. The allowance is paid to the mother to provide the greatest assurance that the money will be spent in the interest of the children. This system places the purchasing power for basic-necessity items in hands where it will be spent for manufactured goods and agricultural products, thus providing a continuous market. Under the Canadian system as it now operates, millions in family allowances are paid out monthly to more than a million and a half eligible families. The Canadian program is considered highly satisfactory, not only by people who are recipients but by citizens in general and by industry.

[1] Great Britain's family-allowance plan was adopted in June, 1945. Allowances begin with the second child. New Zealand's plan was adopted more than thirty years ago, and Australia's in 1941.

The Children's Charter for Canada reads:

Canada's future depends on its children. They are the country's greatest asset. Healthy and happy children, reared in an atmosphere of security, take their place as active and productive members of society.

Yet under present conditions, the major burden of raising the nation's children falls on less than one-fifth of the working population. The value of the child to the community bears no relation to the father's work or income. Each child in the family means increased expenses without providing additional funds whereby the expenses can be met.

Family allowances help Canadian parents meet this financial burden. Money for the child goes directly into the home, the centre of the child's life, where he is fed, clothed, sheltered and cared for. It goes to the parents who know the individual needs of their family better than anyone else.

As the years go by, family allowances can help to reduce sickness, disease, crime, illiteracy, inefficiency, and other social ills that have their roots in child unbringing. Since they are given to people who spend the money, they create a continuous demand for necessities which will result in increased production and employment.

Family allowances provide a simple, fair and effective way to ensure a greater measure of well-being to Canadian citizens of the future. Family allowances are an installment in social security.[2]

Whether the United States should adopt a similar program, or some entirely different one, is a vital matter for public discussion, but certainly it must be recognized that the United States has not as yet provided sufficient security measures to guarantee the child in the low-income family adequate nutrition, decent housing, medical care, or even for that matter the equality of privilege for education beyond the grade school. These certainly are welfare ideals to be sought.

The United States has already gone a long way in helping carry the burden for the care of young children, but could go much further. For example, we have made public education a social responsibility; parents do not have to pay the cost. The school lunch has gone a step further in helping to lift a burden from the parents' shoulders and in guaranteeing adequate nutrition. In prosperous communities the textbooks are provided, lifting another burden from the shoulders of parents with children. Every city today provides playground space to compensate for the fact that the average parent with children cannot provide a lawn for play space as he once did in the country and as he still does in the small town.

Should the nation not go further and guarantee that every child will have complete medical care, provided through some system of health insurance or through tax-supported medicine? Certainly the

[2] Minister of National Health and Welfare, *Family Allowances: A Children's Charter* (Ottawa, Canada, 1957).

average couple with children cannot now carry the load and guarantee adequate medical care. Should the nation assure every child an adequate diet by making available protective foods—milk, citrus fruits, green vegetables—by a food-stamp plan or some other such device? Should the nation give more attention to public housing, so that every child will have at least a reasonable shelter? Should the nation make greater concessions on the income tax to workers with children?

Certainly it is clear that the burden of caring for children is now too much a personal responsibility and not enough a social responsibility. The bachelor and the single woman have all the advantage from the standpoint of earning an income and living from it. In a competitive economic order based on wages and salaries, the larger the family, the greater the economic risk.

HEALTH INSTITUTIONS

Health institutions, although much less formal than some other institutions, have the same type parts as far as the culture is concerned. The nonmaterial culture traits consist of such things as the diploma and medical degree, which permit members to practice. These certificates vary in importance. A certificate from the American College of Surgeons, for example, admits to high quality of surgical performance. In the field of attitudes are those centering around the ethics of the profession. The profession presumably calls for the highest kind of public service and public trust. It deals with matters of life and death and must render decisions concerning the patient's welfare in areas where the patient has insufficient training to evaluate decisions made.

A profession, by definition, is a kind of work which requires such a high degree of skill and knowledge that the public is not competent to judge the quality. If one is going to trust his health, and often his life, to a person in the medical profession, he must be assured that person has passed the high standards of entrance which make him the kind of person whose judgments with regard to one's welfare can be trusted.

In the field of utilitarian culture traits, modern medical science has made the most marked progress during recent centuries. In the field of technology it has long ago left behind the horse and buggy days. Modern medical technology requires specialists highly trained in particular aspects of health and diagnosis. Rather than the old private practitioner's office being adequate for diagnosis, in our age a lengthy clinical or hospital examination with the best available equipment is required.

Few doctors today are satisfied with the role of the practitioner or general family doctor. These are some of the reasons why the old system is impractical from the doctor's standpoint as well as inadequate from that of the patient: (1) too many patients to treat anyone adequately; (2) no time to keep abreast of new medical discoveries; (3) not enough time for home life and civic activities; (4) many doctor bills go unpaid; (5) the doctor is expected to assume the burden of charity patients; and finally, (6) few health-insurance policies provide for the family doctor.[3]

American health institutions, particularly those aspects having to do with the treatment and cure of disease, are now involved in a conflict of attitudes and goals that is destined to shake them to their very foundations. Although the medical man professes to be a professional man in the true sense, many leading members of the profession have become deeply involved in the competitive profit-making economy of a fee system of payment. Even hospitals have been somewhat affected. Now, when the public believes its interests would be better served through insurance or through tax-supported medical programs, the medical group, as a vested interest group, is fighting a remodeling of the existing system. Since it is the most dynamic aspect of health institutions today, this struggle to create new culture patterns through new systems of medical administration bears further analysis. No better example can be found of the way in which widely acknowledged group needs eventually bring modifications in existing institutional systems.

MEDICAL ADMINISTRATION

Institutional Folkways. The current system of medical practice roots in the tradition of the family doctor of the primary group of yesterday. He was the man who knew all the family secrets and who was the family counselor, not only on health matters but also on many other matters of personal importance such as marriage and family problems. He developed many loyalties, and about him grew up much folklore. His devotion, his tireless effort, his sacrifice of self-interest, his willingness to care for patients whether they had money or not, made of him an imposing figure.

With the development of metropolitan culture, the loyalty of the

[3] William A. Dunnagan, "Why I Stopped Being a Family Doctor," *Look,* Aug. 21, 1956, pp. 35–37.

medical profession to the individual and to the family is rapidly disappearing. People have died in their homes in metropolitan centers because doctors refused to answer a home call for help. Clinics, laboratories, and hospitals have multiplied. Often sponsored by doctors themselves, they are fast replacing the private practitioner in urban areas. The family doctor who is capable of diagnosing all the ills of the family members and in meeting all their medical needs is a rarity in the great city. Many rural communities, however, still depend upon him.

The general drift away from the older folkways of medical practice is in response to the technicways of modern medical care on the one hand, and to the impersonality of contacts in the metropolis on the other. It is a natural and inevitable trend.

The Lag in Medical Administration. It has long been evident to population students, welfare workers, and to the more informed public that the nation's highly effective system of medical technology and highly trained staff of medical experts are not netting the American public the maximum benefits in terms of physical well-being. For a nation with a democratic philosophy of life and an abundant material resource, we have an amazing amount of ill health,[4] a high rate of physical disability,[5] a shockingly high maternal death rate[6] and a lower expectation of life[7] than might now be attained by a more intelligent use of medical talent and life-saving medicines and machinery.

Many of these failures to achieve what might be achieved in the way of health and long life must be blamed on the fee system for medical care, an outmoded system in an age of machine efficiency. Among the liabilities of this system are: (1) Fees have become so

[4] A canvass of over two million persons in 1935–36 revealed that during one year there were 124 acute illnesses and 48 chronic illnesses for every 1,000 persons. Each ill person was disabled for an average of 9.8 days in one year. *People and Resources,* National Resources Planning Board (Washington, D. C., 1940), p. 32.

[5] Of some 14,000,000 draftees who were examined by the Selective Service for World War II, only 2,000,000 were up to reasonable standards; 3,500,000 were hopelessly unfit; 2,250,000 were remedial 4-F; and 6,500,000 were accepted despite physical defects. One million were discharged for defects which were discovered or which developed after induction.

[6] Paul H. Landis, *Population Problems* (2d ed.; New York: American Book Co., 1954), p. 479.

[7] In 1940, life expectancy at birth of the white population of the United States was 63.8, lower than the average expectancy in New Zealand and the Netherlands. *International Vital Statistics* (U. S. Census, 1940), pp. 430–32. By 1947, the life expectancy for white females in the United States had reached 70.5, but in New Zealand the expectancy was 71.6 and in the Netherlands, 71.5. For further comparison, see Paul H. Landis, *Population Problems* (2d ed.; New York: American Book Co., 1954), chap. 7.

high that the average citizen cannot afford to pay for emergencies that arise in the health care of his family. The security of every middle-class family is threatened should any member of the family suddenly require one or more operations with the attendant hospital cost. (2) A year's sickness of the breadwinner may be a major catastrophe, placing the family in an economic situation from which it will not be able to recover over a period of many years. It may consume all the family capital and savings and place them in a position where they may never be able to advance beyond meeting the current needs and paying medical debts. In many families an invalid member mortgages the lives of one or more family members. (3) The

FAMILIES WITH VOLUNTARY
HEALTH INSURANCE

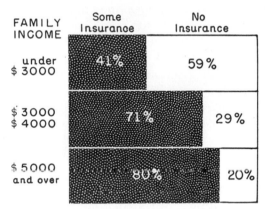

FAMILY INCOME	Some Insurance	No Insurance
under $3000	41%	59%
$3000 $4000	71%	29%
$5000 and over	80%	20%

Health Insurance Related to Income

Those whose risk is greatest have the least coverage. Is this an area for social policy?

masses of the American public never have adequate medical care because they will not accept care on a charity basis and cannot afford the expensive diagnosis that the clinical examination or a period in the hospital may require. (4) Medical technology has become so elaborate that the average practitioner is unable to make a reliable diagnosis. Failure to diagnose adequately, greed, and other factors result in some 9,000,000 needless operations annually in the United States. These operations are an economic burden and often are a severe shock to the nervous system. (5) The above suggests that the present fee system is subject to exploitation by many unethical members of the medical profession. Fee-splitting, long a common practice, is on the increase.[8] (6) The private system of medical care now, as always, emphasizes cure rather than prevention. Medical examinations and diagnoses are expensive and the average citizen therefore goes to the doctor as a last resort after he has been troubled with pain over a period of time. Often this is too late, explaining in part numerous needless deaths that occur annually. The medical profession as such is almost completely involved in a program of cure, neglecting prevention.

Only through the United States Public Health Service, with its quarantines, examination of food and water supplies, and control of communicable diseases, has there been any appreciable attempt in medical programs of the nation to prevent disease. One cannot help wondering whether these preventive measures, for which we have spent about one cent of each dollar through the United States Public Health Service, may not have given more in the way of health than the ninety-nine cents we have spent for private medical care, which is often a belated attempt at cure.

The continued emphasis on the profit motive in medical care has produced a serious lag in the effective development of the Public Health Service itself. It is estimated that there are 200,000 needless deaths a year in the United States because of a dearth of Public Health officers trained adequately for their work.[9] Under the semi-profit motivated system of medical practice, it is almost impossible to attract public-spirited men of high caliber to the salaried practice of preventive medicine. Because of weak leadership in this field, local public health budgets are inadequate. Water, milk, and other food supplies are inadequately guarded in most towns and cities. Sanitation is often inadequate.

Emerging Patterns. Change in the system of medical administration has been in process for several years. As in the case of any institutional change, it began in dissatisfaction which led to experimentation with new patterns of meeting human needs.

Cooperative groups were formed to pool funds to meet the emergencies of medical, and particularly hospital, expense. Some industries developed insurance funds for their employees and most colleges developed health services financed by assessments collected with student fees. The government during the Depression Decade

[8] In 1946, and again in 1948, the government filed antitrust suits against optical companies and several thousand eye specialists for participation in rebate systems "which took hundreds of thousands of dollars from unknowing patients." (Associated Press releases.)

[9] Jack H. Pollack, "The Shame of Our Local Health Department," *Collier's,* Jan. 27, 1949, p. 13.

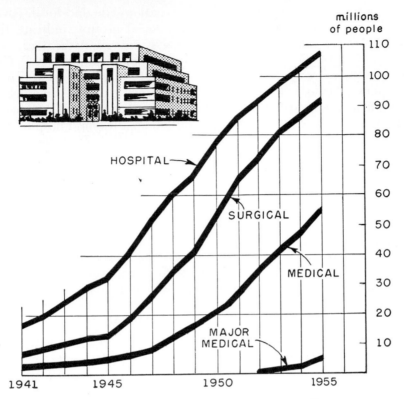

Hospital, Surgical, and Medical Expense Coverage in the United States, 1941–1955

Seventy per cent of the American people had insurance coverage of one sort or another by 1958. The Blue Cross hospital plan, sponsored by the American Hospital Association, was by far the most extensive as far as membership was concerned, although less complete in medical coverage than some others. It had more than 50 million subscribers. Even the medical profession was sponsoring a prepayment plan for clients called the Blue Shield Plan, for surgical benefits. It had more than 36 million subscribers.

developed hundreds of cooperative prepayment medical care plans through the Farm Security Administration[10] as a means of guaranteeing repayment on their loans, for they learned that in low-income farm families a medical bill was often the extra burden that defeated the farm family economically.

[10] Up to the beginning of World War II the Farm Security Administration had developed medical programs in 1,000 counties, one-third of the counties in the United States. Some 120,000 families, representing 630,000 persons, were covered by these group medical care units.

Numerous public-opinion polls, both nationwide and local, covering various occupational, income, and social groups, indicate that most American people want some better system of medical administration than that now existing under private medical practice.[11] They also want much more than they are getting through the usual private insurance scheme, with its relatively high cost for limited medical or hospital service. Most of the public, if they had their choice, would have a prepayment plan covering complete medical and hospital care and dental service.

When agitation for change, and change itself, becomes so extensive, one can be certain that the patterns of health institutions will in time become reorganized into new uniform patterns. To date, changes are for the most part random, varied in character, and differently motivated. What will the pattern of medical care be in the years ahead?

As in the case of most institutional change, one can expect a combination of some of the old patterns with new patterns that have to date proved satisfactory on an experimental scale.

NEW SYSTEMS OF MEDICAL ADMINISTRATION

As the public views its health needs, three types of medical administration are within the realm of possibility: (1) continuation of the present fee system and of random voluntary insurance plans of various coverage and for various groups; (2) tax-supported medical care, properly referred to as socialized medicine; (3) nationally sponsored compulsory health insurance, comparable to unemployment insurance, to be operated by the states and the federal government along with other provisions of the Social Security Act. (This plan is improperly referred to as socialized medicine by its opponents.)

Outlook for the Fee System. The present fee system of medical care probably cannot survive alone as the prevailing system as there is too much dissatisfaction with medical care as now organized. That private medical practice and private insurance programs will con-

[11] For the development of public attitudes in this area, see the public opinion polls as reported in the hearings before the Senate Committee on Education and Labor, 79th Congress, on Senate Bill 1606, "A Bill to Provide for a National Health Program," Part I, pp. 66–72. The polls referred to include the Washington Post Poll, *Washington Post*, Jan. 28, 1946, p. 1 col. 4; the Denver University Poll, "What Do the American People Think About Federal Health Insurance?" Denver University National Opinion Research Center, October, 1944; the American Institute of Public Opinion Poll, Aug. 13, 1943, *Public Opinion Quarterly*, Fall, 1943, p. 488; the National Opinion Research Center Poll, June, 1943. Appendix to the Congressional Record, vol. 89, Part 11, p. A3358; the Fortune Poll, *Fortune*, July, 1942, p. 14; and the New York State Commission on Medical Care Poll, 1945.

tinue regardless of modifications in the medical system one must take for granted. It is always so in institutional change.

Outlook for Socialized Medicine. Is socialized medicine a possibility? The view that the health of the American public is a social responsibility in a democratic society has widespread acceptance. The idea that medical, dental, and hospital care should be fully tax-supported is not so generally accepted even though socialized education through the public school system is quite universally approved today. Socialized medicine would make those who work in the public medical agency salaried employees comparable to those now in the teaching profession. It would stress prevention rather than cure. There could exist at the same time a private system of medical care, as in education, which could flourish to the extent that it was patronized by those with the funds to buy its services.

Great Britain, New Zealand, Sweden, Denmark and many other democratic nations have adopted this plan of medical care, thus setting the pattern for a democratic state.

From the viewpoint of tradition, a socialized medical program is within reach, but conflicting interests in the nation will probably make it impossible of attainment in this generation. It has been called "socialistic" for so long by the organized medical profession and made the object of their organized propaganda that many fear it.

The problem is one of such frequent debate that the arguments are fairly well standardized. The negative alleges that socialized medicine would (1) destroy the relationship between patient and doctor; (2) become political; and (3) lead to low salaries and, therefore, attract less competent men than now enter the medical profession. The affirmative contends that (1) the personal relationship between doctor and patient is already gone in urban society, the patient needs scientific medical care, not a friendly counselor; (2) education has not been seriously hindered by political vices, hence why should medical care on a tax-supported basis be; (3) high income is not required to attract strong men to a profession, as is evidenced by university staffs; (4) men are attracted by a career promising advancement in a respected institution where merit leads to promotion and to recognition; (5) under such a system doctors would no longer be bill senders and collectors, businessmen with the overhead of an office and expensive equipment to support, but could devote their energies to preventive medicine, curative medicine, and to research.

This clash of arguments will go on, of course, regardless of the system of medical administration adopted in the nation.

Health Insurance. The most likely compromise measure in the field of medical care seems to be prepaid health insurance. This fits the existing framework of the Social Security Act. It would avoid the problem of direct taxation by requiring worker and employer to share costs by payroll deductions and requiring self-employed persons to pay insurance premiums. By a judicious compromise with the medical profession, it would permit the client to choose his doctor, provided the doctor wishes and his training permits him to be placed on the list of those to whom the client may go for service. And it retains the profit motive of the fee system in part. Doctors would be paid for clients served under a uniform fee scale. By a division of state and federal authority, this system can avoid some of the centralization of a federally dominated bureau.

The insurance program would provide funds for health clinics and medical centers in rural as well as in urban areas. It would put the nation's system of hospitals on a secure economic foundation and would provide for their expansion. It would provide funds for medical schools, for fellowships, and other subsidies for training medical students. It would, for the first time, provide funds for a serious nationwide campaign of preventive medicine, such as the nation has never had with the meager funds that have been available to the United States Public Health Service and other preventive agencies.

Such a program for medical care for the American people was before the Congress during several sessions of Democratic leadership. It was not on the agenda during the Republican regime.

When such a program is adopted, as it seems likely to be, the controversial issues will not be settled, for new institutional changes do not readily find full acceptance. Nor do new administrative ventures always function perfectly from the beginning; in fact, they rarely do. The medical profession will not cooperate fully,[12] since as a body it has repeatedly declared itself against any form of public medical program.[13] A generation of physicians trained under a different phi-

[12] This was the biggest threat to the New Zealand system at the outset. The plan is succeeding, however, in spite of the lack of whole-hearted cooperation between the government and the medical profession. See Hugh McLean and Dean E. McHenry, "Medical Services in New Zealand," *Milbank Memorial Fund Quarterly,* 26:1–34 (April 1948).

[13] When President Truman announced his plan to place this issue before Congress in 1949, the American Medical Association announced a campaign to raise a fund of $3,500,000 to "educate" the public to the "advantages" of the present system of medical care, the fund to be raised by an assessment of $25 on each of the 140,000 members of the association. A group of members of the organization did protest publicly, as they have on previous occasions, indicating that many of the doctors are not in harmony with the stand of the leadership of the organization.

losophy of medical care will have to be brought into the American Medical Association before full cooperation can be expected.

THE WELFARE STATE

In a day of employment by others, when the masses are dependent on wages and salaries for life itself, welfare programs as defined and administered by urban-industrial social orders are among the most essential of all government functions. To deny this is to confess ignorance of the nature of modern economic life.

All industrial societies have had to move in the direction of improving housing by resorting to programs of slum clearance, unemployment insurance, protection against economic losses due to accident or untimely death of the worker, old age pensions, and medical care and family allowances. Totalitarian states, no less than democracies, have had to move in this direction, because industrial society has these hazards no matter what the form of government.

Such ventures on the part of government do not mean the end of private enterprise in America. They do mean that when economic adversity besets private enterprise and the worker no longer has a job, he is able to survive and to maintain his self-respect. In a very vital sense, industrial society can have no other kind of state than the welfare state as so defined.

SUMMARY

Welfare institutions as they exist today are a new type of institution developed to meet man's need for security in an urban-industrial civilization. No longer adequately protected by a primary group and by self-employment, the worker and his family and other socially inadequate groups must have their security underwritten by society through taxation. The Social Security Act of 1935 made a substantial beginning on a national scale. The end will not have been reached until the health, education, and general welfare of children and youth are protected. In the field of medical administration one finds an interesting example of unmet human needs providing the motive power for extensive changes in the customary institutional procedures.

DISCUSSION AND REVIEW QUESTIONS

1. Compare the security of an agrarian economy with that of an urban-industrial economy.

2. How has the trend from the one to the other affected the development of security programs?

3. How has industrialization affected the security of agriculturalists?

4. Discuss briefly the Social Security Act.

5. What is meant by public works? Show how they help meet the need for social security of the worker.

6. Show how problems of insecurity affect the welfare of individuals.

7. Why must welfare programs take youth as well as the aged into account? Cite evidence.

8. Cite evidence to show that welfare programs for children are necessary in our competitive economic system.

9. What are the basic provisions of the Canadian Family Allowance Plan?

10. Do you think such a plan would be appropriate for the United States?

11. Discuss some of the basic culture traits of health institutions.

12. Compare the place of the doctor in rural culture and urban culture.

13. Distinguish between socialized medicine and health insurance.

14. Cite evidence for and against group medical-care plans.

15. Appraise the concept of the "welfare state" for a democratic society.

SOURCEBOOK READINGS

Koenig, Samuel, Rex D. Hopper, and Feliks Gross. *Sociology: A Book of Readings.* Englewood Cliffs, N.J.: Prentice-Hall, Inc., 1956.
  1. Hoyt, Elizabeth E., "Freedom from Want," pp. 174–79.
  2. Truman, Harry S., "Economic Help for the World's Underdeveloped Areas," pp. 179–80.

Lee, Raymond L., James A. Burkhart, and Van B. Shaw. *Contemporary Social Issues.* New York: The Thomas Crowell Co., 1955.
  3. DeVoto, Bernard, "Letter to a Family Doctor," pp. 736–44.

Lee, Elizabeth Bryant, and Alfred McClung Lee. *Social Problems in America* (rev. ed.). New York: Henry Holt & Co., Inc., 1955.
  4. Anderson, Odin W., "Family Medical Costs and Voluntary Health Insurance," pp. 280–81.
  5. Stevenson, George S., "Needed: A Plan for the Mentally Ill," pp. 287–89.

O'Brien, Robert W., Clarence C. Schrag, and Walter T. Martin. *Readings in General Sociology* (2d ed.). Boston: Houghton Mifflin Co., 1957.
  6. Dublin, Louis I., Alfred J. Lotka, and Mortimer Spiegelman, "The Trend of Mortality from Specific Causes," pp. 69–74.
  7. Davis, Kingsley, "Family Patterns Favoring High Fertility in Under-Developed Areas," pp. 74–78.

Schuler, Edgar A., Duane L. Gibson, Maude L. Fiero, and Wilbur B. Brookover. *Outside Readings in Sociology.* New York: The Thomas Crowell Co., 1956.
  8. Henderson, Elmer L., "The Responsibility of American Medicine," pp. 504–10.
  9. DeVoto, Bernard, "Letter to a Family Doctor," pp. 511–19.
  10. Ford Foundation, "Human Welfare," pp. 846–50.

SELECTED READINGS

Knebel, Fletcher. "The Welfare State Is Here to Stay," *Look*, Jan. 25, 1955, pp. 81–84.

Koos, Earl Lomon. *The Sociology of the Patient.* New York: McGraw-Hill Book Co., Inc., 1950.

Landis, Paul H. *Population Problems.* 2d ed.; New York: American Book Co., 1954, chaps. 11–12.

Means, James H. *Doctors, People and Government.* Boston: Little, Brown & Co., 1953.

————. "The Doctor's Lobby," *Atlantic Monthly*, Oct., 1950.

OSBORN, FAIRFIELD. *The Limits of the Earth.* Boston: Little, Brown & Co., 1953.

PRESIDENT'S COMMISSION ON THE HEALTH NEEDS OF THE NATION. *Building America's Health.* Washington, D. C.: Government Printing Office, 1953.

SERBEIN, OSCAR N., JR. *Paying for Medical Care in the United States.* New York: Columbia University Press, 1953.

Social Problems, vol. 4, July, 1956. Medical Sociology, with particular emphasis on problems of mental disease.

FILM LIST

Community Chest—19 minutes—sound
Students of sociology report how welfare organizations in New York organized the community chest and work to solve public welfare needs. *Source:* United World Films.

Institutions—21 minutes—sound
Presents the operation and services of mental and correctional institutions, including a prison and institutions providing for welfare of mentally retarded children. *Source:* Progressive Pictures.

Defending the City's Health—10 minutes—sound
"Brings to life the working activities of the great army of public health workers upon whom so much depends in the matter of living in a city." *Source:* Encyclopaedia Britannica Films.

Make Way for Tomorrow—18 minutes—sound
Considers the problem of an older person, the husband's mother in this case, in the home. *Source:* New York University Film Library.

Old Age and Family Security—10 minutes—sound
Provides a description of federal old-age and survivors insurance and its operation. *Source:* Social Security Board.

Soak the Old—21 minutes—sound
A racketeer organizer exploits an old-age pension movement. *Source:* Teaching Film Custodians, Inc.

Social Security—10 minutes—sound
Gives a valuable and factual explanation of Social Security legislation. *Source:* Teaching Film Custodians, Inc.

Chapter 40

Science and Technology

Trial and error are the lot of man. He learns by tinkering. If one trial out of many turns out successfully, his life improves. Change comes and the old is given secondary place. So it has always been. So it will always be.

As Charles S. Kettering, long in charge of invention and design for General Motors, said on his eightieth birthday: "A child from the time he goes to school is taught that it is very dangerous to fail . . . The inventor fails 9,999 times and if he succeeds once, he is in . . . The one time is the last time you try . . . Just the minute you get satisfied with what you've got, the concrete has begun to set in your head."[1]

An age of science and technology has elevated trial and error to a profession, institutionalized it, and made it pay dividends in human improvement. Science has become formalized trial and error procedure—setting up a hypothesis, testing it, and proving its fallaciousness or workability. The laboratory has become the main instrument of this trial and error routine. Under the ideal conditions of the laboratory, small quantities of materials can be employed to test and try results without the cost, risk, and loss of time involved in large-scale trial and error. The mathematical and chemical symbol, the blueprint and formula, have become the shorthand tools. If a thing works, it may then be carried to the level of technology by way of the pilot plant, which is trial and error on the level of production.

SCIENCE A NEW ASPECT OF INSTITUTIONALIZED CULTURE

Primitives have no science as such and yet they do, of course, have practical knowledge of an exact character which is, in many re-

[1] Quoted by Leonard Gross in *Collier's*, Oct. 26, 1956, p. 6.

spects, closely akin to modern science. Some primitives have re- markable ability to map areas of travel. Many primitives have a sound understanding of plant and animal life, of trade winds, ocean currents, and numerous factors of climate. Some primitives even manifest a great deal of understanding of heavenly bodies. In wres- tling with basic problems of living they arrive at much of the same knowledge that is for us the basis of physical sciences, although its formulation into a system of scientific principles certainly is not present.[2]

Science, as an organized system of knowledge, is a relatively new aspect of culture, the most rational, in fact, yet developed by man. It takes modern man on a perpetual quest to learn the nature of things, to explain how they came to be as they are, and to learn why they act as they do. It has developed a method of approach to un- derstanding the nature of things which early man did not follow. It accepts evidence only on the basis of proof. It may start with hunches or hypotheses, as does myth-making, but proceeds to as- semble evidence. Mental trial and error is a part of the accepted folklore of science.

One of the unique devices developed by the physical and natural sciences is that of working with small quantities of matter and con- cluding from experiments with them what is true of the universe in general. For this type of experiment, the laboratory has come into use. There, where conditions can be controlled and made ideal, par- ticular substances can be isolated and studied. Not only is inorganic matter studied, but by similar techniques the structure of the single cell is studied and its life processes are understood. Instead of draw- ing broad conclusions about the nature of life or of matter, physical science begins with atoms and their parts, and natural science with cells and their structure. Through study of elemental structures, gradually through painstaking effort, is built up a more reliable sys- tem of ideas concerning the natures of matter and life than was ever before available to man.

Yet even today the universe is a mystery. Many of its secrets re- main for man's future conquest. The more science helps man under- stand the world in which he lives, the more man recognizes that he has just begun to learn. Think of developments that are still to be made in the fields of energy, sound, and movement. The mystery of life itself is yet to be solved, even though much is known about how living things function.

[2] Robert H. Lowie, *Are We Civilized?* (New York: Harcourt, Brace & Co., Inc., 1929), chap. 22.

APPLIED SCIENCE, THE BASIS FOR TECHNOLOGY

Science has proved to be more than a device for satisfying man's curiosity about the nature of things. No sooner has he learned their nature than he begins to want to use them to his advantage. Science has, therefore, provided the foundation knowledge by which man reconstructs the world in which he lives, harnesses the energy of matter and of living things, and converts it to his use and convenience.

This huge structure is a light-end fractioning unit of the Humble Oil and Refining Company, Baytown, Texas. Back of such structures lies a vast non-material culture of science, and the precision technology of engineered construction. (Standard Oil Company, N.J.)

At one time, tinkering with the unseen forces of electricity was a venture in scientific curiosity. But no sooner had the nature and the power of electricity become known than man converted it to usable energy. In his tinkering to learn the nature of things he developed gasoline, kerosene, and other fuels which are essential to the modern combustion engine and which have made possible the conquest of space by travel over the surface of the earth at rapid speeds. The horseless carriage made man's domestication of the horse seem like an unimportant achievement. With the airplane, man actually achieved a dream that he has had, no doubt, since he first saw birds flying in the heavens.

Applied science, by virtue of its step-by-step conquest of the environment, and conversion of it to man's use, has helped build an unusually optimistic outlook for Western man. Rather than looking to the past and considering some historic period the golden age, he looks forward to the golden age of tomorrow. Today, when men are already at work on devices for conquering outer space and reducing handicaps of global distance by speed, people no longer laugh or mock or think of putting them in an institution for the mentally ill. They actually believe in such projects, because they know what has already been accomplished in our own lifetime. They wait only scientific achievements which will give man a better understanding of the nature of things and thus provide a foundation for taking advantage of natural laws discovered.

Technology Defined. Applied science is the foundation stone of that aspect of modern civilization known as technology. By *technology* is meant, primarily, the elaborate world of industrial arts and techniques which are the product of applied science and which convert raw materials into material cultural objects. In more common-sense terms it is the field of machine culture which has made it possible for much to be produced through little effort. This world of machine methods and machine equipment which serves man's needs and caters to his fancy has become an element of increasing importance in modern culture. In the area of technology the inventive processes have been most rapid and persistent. Inventions are the route to money-making. Industry therefore finds it profitable to spend huge sums for research in the fields of both applied and pure science, feeling confident that in the long run even the most abstract principle will find application in money-making manufacturing ventures.

The power of a people is measured by its technology, and the level of living is determined largely by it. The United States has more machine power per person than has any nation in the world. Consequently, the people of this nation have the highest living standard on the face of the earth, and the nation itself has the greatest power reserves.

Technology and Behavior. Hours of work, sleep, and recreation are affected to a considerable extent by the technology of a people. As a result of modern lighting devices, man is becoming a more nocturnal creature than in previous cultures. Many primitives never go out after dark at all. In the dim candlelight of another age, Western man tended to "retire with the chickens" and to rise when the rooster crowed, taking maximum advantage of daylight. The life of the modern city is relatively free from daylight requirements and ignores, in part, the cycle of the sun. The larger the city, the later the morning work hour begins and the later the activity of the city is projected into the night. The life of the city is a twenty-four hour life, for certain of its establishments never close.

In many fields behavior is modified by technology even though far removed from the mechanical aspects of life as such. The automobile has broken down the idea of not doing business on the Sabbath, which was once a part of American mores. The radio and television have affected church-going habits, as has the automobile. Many now feel that they do not have to gather at a place of worship in order to satisfy their religious needs. They can select their church service any Sunday morning while sitting comfortably at home, or even while lying in bed.

Man's conception of time and space has been changed by technology. Less than fifty years ago people talked more or less guiltily, but boastfully, of having driven an automobile thirty-five miles an hour. With less compunction of conscience and less pride today, they talk of driving ninety miles an hour. Keeping down speed and increasing limits of safety are the constant quest of those who deal with traffic controls today.

Technology has remodeled man's domestic life. Once he worked at or near home; now, in every industrial society, the machine takes the worker outside the home for his working day. The family has no contact with the work experience of the breadwinner. Children have no natural apprenticeship to the work of their fathers. They must enter the work world by virtue of their own efforts after having achieved adulthood. The work world, as has been discussed elsewhere, is highly specialized, so much so that man becomes an automaton. He lives in a series of work habits formed to fit a repetitive routine. His work is often made up of exacting detail that requires little imagination or little skill beyond that required to learn the initial habit.

The far-reaching implications of technology to the workman of today are suggested in the following description of the industrial worker.

". . . The industrial worker has become one of the most real facts and ominous portents of our existence.

"The industrial worker is the mirror of all industrial men. Both stormy petrel and weather vane, he signalizes the vicissitudes of modern existence under the aegis of machine technics. The steps which lead to this conclusion are clear and unmistakable. They start with the observation that the modern worker, unlike his historic predecessors, is propertyless in the things that really count—production tools. Industrialism is a lop-sided structure, with a heavy concentration of ownership of productive technics in increasingly fewer hands. Operations are mechanized, serialized, massed, having a decreasingly significant amount of productive effort going on outside the walls of the large-scale factory. The worker's approach to production is by way of the wage contract and the time clock. He is productively dependent on some one else; the dependency is called a job; from it he receives a wage; for it his time is clocked, his routine pre-determined, his operations segmented, his creativity fragmented. As long as he has the job, he has 'security'—a poor thing, an affair of bookkeeping, courts, faraway markets, benevolent government, and good luck.

"Propertylessness is the family name of the modern worker. He may own a home, a car, a workshop, a set of golf clubs; but these things yield him no 'income' . . ."[3]

Yet, wherever the machine goes, the worker becomes a king. Where workmanship is removed from the home, a man gains a new status outside the framework of traditions, as a worker, a creator of goods, and in due course the social pyramid is turned upside down with the worker coming to the top and the idle drone drifting to the bottom.

One sees it happening in India, where the untouchable, the one man in India who knows how to work with his hands, most quickly becomes the earner where factories are introduced. Through earning, he raises his level of living and begins to climb in affluence.

The older caste orders of the world cannot survive the onslaught of technology. As women enter the labor market, footbinding disappears, the Moslem veil is rent, and the old restrictiveness of a homebound existence is destroyed. And then, with new liberties come new aspirations and new demands on the part of women. To lighten their age-old burden of too frequent childbearing, the technology of birth control presents itself.

So the impact of technology is becoming world wide, and there is no end to the changes it will bring to the life of men and women throughout the world in the years which lie immediately ahead.

There is another side of the coin, however: the revolutionary technological developments in the area of power. Technological advances

[3] Paul Meadows, "The Worker: Archetype of Industrial Man," *Social Forces,* 25:443 (May 1947).

here can mean human destruction on a scale unprecedented in history; but they can also mean that nations will come to see, as see they must, that the game of war has become too costly and that the new power must be employed to lighten man's burden of want everywhere.

Numerous other examples might be cited of the way technology has affected life, but that is unnecessary. Enough have been suggested so that anyone can quickly, by recounting activities of his daily life and reading, see how much life is geared to technology.

TECHNOLOGY AND HUMAN ENERGY

Throughout the centuries much human energy has been spent in meeting the needs of life. Except in the most hospitable environments leisure has been the possession of few and has been purchased at the expense of many. For each man who enjoyed a luxurious mansion and a leisurely level of living, thousands of slaves toiled, living in misery and want to support their feudal lord in his grandeur. The building of the Great Pyramid literally consumed the life energies of thousands of workers and the Great Wall of China was built by the enslavement of millions of Chinese who toiled their lives away. The Taj Mahal, built by a Mogul Emperor of northern India—"mir-

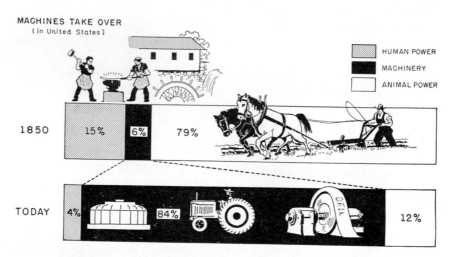

MACHINES TAKE OVER
(in United States)

HUMAN POWER
MACHINERY
ANIMAL POWER

1850   15%   6%   79%

TODAY   4%   84%   12%

Sources of Productive Power in the United States,
1850 and Today

In 1915 there were some 26,000,000 horses and mules on American farms. By 1956 there were fewer than 4,000,000. We no longer mark the ages of man by materials—stone, bronze, iron—but by power—steam, electrical, atomic.

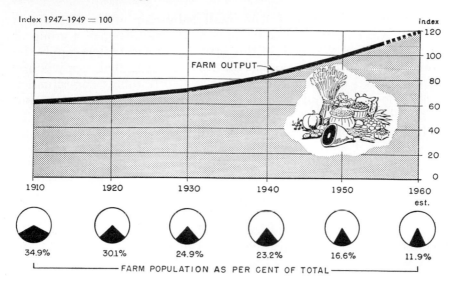

Index 1947–1949 = 100

FARM OUTPUT

34.9%   30.1%   24.9%   23.2%   16.6%   11.9%

FARM POPULATION AS PER CENT OF TOTAL

More Output—Fewer Farmers

In 1935 a farm averaged about 155 acres. By 1950 the average size had increased to 215 acres. Fewer and fewer farmers are feeding more and more city dwellers. In a half-century the number of farmers declined by more than half, but production kept climbing.

acle of miracles," "final wonder of the world"—consumed fifteen years of labor of 20,000 workmen. This was the price of luxury and beauty in an earlier age.

It is not so with the great structures of today. The Grand Coulee Dam, for example, has three and a half times the volume of masonry as the Great Pyramid. Human energy has been replaced by harnessing the energy of steam, gasoline, electricity, and the atom. This energy is substituted for human energy and for the energy of horses and oxen employed throughout the ages to help man toil. The application of energy to the tasks of human living has been a never-ending series of human conquests.

Consider briefly some of the achievements of technology during this century. Take the field of agriculture. Today in the United States, where it once took about eighty-five workers out of each hundred to provide foods and fibers for the people, it now takes only fifteen.

The late 1950's found the nation short of skilled workers in both agriculture and industry. The operation of complicated machines called for skills of a high order in order to protect the investment of the farmer or industrialist. The small baby crop of the Depression Decade was entering the labor market. It was too small a group of workers to meet the need. In this situation of short labor supply the wages of the unskilled approached those of the skilled; many young people lacked motivation to acquire skilled training. This situation will undoubtedly lead to further mechanization and greater output per worker on farm and in factory.

In the field of mining, including oil and gas development, there was a drop of 85 per cent in man-hours required for a unit of production during the period from 1880 to 1939. In the field of manufacturing and the development of public utilities and transportation, there was a drop of one half in man-hours required between 1899 and 1939.[4]

No one in America acquired such fame at the beginning of the technological age as Henry Ford, who took advantage of every device which technology had tried and added new ones, with the aim

Ford's first assembly line represented a long step forward in technological development. This revolutionary method is now applied in medical clinics, stenographic pools, mail-order houses, and thousands of other activities—saving human energy, employing specialized skills, and speeding production. It has contributed considerably to the rising standard of living in the United States and growing aspiration for a higher standard throughout the world. (Ford Motor Company.)

[4] H. Gordon Hayes, "The Narrowing Gulf Between the Rich and Poor," *Harper's,* 195:57–60 (July 1947).

of producing an automobile with the least possible use of human energy so that it could be priced within the reach of the masses. He employed many devices that are at the basis of machine technology today: for example, standardized parts, precision-made and therefore interchangeable, a system originally developed by Eli Whitney in a rifle plant in Bridgeport for the War of 1812. He took over the conveyor-belt assembly system which had been used by the meat-packing industry as early as 1880. He adapted the assembly line to the purpose of assembling an automobile from beginning to finish. The "Tin Lizzy" rolled off the conveyor belt at the end of the line as a completed automobile.

Each job in the assembly of the automobile was broken down into its elementary skills, so that workers could be used to the greatest degree of efficiency. The system had been used before by the Singer Sewing Machine and National Cash Register companies, but was used by Henry Ford for the first time in the construction of a large piece of machinery. Through these various uses of machine devices and labor, he put industrial production on a new level; in fact, laid the foundation for automobile technology. He built automobiles on a mass-production scale with little use of human energy and actually succeeded in making a Model T Ford the possession of the majority of American families. He took the American farmer out of the horse-drawn carriage and ushered in the age of the automobile and year-round roadway.[5]

TECHNOLOGY AND THE EQUALIZATION OF PRIVILEGE

Marxian communism criticizes capitalism because of the wide gulf in wealth between the capitalist and the laborer. Its theory holds that an eternal conflict must exist between capital and labor until labor eventually takes over the management of industry, eliminating capitalism. The facts of capitalistic history in the West refute this theory at every point. Capitalism, the industrial corporation, and technology combined have narrowed the gap between the capitalist and the worker.[6]

Today the rich and the middle class enjoy the same gadgets and living conveniences. The rich have much the same type of cooking and refrigerating equipment, vacuum cleaners, cigarettes, and all the other devices that go into modern living as have the rest of the population. They use the same type of telephones; they go to the

[5] For an excellent discussion of Henry Ford's place in the development of American technology, especially in the automobile field, see Peter F. Drucker, "Henry Ford: Success and Failure," *Harper's,* 195:1–8 (July 1947).

[6] Hayes, *op. cit.*

same schools; to the same universities and colleges, for public education long ago replaced private education for the rich as well as for the masses.

And think for a moment of the equality of privilege that exists in the field of books and magazines, newspapers, and entertainment. For a few cents any man can enjoy superb acting, acting that may exceed the finest stage plays, on the motion-picture screen. And by turning the dial of the radio or television, one or both of which are now a possession of practically every American home,[7] he can listen to or see the finest concerts of the great artists or enjoy the master entertainers of the age, an experience of monarchs and of the privileged alone in previous centuries.

Technology on the farm and in processing plants has made it possible for the masses to enjoy the same canned and frozen foods and bottled beverages. There are, of course, still radical differences in the consumption of certain luxury foods. Examples could be multiplied showing the extent to which equality has been achieved between the social classes in America through industrial technology. Take the matter of electricity. It is now the cheap possession of practically everyone in the city. Through the Rural Electrification Administration of the federal government, it has also become so for the majority of farm families. Take the matter of the automobile and gasoline to propel it. These are now the possessions of the masses, and it is difficult for the rich to outdo even the average man in the lavish appearance of his automobile or in its efficiency. The Cadillac cannot outclass the Ford in beauty. In fact, Ford won the 1949 "beauty contest" among cars.

No doubt it was America's equality in gadgets and conveniences that Franklin D. Roosevelt had in mind when he said the thing that would defeat communism in the end was the Sears and Roebuck catalogue. Certainly no one could look through the Sears and Roebuck catalogue and see the wonderful array of mechanical conveniences priced from a penny to a nickel on up, or see garments offered at low prices that rival the lavishness and finery once the exclusive possession of the rich without acquiring some respect for capitalism and its technological output. And certainly no one can deny that the average woman store clerk, using the inexpensive cosmetics offered by modern technology, can rival Chicago's Gold Coast resident in make-up and in scent. These devices may not cost her as much but they are quite as effective in meeting the ends of women in social relationship.

[7] In 1957 there were 150,000,000 radios in the United States and 75,000,000 television sets.

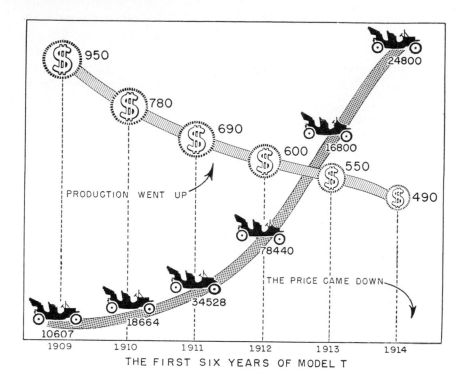

950
780
690
600
550
490
24800
16800
78440
34528
18664
10607

PRODUCTION WENT UP

THE PRICE CAME DOWN

| 1909 | 1910 | 1911 | 1912 | 1913 | 1914 |

THE FIRST SIX YEARS OF MODEL T

Increased Production and Reduced Prices Through Technology

Mass production methods greatly reduced the cost of producing each car by distributing costs over a large number of automobiles instead of a few. In this way, as production went up, the cost to the consumer declined. Henry Ford's assembly line methods began a world revolution in a rising standard of living. (General Motors Corporation)

Modern industry needs a mass market for its goods and, therefore, tends to reduce the cost of production. High wages for workers makes them customers for goods produced. The average working man becomes the mass customer of industry, and industry, in reducing the price of technologically produced goods, makes possible a rising standard of living for the worker.

TECHNOLOGY AND OTHER SOCIAL INSTITUTIONS

No aspect of American social, cultural, or personal life has entirely escaped the influence of the technological regime which has developed so rapidly and become so extensive a part of the American culture pattern. Certainly technology has had a major influence on other social institutions in that it has been a key factor in bringing about a shift in functions between them.

The home has been radically modified by technology, as far as its internal operations are concerned, but perhaps even more significant is the fact that efficient technology in all fields of production has shifted most of the common domestic activities—food preparation, clothes-making, washing, baking, and other such activities—to outside agencies where they are handled by technological devices. The automobile has entirely changed the recreational patterns of families and their vacation habits. For many families it has provided the only place where they really get together for any long period of time. Most technological devices in the field of entertainment have taken recreational activities from the home and assigned them to commercial recreational institutions, although the radio and television have brought to the home a new type of education and recreation.

The development of efficient technological devices in industry has led to such extensive concentrations of power and wealth, capital and management, that many aspects of economic control and management have had to be shifted to government; in fact, one of the major functions of government has become that of regulating and managing, controlling, directing, and restraining business activity.

During World War II the research function of educational institutions and industry was transferred in part to government research centers, where research designed to produce quick results in the field of applied military science was concentrated. Such federalized research centers have become a major function of government, especially in fields of science closely allied to national defense.

Technological devices tend to make and unmake other institutions in the culture. An example in point is the relative decline in the supremacy of the newspaper in formulating public opinion and in influencing the outcome of an election. There was a time when the press practically determined the opinion-forming process on a national scale. Today this function has been pre-empted by the radio and television, which are more influential public-opinion-forming media. These new technological devices have become the main tools of government, not only in democratic nations but also in those with centralized authority. One might go on citing numerous illustrations of the effect of technology in shifting the major functions of social institutions, but these certainly are sufficient to illustrate the point.

A summary statement from the National Resources Planning Boards' report, *Technological Trends and National Policy* is appropriate:

"Very many of the great inventions following the so-called Industrial Revolution have been machines affecting industrial and economic life, namely, gasoline engines, motors, steamboats, chemical and metallurgical inventions. Very often, then, the first great social institution affected by these changes has been the economic organization.

"Later derivative effects impinge on other social institutions, such as family, government, church. Thus, the great economic changes that followed the power inventions modified the organization of the family. Women went to work outside the home. Children were employed in factories. The home gradually lost its economic functions. The father ceased to be much of an employer or manager of household labor, at least in cities and towns. There followed a shift of authority from father and home to industry and State. In cities homes became quite limited as to space. More time was spent outside by the members of the family. In general, then, these changes in industry reacted on the family life.

"In a similar way inventions have impinged upon government. In some industries the nature of invention was to encourage monopolistic corporations dealing in services used by a large number of individuals or other corporations. Hence, governments took on regulatory functions as in the case of the public utilities. Taxation measures shifted from general property, tariffs, and excises on consumption goods to taxes on personal and corporate incomes and on inheritances. In many other ways the government was forced to extend its functions, as in the case of interstate commerce. City governments, especially, had to assume many more activities than those exercised by counties, where wealth was produced largely on farms without the use of power machines.

"Thus, the great inventions which first changed industry produced derivative effects on other social institutions, such as government and the family. Finally these, in turn, have produced still another derivative effect upon social views and political philosophies. The attitude toward the philosophy of laissez faire eventually undergoes change as more and more governmental services are demanded, despite profession of the old faith to the contrary. The philosophy regarding home changes too. It is not so clear under the new conditions of the machine age that woman's place is in the home or that the authority of paternalism in the family is exercised as wisely as it was thought to be in the days of our forefathers. Also attitudes toward recreation and leisure time change, with city conditions and repetitive labor in factories. That these attitudes are so slow to change and are often near the last of the derivative effects of invention may appear surprising. It is true that these new attitudes always appear quite early with some few advanced individuals, leaders, and martyrs. The social philosophies of the mass of citizens do not change so early. Observation seems to indicate that the ideational philosophies hang on, become subjects of reverence, and are in general the last to change in any large way.

"In concluding the observations of the way technologies exercise influence, an invention may be likened to a billiard ball, which strikes another ball, which in turn strikes still another, and so on, until the force is spent. Changes are started on one institution which impinge on others, and those on still others. There is great variety in these sequences; but in the past in many important cases the change occurred first in the technology, which changed the economic institutions, which in turn changed the social and governmental organizations, which finally changed the social beliefs and philosophies. This conclusion does not preclude, of course, the importance and prevalence of other social forces originating from sources other than invention and following this or other sequences."[8]

TECHNOLOGY AND ATTITUDES TOWARD PROGRESS

In the modern world technology is at the focal point of cultural change, for technology requires man to change in many other spheres. As has been pointed out, attitudes toward innovation are important, both to the invention of new devices and to the borrowing of culture traits of other people. An attitude of tolerance toward the new has been achieved in the Western world, probably in large part because technological change produces such irrefutable improvement in the devices with which man works. In the field of technology, the old quickly becomes obsolete and often valueless. Many great industries junk millions of dollars' worth of machinery each year as a new model is produced. Sometimes great factories are built and hundreds of thousands of dollars' worth of machinery for making new devices is scrapped before it is ever used, because some competitor develops a more efficient method.

One reason that technology improves so rapidly, as has been pointed out, is that it is so closely identified with the prospect of profit-making in a competitive economic system. Nonetheless, the

8 W. F. Ogburn, in *Technological Trends and National Policy*, National Resources Planning Board (Washington, D.C., 1937), pp. 9–10.

attitude favoring change which comes from experience with technological devices undoubtedly carries over to other devices, making for greater tolerance toward the new than has been customary in most societies.

Most cultures of the world have been and are fatalistic in their approach to life. History teaches them that what has been must continue to be. Resignation rather than hope becomes the philosophy of the masses. The West has undertaken the difficult task of teaching the "underdeveloped areas" that through technology life can be made over, the future remodeled, and life made secure from hunger, pestilence, and untimely death. It will take much patience, for those unaccustomed to the new model lack Western man's object lesson in the improvability of life through inventive effort.

Technology brings problems. That one cannot deny. Improvement in human culture is never easy. The phrase, "technological unemployment," has been coined to describe a typical problem. Many an experienced workman has lost his job because of shifts in techniques. He did not have the skill to take over the new job, so a younger man was put in his place. In many other cases the machine has so completely replaced him that industry no longer requires his service. The replacement of persons by machines has been an epoch in American history. During this century millions of men have been pushed aside by the iron man. This is a part of the price paid for a machine age and for technological civilization. This is a price paid for labor-saving and for the luxury of a high level of living.

The latest word and latest fear in production is *automation*. Automation not only provides for assembly-line methods of machine operation without human hands, but also computation and problem-solving by electronic brains. This new step in freeing man from toil again brings the spectre of human unemployment onto the horizon. But will it mean this, or merely that more and more skilled workers and engineers will be needed to produce the new devices and supervise their operation? If one is to read the lesson of history, the latter will be true, after perhaps a temporary transition period.

But the very problems which arise from the rapid change that technology produces has forced Western nations to have more foresight than has been customary in human history. The changes that a machine produces are so profound and extensive that a technological civilization must be above all else a civilization which believes in and practices social planning. Quick change presents the possibility for man to improve his life by pointing change in the direction which he wishes his civilization to go. For this reason new ideals and goals for human improvement, which in more static cultures might have taken

centuries or might never have come at all, can be achieved in a few years.

Whatever the problems technological institutions impose, technology is here to stay. The rapid pace of change with its constant demand for adjustment and adjustability will become world wide, for a world of increasing population pressure, a world in close contact which mirrors the level of living of every people before every other people, has no choice but to move ahead as rapidly as possible in the direction of creating technological culture everywhere. This is the key to improvement of man's lot and life. There is no other choice.

The summer of 1955 saw the world's first "Atoms-for-Peace" Conference held in Geneva. At that conference more than 400 scientific papers covering some ninety basic theoretical problems of the new nuclear science were presented. At the same time in Geneva an "atomic fair" was held in which nations presented samples of their technology employing atomic power.

Time (Aug. 15, 1955), reporting these exciting landmarks in history, pointed out how even the poorest, most desperate parts of the world could see that the atomic age is not just a menace, "but hope, a new start, a new future." For scientists and technicians foresee cheap energy for power-starved countries within the next decade. "The magic of radio isotopes is already enhancing medicine, indus-

Will It Destroy an Old World

or Create a New One?

There is energy here to do either. The outcome will depend on the skill of governments in working out harmonious relations between peoples of the earth. "Atoms-for-peace" projects emphasize the constructive aspect of this new force. The hope of mankind lies in the creative use of atomic energy —in its being harnessed to lift age-old burdens from man's shoulders and provide a more abundant life for people everywhere. (AEC, Joint Office of Test Information)

try, agriculture, food storage. No possibility is too small or too big. The atom can ultimately move mountain ranges, drain seas, irrigate deserts, transmute poverty into plenty, misery into mercy."

The following remarks on the influence of technology were written by sociologist William Ogburn over a decade ago.

". . . One invention, in a more or less stationary world, might not have a great effect on our future. But there are 50,000 patents a year. And they are increasing in number. A half-million patents a decade produce a terrific impact on society, starting a turbulent torrent of change.

"These changes will make the future quite unlike the past. The 1940's are vastly different from the 1890's, or even the 1920's. The 35 years that are ahead for the average reader of these lines will be even more different. Patents to the number of two million may be expected during this period. History does not repeat itself in an age of change. Hence we should look forward rather than backward. Imagine yourself driving 80 miles an hour across rough country in a veil of mist. You would need to look forward with all the concentration possible. Would you spend your time and energy looking backward? Yet this is what humanity is doing as it is carried along by a rapidly moving civilization. The universities, colleges, and schools are abundantly supplied with teachers of history, but not one has a professorship for the study of the future. It is, of course, easier to remember the past

701

than it is to read the future. Yet we can see the future unrolling in the technology of the present, just as the modern age is the product of yesterday's advances. . . .

"The inventor of the automobile has had more influence on society than the combined exploits of Napoleon, Genghis Khan, and Julius Caesar."[9]

SUMMARY

Science has made possible a technological age which readily permits converting natural objects into cultural objects of many forms and usages. Machines have replaced the labor of slaves and given man an abundance of both leisure and goods. Technology has helped equalize the great gulf between the rich and poor, the favored few and the masses. A technological civilization has forced revisions in the habits of the individual and in the patterns of social institutions. It has made man change-minded and given him the tools whereby he can realize, in a short space of time, his dreams for improvement. In science and technology lie both the threat of man's destruction and his fondest hope of utopia.

DISCUSSION AND REVIEW QUESTIONS

1. Indicate how science has changed man's approach to problem-solving.
2. Discuss science as a new aspect of culture. How is it related to technology?
3. Define technology and show how it has replaced human energy by machine energy.
4. Discuss the effect of technology on human psychology; on social structures.
5. Compare technology in its effect on agriculture and industry.
6. What is meant by automation? What do you think its effects will be on job opportunities? on leisure? on human comfort?
7. Show how technology has been a factor in equalizing privilege. Do you feel this offers promise to underdeveloped areas of the world?
8. Discuss the effect of technology on other social institutions.
9. Do you have faith that new energy released from the atom will in the end work more toward improving human well-being than toward destruction?

SOURCEBOOK READINGS

GITTLER, JOSEPH, *Social Dynamics*. New York: McGraw-Hill Book Co., Inc., 1952.
     1. OGBURN, WILLIAM FIELDING, and others, "The Social Effects of a Single Material Invention: The Radio," pp. 260–65.
LEE, ELIZABETH BRYANT, and ALFRED McCLUNG LEE. *Social Problems in America* (rev. ed.). New York: Henry Holt & Co., Inc., 1955.
     2. DEWHURST, J. FREDERIC, and associates, "The Rising Tide of Energy," pp. 59–65.
     3. WHITNEY, VINCENT H., "Some Sociological Consequences of Atomic Power," pp. 65–67.

[9] William Fielding Ogburn, "Machines and Tomorrow's World," Public Affairs Pamphlet No. 25, 1946.

SCHULER, EDGAR A., DUANE L. GIBSON, MAUDE L. FIERO, and WILBUR B. BROOKOVER. *Outside Readings in Sociology.* New York: The Thomas Crowell Co., 1956.
    4. ORWELL, GEORGE, "Ignorance Is Strength," pp. 833–45.
WILSON, LOGAN, and WILLIAM L. KOLB. *Sociological Analysis.* New York: Harcourt, Brace & Co., Inc., 1949.
    5. MÜLLER-FREIENFELS, RICHARD, "The Mechanization and Standardization of American Life," pp. 146–51.

SELECTED READINGS

ALLEN, FRANCIS R., HORNELL HART, DELBERT C. MILLER, WILLIAM F. OGBURN, and MEYER F. NIMKOFF. *Technology and Social Change.* New York: Appleton-Century-Crofts, Inc., 1957.

BOGART, LEO. *The Age of Television.* New York: Frederick Ungar Publishing Co., 1956.

BURCK, GILBERT. "The American Genius for Productivity," *Fortune,* July, 1955, pp. 86 ff.

COWLES, GARDNER. "What the Public Thinks about Big Business," *Look,* Feb. 8, 1955, pp. 19–21.

DRUCKER, PETER F. "America: Next Twenty Years," *Harper's,* "I. The Coming Labor Shortage," Nov., 1954, pp. 67–78; "II. The Promise of Automation," April, 1955, pp. 41–47; "III. The New Tycoons," May, 1955, pp. 39–44.

GIEDION, SIGFRIED. *Mechanization Takes Command.* New York: Oxford University Press, 1948.

GILFILLAN, S. C. *Sociology of Inventions.* New York: Follett Publishing Co., 1935.

HERSKOVITS, MELVILLE J. *Man and His Works.* New York: Alfred A. Knopf, Inc., 1949.

HOCKING, WILLIAM E. *The Coming World Civilization.* New York: Harper & Brothers, 1956.

HUGH-JONES, E. M. (ed.). *The Push-Button World: Automation Today.* Norman: University of Oklahoma Press, 1956.

JUNGK, ROBERT. *Tomorrow Is Already Here.* Translated by Marguerite W. Aldman. New York: Simon & Schuster, Inc., 1954.

MACMILLAN, R. H. *Automation, Friend or Foe?* Cambridge, England. Cambridge University Press, 1956.

MAYO, ELTON. *The Social Problems of an Industrial Civilization.* Cambridge: Harvard University Press, 1945.

MEADOWS, PAUL. *The Culture of Industrial Man.* Lincoln: University of Nebraska Press, 1950.

MILLER, DELBERT C., and WILLIAM H. FORM. *Industrial Sociology.* New York: Harper & Brothers, 1951.

OGBURN, W. F. *Social Change.* New York: The Viking Press, Inc., 1950.

———. "Technology and Environment," *Sociology and Social Research,* 41:3–9 (Sept.–Oct. 1956).

OGBURN, W. F. (ed.) *Technology and International Relations.* Chicago: University of Chicago Press, 1949.

———. *The Social Effects of Aviation.* Boston: Houghton Mifflin Co., 1946.

OGBURN, W. F., and MEYER F. NIMKOFF. *Technology and the Changing Family.* Boston: Houghton Mifflin Co., 1955.

ORWELL, GEORGE. *Nineteen Eighty-Four.* New York: American Library of World Literature, 1950.

POTTER, DAVID M. *People of Plenty: Economic Abundance and the American Character.* Chicago: University of Chicago Press, 1954.

RUSSELL, B. "The Next Eighty Years," *Saturday Review Reader No. 2*. New York: Bantam Books, Inc., 1953, pp. 20–30.

SCHRAMM, WILBUR (ed.). *The Process and Effects of Mass Communication*. Urbana: University of Illinois Press, 1954.

SELDES, GILBERT. *The Great Audience*. New York: The Viking Press, Inc., 1950.

SIEPMANN, CHARLES A. *Radio, Television and Society*. New York: Oxford University Press, 1950.

STALEY, EUGENE A. *Creating an Industrial Civilization*. New York: Harper & Brothers, 1952.

THEODORSON, GEORGE A. "Acceptance of Industrialization and Its Attendant Consequences for the Social Patterns of Non-Western Societies," *American Sociological Review*, 18:277–484 (Oct. 1953).

WHYTE, WILLIAM F. (ed.). *Industry and Society*. New York: McGraw-Hill Book Co., Inc., 1946.

FILM LIST

Hold Your Horsepower—15 minutes—sound—color
A Walt Disney treatment of the development of man's ability through the ages to increase his use of horsepower. *Source:* Walt Disney.

Science and Agriculture—9 minutes—sound
Interdependence of science and agriculture in modern civilization. The soy bean is studied from its cultivation in China through its culture and use in the United States. *Source:* Encyclopaedia Britannica Films.

Story of Dr. Carver—10 minutes—sound
Story of a Negro slave boy, George Washington Carver, who received an education and became a scientist whose discoveries influence man's welfare in many fields. *Source:* Teaching Film Custodians, Films.

Valley of the Tennessee—30 minutes—sound
Founding and development of the TVA with particular emphasis on the change it brought to the lives of the farmers. *Source:* Office of War Information.

Machine: Master or Slave?—14 minutes—sound
"Considers the problems that management faces in its approach to the human and financial factors involved in technological progress." *Source:* New York University Film Library.

Trees and Men—44 minutes—sound
Covers the "story of logging and reforestation in the Pacific Northwest, with scenes in various camps and mills and historical sequence of the development of the Westward March from 1850." *Source:* Weyerhaeuser Sales Company.

Appendix

Anti-Defamation League of B'nai B'rith, New York, N. Y.

Antioch College, Yellow Springs, Ohio.

Association Films, Inc., New York, N. Y.

Athena Films, Inc., New York, N. Y.

Australian News and Information Bureau, New York, N. Y.

Austria State Office of Education, Vienna, Austria.

Brandon Films, Inc., New York, N. Y.

British Information Services, New York, N. Y.

Castle Films Division, United World Films, Inc., New York, N. Y.; Chicago, Ill.; San Francisco, Calif.

Chicago Board of Education Film Council, Chicago, Ill.

China Film Enterprises of America, Inc., New York, N. Y.

Coronet Instructional Films, Inc., Chicago, Ill.; New York, N. Y.

Encyclopaedia Britannica Films, Inc., Wilmette, Ill.

Film Forum Foundation, Spokane, Wash.

Films, Inc., New York, N. Y.

General Electric Company, Schenectady, N. Y.

Harvard Film Service, Graduate School of Education, Cambridge, Mass.

Ideal Pictures Corporation, Chicago, Ill.

International Film Bureau, New York, N. Y.

International Theatrical & Television Corporation, New York, N. Y.

Look magazine, New York, N. Y.

March of Time Forum Films, New York, N. Y.

McGraw-Hill Book Company, Inc., Text-Film Division, New York, N. Y.

Mental Health Film Board, New York, N. Y.

Museum of Modern Art, Film Library, New York, N. Y.

National Association of Manufacturers, New York, N. Y.

National Conference of Christians and Jews, New York, N. Y.

National Education Association, Washington, D. C.

New York University Film Library, New York, N. Y.

Office of War Information, Bureau of Motion Pictures, Washington, D. C.

Post Pictures Corporation, New York, N. Y.

Progressive Pictures, Oakland, Calif.

Psychological Cinema Register, Pennsylvania State College, State College, Pa.

R.K.O. Radio Pictures, Inc., New York, N. Y.

Sarah Lawrence College, Bronxville, N. Y.

Simmel-Meservey, Inc., Beverly Hills, Calif.
Social Security Board, Washington, D. C.; New York, N. Y.
Teaching Film Custodians, Inc., New York, N. Y.
United Electrical, Radio and Machine Workers of America, New York, N. Y.
United World Films, Inc., New York, N. Y.
University of Iowa, Iowa City, Iowa.
United States Department of Agriculture, Washington, D. C.
Walt Disney, Hollywood, California.
Weyerhaeuser Sales Company, St. Paul, Minn.
Young America Films, Inc., New York, N. Y.

Name Index

Subject Index